Teaching
The Social Studies
What, Why, and How

Miss Higgins

RICHARD E. GROSS
Stanford University

WALTER E. McPHIE
University of Utah

JACK R. FRAENKEL
San Francisco State College

INTERNATIONAL TEXTBOOK COMPANY
Scranton, Pennsylvania

Standard Book Number 7002 2210 3

Preface

This book contains a representative sampling of the best thinking—old and new—on social studies curriculum and instruction. The social studies comprise a field wider and more diverse than any other broad-field disciplinary area. It is nearly impossible for one author, or three—for that matter, to have the rich background, highly specialized competencies, and grasp of the rapidly expanding knowledge in the field that is available to the readers of this volume. The editors have selected, in light of their extensive experience in the secondary as well as in the elementary grades, the kinds of articles that would have been most valuable to them as neophytes in the social studies classroom. Indeed, a large number of these readings have been systematically rated over a period of years by the editors' student-teachers and beginning interns as readings of "most practical value" for such individuals as themselves. Thus, we present many discerning articles, rich with valuable teaching suggestions. Some of these are from out-of-print sources, and many are not readily accessible. In total, the contents of *Teaching the Social Studies: What, Why, and How* contain much of the sound theory and instructional wisdom available in this demanding subject area.

No one book in this field today can possibly carry all the information that may be needed by either prospective or practicing teachers; but our inclusions focus upon most of the essentials, thereby enabling instructors to employ this volume as a basic text for the special-methods class. Reflecting this purpose, the majority of the readings center upon the all-important "how" element of the instructional process. When used in conjunction with the excellent professional publications of the National Council for the Social Studies, this book provides a most complete package of resources for social studies instruction.

Our selections naturally reflect the views of the editors, as to important strategies and tactics of successful teaching. We have, however, left each author to speak fully for himself or herself. In the complex field of the social studies, as in the profession of education itself, "right" answers, to tally and forever true, do not exist. This is especially true in connection with the curricular emphases and organizational patterns that have been advocated. Accordingly, the editors have attempted to present differing viewpoints, particularly in Parts I and III of the volume.

In the next decade, teachers of the social studies will play a major role in shaping the directions as well as the substance of the emerging field. The conclusions which they reach in relation to issues reflected in the queries posed in our introductory remarks to each section, and raised and discussed in the readings, will ultimately determine both the form and the efficacy of the new social studies programs in American schools. Toward this end we urge that the ideas presented in this book be recognized as both tools for practice and guidelines for the theory that must be joined in attaining a truly viable socio-civic education.

RICHARD E. GROSS
WALTER E. McPHIE
JACK R. FRAENKEL

January 1969

Contents

Contents ix

Cross-Reference Chart
for Use with Current Textbooks in Social Studies Education

Handbook For Social Studies Teaching, Third Edition, Association of
Teachers of Social Studies of the City of New York, New York,
Holt, Rinehart and Winston, 1967.

1—IA, IC	6—IIC-5	10—II-D
2—IIB	7—IIC-1, IIC-2,	11—IIA, III
3—IIC-1, IIC-3	IIC-3, IIC-4	12—III
4—IIB, IIC-1, IIC-3	8—IIC-2	13—IIA, IIB, IIC-1,
5—IIC-5	9—IIC-6	IIC-3, IIC-5, IIC-6

Hunt, Maurice P., and Metcalf, Laurence E., *Teaching High School
Social Studies: Problems in Reflective Thinking and Social Understanding*, Second Edition, New York, Harper and Row, 1968

1—IA, IB, IC	8—IIC-1, IIC-3	13—IB, IC
2—IC	9—IIC-1, IIC-3, IIC-5	14—IB, IC
3—IIC-1	10—IIC-1, IIC-2, IIC-3,	15—IB, IC
4—IIC-1	IIC-4, IIC-5	16—IB, IC
5—IIC-1	11—IID	17—IB, IC
6—IIC-1, IIC-4	12—IA, IB	18—IB, IC
7—IIC-1, IIC-3		19—IB, IC

Kenworthy, Leonard S., *Guide to Social Studies Teaching*, Second
Edition, Belmont, California, Wadsworth, 1966

1—IA	5—IIC-6	9—IID
2—IC	6—IIB	10—III
3—IA, IC, III	7—IIB	11—IIA, III
4—IIA, IIC-1, IIC-2,	8—IA	12—
IIC-3, IIC-4, IIC-5,		
IIC-6		

Krug, Mark M., *History and the Social Sciences: New Approaches to the
Teaching of Social Studies*, Waltham, Mass., Blaisdell, 1967

1—IA, IB	6—IIC-1, IIC-3	10—IIC-1, IIC-3
2—IA, IB	7—III	11—IIC-3
3—IA, IB	8—IIC-3	12—IIC-3
4—IA, IB	9—IIC-3	13—IIC-3
5—IA, IB, IIC-3		14—IIC-3

Lewenstein, Morris R., *Teaching Social Studies in Junior and Senior High School*, Chicago, Rand McNally, 1963

1—IA,	6—IA, IIB	12—IIC-1, IIC-2, IIC-3, IIC-4
2—IB, IC	7—IA, IIB	13—IIC-1, IIC-2, IIC-3, IIC-4, IIC-6
3—IB, IC, IIB, II-C-2, IIC-3, IIC-4	8—IA, IIB	14—IID
4—IIB	9—IA, IIB	15—IIA
5—IA, IIB	10—IIC-1, IIC-2, IIC-3	16—III
	11—IIC-1, IIC-2, IIC-3, IIC-4	

Massialas, Byron, C., and Cox, C. Benjamin, *Inquiry in Social Studies*, New York, McGraw Hill, 1966

1—IA, IC	6—IIA, IIC-1, IIC-2, IIC-3	10—IIC-1, IIC-2, IIC-3, IIC-4
2—IA, IB, IC	7—IIC-1, IIC-4	11—IID
3—IIC-1, IIC-3, IIC-4	8—IB, IC, IIC-4	12—III
4—IIC-1, IIC-3	9—IIC-1, IIC-6	13—III
5—IIA, IIC-1, IIC-2, IIC-3, IIC-4		14—III

McLendon, Jonathan C., *Social Studies in Secondary Education*, New York, Macmillan, 1965

1—IB, IC	8—IB	15—IIC-3
2—IB, IC	9—IIA, IIC-5	16—IIC-2
3—IB, IC	10—IIB	17—IIC-2
4—IA	11—IIB	18—IIC-2
5—IA	12—IIC-2	19—IID
6—IA	13—IIC-2, IIC-3	20—III
7—IA	14—IIC-3	

Moffatt, Maurice P., *Social Studies Instruction*, Third Edition, New Jersey, Prentice-Hall, 1963.

1—IA	8—IIA, IIC-1, IIC-3	14—IA, IB, IIB, IIC-3
2—IA	9—IIC-2	15—IA, IB, IIB, IIC-3
3—IB IC, IIC-6	10—IIA	16—IIA, IIB, IIC-2, IIC-3
4—IIA	11—IA, IB, IIB, IIC-3	17—IIC-6
5—IIA, IIC-5	12—IA, IB, IIB, IIC-2, IIC-3	18—IIC-6
6—IIA	13—IA, IB, IIB, IIC-3	19—IIB, IIC-3, IIC-6
7—IIB		20—II-D

Oliver, Donald W., and Shaver, James P., *Teaching Public Issues in the High School*, Boston, Houghton Mifflin, 1966.

1—IA, IB	6—IB, IIC-1, IIC-2,	9—IIC-1, IIC-2, IIC-3,
2—IC, IIC-4	IIC-3, IIC-4	IIC-4
3—IB, IC, IIC-4	7—IIC-1, IIC-2, IIC-3,	10—IID
4—IC	IIC-4	11—IID
5—IA	8—IIB, IIC-1, IIC-4	12—IB, IC, III

Wesley, Edgar B. and Stanley P. Wronski, *Teaching Social Studies in High School*, Fourth Edition, Boston, D. C. Heath & Co., 1958

1—IC, IIA, III	11—IIC-2	21—IIB
2—IA, IB, IC	12—IIC-1	22—IIB
3—IB	13—IIC-6	23—IIB, IIC-3
4—IB, IIB	14—IIC-6	24—IA, II-B, IIC-3
5—IB	15—IIC-2	25—IA, IB, IIB, IIC-3
6—IA, IB, IIA, IIB	16—IIC-6	26—IA, IB, IIB, IIC-3
7—IIC-5	17—IIC-3	27—IA, IB, IIB, IIC-3
8—III	18—IIC-6	28—IA, IB, IIB, IIC-3
9—	19—IIA, IIB	29—IID
10—IIC-1	20—IIB, IIC-3	30—IID
		31—II-B

ELEMENTARY

Clements, H. Millard, William R. Fiedler, and B. Robert Tabachnick, *Social Study: Inquiry in Elementary Classrooms*, Indianapolis, Bobbs-Merrill, 1966.

1—IA	6—IIA	11—IB, II-B IIC-3
2—IIC-1, IIC-3	7—IIA, IIC-1	12—IB, IIB, IIC-2, IIC-3
3—IA, IB	8—IIA, IIC-6	13—IB, IIB, IIC-2,
4—IIC-1	9—IIB	IIC-3, IIC-6
5—IIC-2, IID	10—IB, IIB, IIC-3	14—IB, IIB, IIC-1,
		IIC-2, IIC-3, IIC-4

Douglas, Malcolm P., *Social Studies: From Theory to Practice in Elementary Education*, Philadelphia, J. B. Lippincott, 1967.

1—IA, IC	5—IIB	10—IIC-2
2—IA, IB	6—IIA, IIC-1, IIC-3	11—IIC-2
3—IA, IB	7—IA, IB, IIC-3	12—IIC-2
4—IB, IIC-1, IIC-2,	8—IA, IB, IIC-3	13—IID
IIC-3, IIC-4	9—IA, IB, IIC-1, IIC-3	

Dunfee, Maxine and Helen Sagl, *Social Studies Through Problem Solving*,
New York, Holt, Rinehart and Winston, 1966.

1—IA	6—IIB, IIC-3	10—IIB, IIC-1, IIC-2
2—	7—IIB, IIC-3, IIC-6	11—IIB
3—IIB	8—IIB, IIC-6	12—IID
4—IIC-1, IIC-3	9—IIB, IIC-3	13—III
5—IIC-2		

Estvan, Frank J., *Social Studies in a Changing World, Curriculum and
Instruction*, New York, Harcourt, Brace and World, 1968.

1—IA	7—IA, IB, IC	13—IIC-I, IID
2—IA	8—IA, IB, IC	14—IIC-2, IID
3—IB, IC, III	9—IIB	15—IIC-2, IID
4—IB, IC, III	10—IIB, IIC-I, IID	16—IIC-2, IIC-4, IID
5—IB, IIB	II—IIB, IIC-2, IIC-3, IID	17—III
6—IB	12—IIB, IIC-4, IID	

Jarolimek, John, *Social Studies in Elementary Education*, Third Edition,
New York: Macmillan, 1967.

1—IA, IB, IC	7—IIC-2	12—IA, IB, IC, IIC-1, IIC-3
2—IIB	8—IIC-1, IIC-2, IIC-3, IIC-4	13—IA, IB, IC, IIC-1, IIC-3
3—IIA, IIB	9—IIC-2, IIC-3	14—IB, IC, IIC-3
4—IIC-2	10—IIC-2, IIC-3	15—IA, IB, IC, IIC-3
5—IIC-5	11—IA, IB, IC, IIC-1, IIC-3	16—IID
6—IIC-1, IIC-2, IIC-3		

Joyce, Bruce R., *Strategies for Elementary Social Science Education*,
Chicago, Science Research Associated, Inc., 1965

1—IC	7—IIC-1	12—IIC-3, IIC-5, IIC-6
2—IA, IB, IIC-1, IIC-3	8—IIB	13—IIC-2
3—IA, IIC-1, IIC-3	9—IB, IC, IIB, IIC-3	14—IID
4—IA, IB, IIC-3	10—IIB, IIC-3	15—IIC-5
5—IB, IIC-1, IIC-3	11—IIC-3, IIC-6	16—III
6—IIC-1, IIC-3		

Michaelis, John U., *Social Studies for Children in a Democracy: Recent Trends and Developments*, Fourth Edition, Englewood Cliffs, New Jersey, Prentice-Hall, 1968.

1—IA, IC, III	7—IIB	13—IIC-3
2—IC	8—IIC-1, IIC-2	14—IIC-1, IIC-2
3—IIC-1	9—IIC-2, IIC-6	15—IIC-2
4—IA	10—IIC-6	16—IIC-3
5—IA, IB, III	11—IIC-6	17—IID
6—IB, IIC-3	12—IIC-2	

Ragan, William B. and John D. McAulay, *Social Studies for Today's Children*, New York, Appleton-Century-Crofts, 1964.

1—IA	7—IA, IB	12—IIC-6
2—IA	8—IIC-5	13—IIA
3—IA	9—IIB	14—IID
4—IC	10—IIC-2	15—IID
5—IIB	11—IIC-6	16—III
6—IB		

Wesley, Edgar Bruce and William H. Cartwright, *Teaching Social Studies in Elementary Schools*, Third Edition, Boston, D. C. Heath, 1968

1—IA	8—IID	15—IIC-2, IIC-6
2—IA, IB, III	9—IA, IB	16—IIC-6
3—IC	10—IIB	17—IIC-6
4—	11—IIB	18—IC, IIC-3
5—IB	12—IIC-2	19—IID
6—IIA	13—IIC-1	20—IID
7—IB	14—IIC-5	21—IID

part I

What and Why?

IA. What Are the Social Studies and How Do They Relate to the Social Sciences?

In America the term "social studies" has for over sixty years raised considerable debate among academic scholars and professional educators, as well as among questioning laymen. Despite some variations in definitions and conceived purposes, most conceptions of the nature of the social studies have seemed to crystallize around two extremes.

At one extreme are those who equate the content of the social studies with that of the parent social science disciplines. Advocates of this view hold that the social studies are essentially microcosmic versions of history, geography, political science, economics, and the other social sciences. They believe that teachers in the schools should ask similar questions and follow similar procedures of inquiry as do practicing scholars in these disciplines. They warn that unless such a procedure is followed, the students will not have a clear and adequate understanding of the social world, let alone of the nature of the social science disciplines. The prime purpose here is to develop young, objective, social analysts.

Those who disagree with this position hold that the social studies, instead of being minor replications of the parent subjects, are, rather, carefully selected aspects. These advocates argue that the task of social studies curriculum planners and teachers is to select from the disciplines that data necessary to accomplish the objectives of the school and society. They emphasize the use of those portions of the parent subjects which will help attain their purposes, arguing that the function of the social studies is not to produce miniature social scientists but moral and intelligent citizens who are able to use their knowledge to make their world more meaningful and to work for worthy human ideals.

Both the social sciences and the social studies are in flux. Indeed, the social studies with their focus upon contemporary affairs and attention to youth needs, as well as their applied nature, should probably be changing even more than their parent disciplines. But generally they are not. Traditionalists in the schools maintain a spirited rear-guard action against innovations; some continue to question even the concept of the social studies. Among the social sciences, however, new directions are the order of the day—although it must be admitted that there are academicians who resist new emphases and approaches.

Disciplinarians from each of the social sciences are actively redefining their subjects. They are attempting to identify key generalizations accruing from research and are delineating the processes and relevant skills whereby their subjects become meaningful and purposeful to students of society. Some academicians see progress resulting from the extension of their subjects down into the elementary grades and want the high schools to offer electives or even to require courses in their particular specialties. Others prefer topical or problem-type courses or curricula in which the content and methods of a number of the relevant social sciences are brought to bear on a given issue.

Today almost no one calls for amalgamated offerings entitled "social studies." Many social scientists believe that a broadfield social studies course, often with a single social study title, is preferable to a narrowly conceived or "pure" course in history, geography, government, or any other social science. Multidisciplinary explorations and interdisciplinary approaches to the resolution of social problems are increasingly common. It is also true that the geographer, the anthropologist, the economist, and the historian, for example, can each claim his subject as the ideal base for social education. In the years immediately ahead, one great challenge in the lower schools will be the bringing of the social studies into line with the new departures and discoveries of the social sciences. Much more research, however, is needed before we can be certain as to the best base and the most appropriate scope and sequence of social learnings. Until then, every specialist is obliged to be a generalist. Academic borders seldom exist in the world of interaction outside the school. It was Lancelot Hogben who explained so fittingly that the boundaries of his province are the last thing the scientist discovers, and that when he has discovered them, he has set the limit to further progress!

The articles which follow discuss in varying but related degree the nature of the social studies and the social sciences. Can you differentiate between the two? In what ways are they related?

JOHN DEWEY

*John Dewey wrote this late in his career, after he had become
Emeritus Professor at Teachers College, Columbia University.*

1. What Is Social Study?*

In the new proper emphasis upon social studies, the primary problem,
it seems to me, is to determine the scope and range of the subject-matter
designated by "social." More definitely, the question is: how far that which
is social can be separated and treated by itself, and how far the social is a
limiting function of the subject-matter of all studies—what philosophers
might call a category by which all materials of learning are to be interpreted. This is of course a restricted sense in which it is correct enough to
isolate social materials. Questions of family life, of politics and economics,
of war and peace, are obviously social questions. The problem I am raising
is how far such materials can be understood and be educative in the full
sense without a background of study of matters which lie outside of the
social as thus limited.

No one would deny, I suppose, that many political questions at the
present time have economic roots. Issues of the relation of capital and
labor, of concentration and distribution of wealth, of economic security and
unemployment, occupy the attention of our legislative bodies. They are
primarily economic questions but they find their way into political action
because their impact upon human relations and their public consequences
are intense and widespread. Can the student stop when he has traced these
political themes to their economic sources? Or does understanding of the
economic situation demand going further?

It would probably be admitted on all hands that the present economic
situation is a historical development, and that while present facts may be
amassed in quantities, the information thus gained needs to be placed in an
historic setting if it is to be intelligently grasped and used. Many, perhaps
all, of the economic questions have also definitely geographical aspects.
The problem of the farmer comes to mind, for example, and that of the
railways as means of distribution of products. So does that of soil conservation and reforestation. The question of the distribution of population,
of congestion in industrial and commercial centers, is another aspect of the
same general question. Careful studies show that in recent years there have
been a number of great regional migrations which have left certain large
regions in a state of relative desolation while the burdens of relief, hos-
pitalization, etc., have been greatly increased in the areas to which they

Progressive Education, XV: 367–69, May 1938. Used by permission.

have gone. That miners live and work where there are mines and lumbermen work where there are still forests, as well as that farmers live on farms, and that certain centers are what they are because of facilities of transportation and need for reshipment of products, are obvious facts. But they raise the question how far are social studies to be conducted in the light of fundamental geographic and physiographic knowledge?

The reference that was made in an earlier paragraph to the historic context of economic questions suggests in turn the scientific background. The industrial and commercial change which has taken place in the world in the last century, in the past forty years, is the product of the great change which has taken place in physical, chemical and, more recently, biological science. The prime factor in the economic and political history of this period is what is known as the industrial revolution. The story of that revolution is the story of new technologies in the production and distribution of goods, which are themselves the result of a scientific revolution. Any vital comprehension of existing economic and political issues demands insight into processes and operations that can be grasped only through understanding of fundamental physical and chemical operations and laws. I will not press the point further, though it might be extended into the subjects of literature, the fine arts and mathematics. The obvious objection that may be made to what has been said is that if it is accepted it swells the social studies beyond all limits; that they have so many ramifications and absorb so much of other studies that teacher and student alike are confronted with an unwieldy, unmanageable mass. The objection, when it is analyzed, brings us to the other aspect of the educational question.

When I asked how far the social is from an educational point of view the limiting function of all the studies, the question I had in mind was whether such subjects as, for example, the history, geography and natural science already mentioned can be isolated, so as to be treated as independent subjects; or whether from the beginning and constantly they should be treated in their social bearings and consequences—consequences in the way, on one side, of problems and on the other side of opportunities. The human and cultural is after all the embracing limit to which all other things tend. In the higher reaches of school education there must, of course, be provision for training of experts and specialists. In them, a certain amount of relative separation of subjects from their social context and function is legitimate. But it is a fair question whether society is not suffering even here because the expert specialists have not the educational background which would enable them to view their special skills and knowledge in connection with social conditions, movements and problems.

But the particular point I would make is that in any case we have carried the isolation of subjects from their social effects and possibilities too far down the educational scale. From the psychological and moral standpoint it may be urged that for most boys and girls the material of studies loses vitality, becomes relatively dead, because it is separated from situations, and that much of the need which is felt at the present time for resorting to extraneous devices to make subjects interesting or else to coerce attention is a necessary effect of this isolation. Natural docility leads to acceptance. But underneath, there is the subconscious questioning, "What does all this mean? What is it for? What do the studies signify outside of the schoolroom or do they only belong there?"

The problem of congestion of studies and this version of aims with resulting superficiality is a pressing one today. The progressive and the reactionary agree in this one thing on the negative side. Both insist that there is lack of unity of aim, that there is dispersion and confusion. As far as I can see, the one hope of obtaining the desired unification is that which has been suggested. The natural focus, the assembling point, of the various studies is their social origin and function. Any other scheme of unification and correlation seems to me artificial and doomed to only transitory success. Progressive education has reached a point where it is looking for a lead which will give coherence and direction to its efforts. I believe it will find it here and that in the end emphasis upon social studies as a separate line of study may only add to the confusion and dispersion that now exist! Not because they are not important, but precisely because they are so important that they should give direction and organization to all branches of study.

In conclusion, I want to say that in my judgment what has been said has a definite bearing upon what is called indoctrination, or, if one prefer, teaching, with respect to preparation for a different social order. Social studies as an isolated affair are likely to become either accumulations of bodies of special factual information or, in the hands of zealous teachers, to be organs of indoctrination in the sense of propaganda for a special social end, accepted enthusiastically, perhaps, but still dogmatically. Young people who have been trained in all subjects to look for social bearings will also be educated to see the causes of present evils. They will be equipped from the sheer force of what they have learned to see new possibilities and the means of actualizing them. They will be indoctrinated in its deeper sense without having had doctrines forced upon them.

EARL S. JOHNSON

Visiting Professor of Education and Social and Philosophical
Foundations, University of Wisconsin, Milwaukee

2. *The Social Studies versus the Social Sciences**

That an issue has arisen in the teaching of social knowledge in the secondary school which provokes an alternative as drastic as that stated in the title of this paper is, if taken literally, a symptom of deep intellectual confusion.

It is, in my view, a sad and tragic augury that we are now told by some that we must choose between the parent social science disciplines and the social studies. Such an "either-or" I categorically reject.

Let it be noted, however, that because I am against a return to the classic disciplines, now to be named high-school subjects and taught as such, I do not indorse a good deal of what now goes on under the aegis of the social studies. That term, as well as not a little teacher performance under it, has, not without considerable justification, been said to be "vague, murky, and too all-inclusive."

What the author of that indictment meant, in fine, I am not certain, but agreement, in whole or in part, with such a characterization does not, in my judgment, warrant the substitution of the separate and separated disciplines for the social studies. I look upon such a recommendation as a pedagogical *non sequitur*. A more sensible and more defensible alternative would be to cure the social studies of their vagueness, murkiness, and too all-inclusiveness, if on examination it may be established that they really are beset by these ills.

The invitation to return to the parent disciplines does, however, intrigue me. It reminds me of the quality of arguments posed by Hillaire Belloc in his *The Crisis in Civilization* which he would resolve by a return to the Middle Ages. Belloc's book bespeaks a nostalgia for some form of "the good old days"—as does the invitation to return to the classic disciplines.

I might be willing to return to the disciplines if that were either possible or profitable. But the world in which the parent disciplines would be either possible or profitable as high-school subjects, and taught as such, we have not had for a very long time in this Republic: certainly not since

**School Review*, 71:389–403, Winter 1963. Used by permission.

the days of Andrew Jackson. Thomas Wolfe was right: "you can't go home again," for home is not what it was and we are not what we were.

But let me say what the two immediate origins of my present concern with the social studies are. The first I view, in part, with alarm, surprise, and dismay. It is Professor Charles Keller's article in the *Saturday Review* for September 16, 1961: "Needed—a Revolution in the Social Studies." The second is the volume, *The Social Studies and the Social Sciences*, done by an able and perceptive team of social science scholars under the joint auspices of the American Council of Learned Societies and the National Council for the Social Studies, and published in 1962 by Harcourt, Brace and World.

I find myself in hearty agreement with a great deal of Keller's diagnosis. It is with that part of his prognosis which I infer as the abandonment of the social studies in favor of a return to the disciplines with which I totally disagree. It is, in my view, a substitution of elegance for usefulness. The language on which I base my inference is this: "History and the social sciences are subjects with disciplines. . . . Subjects as such have disciplines that will help to develop students' minds . . . the study of history and the social sciences should begin in the fifth grade when they can be subjects with disciplines."

I should be ever so happy to learn that I had misread Keller, but in any case I do not wish to make a whipping boy of him. I find in his position, and *in his language*, a pathetic misunderstanding (or is it an *un-understanding*?) of the social world in which high-schoool students live and in certain pedagogical principles which permit teachers to deal, realistically, with that world.

The volume, *The Social Studies and the Social Sciences,* has put me deeply in debt to scholars who have refreshed my mind about the structure, substance, and methods of the several social science disciplines and made clear the bearing of their comprehensive and critical elaborations on the aims which we either have or ought to have served in our teaching of the social studies.

I find in this book a reasoned and temperate invitation for us to reflect on the need for revision, not the abandonment, of the social studies. Such upgrading or revision ought to be approached, as both Bernard Berelson in the "Introduction" and Lewis Paul Todd in the "Afterword" make clear, from the perspective of what aims we wish to achieve and what changes in the present organization and practice of the social studies would appear to be most appropriate to these aims.

I now intend, as you have already surmised, to bring under quite rigorous criticism the proposal that we abandon the social studies in favor of a return to the traditional disciplines. In this endeavor I swear an oath of good will whether or not, to anyone's satisfaction or dissatisfaction, I score a hit, a near-miss, or only waste my powder and shot and your time.

The issue is clear: It is the nature of a general education appropriate to the abilities of young people in the high school. The role of social knowledge in such an education at that level is to make its unique contribution to students becoming cultured persons. This requires their sensitive appreciation of the great adventure in which they live and will live and of which they are a part, their becoming knowledgeable about it and skilful in it, dedicated to it, and concerned to discover how they may make their own best contribution to it and, in doing so, come to the fullest and richest development of their intellectual and spiritual potentials which that dimension of experience allows. If you ask me to specify the chief aim which social knowledge should engender, I would answer: improvement in judgment about values.

To achieve such a generalized aim, with the many more definitive and operational aims in terms of which it might be realized, the traditional disciplines are inappropriate. They are inappropriate because they do not and cannot, taken singly or in any sequence, speak to or "fit" the student's "life-space" or "area of experience"—these, obviously, plural in number. These are situations of choice and personal judgment and all the phases of individual and collective life viewed from the perspectives of the related social processes about which Leon C. Marshall writes.[1]

It is in and by such thought-and-action configurations as these that high-school students and, for that matter, all of us live. We do not live either in or by the configurations or structures which, respectively, inclose the areas of the classic social science disciplines.

In this view, it is my position that none of the disciplines taken singly "give the student his world." Correlatively, none of the disciplines taken *seriatim* are adequate means to such an end. To suppose that an effective synthesis of the data and methods of the several disciplines might thus be brought about, with the result that operational meaning and significance would be given to students in such contexts, strikes me as fanciful as the view that history, conceived as "one damned fact after another," would give them a sense of the ethos or *Zeitgeist* of an historical epoch.

My argument thus far may be summarized in the comment that the experiences of human beings do not come wrapped in six or more packages, each bearing the label of, or containing only the substantive data of, one of the social science disciplines. Nor, to change the figure, can the meaning and significance of human life be known by experiences being submitted to a sum of analyses under any number of disciplines undertaking the task in sequence. When such a "sum of" or "in sequence" approach is espoused

[1]Leon C. Marshall and Rachael Goetz, *Curriculum Making in the Social Studies: The Social Process Approach* (New York: Charles Scribner's Sons, 1936).

it is, I am quite sure, premised on the view that the student is able to take appropriate data from each of the disciplines as they pass in review and pattern them into operationally useful knowledge, germane to his "life-space" or "area of experience" as I have used those terms. There is little evidence that any but the most exceptionally brilliant students can effect such patterns of knowledge. It is for this reason that the teacher of the social studies is obligated to teach these patterns. Over forty years of teaching and working with young people in high school, college, and the graduate school convinces me of the wisdom of this view.

The position which I take in this matter traces to the abstract, partial, and fictional nature of the classic disciplines. That they differ among themselves in these respects is readily admitted. Economics is the most abstract, partial, and fictional, and probably sociology, at least as I conceive it, the least so. Geography would, in my view, fall into a class much less abstract and fictional (all disciplines are, in varying degrees, partial) and thus occupy a quite marginal place in the family of such disciplines. History falls completely outside the terms of reference which I am now using and enters, in no way, into the account I am now rendering. It constitutes a somewhat special case but can, in my judgment, be subject to the criteria on which I am insisting for the three disciplines which are my central concern, namely, economics, political science, and sociology, that is, the "policy sciences."

I am now obligated to say why I use the terms "life-space" and "area of experience" as my major datum and bench marks in the theory which I am sharing with you. I owe my use of, and my affinity for, these terms to Kurt Lewin and John Dewey, although I do not recall that Dewey ever used the latter term verbatim. (Lewin's use of the term "life-space" may be found in his *Resolving Social Conflicts*.) In *The Child and the Curriculum* Dewey remarks on the "need of restating into experience the subject-matter of the studies, or branches of learning." "It must," he writes, "be referred to the experience from which it has been abstracted. It needs to be psychologized, turned over, translated into the immediate and individual experiencing within which it had its origin and significance."[2] To this I add a brief extract from Dewey's *Democracy and Education*: "in the degree in which what is communicated cannot be organized into the existing experience of the learner, it becomes *mere* words . . . lacking in meaning."[3] It is my wont to insist that knowledge must be not only transmitted but also transmuted. This concern I find explicit in both of Dewey's observations.

To these remarks of Dewey I wish to add what I suppose might be

---

[2]John Dewey, *The Child and the Curriculum* (Chicago: University of Chicago Press, 1956), p. 22.

[3]John Dewey, *Democracy and Education* (New York: Macmillan Co., 1916), p. 221.

called one of George Herbert Mead's most profound aphorisms, namely, that "thinking is not a field or realm which can be taken outside of its possible social uses." When, as Mead's student thirty-seven years ago, I heard him say this, I did not understand what he meant. Now that I have "had an experience"—indeed hundreds of experiences as a teacher—I understand.

But enough of theory; now to its practice. I now share with you my image of two teaching (really, teaching-learning) enterprises which will illustrate what I mean by my terms, "life-space" and "area of experience." The first is proposed for the freshman year; the second for the senior year.

Although titles are not very important, I have called the freshman course (designed for two semesters), "The Family and the Community." This is hardly an exciting title—even perhaps a trifle dull. But it covers two areas of experience with which I am concerned and in which ninth-graders are caught up and about which they are, many at least, mixed up.

The course takes its content, organization, and focus from the socio-psychological characteristics and status of high-school freshmen whose ages usually range from thirteen to fourteen—the first two years of the "teens." These two, and the early following years, are marked by emotional stress and strain, and the indecision and confusion which attend the early growing away from parental and familial controls. In these years boys and girls find themselves in a more or less rebellious state of mind toward their parents, as well as toward most rules except those of their own making.

This age group may be characterized as "transitional" or "marginal." Its members are in the process of seeking emancipation from parental controls, but they are not yet "at home" in the social world outside those controls. They have, to a greater or lesser degree, begun to reject parental controls but have not yet been *accepted by nor accepted* the control systems which are non-familial. (In a good many ways the non-familial world of control systems is not organized to either understand or help them make the transition.) Their acceptance *by* or *of* this new world of social rights and obligations will, of course, come about slowly in the process of their growing both up and out, that is, biologically and sociologically.

Hence the course is designed to give understanding of, and insight into, this transitional phase of growing up and out. It is rationalized in terms of the observation of the great Danish educator, churchman, and statesman, Bishop Gruntwig: "the only thing which can save this generation is the spectacle of its own condition." Thus the course would rest its case on understanding and insight, not on moral injunctions. It is the latter from which boys and girls of this age group are seeking emancipation. What they want and need is light on their status—their "own condition." From this will come the appropriate moral insights. If not, the school can do little to help them.

The transitional experience in which this age group is caught up lies between two poles, each of which symbolizes an idealized social situation—"ideal types," we call them. These poles may be designated as *family* and *public*.[4] To the ideal-type situation named *family* the following characteristics are assigned: status given, judgments accepted, intimate personal relations, and self-organization unconsciously achieved. To the ideal-type situation named *public* these characteristics are assigned: status earned, judgments self-made, impersonal relations, and self-organization consciously achieved.

The ultimate focus and purpose of this course would be to clarify the processes and problems associated with students' transitions between these poles. The difficult part of the teacher's task would be to insure, as far as possible, that the students' sense of continuity with their familial world is maintained while, paradoxically, this same continuity is challenged, if not "broken" in many ways. Thus both continuity and discontinuity of students' self-conceptions, even their characters, are involved in the growing-*up* and growing-*out* experience which this enterprise is designed to analyze and clarify.

Helpful perspectives and insights on such a transition experience may be gained through cross-cultural and intercultural studies of two kinds. First, anthropological materials would provide an account of how this transition experience is met within primitive cultures. Such materials would treat with age and maturity groups and their corresponding statuses and roles. The strategy involved and intended would be that of an indirect and round-about approach to the situation which this age group faces in *its* culture. It is hoped that the students might thus come to see themselves in the mirror of a similar age group but in a simpler culture. Of special importance would be the study of *rites de passage*, the ceremonial observances at phases or "passages" from pre-teen to teen and post-teen years. Thus they might come to see the significance of such experiences as christening, confirmation, the taking of pledges or oaths of various kinds, "the first long pants," the first date, and the like. Second, historical materials would provide interesting accounts of the relations of parents and children in the American family at the turn of the century. Such materials would, one might hope, shed light on significant changes in the organization of family life, parent and child roles and statuses, the relation of the father's occupation to home life, the amount, kind, and ways of spending leisure time, that is, *en famille* or by age and sex groupings, and similar matters.

The focus of attention in these contrasting cultural settings would be the study of the relation between one's culture and the discipline, definition, and direction of native impulses—call it "original human nature."

[4]See my *Theory and Practice of the Social Studies* (New York: Macmillan Co., 1956) for a discussion of these terms.

The nature of this relation might be even further clarified by comparing insect and human communities. Here the focus would fall on the difference between social organization based entirely on instinctive and hereditary factors and that based on these greatly modified by cultural factors.

Studies such as these would preface intensive and extensive studies of the modern family. These studies would be more difficult and more controversial. No longer would the objectivity associated with the exotic-primitive and historical approaches be possible. But, if this age group is to understand its position vis-à-vis its own family life, such studies ought not to be foregone. They might well include a variety of types, for the American family is no cultural monolith. Among them are the following: the suburban family, the rural family, the slum family, and perhaps a typical southern-rural Negro family. It is anticipated that such studies would challenge the naïvete or smugness which often characterizes the attitudes of this age group.

Studies of the contemporary family would lead to inquiries into the nature of the relations which obtain now—and in the historical period just studied—between the family and the state which is the most formal and legal manifestation of "the public." Here the context would be provided by the difference between sentimental-kinship (*Gemeinschaft*) and utilitarian-territorial (*Gesellschaft*) types of social organization. This age group has just begun the transition from sentimental-kinship to utilitarian-territorial social contexts and types of social controls and is deeply involved in the difficulties of this transition. In them, as I have observed, it is caught up, and mixed up! (Needless to say that here, as well as in my remarks on the course for the senior year, I am using a kind and level of discourse which is designed for sophisticated readers, not for ninth- and twelfth-grade students. At those grade levels the language, like the subject matter, would have to make sense in the "life-space" or "area of experience" of the students.)

Such a polar and transitional view of the experiences of this age group would permit, even require, consideration of such concepts as these: love and justice, custom and law, status and contract, freedom and restraint, and private and public. Each pair would, obviously, require elaboration in terms and at the levels which would make sense to the students. Thus, in Dewey's terminology, their meaning would have to be "*psychologized*, turned over, translated into the immediate and individual experiencing within which [they] had their origin and significance."[5]

Thus *family* and *public* would become related in ways useful to those whose present life course newly and strangely runs between these poles. Correlative to the study of such pairs of concepts (and social situations)

[5]*The Child and the Curriculum* p. 22.

would go the study of situations and events which would permit practical understanding of such terms as leadership, policy, compromise, loyalty, propaganda, judgment, authority, and rights and obligations.

To the degree that the prosecution of such studies would involve acquaintance with the formal aspects of government, the study of its structures would always take second place to the study of its functions. Indeed these would be related as means to ends. "In the large," such structures and functions would be viewed as public rather than private agencies for social control. "Government," in all instances and perspectives, would be interpreted as "what some given policy-and-control-making and power-wielding group *does*, upon what *authority*, to what *welfare ends*, and subject to what kinds of *review* and popular *control*."

Among the specific aims of such an enterprise, the following may be named: to reveal to this age group some of the representative schemes of organization of the control patterns and processes in the non-familial world and how these affect the rights and obligations of all concerned; to show the inappropriateness and ineffectiveness of attempting to deal with secondary-group (i.e., public) situations with primary-group (i.e., familial) means and attitudes; to provide a view of "government" in wider and more useful ways than the typical "civics" book permits, that is, in its all too frequent legal-formal and constitutional approach; to reveal the difference between love as a motivating principle and justice as an organizing and power principle, as well as their appositive rather than opposite bearing on each other; to show that new and more "public" situations require new and different but no less demanding concepts of loyalty and dedication than those required in old and more "private" situations; to reveal that restraints may both increase and decrease freedom depending on their use; to show that the growth of the functions of the state is to be justified in terms of the greater security and dignity of persons and the community at large but only when such uses or ends can be shown actually to be their aim and consequence; and, in the service of such objectives as I have noted, to exploit to their maximum usefulness to the present experiences, individual and collective, of all those who "belong" to this age group.

A distinction which is implicit in the foregoing needs now to be made explicit. I speak of the difference between *method* and *technique* in teaching. By *method* I mean the teacher's scholarly knowledge, insight into its significance for those being taught, and skill in the means of critical inquiry. By *technique* I mean what the teacher does in order to adapt such scholarly knowledge, insight and skill to the subject matter so that those being taught will grow in knowledge, insight, and skill.

Now, a brief description of a course for the senior year. It is also conceived of as a two-semester enterprise; its title, "Social Knowledge and Social Policy."

It would seek to give students an understanding of the fact that social problems have their origin in conflicts in values. It would, perhaps, be intellectually the most rigorous and ethically the most penetrating course in the social studies curriculum. For this reason it is scheduled for the year by which students may be presumed to be ready for a learning experience of such a nature and be not too greatly upset by it.

It would seek to shed light on the nature of both private and public values and value systems, and the use and limitations of the tools of scientific inquiry in resolving value conflicts. The course content would consist of a selected few of the major problems of social policy which the Western world faces and will, in the foreseeable future, continue to face. It would seek, then, to deal with the present and the "shape of the future" rather than with what someone has called "disappearing difficulties."

Although some freedom might be given students to nominate the problems to be studied, the method of their analysis would permit no options. The range of problems should permit a sampling suggested in such as these: population and natural resources, the integrity of the family, unemployment (especially as it traces to technological factors), civil liberty, mental health, and peace.

The course would find its major context in the dual mores of our civilization: the *organizational* mores which the prevailing institutional apparatus and its values represent, and the *humanitarian* mores which are dedicated to bring about those changes in the organizational mores which would narrow the gap between our declared values and the service, both individual and institutional, which we render them.

Students would learn the nature of and the difference between three kinds of problems: (1) problems of effective means or problems of technology; (2) problems of knowledge or the relation between variables; and (3) problems of social policy, that is, the issue of what ought to be done.

The course would seek to make clear the difference between humanistic "oughts" and the facts of social reality as reliable knowledge, provided by the social science disciplines, reveals that difference. It would likewise seek to clarify the role of both persons and institutions in the onset, effects, and resolution of social problems and seek to make clear the pervasive nature of the "value problem," namely, the problem of discriminating between alternative value choices. In such a context it would undertake to expose the major fallacies entertained and practiced by those who hold to simple "answers" respecting both the cause and the resolution of social problems.

So conceived, the course would try to engender an abiding interest in social problem analysis; develop that unique balance between zeal, skill, dedication, and patience necessary for penetrating problem study and related social action; and develop critical awareness of society's need for more dedicated and knowledgeable persons, and more effective social institutions.

In such patterns as I have proposed, the course would draw upon and draw together materials and methods from the major social science disciplines. Thus social studies rather than the social disciplines would be shaped and taught. Students would be exposed to, and required to think with, the concepts primarily of economics, political science, and sociology and how these concepts complement one another in social inquiry.

The division of labor among these three disciplines would correspond to the distinctive tasks to which they address themselves: for economic analysis the relation of scarce means to unlimited wants or desires; for political analysis the problem of consensus, the process of achieving it and making it effective; and for sociological analysis the problem of elaborating the institutional forms as means through which past and present move to future in the lifetime of a society. Thus, the unity as well as the division of labor of the scholarly social disciplines would, I hope, be brought to student awareness and understanding.

An abundance of textual and fugitive materials is available for such an enterprise. But, because of the contemporary focus of the inquiries which would be advanced, firsthand experience in the community would be maximized.

Let me now submit for your reflective criticism the following commentary on the image of some social studies which I have sought to share with you. I have been careful not to confuse the scholar's form or structure of knowledge with the substance and method abstracted from it for the purposes in mind. In doing this I do not understand that I have depended any less on intellectually firm and reliable sources, even though I have not counseled that the "received" and classic disciplines be taught as such. I have sought to make values and their study integral parts of the enterprises and hence have not needed to devise some pedagogical *deus ex machina* to bring them on stage. I have, throughout, sought to "speak to the students' condition" by drawing on, and drawing together, the most reliable knowledge and skills available.

Whatever be the limitations of the theory and practice which I have shared with you, it represents a venture in general education, the road to which is synthesis. I wish now to share with you the most perceptive and boldest statement about synthesis which I know. I give you, too precious to be spoiled by my paraphrase, the language of Hoyt Hudson, late professor of humane letters at Stanford University:

> The synthesizer lays himself open to attack from every quarter and by a variety of weapons. The specialist is safer, for he can be attacked only at a single point and by one sort of weapon. What the specialized

critic overlooks is that his very safety is dangerous, so far as it depends on isolation, and that the synthetic thinker runs his hazards (of superficiality, of confusion, of categories, of false analogy) in the interest of a high cause—namely, the relief of man's estate. . . . It is surely not exorbitant to suggest that one goal—perhaps the highest—of any specialized group of thinkers should be the discovery of ideas and principles which may be added to man's common stock, with applications that transcend the field of their discovery. Hence, I am inclined to say, at the risk of sounding unscholarly, that a serious attempt to find effective relations among fields of study and knowledge is more praiseworthy than a denial, whether explicit in a statement or implicit in practice, that such relations exist. . . . No specialized mode of knowing, any mode short of the most full and most complete understanding possible, can be considered adequate—adequate either to the mind of man or to the problems of his life on earth.[6]

A test of synthesis has been proposed by Gordon B. Turner in his Foreword to *The Social Studies and the Social Sciences*. He asks, "Can the social studies program be designed simultaneously to provide knowledge about man and society and to make students aware of the general concepts and unity of social science?" I am sure such a program can and ask that my two-course patterns be tested by those very criteria.

[6]*Educating Liberally* (Stanford, Calif.: Stanford University Press, 1945), pp. 42–43.

ROBERT REDFIELD

*The late Robert Redfield was a Professor of Anthropology at the
University of Chicago*

3. The Social Uses of Social Science*

The subject of my remarks ... might be expressed as a question for
which three different forms of words suggest themselves: What beneficial
functions may social science hope to perform in our society? What is the
task of social science? Why have a social science?

Institutions are good not only for what they are but also by reason of
what we strive to make them. I think, then, not only of what social science
is, but also of what it might be. I think of social science as one of many
institutions that contribute toward the making of the life we want and that
could do it better than they do. I would review the functions and the goals
of social science as I would review the functions and goals of medicine, the
fine arts, or the press.

The social uses of medicine are to reduce human suffering and to prolong life; this is well understood, and it is clear that to great degree medicine performs these functions. The social uses of the press are to tell people,
truthfully and comprehensively, what happens around them, to provide
forums for public discussion, and to reflect and clarify the ideals of our
society. It is more or less well known that this is what our press is expected
to do, whether or not it does it as well as it should. But the social uses of
social science are not, I think, so generally recognized. People do not
know, at once, why there should be social science or even what social
science, ... to make clear its nature and its usefulness.

It will not be necessary for me to say much about the nature of social
science. It is a group of disciplines that provide descriptions of human
nature, human activity and human institutions. These disciplines are scientific, first in that they are concerned with telling us What Is, not What
Ought to Be; and second, in that they exercise objectivity, pursue special
knowledge and move toward systematic formulation of this knowledge. So
they strive for descriptions that are more illuminating, valid and comprehensive than are the corresponding descriptions of common sense.

You will readily understand that I have in mind the social sciences that
one meets in the catalogues of graduate schools and in the membership of
the Social Science Research Council. Just which of them are to be included

*University of Colorado Bulletin, May 24, 1947. Used by permission.

in any roster of the social sciences does not concern us here; the existing division of labor as among the special social sciences is not wholly defensible and may not endure. I am not thinking of ethics, which is the criticism and organization of principles of right conduct. I am not thinking of the social arts and professions, such as law or social service administration, which are ways of acting on people to get certain results. I am thinking of the application of the scientific spirit toward the description and explanation of man in society. I am asking how its application there serves the common good.

A further limitation of my subject is required. History is not in my mind today. The social uses of history have a special and important character which I shall not discuss. History, being a content of preserved and considered experience, has those social uses which memory and tradition have. From history, as from memory, we expect "a knowledge of our own identities," "orientation in our environment, a knowledge of its usual uniformities, including . . . some knowledge of the characters with whom we must deal, their strengths and weaknesses, and what they are likely to do under given circumstances." Further, " . . . we all hope to draw from past experience help in choosing successfully between the alternatives offered by present events." These social uses of history have been recently summarized by Garrett Mattingly,[1] from whom I quote these phrases. Today I am thinking of that social science which is analytical rather than historical, which seeks to understand a social problem or which describes the general characteristics of some class of social phenomena. How does such social science serve the common good?

The familiar answer is that social science tells us how to do what we want to do. The reply is that the understanding that social science gives can be applied to the purposes of society. The descriptions of social science lead to more effective practical action than would be possible without social science. Social science, is, from this point of view, like physics or biology. Just as those sciences reach understanding and explanation of the physical and the organic worlds which lead to practical applications in engineering and in medicine, so social science reaches understanding of man in society which leads to practical applications in social action.

Surely it is true that social science does this. It does tell us how to do what we want to do. It tells us some things that common sense does not tell us or does not tell us nearly so well about how to select people to pilot airplanes or to perform other special tasks, how to predict the consequences of a given tax policy, or how quickly to discover fluctuations in the opinions of over a hundred million people on current issues. The competence of social science to guide useful social action has grown greatly in a few

---

[1]"A Sample Discipline—The Teaching of History" (address delivered at the Princeton University Bicentennial Conference, February 20, 1947).

years. The contributions of social science to the national effort at the time of World War I were almost limited to certain studies of prices, to the work of historians in war information, and to developments in mental testing. The contributions of social science in connection with World War II were so numerous and varied that a mere list of them would fill many pages. In the army and in the navy, and in scores of civilian agencies, social scientists were employed for the reason that their efforts as social scientists were recognized as helping to win the war or the peace. This direct service to the community, through the application of their special knowledge, continues in the efforts of social scientists after the war. Of the many fields of research which have already found practical justification I mention three: the understanding of problems of morale and of human relations in industry; the prediction of human behavior in regard to the stability of marriage, criminal recidivism, and certain other kinds of behavior where dependable prediction is useful; and the analysis and control of communication made to mass audiences through print, radio or screen. Social science had indeed so well established its usefulness in certain fields that specialized technicians are recognized in those fields—professional appliers of social science knowledge. I mention clinical psychiatrists and city planners.

The question I asked appears at once to be answered. Why have a social science? Have it because it is useful. Have a social science because it gets things done that society wants done. According to this answer social science has the same nature and the same justification that physics and chemistry have. It is supported by society as physics and chemistry are supported by society: because what is learned can be directly applied to the service of mankind. Society less and less can take care of itself; more and more is it true that conscious decisions are required in the management of human affairs, and social science provides guidance in the making of these decisions, just as biological science provides guidance for decisions as to health and hygiene. This is the simple answer that is often made.

I will state my own position at once. I think that this is a true answer but that it is far from a complete answer. I think social science is notably different from physics and chemistry, and that its social uses are not exhausted when one has recognized the practical applications of social science. I think that social science has other important social uses in the testing and in the development of social values.

What has social science to do with the proving and making of values? What is its role in regard not merely to the valuation of a means to reach an end sought, but also to the more ultimate values of society?

The plainest values with which social science is concerned are those necessary to science: objectivity, honesty, accuracy and humility before the facts. To the preservation and cultivation of these the social sciences are devoted. In the course of carrying out research the social scientists invent and promote means to realize them. In doing so the social scientist shares with the physicist and the biologist the effort to maintain and extend the common morality of the scientific mind. It is, moreover, a morality quite consistent with the morality which the citizen who is not a scientist, may embrace. Honesty, accuracy, humility before the facts, and faith in the power of truth to prevail in Milton's free encounter are virtues in their own right. Science is one of the institutions that contribute to the cultivation of these virtues.

In the work of cultivation of these values the position of social science is critical because it is by no means sure that even our free and liberal society will allow the extension of the scientific spirit to the study of social problems. Many people do not understand that it is useful to society to extend it there. While the usefulness of physics and biology is generally acknowledged, the scientific study of many social problems is popularly regarded as either futile or dangerous. This is because many of the subjects studied by the social sciences are protected from rational examination, for the general population, by tradition, sentiment and inviolable attitude.

In short, the subject matter of social science is not morally indifferent. It is morally significant. The social scientist himself, and his neighbors and fellow citizens, are also concerned with that subject matter. They have convictions, prejudices, sentiments and judgments about the tariff, party politics, relation between the sexes, and race relations. All of these things the social scientist studies, and what he has to say about them in the course of his trying to improve our understanding of them encounters these convictions, prejudices, sentiments and judgments. They are all "tender" subjects. People feel a sense of distress if their convictions or assumptions on these matters are challenged or controverted. Often they are distressed at the mere looking at these subjects objectively. Some social scientists study such subjects as the relations between husband and wife or the attitudes people have toward racial or religious minorities or the profit motive in economic activity. It makes some people uncomfortable to hear that these subjects are being studied with critical impersonality. The social scientist is then resented or distrusted. If, furthermore, his descriptions or conclusions appear inconsistent with the more sacred values of the community, a cry may go up that the social scientist be restrained or that his publication be suppressed or that he lose his job.

Therefore social science is the test case of the vitality of those ideals I have mentioned which are common to all science and which play so large a part in the freedom of the modern mind. The scientists as a whole understand this. In discussions which are now going on as to the drafting of a bill for a national science foundation, it appears that almost all the scientists, natural scientists as well as social scientists, think that if government money is to be provided for the support of science, social science should be included. On the other hand, with similar unanimity the scientist understands that Congressmen are much less likely to provide such support for social science than for natural science. The scientists see that science is one way of looking at the world around us, a way applicable to men and society as it is applicable to molecules and cells. They feel this common morality of the scientific mind, and respect the usefulness of social science in not only making useful social inventions but also in developing this morality throughout society. But they also know that people who are not scientists do not see it that way, and imagine social science to be political propaganda or doctrine, or speculative futility. These scientists perhaps realize what I believe to be true: that that freedom of the mind to enquire, propose, test and create which is so central and precious a part of the more ultimate values of our manner of life may, in a military or reactionary trend of events, be first tested and won or lost in our country in the freedom of social science.

In effect social science is a new instrument, not only for the getting of certain specific things done in the management of society, but for the clarification and development of our more ultimate values. The social uses of social science are not exhausted when we have said that social science can improve the efficiency of industrial production or test the aptitudes of young people for one kind of occupation rather than another. Social science is one of the ways to form our convictions as to the good life. This it does not as preaching does it, by telling us what the good is and what our duty is. It does not do it as ethics does it, by examining central questions as to the nature of conduct and by criticizing and formulating systematic rules of conduct. It does it by remaining science. It does it by making clear to us where our choices lead us and what means must be employed to reach what ends. It does it by extending our understanding of where our ideals are in conflict with each other. And it does this through those intensive studies of particular societies and particular men which are not ordinarily carried on in ethics and which are outside the powers and the responsibilities of the preacher.

An example may make this clear. Recently a study of the Negro in the United States was made by Gunnar Myrdal, a Swedish social scientist. The resulting books are not sermons nor are they analyses of the principles of conduct. They are descriptions of the Negro in American business, government and social life. They are also descriptions of the white man in his positions toward the Negro in American life. These books do not tell us didactically what we ought to do. The propositions that make up the books are Is-propositions not Ought-propositions. Nevertheless the book can hardly be read carefully by anyone without some effect upon the reader's system of values, his conceptions of duty, justice and the good life. The effect is enhanced, in this particular case of social science research, because the authors took for their problem the relation of the Negro's place in our society to the ideals of freedom, liberty and democracy which are genuinely held in our nation. They were interested in finding out what effect, on the white man especially, results from the presence of practices and institutions inconsistent with these ideals. The book does not argue for any norm of conduct. It just tells about norms in relation to customs and institutions But any American reader, at all thoughtful, finds himself understanding better than he did the choices that are open to him: less democracy, liberty and equality, and race relations as they are; or more democracy, liberty and equality, and a change in race relations. Or, as a third possibility, he learns something of the effects on his state of mind if the inconsistency persists. And this increased understanding is a leaven in those workings of the spirit which lead to the remaking of our system of ideals.

I think it is self-delusion for a social scientist to say that what he does has no concern with social values. I think that people are right when they express their feelings that social science does something to the values they hold with regard to such particular institutions as restrictive covenants or the tariff. For one thing social science tests those special values, by showing what they cost. It hears the people say, We want freedom. Social science listens, studies our society and replies, Very well, if you want freedom, this is what you will pay in one kind of freedom for enjoying so much of another. To every partisan the social scientist appears an enemy. The social scientist addresses himself to the question, How much security from idleness and want is compatible with developed capitalism? and equally to the question, How much political and civil freedom is compatible with socialism? To partisans on both sides he appears unsympathetic and dangerous.

For social science, along with other science, philosophy and the general spirit of intellectual liberty, is asserting the more general and comprehensive values of our society against the more limited and special interests and values. It hears society say, We believe in the right of the human mind to examine freely, to criticize openly, to reach conclusions from tested evidence.

Very well, replies social science, if this is your desire then you must endure pain of the examination and the testing of the particular customs and institutions which you hold dear. Social science says to all of us: Except where your special interests are involved, you recognize that mankind has passed the period in which he took his ethical convictions from his grandfathers without doubt and reflection. Now we have to think, investigate and consider about both the means and the ends of life. Social science is that science, which in other fields you so readily admire, directed to human nature and the ways of living of man in society. By your own more general convictions you have authorized and validated its development.

It follows that the successful functioning of social science is peculiarly dependent upon education. The realization of the social uses of social science depends closely upon the dissemination of the findings of social science and of the understanding of the very nature of social science among all the people. So a responsibility falls upon you and me who have thought something of the matter to make social science known to all. It is for us to make it clear to our fellow citizens what social science is and why its development is so needed today.

Social science does not need to be sold to the people. It needs only to be explained. There never was a time when social science was more needed than it is today. The extreme peril in which we live arises from the small political and social wisdom we have in the face of our immensely dangerous material strength. We should have more control over the physical world, yes, surely; but it is far more necessary that we learn to control the relations among men. We know now that we can destroy one another and the fruits of civilization, and we are far from sure that we can prevent ourselves from doing so. If social science could effect an improvement of our chances of preventing it of no more than one percent, a great expenditure in social science would be justified.

In explaining social science it needs to be said that social science is not only a box of tools. It is also a light. The social scientist is not only a sort of plumber to the circulatory and other ills of society; he is also, at his best, a source of understanding and enrichment. It should be pointed out that the test of good social science is not only: Will it work? There is another test: Does it make sense? For social science also justifies itself to the extent to which it makes life comprehensible and significant. That social science, also, has worth which, though it solves no problem of unemployment or of selection of competent administrators, shows men the order and the pattern of their own lives. Good social science provides categories in terms of which we come to understand ourselves. Our buying and selling, our praying, our hopes, prejudices and fears, as well as the institutions which embody all these, turn out, under the light of sound social science to have form, perspective, rule. Shown the general, we are liberated from the tyranny of the particular. I am not merely I; I am an instance of a natural law.

To say this is not to say that social science should be speculative or philosophical. The significant generalization may first appear in a flash of insight. Or illuminating generalizations may be built up out of many detailed observations. Out of the innumerable painstaking studies of particular facts, in biology, anthropology and sociology, emerges now a broad conception of society, inclusive of ants, apes and men, and the notion that the mechanisms of evolution operate through, not merely individuals, but the social groups themselves. This but illustrates the fact that comprehensive general understanding of society is often the work of many men over much time.

So we will praise social science both as a practical servant of mankind, useful as biology and physics are made useful, and also as a handmaiden of the spirit. It has on the other side some of the social uses of the humanities. It makes a knowledge which helps to define the world of human relations in which we live, which makes clear to ourselves our place in a social cosmos. Social science is not essentially a series of inventions to be applied. The inventions come, and they are useful. But primarily social science is a chain of understandings to be communicated.

And we will make it clear that in this work of increasing understanding, there is a moral commitment and a moral purpose. Social science is objective in that it cultivates deliberate consideration of alternative explanations, demands proof, and submits to the conviction which facts compel. But it is not indifferent. It will not tolerate cynicism. It expects responsibility from its followers, responsibility to use special knowledge for the common good and to act on convictions reached by reason and through special knowledge. It demands that the values that are implied in the conduct of its work be declared. It commits itself to the use of man's rational nature and the methods of modern empirical investigation to the service of society. The service is one not only to the strength of the social body. It is also a contribution to its soul. Social science is a proving ground of values. It is a means to wisdom. Let us, who are social scientists, so conduct our work as to make it yield more of the wisdom the world so sorely needs. Let all of us, who know something of social science, explain that this is its purpose, its highest ideal.

SHIRLEY H. ENGLE

Professor of History Education and Associate Dean,
Indiana University

4. World History in the Curriculum*

The concern of world history is all mankind. The scope of world history is man throughout all time, living in a universe the limits of which are even yet unknown, and in a great variety of cultures each the invention of men. The particular contribution of world history lies in the broad view of humanity as a whole which it affords. Among the major concerns of world history are the following: the broad lines along which the development of human society proceeds, the role of both continuity and change in human society, the significances of uniformity and variety among human institutions, the persistent problems faced by all human societies, and the resources for improvement in human affairs. In this connection a persistent defect of the world history course has been its failure to take the broad view. Too frequently the course bogs down in the effort to cover and to remember a great mass of detailed information heedless of the general ideas and broad vistas to be drawn from and tested against such information. Or, in the world history course it may be erroneously assumed that the history of Western civilization is the same as the history of mankind.

The claim for world history is frequently put as being that of giving a world perspective to the way in which we view human affairs. Perspective may be correctly taken to mean the construction in the mind of a kind of total picture, map, model, or comprehensive theory of human society throughout all time, somewhat after the grand manner of a Toynbee, Pareto, Hegel, Spengler, or H. B. Wells. The model may take the form of a series of substantive statements or summary sentences each of which makes a truth claim; that is, asserts that something is the case. Truth claims may be either classifications, testable propositions, or evaluations.

A classification associates a set of relationships or meanings to a key term in our own or another language. Classification is a necessary tool of clear thought and communication. Classificatory terms provide the framework for a model of human behavior. Important classificatory terms include, among others, civilization, progress, freedom, democracy, nationalism, imperialism, capitalism, socialism, constitutionalism, etc. It should be remembered that a classificatory term, while serving as a short

Social Education, XXIX:459–63, November 1965. Used by permission.

cut or convenience in thought and communication, never exhausts all the meanings which may accrue to the set of relationships represented by the term. Definitions are never final, to be settled by reference to a dictionary, but are correctly thought of as dynamic instruments whereby a set of relationships held temporarily to be constant may be probed for deeper meaning. Thus freedom or equality or imperialism may not be defined once and for all, and our notions of what is democracy or civilization may change with experience.

Testable propositions are descriptive or explanatory claims that something is the case in the world in which we live. Such statements are verified by observing the real world or by reading to see what others have observed. A testable proposition may be said to be validated when the claim made is found without exception to fit the reality. The process of testing such a claim is akin to the experiment which a physical scientist carries on in the laboratory, except that in observing human behavior, especially behavior in the past, we are seldom privileged to set up a controlled experiment. Our objective is to arrive at the truth; that is, to get a true picture of how human beings behave and for what causes. Such statements as the following illustrate testable propositions: (1) History demonstates that man may act from moral conviction as well as from material wants and needs. (2) Change has been common to all human societies, but the rate of change has increased markedly in recent years. (3) Both peaceful co-operation and human conflict are part of man's historical experience. (4) Geographic variations explain in part the variations in human societies. (5) The cultures of different societies differ widely but serve comparable functions. (6) The members of a society from time to time invent technical improvements or borrow them from other societies. (7) Technical improvement in a society sets in motion a chain reaction which eventually works to modify all of the institutions of the society. (8) Science and technology have allowed men to control and change their physical environment rather than to adapt to it.

Evaluations are statements which place a relative value, rate, or grade on something. Such statements usually use words such as good, bad, better, worse, ought, should, and must, or words connotating a value rating as beautiful, ugly, moral, immoral, etc. That evaluations constitute an important part of one's image of society is fairly obvious. What is not so obvious is that evaluations may be adjudged true or false providing the criteria to be used in the judgment are agreed upon and providing comparison is made of the criteria to the facts of the case. To say that a thing is good or beautiful is meaningless unless the criteria for goodness or beauty are agreed upon. Once the criteria are accepted, the value of a thing is open to critical apprasial. If it is agreed that optimum freedom for every individual is the criterion, then states rights doctrine can be studied objectively and adjudged critically on the evidence, that is, on the facts of the case.

Out of key statements such as these, a comprehensive and ever-correcting model or picture of human society may be built. The model which emerges can be seen to include both descriptive and evaluative elements, that is, statements of what has been or is the case, statements of what is possible, and statements of what ought to be the case. The model will trace and even forecast lines of possible and desirable development, and it will suggest lines of attack on the persistent problems of society. The model will afford explanations and/or theories of why human beings behave as they do, and therefore it should enable us to predict with a fair degree of accuracy how human beings may be expected to behave in the future under a variety of conditions and circumstances. For example, it may be predicted that people will respond with loyalty to any society which rewards them in just measure for their contribution to the society. In contrast, people will eventually flout the institutions of a society which brings them no personal satisfaction or reward. To the extent that the model encompasses the broad goals of all mankind, we may venture to evaluate the performance of a particular human society, including our own. To the extent that we are able to explain why men behave as they do, our model should enable us to control or work to improve the lot of mankind.

In all these connections it should be recognized that a model may be theoretical, in part or wholly, as well as factual. The physical scientist is well aware that an important way to doscover the truth is to set up a theoretical model, based on an educated guess, and then build an experiment or make observations to verify or correct the theory. Theory building may play quite as useful a role in social science as in chemistry. Classical economic theory may be taken as a prime example of how a carefully spun theory, though factually inadequate in many respects, aided immeasurably in clarifying the real nature of man's economic activity. Toynbee's grand design is by no means totally accepted by historians today, but it has served most usefully to drive the study of history back to basic considerations. Deliberate theory building will work to expand the comprehensiveness and depth of historical study as well as to add the element of romance and adventure to the pursuit of scholarship.

Not to be ignored in this respect is the fact that the student will bring with him to the world history course his own concept (or model) of how human affairs are ordered. While this model may be factually inaccurate and restricted in scope it is nonetheless real to the student, representing for him the level at which he presently understands humanity. The student may have come to believe, human nature being what it is, basically self serving and pugnacious, that the peoples of the world respect only the rule of force, that wars are inevitable and that our first concern must be defense (being able to drop the bomb first). With such a model in mind he has probably decided too on a career in the army (the only safe place). Such a home-grown model is not to be lightly treated or ignored. Rather, a patient effort should be made to bring the student's ideas out into the light of day so that he may correct and expand his model on the basis of the new experience which the world history course affords.

If world perspective is our goal, the search for the broad meaning of factual episodes in history must pervade study continuously from the very beginning. It is not at all likely that perspective will miraculously emerge at the end of a tedious process of memoriter learning, the goal of which is to master the answers to poorly related and only secondarily important questions. Instead, we will need to ask the really important questions, the main questions, at the very outset and repeatedly throughout the study. Illustrative of such questions are the following: (1) What changes has human society undergone in the past, what changes is it presently undergoing, what changes are likely in the future and why? (2) What major variations are distinguishable within and without the main stream of human development and how are these to be explained? (3) What are the goals common to all human societies? (4) In the face of common goals how can we account for and justify the great variety of human institutions? (5) How do the goals of a society relate to the religious, philosophical, scientific, and aesthetic thought in the society? (6) How do different societies relate themselves differently to their physical environment? (7) Who can be rightly called civilized man? (8) By what criteria may we judge the state of excellence of a human society?

Questions like these invite theorizing and speculation and afford the framework on which myriad details may be arranged. It is in the persistent pursuit of these and other such broad questions that the progressive development of a world perspective lies.

WORLD HISTORY AND THE SOCIAL SCIENCES

World history bears a necessary reciprocal relationship to the social sciences. Each feeds upon the other. The contribution of world history lies in the overview of events which it affords and the broad theory which it suggests for explaining and perchance improving society. At the point of action, history represents the need to pull together fragments of information so that thinking and action may proceed in some synthesized and unitary manner.

In a restricted sense, history is concerned merely with remembering (aided by historical research) and recording events sequentially in time. Historical sequences have usually been reported under such general headings as continental, regional, national, period, or cultural history. Until very recent times the state of historical scholarship has been quite as much speculative as scientific, allowing only the more obvious common-sense explanations of events based on the too-naive assumption that all men are rational and logical beings and, further, that the reasons given by men in their public and private utterances were the real reasons behind their behavior.

The perplexing social problems triggered by the industrial revolution and the social, political, and colonial upheavals of the last century or so stretched the credulity of historical explanation to the exhaustion point and social science was born. In contrast to history, but taking its cues from historical narrative, the new social sciences attempt to analyze and describe human cross-sectional interrelationships on other than historical grounds. The search is for patterned relationships internal to the cell, unit, system, group, community, or culture. Such analysis has rapidly advanced our knowledge of human behavior, revealing among other things that basic human psychological needs, social or reference group pressures, and culturally induced and transmitted habits of acting and thinking are important, if not the determinate factors in human behavior. Thus while history is not ruled out as a factor in causation (some events seem almost a matter of chance or accident) it is no longer held to be the sole or even the most important factor. And historians as never before are turning to the behavioral sciences, particularly to anthropology, psychology, and sociology for the conceptual framework in which to interpret and explain human behavior.

Today, fairly sophisticated theoretical models of special aspects of human behavior are provided by the special sciences of social psychology, cultural geography, cultural anthropology, and sociology, as well as by economics and political science. Limited models are of great usefulness in explaining particular aspects of human behavior, but any statement attributed to a limited model is valid only if qualified by the antecedent statement, everything else remaining equal. The synthesis of behaviors in a given complete episode is still ruled by the gross kind of analysis which only the historian and perchance the citizen, in his innocence, will undertake.

Reference to the various social science has reduced considerably the gross error in historical study. Modern historians are not so likely as were their predecessors to allow cause to oversimplify factors like geography or perverse human nature. Particularly useful in this respect has been the contribution of the anthropologist whose theoretical model, "the culture concept," has become the common denominator in the context of which all informed discussion of human behavior now takes place. In short, knowledge of the "cultural model" is now a necessary tool of historical study.

An important question with respect to the place of world history in the curriculum is therefore that of how it is to be related to the social sciences. Three alternatives may be suggested as follows: (1) World history may be made the integrating subject in the curriculum, incorporating into its content appropriate elements of criticism from the social sciences. (2) World history may be supplemented by units in the basic social sciences. And (3) world history may be incorporated into a carefully contrived sequence of social studies experiences extending from grade 1 through 12.

WORLD HISTORY AS THE INTEGRATING SUBJECT

Because of its broad scope, world history is more suited than any present subject to serve the role of integration in the social studies curriculum. However, if world history is to serve this role it would need to be thought of minimally as a two-year course, the content of which would be broadened to include the whole gamut of human activities—scientific, philosophic, religious, and aesthetic quite as much as political and economic. Further, at times, the narrative would need to be slowed down or brought to a complete halt to focus attention exclusively on important human institutions or ideas, and the pace of the whole course would need to be a more deliberate one to allow at times for study in greater depth and for the cultivation of criticism. Possible components of such a course might include the following: (1) A study of the origins of the races of men with possibly some cross reference to an isolated contemporary primitive society; (2) a quick survey of the centers of civilization, somewhat in the Toynbee manner, to get a basic concept of the phenomena of change in human affairs, to provide a broad time frame of reference into which subsequent units of study could be fitted, to get some initial concept of the phenomena of commonality as well as variety in human development, and to face seriously for the first time the question of what is civilization and who are civilized men; (3) the study in some depth of selected peoples of a cultural region, nationality, and imperial complex, raising in each case questions as to common and varied life purposes and goals, economic ideas and practices, family and community life, religious ideas, educational provisions, aesthetic expression, and place in history; (4) the study in some depth of (and an attempt to appraise) major changes, movements, developments, and trends in world society; (5) the identification and critical analysis of persistent high-level problems and ideational conflicts in world society including, among other, problems of continuity and change in human societies, changing human goals and institutional redevelopment, population and food, technological development, war and peace, technological change and moral breakdown, nationality or the rise and decline of nations, the struggle for freedom and individual integrity, coping with cultural and ideational differences, etc.

With imagination and the resolve to cultivate to the utmost the critical capacity, such a course could go far to integrate the social studies curriculum.

SUPPLEMENTARY UNITS IN THE BASIC SOCIAL SCIENCES

As has been indicated earlier, "culture," in the anthropological sense, is coming to be recognized among social scientists as the basic model against which all human behavior may be understood and explained. The people of a single culture are seen as the social unit wherein all human behavior gets its meaning and integrity. The culture sets the conditions under which the individual establishes his individuality. The culture determines the degree of control which the society will exercise over its physical environment. The culture is the mechanism of social continuity; it is also the mechanism of social change. Culture is never completely understood except through the eyes of people who have been nurtured in that culture. Hence historical study is sure to miss the mark unless it is carried on in a full awareness of the fact of "culture," which suggests the appropriateness of appending to the world history courses introductory units in the basic social sciences, particularly units in cultural anthropology, social psychology, and cultural geography.

Thus the comparative study in some depth of two or three contemporary primitive societies, much as the anthropologist would study them, will afford to the student of world history a necessary insight into the nature of a culture and a realization of the real extent of cultural differences. Such an insight is a basic tool in understanding, explaining, or interpreting human behavior in whatever place, time, or circumstance. If time allows, case studies in individual accommodation to social norms will help the student of world history to better account for the behavior of individuals as, buffeted by social norms and struggling to maintain his individuality, he is caught up in a sequence of historical events. Lastly the well known tendency for students of history to lay too much to geographic determination might be allayed by comparative case studies of the people of a variety of cultures as they interact with and work to control their environment.

WORLD HISTORY IN UNIFIED SOCIAL STUDIES

A third and more daring alternative would build world history into a carefully contrived sequence of broadly conceived social studies experiences beginning in the first grade, or even kindergarten, and continuing through grade 12 or 14. Units of study would focus at each grade level on a relatively small number of key ideas, concepts, or models of human behavior in the illumination of which materials from history and from the social sciences would be used in a balanced and related manner. The key ideas would be the same from grade to grade, but the quantity and difficulty of materials used would increase from grade to grade. If, under these circumstances, world history should survive as a separate course, it would probably become a rather sophisticated study of historical problems of the kind in which historians are concerned as research scholars.

Key concepts, around which such a unitary study of human societies might be organized would include, among others, the following:

a. The concept of culture, including the way in which a culture is preserved and /or changed.
b. The concept of man in a culture interacting with the forces of nature, including both man's dependence on nature and his increasing control over nature.
c. The concept of social group, including the relation of the group to the development of the individual.
d. The concept of economic organization, including: the relation of economic organization to human goals and to developing technology; division of labor and corporate production; growth through economic planning, capital saving and investment.
e. The concept of political organization, including the nature of political rights and responsibilities and means of political control.
f. The concept of freedom in relationship to personal security and social control.
g. The concept of growing interdependence between individuals and groups.
h. The concept of science and the scientific approach to knowing.
i. The concept of the suprarational including religion, aesthetics, and philosophy.

As the study of world society proceeds, the study may be expected to become more mature and withal more concerned with the *ought* in human society. Concern for the recurring problems of societies will increase. Broad goals toward which all human societies move will be more clearly identified. The potentials for change and improvement will be assessed. New goals within the range of the possible will be suggested. New oughts will be proposed. Toward the latter stages, study may well become almost completely concerned with the recurring problems found in some form of every society. Really mature students of world history may well begin a new unit of study, involving most usually a fairly current society, with an appraisal of its prospects for survival. Though the efforts to cate-

gorize the persistent problems of mankind may never be entirely successful (since problems, like other components of behavior, are complex and
never can be made to fit in neat packages) rough categories may be arrived
at and serve the useful purpose of focusing attention on important problem areas and make comparisons and evaluations between cultures possible. The following list, which bears a rough approximation to the basic
concepts included in the model, is timorously suggested:

a. How do we preserve that which is good in our society and still provide for criticism, change, and improvement?
b. How can we make maximum use of our natural resources to
   improve conditions of living and conserve our resources for
   the benefit of future generations?
c. How can we live in harmony within groups and still escape the
   blind prejudice, biased opinion, and stultifying restraints imposed on individuals by groups; how can we resolve conflict
   among groups with varying backgrounds, interests, and points
   of view?
d. How can we best organize ourselves for the maximum production and enjoyment of economic goods?
e. What political institutions best insure that rights will be protected and that government will be responsible to the people?
f. How do we reconcile individual freedom with social control,
   especially in a period of growing interdependence?
g. How can we best use science as a tool for social improvement?
h. What is the proper role of religion, philosophy, and aesthetics in ordering human living?

THE PREPARATION OF WORLD HISTORY TEACHERS

The introduction of this critical and more scientific element into the
study of world history would require a very different preparation of world
history teachers than is current at present, for such teachers would need to
be steeped in the content of cultural anthropology, cultural geography,
and social psychology—not to mention sociology, economics, and political
scieice, as well as to have a comprehensive command of the history of
man (not merely that of Western man). Further, such teachers would need
to have more than a passing acquaintance with the systematic and analytical methodology of the social scientist, as well as the more simple and
pseudo-scientific methodology of the historian. This is a tall order in
teacher preparation, but a necessary and, I think, not an impossible one.
Further this process of teacher preparation could begin with the retreading
of existing world history teachers whose intellectual horizons and capacity
for criticism need to be lifted by introduction to the systematic social sciences.

WILLIAM H. CARTWRIGHT

Professor of Education, Duke University

5. Selection, Organization, and Placement of Subject Matter in American History*

American history is the only subject among the social studies that is studied by all American students in both elementary and secondary school. Further, the study of American history at both levels is required by the force of law. In many states such a requirement exists also for American government, and some states require some others of the social studies of all students in elementary or secondary school. But in general, while elementary schools or teachers may decide for themselves whether or not to include in their curriculum concepts drawn from anthropology, sociology, economics, or psychology, they must teach American history. The high school student may study civics, geography, economics, sociology, psychology, or the history of parts of the world outside the United States for a variety of reasons: the local school board may require the subject; the student may be interested in it; his parents may insist on it; the counselor may urge it; or it may be the only subject that the student thinks he can pass. One or more of these conditions may be true in the case of American history, but regardless of them or others, the force of law compels the study of American history.

The fact that the study of American history is required everywhere by state action in both elementary and secondary school should give some pause to the teacher, the supervisor, and other curriculum makers. The reasoning that brought the lawmakers to this determination must be a conditioning factor in the selection, organization, presentation, and placement of American history in the curriculum. And that reasoning is clear. The lawmakers believed that knowledge of the history of this country is necessary to effective citizenship. That belief was set forth by Jefferson and others of the Founding Fathers. No other argument for the study of American history has been stated so frequently, so consistently, and so forcefully throughout the national period. Many other benefits should come to both

---

*Drawn upon an article in *Social Education*, XXIX:435–44, November 1965. Used by permission.

the individual and society from the study of American history. Several of them will be referred to in this paper. They are not in conflict with the development of effective citizens, rather they support that development. However, common sense and wisdom, as well as a sense of duty, demand that we recognize that in the teaching of American history we are concerned not only with the pronouncements of historians and educationists, but also with a mandate from the American people as embodied in their governments.

PLACEMENT IN CYCLES

Let us discuss the placement of American history in the curriculum before we consider the other three matters assigned to this paper. One reason for so doing is the consideration just emphasized. Another is that the selection and presentation of subject matter (and perhaps its organization also) must be viewed in the light of the maturity and previous knowledge of the learner. It is a commonplace that American high school graduates have studied the history of their country at three levels of instruction: the middle grades, the upper grades or junior high school, and the senior high school. Most often it is required in the fifth, eighth, and eleventh grades. The college student is likely to have a fourth course. As Professor Joseph Strayer has said, if school courses are taught properly, there should be no need for the college survey course. In fact, Princeton University did away with its general course in American history several years ago. But the three-cycle approach in the schools has much to recommend it, and probably no fundamental change should or can be brought about in the general practice of placement there. The importance and complexity of the subject are not to be gainsaid. Three years are not too long a time to devote to it, yet a three-year course at one level can hardly be conceived. The curriculum at each level has other essential concerns, and the study of American history can neither be delayed until adolescence nor completed before its onset.

The fifth-grader has gained enough knowledge and experience, both in and out of school, to profit from and appreciate the study of many aspects of his nation's history. Without such study he can hardly develop the sense of belonging that is necessary to his own stability and that of society. The eighth-grader has grown and learned enough to justify both a reconsideration of some of his earlier study of national history in the light of that growth and learning and an extension of his study into more complex matters. The eleventh-grader, nearly ready for college or the assumption of an independent role in society, can scarcely afford to forego earnest efforts to comprehend his relation to his developing land and people and their mutual dependence on one another and on other nations.

Agreements to expand or shift one of the cycles of American history into an adjoining grade may be successful, and substantial changes in emphasis may be brought about in one or more of the cycles, but the elimination of any of them is not to be feared or hoped for except for scattered or temporary "experiments." The cycles are fixed by tradition and have popular support. It is difficult to get complete data about middle-grades offerings, yet American history is clearly there. It is listed as one of the most frequent fifth-grade offerings in each of six recent textbooks on the teaching of social studies in elementary school. And with few exceptions the arguments about it are not concerned with its elimination, but with emphases and the manner of its organization. Some people have suggested the elimination of the junior high school course. But its place seems secure. Howard R. Anderson showed that in 1946–47 practically every American student studied United States history for at least two semesters in the seventh and eighth grades.[1] Grace S. Wright's report of last June for 1960–61 showed more students enrolled in United States history in the seventh grade, more than half a million more than in geography, and more than a million more than in either state history or something called simply "social studies." [2] In 1960, Richard E. Gross and William V. Badger asserted in the *Encyclopedia of Educational Research* that, "there is greater unanimity throughout the United States on the desirability of this eighth grade offering than is true of any other social studies course or emphasis at any other grade level."[3] If there is an exception to their statement, it must be the senior high school course in American history. Here, again, Howard Anderson's report showed that practically all high school students took a year of American history in 1946–47, and Grace Wright's report showed more high school students enrolled in American history in 1960–61 than the total number of eleventh-graders. Curriculum situations as firmly fixed as the three cycles of American history could not be eliminated easily even if large segments of the educational leadership did not support them. But many leaders do support them. And, beyond these arguments, one of the surest ways to bring the legislatures into the curriculum-making process could be to get a movement under way to reduce the emphasis on American history.

ORGANIZATION OF CYCLES

The continuation of the three-cycle approach to American history requires that the cycles be planned so that there is no needless duplication

[1] U.S. Office of Education, *Teaching of United States History in Public High Schools*, Bulletin 1949, no. 7 (Washington, D.C.: Government Printing Office, 1949).

[2] U.S. Office of Education, *Summary of Offerings and Enrollments in High School Subjects 1960–61*, Preliminary Report (Washington, D.C., June 1964).

[3] "Social Studies," in Chester W. Harris, ed., *Encyclopedia of Educational Research*, 3d ed. (New York: Macmillan Co., 1960), p. 1301.

among them. This is not to say that there will be no planned reuse of knowledge and skill gained previously. The cyclical approach should demand the use of earlier learning to support new learning, reconsideration at *a more advanced level* of facts and ideas that are already somewhat familiar, and the development of new understanding and skill. The Committee on American History in Schools and Colleges, in 1944, made useful suggestions for differentiation among the cycles.[4] Despite the fact that its report is more than 20 years old, no more recent body of comparable stature has made significant additions to its proposals. The Committee recommended that differentiation be achieved through changing emphasis in central theme and in chronology, although all three cycles would give some attention to the whole period of American history. Thus in the middle-grades cycle the emphasis would be on how the people lived, and two-thirds of the time would be allotted to the period before the establishment of the government under Washington. The junior high school cycle would emphasize the growth of a free nation, with two-thirds of the time allotted to the century from 1776 to 1876. The senior high school cycle would emphasize a democratic nation in a world setting, with at least half the time devoted to the period since 1865.

American History in Schools and Colleges still makes much sense, and many teachers would improve their courses by adopting its proposals. The middle grades might well follow its recommendations. But too much has happened since 1944 for its proposal for chronological division between the two upper cycles to remain valid. At the least, the date for division in emphasis should be much later than 1865. More radical would be an outright division of the two cycles into courses dealing with distinct chronological periods. Several states are reported to be making plans for the junior high school course to stop with the Reconstruction and for the senior high school course to begin there, with only a brief review. One "illustrative desirable pattern" suggested in the "Social Studies in the Comprehensive Secondary School," a 1961 position paper of the National Association of Secondary-School Principals, would have the junior high school course stop in 1876 and the senior high school course begin there. Another such pattern in the same document would have the same kind of break between the two courses come in 1870. There is, in fact, a greater difference in content among the cycles than is often assumed. The authors of textbooks were shifting their emphasis throughout this century. By 1950, more than three-quarters of the typical text for the middle-grades cycle was devoted to social and economic matters, as was the major part of the typical text for the junior high school cycle. Only in the senior high school was more than half of the typical test given over to matters of poli-

[4]Edgar B. Wesley, director, *American History in Schools and Colleges* (New York: Macmillan Co. (1944).

tics and foreign affairs. Nevertheless, much needs to be done in many class-rooms both to eliminate much unnecessary duplication between the upper two cycles and to give adequate treatment to the phenomenal and cata-clysmic developments of the twentieth century. October finds too many senior high school classes still discussing the European backgrounds of the period of exploration. And far too many have not yet completed their study of the Civil War in March. Perhaps such matters can be remedied only when the senior high school course of study and textbook begin, as has been suggested, with the post-Civil War unit. Yet, no period or topic in American history can be taught without reference to others. Professor Strayer puts the case for the cyclical approach well. He says that American history can be divided into four periods that differ significantly in political, social, and economic development: colonial, early national, industrialization, and emergence of a world power.

> A good deal can be done with the first two periods in elementary school and junior high school; the last two can be treated fully only in senior high school. This is not to say that nothing should be done with the twentieth century in the lower grades, or that a certain amount of repetition is undesirable. In fact, repeated coverage of a period with the introduction of new ideas and new materials is the only was in which a historical period can ever be fully understood. Nevertheless, the earlier periods should be emphasized in the lower grades and the later periods in senior high school.[5]

Aside from the unnecessary duplication that too often exists among the cycles of American history, such duplication between other subjects and American history should be avoided. This kind of duplication is often present, and it receives even less attention than that among the cycles. It takes place between state history and the junior high school cycle, which commonly are taught in successive years. In particular, the study of the Civil War in one year often can hardly be distinguished from that in the other. In some schools the Constitution is taught in almost identical fash-ion in the junior high school cycle of American history, civics, senior high school American history, and for the fourth time in twelfth-grade govern-ment or problems. The treatment of two World Wars and the complex world relations of the past half century is often very much the same in world history and senior high school American history. In these cases, as in the cycles of American history, it is desirable and necessary to use pre-vious knowledge as a foundation for further learning, but it is wasteful to have outright, unplanned duplication. Such duplication can be avoided only

[5]Joseph R. Strayer, "History," in *The Social Studies and the Social Sciences,* spon-sored by the American Council of Learned Societies and the National Council for the Social Studies (New York: Harcourt, Brace, and World, 1962), p. 28–29.

when all social studies teachers are reasonably familiar with the entire twelve-grade program. And it must be said that this happy condition is a rare phenomenon in American schools. Even under it, the problems caused by overlapping of content between required and elective courses are difficult to solve, for the adjustment must be made largely in the elective courses, sometimes to their detriment. But where the overlapping is among required courses, careful planning can bring about true application of the sound theory behind the cyclical approach.

ORGANIZATION WITHIN CYCLES

To open a discussion of the organization of content within the cycles reminds one of a barrel of fishhooks. There are those who support a chronological and those who prefer a topical organization. Some advocate approaching the matter through problems and some through social processes. Some believe that the task can be performed most effectively through teaching American history as a separate subject; some believe that the social studies should be formed into a single subject; some advocate combining the social studies with other subjects so as to bring about a core curriculum or a humanities course. Some advocate one of these approaches at one grade level and a different approach at another grade level. Some would use the same approach at all grade levels. The same arguments and counterarguments seem to be advanced by the most expert and the least expert, the most expert disagreeing among themselves on the same issues and in the same ways as do the others, but, presumably, for better reasons. On these matters, while there is strong feeling, there is little certain knowledge. In this situation, it hardly behooves the writer of this paper, or a supervisor, to dictate a specific form of organization to a school or to a competent teacher. Yet some consideration of the arguments will be valuable to all curriculum makers.

Those who believe in a chronological organization say that only such an approach can tell the story as it was taking place and can make it clear that an individual or group always is contending with many problems at the same time. It is countered that chronological history easily degenerates into a mere chronicle of names, dates, and events, many of which have no relevance to the present or the future. The proponents of a topical approach contend that it provides for study of the relevant and significant and that it allows the student to concentrate on a particular topic until he understands it well. The supporters of a social process approach use the same arguments, and add that organization by social processes provides topics of importance to all people at all times and places. The advocates of a problems approach use all these arguments, and add a psychological one; namely, that learning takes place only when there is a problem to solve. Opponents of these approaches argue that their use brings about a loss in the advantages alleged for a chronological organization, often leads to the omission of important matter, and introduces the bias of those who select the topics, processes, or problems to be studied. They say, further, that while there must be a problem in order for learning to take place, the problem may be simply the learning of important knowledge and skill, and that one of the tasks of the teacher is to create situations in which students solve that problem.

Those who support the organization of the curriculum into separate subjects say that these subjects have resulted from the best efforts of scholars and teachers to devise means for learning about society, that it is not efficient for students to study all of society at the same time early in their learning career, but that by successive study of various aspects of society from the point of view of various disciplines they will eventually be able to view it as a whole. The advocates of fused social studies or a core curriculum say that we live in a total society, not in a discipline, and that the curriculum should take account of that fact; that the boundaries between the subject are artificial; and that only through an interdisciplinary approach can the curriculum provide for meaningful study of the development and problems of society.

All of these arguments, and others that might have been given, have some validity. Yet, in our present state of knowledge about learning, none of them is conclusive. Sound planning or unsound planning, effective teaching or ineffective teaching, can be carried out under any of the proposals. The negative arguments will be useful to teachers and supervisors as warnings against weaknesses in any approach. Whatever organizational plan is adopted careful consideration of the others will be useful in evaluating it. If a chronological approach is used, checking the course of study against others organized by topics, processes, or problems will help in emphasizing the relevant. If one of the latter three approaches is employed, checking against a chronological course of study will help guard against omitting matters of significance. And a word of caution is in order with regard to the meaning of "relevant" and "significant." It will not do to teach only those parts of American history that seem most relevant to the present. It is often true that nothing is older than yesterday's headline. Henry Johnson's test of enduring value is the fundamental test. What seemed relevant *then* to the people being studied may have as much relevance for the future as what seems relevant now to us.

Where American history is taught as a separate subject, it must be recognized that it may carry special burdens and obligations. To the extent that it is the only subject among the social studies to be required of all students, it must, as Strayer says, "carry most of the load of giving the students essential ideas about the nature of human society, and the skills and attitudes needed to deal with human problems." This is likely to be the case of the senior high school. In the junior high school and elementary school this load can be shared with whatever geography, world history, and state history are required. Fortunately, there are no rigid boundaries around any of the social studies. Historians, themselves, in their own scholarly endeavors, are finding it more and more necessary to be familiar with and to draw on the findings and procedures of other disciplines—anthropology, economics, geography, political science, and sociology, as well as art, literature, music, and social psychology. Knowledge in these areas will be helpful to the curriculum maker and teacher of American history. The essays by scholars in the several disciplines continued in *The Social Studies and The Social Sciences,* in *High School Social Studies Perspectives,* and in *The Social Sciences: Foundations of the Social Studies* were designed to help those concerned with the curriculum and should be read by them.

Where the social studies are fused, or combined with other subjects, as is often the case in the middle grades and sometimes the case in junior high school, curriculum makers and teachers have a responsibility, not only to the laws and regulations of the state but also to the reasoning behind those laws and regulations, to see that American history is taught and its values gained. There is as little sense in correlating for the sake of correlation as there is in teaching history for the sake of history. Just as it is true that where American history is a separate subject it must be broad in scope, so where the subjects are combined, American history must have an important place, not only as incidental support for nonhistorical topics, but as history in the form of historical units and historical parts of units. The reason for organizing instruction in American history is to facilitate the attainment of our objective. The main objective is to help rear people who understand their society and their relation to it, and who have the knowledge, skill, and purpose necessary to make them effective members of that society as well as better persons.

SELECTION OF CONTENT

Consideration of the main objective provides guidance in the selection of content for school American history. The question to be answered is, What can these children or youth learn from the study of American history that will contribute most effectively toward the attainment of that objective?

The content must be such that the students concerned can learn it with a reasonable amount of effort. But this statement is helpful only in a negative way. There is so much content in American history that students could learn at any age that they have time to consider only a small portion of it. And, any tasks that we give them prevent them from undertaking others. Most middle-graders, and most high school students, can memorize a list of a hundred names, another of a hundred dates, and another of a hundred places. But probably teachers should not make such assignments. There are more important, more useful activities than memorizing such lists. It is not that facts are unimportant; they are the principal materials required for the construction of useful generalizations. As William James said, no one sees further into a generalization than his own knowledge of the details permits. But it is hard to make a significant generalization out of the names of the capitals of the 50 states.

Good citizenship requires desirable action. Desirable action rests on sound attitudes. Sound attitudes must be based on intellectual generalization and controlled emotion. These in turn must be achieved through facts and skill in getting and using facts. The study of American history should contribute to the development of all of these attributes. The content of school history should be chosen with a view to its contribution toward them.

Good citizens are loyal to their government. They seek, through the orderly processes of law, to perpetuate that which is good, and to change that which needs improvement. Through the study of their history they find examples of personal and social action, some of which they want to emulate and some of which bring shame. Even at the simplest level, knowledge of a common past is essential to lasting social organization. This principle is followed by all social organization. It is essential to a nation-state. To the question, why teach about Christopher Columbus, John Smith, William Bradford, George Washington, Thomas Jefferson, Abraham Lincoln, Robert E. Lee, George Washington Carver, Theodore Roosevelt, and Woodrow Wilson, one good answer is that is would be impossible to conceive of our country without them or a good American who does not respond warmly to them. The same could be said for the Mayflower Compact, the Maryland Act of Toleration, the Declaration of Independence, the Constitution, the Gettysburg Address, and the Four Freedoms. The case can easily be made for such examples as these, but they are not enough, and this case by itself is not complete.

The study of American history should provide a guide for social action. As a course of study is packed with specific facts, it becomes necessary that most of these facts are chosen because they support needed generalizations. And as the course becomes loaded with generalizations, it is necessary that they be supported by adequate details. Space does not allow for extended illustrations in this paper, but here is one.

There is general belief in this country that consideration of national origin, religion, and race has no place in the voting booth or the employment office. For this belief to be implemented, there must be action by citizens who respect officials and workers for what they are and do without regard to national origin, religion, or race. Such respect can be based on generalization as well as on emotion. And the generalization, to be well founded, must rest on specific facts.

Let us suppose that the junior high school teacher of American history is teaching a unit on the Westward Movement. Part of the unit is the story of the "Dark and Bloody Ground," the settlement of Kentucky and Tennessee before, during, and immediately after the American Revolution. It is an exciting story, and useful in many ways, only one of which concerns us here. Of course, the students will study persons and learn some names. By selection of materials, the teacher sees that his students learn more than the names and exploits of the people involved. The student will discover that Daniel Boone was a Welsh Quaker, that John Sevier was a French Huguenot, that James Robertson was an Ulster Scot, that Jost Heit was a German Pietist, that Catholic Highland Scots and French, and men and women of English origin and varying faiths were involved, as well as Indians and Negroes. These details, and similar one from other episodes in other units, will go far toward helping children to establish a generalization that moralizing probably cannot establish; namely, that people of many differing national, religious, and racial origins worked together to build the nation. And it must be added, lest we grow too proud, there were good-for-nothings and blackguards of various origins who wrought damage as individuals and conspirators. These generalizations, it may be hoped, will contribute to right attitudes and desirable actions.

It may be charged that what has just been described is a perversion of history to a subject for undesirable indoctrination, that the teachers should "let the facts stand for themselves." The answer to the charge is at least threefold. In the first place, no suppression or distortion of the facts was required to establish the generalization. In the second place, the generalizations, attitudes, and action concerned have the support of the overwhelming majority of the American people and their curriculum markers, and the endorsement of every branch of our government. It would be a very different and unethical action for the teacher to seek to establish his own brand of politics or religion. In the third place stands a counter question: What facts are to stand by themselves? There is a myriad of facts about American history. A professional historian of the United States may, in the course of his training, take a survey course in American history and follow it with several specialized courses, one of which may be a course in the frontier in American history. These in turn may be followed by several year-long seminars, in one of which he devotes his full time to the settlement of the Shenandoah Valley. He emerges from the seminar knowing that he has dealt with only a small portion of the facts related to the settlement of the Valley and is thankful that the settlers there had no hostile Indians with whom to deal. After he has devoted a few years to the preparation of a specialized volume, he shudders at the thought of writing a school textbook that presumes to cover all of American history. He may undertake the task, but one of his major problems is to select the facts that will establish the big generalizations he considers vital. If any other curriculum makers, including teachers and supervisors, do not have the same problem, it is because they do not recognize it. There are too many facts about American history for those to be taught in one of several subjects taken by a student, during a single school year of 180 or 200 days, to stand by themselves. Either they will be selected in accordance with some principles, or they will be selected without regard to principle. In the latter situation, there is little reason for society to mandate the study of American history by all its young people.

The nature of the generalizations that this writer believes should make up the stuff of school history has been indicated in another place by a series of questions. School history must treat of how people

> . . . met and solved, or failed to solve their many problems. How did they overcome, adjust to, or become overwhelmed by the physical characteristics of the regions in which they lived? How did they force nature to yield its riches, exploit these riches while yet conserving them, or lose the material basis of their society through failure to conserve? How, in modern times, has the dizzying pace of the acceleration of material progress become one of mankind's greatest problems and what subproblems does that acceleration pose? What ways have men tried for organizing their economic activity, and how well have they succeeded? What systems have been developed for governing people and with what sub-problems does that acceleration pose? What ways have men tried for organizing their economic activity, and how well have they succeeded? What systems have been developed for governing people and with what success? Under what conditions has human liberty thriven or succumbed? How have men learned to work together peaceably to their mutual advantage? What causes have led them to conflict, and what means have they employed to eliminate conflict or its causes? What institutions have civilizations found necessary to their existence and strengthening? What forms have these institutions taken and what successes or failures have they had? What personal and societal values have people developed as guides to their activities? What means have people taken to bring up their young so as to preserve and enlarge their heritages?[6]

[6]"Clio: A Muse Bemused." *Indiana Magazine of History* (June 1963), p. 129–130.

Strayer suggests that at strategic points in a course in American history,

> ... the student should be asked to consider the questions: What is an American? How did these people view themselves? What did they believe were their greatest accomplishments—and greatest failures? In what ways did they feel that they differed from other people?[7]

And he suggests that the same sort of question be raised at the end of the course.

> What is an American? What do we think we stand for? What sort of a society and world do we want? How do we think we are going to get it? How has our past conditioned our present? How can we make our present serve as a basis for the future we desire?[8]

The answers to these questions have meaning for future social and personal action. The questions do not provide a basis for organizing a course of study. But they will be of value in checking the adequacy of that course, and they should help in the selection of content for it.

[7]Joseph R. Strayer, *op. cit.*, p. 29.
[8]*Ibid.*, p. 34.

ROBERT E. CLEARY

Associate Professor of Government,
American University

DONALD H. RIDDLE

Professor of Government and Dean
of the College of Police Science,
City University of New York

6. Political Science in the Social Studies*

THE STUDY OF POLITICAL PHENOMENA

A democratic people must understand and appreciate the character of their society, its goals and purposes, its limitations, its methods of operation, and the boundaries of reasonable choice in their nation and the world of which they are a part. Every country requires people with certain kinds of knowledge and particular skills, but if a democratic nation is to exist, its citizens must have an understanding of their political system and its setting. The people of a democracy play an active role in public affairs. At times, they virtually set national policy. As a consequence, they must be acquainted with ways of gathering, ordering, and using knowledge about matters political.

In the complex world of the twentieth century the elementary or secondary school social studies teacher has an extremely difficult job to perform. The editors of this yearbook feel that the discipline of political science can be of considerable assistance to teachers of social studies courses. Political science is an intellectual discipline that is primarily concerned with the question of how man governs himself. It includes the analysis of informal interaction within government, interaction among governmental officials, individual citizens, and interest group representatives; along with the study of the visible organizational structure of government.

Political science is concerned with the study of government, but it is by no means restricted to the study of the formal structure that is usually called government. Students of political science go beyond the study of governmental structure to concern themselves with the processes and the goals of politics: with techniques of government, methods by which decisions are made, and the bases of decisions. In so doing they pose questions such as: Who has the ability to influence others in the determination of policy choices on matters of public concern, and to secure the enforcement of his

*Yearbook of the National Council for the Social Studies, no. 36 (Washington, D.C.: N.E.S.S. 1966), chap. 1.

policy preferences through government? How is such influence exerted? For what purpose is it employed? In other words, who has power in a given situation, how is it exercised, to what ends, and with what results?

Students of American politics should supplement their study of governmental structure through analysis—even if only on an elementary level—of such topics as the nature of the American party system, the role of political parties, party operation, voting behavior, the role of the independent voter, interest groups, the role of a particular interest group, public opinion, political campaigning, and the nature of representative government. It is also useful to examine the social structure of a society, for often goals and means alike are influenced or determined by it. Class discussions, library research, and individual involvement on topics such as those presented here allow attention to the nature and the purpose of the political process, as well as emphasis on political behavior, thus amplifying the study of the "who" and the "what" of government with the "how" and the "why."

Political studies of this nature do not focus on factual knowledge for its own sake, but attempt instead to use facts to help achieve understandings. After all, facts as such are easily forgotten. They also become obsolete rather quickly in our constantly changing world. Furthermore, any body of knowledge encompasses more information than can possibly be learned in a school year or, for that matter, in a lifetime. In recognition of these facts, social studies courses with a political content are increasingly concentrating on central ideas, basic generalizations, and methods of inquiry that will be of assistance in the development of understandings and appreciations.

Political analysis in the elementary and the secondary school increasingly involves an attempt to help students develop a way of thinking that will give them the knowledge and the techniques necessary to arrive at reasonable answers to given questions. Such tasks as forming generalizations, making inferences, predicting possibilities, and explaining new phenomena involve skills that can be developed with practice. These skills take time to mature, but students can learn to group and to classify facts and to make generalizations on the basis of the evidence available.[1]

Along with the functioning and the processes of American government, the role and the purposes of government in our nation might well be emphasized in this connection in elementary and secondary school. History indicates that it is impossible for any society to maintain itself over a long period of time if it fails to pass a major portion of its basic heritage on to at least some key members of the younger generation. As a result, every nation must build an effective method of transmitting a deep appreciation of its underlying values to the young people who will be its future leaders.

[1]For a good discussion of these points see Hilda Taba, *Curriculum Development: Theory and Practice* (N. Y.: Harcourt, Brace and World, 1962), chap. 12.

Political studies in the United States have long been concerned with the necessity to help young people acquire certain knowledge, attitudes, and understandings with regard to the nature of their national community. Yet many American students have never undertaken an examination of the functioning and the processes of government in the United States, or a meaningful treatment of the underlying values and goals of the American society in a conscious effort to familiarize themselves with the roots of our heritage and the reasons for our basic beliefs. As a result, many Americans cannot place a specific situation in the perspective of a total picture by relating it to the overall goals of America. How many of our readers' students, for example, can even outline what the basic goals of the United States as a nation might be? Do we want an orderly society? How much order is desirable and how far should the government go in enforcing order? Do we want a society in which government interferes with individual action only when interference is absolutely necessary? When is interference absolutely necessary? Do we want a society that reaches a balance between the needs of order and of individual freedom? How do we reach such a balance? Do the people make decisions of this nature in a democracy? If so, can the majority override the rights of the minority? If not, are we a democracy? In sum, what might our goals be, and how can we attain them?

One basic listing of American goals can be found in the Preamble to the Constitution of the United States:

> . . . to form a more perfect union, establish justice, insure domestic tranquility [i.e., order], provide for the common defense, promote the general welfare, and secure the blessings of liberty to ourselves and our posterity. . . .

Such goals, however, penetrating as they are, are not self-defining. Does liberty include equality, or does promoting the general welfare include federally paid rent supplements in private housing? Furthermore, the goals may conflict with one another. An attempt to insure domestic tranquility can collide with the need to secure liberty. A political studies program might well include, therefore, an emphasis on the nature, the extent, and the interrelationships of equally desirable but conflicting American goals.

Careful attention to the question of how our basic national goals can be achieved and preserved also seems to be in order. What are the responsibilities of the individual citizen in this regard? What limits on conduct should he recognize? What positive obligations must he accept? Is it enough for him to obey the law and to pay his taxes? Moreover, what is his responsibility in so far as obeying the law is concerned? Should he, for example, refuse to buy merchandise offered for sale on Sunday in violation of a local blue law? Then, is there a higher order of responsibilities beyond observance of the law, particularly for the citizen in a democratic society? Must he vote? Keep informed on political affairs? Participate in party politics? Act in the general interest rather than in the specific interest? What does action in the general interest mean? Supporting zoning regulations that will limit the value of property the citizen owns? Supoorting the reduction of tariffs when this will hurt his business? Supporting foreign aid when it will increase his taxes?

Queries of this nature are the heart and soul of government and politics, and should constitute a basic part of any political studies program. It is extremely difficult to teach about values and goals in a complex society, particularly one that is undergoing rapid technological and social change. There are no final answers to questions like those cited above. This is no excuse, however, for ignoring such queries. After all, people are more likely to be able to arrive at reasonable answers to these questions if they have some understanding of the nature of the political process, of political behavior, and of the purpose of government and its role in their nation.

Yet social studies courses often ignore or deny problems like graft in government, civil rights and civil liberties violations, and the informal control exercised by powerful economic groups over a number of governmental decisions because of a fear of controversy. Controversy is the very essence of politics, however, and pupils must learn that there are honest differences of opinion on most political matters even among the well informed. In so doing, they should also learn to analyze problems, to evaluate arguments, and to come to their own decisions on recommended courses of action. This does not mean the classroom presentation of a controversy should insure that "equal time" is given to each of two competing sides. One argument may be more complex than another and may require a greater amount of time to present. Furthermore, there are not usually two sides to a controversy, but three, or seven, or even more that may well require at least a summary presentation. Reasonable discussion of possible alternative choices in a given situation, however, is basic to education as well as to democracy.

A few teachers attempt to handle controversial political problems by dressing up reality to paint a picture that is more attractive than what actually exists. Teachers should be wary of this temptation to give students "final" answers based on hope, particularly in situations laden with political and emotional overtones. A thinking individual is more likely to be the product of an education in which he is allowed to study relevant information and come to his own conclusion than of an environment in which an attempt is made to provide him with specific but necessarily limited answers. Scarcely an American is unfamiliar with the Pledge of Allegiance, but how many citizens can rationally apply in specific situations those words in the pledge that refer to our basic rights as citizens? It seems clear to us that the individual who has developed the ability to think analytically and who has an understanding and an appreciation of the basic values of America should be better able to apply such overall principles in a sound manner than someone taught by rote and indoctrination.

Moreover, the majority of American students have at least a nodding acquaintance with the truths of politics by the time they reach high school, and some are already developing a cynical attitude toward government. An attempt to persuade them that government is ever benevolent is merely likely to feed their cynicism and convince them that the teacher is part of the "system." What has been termed "the milk-and-water moralism" of the average civics text is frequently self-defeating.[2] Defects in the American system must receive recognition in the study of politics, but emphasis should be placed on the overall validity of our political arrangements, with weaknesses being handled as deficiencies that require correction. If our system of representative government is basically a valid method of achieving order with justice, greater attention to controversial issues in the classroom should result in a better appreciation of American politics on the part of all concerned.

The full and frank discussion of various social problems and of possible ways of resolving them should, therefore, be encouraged. The excesses of the McCarthy period in the early 1950's, as well as the prevalence of trial by newspaper in modern America, well illustrate that we cannot ignore controversial political issues if we are to maintain our basic values. Nevertheless, in many communities it is extremely difficult for a teacher to discuss the activities of interest groups, or the problem of illegal arrest, or even a liberal interpretation of the clause "to promote the general welfare." Those who may suffer from changes stemming from such discussions are frequently powerful enough to block debate on these matters. As John Jarolimek puts it in Chapter XV, "Not many teachers wish to personally fight the cause of freedom, to appear before school officials to respond to charges, or to become the objects of local controversy and publicity. As a result, the teaching of political matters has, through the years, been formal, bookish, and often not very interesting. . . . No one can contest such teaching; besides, the correct answers can be found in the book. It is unfortunately true that the main emphasis in political studies at the elementary school and junior high school levels has been and continues to be descriptive." The material emphasized in this kind of situation, however, often has little relationship to the overall objectives of political analysis. Understandings are not likely to result from study which overemphasizes

[2]Norton E. Long, "Political Science," in *The Social Studies and the Social Sciences* (New York: Harcourt, Brace and World, 1962), p. 97.

description at the expense of investigation. The school is an agent of behavior change—in a desirable direction, it is hoped—as well as a guard-
ian of our heritage and ought to be allowed to attend to both these tasks.
The teacher should recognize that the alternative is another nudge by
the school—and by the teacher himself—toward cynicism or apathetic
withdrawal.

An emphasis in our schools on the free and open discussion of the basic
goals of America and the ways that such goals might best be implemented
is necessary in order to allow students the opportunity to obtain a better
understanding of our political system. We believe that the traditional civics
course is completely inadequate in achieving the objectives of American
political studies. The typical such course is too often a dreary collection of
unrelated facts which do little to help achieve student understandings.
Either a much broader course in government or a full treatment of political
issues in a problems of democracy course is much to be preferred. Among
the problems which might well be treated at length in such courses are the
extent of civil liberties in the United States, along with limitations on their
exercise; the role of Negroes in American society and their rights; the
meaning of the phrase "due process of law"; the basic goals of the United
States in international affairs; the ability of the American system to reconcile the interests of the diverse and conflicting groups in American society;
the desirability of changes in the system as it operates; how the people of
the United States go about handling issues of this nature; and the role of
Congress, the President, and the Supreme Court in dealing with them.

In discussing matters such as these we are attempting to help educate
individuals who are more than passive observers, who do more than mouth
the right slogans without having an understanding of how to apply them in
specific situations. In doing so, of course, we must exercise caution. We are
not trying to teach specific attitudes or beliefs in and of themselves. We
must draw a distinction between indoctrination and education, between attempts to implant ready-made conclusions and attempts to get individuals
to think for themselves. It is sometimes argued that the demands of good
citizenship require we "teach the virtues of democracy" along with the
drawbacks of communism in our schools. This misses the point that in
attempting to infuse a respect for freedom we may effectively destroy
freedom. How can we tell people to "appreciate the American way of life"
without violating the free and open consideration of issues that are
essential to that way of life? A true appreciation of the nature of freedom
is not learned very easily. Freedom must be examined, discussed, and even
lived if its meaning is to be understood. Rote learning and memorization of
its principles are not likely to result in their comprehension. An atmosphere in which the individual can question, experiment, and investigate is
of prime importance. The mere learning of facts will not develop desirable

attitudes, for facts are simply tools which an individual employs to discover the larger and vastly more important ideas that are vital in a free society. We should not, therefore, be afraid to allow students to examine issues and draw their own conclusions. If we have taught them how to acquire knowledge and how to analyze it critically (even at relatively low levels of sophistication) they are more likely to make sound choices and reach defensible conclusions. They will also know how democracy works and will be able to help actively to preserve it.

THE OBJECTIVES OF POLITICAL STUDIES IN THE SCHOOL CURRICULUM

The social studies teacher has a responsibility to acquaint students with methods of gathering information, as well as with the uses of knowledge—with ways of understanding, viewing, and evaluating the world in which we live. He is expected to go beyond facts, to be able to place discrete information in perspective by giving it order and by fitting it into a structure which will assist in understandings and appreciations. Above all, he must help students develop habits of critical thinking about political phenomena which will enable these future citizens to participate meaningfully in the political life of their society.

A basic controversy exists, however, over the primary purpose of political studies in elementary and secondary school. The editors of this yearbook feel that politics should be studied, in the final analysis, for the same reason other areas of knowledge should be studied: to acquaint an individual with information, to allow him to expand his ability to reason, to give him every opportunity to be a thinking, functioning individual—in short, to allow him to become an educated man. Within this framework, a second order goal of political studies is to acquaint students with the nature of government and politics, especially American government and politics.

A number of educators have argued that the immediate objective of political studies in the schools is carefully oriented toward a related but somewhat different goal. Good citizenship is so important to our nation and is so difficult to structure, it is declared, that the making of good citizens must be the immediate objective. While the editors sympathize with this argument, they disagree with it. Good citizenship is extremely important in a democracy. Americans are far from agreement, however, on what it involves. Who is to define good citizenship? One man's good citizen is another man's criminal. What about civil rights demonstrations, sit-ins, and the whole role of peaceful protest in American society, for example? Even if good citizenship were to be defined, how can it be attained? Not only is the concept a nebulous one, but it involves attitudes and values that are extremely difficult to structure. It may even be self-defeating in many situations to attempt to structure them.[3] Moreover, good citizenship is likely to be influenced more by developments outside the school than by those in the classroom, for academic instruction plays only a small role in the formation of the attitudes and habits of citizenship (See Chapter XIV on political socialization.)

To the extent that the values of citizenship can be developed in the classroom, it is the belief of the editors that an honest inquiry into the nature of government and political interaction is more likely to result in good citizenship than a controlled attempt to develop particular attitudes and ideas. Good citizenship is a goal of political study, yes, but it is our feeling that the way to achieve this goal is through an effort to enlarge student horizons. In this sense there is nothing unique about the study of politics as compared with other social sciences, and no need to orient instruction to conform to a particular mold.

What, then, is the place of political science as a discipline in the elementary or the secondary school classroom? A number of educators and political scientists have argued in recent years that pre-college students should become familiar with the nature of political science as a discipline. For example, Jerome Bruner, is his book on *The Process of Education*, develops the thesis that the structures of the various intellectual disciplines should form the framework for the elementary and secondary school curriculum.[4]

Evron M. and Jeane J. Kirkpatrick, in their article on political science in *High School Social Studies Perspectives*, argue that:

> One of the most important responsibilities of the secondary school teacher is to inform students about the existence of a field of inquiry into government and politics and to give them some indication of the complexity and difficulty of many public problems. . . . [While it is not] possible to make political scientists out of secondary school students . . . it is possible to teach secondary school students something about political science: what it is, what it does, the complexity and the difficulty of the problems it deals with.[5]

Norton Long, in his chapter on political science in *The Social Studies and the Social Sciences*, declares that education in the social studies has a threefold objective: acquainting students with factual knowledge and a

---

[3]For an excellent discussion of the complexity of desirable civic attitudes see Gabriel A. Almond and Sidney Verba, (*The Civic Culture: Political Attitudes and Democracy in Five Nations* (Boston: Little, Brown and Co., 1963).

[4]Jerome Bruner, *The Process of Education* (Cambridge: Harvard University Press, 1960).

[5]Evron M. and Jeane J. Kirkpatrick, "Political Science," in *High School Social Studies Perspectives* (Boston: Houghton Mifflin Co., 1962), p. 122.

means of ordering it, imparting an understanding of the methods of inquiry and verification, and imparting an appreciation of the basic values of our society.[6]

Bruner feels, then, that the disciplines should provide the framework for social studies education, the Kirkpatricks believe pupils should know what political science is, and Long feels that the student should be acquainted with the broad outline of political science as a discipline along with its methods of inquiry. The editors agree, but only with an important qualification: students should know what political science is and they should be acquainted with its scope and methodology, but they should also know what it is not. One thing it is not is a unified science with an agreed-upon structure, in Bruner's use of the term. Political science *may* provide a useful framework for political studies in the elementary and the secondary school. There are a number of approaches and concepts which *can* provide unity and give order to political studies (See Unit I of this yearbook). The focus of study, however, should not be on political science as a discipline. The main ideas of the discipline might form the framework for study, but the overall purpose of social studies education is not to acquaint young people with the existence of various disciplines such as political science. Rather, within the framework of a cultivation of the intellect, the purpose of political studies is to acquaint young people with an understanding of the nature of government and its methods of operation.

As Long points out, the social studies educator is attempting to acquaint students with various means of pursuing knowledge, ordering it, and evaluating it. It is not information about political science *per se,* however, which is central to the elementary or the secondary school student. With rare exceptions, he is not a scholar attempting to expand the boundaries of knowledge. Instead, he is attempting to expand *his* knowledge about and understanding of government and politics. In this endeavor political science is a tool to be used by the teacher according to the capabilities of the students concerned. Knowledge and understanding are best imparted in a framework, rather than in bits and pieces. Political science can offer a framework that students might employ to organize their study of government. (Actually, it presents a choice of frameworks for such a purpose.)

As students expand their horizons and develop their understandings of the political world, it is likely, then, that they will gradually become acquainted with the existence of the discipline of political science, as well as with some of the leading methods of inquiry used by political scientists. This is desirable, for students should know that the discipline exists and should have an idea of how political scientists are attempting to expand their understanding of government. It is our feeling, however, that this is

[6]Long, *op. cit.,* pp. 88–89.

not a goal in itself at the pre-college level, but a means to an end—the improvement of the political understanding of the average student. In doing this, social studies teachers might well utilize much of the information and many of the techniques of political science. A primary by-product of such an emphasis is quite likely to be the development of better citizens who are knowledgeable about their rights, their duties, and the limitations of reasonable choice in their society and their world.

HENRY WARMAN

Professor of Geography, Clark University, Worcester, Mass.

7. Geography in the Curriculum*

A geography program including the most meaningful content, modern methodology, and excellent teaching necessarily operates within a conceptual framework. Geography studies, *per se,* should deal with the "writings on the surface of the earth"—those inscriptions done by man, by nature, and by society. The substantive, meaningful, content draws upon the "trilogy" of Geography, namely, the physical environment, the cultural environment, and people. An approach through the people involving a study of the impacts these two-legged creatures have made and are making on both the physical and the cultural environment seems best at present. Such an approach, followed by intensive study geared to the fifteen concepts to be mentioned later in this paper, will enable educators to give that life to Geography's role in education which will be apropos not only for our time but will have the greatest lasting value. The creation of a conceptual framework will enhance the feasibility, the longevity, and the meaningfulness of Geography studies throughout the curriculum and in later life.

If education be likened to a magnificent garment supplying color, comfort, and joy to the wearer and viewers, then one may assume that the cloth is woven of superb materials, the strands of the warp—holding together, yet also basic to the finished product—need be of a conceptual nature. These conceptual strands in the geography garment will have woven across and through them the woof of fine materials fashioned out of field work, geographic writings, maps, and pictures at all grade levels. The most colorful, the most appealing and, one might venture to say, the most useful are those warp and woof threads made of "Man-Society" materials. Put more simply, they are the stuff of human-cultural Geography. Today the generative power of the cultural Geography approach is tremendous. (Some would say that it is tremendously lopsided!). I shall return to this later, but at the moment I might say that if it is lopsided then the trilogy of Geography referred to above is not being used to view and assess the "earth writings" and their distributions. But let us return to the generative power of the cultural Geography approach.

Educational Forum, XXI: 167–72, January 1967. Used by permission.

GENERATING POWER OF THE CULTURAL
GEOGRAPHY APPROACH

The thought-stimulating potentials of Geography in studies of what man and his cultural heritage have made, and will make, in places near and far may be viewed in the light of several significant concepts. Among these concepts, which I like to think of as warp threads, those long strands running through the geography garment, the curriculum if you will, are the following:

1. The concept of the Life-Layer
2. Man the Ecological Dominant
3. Culturally-Defined Resources
4. Continual exercising of the Law of Comparative Advantage
5. Perpetual Transformation

These five concepts certainly are not peculiar to the discipline of Geography. Each one, however, undergirds, envelopes, and has implicit goals for the selected Geography subject matter—the content and the methods—proposed later in this paper. Each one poses challenges to man, and the content of the Geography offerings illustrates *where* primarily, and *when* secondarily, man has been dealing or is dealing with them.

A quick appraisal of each of these cultural Geography strands, these "thought generators," may be helpful. The first, the Life-Layer, calls for a study of the choice and not-so-choice areas of the earth where mankind has nestled down. Man is a surface creature, although he has probed downward into the lithosphere and rocketed upward through the atmosphere. He operates for the most part in a relatively thin layer, or earth shell, where land, water, and air are responsive to his efforts. The areal (horizontal) extent of his surface home is the basis for population studies, and these become more complex from grade level to grade level. The usefulness to him of what is below and on the surface leads to studies of mineral wealth and agricultural practices and production. His probing upward and around lead into weather and climate studies of that great thermodynamic engine, the atmosphere, and of space beyond our planet's changing positions. In this geography garment which teachers weave—in the curriculum itself—the complexity of the great ocean of air needs to be viewed as colorful threads in the woof, crossing at frequent intervals the other conceptual strands of the warp.

The second and third concepts, namely, *Man—the Ecological Dominant* and *Culturally Defined Resources,* are fraught with ideas as well as actual cases showing man and the alterations he has made in his particular part of the *Life-Layer.* Through time he has stood out as the chooser, the decision maker, the *Ecological Dominant.* His decisions and consequent actions have been reflected in the cultural milieu he has devised and which often, in turn, affects him. Perception studies—what a person sees as the environment through his cultural glasses or filters—are at present a widening avenue of research in Geography. In such studies the cultural impactors in a place often have more meaning than the physical impactors.

A study of *Resources—Culturally Defined* probably is done best in a Geography course which deals with Economics as both ways of life, in some instances, and as ways of making a living in others. A mere catalogue treatment of products—where, what and how much at given times—may lose the man-cultural aspect referred to above. The second, third, and fourth concepts (No. 4 deals with the exercising of the *Law of Comparative Advantage*) all call for an intimate look at man himself and by man himself at the Cultural Resource base. Erich Zimmerman has put it succinctly. He states, "Resources are not, they become." As teachers I am sure we all strive to apply this to the human resources before us in the classroom.

The fourth concept along with the idea of developing human resources also directs our study to a closer look at the composition of the population of an area, whereas concepts 1, 2, and 3 deal largely with how many and where. Distribution (place) studies of age, sex, stocks, races, education, *mores* of different peoples give insight into their competency to make the "correct" decisions; to exercise wisely the *Law of Comparative Advantage* in their particular part of the *Life-Layer*. Geography units on Urbanization and Urban Planning certainly call for recognition of many of the foregoing points. But at all levels of learning the decisions by man, evidenced in the attributes of a place, are very significant parts of the Geography learning and teaching units.

Let us turn to the fifth concept. This concept, *Perpetual Transformation,* may be illustrated of course in erosion cycles, vegetation transformation, natural disasters, and sequent occupance studies. Cultural Geography studies, carefully selected as to time intervals and place attributes, go far beyond the physical environment phases of Perpetual Transformation. They might include the Tigris-Euphrates "heartland," Inca Empire, the Iroquois Nation, Southeast Asia "Shatter" Zone, and even the Atlantic Seaboard's thirteen colonies. They might even include (in fact, I recommend) a sequent occupance study of the area enclosed by a circle drawn on a half-mile radius with the school as the center. We need more such work; few graduates of our public schools have looked at America "close-up." As geographers we probably do too much telling of what is there when our charges could be directed to look for themselves. However, I am suggesting more than a look only at today's cross-section through time; several cross-sections will indicate that "there is a Geography for every time."

Such studies or units of necessity will need to include considerable discussion of the physical environment which has developed through time. A major point, however, in several, perhaps all, of the studies would be that civilizations which at one time thought they "had it made" are no longer in existence. A look to the future by citizens of my own country, the United States (not yet 200 years old!) might be colored by this sobering thought. Planned use and wise conservation of key resources such as water, air, soils, and even people make fine units in Geography here.

Inherent in the studies already suggested and to be suggested later are two concepts—two major strands in the curriculum garment's warp. They both involve using maps to learn from and using maps to express learnings. Without the latter opportunity (and frequently we forget this) a new map would never be made. The two related concepts are (No. 6 on a list if you are keeping one) *The Round Earth On Flat Paper* and No. 7 *Regions and Regionalizing.* The desires, the aims, and devices of geographers have been to portray graphically their area of learnings, and thus to learn from their portrayals. The heritage of maps is a precious one. To block off the world into understandable parts is an integral part of Geography. Such endeavor calls for a graphic device—the map. It provides a common language for the world's people. It is an outgrowth of concept (7) *Regions and Regionalizing.* Let us see how important this strand is in the Geography garment as worn by educated people.

CONTENT AND METHODS LINKED TO TOOLS

The cultural-impactors-approach to Geography eventually faces the problem of how best to portray the areas or regions involved in the study. Reflection and considered judgment are necessary before the significant attributes of a place may be mapped. The key word is of course "significant." Just what is significant? Are there single or multiple criteria which need consideration and weighing? Indeed, the graphic portrayal of those parts of the globe selected for geographic study, both physical and cultural, has just as much perpetual transformation in it as any other concept. One may ask, "Given a region what is its human envelope? How do I show it?" Or one might reverse this and say, "Here are indications of man's imprints on the earth's surface. How do I go about regionalizing them?" Place and the significant attributes thereof are core themes in such regionalizing. Of all strands in the warp this is a very strong, if not the strongest, one.

Finally we come to concepts deemed basic to all geography study.

The words *area* and *areal* run through practically all geography accounts. "Areal," an adjective, precedes nouns of great importance. "Area" a noun has a "stand-patness" of its own. Let us look first at the nouns associated with the word "areal."

Geography calls for studies of (8) areal distribution, (9) areal differences, (10) areal likenesses, (11) areal uniqueness, and (12) areal relationships. These studies may be of single items, i.e., of climate, land forms, soils, wheat, coal, transportation route, or the rest of the so-called physical factors. However, studies of truly meaningful geographic regions, fraught with ideas as well as content or straight factual information, are of those areas which contain the "trilogy" referred to in the introduction: physical attributes, cultural attributes, and people. The challenge lies in drawing the significant *relationships* among them.

Along with the drawing of relationships there is a necessity to recognize two final concepts, two lengthwise strands in the Geography garment and in the curriculum covering, or garb as a whole. One is the concept of (13) *Spatial Interaction* and the other is (14) *Relative Location*. Relative location is concerned with building a "mental atlas" in the minds of learners; spatial interaction implies movement and inter-connections which today occur in seven directions. They are North, South, East, West, Up, Down, and Around (or in orbit). Present-day studies in Geography include the horizontal activities of trade and transport, the vertical actions of the hydrologic cycle and turbulences (storms) in the atmosphere, the dissemination of ideas concurrent with the mobility of people. All these inter-activities inevitably lead us back to the concept of (15) *Globalism*. The earth is viewed as the home of mankind and that home represents, or ought to represent, a unity of many physical and cultural diversities. Finally, it becomes the ultimate in the study of regions; it *is* the number one region. It also is our sub-region in a Universe. Planetary Relations, highlighted so often in courses of Geography at various levels of learning, take on new zest when viewed in such a context—the concept of the Globe as our number one region for study. But what makes us think that it ends there?

Relative Location implies the question: Where do I stand (or you, or we) in relation to other people in their "standing places"? What is the world of a first grader? What is your world? My world? May I develop this by quoting from a recent newspaper column written by Julian F. Grow in the Worcester (Mass.) *Evening Gazette.*

> The frame of reference of the astronomer studying the universe is based on his unit of measure, which is a light year. The measure for a shipping clerk sorting outgoing mail may be an entire state. A bombardier's measure might be a town, a taxi-driver's could be maybe a city block. A newspaperboy's measure is the width of a front porch, a pitcher's is the width of the plate and knee to shoulder-high. A seamstress has a measure of about one half inch, a carpenter one sixteenth, a machinist a thousandth, an engineer a millionth. A physicist works in sizes smaller than atoms are high.
>
> What makes us think it ends there?

Conversely we can go the other way, from the small to the big and again quote Mr. Grow:

> The world of the germ, the environment that contains most of the things that the germ must worry about, could be the bloodstream of a mite. The world of the mite could be the back of a flea. The world of the flea is a dog's fur. The world of the dog is his master's home. The world of his master is, most likely the community and state in which he lives.
> The world of the state is, of course, Earth. The world of Earth is our particular solar system. The world of the solar system is our galaxy, and the world of our galaxy is the universe we are just beginning to perceive.
> What makes us, any more than the germ, think it ends there?[1]

Let us reflect on the foregoing quotation and the fifteen concepts presented in this paper. What subject throughout the curriculum, actually permeating it, provides the most efficient vehicle to acquaint the new generations with their "worlds"? The conceptual strands referred to earlier as the warp of a magnificent Geography garment woven through and across at different grade levels with woof materials taken from the vast trilogy of Geography possess a strength, a durability, and a singular quality which almost demand a place in the curriculum. To deny such a place will mean an appalling increase in geographic illiteracy which in a world looking to the North American continent's people for leadership may well prove to be disastrous. We do not want the germ or the atom, if they can talk, to say at some future date, "It *did* end here."

[1]Aug. 31, 1965, p. 7.

JOHN E. MAHER

*Senior Economist at the Joint Council on Economic Education
and Director of its Developmental Economic Education Program*

8. Economics: Conceptions and Misconceptions*

A commuter to Manhattan pays his fare and boards the 7:10 train from Chappaqua, a 90-minute ride to Grand Central. To the sociologist, this little event may symbolize the great removal of people to residences far from their places of work, and a profound change in cosmopolitan culture. The political scientist, on the other hand, may view this event as representing the shift of political influence from rural regions and from urban centers to the new suburban communities where redistricting is giving increasing political weight to these growing areas. Again, the traffic engineer may see the commuter on railroads and on rapid transit systems as the answer to the cities' problem of motor vehicle congestion. The economist may be struck by the special importance of maintaining passenger rail service in the face of relatively declining passenger revenues and rising costs and the severe competition between rail transportation, busses, and private passenger automobiles.

In reciting the different inferences that may be drawn from what appears to be the same behavior, we underscore the fact that different areas of learning are fruitfully depicted as different perspectives on the same phenomena. Just as we may say that a human being is a composition of chemicals, a soulful creature, and a psyche, so we recognize that chemistry, theology, and psychology are among the appropriate modes for understanding him. Thus, it can rarely be *what* a discipline concerns itself with, but rather *how* it views its material and how it analyzes that distinguishes it from other disciplines.

The economic view of reality sees in human behavior the need to cope with the problem of resources that are scarce in relation to the objectives that they may be used to attain. Whether these objectives are the limited wants of a hermit or a Robinson Crusoe or the more varied wants of a modern industrial worker or an affluent executive—the means of satisfying our wants are scarce relative to the extent to which we should like those wants satisfied. Thus arises the economic problem: how to allocate our scarce resources as best to satisfy our wants. Whether we are studying primitive man or the economy of a modern Western state, a monastic order

Social Education, xxx:229-31, April 1966. Used by permission.

or a business enterprise, an individual or a nation, the fact of scarcity pervades and conditions human behavior.

To grasp better the nature of the problem of scarcity, we must understand the system of relationships that leads from resources to the satisfaction of human wants. This kind of system is highly general and, we may hope, generally useful to analysis. It is useful whether we consider a child's attempt to use scissors and paste to make valentines, a grocery store's effort to schedule the hours of its cashiers, the steel industry's program to compete successfully in foreign markets, or the nation's plan to achieve full employment. All of these forms of behavior have fundamental, economic features in common.

The features that are common to virtually every economic activity include, principally, *resources* used in a process we call *production*. From production we get *outputs* (valentines, groceries, steel, national income) that are transformed through a process called *consumption* (use by consumers). The consuming of outputs satisfies *wants*; this satisfaction is the objective of the system.

Now this simplification of economic activity does not pretend to do justice to the plurality of processes and objectives that are included in most economic analyses. Yet it serves as a generalization that makes systematic analysis easier to approach. Moreover, it leads to the important notion of efficiency. If the achievement of the objective of any system is to be rationally pursued, then the system must be governed by an appropriate criterion of efficiency. Roughly stated, this criterion is: Getting the most satisfaction from the employment of resources.

The accompanying diagram is a schematic representation of those features common to virtually every economic system, using "system" in a broad sense. Those familiar with the textbooks of a few years ago will recognize the way in which the figure draws upon earlier ways of thinking about economics. Reading upward from the box at the bottom, we see that

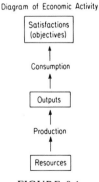

FIGURE 8-1

economic activity includes resources, which are transformed by a process we call production, into outputs. In turn, the outputs are transformed, through a process we call consumption, into the satisfaction of human wants. And these five steps or stages are all held together by relationships which make of them a system. This is true whether we speak of the gross national product of the entire economy or the rendering of haircuts by the local barber. The relationships are principally a set of prices, a set of technical production combinations (the ways in which steel, glass, rubber, and other materials are combined, say, in the making of automobiles), and relationships guiding the consumer in the uses to which he puts the goods and services he wants. If this entire system, running from resources to satisfactions, is to operate efficiently, a standard of performance, earlier alluded to, is essential. Usually, we express this as maximizing satisfaction.

In a properly balanced social studies curriculum, economics makes an important contribution to education. Its wide applicability and its coherence as a body of knowledge makes of the discipline a powerful mode of inquiry.

As an appreciation of the kind of thinking toward which economic understanding should strive, we may refer to Whitehead's definition of style which he called the "ultimate morality of the mind":

> Finally there should grow the most austere of all mental qualities. I mean the sense for style. It is an esthetic sense based on admiration for the direct attainment of a foreseen end, simply and without waste. . . .
>
> The administrator with a sense for style hates waste; the engineer with a sense for style economizes his material; the artisan with a sense for style prefers good work. Style is the ultimate morality of the mind.[1]

The mind exposed to economic inquiry, we may hope, will achieve a sense of style. There can, of course, be no pretension that all children should be turned into economists, but it is equally true that no civilized mind should be without the ability to assess the economic dimension of human life.

We have defined economics in the most general terms as a perspective, a mode of inquiry, a special appreciation of human behavior. Other disciplines may similarly be thought of as various perspectives, differing from one another according to the principles upon which the perspectives are organized. If we base our economic understanding upon this view of economic learning, then we avoid some of the worst pitfalls that confront those in education. Three of these pitfalls are worth more detailed consideration. I call these three misconceptions of economic science the "nuts and bolts" approach, "that's what *you* say," and "the worrybird." Let us take these up in order.

[1]Alfred North Whitehead, *The Aims of Education* (New York: Macmillan Co., 1929), p. 24.

"NUTS AND BOLTS"

If you lay out the component parts of an automobile, you will have an engine, carburetor, distributor, wheels, crankshaft, and a lot of nuts and bolts. But these parts from which you could make a vehicle are not an automobile; rather, instead of an automobile, you have a pile of nuts and bolts.

The same is true of economics. Too often, many teachers and their students are misled into thinking that economics consists of the component parts of study; i.e., the table of contents of a typical text in the subject. In this way economics may come to be thought of as international trade, money and banking, business cycles, labor relations, and a host of other areas of applications. But this, of course, is not economics. This is not what makes it a peculiar mode of inquiry of the discipline, nor does it reveal its essential structure.

Carried further, the nuts-and-bolts interpretation of economics sees the discipline not only as areas of application, but even as specific, detailed, and superficial symbols of economic behavior. Along these lines, economics becomes the operation of a cash register, writing a money order, answering the telephone, and going out to lunch.

Just as chemistry is not beakers, test tubes, and Bunsen burners; physics is not cyclotrons and cloud chambers; so, economics is neither the things it uses, nor the things it studies.

Our illustration of the commuter boarding a train shows that human behavior exhibits simultaneously economic, political, sociological, and other aspects. It is not an event or a fact that is peculiarly economic, but the angle from which this fact or event is viewed. Economics is a way of organizing observations. This notion carries with it the implication that there are generally not such things as economic institutions or organizations, but rather there are institutions and organizations which, when viewed from a certain angle, display an economic aspect. Thus, neither the AFL-CIO nor the National Association of Manufacturers is solely a political, economic, or social organization, but all of these things together.

"THAT'S WHAT YOU SAY!"

Equally dangerous to sound thinking in economics is the view that economics is a matter of opinion. Some would defend this spurious notion by saying that if economics were not a matter of opinion, all economists would agree among themselves and there would be no dispute over economic policy.

Disputes, of course, do not signify the extent or nature of agreement on basic principles. Medicine, for example, is usually considered both an art and a science. No one would think of arguing that the scientific basis of medicine is questionable because different doctors are sometimes required to consult on a given case. Consultation and disagreement may arise in economics, as in medicine, because different interpretations are placed on facts, because different objectives are sought by practitioners, or because, while there is agreement on facts and on objectives, there remains contention over the appropriate methods to be used for achieving the best results. Furthermore, differences of opinion over methods may arise, not because of any disagreement on principles, but rather because certain methods entail consequences that one group finds acceptable and another finds objectionable.

The view of economics as a matter of opinion is largely fostered by those who are ignorant of the subject. Their reasons for promoting this view may be innocent or, on the contrary, may be an attempt to persuade the public of political views that are, in fact, without economic foundation. Critics of economics from both the far right and the far left are often discovered persuading their constituents that economics is a matter of opinion. The reason is usually pretty obvious. If you wish in simplistic fashion to argue for the abolition of private property, or the banking system, or the public schools, then you will, indeed, require an unscientific argument. If the simplistic argument is largely based upon economics, it will have to be bad economics. And the only time a bad economic argument can be successfully advanced among any but the most economically illiterate is when it is forcefully coupled with the spurious notion that, after all, economics is only a matter of opinion.

Of course, economics is not a matter of opinion. The wide consensus on the nature of the subject is clearly shown in economics textbooks. No matter what the topic under consideration, it will be found that the same general principles are applied to each. Similarly, the economist, whether hired by business, labor, or the colleges and universities, will have been exposed to the same orthodox training and will bring the same professional standards to bear, no matter in whose employ. Of course, it is true that economic "rationalization" may be offered by economists according to their own interests. But this is no different from the behavior of engineers, chemists, and others who bespeak different philosophies depending in part, upon their outlook and position in society. In no case, however, need one call into question the underlying principles that unify each of the sciences.

"THE WORRYBIRD"

In recent years, both the natural and the social sciences have enjoyed great stimulation from the development of a "problem-solving" approach to teaching and learning. No one can doubt the benefits derived from applying general principles to concrete situations. The student and teacher engaged in common enterprise find that the hope for solution is a powerful inducement to study, and that problems that can capture the imagination serve to enliven and enrich the process of education.

Despite the value that derives from solving problems, there are difficulties that can be encountered in using the problem-solving approach in teaching and learning. One difficulty in particular is that a method of solving problems will be confused with the discipline itself. For example, consider the following rough outline of how a problem in the social sciences might be attacked. In descriptive fashion, the student might be urged to follow these steps:

1. Identify the problem.
2. Gather pertinent facts about the problem.
3. Analyze the alternative solutions to the problem.
4. Introduce the objective toward which a solution should point.
5. Determine which alternative solution approaches most closely the objective.
6. Arrive at a judgment as to the best solution.

I have deliberately avoided attempting to work out in detail the logic that underlies this approach and have not taken care to spell out some intermediate steps that might intervene. Yet I think this readily suggests the kind of method that has gained acceptance in the social sciences. But if we ask ourselves, "Has this method of problem solving anything special to do with economics?" the answer must be, "No, it has not." The same steps may be indifferently applied to political science or sociology or chemistry, physics, astronomy.

The fact is that logical reasoning plays an important role in all disciplined inquiry. But logic itself is not a definition of these disciplines, nor is the use of logic in problem solution peculiar to any particular field of inquiry. Therefore, we must guard against the danger of substituting a particular chain of reasoning for the special mode of inquiry that is economics.

The learning of economics is advanced when the particular aspect of human behavior that is *economic* is understood. There is a body of economic principles underlying the perception that we call economics, and certainly, when these principles are understood, and when, in addition, the use of logic is brought to bear, the students' appreciation of economics is greatly enhanced.

There are, of course, other misconceptions as to the nature of economics that would be worth noticing in a more extensive treatment of the subject. One of these which plagues economists themselves is the odd idea that economics is a branch of applied mathematics. We cannot here take up this more complex problem, nor another; namely, that economics is in some fashion especially concerned with "material wants" or "material satisfactions." This latter myth was exploded some 30 years ago by Lionel Robbins,[2] and yet we often encounter the deviant and, indeed, sometimes self-contradictory notion that economics has a special preoccupation with the material world.

In conclusion, we may re-emphasize the fact that economics is essentially a way of organizing special observations upon human behavior. The principle underlying the method of organization is the condition of scarcity which shows itself to us in the fact that typically the resources at mankind's disposal are not adequate to meet all its wants and that, therefore, people must choose between alternative uses to which these resources may be committed. Economic man, depicted historically as a creature of unlimited wants and voracious appetite, was never a real person nor a really typical person. And economics does not depend upon assumptions about this historical fiction. For the "economic problem" confronts all people both within and without their forms of social organization. Economics is not the topics of which it consists, nor is it a matter of public or private opinion, nor a general method of solving problems.

To the extent that we can convey the meaning and usefulness of economic science, to that extent shall we be able to contribute to the advancement of the education of the student toward the attainment of that ultimate morality of mind which Whitehead calls style.

---

[2]*An Essay on the Nature and Significance of Economic Science,* 3d ed. (Washington, D.C.: The Brookings Institution, 1962).

RICHARD L. WARREN

*Research Associate, Stanford Center for Research and
Development in Teaching*

9. Anthropology and the Social Studies*

An assessment of the condition and outlook of the social sciences today reveals an accumulation of scholarly material rich in potential application to the social studies program. For those directly concerned with the social studies curriculum the process of digesting and sifting "new viewpoints" is both boon and burden. A towering amount of research awaits incorporation—research in history, geography, political science, economics, and sociology. To these fields one may add anthropology, a discipline which has in common with the social studies many problems and concerns. The mutual interests of the two fields are given explicit consideration in an article by George Spindler.

> No one student of human behavior can hope to master this great and heterogeneous mass of interests centered in man. But an anthropologist carries with him the obligation to be aware of these interests, even in the pursuit of his specialty, and this awareness affects the way he deals with his realistically limited studies.
>
> It is by virtue of this very generalizing, holistic breadth that anthropology is particularly relevant to the teacher of the social studies. By implication, if not by definition, social studies comprises an equally broad range of interests.[1]

It is only in the past few decades that attention has been given to the relationship of anthropology to education in general and to social studies in particular. As a discipline anthropology itself is relatively new, and its structure is still apparently in the process of being "shaken down." So there would be reason to argue that any effort to relate anthropology to another field is premature. Furthermore, what at first glance might seem to be a logical and fruitful development contains some risks. There is the danger that anthropology might be seized upon and appropriated as an exotic panacea to the problems of the social studies curriculum. There is the pos-

---

*Based on an article in *California Social Science Review*, 2:10–16, March 1963. Used by permission.
[1]George D. Spindler, "New Trends and Applications in Anthropology" in Roy A. Price, ed., *New Viewpoints in the Social Studies,* National Council for the Social Studies, 28th yearbook (Washington, D. C., 1958), p. 116.

sibility that the concepts and generalizations of cultural anthropology in particular, evolved through years of careful field work, study and observation, will be skimmed from the surface and applied in a loose, academically irresponsible manner. Nevertheless, the movement to relate anthropology to the social studies is accumulating an increasing number of helpful and careful analyses.[2]

Weingrod suggests several relationships between anthropology and social studies. There is first of all a method, comparison, which is a useful tool for looking at and making sense of the facts of the universe, certainly not unique to anthropology but given special treatment by it. There is the lesson that no single course can illuminate the human whole and that there are alternative ways to live, no less dignified nor noble than our own. There is, he reminds us, the insistent obligation to separate the biological from the nongenetic in human affairs. Finally there is the recognition that cultures are functionally related, whole things.[3] These are all considerations of important consequence for the social studies. A veiwpoint which reenforces this assessment is expressed by Chilcott.

> Not only do students need to learn more about other peoples but they need to understand more about themselves. The humanizing nature of anthropology gives the student an idea of his place in the world, both natural and social. He becomes aware of what is involved in his being a human. Through a study of the standards of adulthood in other cultures, the student learns what standards he must meet in order to be an adult in his own society.[4]

There is then good reason to explore the possible articulation of anthropology with the social studies. Efforts in this direction are naturally in an embryonic or experimental stage. Indeed, the absence in the thirty-first yearbook of the National Council for the Social Studies of any formal consideration of the relationship of anthropology to the teaching of American History (geography is the only social science whose relationship to history is given special treatment in this volume) suggests that its relevancy to social studies is still raw and undefined.[5]

---

[2]See, for example, John H. Chilcott, "A Proposal for the Unification of Secondary School Courses through Anthropology," *Clearing House,* 26:387–93, March 1962; Solon T. Kimball, "Anthropology and Education," *Educational Leadership,* 13: 480–83, May 1956; Anthony Leeds, "Considerations Regarding Anthropology in High School Curricula," *Human Organization,* 20:134–40, Fall 1961; Robert Redfield, "Study of Culture in General Education," *Social Education,* 11:259–64, October 1947; Alex Weingrod, "Anthropology and the Social Studies," *Social Education,* 20:5–9, January 1956; and Raymond H. Muessig and Vincent R. Rogers, "Suggested Methods for Teachers," in Pertti J. Pelto, *The Study of Anthropology* (Columbus, O.: Charles E. Merrill Books, Inc., 1965).

[3]Weingrod, op. cit., pp. 8–9.

[4]Chilcott, op. cit., p. 389.

[5]William H. Cartwright and Richard L. Watson, eds. *Interpreting and Teaching American History,* National Council for the Social Studies, 31st Yearbook (Washington, D. C., 1961).

A variety of experiments in this area are going on at different levels of the curriculum and in different forms.[6] They generally fall into two categories: (1) a specialized course in anthropology at the high school level, and (2) the integration of certain anthropological materials and concepts into a traditional social studies program.

So far as this writer knows, only a relatively small number of courses in anthropology are being offered at the high school level, and most of these are to be found in private schools—a result probably of a predominantly college-bound student population and the attendant interest in experimenting in specialized curricula offerings for such a group. Verde Valley School at Sedona, Arizona, requires a course in anthropology of all ninth grade students.[7] The course includes the study of the concept of race, the structure and function of language, three simple cultures, a subculture in the United States, and an industrial society in Europe. A significant supplement to the formal instruction is a three-week field trip which the entire student body takes into Mexico to study different aspects of Mexican culture and a trip in which the students live and work for several weeks on an Indian reservation.

At Francis W. Parker School in Chicago a semester course in cultural anthropology is offered to seniors on an elective basis.[8] The basic text is George P. Murdock's *Our Primitive Contemporaries,* and it is supplemented with a variety of monographs, films and recordings. Germantown Friends School in Philadelphia offers a full year's elective course at the ninth grade level.[9] It includes the study of evolution, prehistory, and the ethnology of selected simple societies. All the course descriptions cited here place considerable emphasis on the discussion of assigned material with particular attention to cross-cultural implications and self-understanding.

Where anthropology is conceived as a vehicle to infuse the social studies curriculum with materials and concepts which will dramatize variety and unity in human behavior, there is naturally a wider range in the nature of the experiments. The elementary social studies curriculum has for years, of course, utilized materials which could be classified as anthropological even though there has been no conscious effort—or need—to label them as such. The traditional unit on the American Indian, the study of

---

[6]This material was gathered over a period of several years through a perusal of relevant journals, through correspondence with individuals and through attendance at a National Science Foundation Summer Institute in Anthropology held at the University of California, Santa Barbara, in 1961.

[7]Zdenek Salzmann, "On the Anthropological Aspects of Education at Verde Valley School," *Newsletter,* 30:1–4, January 1961.

[8]Jack L. Ellison, "Syllabus of the First Semester of Twelfth Grade Social Studies," mimeographed, Francis W. Parker School, Chicago, Illinois, September 1961.

[9]Howard C. Platt, "Anthropology in Secondary Schools," *Independent School Bulletin,* May 1952.

"Peoples of Other Lands," and related units have carried with them, under the guidance of a competent teacher, valuable cross-cultural learnings. In the past few years, however, units have been developed which make explicit their anthropological content. The Castro Valley School District makes use of a unit at the sixth grade level which emphasizes a comparative cultural study of the races of man; in this case the four cultures selected are Japanese, Eskimo, Central African, and modern American.[10]

Another kind of unit was organized by teachers at the Alexander Hamilton Junior High School in Seattle, Washington. Called "An Introduction to Elementary Anthropology," its primary goal is "to promote a better and more complete understanding among both pupils and teachers in the social studies and science fields."[11] The emphasis in this particular combination lay on eugenics and evolution, euthenics and ecology.

Certainly the most ambitious experiment in this area and one that has received considerable attention is the social studies curriculum at the Edsel Ford High School in Dearborn, Michigan. The first semester of the sophomore year is organized around the general subject, Culture; the second semester and entire junior year are devoted to The American Society and Culture in Today's World and the first semester of the senior year to Persistent Problems of Our Society.

The sophomore semester course is not unlike the special courses described and categorized as anthropology. The objectives of this particular course are stated as:

(1) An understanding and a working vocabulary of terms pertinent to the social studies;
(2) An understanding of the unity of culture with the ability to identify its component parts;
(3) An understanding of the interrelationships of the institutions and customs which make up a culture;
(4) An understanding of the value system which holds the culture together and makes the behavior of the people meaningful;
(5) An understanding of the causes of cultural change.[12]

The primary subject matter for the development of these and related understandings is material on three societies: the Andaman Islanders, the Hopi, and the Baganda. The organization of the curriculum is, of course, cumulative in its direction; these understandings are brought to bear on the

[10]Curriculum Bulletin No. 7, Castro Valley School District, Castro Valley, California, February 14, 1961.

[11]Ralph S. Henry and Robert L. Gantert, "An Introduction to Elementary Anthropology," Alexander Hamilton Junior High School, Seattle, Washington, 1961.

[12]H. B. Hoffenbacher, "American Society and Social Problems," in Richard E. Gross and Leslie O. Zeleny, *Educating Citizens for Democracy* (New York, Oxford University Press, 1958), pp. 221-22.

subject matter of subsequent courses which are constructed out of topical units—similar to what can be found in many social studies programs.

Another approach involves the use of anthropological concepts to develop a systematic study of human behavior within the framework of a sophomore course in world history. A variety of selected materials, i.e., Margaret Mead's collection *Cultural Patterns and Technical Change,* are being used in the University of Chicago's Laboratory School to develop the following concepts which are then applied to the study of a standard textbook in world history:

1. Ethnocentricism
2. Culture Concept
3. Values
4. Status and Role
5. The function of the basic institutions:
   a. family
   b. religion
   c. government
   d. economics
6. The problem of cultural change:
   a. cultural lag
   b. vested interest[13]
   c. cultural diffusion

A significant development is also taking place in the production of materials appropriate to various grade levels. In this regard the work of the Anthropology Curriculum Study Project in Chicago,[14] the Anthropology Curriculum Project at the University of Georgia,[15] and Educational Services Incorporated[16] is particularly relevant.

Final mention should be made of a project carried out over a two year period by the Palo Alto Unified School District. The purpose of the project was to "develop a total school program which will help children to develop constructive and mutually satisfying relationships with people of diverse cultural backgrounds."[17] The heart of the project was the thorough preparation of selected teachers for effective cross-cultural teaching, and the project proposed to test, among other things, the following hypothesis:

> Teachers who have had systematic training in the theoretical constructs and methods of anthropology, who have systematically analyzed

[13]Philip E. Montag, "Notes," mimeographed, University of Chicago Laboratory School, Chicago, Ill. 1961.

[14]Anthropology Curriuclum Study Project, 5632 S. Kimbark Avenue, Chicago, Ill.

[15]Anthropology Curriculum Project, University of Georgia, Athens, Ga.

[16]Educational Services Incorporated, 12 Garden Street, Cambridge, Mass,

[17]Intercultural Education Project, Palo Alto Unified School District, Palo Alto, California, March 1962, p. i.

their implications for education, and who have in addition had direct field experience in which to test and organize the anthropological constructs, will have greater success in educating children for cross-cultural understanding than will those teachers who have received only academic training in anthropology, or those who have had no such training.[18]

The format for the experiment was a year's preparation involving language training and seminars in the cultural determinants of human behavior, followed by a year of residence in a foreign country. It was hoped that the teachers involved would become more adept at handling cross-cultural material in the classroom and would through publications and personal contacts diffuse the impact of their experience throughout the school system.

The programs described here indicate a serious interest in and appreciation of the value of anthropology to the social studies. Since most of them are rather new, a systematic evaluation of their success may not be possible. Nor do the program descriptions give any indication of the background and training of the personnel directly involved in the programs. With what skill the materials and concepts of anthropology are being utilized in the classroom is an important question, the answer to which is obviously impossible to obtain at this point. The variety of the programs emphasizes, however, the need for continuing examination of this development.

Professor Spindler has provided a framework for one kind of examination in his discussion of six major anthropological interests: human evolution, culture history, cultural values, cultural change, culture and personality, and national character.[19] Brief consideration will be given to some of the "points" in the social studies program at which these interests can make or are already making contacts, however tentative or superficial such contacts might be.

Notwithstanding the hesitancy of some teachers to confront in a classroom the facts of evolution, this subject is probably given more considered treatment than any other of these interests. The biological aspects of evolution are traditionally the responsibility of the science department, and it may well be that in many schools the treatment of prehistoric man is limited exclusively to the biology course. But there is an obvious, natural correlation with the social studies curriculum contained in the world history course. The first chapter of many textbooks touches in a cursory manner on prehistoric man. If the interest and background of a teacher were appropriate, the introductory material of world history could be expanded into a fascinating study of the interacting forces of biology and culture in man's evolution.

[18]*Ibid.*, p. 2 (Overseas Project section).
[19]Spindler, "New Trends," p. 117.

As a matter of fact, the subjects of human evolution and culture history not only can find points of contact in the social studies curriculum, but they also are potentially capable of rehabilitating the early stages in a world history course. As the dramatic and complex events of contemporary history thrust themselves into the course, the study of ancient history becomes more of a "problem," particularly that of the ancient Near East civilizations. Somehow they are becoming increasingly more remote. If these civilizations were treated less as a beginning point and more as a climax to a dramatic period in man's development, the cause of anthropology and social studies would be better served.

Cultural values are given both explicit and implicit treatment in the curriculum. The revered documents of American history, for example, which give expression and sanctification to many of our values, are considered important points of study in the classroom. Furthermore, the contemporary attention to and concern for a definition of an American creed or value system—which ranges in weightiness from the very scholarly analysis to the "This I Believe" syndicated feature in the daily newspaper—has surely increased the exposure of students to values. This doesn't mean that values or value systems are approached in an anthropological way—that, for example, the covert, implicit, unverbalized values and sanctions are rooted out of the observable in interpersonal behavior—except in a necessarily superficial, limited way. But it does indicate that, again, a lively point of contact exists.

Closely related to cultural values in the social studies is the consideration of national character. Here again the sensitivity to the historical uniqueness of the American experiment—nurtured, it seems to me, quite consistently in the classroom—and the awareness of our international conflicts and commitments both serve to heighten the student's consciousness of national character even though it may have a strong ethnocentric quality. While the danger of superficial or even incorrect generalizations is omnipresent, we continue to discuss in the classroom why they behave like Russians, or Germans, or South Vietnamese, or Southerners.

Cultural change is an anthropological interest that has literally exploded its way into the curriculum. We date, I suspect, our contemporary appreciation of the prospect and impact of cultural change from the first atomic explosion in 1945. The events of the day continually remind us of the presence of cultural change, whether it is the triumph of a space orbit or the disaster of a Belgian Congo. History is change, and in a sense the entire social studies curriculum is about cultural change. But it is seldom considered at a social-psychological level—the level at which the "ugly American" concept, for example, could best be comprehended.

A final anthropological interest identified by Professor Spindler is that of culture and personality, and here I would like to quote at length from his statement.

> For the social studies teacher the personality and culture development in anthropology has produced a host of potentially useful interpretations of human behavior and of the reasons behind the behavior. If the social order within any society is maintained and supported by the psychological version of cultural norms built into the individual members of the society as they grow up, then it means that we have to understand these processes, to understand how society works and how a cultural heritage is retained and passed on. It is possible that social studies programs have tended in general to deal more or less exclusively with the formalized end-products of human behavior. . . . But it seems clear that eventually the psychological, or more properly speaking—the psycho-cultural approach (to denote the joining of the two interests) will need to be incorporated into the social studies offerings if the instructional program is to keep pace with the discoveries made available by the social sciences.[20]

Incorporate the psycho-cultural approach into the social studies. Make use of the interpretations of human behavior which have sprung from the personality and culture development. The appeal is immediate; the heart of social studies is history, the history of people, of human behavior. Of all the anthropological interests, that of culture and personality has perhaps the greatest import for the social studies. Yet in its present specialized and evolving form it is the interest that is probably least available. Concepts such as cultural heterogeneity and personality, caste and personality, and socio-cultural sources of aggression[21] are obviously relevant to the scholarship which gives substance and direction to the social studies curriculum. It may be that the contribution of culture and personality should remain at this level.

Yet the conditions of American society and the developments in international affairs demand of the younger generation an increased understanding of themselves and the world. Cold war, social upheavals, and accelerated technological change are rendering the pat, textbook teachings about causation and human behavior quite inadequate. However important groups and nations are in explaining the record of mankind, it is rather the personality in a dynamic cultural setting which encompasses the forces that give substance and meaning to man's behavior. It may well be that this anthropological interest will prove in the future to be of primary importance to the social studies.

[20]*Ibid.*, pp. 137–38.
[21]John J. Honigmann, *Culture and Personality* (New York: Harper and Bros., 1954).

JAMES H. SCHALL

Chairman, Sociology Division, Social Studies Department,
Upper Darby Senior High School, Pennsylvania

10. Sociology in the High School Curriculum*

The increasing interest in the inclusion of such subjects as sociology, anthropology, and psychology in the high school curriculum has prompted the writer to attempt to get into the record the work which Upper Darby (Pennsylvania) High School has been carrying on for at least 25 years in these areas. As one reads the professional literature concerning the innovations in the social studies curriculum—interdisciplinary approaches, broader elective offerings, and so on—it would appear that Upper Darby has been something of a pioneer in these fields.[1]

As Chairman of the Sociology Division (which operates within the Social Studies Department at Upper Darby), it was gratifying to the writer that for the 1963-64 school year close to 300 students out of a senior class of 600 elected this subject from a list of five senior social studies electives, and that well over 300 are enrolled for this course for the 1964-65 academic year. The assignment of four teachers has been necessitated in order to handle this load, the writer teaching six sections, and the other three men teaching two or three sections each.

In the sociology course an attempt is made to introduce the student to the science and the art of human relations on a high academic level, building upon the knowledge he has acquired in the other social sciences in his previous school years. It is probably laboring the point to say that sociology must be studied in the light of history, government, economics, geography, psychology, and even biology, and that correlations must be made and relationships shown between sociology and other social sciences.

We at Upper Darby attempt to aid the student in understanding the major social forms of which he is a part, and in making satisfactory personal, social, and civic adjustments to our time. We insist on critical thinking based on observation and accumulation of data. And no controversial issue,

---

*Social Education, xxix; 296-98, May 1965. Used by permission.

[1] As long ago as 1926, Ray G. Wallick, then a member of Upper Darby High School's Social Studies Department, initiated a course in sociology as one of the social studies electives in the senior year. In subsequent years (until his death in 1958), Charles L. Wood, Head of the Social Studies Department, was largely responsible for the development of the course and the growth of its popularity. The present Department Head, Clayton Shenk, is continuing the good work, and it is from him that the present writer received his appointment as Chairman of the Division of Sociology.

no matter how fraught with emotion or bias is buried or hushed up as too hot to handle. To ignore such issues, we feel, performs a distinct disservice for the student. If any enlightenment is to come to a student on a particular issue, it will not be when that issue is buried in the dark cellars of an institution too cowardly to face it. In a world that stresses the practical, the pragmatic, and the materialistic, we make no apologies about attempting to build idealism. We collide head on with prejudice, bigotry, intolerance, narrow dogmatism, and provincialism in students, their parents, and even some teachers; and we try to wear away these restrictive attitudes by attrition through the patient presentation of facts.

Our goals are to achieve a real appreciation of human values and problems, their origin, development, and possible solution; to achieve a meaningful appreciation and understanding of our own culture, our strengths, weaknesses, present problems, and possible future; to achieve a significant understanding of the interdependence and vulnerability of all peoples in a shrunken world in an atomic age; to encourage alignment with the constructive forces at work in the world; to develop powers of analytical judgment, responsibly applied; and, finally, to whet the natural curiosity and inquisitiveness of young people to seek more and more knowledge and to ask more and more questions. The instructor is never at a loss regarding the posing of questions for discussion; the students raise hundreds of them throughout the year. (It is interesting to note that a very high percentage of our graduating classes plan to enter some field of social service as a career.)

We encourage personal initiative by assisting students in organizing their own work and mental discipline and in conducting supervised and unsupervised research. Liberal use is made of classroom lecture and discussion. Materials are derived from many different sources. We do use textbooks, *Sociology* by Ogburn and Nimkoff, and Broom and Selznick's text, *Sociology*, with adapted readings, used on many college campuses as texts, but no attempt is made to march lockstep through these texts. Liberal use is also made of excellent films and filmstrips, tape recordings, and records, all of which serve as springboards for discussion as well as for the presentation of data. Current books, magazine articles, television shows, movies, and radio programs provide the class with a well-stocked social laboratory where they will find subject matter or ideas pertinent to the areas being studied in class, and where they can bring to bear the powers of critical judgment and analysis which we are encouraging. Student committee work and debates are also utilized to some extent.

Each student is required to prepare one research paper each report period (four in all) containing a minimum of 1500 words each and no less than three acceptable references (encyclopedias excepted), following accurately the instructions for the proper format in research paper preparation. Hundreds of new technical words are introduced and explained in the course of the year, and the student is required to keep a running glossary and to familiarize himself with the proper use of this new vocabulary.

Space does not permit us to list here the dozens of books and periodical articles used in this course, nor the 30-some films that have been ordered for use in the current year. Suffice it to say that resources are more than ample and the problem really is not what to include in the course, but what to leave out.

The sociology course at Upper Darby is offered in two ways: (1) a full year sociology course, meeting four times per week (soon to be expanded to five times per week); and (2) a course entitled Sociology-Economics, in which 36 hours of economics is offered to satisfy the new State of Pennsylvania requirement in economics. Those taking the full-year course in sociology must take either the full-year course in economics or some other combination social studies elective which includes the 36 hours of economics necessary to meet the state requirement.

The writer has found it necessary to revise and refine his course in sociology a little each year in order to meet more adequately the goals and objectives mentioned earlier. It must be remembered that this is a survey course and is not to be interpreted as anything else. The time allotted to each unit is approximate and flexible, adaptable to any exigencies which may arise. The reader should bear this in mind as he examines the outline of the course.

OUTLINE

Unit 1. Introduction (one week). This includes an introduction to sociology as well as discussion of the requirements and procedures for the year; also discussion of the desired personal attitudes and interpersonal relations within the class.

Unit 2. Psychology and Social Psychology (six weeks). This unit describes the relationship between psychology and sociology. It discusses various types of human behavior (neurosis, psychosis, mental deficiency, and anti-social personalties), showing how the discipline of psychology explains these phenomena, as well as the socio-cultural causations of the human behavior. Some of the basic tenets of social psychology and social process and social change are discussed, with some work on propaganda analysis.

Unit 3. Social Structure and Class System (two weeks). Here the work of Warner, et al., is freely drawn upon. The class is asked to make an analysis of its own community with regard to social structure and class system.

Unit 4. The Family (four weeks). This unit presents the history of the human family, with its sub-human forerunners, together with the various forms of human marriage and human family. Other topics of discussion are the functions of the family, the American family in transition, mate selection and success in marriage, and preparation for parenthood.

Unit 5. Culture (five weeks). This is really a presentation of the basic concepts of physical and cultural anthropology. Among the topics taught are organic and superorganic evolution, early human cultures and the origins of civilization, processes of cultural change, resistances to cultural change, and ethnic and racial classification and comparisons.

Unit 6. Social Problems (nine weeks). Emphasis in this unit is placed on the general state of our society with reference to its many social problems. Because there isn't time to cover all the problems, selection is made for formal presentation of such topics as crime and delinquency, intergroup relations and prejudice, world population, poverty, alcohol, gambling, and narcotics. Other problems are brought out by the students as a result of their research and oral reports in class.

Unit 7. Religion (seven weeks). This unit is saved for near the end of the year for several reasons. It always revives interest on the part of any student whose enthusiasm may have lagged. Young people love to discuss religion and seem to become more personally involved in this unit than in any other. Too, it is felt that a background of sociological and anthropological knowledge should be accumulated before handling the subject of the sociology of religion. We discuss what it is and why it is, its history and evolution. We draw interesting analogies between so-called primitive religion and the religions of the United States. Not only the sociology of religion, but the psychology of it is discussed freely and frankly—from an academic, of course, not a sectarian point of view. We do not ignore the relationship to and the conflict with science. The beliefs of the major religions of the world are presented, along with the status of religion in our own society.

Curiously, we find that many students learn more about religion, including even their own individual religious groups, from this course than they do from their own churches. The writer never ceases to be amazed at the religious illiteracy on the part of so many students, and the ignorance which they manifest concerning religion and its role in a society. Even more amazing is the lack of knowledge demonstrated concerning even their own professed religious affiliations. Despite their misinformation or lack of information, however, the students will argue more vociferously on this subject than on any other. I am sure this experience is common to most teachers.

Unit 8. Social Reconstruction (two or three weeks). This unit concerns itself with a brief history of utopian thought, current ideas concerning social and economic planning and reconstruction, and an appraisal of past and present plans and theories.

For those students not electing the full-year sociology course, but rather the sociology-economics combination, the final nine weeks is devoted to economics. The units on social problems and religion are condensed and telescoped somewhat so that the economics unit can occupy the entire final report period. Our general approach is a study of comparative politico-socio-economic systems: fascism, socialism, communism, and capitalism. Mention is made of their historical backgrounds, their major doctrines, the philosophical ideas upon which they are based, what life is like under these systems, and evaluation and appraisal of them. Emphasis is on the economic aspects of each system, realizing that we cannot ignore the political and social causes and effects of economics. Stress is placed on capitalism, and a strong unit on investments and the stock market is included. Interest, discussion, and debate is lively in this unit; in fact, we structure formal debates on highly controversial economic issues, and never seem at a loss to find students who will take the unpopular or unconventional side of any particular issue.

The appeal of the sociology course to our students is tremendous. It seems that at last they are discussing maturely and in some depth the things they really want to know about—what makes the individual behave the way he does, and what makes society tick. Innumerable students return to visit after graduation and remark how much more they enjoyed this course than any other they had taken in school, and a few express their appreciation for the "stretching" their minds were given. But perhaps the most revealing factor, and surely the most rewarding the writer has observed, has been that upon graduation day the commencement speeches seldom if ever deal with mathematics, science, or foreign languages. Almost invariably the students build their speeches around and upon material drawn from their social science classes, especially sociology. They make these selections spontaneously without any suggestion or prodding from our department, and the sensitivity to human problems which they express, their fairly mature discernment, their insight, and their liberality are sources of satisfaction to any social science teacher.

E. OHMER MILTON

Department of Psychology, University of Tennessee

11. Psychology and the Social Studies*

As a college professor with some fifteen years' experience in attempting to impart certain principles from academic psychology to young adults, I must confess that I am genuinely puzzled about the matter of introducing the subject in a somewhat formal manner into the social studies portion of the curriculum, grades one through twelve. Some consolation is provided, however, by the fact that I need not be concerned in too great detail with the "how" of accomplishment; this must be left to others. Moreover, judging by the fact that, throughout its history as a specific discipline, there has been little attention to the introduction of psychology into the elementary grades particularly, almost all psychologists must have some reservations. For the most part and for reasons which are not clear, psychology has been a college subject, although in the past few years it has gained increasing favor in secondary schools as an elective subject.

I do not presume to speak for my colleagues; any one or all of the 23,000 American psychologists might emphasize different portions of our field;[1] a complete presentation of our views and activities would require several volumes.

THE FIELD OF PSYCHOLOGY

All through the ages man has sought to understand himself and the world about him—especially the latter. Perhaps this has been a dominant urge because man can reflect upon the past, take account of the present, and contemplate the future. Until very recently, however, his own behavior has largely been thought to be the result of, or explained by, forces beyond his own control—divine intervention, magic, instinct, and heredity. Indeed, belief in such forces seems to persist for the great majority of persons. Favorite topics for both high school and college students are hypnosis and extrasensory perception. We may have held tenaciously to mysterious "explanations" about human behavior as ways of relieving ourselves of responsibility for our eccentricities and shortcomings. Mother

*Excerpted from John U. Michaelis and A. Montgomery Johnston, eds., *The Social Sciences: Foundations of the Social Studies* (Boston: Allyn and Bacon, 1965), Chap. 8 (Used by permission.)

[1]For example, see W. J. McKeachie, "Psychology," in *The Social Studies and the Social Sciences* (New York: Harcourt, Brace and World, 1962), pp. 171–90.

undoubtedly comforts herself about her role in little Joe's inadequate school performance when she says (after reluctantly deciding his teacher is not to blame): "His father's folks were just the same." Yet all of us are interested in varying degrees in finding out what is true about human behavior —at least as the "truths" apply to the *other fellow*.

Now it seems safe to assert that truth about human behavior is the most elusive of all truths. Partly for this reason, psychologists' aspirations in discovering truth are rather modest ones. Most of our efforts are directed toward discovering those things about human behavior which appear to be true at the moment—our methods of investigation require this. For the most part, we leave the task of adding together tiny increments of truth which may lead to ultimate truth to the philosophers and historians. Also, since the discipline is so young, there has not been sufficient time to permit the bringing together of many diverse points of view and apparently isolated findings.

Though our goals about truth are limited, as one examines reports of psychologists on behavior it is evident that psychology in the 1960's is an extensive field. During its history of only seventy-five years, with the greatest growth occurring since World War II, its concerns have broadened from those of observing the rather simple problems of differences in reaction-time among people to the social issues of the moment to the behavior of man in space. With all these complex problems and many others, the experimental method, with special attention to the unique problems which are created when man studies man, has been viewed as the ideal means of studying behavior. It is also evident that the boundaries of psychological knowledge are no longer clear-cut and distinct from those of many other fields. Today there is much overlap with such areas as biology, anthropology, sociology, psychiatry, physiology, and physics.

Almost all aspects of behavior are studied by psychologists. One way of gaining some indication of the areas of special interest in the field is by examining the titles or names of the Divisions of the American Psychological Association:

General Psychology
The Teaching of Psychology
Experimental Psychology
Evaluation and Measurement
Developmental Psychology
Esthetics
Clinical Psychology
Consumer Psychology
National Council on Psychological
    Aspects of Disability
The Society of Engineering Psychologists

Personality and Social Psychology
The Society for the Psychological Study
    of Social Issues
Psychologists in Public Service
Consulting Psychology
Industrial Psychology
Educational Psychology
School Psychologists
Counseling Psychology
Military Psychology
Maturity and Old Age

THE IMPORTANCE OF LEARNING

If there is any single message which psychology has to convey at the moment, it is that of the tremendous role which learning plays in determining the behavior of man, rather than that of forces beyond his control. Psychologists are not noted for agreement about specifics in scientific affairs, but they do agree about the overshadowing importance of learning as the major determinant of human behavior. Perhaps the earlier this message is brought to children in a manner they can grasp, the better for us all.

George A. Miller of the Harvard Center for Cognitive Studies summarizes the magnitude and profundity of the learning issue in this manner:

> Our entire way of life is predicated upon our ability to learn. Not only do we rely on learning to give us the basic skills with which we earn our daily bread, but also to educate our children for citizenship in a free society. It is a solid axiom of the great liberal tradition in England and America that education is the best tool for social progress. We believe that people learn their system of values, learn to love themselves and others, learn to channel their biological drives, even learn to be mentally ill. When we begin to analyze the learning process, therefore, we are probing the ultimate source of our humanity. . . .[2]

This view notwithstanding, there is a tenacity with which people hold to false explanations about humans; such tenacity is reflected in this comment attributed to George Bernard Shaw (source unknown):

> There is no harder scientific fact in the world than the fact that belief can be produced in practically unlimited quantity and intensity, without observation or reasoning, and even in defiance of both by the simple desire to believe founded on a strong interest in believing. Everybody recognizes this in the case of amatory infatuation of the adolescents who see angels and heroes in obviously (to others) commonplace or even objectionable maidens and youths. But it holds good over the entire field of human activity.

To our great advantage as educators and teachers, of course, is the fact that beliefs are also learned. In the past, beliefs about magical and other mysterious forces have been learned by successive generations of children; to a large extent, this appears to continue for the great bulk of the population. Currently, though, information is available from which sounder understanding of the determinants of behavior can be learned.

The importance of learning in man's behavior is far more than an aca-

[2]George A. Miller, *Psychology: The Science of Mental Life* (New York: Harper and Row, 1962), p. 212.

demic matter. If we fully accept it as being true, then we must also accept the responsibility for improving man's lot that accompanies it.

CONCEPTS AND GENERALIZATIONS

There are several concepts and generalizations from psychology that well may be given attention in the social studies. The following generalizations about man (detailed at greater length in the Psychology section of the Appendix) seem to have special relevance to instruction at all levels:

Behavior is caused. . . . Each form of behavior exhibited by the individual has a pattern of causes which are multiple, complex, and interrelated . . . .

Human behavior is purposive and goal-directed. The individual may not always be aware of basic purposes and underlying needs that are influencing his behavior . . . .

Behavior results from the interaction of genetic and environmental factors . . . .

As a biologic organism the individual possesses at birth certain physiological needs, but the methods of satisfying these needs and their subsequent development are to a great extent socially determined by a particular subcultural unit.

Through the interaction of genetic and social and physical environmental factors the individual develops a pattern of personality characteristics.

Individuals differ from one another in personal values, attitudes, personalities, and roles; yet at the same time the members of a group must possess certain common values and characteristics.

Each of the social groups to which an individual belongs helps shape his behavior . . . . The behavior of any individual reflects in many ways the influences of group pressures.

Socialization processes (for example, child-rearing practices) differ markedly in different social classes, groups, and societies. Personality structure and behavior are largely influenced by these practices.

Other especially important generalizations for educators are: (1) Since perception is selective, each person not only tends to see the world differently, but each tends to interpret and react to stimuli differently (one reason for confusion in knowledge). (2) Motivation is primarily a function of social learning. Middle-class children, for example, are motivated for academic achievement, while lower class children are not. (3) Intelligence levels, as measured by tests, are not fixed and static. That is, for a given child, I. Q. scores can vary considerably over a period of time. (4) The first few years of life are of profound importance in determining a child's later adjustment.

Again, the importance of learning should be noted in each of the above generalizations. Research during the past few years has suggested that learning may possibly occur in the human organism even prior to birth.

. . . .

PSYCHOLOGY IN THE SOCIAL STUDIES

I cannot overlook this opportunity of having a very few words about the "how" of introducing psychology into the elementary and secondary curricula, It seems that many of the generalizations which have been mentioned and the difficulties of experimental investigation could be introduced as early as the primary grades. At least one study has shown that children at that level are seeking psychological information. An especially effective vehicle for the introduction might well be much of the work that has been undertaken in perception. Excellent discussions can be found in almost all introductory textbooks. Furthermore, illustrations of simple and easy to make materials for demonstrations and experiments are contained in those sources. "Seeing is not believing," or selective perception would be a helpful truth to convey. Also certain principles of learning could be introduced via "how to train pets."

There have been at least two recent reported instances of the subject having been taught in a more or less deliberate fashion in two elementary grades. Reactions and comments of those youngsters should provide instructive guidelines for all those individuals who are thinking about and planning further development of the social studies portion of the primary curriculum.

In 1956 a formal course was offered—two terms in length—to a group of eighth graders. One of the questions asked of the students was, What do you expect to accomplish in this course? A preponderance of the replies indicated concern about "why people act as they do" for example:

> . . . to try to find out about myself and why I do the things I do . . .
> . . . to find out why some people are nice and why some are hotheads . . .
> I want to learn how to get along with people.
> I think I may be able to overcome some of my problems by knowing more about them, such as, when I get up in front of a group I get very nervous.
> I hope to find out what makes people have the emotions they have, such as being angry, doing things they know they shoudn't do, etc.
> . . . to find out why people behave in a certain way, why there are personality clashes and restlessness in class.

Further, some of their questions reflected interest in the sorts of problems with which psychology has been most concerned traditionally:

. . . to try to find out why people are different from each other.
. . . to find out why some are musically inclined and some can't even read music.[3]

Recently a school psychologist was asked to talk to a fourth grade class on "Psychology as a Science" as part of a unit in science. Reception of the presentation was exceptionally enthusiastic and led to a return engagement for the speaker later in the year. Whereas these children's questions were much broader in scope then those of the eighth graders (at age ten or so children haven't learned about the artificial boundaries of knowledge), their concerns were also mostly about "why people act as they do"; by way of illustration and *uncontaminated* by grammatical corrections:

Why does my brother tease me.
Why does father yell at you.
Whey is my sister a peast.
What makes a chiled winey in the morning.
How come boys and girls when they go into the first grade think they are jerks?
Why do people fight?
How comes a man is King of the family.

These children also exhibited some interest in the more traditional aspects of the field:

Why do cat's eyes get bigger when it is dark.
How come some people are smart and some arn't.
I stepped on a nail and it didn't hurt why didn't it hurt.
What part of the head lets you see.
What makes people go to sleep?
Could you kid become a genus after she or he has have many years of college?[4]

Perhaps the most obvious conclusion to be drawn from the queries and reactions of the children in these two grades is that primary youngsters do have important questions and exhibit curiosity about matters for which the field of psychology may have something to offer. The observation that children are curious about causation in human affairs will certainly come as neither a surprise nor as any enlightenment to teachers or to others who have worked extensively with them. An interesting paradox about formal education, however, is brought into sharp focus: throughout the public school era children are taught forthrightly about all aspects of the world—geography, history, mathematics, language, and so on. But they

[3]Joseph B. Patti, "Elementary Psychology for Eighth Graders," *American Psychologist,* 11:194–96, April 1956.
[4]Robert Belenky, "Psychology in a Suburban School System," *American Psychologist,* 18:669–70, October 1963.

are not taught directly about human behavior. Yet, in the final analysis, man's behavior is the basis of all other subject matter. Mathematics, to mention only one discipline, is nothing more than a series of abstractions which man has devised for his convenience in dealing with the world. In view of the fact that mathematics is often referred to as the "exact science" (somewhat incorrectly) it is interesting that man has changed it so much in the past few years.

ROLE OF PSYCHOLOGY

There is no intended implication here that other disciplines have nothing to contribute with respect to understanding man, but rather only the emphasis that psychology is the one field in which understanding of behavior is the prime concern. Of some importance, too, is the fact that the interests of children in many facets of behavior have been disregarded, at least in the early grades.

It would appear likely, also, that children "know," in a sense, a great deal about psychology. After all, most of them have been exposed to radio and television and all of them have had contact with at least a few people— such experiences having led them to form judgments and opinions about human behavior in general. Regrettably, popularized presentations of subject matter are not always the best, and contact with a few persons in a limited number of situations does not usually give a proper basis for broad valid generalizations. Thus it seems reasonable to suppose that adults have brought from childhood many false notions and distortions about human behavior (if college students are any sort of representative sample, that is more than supposition). Not long ago a woman asked a newspaper columnist: Can mental illness be caused by sleeping in metal hair curlers? Not only does that question reflect gross ignorance about psychology but about anatomy and physiology as well. Many of us can attest to the difficulties encountered in attempting to alter many of the incorrect ideas of college students as well as those of older adults.

Finally, in view of the fact that the boundaries of all knowledge are becoming less distinct, psychology should not be introduced in separate units. Instead, there should be combination and integration with material from other subject matter areas. It has always seemed strange to me that, on the one hand, throughout formal education we beseech students to integrate subject matter from various sources; while on the other hand, we create conditions for learning which seem to hamper or prevent integration—namely, the presentation of information in neat and discrete, but artificial, parcels. This, of course, should not preclude the offering of an elective course in psychology in high schools as a capstone to the many important concepts and generalizations that have been introduced earlier in the program.

immature for an advanced course in American constitutional law. He is intellectually immature in the sense that he is intellectually unprepared to take advanced work in political science. Again, some American parents are amazed to learn that in some schools boys and girls of eight and nine are taught to read and speak French or German. These parents may regard their own children of a similar age as too immature for such instruction; yet, strangely enough, they do not find it unusual that their children began speaking English—recognized by linguists to be a most difficult language—by the age of two.

Concerning the maturity required for philosophy, then, while pupils may not be ready for a serious, detailed presentation and just appraisal of elaborate philosophical systems, they may be ready for a more elementary critical analysis of basic philosophical problems. No one is suggesting that Kant's *Critique of Pure Reason* or Spinoza's *Ethics Demonstrated in the Geometric Manner* be required reading for fifth- or sixth-grade pupils, for works of this sort presuppose some acquaintance with other philosophical writings, and are difficult even for professional philosophers. But why should it be assumed that until a student is ready to cope with the most complex of philosophies he is not ready for any philosophy? No one makes this assumption concerning other areas of study. The student does not begin his study of history with European historiography or the diplomatic history of the United States, nor does he begin his study of psychology with a course in physiological psychology or advanced psychometrics.

It is sometimes argued that the learning process in philosophy is different from that in other disciplines. The pupils' learning in the sciences, for example, is said to be analogous to their learning to swim. They play along the shore in shallow water and are not permitted into deeper water until they have learned to swim. Their grade school days, then, are a playing along scientific shores, a getting used to scientific waters. In the high school they are given a chance to swim, but only in shallow waters, and not without the close supervision of the teacher. Only in college do the students ever really get the chance to venture into the deeper waters of any science and swim on their own. To be sure, some pupils never go beyond the getting used to the water, for they never succeed in swimming in the science; they never cease crawling along the bottom, and so they never get into the theoretical structure of science. Some, of course, get in over their heads and drown. Consequently, the teacher must be both life guard and swimming instructor. The pupils must be kept close to the shore, and on occasion rescued from deeper waters, until they have learned to swim.

Now the difference between science and philosophy, it is said, is that in learning philosophy there can be no playing in shallow waters. The student cannot wade gradually into deeper and deeper waters, for there is a sharp drop off at the water's edge. There is no getting used to the water here; when the pupil jumps in he is immediately over his head and must swim or drown. Very few high school students are mentally tall enough to have both their head above the water and their feet touching bottom, and to toss a grade school pupil into such water is almost surely to invite a drowning.

Therefore, some persons would have us erect signs around philosophy, signs reading "Danger, Deep Water." "Danger, Tricky Currents," or "Beware of the Undertow." Now it may be that all of these signs have their place, not only beside philosophy, but around scientific waters as well. However, the opponent of philosophy commits the logical fallacy of composition; he mistakenly attributes the characteristics of a part of philosophy to the whole. He sees only the deep end and overlooks the shallow end of the pool. I should like to argue that there can be a "kiddies' pool" in philosophy just as there is in other disciplines. There can be a getting used to abstractions, philosophical ideas and critical analysis; there is an important elementary training period here as in the sciences.

THE ROLE OF PHILOSOPHY IN THE
SOCIAL STUDIES PROGRAM

There is no reason why the beginning student must jump into philosophy by way of either a specific philosophical system or courses that have as prerequisites an advanced knowledge of both philosophy and some other subject matter. The proper place to begin is with the basic philosophical problems, and these can be treated on an elementary level. Moreover, they can be related to topics in ethics, religion, aesthetics, and the social sciences with which pupils are already familiar; for example, the difference between right and wrong, the meaning of freedom, the existence of God, the censorship of art, the source of human dignity, the role of authorities in a democratic society, and the difference between truth and falsehood.

Logic also can be introduced on every level. Even grade school pupils can be taught to distinguish between correct and incorrect patterns of deductive and inductive reasoning in the social studies as they do in mathematics and science education. They need to recognize the simpler types of formal and informal fallacies such as the syllogistic (formal) fallacies of the undistributed middle term, of drawing an affirmative conclusion from a negative premise, and of exclusive premises, and the informal fallacies of appeal to force, of argument from ignorance, of argument directed to the man, of appeal to pity, of appeal to the people, of false cause, of amphiboly, of accent, of division, and others that are discussed in the standard introductory texts to logic.

Perhaps a few examples will make it clear that an understanding of these fallacies is not beyond the grasp of young boys and girls. The following is an example of the fallacy of the undistributed middle term:

All Communists are persons who criticize our present foreign policy. All demopublicans are persons who criticize our present foreign policy. Therefore, all demopublicans are Communists.

Notice that in both premises the term, "persons who criticize our foreign policy," which provides the link between "demopublicans" and "Communists," is undistributed in that in neither premise are we talking about *all* persons who criticize our present foreign policy. One might just as well argue that since all dogs are animals, and all cats are animals, then all dogs are cats. Both arguments have the same form. Obviously, the conclusion does not follow. Our next example is an instance of the fallacy of appeal to force:

It should be obvious to you, Mrs. Brown, that it is your turn to stay after school today. I say that it is, and I am the principal. You want to stay on here next year don't you?

In this argument the conclusion is not proved by the premises, because the premises are logically irrelevant to the truth of the conclusion. But because of the threat of force the conclusion may be accepted. As in all fallacies of relevance, the argument gets its persuasiveness from the psychological, rather than logical, connection between the premises and the conclusion. Our final example illustrates the fallacy of division:

Dogs have been hunters for thousands of years, so my dog Spot should really catch lots of rabbits.

Quite the contrary, Spot couldn't care less for rabbits. There is an ambiguity here; the properties of a class, dogs, have been identified with the properties of a member of the class, Spot, but the class may have characteristics which its members do not possess. As in all fallacies of ambiguity, the force of the argument is dependent upon our inattention to subject matter, our carelessness.

The teacher will find that most elementary logic texts contain explanations and examples of each of the specific types of formal and informal fallacies.

That our schools will turn out full-fledged philosophers is not to be expected—nor will essays of this sort produce professional teachers of philosophy. The most that we can hope for is that the students will gain an awareness of and appreciation for philosophical problems and be more careful and accurate in their thinking, arguing, and decision-making.

It is a mistake to assume that philosophies and philosophical problems are found only in philosophy classes, for philosophies are not something given to students by teachers of philosophy. By the time the child has reached the sixth grade he has at least the beginning of a philosophical point of view, and by the time he has reached the senior year of high school or the freshman year of college what was earlier a flexible philosophical outlook has pretty well solidified into dogmatism. As a matter of fact, the average sixth grader is closer to being a true philosopher than is the college freshman,[2] for the sixth grader has a more open mind, his point of view has not crystallized; at least the crust is easier to break. Philosophies are things neither given to, nor forced upon, students by teachers of philosophy; they belong to the cultural inheritance of the student. Ideas concerning the good and the bad, the real and the unreal, the true and the false, the nature of man and God, are absorbed by the student long before he gets into his first philosophy course. The unfortunate thing is that by this time he may be unable to philosophize; his natural curiosity for diverse philosophical points of view has died as the dominant beliefs which he acquires from his society—and which that society tends to require of him—have become fixed. The task of the teacher is to make the pupil aware "that there really are many different, defensible answers to many different, important, intelligible questions; that the world in which he lives is not a single, one-dimensional object, toward which one simple-minded, clear-cut and culturally ordained attitude alone is appropriate."[3] That this comes as a staggering discovery to many college students is a discredit to our elementary and secondary schools.

Strangely enough, such staggering experiences are sometimes given as a reason why courses in philosophy should not be taught even to college freshmen, let alone high school students. Not only are such students intellectually too immature for philosophy, says the opponent, they are apt to be emotionally immature as well. Philosophy courses do prove unsettling to some students, even to some graduate students, but this is because they have learned not to be philosophers; at an early age they ceased to philosophize, and so it comes as a shattering experience to them to learn that there are respectable answers in disagreement with theirs to problems which they have ceased to regard as problems. They need to be roused from their complacency. As Joseph Wood Krutch says, "Unless education to some extent maladjusts the educated man to life as it is lead [sic] it can neither improve anything nor even change anything."[4]

[2]Cf. Clifton Fadiman's statement in *The Instructor*, 66:42, January 1957: "I should like to set before you what may seem a crackpot notion. The notion is that the best place to teach philosophy is not the university but the elementary school; and that the ideal student of philosophy is the child from eight to twelve."

[3]"The Teaching of Philosophy in American High Schools," p. 93.

[4]Joseph Wood Krutch, *More Lives Than One* (New York: William Sloane Associates, 1962), p. 340.

Rather than being a reason for postponing the teaching of philosophy, emotional immaturity should be a reason for introducing pupils to it early. The sixth grader will not be at all disturbed at finding that there are really many different, defensible points of view concerning the good, the true, and the real. He may, indeed, find the whole affair charming, but if he has to wait six or seven years, the discovery may have traumatic effect.

Apart from the influence of logic in helping the student to think clearly and correctly, the most important contribution that philosophy can make to the social studies program is to help the student to become aware, if not to appreciate, that there are diverse philosophical points of view on the nature of truth, freedom of will, the existence of universal moral laws, the nature of man, and so on. The role of the teacher is not to give the student a philosophy, but to keep him from developing a narrow philosophical provincialism, to keep his philosophical outlook flexible.

The normal child is not only curious but also, I think, inclined to dogmatism. His attitude is not to take the answers given to his questions as tentative and provisional but as absolute, ultimate, and final. For the very young child the mere fact that a statement has been made is enough to make it true, the mere fact that something is done enough to make it right. And when such statements are made by those in authority, parents, ministers, and teachers, they are beyond question, beyond review, absolutely true. The student cannot help but feel uneasy and dissatisfied when he is later asked to mistrust "absolute truths" and to accept all explanations as hypotheses, as tentative solutions to problems.

I suggest that the teacher's role is to lead his pupils away from dogmatism to thoughtful open-mindedness. Dogmatism is a form of arrogance and pride, a vice, concerning knowledge claims. Thoughtful open-mindedness, on the other hand, is a healthy skepticism, a form of humility; it is modesty with respect to knowledge claims. Such an approach is not only Christian—since humility is a Christian virtue and pride a vice—but democratic as well, for the dogmatist is not likely to be tolerant and respectful concerning the beliefs of others, while the thoughtful skeptic in being humble cannot help but be tolerant and appreciative of the beliefs of others, even though he is not persuaded to accept and adopt them. Religiously, humility is the feeling one has when he sees his place in the Universe as a whole, only one of the many children of God. Politically, it is the feeling of the democrat who is aware that his voice and his demands are those of only one citizen among the many within the state. In contrast, the dogmatist is one who arrogantly asserts that he is first among the children of God and demands that his voice alone be heard within the state.

Thus with respect to its role in the school, philosophy may be defined as the attempt to introduce the virtue of humility into pupils whose normal curiosity tends to be smothered by the vice of dogmatism. And now a word of warning: when dogmatism has been destroyed, nihilism rather than open-mindedness may take its place. The student may foolishly conclude that it really does not matter what one believes: a person may be an idealist and believe that reality is of the nature of mind, or he may be a materialist and believe that reality is matter; he may be a hedonist and believe that good is pleasure, or he may be a logical empiricist and believe that all ethical judgments are mere expressions of emotion; he may be a pantheist and believe that all things are a part of God, or he may be an atheist and believe that there is no God; he may be a democrat and believe that human dignity is best achieved in the state wherein the people are given freedom to govern themselves, or he may be a totalitarian and believe that the state is supreme and that man's sole purpose is to serve the state. Some may feel that it really makes no difference which side one takes or whether he even takes a side, for there is no objective or real ground of truth and of moral principles. Thus the student may think that the reason he should tolerate other beliefs is that beliefs are not important enough to disagree with.

The point is that beliefs matter very much! Beliefs of others are to be tolerated not because they are unimportant but because they are important; and they are important because they may contain aspects of the truth. There may be infallible truths, but fallible human beings select them and interpret them; so we cannot be absolutely sure regarding any belief, although we can be more sure of some than of others. The teacher's task is to help the student explore the reasons for accepting various philosophical beliefs, to discover their hidden assumptions and implications for action, and to ascertain their compatibility with other beliefs that are accepted as true. Thus the teacher's task is two-fold, to help the student see that there may be good reasons for each of the diverse philosophical positions, but that this is *not* itself a good reason for refusing to take any position at all.

It is to be expected that pupils will accept the skeptical attitude with more grace than will many of their parents in discovering that their children have been led to develop it. Parents are notoriously dogmatic and are rather sensitive to "dangerous" doctrines and free thinking. Some demand the democratic right to deny their children the right to think for themselves! Because of this, some teachers will prefer to let sleeping dogs lie, and in this case, let sleeping pupils sleep; there will, however, be less growling from dogmatists and less danger of being bitten by them, if philosophical considerations are introduced on the elementary level rather than waiting for high school and college. The emotional immaturity of parents may not be challenged unless the child becomes emotionally disturbed, and this is less likely if the child is introduced to philosophy early.

The teacher's position is not an easy one. He has a duty not only to parents but also to his students and his state. As a teacher his first duty is to his student. He must assist in the growth of his pupil, and this is to say that he must help the pupil to become a free, responsible human being, to realize his dignity as a rational individual. And in a democracy this is precisely the teacher's duty to the state.

In a healthy, growing society differences of opinion are to be expected and even encouraged. In a democratic society it should be no disgrace that one's beliefs are in disagreement with those of his neighbor, but it should be a cause of alarm if such disagreement were discouraged. Controversy ought to be encouraged, for our "social truths" are hammered out and continuously tested in controversy. In the conflict of open discussion our democratic ideals are given renewed life, and we as a people are strengthened through a renewed commitment to them. Without such free and open discussion our ideals become mere empty platitudes having no influence on our behavior either as individuals or as a people and may soon be forgotten.

If philosophy serves no other purpose than that it stimulates thoughtful controversy, this would be enough to warrant its inclusion in the social studies program, for in such controversy not only are ideas tested but the conditions are provided for the growth of young, curious minds. The basic test of any school is that the students should leave with as much curiosity as, and considerably less inclination toward dogmatic authoritarianism than, they began with, and philosophy should help the school to meet this test.

STUART C. MILLER

Associate Professor of Social Science, San Francisco
State College

13. The Interdisciplinary Approach to Teaching Social Studies*

The central position of history in the high school social studies curriculum is now being seriously challenged by the historian's academic cousins in the social sciences. Their silence, or relative silence, until recently has been due, in part, to the theory that history offered the best synthesis for all of the social sciences. The very nature of history makes it easier to fuse useful concepts and theories from many fields as the story of the development of man and society is unfolded. Since all of the social sciences could not be taught in the high school, this seemed to be the best compromise. Today, few social scientists believe that any real fusion takes place in the geography and history courses which make up the bulk of the curriculum. Unlike many of the popular critics of this curriculum, they refuse to take the title of a course at face value. They know that upon closer examination a course entitled "Understanding Current Problems in Our Country" is apt to be a standard course in American history. My own experience indicates that Arthur Bestor's "social stew" exists more often in curriculum theory than in the classroom.

But the rebellion has gone far beyond this. These social scientists no longer want any fusion, but separate courses in their own disciplines. Too often the fusion of economics, the economist argues, is at best superficial, and taught by someone illiterate in this discipline. More often than not it is economic history and not economics. Inflation, for example, may be dutifully mentioned at the appropriate time in the history of the Western world, but rarely is any attempt made to conceptualize it from the point of view of the economist, illustrating the relationship between the economic variables involved. It is no wonder that "inflation" has been used so effectively to frighten voters into supporting a program that virtually starves the public sector. Generations of Americans have been taught that inflation is an unmitigated evil instead of understanding that a certain amount of it is probably a necessary evil in an expanding economy. There are many such examples in economics. The Federal Reserve System

Social Education, XXVIII: 195–98, April 1964. Used by permission.

is taught frequently by having the students memorize districts and how many directors there are for each Federal Reserve Bank, etc., without once mentioning its relationship to the need for an elastic supply of money. When the latter is pointed out, too often the mechanics of controlling bank credit and the amount of money in circulation is erroneously presented, attributing control to its discount rate rather than its open market operations. Budgets may be mentioned when the history teacher gets to the New Deal, or in discussing current events, but rarely is fiscal policy discussed as a possible stimulant for economic growth. As a result, the economist is demanding, and getting, a separate course on the high school level, and a greater share in the training of high school teachers.

The behaviorists, anthropologists, sociologists, and social psychologist have even gone beyond simply a demand for a separate course. They often argue that history is not a social science at all and does not offer the best possible synthesis for these disciplines. Professor Chilcott has put in a bid for anthropology, and Professor Donald Oliver for social psychology to displace history in this role. Their disciplines, it is argued, would not ignore history but would focus on contemporary society, and more efficiently achieve that often stated goal in teaching social studies: to develop an understanding of the political, economic, and social world in which we live.[1]

The fears and complaints of these social scientists are not without justification. The teacher of social studies receives the bulk of his training from historians who frequently manifest a kind of siege mentality in rejecting any kind of influence from the behavioral sciences. Thus it is not simply ignorance of the disciplines when a teacher refuses the aid of any of their analytical tools, but a strong bias against such "sociological jargon." If the curriculum for training teachers requires some exposure to them, the historian tells the student to equate it with their education courses as utter nonsense, and certainly to leave it outside of their history classrooms. Perhaps, some of the very exciting history being written using behavioral concepts by such traditionally trained historians as David Potter and Lee Benson will alter this in the future.

The teacher of social studies should take a second look at the possibilities of an interdisciplinary approach to history. Actually he fuses concepts given to him by the geographer and political scientist all the time. He would consider this a legitimate part of history. But it might be that the behavioral sciences can offer him concepts and theories which will enable him to organize and explain historical data more efficiently. History courses in grades 10 and 11 already encompass more material

[1]J. H. Chilcott, "A Proposal for the Unification of Secondary School Courses Through Anthropology," *Clearing House*, 36:391, 1962; Donald Oliver, "The Selection of Content in the Social Studies," *Harvard Educational Review*, 27:294–301, 1957.

than can possibly be covered with any meaning in a single year. The teacher frequently presents huge doses of factual and descriptive material, more closely resembling antiquarianism than history, simply because he does not know how to conceptualize the material. A model like W. W. Rostow's stages of economic growth could provide him with a useful conceptual scheme upon which to hang his facts and show important relationships between political, economic, and social variables. Or the theory of "status politics" may be worth the time needed to develop it in class if it affords a clearer explanation of the behavior of the abolitionists, and McCarthyites. Historians such as David Donald and Richard Hofstadter have, in fact, used this last concept to interpret these movements.

In teaching a high school history course it behooves the teacher to examine the different ways in which anthropologists and sociologists have conceptualized social change. As an example, let us look at one possibility. We often hear of the dichotomy between "heroes" and "social forces" in explaining change. But these social forces are rarely spelled out in the classroom. They remain vague and almost mystic to the student. Max Rafferty's recent lamentation over the disappearance of the hero from the classroom has little relationship to reality.[2] True, Nathan Hale and John Paul Jones may be missing, but that is only because we have so much more history to cover; and other types of heroes—industrial, technical, and political ones—are deemed more important. It is not unusual for even bright students to arrive at college under the impression that Andrew Jackson brought about mass democracy, T. R. broke the trusts, and F.D.R. was the cause of the New Deal.

How can the behaviorists help us to get across a more realistic view of social change? For one thing, they are more interested in social forces than individuals and spell out the important sources of change. Generally they are divided into six categories: Technological change, population change (size, migration, and distribution), changes in natural resources, changes in neighboring communities, natural occurrences, and lastly, ideas. The last category is seriously debated by some who view ideas more as a rationale for change already occurring than as a source of change. These forces first affect our value system which leads to institutional change, the behaviorist contends. The teacher might justifiably ask which of the myriad definitions of social values and social institutions he should use. Certainly a study of these definitions leads to a good deal of semantic confusion. My advice would be to use the one best understood by himself, and best suited for classroom use. I would define social values as an emotionally charged preferential list of cultural products, standards or ideas which the people of a society prize not only for themselves, but

---

[2] Max Rafferty, "What's Happened to Patriotism?" *Readers Digest*, October 1961.

for the group and the descendants of that group. These products and patterns of behavior and belief have importance in themselves over and beyond their practical utility; e.g., Christianity, individualism, democracy, Shakespeare, the automobile. Social institutions I would define as formal groups engaged in behavior directed at meeting the basic needs of man or society. Putting across these concepts requires illustration by the teacher, but their utility in a history course may be worth the time invested.

Armed with such a conceptual model of social change, the teacher can efficiently explain a good deal about both the past and the present. It can be introduced at almost any point and used again in later units. The two broad areas through which it cuts most efficiently in American history are Westward expansion and industrialization. The student can more readily visualize how values would undergo change as a result of migration, rapidly expanding economic opportunity, and adaptation to new conditions. For example, the values associated with egalitarianism, individualism, mass democracy and social mobility can be explained in terms of people migrating ahead of many of their social institutions. The lack of occupational specialization, one of the key determinants of social stratification, made equality a reality to begin with along the frontier. Since these pioneers had to serve as lawyers, judges, doctors, and preachers at one time or another, they were less in awe of the authentic professional with traditional training once he did arrive. The potential abundance and wealth of the West enhanced the value placed upon the self-made man and again lessened the esteem of those upper classes of inherited wealth. There is no end to the available travel books and diaries to illustrate this in the classroom. Reverend Bayard Rush Hall, a Union and Princeton graduate who went out to the Iowa territory, quoted one Westerner who paused outside of his house to exclaim to a friend: "Well thats whar thet grammur man lives that larns 'em latin and grandlike things. Allow we'll oust him yet." Hall also quoted a circuit rider's sermon to illustrate his resentment of the presence of a formally trained minister in the territory:

Yes, bless the Lord, I am a poor humble man—and I don't know a single letter in the ABC's, and couldn't read a chapter in the Bible no how you could fix it, bless the Lord! I jest preach like old Peter and Pall by the Speret. Yes, we don't ax pay in cash nor trade neither for the Gospel, and aren't no hirelins like them high-flowered college larned sheepskins.

De Tocqueville said a good deal about the American's predilection for equality, even at the expense of freedom if necessary.[3] This insight can help to explain both the populists and the McCarthyites. What better way

[3]Alexis de Tocqueville, *Democracy in America* (New York: Vintage Press, 1954), 2:99–103.

to explain the Wisconsin Senator's reckless attacks upon the very pillars of our society, such symbols of authority and inequality as *The New York Times,* Harvard, Yale, and Princeton, the National Council of Churches, and the State Department, or his preoccupation with traitors who were born with a silver spoon in their mouths?[4] There was more to McCarthyism than this, to be sure. "Status politics," ethnic considerations (German and Irish) and isolationism all help to explain this phenomenon, but the strong egalitarian motive in our society can also help to account for it.

What institutional change resulted from this alteration in values associated with the frontier? Well, the more democratic manner in which presidential candidates were nominated and elected, the spoils system and log cabin campaigns all reflect these new values. Rather than the popular conception of Jackson bringing this about, it was due to social forces of which Jackson took advantage. He was a backcountry aristocrat, a "nabob" in Tennessee who fought the democratic forces of Grundy and Carroll, and a Mason as was Van Buren, who originally opposed the nominating conventions initiated by the Anti-Masonic party, the real party of egalitarianism. No period in our history, perhaps, better illustrates that the "hero" cannot alter these forces, but only use them more efficiently than can others.

There were other important institutional changes: land grant colleges with an emphasis upon practical subjects; frontier revivalism and the creation of new sects around personalities such as William Miller and John Smith; the breakdown of the authoritarian structure of the family. Perhaps the most important result was our inability to nominate and elect a really strong President after Jackson until the twentieth century with the lone exception of Lincoln, who could be considered almost an accident.

One important result of such an approach is that it breaks down the dichotomy between Western migration and industrialization. The values of the frontiersman were remarkably similar to those of the early industrialist. The former we forget bought land for speculation, too, and behaved as a good capitalist. In fact, one could view the industrialist as simply another type of pioneer, and industrialization as an economic frontier. If we view both as a social process, we can salvage some of the Turner thesis.[5] Of course, the student has to understand that the results are only intelligible

[4]Martin Trow, "Small Businessmen, Political Tolerance and Support for McCarthy," *American Journal of Sociology*, 64:279–80, 1958. See also S. M. Lipset, "The Sources of the 'Radical Right,'" in Daniel Bell, ed., *The New American Right* (New York: Criterion Books, 1955), pp. 166–219.

[5]See George Wilson Pierson, "The Frontier and American Institutions," *New England Quarterly*, 15:224–55, 1942. For an excellent criticism of the Turner thesis and an attempt to salvage it as a migration thesis, see also David Potter, *People of Plenty* (Chicago: University of Chicago Press, 1954), chap. 7.

if he keeps in mind the values brought to the frontier: the democratic beliefs of the radicals in the Revolution which, in turn, can be traced to seventeenth-century England, the Puritan emphasis upon an emotional experience of conversion, and the "Protestant ethic."

This conceptualization of change can constantly be referred to in later units. The student should be asked to analyze later changes in terms of these traditional sources of change. In looking at the New Deal, he should be able to see its relationship to technological changes known as the industrial revolution and accompanying migration to urban centers, and to visualize how these social forces would alter values and lead to institutionalized change. The less obvious and less concrete changes brought about by industrialization are too often overlooked in the classroom. The student should be made aware of what migration into the city meant in terms of total dependency upon wages; lack of personal satisfaction and identification working on an assembly line; effect of the premium placed upon physical space; the transition of the family from a producing unit to a consuming one. I have witnessed lessons in high school classrooms on the standardization of goods without a single mention of the concomitant standardization of life itself, or on increased economic specialization without the direction of the students' attention to the fact that this increases the dependency of members of society on each other to satisfy their wants. The booms, crashes, panics and depressions are recorded in the classroom in good chronological order without any consideration of how it must have increased the feeling of insecurity as men faced more abstract, comples economic forces over which they had less control. Taught correctly, the student quickly sees how technological and ecological changes can greatly alter values. The response was a collectivistic one on all levels. That is, the industrialist formed pools and then trusts to mitigate the effect of competition and business cycles. The distributors formed associations and were perhaps, more instrumental than any other group in bringing about railroad regulation and the Interstate Commerce Act. The workers formed unions and the farmers cooperatives. All of these organizations sought government aid, both state and federal, at one time or another. The very density of population in cities would necessitate greater group cooperation in areas such as crime prevention and fire and health controls. All this would have to affect values associated with rugged individualism. With such an understanding, it would be difficult for the student to view the New Deal as a betrayal of Jeffersonian liberalism, or a left wing plot hatched in the economics department at Harvard.

Current events can be analyzed with the same conceptual model. For example, the student could be asked to analyze today's increased Negro militancy in terms of these traditional sources of change. It would be difficult for him to view it as the result of a Yankee or Communist plot. A more fruitful approach would be apparent in the migration of Negroes into cities during the two world wars. In the cities the Negro is less dependent upon the white man than he was as a sharecropper, and even has greater economic power as a consumer due to his higher wages. All this will alter his values. He no longer accepts Uncle-Tomism or displaced aggression against his own, or humor as the only responses to Jim Crow. He is now in a position to demand more, and the timing of this demand at the very moment when we are competing with Soviet Russia for the allegiance of the underdeveloped world inhabited largely by non-Whites sensitive to the racial issue, has put the whites in a position which makes it difficult to refuse him his demands. Lastly, ideas associated with Christianity and democracy have afforded him powerful arguments with which to irritate the conscience of the white man. In other words, traditional sources of change, i.e., migration, effect of neighboring states, and ideas, have altered to a degree the values of both the Negroes and the whites on this issue. With this understanding, the debate, fostered largely by the White Citizens Council, over whether or not Martin Luther King is a card-carrying Communist becomes totally irrelevant.

Medicare may well be "creeping socialism," but the student is made aware that changing values are behind it and not a left wing plot pulling the wool over our eyes. Since 1880 the percentage of people over 65 in our population has increased from 3.4 to 8.1 in 1950[6] This means that more families support people over 65 whose social security checks hardly begin to cover their medical bills. A few heavy bills from a nursing home will quickly alter their attitudes toward a collective plan which will offer them relief. Increased medical costs are in turn partially due to technological changes in the field of medicine.[7] If they continue to increase at the same rate, it is not inconceivable that our values will change enough to permit some sort of health plan similar to the one in the United Kingdom. If it comes, it cannot be attributed simply to the administration that initiates it, but to social forces now in operation.

This is, of course, only one of the many possibilities in utilizing the approach of the anthropologist and sociologist to social and cultural change. It can provide the teacher with a valuable pedagogical tool permitting him more efficiently to organize a mass of material. It also is a better approach to the period discussed than the usual broad coverage that includes "locofocos," "barnburners," "hunkers," and such, in that it

---

[6]Warren Thompson, *Population Problems* (New York: McGraw-Hill Book Co., 1953), p. 95.

[7]See *The New Republic*, November 9, 1963, pp. 9-12. Almost this entire issue was allocated to an excellent discussion of the problems facing both the doctors and the patients (pp. 5-43).

more clearly illustrates cause and effect relationships. Moreover, such a conceptualization avoids the liberal or conservative indoctrination that often takes place in the social studies classroom. The teacher does not have to assign moral values to these events but simply stick to the cause-and-effect relationships, much the same way a teacher of physics would do. It is immaterial whether the teacher approves or disapproves of the current Negro militancy. Given the social forces that have brought it about, there is little we can do beyond slowing down or speeding up the social process by which Negroes are achieving equal status. One can discuss plans to make this transition more orderly and less costly for all concerned,[8] but we cannot prevent it. Lastly, this conceptual model not only provides the student with too much sophistication to swallow a silly conspiracy theory of history and social change,[9] but it also equips him to anticipate change. In other words, such a model may help him to see what Robert Heilbroner calls "the forward edge of history."[10]

[8]For example, see Morton Grodzins, "The Metropolitan Area as a Racial Problem," in Earl Rabb, ed., *American Race Relations Today*, (New York: Doubleday and Co., 1962, pp. 85–123. See also Ingle Dederer Gibel, "How Not to Integrate the Schools," *Harper's*, November 1963.

[9]This is not to imply, of course, that the teacher using a strictly disciplinarian approach inculcates such interpretation. But it does suggest that the usual bland description of the past with little real analysis leaves the student more vulnerable to the plot thesis of either right or left wing variety, depending upon his own political predilections.

[10]Robert Heilbroner, *The Future as History* (New York: Harper and Bro., 1959), pp. 13–58.

EDGAR BERNSTEIN

*Associate Chairman of the Freshman Project, Laboratory School,
University of Chicago*

14. Structural Perspectives: The Social Science Disciplines and the Social Studies*

Although important advances have been made within the social sciences toward developing insights for clarifying and analyzing the realities facing man, all too many people continue to lack an understanding of the forces affecting their lives and come to feel that they exist as individuals in a difficult world not of their own making. Social studies education could accept the responsibility for making available the *perspectives* from the social science disciplines by which the individual can begin to explicate his enigmatic world. By delineating and coordinating these perspectives, and by making them central to an *integrated social studies curriculum* for the high school, an important step might be taken toward making available to the young, and thereby to the future, some of the advances in knowledge now available in the sciences of man.

The idea of an integrated social studies curriculum is not new. Not a few historians see such a curriculum in a well-wrought history sequence, and some cultural geographers find this curriculum available in a thorough study of their discipline. Beyond reflecting dedication to their respective fields, there is truth in what these experts say. When one attempts a survey of all the social sciences, one is struck by the frequency with which each discipline claims a significant similarity and important relation to many, if not all, of the other social science disciplines. While one may be reluctant to label any one of the disciplines an integrated social studies curriculum, one cannot take exception with the recognition of the underlying interrelationship of the various fields encompassed in the social sciences. But organizing a curriculum which makes explicit these relationships is difficult. There is something symbolic about the names of courses presented to students as world history, economics, geography—the specialization indicated by the course title suggests the single dominant set of perspectives of each course. An historian and a geographer find it difficult to give each other his proper

Social Education, xxix: 79–85, February, 1965. Used by permission.

due in a single course. Each is dedicated to the full coverage of his field, and often can do little more than suggest the relationship of his field to other social sciences. The expert concentrates on the significant and unique perspectives that his field has to deliver to students to aid them in understanding the societies which are a part of the world in which they exist. (The problem becomes more complicated when the specialist is quietly convinced of the dominant importance of his own field over the others.)

Yet each discipline presents important and unique ways of explicating the individual's world, and it is important that students have all of these views presented to them by the time they complete high school. For some, this may be their only opportunity to gain the insights of each of the fields of the social sciences because they will not go on to higher education. And it would seem desirable for those who do go on and who may come to specialize in one of the social sciences to have some initial contact with the viewpoints and tools of each discipline early in their school career to provide the initial interest in, and to set a base of understanding for, ensuing studies.

The conviction that high school students should have contact with the several social science disciplines raises problems of implementation. Attempts to give full coverage to some of the disciplines will necessarily lead to the exclusion of others. A course in economics will absorb the time necessary to present a course in sociology. Unless one thinks seriously of requiring of every student a course in each discipline—a solution which not only is unrealistic about the amount of time available in the school years, but also is pedagogically unsound—the inclusion and exclusion of disciplines will be by an arbitrary priority established on the basis of the choice-maker's bias and training. Even were it possible to require the study of the full complement of disciplines, the problem of the coverage of historical content would not yet have been allowed for, and this is in itself a mammoth consumer of time.

One must question also whether students, required to take a course in any of the disciplines, can have the internal involvement and motivation which seem to be requisite for effective absorption and internalization of the ideas and concepts of these disciplines. For younger students particularly, it is to be seriously questioned whether that necessary motivation would be sufficiently present in a *required* course entitled economics, anthropology, or geography; such motivation might be more likely in students who have already had some contact and training in these areas and who come to them with an already established interest.

It is also questionable whether high school students, especially in their first two years, have the intellectual sophistication which would enable them to deal with the full theoretical development of any of the social science disciplines. Those disciplines that are attempted at the lower levels of high school have to maintain both a pace and a simplicity designed to allow for children of this age. At best they must be a somewhat watered-down and not totally adequate development of the disciplines.

Because of the limitations on the offerings of "pure" social science disciplines that can be made to high school students, one is tempted to the conclusion that any effort to construct a curriculum for the high school level which includes understandings of all the social science fields is doomed to fail. Either it cannot be done, or if it is done it will be partial and inadequate. Yet it may be possible to deal with the difficulties involved in constructing and presenting such a curriculum. To do so would require agreement on the following points regarding such a curriculum:

A. All students will be presented with the basic frameworks of every social science discipline without displacing important historical and contemporary content. These presentations will be less than the full development of the highly sophisticated bodies of knowledge contained in each social science discipline; nevertheless the significant and basic ideas of each discipline will not be jeopardized.

B. Provisions will be made through advanced courses in the social science disciplines for students with high interest and motivation to pursue the study of a particular discipline in order to develop a full and sophisticated understanding of the knowledge and ideas of that field.

A curriculum with the above characteristics would make use of:

1. The conceptual frameworks characterizing each of the social science disciplines, and the basic conceptual framework underlying the social sciences as a whole. These two types of framework will be referred to respectively as *discipline perspectives* and *basic perspectives*; together they will be grouped under the heading of *structural perspectives*.

2. The concept of the spiral curriculum presented by Bruner.[1] The work of Piaget and Inhelder,[2] has suggested that if one constructs a base of understandings at an early level, the teaching of those understandings in a highly complex, fully developed and sophisticated way at a later level will be facilitated. Thus, if freshman students develop a feeling for some of the concepts of economics without requiring that these be presented in a formal economics course, they will be prepared at a later level to deal with a fully developed course in that discipline at a highly theoretical level.

The following sections represent an attempt to begin to delineate the *structural perspectives* of the social sciences, and to suggest how these can be organized into an integrated social studies curriculum for the high school which makes use of the concept of the spiral curriculum.

[1]Jerome Bruner. *The Process of Education* (Cambridge: Harvard University Press. 1960).

[2]Jean Piaget. *Logic and Psychology* (New York: Basic Books, 1960).

TOWARD A DELINEATION OF THE
STRUCTURAL PERSPECTIVES

The Basic Perspectives

The social sciences focus on man in society through the study of history and the contemporary world. Basic to this study is the concept that social phenomena result from a *multiplicity of causal factors*. There are three sets of determinant factors involved in this multiplicity: geographic, biological, and cultural. The *geographic* deals with the effects of the natural environment on man and his society. This set would include the factors of climate, topography, natural resources, and location. The *biological* factors consist of the requirements for survival of the human body—at base, food, air, water and people. Man is essentially a biological being—so is he born into the world and so does he remain. As he grows within his society, he incorporates into his own unique essence the attributes of that society. He develops therefrom a personality which is moderated by his own particular eugenics as well as by the universal biological needs with which he is born. But, though the personality products of society differ from individual to individual, the biological universals remain constant and ever present.

To deal with the geographic and biological determinants, man created culture, and *cultural* forces have come to form the most profound set of determinants of all. It is through the device of culture that man has, with increasing success, met the forces of biology and geography. The story of man might be viewed as the history of the extension through society of the knowledge and understanding which have enabled him to deal with the forces of nature and the needs of the human body with increasing success. The emergence of civilization must in part be so viewed (though the appearance of civilization was also a response to cultural factors).[3] But though man has become increasingly knowledgeable and facile in relation to the natural and biological forces, he has proceeded much more slowly in expanding his understanding of the cultural forces, of the effects of society on society and on the individual. Yet he has proceeded, and to such a point that today attempts to analyze social phenomena without considering the social forces which impinge upon these phenomena are inadequate.

Though the distinctions between geography, biology, and culture provide useful ways of looking at social phenomena, they are not isolable in reality. For from the time that man moved from isolation into the simplest society, he moved into the midst of the highly complex multiplicity of forces which man has faced ever since. Perhaps the theoretical "primal man" dealt only with his biology and natural surroundings, but when he

---

[3]V. Gordon Childe suggests that the first civilizations in Europe and the Middle East appear at a time when a high degree of cultural interchange among many societies was in progress (i.e., cultural determinism). See V. Gordon Childe. *Social Evolution* (Cleveland: World Publishing Company, 1963).

took a mate he began to construct and to partake of a culture and to transmit that culture to ensuing generations. The directions the primal figure initiated somewhat determined a line of development for those that followed him. The cultural divergencies that exist between societies isolated over time may be due to the fact that a number of primal figures, faced with essentially universal problems of biology and with particular versions of the geographic forces, dealt with these forces each in their own peculiar ways and thus determined the differential directions of the societies which followed them. Maintaining their isolation, these societies retained and expanded their cultural uniqueness.

Once established, culture took its place among the other forces which determined the direction and development of man's progress thereafter. Not only did the development of the rude hand ax enable man to kill animals more effectively to satisfy his need for food, it also helped to set the direction of technological development for hundreds of generations to follow. The primitive genius of Paleolithic times was he who could refine and improve upon the use of stone for weaponry and toolmaking. It must have taken a genius of the *genre* of Newton, Galileo, or Einstein to see so far beyond the given cultural practices that he could recognize the value of argiculture as a means of dealing with his need for food. This cultural invention in turn set the line of development for some thousands of years so solidly that it still maintains today. The impact today of industrial societies upon agricultural societies is the impact of culture upon culture. The oft-discussed effect of industrial societies upon their own members is again evidence of the profound force which is culture. Yet culture does not exist in a vacuum divorced from the individual man or from his environment. Society has its heavy effect on the individual, but the individual plays back in turn upon society as he may upon his natural environment. The concept of multi-causality requires that the complex interplay between man and his social and natural environments be recognized. The *basic* perspectives of *geography, biology,* and *culture* provide partial ways of viewing and analyzing the multi-causal nature of all social phenomena, whether they be economic, political or sociological. It is suggested, therefore, that the perspectives of multi-causality and of its sub-parts form the underlying strata of all the social studies and are basic to those studies.

THE DISCIPLINE PERSPECTIVES

Geography

Much of the study of geography in the past was given over to the study of the physical laws which govern the natural environment. Predominantly the concern was for an understanding of the mechanics and the distribution of the physical environment, and it has been appropriately termed "physical geography." In such a study, man and his society could be almost peripheral. This approach to geography might be interpreted as a study of the interplay among the various geographic determinants. Its place within the social sciences is certainly open to question. Recent developments in geography have produced an area which is known as "cultural geography." This approach to geography pays due heed to the existence of man and his society. To the extent that such a study moves away from the predominant concern with physical geography (which properly belongs in the physical sciences), to that extent does cultural geography come increasingly into the ranks of the social sciences. But as it emphasizes a study of culture and the role that culture plays in determining the land-man relationship, then its concern is with the much broader province appropriate to the *total* social studies curriculum which elaborates the complex interplay of all the conditioning factors and puts a primary emphasis on the study of culture. But it is a study of culture which recognizes the importance of geographic factors in social phenomena. The full understanding of the geographic determinant itself must, of course, continue to derive from the physical geography discipline (and from the other physical sciences).

Clyde Kohn of the University of Iowa sees as the characteristic viewpoints of geography a study of the location and distribution of things.[4] This suggests the unique geographic perspective which can be brought to bear on a unified social studies curriculum—that of *space* or *place*. Social phenomena (the ongoing interplay among the three determinants) occur in a location or in sets of locations, and the geographic perspective gives the means of demarcating the location and distribution of these phenomena.

Economics

Economics concerns itself with the means and the methods which man and his societies use to make a living through the use of the natural environment. Man's relationship to his geography, when it has not been poetic—i.e., aesthetic or religious—has been essentially economic. The forces of geography play a major role in conditioning the way man is able to satisfy his basic biological needs. But these factors do not alone fully define the economic condition. To view some aspect of man's history as being solely economically determined—as a response to biology and geography—ignores the impact of culture upon man. The views of Smith, Ricardo, and Malthus helped make their field into "the dismal science" by ignoring the fact that the various economic forms of societies are culturally as well as biologically determined. Economics has been seen as a field which studies

---

[4]"Basic Notions of Geography and Their Development in the Classroom." (Address presented at the 43rd Annual Meeting of the National Council for the Social Studies, Los Angeles, November 29, 1963).

the relationship between limited means and unlimited wants.[5] Limited means could refer to cultural as well as geographic limitations. The contemporary "have not" societies which lack the technical knowledge for making use of methods available to them to achieve the higher standard of living which they demand is [sic] an example of this.

The relationship between limited means and unlimited wants is made meaningful in the social studies curriculum through the application of the economic perspective to such things as the study of the relation between a society's economic system and its geographic surroundings (the interrelation between culture and geography), and to the study of the relation between a society's economic and political and social institutions (which examines the impact of culture upon itself).

Political Science

It has been stated that among the main concerns of political science are "the history, agencies, processes, structure, functions, composition, rationale, influence, successes, and failures" of governments.[6] Perhaps the underlying concern which sets the perspective of political science is "the problem of consensus, the process of achieving it and making it effective."[7] Both consensus and process cut across the whole domain of society, and can affect society's use of the natural environment as well as the ability of the individual to satisfy his needs and wants. The political science perspective furnishes to the social studies curriculum the means of examining the effects of culture upon culture, of the political institutions as they affect and are affected by other social institutions and the individual; they can also clarify how politics react to and act upon a geographic environment. As with the other disciplines, political science can furnish means for interpreting the interplay among the three basic determinants.

Sociology

As the "empirical scientific study of the structure and process of systems of interaction among humans,"[8] sociology scrutinizes patterns of hu-

---

[5]*Economic Education in the Schools,* Report of the National Task Force on Economic Education (New York: The Committee for Economic Development, 1960), p. 14; Ben Lewis, *"Economics, " in The Social Studies and the Social Sciences,* Sponsored by the American Council of Learned Societies and the National Council for the Social Studies (New York: Harcourt, Brace and World, 1962). p. 108.

[6] Evron M. and Jeane J. Kirkpatrick, "Political Science," in Erling M. Hunt, *et al. High School Social Studies Perspectives* (Boston: Houghton Mifflin Co. 1962), p. 104.

[7]Earl S. Johnson. "The Social Studies versus the Social Sciences," *The School Review,* 71:401, Winter 1963.

[8]E. Merle Adams, Jr. "New Viewpoints in Sociology," in Roy A. Price, ed. *New Viewpoints in the Social Sciences.* 28th Yearbook National Council for the Social Studies, Washington D.C., 1958), p. 97.

man behavior in social interaction. Put another way, sociology examines the institutional means by which a society interacts with the triumvirate of forces working upon it. Thus, at one level the institution of the family is seen to be constructed of certain roles which carry definite prerogatives, expectations, and benefits *vis-à-vis* other members of the family. At the same time the family has long been recognized as the first social organization invented by man in an attempt to expand his ability to satisfy his biological needs, and to meet more adequately the forces of nature. As society grows, the family becomes a technique for relating to that society. In the same way the sociological perspective is applicable to the local community as well as to the total society.

Anthropology

Sometimes termed the "science of culture,"[9] anthropology is seen by Robert Redfield as a field "organized around an interest in man seen as something with the characteristics of all life, and around an interest in man seen as something human—a quality not shared, or very little shared, with other forms of life. The quality that induces the second polarity—humanity —is manifest in three basic forms: as it appears in individuals (personality), in persisting social groups or societies (culture), and in all socialized members of our species (human nature)."[10] This bespeaks the broad range of materials to which anthropology addresses itself. Anthropology approaches these materials through a perspective that views human reality in its totality—"holistically"—and this totality is culture. By this integrative perspective anthropology can bring together the understandings provided by the specialized social sciences of political science, economics, and sociology.

In addition, the "functional" perspective used by some anthropologists[11] sees culture or society as an organization of things designed to achieve certain ends. The ends may be biologically or culturally based and the means may be either internal or external to the culture. This functional model justifies the expectation one would have of the "science of culture"— namely, that it specializes in explicating and clarifying the complexities and intricacies of cultural determinism. In essence, anthropology brings this perspective to bear on the disciplines of economics, political science and

[9]Meyer F. Nimkoff. "Anthropology, Sociology and Social Psychology," in *High School Social Studies*, p. 36.
[10]Robert Redfield. "Relations of Anthropology to the Social Sciences and Humanities," in Sol Tax, ed., *Anthropology Today* (Chicago: University of Chicago Press, 1963), p. 456.
[11]Ibid., p. 454–64. Redfield discusses the wide disagreement on the appropriate perspectives to be used in anthropology and indicates the variety of "models of anthropological thought" which are in use in the field. They include the causal model, the functional model, the aesthetic model, the logical model, and the symbolic model.

sociology, and then provides the integrative perspective to relate the separate insights offered by these other disciplines.

The Role of History

History has an important role in the social studies curriculum herein envisioned. First, this is so because historical data stand as the record of societies' developing experiential repertoire—conscious and unconscious. As such, history itself is seen as a major cultural determinant. It becomes a profound analytical tool for explaining the present. One cannot fully comprehend the contemporary American society without considering its historical antecedents any more than one can make sensible the dazzling achievements of the ancient Egyptian civilization without understanding the Neolithic developments on which it was based. History is important also because it provides a laboratory of materials with which to develop an understanding of the *structural perspectives* of the social sciences, and, in turn, history gains meaning through the application of these perspectives. Without them, history remains a reportorial craft. And, finally, history brings to the unified social studies curriculum the unique perspective of *time*. As geography does with place, history sets the location and distribution of social phenomena over time.

Selection of historical materials is, and no doubt will remain, an insoluble problem, for it is obvious that not all history can be dealt with adequately. Erling M. Hunt's review of the historical development of the social studies curriculum in this country over the past decades[12] indicates the constantly changing emphasis during this time as to what constitutes the appropriate content for the curriculum. No doubt emphases will continue to vary. Criteria for selection of historical studies should be based on the dual role seen for history in the social studies curriculum. Studies of history should pinpoint the vital antecedents of contemporary civilizations, and the material should lend itself to the development of the *structural perspectives* outlined earlier.

The above formulation of the *structural perspectives* leads to some generalizations which are helpful in looking toward the construction of an integrated social studies curriculum. First, there is a clear interrelatedness among the social science disciplines. The concerns of each discipline invade the domains of the others. Second, there is a tendency for each discipline to view a particular body of content as peculiarly its own—i.e., as part of its discipline. This conception breeds the feeling of separateness among the disciplines. Thus, anthropology tends to "own" the histories of primitive

[12]Erling M. Hunt. "Changing Perspectives in the Social Studies," in Hunt, *et. al.*, *High School Social Studies* pp. 3–28.

societies, and economics sees as its purview material dealing with the market place. Yet clearly each of these can quite profitably apply its particular perspective to the content associated with the other field—one can study the economics of a primitive society or the culture of the market place. The same history can, in fact, be studied through the perspectives of any of the disciplines. Redfield has pointed out the disagreement that exists as to whether anthropology is a field that addresses itself to the writing of histories or the writing of science. The question might fairly be applied to all of the social science disciplines. It would seem clear that it is the characteristic frame of reference each of the disciplines brings to bear upon the study of man in society which provides its valid distinctiveness, rather than the histories to which it is related and on which it traditionally concentrates. The content itself belongs to history and geography: to history as the record of social phenomena organized according to time, to geography as the record of social phenomena organized according to space. Economics, political science, and sociology concentrate on specialized aspects of social phenomena. As Kluchhohn suggests, "Sociology, economics, and government study man's actions and their result."[13] This focus makes them well suited to develop fully an understanding of aspects of cultural determinism. It is anthropology which suggests that political, economic, or social phenomena in time and place are partial aspects of the total picture. From anthropology comes the concept of the functional model of society, leading naturally to the study of man and society as both means and ends, and to a study of those means and ends through the perspectives of the various disciplines. And it is left to anthropology to suggest the integration of these singular aspects into an holistic view.

As the geographic determinant will be clarified by physical geography and the other physical sciences, and as the biological determinant will also be clarified by the physical sciences (and the social science of psychology),[14] so will the cultural determinant be clarified through the perspectives available in anthropology and the other social sciences.

STRUCTURAL PERSPECTIVES AND THE
SOCIAL STUDIES CURRICULUM

Let us now consider a social studies curriculum based upon the underlying *structural perspectives* delineated previously. It is set up for four

[13]Clyde Kuckhohn, *Mirror for Man* (Greenwich, Conn: Fawcett Publications, 1960), p. 224.

[14]Though psychology has not been discussed in this paper, its inclusion in the curriculum might seriously be considered—it affords clarification of the individual's relation to his social environment.

levels, and the criteria for inclusion of content and disciplines to be taught at each level are:

1. Disciplines which are most appropriate to the development of the basic perspectives.
2. Historical and contemporary studies which present opportunities to develop both the basic and the discipline perspectives.
3. Historical materials which supply significant historical antecedents to the present.

First and Second Levels

The basic and discipline perspectives are introduced at the first level and developed at the second level. *Both levels are required of all students.*

At the first level, pre-history, ancient history, and contemporary world geographic regions are studied with an emphasis on the perspectives of economics and geography, and both content and disciplines are used to introduce an awareness of the interplay between the forces of geography, biology, and culture. A study of the social, technical, and economic inventions of the Paleolithic era could effectively dramatize man's response to geography and biology. A geographic micro-study might introduce the idea of multi-causal determinism. At this level, students learn to think economically and geographically about man in society. They begin to become aware of the multiplicity of forces affecting him and to appreciate the impact of geographic forces on social phenomena.

At the second level, a continuing examination of world history from Greece through the modern world is pursued, emphasizing the perspectives of anthropology, political science, and sociology. Both the content and disciplines are used to develop and refine the basic perspectives introduced at the first level. The emphasis on anthropology at this level makes possible a full development of the concept of cultural determination. The portrayal of history as a major cultural determinant would be quite effective here.

By the time students have completed the second level they should have an understanding of the basic perspectives of multi-causal determinism and its sub-parts (with a particular emphasis on cultural forces). They should as well be aware of the perspectives of each of the disciplines—that is, be able to look at social phenomena anthropologically, economically, geographically, politically, sociologically, and historically. And they should have knowledge of the significant eras of world history and a familiarity with the contemporary world geographic regions.

Third Level

This *elective* level is open to all students interested in further investigations of the social studies after they have demonstrated mastery of the above learning and thus have the necessary groundwork for confronting the sophisticated conceptual frameworks of the social science disciplines. Having come to understand the multi-various ways of viewing and explaining man in society, they are in a position to choose among selected areas of content (Africa, the U.S.S.R., Moslem history, the history of the British Empire, U.S. problems, etc.) which would be studied through the eyes of every one of the discipline perspectives. To achieve this, third-level course content would be analyzed by experts in each of the disciplines. Separate periods of the school year would be given over in every third-level course for the development of analyses of the same content through the fully developed perspectives of each of the disciplines. Area studies and special historical studies presented at this level should serve the following purposes:

1. The development and refinement of the specialized perspectives of each of the disciplines (At the first two levels students learned to view society economically, sociologically, etc.; at this level the studies are clearly designated as Economics and Anthropology, and the theoretical frameworks of the disciplines are closely articulated and developed).
2. The reinforcement, through application, of the perspectives of multi-causal determinism.
3. The pursuit, in depth, of significant historical and contemporary studies.

Having experts in anthropology, political science, sociology, economics, and geography deal with the *same* content each from his own discipline perspective would serve the above purposes. And it would avoid that total compartmentalization of the social studies which tends to breed the erroneous view that a single perspective is sufficient to the task of social analysis.

Fourth Level

Students who have demonstrated competence with the basic perspectives and with the perspectives of the disciplines are in a position to move on to the fourth *elective* level. Here tutorial research courses provide them the opportunity to undertake special studies of their own interest, in which they are able to apply the perspectives with new and perhaps original meaning. These courses can be either content or discipline oriented.

The accompanying diagram illustrates the social studies curriculum plan set forth in this paper.[15]

[15]The plan presented is for a secondary school curriculum but, with modifications, it could be conceived of as an eight- or twelve-year curriculum. In any case, it provides opportunities for differentiation of instruction. Those who are able to move quickly from level to level may do so as they demonstrate competency, and those requiring more time at a given level should have it provided.

	CONTENT AND DISCIPLINES		STRUCTURAL PERSPECTIVES	
Fourth Level Tutorial	To Be Arranged by Teacher and Student		Application of These	
Third Level Required	Selected Historical and Area Studies	Anthropology Political Science Economics Geography Sociology ⎫⎬⎭	Development and Refinement of every *Discipline perspective*	Application of *basic perspectives* (of multi-causality and its sub-parts)
Second Level Required	World History from Greece to the Modern World	Anthropology Political Science Sociology ⎫⎬⎭	Development of *discipline perspectives* (with emphasis on viewing social phenomena anthropologically, politically, and sociologically)	Development of *basic perspectives* (of multi-causality and its sub-parts)
First Level Required	Prehistory Ancient History Cultural World Regions	Economics Geography ⎫⎬⎭	Introduction to *discipline perspectives* (with emphasis on viewing social phenomena geographically and economically)	Introduction to *basic perspectives* (of multicausality and its sub parts)

It should be noted that care has been taken to introduce each of the perspectives at one level, and to develop and refine it at a later level. At the introductory levels, students become aware of, and gain experience with, viewing social phenomena through each perspective. Though this does not constitute a full articulation of each one, it provides the students with a feeling for it which prepares them for the subsequent fuller development of that perspective at a later level. By the end of the third level, students will have gone through the process of introduction, development, and refinement for every perspective. In addition, students will have had by then ample opportunity to apply the basic perspectives underlying the entire social studies field. For those students able to achieve the fourth level, the opportunity for specialization in one selected discipline becomes possible and reasonable. Students will approach this fourth level with a broad enough base of preparation in a discipline to make intense concentration in this area effective and meaningful. And this specialization will come only after a solid confrontation with the *totality* of the social studies. This same totality will have been presented, if less thoroughly, to students whose studies do not extend beyond the second level.

One must, of course, avoid an overformalization of the above scheme. At, best, the perspectives used for each of the disciplines need to remain somewhat tentative and subject to change, reinterpretation, deletion, or expansion as new knowledge in the various fields dictates. A limited and confining interpretation of the perspectives could lead toward a singularity of intellect by which everyone viewed man in society in a unitary and unimaginative way. Also, the perspectives should not be implemented in such a way as to constrain the possibility of new insights by the student into the social studies material with which he deals. The *structural perspectives* make possible a variety of insights into the realities which can and *should* be interpreted in more than one way. Bruner has written that the educational process

> transmits to the individual some part of the accumulation of knowledge, style and values that constitute the culture of a people. In so doing, it shapes the impulses, the consciousness and the way of life of the individual. But education must also seek to develop the processes of intelligence so that the individual is capable of going beyond the cultural ways of his social world, able to innovate in however modest a way so that he can create an interior culture of his own. For whatever the art, the science, the literature, the history and the geography of a culture, each man must be his own artist, his own scientist, his own historian, his own navigator. No person is master of the whole culture . . . each man lives a fragment of it. To be a whole, he must create his own version of the world, using that part of his cultural heritage he has made his own through education.[16]

But the disposition to arrive at and make use of the insights into the problems of the individual and of his society which social studies education can provide will be determined by an individual's subjective self. Surely a distinction must be made between the intellective self which learns ideas, and the subjective self which determines to such a great extent what can be learned, how and how well it is learned, and to what ends the learning is put. Social studies education must deal with both "selves." The student should be encouraged to do more than memorize and apply the *structural perspectives* as our wisdom suggests; he can be allowed to discover the experiment with them in ways that reinforce his own sense of competency in confronting the untried and unknown. Used in this way, the *structural perspectives* can lead the young toward the realization that man, to achieve freedom from subjugation to the forces of nature and the needs of the body, need not lose his identity to the instrument which he has created, that social forces can be understood and dealt with as are the geographic and biological forces. Perhaps such a vision will help the young to see that the problems facing mankind are not necessary beyond the ken and ability of man.

[16]Jerome S. Bruner, *On Knowing: Essays for the Left Hand* (Cambridge: Harvard University Press, 1962), pp. 115–116.

IB. What Content Should We Teach?

In the field of the social studies, there is an overabundance of potential subject matter. Each year provides increasing amounts of knowledge which may be included in the curriculum. With the burgeoning results of research and development, the problem of selection looms ever more important. But once we have made our selection, many choices still remain. The tendency has been to include as much of the story as possible, to cover the ground, to be comprehensive. It has been deemed dangerous to leave anything out that the student may possibly need to know at some unspecified later date. In most instances, however, these inclinations have led to wide-flung, superficial surveys which rob the courses of depth, color, humanity, intriguing interconnections, and individualized appeal. The shallow attempt to serve as many as possible with as much as possible has usually satisfied no one.

In the rush to touch upon a host of items, the teacher may neglect adequate attention to essentials, may inhibit vital student investigation and discovery, and, above all, may make potentially exciting social study a deadly bore. It has been suggested that the content taught also indicates the manner in which it should be approached and learned. This dictum calls for greater attention from educational researchers. If the psychologists and other social scientists who hold this "structural" view of subject matter are correct, it imposes further guidelines or limitations upon the selection and ordering both of the course of study and of each lesson.

Meanwhile, we must be clear on our criteria for curricular inclusion; we must explore the evident priorities in instruction; we must decide to what extent the social studies program equates with general education and then decide if and how that "common" education should be varied for different pupils. Toward these ends we should carefully examine the social science disciplines to try to ascertain the fundamental contributions of each to our purposes.

Traditional content and traditional subject matter approaches have tended to characterize the social studies. For certain learners, under inspired instructors, this has sufficed. But today's schools must complete with increasingly attractive appeals for the student's time and energy; teachers now face a more critical and pragmatic clientele. Youth demand a program of instruction that will serve evident purpose, and they mean a fairly immediate and direct purpose. The last entry in this set of readings reveals the heritage of most of the so-called new ideas in education. Consider, for example, among other "modern" ideas, the "spiral" curriculum of expanding experiences. It was anticipated almost a half-century ago by one of our educational prophets who foresaw the need for a much more vital and timely social studies program and who outlined the principles he saw as fundamental in resolving the issue of what content we shall teach.

In reading the following entries, ask yourself how the suggestions made might lead to a changed curriculum. Which of the described approaches, views, or emphases would you endorse, and why?

DONALD W. OLIVER

Professor of Education, Harvard University

15. Categories of Social Science Instruction*

INTRODUCTION

Social Science instruction is notorious for its multiplicity of objectives and the vagueness of relationship between objectives and the actual instruction carried out to achieve them. In the last sixty years there have been at least five major efforts to order the field and provide guidelines for a defensible social studies program. Investigators attempting to rationalize this field have generally begun with the question: "What should the social studies be?" In this paper we shall try a different tack: an intuitive categorization of approaches now commonly observed in practice or described in the literature and an analysis of some general elements of approach by which different social studies programs may be more systematically distinguished.

First, a note of caution. This process of categorizing or stereotyping approaches runs the risk of considerable distortion and error. We feel the effort worthwhile, however, if only it provokes other curriculum workers to seek greater clarification of essential elements that actually relate particular social studies programs to the general objectives toward which such programs strive.

The categories we shall discuss are: the wisdom approach, the social science disciplines approach, the harmonist approach, the great image approach, the jurisprudential approach, and the civic action approach. Although there is some deliberate effort at caricaturization we are concerned that each approach get reasonably fair treatment.

APPROACHES

(1) The Wisdom Approach

The wisdom approach is concerned mainly with the transmission of established knowledge in the social sciences. The essential justification of this approach is a vague but simple prediction: knowledge is good because it leads to understanding and wisdom. When one questions more deeply

*High School Journal, 43:387-97, April 1960. Used by permission.

which segments of this large body of available knowledge will make the greatest contribution to wisdom, we are generally told that all knowledge is important—one shows wisdom by referring back to a "total historical picture." The rather astonished questioner might exclaim, "How can you teach all history?" The answer is already in the curriculum. Not only is all history taught, it is often taught in one year under the rather inclusive title "world history." The method of scholarship by which this feat can be carried out depends on two principles: the materials must be dealt with on an extremely high level of abstraction; and no more than a single interpretation of events can be treated.

Although there is little evidence that the accumulation of historical, or any social science information in a high school setting has a permanent effect upon the student's later thinking, proponents of the wisdom approach continue to assert that the knowledge is, in fact, applied at some later undetermined time "when it is needed." The question may be asked: When will this time come? Elementary school teachers will often assert that it comes in high school. High school teachers say it will come in college. Teachers of the survey course in college say it is needed in graduate school. From one point of view this set of answers is quite reasonable: the wisdom approach is most valuable for students who will eventually become professional scholars.

There are, of course, some conditions which tend to cast doubt on the notion that the general accumulation of social science knowledge will make the student wiser in his later approach to political and social issues. First, the conditions in which such knowledge is learned differ so markedly from the conditions under which it might later be used, that the student may not know when to apply particular items of knowledge. That is, the student may need training in the application of this knowledge as well as prodding to accumulate the knowledge in the first place. Training in application is rarely carried out, however, since the wisdom teacher is frantically working to cover all the ground necessary for the student to see the total historical picture. A second problem is that the time between initial learning and potential application is often so great that the major effects of such learning may be washed away before there is any chance at application. A third difficulty relates to the problem of deciding exactly what to teach. Simply making the general assumption that historical or sociological knowledge may some day be useful in interpreting one's society offers no criteria for selecting content. As noted above, when faced with this problem the wisdom teacher often solves it be treating tremendous areas of content in a swift and superficial way, the superficiality being defended on the grounds that memorization is preliminary to application, which will take place somewhere else at some other time.

In summary, the wisdom approach tends to deal mainly with a broad base of factual knowledge, usually history. It tends to avoid discussion of the research methods in the social science disciplines from which this content originates. For its justification it talks either about broad general objectives such as "teaching a sense of history," or about very specific goals, such as the major points of the Missouri Compromise. It is based on the assumption that knowledge promotes wisdom and sets up fairly arbitrary standards regarding exactly what knowledge will, in fact, fulfill this function.

(2) The Social Science Disciplines Approach

The disciplines approach is mainly concerned with the proof process by which valid pictures of man and society are painted, and with the explanation of historical or sociological events through the identification of a particular constellation of antecedent conditions in society.

In teaching the student this approach, the methods of scholarship and the analytical concepts by which one arrives at such explanations are fully as important as the findings themselves. The central purpose of existing knowledge, both factual and theoretical, is to discover new problems which might fruitfully be investigated. In this approach there is respect for a tradition of scholarship, but not unquestioning adherence to the products of scholarship, as tends to be the case with the wisdom approach.

In teaching the social sciences as disciplines, the instructional procedures are generally patterned after natural science teaching. Methods of observing and recording important events, as well as the use of theoretical tools for the interpretation of these events are emphasized fully as much as knowledge of currently available findings. A laboratory is necessarily involved. At the present time this approach is used most comonly at the university graduate level.

Many simple skills of scholarship are, however, often taught, as early as the elementary school. In fact, the term "skills" is common in the social studies to describe elementary mechanics of scholarship. It should also be noted, that the research skills taught on the high school level are almost exclusively limited to the analysis of documents, the behavioral sciences with their use of direct observation and quantitative inference being pretty well excluded.

(3) The Harmonist Approach

In contrast to the wisdom approach, the harmonist approach does not focus as much upon historical or social science content, but rather upon the learner. It is mainly concerned that the learner "grow" with a minimum of frustration. Growth is usually defined in social terms, probably best summarized by the term "living together."

In the harmonist approach there is emphasis upon cooperation, group work, pupil-teacher planning, "democracy in the classroom." There are strong sanctions against any kind of aggression or competition. The spirit of the classroom is equality and friendship.

It is hazardous to assume that, because the harmonist teacher emphasizes the importance of the immediate social situation in the classroom, he does not treat traditional historical content. He often treats much the same content as the wisdom teacher. The content, however, in contrast to the wisdom aproach, has immediate utility in the classroom as well as later in life. It is used to illustrate good and evil. Evil is represented as competitive greed. Good is represented as cooperative planning and group solidarity. It deals explicitly with values. Each historical incident carries a message: Columbus and his men worked together and found a new world; Washington and his men worked together and won a war, etc. There is obviously an explicit principle of content selection and emphasis here. Certain historical situations are clearly more appropriate for teaching a harmonistic value system. Some teachers and schools have mixed in or substituted life adjustment content for the historical content. In these cases, harmonistic values are taught directly through personality analysis, rather than through the use of historical analogy. The essential ingredient of the approach is the same, however: teaching a doctrine and method by which to achieve harmonistic human relations.

(4) The Image of Greatness Approach

The central objective of the great image approach is to provide young people with inspiring symbols which dramatically present basic human problems and the particular cultural solutions of our own society. These symbols can then bind the culture together by suggesting that the problems of socialization and survival have a uniquely appropriate solution: that solution found in our own culture. Thus the image of greatness approach focuses upon the problem of cultural integration, as does the harmonist approach, but finds a different solution. While the harmonist indoctrinates the child with the values of mutual love and tolerance, which are to be translated into action in the immediate classroom situation, the great image approach projects the child into historical problem situations, and leads him to historical solutions—whether these solutions involve harmony or war.[1] The content of the great image approach is essentially dramatic narrative history to provide a national image consistent with the values, ideals, and aspirations of our culture. The ultimate objective of the great image approach is to make the student see and feel a sense of historical reality which somehow binds him with his fellow compatriots. In contrast to the wisdom

---

[1] It may be noted that some teachers react against the great image approach by debunking symbols of the American past: wars are fought for personal greed, territorial expansion led to inhuman treatment of the Indians, etc.

approach, the image of greatness conception of history is narrative and concrete, rather than analytical and interpretive.

Before scientific history became established as a discipline, the concept
of history as great literature was very close to the great image ideal. Many
formal courses in history were undoubtedly introduced into school curricula
with the great image spirit in mind. Modern historians have, however,
moved in the direction of "objectivity" and interpretation (the "new history") which has had an erosive affect on the great image conception.

(5) The Jurisprudential Approach

Of the four approaches discussed above, the wisdom and discipline approaches are more concerned with the validation or existence of accurate
factual knowledge, and generally less concerned with value judgments. The
harmonistic and great image approaches are heavily laden with emotive
content than with the value judgments such content might support.

The jurisprudential approach makes a deliberate effort to bridge the
gap between knowledge and value. It presumably teaches the student to deal
with disputes arising out of the value one places on his own definition of
personal liberty, and the restrictions on this freedom imposed by law and
governmental power. As the jurisprudential teacher sees it, the underlying
problem behind the settling of such disputes is that man must judge what is
good for man. To circumvent this difficulty a system of law is created which
somehow stands "above men," a system commonly labeled constitutionalism. Underlying the concept of constitutionalism is the belief that through
the use of reason, men of good will can transcend the petty interests of individuals and private groups. This faith in reason as a method of controlling
controversy is the spirit underlying what we are here calling the jurisprudential approach.

Three ingredients are common to this approach: the initial focus upon
a disputed normative claim; the use of carefully defined intellectual procedures by which evidence must be reviewed and weighed before decisions
involving personal freedom can be made; and training in the use of persuasive argumentation as well as disciplined reason to deal with political problems.

The positive element that lies behind the jurisprudential concentration
on the disintegrative forces in society is, of course, the protection of individual liberty. Contemporary as well as historical situations may be chosen
to illustrate the basic dilemmas created by society's attempt to maximize
individual liberty while at the same time maintaining a level of equality
consistent with an acceptable standard of human dignity.

This concern with dilemmas that plague man in his effort to live peacefully with himself and his fellow men is based on a number of assumptions
about the nature of man and society. It assumes that there are inevitable

conflicts of interest competing within the individual, conflicts of interest among groups within society, conflicts of interest among societies. It assumes that these conflicts are built into the nature of man. The danger of these assumptions is obvious. Conflicts of interest may not be "inevitable." The governmental procedures set up to deal with these conflicts, procedures which the jurisprudential approach values and dwells upon, may only be stopgap measures to mark time until man can be more fully humanized or civilized. Perhaps education should direct itself at this humanizing function, which is exactly what the harmonist does. In short, the danger of the jurisprudential approach is its conservatism. It is working to conserve an existing legal and constitutional system of government, to conserve our existing conception of the relationship between reason and emotion. It structures a specific framework of the world for the student much more so than the wisdom approach. It tends to be pessimistic about man's capacity to find inner peace within himself and outer peace with his society.

Although quite different in orientation, there is obviously a good deal of common ground between the disciplinary approach and the jurisprudential approach. This common area is the use of the so-called scientific method to analyze and support claims. There is, however, a considerable difference. The disciplinary approach is concerned with the ordering of valid knowledge within some explanatory framework. The purpose is to discover (or create) order in nature; to demonstrate that there is a predictable or rational order to the social world. A problem occurs in the disciplinary approach when one or more reported events are found to contradict an existing theoretical scheme. The jurisprudential approach begins with a conflict of interest, a conflict between the way two individuals or groups define personal liberty. It is essentially a conflict in feeling, in attitude, although there is often a conflict in the way a particular societal situation is actually described because of the distorting influence of personal feelings.

A disciplinary problem is terminated when new knowledge is found to fit an existing order of the world, and existing theory, or when an old theory is reconstructed to allow new knowledge to fit within its structure. A jurisprudential problem ends only when there is a change in attitude: either acceptance of a new definition or "right," or acceptance of the fact that one must abide by an alien definition until others can be persuaded to legislate our viewpoint. This is not to say that factual knowledge is not needed in the analysis and understanding of a jurisprudential problem, but the knowledge is directed toward the confirmation of an attitudinal or moral position, not toward the confirmation of a testable hypothesis in a social theory.

(6) The Civic Action Approach

Up to this point the approaches discussed have relied heavily upon the traditional artifacts of school learning, i.e., classrooms, laboratories, books, and documents. In contrast to approaches already discussed, however, the civic action approach leaves the classroom and deals directly with the action implications of content introduced in the classroom. In the words of Gross:

> A good citizen is not only one who knows and understands what to do within the framework of community expectations and tolerances, but one who has the integrity and moral courage to carry out his convictions through appropriate action. Action is not necessarily needed to conform to existing community expectations, but action is needed that will result in desirable changes in community living consistent with the spiritual and human values and goals that have been sought and cherished at an incalculable price of human struggle and sacrifice down through the few centuries of American life.[2]

Gross goes on to give a number of examples of the civic action approach:

> High school students of the Clover Park Schools, Tacoma, Washington helped to organize and conduct a population survey in the fast-growing suburban area in order to help local civic leaders with the community zoning and expansion program.
> . . . Willamette High School students, Eugene, Oregon, in cooperation with the State Board of Health, made a survey of sanitary conditions in restaurants, motels, and trailer courts in the local area and made a report to the Board of Health on conditions as they found them from information collected firsthand.[3]

The civic action approach has been stimulated by the efforts of such groups as the Citizenship Education Project of Teachers College, Columbia University. Its basic purpose is to combine both knowledge and action in a training program to develop civic competence. It centers both upon the immediate problems of school and community, as well as involving students in national, or international affairs, through such devices as mock legislative sessions at the state capital, or mock U. N. sessions.

*   *   *   *

Underlying Elements Which May Distinguish Approaches to Social Science Instruction.

The first part of this paper loosely described a number of approaches to social science instruction which we believe are commonly observed in classrooms or discussed in the literature. These were described as "pure types" or caricatures to emphasize the essential qualities of each.

---

[2]Richard E. Gross, and Leslie D. Zeleny, *Educating Citizens for Democracy* (New York: Oxford University Press, 1958), p. 399.
[3]*Ibid*

An additional procedure can come out of such an intuitive categorization; the identification of underlying elements which may be used to describe any concrete program of instruction. These elements tend to get us away from the stereotyping operation in which we indulged above. Below are four elements of approach which seem useful in analyzing instruction in the social studies:

1. Necessity of a Total Historical or Chronological Contest. To what extent is the approach concerned that some complete historical or chronological picture be presented, or with what we might call historical integrity? To what extent is the assumption made that certain areas in history cannot be cut apart and presented out of a total historical context. On this dimension the wisdom and great image approaches are certainly much concerned with chronological integrity, with a total picture. The disciplinary approach even within history is less concerned with broad fields of historical interpretation than with much more precisely defined historical mysteries, e.g. the effect certain mining interests had on the Montana Legislature between 1880 and 1900. The jurisprudential approach uses historical knowledge to interpret either past or contemporary conflicts in public policy, but not necessarily within a national or world historical framework. It certainly violates the idea of total historical context. The civic action aproach is clearly committed to contemporary issues, although not necessarily out of historical context.

2. Proof Process. To what extent is emphasis placed upon the systematic use of evidence to test the validity of existing knowledge or to explore new knowledge?

With respect to this element, clearly the disciplinary approach and the jurisprudential approach have much in common, and both differ radically from other approaches. The wisdom, harmonistic, and great image approaches generally use authority, either the teacher or the writer of a text, as sufficient evidence of "truth."

3. Utility of Knowledge. To what extent is instruction concerned that the student find some immediate utility or application of the knowledge or values which have been taught?

The disciplinary approach shows the least concern for immediate utility in what is learned: knowledge is good simply because its quest demands exciting intellectual operations. The jurisprudential approach, and its logical consequence, the civic action approach, both tend to show considerable concern for the immediate utility of knowledge in giving direction to policy decisions about contemporary political and social issues.

4. Use of Value Judgments and Emotive Language. To what extent is there some effort, either through indoctrination or the deliberate use of loaded languages, to deal with values and the use of knowledge to support values?

The great image harmonistic approaches clearly have indoctrination as their goal. The jurisprudential approach deals with the personal values of freedom and fair treatment, but demands that the consequences of carrying out specific decisions based on these values be explored empirically. The disciplinary and wisdom approaches are least concerned with the explicit use of value judgments.

The Gap Between General Objectives and Specific Methods: A Note on the Utility of the Broad Approach.

The process of curriculum analysis and building in the social studies has tended to operate on two distinct levels. The general objectives level describes such goals as "making good citizens," "teaching students to think critically," "making the student appreciate his cultural heritage." A second level describes specific items of content as well as ways of presenting content, which will presumably carry out these general objectives. As we see it, there is usually only a vague and unexplained relationship between the general objectives and the specific content. From our point of view, curriculum rationales rarely answer adequately such questions as: Why is American History a more appropriate road to good citizenship than learning the major cases in constitutional law? Why is learning world history a more appropriate road to critical thinking than a course in applied logic or rhetoric? There is usually no clear statement of the relationship between the broadest and most general of objectives and the items of content selected to achieve these objectives.

Looking at social studies programs in terms of broad approaches, we think, forces the curriculum builder to consider difficult questions of content selection not ordinarily faced. Defining such an approach requires that specific items of content be related to specific attitudes, beliefs, or intellectual operations, which in turn must be justified by their implication from more general objectives of the individual and society. Such definition makes salient difficult choices in content, which have long been submerged in the field of social studies curriculum development.

For example, the jurisprudential approach is necessarily less concerned with presenting a clear and integrated historical picture of one's culture than the wisdom approach, and is more concerned with the justification of value judgments and the validation of generalizations which tend to support these value judgments. Skill in critical thinking to validate generalizations is inappropriate for the wisdom approach; specific methods for teaching students how to organize and memorize large segments of chronological history are inappropriate for the jurisprudential approach. If one is concerned that the student have both a sense of historical integrity as well as facility in critically dealing with the classic dilemmas of liberty versus order, or liberty versus equality, we may need two different approaches at two different times. Or perhaps the objectives of these two approaches are, at points, inconsistent with one other, and actually work toward contradictory learning outcomes.

It is our position that progess in the discovery of effective materials and methods of presentation in the social studies will begin to come when the gap between general objectives and specific content is filled by more carefully defined broad approaches. These approaches, when described and rationalized, can then lead to explicit hypotheses relating specific programs of instruction to the way we want the student to think and act as a result of these programs. Such hypotheses are testable. Without greater concern for clear definition of the broad approach or broader elements of social science instruction we may be endlessly hung up on philosophical arguments over high sounding but vague objectives on the one hand or untestable claims about the effectiveness of specific materials or methods of instruction on the other, with no intervening constructs to relate specific method and content to general objective.

JOE PARK

Professor of Education, Northwestern University

16. Three Views of the Problem of Instruction*

The problem of instruction may be viewed in three ways. Some choose to think of it primarily in terms of the child's interests. Others mainly conceive of instruction as the imparting of subject matter or the training of the mind. Still others believe the problem of instruction is the attempt to teach significant subject matter to pupils who are genuinely engaged in the learning process.

Perhaps the most famous advocate of the first view was Rousseau (June 28, 1712–July 2, 1778). In *Emile* he stated what he believed to be the most important rule of education: "Do not save time but lose it." What he meant was that between the time of birth and age twelve the pupil passed through the "most dangerous period of his life" and that considerable care should be taken not to teach him things which he did not need to know or that he could not understand. It was the time when "errors and vices spring up, while as yet there is no means to destroy them." He believed that by the time the means of destruction were ready, the roots would have gone too deep to be pulled up. In *Emile*, Rousseau wrote, "man must know many things which seem useless to a child, . . . try to teach the child what is of use to the child and you will find that it takes all his time. Why urge him to the studies of an age he may never reach, to the neglect of those studies which meet his present needs? . . . A child knows he must become a man; all the ideas he may have as to man's estate are so many opportunities for his instruction, but he should remain in complete ignorance of those ideas which are beyond his grasp. My whole book is one continued argument in support of this fundamental principle of education."[1]

Rousseau was protesting against the times in which he lived. He pointed out that children were thought of as miniature adults who were to have poured into them meaningless subject matters such as the catechism, foreign language (memorized but not understood), foolish fables and the like. He was calling attention to the desirability of considering the "nature" of the child in the learning process. He was demanding that "emotion and experience," the real teachers, be given a chance to educate

*Social Studies, 52:54–58, February 1961. Used by permission.
[1]Jean Jacques Rosseau, *Emile,* Everyman's Library no. 518 (London: J. M. Dent and Sons, 1911), p. 141.

the child. Let the child's capacity to reason accompany learning and then the child will be able to detect the tempter, the charlatan, the rascal or the fool. Philosophy, history, literature, political theory all were to be studied by the youth after he had gained the power of reason, which is so necessary to their understanding.

For our purposes, what needs to be noted here is that Rousseau's ideas formed the basis of the philosophy of education that has come to be known as the "romantic wing of progressive education." These educators stress the child's nature, seek out his interests and follow them, slavishly, in many instances. Much is made over the "needs" of the child. The problem of instruction is seen to be mainly getting the learner involved in an activity of personal interest and meaning to him. While there is some merit in this position, it is one-sided. The significance of the content is not given due consideration and the function of the teacher as director of the learning process is minimized. In the opinion of Herbart, Rousseau liberated the pupil but made a slave of the teacher.[2]

Whereas the child was the chief concern in the romantic notion of instruction, subject matter is the main interest of another group. These persons think of the problem of instruction as "training the mind," "teaching the facts," or "memory." Recently a school board member, when asked to indicate what kind of classroom activity he most desired in his system replied, "memory." He meant that he wanted to see the students of his small town trained in the subject matter contained in the textbooks until they could spout answers to almost any question that might be put to them.

Harry Golden voiced much of the same sentiment in a recent article that appeared in the *Chicago Tribune.*[3] Mr. Golden, the author of *Only in America* and editor of the *Carolina Israelite,* whom many have admired for his insights into the problem of desegregation, charges that "No one reads books any more." Challenging the entire ideal of progressive education, he urges that the educational system of America wake up to the danger of letting pupils do what they want. "Today it is a big joke," he writes. "You watch them running from classroom to classroom and it's all a fake. They know nothing. Nothing at all." Golden then dares the American public to go into these high school classrooms and ask seniors such questions as (1) Who was the Marquis de Lafayette? (2) Who was Jean Valjean? (3) Name four members of the United States Supreme Court. (4) Who was the first man to circumnavigate the globe? and (5) What do we call the series of letters written by Alexander Hamilton, John Jay, and James Madison which helped bring about the United States of America? If you find more than three per cent of the students answering these questions cor-

[2]William J. Eckoff, *Herbart's A B C of Sense-Perception and Minor Pedagogical Works* (New York: D. Appleton and Co., 1896) p. 23.
[3]*Chicago Sunday Tribune Magazine,* September 28, 1958.

rectly, Mr. Golden asks you to notify him immediately so that he can begin his journey from Charlotte, N. C. to Atlanta, Georgia, pushing a peanut with his nose all the way.

What the school board member and Mr. Golden both may know, but have forgotten to mention, is that textbooks are the means to an education. They are not the end. They have failed to see that the desire of the pupil to learn, to want to continue to learn is important, possibly more important than any one set of facts that can be learned. Where is the cultivation of the ability to inquire in this scheme of educational values? Is not much of our knowledge really misinformation? It was James Harvey Robinson who reminded us of this possibility when he said:

> And now the astonishing and perturbing suspicion emerges that perhaps almost all that has passed for social science, political economy, politics, and ethics in the past may be brushed aside by future generations as mainly rationalizing. . . . This conclusion may be ranked by students of a hundred years hence as one of the several great discoveries of our age.[4]

There is a third way of viewing the problem of instruction. It seeks to balance the two elements stressed in the positions discussed above, and it adds an additional consideration. It was John Dewey who wrote:

> The problem of instruction is thus that of finding material which will engage a person in specific activities having an aim or purpose of moment or interest to him, and dealing with things not as gymnastic appliances but as conditions for the attainment of ends.[5]

What did Dewey have in mind when he wrote this? What is the meaning of this passage for the classroom teacher?

To the great surprise of many, Dewey began by indicating that the problem of instruction first of all involved finding material; i.e., subject matter. Subject matter consists of facts "observed, recalled, read, talked about, and the ideas suggested, in course of a development of a situation having a purpose." Thus Dewey thought of subject matter in terms of its use in a process of investigation. He saw the educator's part in the educative enterprise as one of furnishing stimuli to the learner and directing the learner.

> In the last analysis [he wrote] *all* that the educator can do is modify stimuli so that response will as surely as is possible result in the formation of desirable intellectual and emotional disposition. Obviously studies, or the subject matter of the curriculum have intimately to do with the business of supplying an environment.[6]

[4]James Harvey Robinson, *The Mind in the Making* (New York: Harper and Bros., 1921), p. 47.
[5]John Dewey, *Democracy and Education* (New York: Macmillan Co., 1916), p. 155.
[6]*Ibid.*, p. 212.

Increasingly, subject matter has become isolated from the business of life. It is aloof from the habits and ideals of the society that established the school. Consequently children frequently see no connection between subject matter of the classroom and the matters of society. This prompts children to ask, "Why must I study this?" What is the use of this stuff?" In reality the use of the "stuff of instruction" is threefold. (1) It is to help the child assimilate the complex civilization of which he is a part. (2) It is to help the child to discover that his civilization has been encumbered with that which is trivial, perverse and dead, and that it is his task to bring the weight of his knowledge and influence to bear upon their elimination. (3) Finally, it is the purpose of instruction to help the pupil escape from the limitations of his environment and to come into living contact with a broader environment. The Protestant needs to encounter the Jew, the Catholic should learn of the ways of the humanist. The Republican needs to understand the Democrat, and vice versa. It hardly needs to be added that the Russian should know the American and the American the Russian, or that the Frenchman needs to understand the Algerian and vice versa.

When engaged in the art of teaching, the instructor needs to have subject matter at his finger tips. The more he knows about his subject the more he can release his attention from his notes and direct his thinking toward the child, and the process of inquiry in which the child is engaged.

As for the child, he needs to be kept moving "in the direction of what the expert knows. Hence the need that the teacher know both the subject matter and the characteristic needs and capacities of the student."[7] Dewey conceived of the child as a product of biological and cultural continuity. Each child has certain potential for growth and it is the function of the school to take the pupil from where he is toward the thinking of the expert as rapidly as possible. The child is to be interested in instructional materials by causing him to see the meaning or significance of the material.

Interest to Dewey resided in things "between." By this he meant that it was the task of the teacher to discover objects and modes of action which were connected with the "present powers" of the students. These "objects and modes of action" were but another name for subject matter and to the means for handling it. Interest was to come from matters of importance, not from "pleasant bait" or "soft pedagogy." To attach "seductiveness to material otherwise indifferent" deserved, in the opinion of Dewey, "to be stigmatized as 'soft' pedagogy; as a 'soup-kitchen' theory of education." Because learning takes time, pupils should learn to discipline their actions. Thus, said Dewey,

> A person who is trained to consider his actions, to undertake them deliberately, is in so far disciplined. Add to this ability to endure in an

[7]*Ibid.*, p. 216.

intelligent course in the face of distraction, confusion, and difficulty, and you have the essence of discipline. Discipline means power at command; mastery of the resources available for carrying through the action undertaken.[8]

This is "intellectual discipline" of which we hear so much, but see so infrequently defined or demonstrated. Intellectual discipline is learned through a course of instruction in which the student is placed in contact with vital subject matter and deals with this matter in a systematic and intelligent manner in the face of hard work, difficulties in finding ready answers and in spite of distraction, the confusion of detail, apparent conflicting generalizations and the absence of final and "absolute" solutions.

> Intellectual *thoroughness* is thus another name for the attitude we are considering, [he wrote]. There is a kind of thoroughness which is almost purely physical: the kind that signifies mechanical and exhaustive drill upon all the details of a subject. Intellectual thoroughness *is seeing a thing through*. It depends upon a unity of purpose to which details are subordinated, not upon presenting a multitude of disconnected details. It is manifested in the firmness with which the full meaning of the purpose is developed, not in attention, however 'conscientious' it may be, to the steps of action externally imposed and directed.[9]

The third element in instruction, as Dewey saw it, was the "conditions for attaining ends." Perhaps the best way to go at this matter is to say that for Dewey the method of education was the method of science.

Dewey believed that for life to continue it was necessary for the living thing (in this case man) to continue its activity and behavior through both adapting to and changing its environment of which it is a part. As a result experience must involve doing, acting, changing. An organism does not merely exist in a state of inactivity waiting for something to happen to it. Experience includes both sense stimulation and orderly investigation.

One may burn his hand as he attempts to snuff a candle with his index finger or thumb. This burn does not represent experience until there is a connection made between the lighted candle, the heat produced by the flame, the burn, and the pain. When the burn is seen to be the possible cause of pain, and when the burn is seen to be caused by too close contact or too slow reaction time, one can prevent a burn from the candle by limiting the amount of time the hand is in contact with the heat produced by the flame. Dewey summed up the whole affair in *Democracy and Education* when he concluded that: "(1) Experience is primarily an active-passive affair; it is not primarily cognitive. But (2) the *measure of the value* of an experience lies in the perception of relationships or continuities of which it leads up."[10]

[8]*Ibid.*, p. 151.
[9]*Ibid.*, p. 210.
[10]*Ibid.*, p. 164.

The establishment of the relationships of which he speaks can most satisfactorily be bought about by the systematic applications of the steps involved in the scientific method, or the reflective process. Thinking becomes the intentional endeavor of a person to find specific connections which exist between something that happens to him, or that he does, and the consequences which result. Reflective thinking is the process used to establish the connection that completes the act of experiencing. In a word, reflective thinking stands between perplexity and confusion and the post-reflective stage of mastery, satisfaction and application. This process includes normally:

1. Perplexity, confusion, doubt, due to the fact that one is implicated in an incomplete situation whose full character is not yet known. This is called a problem situation.

2. A conjectural anticipation—a tentative interpretation of the given elements, attributing to them a tendency to effect certain consequences (hypothesis).

3. A careful study of all attainable considerations which will define and clarify the problem at hand (the rightful place of facts).

4. A consequent elaboration of the tentative hypothesis to make it more precise and more consistent, because squaring with a wider range of facts (reasoning).

5. Taking one stand upon the projected hypothesis as a plan of action which is applied to the existing state of affairs (application by overt action or means of imagination).

This reflective process which we have been describing, Pierce called the "laboratory habit of mind." It is the means by which students can discover the meaning of facts in a context of problem solving. It is the habit of mind we wish to have our students to carry with them as they leave school for it represents the means by which they can continue their education. It is the means for beginning to think like the expert. It is the method of the expert.

Thus it is concluded that this third concept of the problem of instruction involves the following steps:

1. The teacher determines what material is of most significance in his field.

2. The teacher estimates the potential of his students. He estimates their past experiences and learning potential.

3. Finally the teacher proceeds to lead the students. He does this by engaging them in a process of inquiry to which they are committed, i.e., interested. In the course of the investigation, the students handle the subject matter as they solve problems, using the methods of science.

This third view of instruction would appear to be more sound than the other two because it is more comprehensive. It takes into consideration the subject, the child, and the methods of science.

HAROLD O. RUGG

*The late Harold O. Rugg of Teachers College, Columbia University
was one of the leaders of the Progressive Education Movement.*

17. On Reconstructing the Social Studies*

Our primary purpose is: agitation, discussion by teachers, administrators and specialists of the need of more scientific construction of school courses. It is only by joint and sympathetic discussion of actual evidence concerning existing practices that minds will come together on programs of procedure for reconstruction.

In connection with the organization of social studies material we feel we are making definite use of scientific procedure. My earlier article (May, 1921) showed that there has been a tendency in the organization of social studies courses to ignore contemporary thought on the psychology of learning. The first step, therefore, in organizing a course of study is to set forth hypotheses concerning principles on which that material can be graded and organized. We have arrived at a number of rather important hypotheses and are now framing our experimentation with a view to their confirmation or refutation. I can merely enumerate some of these hypotheses.

I. All units of work shall be presented definitely in problem-solving form (as contrasted with the narrative, factual, compartment method, with questions at end of chapter which courses now employ). Factual settings are grouped around *problems* stated so as to force an attitude of further inquiry.

One of the most important implications of this principle is that all economic, industrial, social and political material shall be woven together in *one course,* as contrasted with three or more in current practice—history, geography, civics, economics, etc.

There are important psychological and administrative reasons for this.

II. At the present time, great gaps occur in the continuity and progression of history, geography, and civics courses. History is taught in certain grades but not in all; geography in but few. It is one of our central theses that there should be one continuous social studies course from the first grade to the twelfth, hence we are assigning material to each grade (tentatively working from the fourth) in such a way that the discussions of one

*Excerpted from *Historical Outlook*, XII:253, October 1921. Used by permission.

grade shall be continuations of those of earlier grades but on more mature levels because of the increased maturity of the children.

III. Problems shall be based (not solely on the spontaneous interests of particular pupils) but on: 1. common experiences of children of that mental and social age; 2. personal appeals where possible, *e.g.* "What would you do if—etc.?" 3. alternative proposals where possible, to force comparison and systematizing of facts; 4. intellectual opposition to obtain interest; 5. much concrete human detail to obtain interest.

IV. Constant practice shall be given in analyzing, generalizing and organizing, as material that pertains to the "problems" is collected and studied. We are applying laws of habit-formation to analytical thinking in the social field. The important generalizations in each field must be discovered and such a considerable amount of activity provided for pupils (excursions, collecting facts, making maps, making notes of observations, writing reports, etc.) that much practice will be given in analyzing, generalizing and organizing.

V. Problem-situations shall be presented *first through current affairs. Only those historical backgrounds* shall be developed which specialists in the validity of historical materials in each field (government, economics and social relations) decide are *crucial for clear thinking about contemporary matters.* Thus, history is not regarded as a "content" subject;— only geography, government, economics, industry, anthropology, sociology, psychology are that. An article setting forth this theory will be published this year.

VI. Historical backgrounds, involving a grasp of "time sequence, " "continuity," or "development" of contemporary institutions and activities, are presented through "sharp contrasts." Sequence should move very rapidly in lower grades, somewhat more slowly in high school. Backgrounds are extensive, "thin," moving rapidly, and very concrete, in, say, the fourth and fifth grades, becoming gradually more intensive, detailed, abstract and moving more slowly in the junior and senior high-school grades.

VII. Problems, or the examples of generalization and organization which contribute to them, should recur in many grades, organized on an increasingly more mature level. Thus, some form of "layer" scheme may prove to be most effective to provide sufficient repetition.

The scientific construction of a course of study demands the most elaborately controlled-experimental teaching in the class room. Current programs must be really experimented upon. An important step is the critical observation and measurement of material taught children in the class room. However, the great need at the present time is new continuously-organized courses of study which are proven by observation and measured results to be teachable in the different grades.

IC. Why Teach the Social Studies: Some Aims and Goals

Many of the readings in the foregoing section were at least implicitly addressed to the question: "What are the purposes of the social studies?" It is evident that because of the scope of the field it has much to contribute to the schooling of youth. The central role of the social studies in both general education and civic education also indicates the breadth of possible aims of social education.

It would seem that a clear delimitation of prime purposes and the subsequent identification of a manageable number of related specific goals are in order. Such action will necessitate scrutiny and thought as to means as well as ends. It has been suggested, for example, that the usual objectives should include the methods or processes of the disciplines. It is claimed that so far these have not been evident in typical teaching and instructional materials. These considerations will also lead to a questioning of the relevancy of the disciplines themselves. In a dramatically changing era with a burgeoning demand for new knowledge and skills, presently underrepresented subjects and areas may have as much or more to offer than some of the traditionally dominant social sciences.

A further issue concerns the degree that the social studies are to be used purposefully to build attitudes. A serious rift exists between some social scientists who desire, above all, to develop "value-free" social investigators and the forces in society that envisage the school as primarily a carrier of traditions and loyalty, as a conservator of the virtues of the American way.

The social studies teacher often concludes that he has responsibilities in both camps. His dilemma is to properly satisfy the worth-while ends reflected in each outlook. To build open-minded, searching youth who also value ethical behavior and will so act is the challenge to education in a free society. From lay leaders such as Jefferson to theorists like John Dewey, we have a heritage that views the school as the "midwife of democracy." The social studies rest at the core of American education, whose fundamental aim, to again quote Dewey, is to help create a society that will be "true to itself."

Under this guideline the professional responsibility of the social studies instructor is to have a sound base for deciding upon the knowledges, skills, and attitudes to be emphasized. Under a system of schooling such as ours, the teacher has the serious duty of selecting many of the specifics of instruction. He must be certain that he has a valid rationale—that he knows why he is doing what he does.

As you read the following articles, ask yourself which elements or emphases promise to best help students to function most effectively in their immediate, throbbing world. How do the content and materials available square with these prime purposes? In what particular ways can we help students attain the desired goals? With which of the goals expressed in these readings would you agree? disagree? What other goals (besides those described in these readings) might be suggested?

COMMITTEE OF THE NATIONAL COUNCIL FOR THE SOCIAL STUDIES

Including Jack Allen, Howard Anderson, William Cartwright,
Dorothy McClure Fraser, John Haefner, and Samuel McCutchen

18. The Role of the Social Studies*

The social studies are concerned with human relationships. Their content is derived principally from the scholarly disciplines of economics, geography, history, political science, and sociology, and includes elements from other social sciences, among them anthropology, archaeology, and social psychology, The term *social studies* implies no particular form of curricular organization. It is applicable to curricula in which each course is derived for the most part from a single discipline as well as to curricula in which courses combine materials from several disciplines.

The ultimate goal of education in the social studies is the development of desirable sociocivic and personal behavior. No society will prosper unless its members behave in ways which further its development. Man's behavior tends to reflect the values, ideals, beliefs, and attitudes which he accepts. As used here, beliefs are convictions which tend to produce particular behavior in given circumstances. In authoritarian societies, the behavior desired by the rulers is brought about by fiat, threat of punishment, and manipulation of the emotions. In a free society, behavior must rest upon reasoned convictions as well as emotional acceptance. Knowledge and the ability to think should provide the basis on which American children and youth build the beliefs and behavior of free citizens.

Not all of the knowledge included in the social sciences can be used for instruction in the social studies. Indeed, the accumulation of knowledge in the social sciences is so vast that only a small fraction of it can be dealt with in a school program. Equally important, many of the concepts in the social sciences are too difficult to be grasped fully by children and youth. Since curriculum-makers must, therefore, decide what materials to include and what to omit, criteria for selection have to be adopted. The basic criterion put forward in this document is that those curricular materials should be included which will be most useful in developing desirable behavior patterns for a free society. Consequently, the knowledge included in the social studies will be related to important generalizations

*Social Education, XXVI;315-27, October 1962. Used by permission.

about human relationships, institutions, and problems, together with sufficient supporting facts to insure that these generalizations are understood. Instruction will also stress the methods used by social scientists in seeking truth. Some mastery of the methods of scholarly inquiry will enable citizens to make intelligent judgments on the important issues which confront them.

To use knowledge effectively, the student must develop a variety of skill in locating and evaluating sources of information, in observing, in listening, and in reading. To make knowledge socially useful, one must be able to think reflectively about data and conclusions derived from them. One must also be able to express his views orally and in writing, and have the will and ability to take part in the work of organized groups.

A number of considerations grow out of the brief description of the social studies and what they are good for. Instruction in the social studies is part of the education which should be provided to everyone. The kinds of behavior, beliefs, knowledge, and abilities mentioned in this statement are needed by all members of a free society. To attain the goals suggested, a comprehensive program of instruction in the social studies is required throughout the elementary and secondary school. In addition to the required program, elective subjects in the social studies should be provided so that individuals may pursue and develop special interests. The effectiveness of the social studies program is impaired if it is assigned a host of extraneous responsibilities. Instruction related to home and family living, personal health, and driver education, for example, has been included in the school program by decision of the public. But it is generally accepted that this type of instruction can best be handled by teachers outside the field of the social studies.

The complex task of teaching the social studies involves a heavy responsibility. The effective teacher must have some understanding of all of the social sciences. A comprehensive program for the education of young citizens clearly cannot be limited to instruction in one social science. It is also clear that in a world of rapid and continual change it is impossible to prescribe a fixed and immutable content for the social studies. Even though most of the information currently taught will remain valid and useful, the total body of content will require frequent updating and sharpening as new problems arise and new ways of dealing with persistent problems are discovered.

In summary, this statement includes four major considerations: (1) The ultimate goal of education in the social studies is desirable sociocivic and personal behavior. (2) This behavior grows out of the values, ideals, beliefs, and attitudes which people hold. (3) In turn, these characteristics must be rooted in knowledge. (4) For the development and use of knowledge, people require appropriate abilities and skills. The perpetuation and improvement of our democratic way of life is dependent upon the development of individuals who achieve these goals.

THE BEHAVIORAL NEEDS IN A FREE SOCIETY

Behavior is the reaction of an individual in any situation. Most behavior is learned in a variety of ways in the society in which the individual grows up. Some kinds of behavior are not acceptable in a democratic society at any time. It is also true that the process of historical change may demand new ways of acting.

In approaching the problem of behavior the school recognizes that in a democratic society responsibility for appropriate behavior must be assumed by individual members. A democratic society depends upon self-discipline and upon societal discipline approved by a majority. In any free society individuals must be willing and able to participate effectively in the solution of common problems. They must also be willing at times to arrive at decisions reflecting compromises among different points of view. Such compromises are acceptable when they help society to advance toward desirable goals, but the compromises must not result in the sacrifice of those inalienable rights, principles, and values without which democracy cannot survive. While it is true that other institutions share in the responsibility for the development of desirable behavior by members of society, it is also true that education has a great responsibility in shaping the behavior of individuals.

Among the behavioral patterns which may be identified as essential for the maintenance, strengthening, and improvement of a democratic society are the following:

1. Keeping well informed on issues which affect society, and of relating principles and knowledge derived from the social sciences to the study of contemporary problems.
2. Using democratic means in seeking agreement, reaching solutions, and taking group action on social problems.
3. Assuming individual responsibility for carrying out group decisions and accepting the consequences of group action.
4. Defending constitutional rights and freedoms for oneself and others.
5. Respecting and complying with the law, regardless of personal feelings, and using legal means to change laws deemed inimical or invalid.
6. Supporting persons and organizations working to improve society by desirable action.
7. Scrutinizing the actions of public officials.

8. Participating in elections at local, state, and national levels and preparing oneself for intelligent voting in these elections.
9. Opposing special privilege whenever it is incompatible with general welfare.
10. Being prepared and willing to render public service and to give full-time service in emergencies.
11. Engaging in continual re-examination of one's personal values as well as the value system of the nation.

The responsibility for the development of patterns of democratic behavior in pupils falls in large measure upon the social studies program. Behavior grows from the intellectual acceptance of new ideas, changes in attitudes, and the formation of a personal commitment to values which are basic to our society.

THE BELIEFS OF A FREE PEOPLE

Values may be defined as the beliefs and ideas which a society esteems and seeks to achieve. They inspire its members to think and act in ways which are approved. To the extent that actual behavior is consistent with the values claimed, a society is meeting the standards it has set for itself.

A fundamental premise of American democracy is that men and women can be taught to think for themselves and to determine wise courses of action. In choosing a course of action they need to take into account the values which are basic to our society. These values are rooted in the democratic heritage and provide a stabilizing force of utmost importance.

In meeting new situations Americans not only must consider whether possible courses of action are consistent with democratic values but they may need to re-examine the values themselves. Although the basic values of American democracy are permanent, secondary values are subject to change. Furthermore, there is always need for adjustment whenever one value is in conflict with another, as, for example, liberty and authority.

Other agencies than the schools obviously have responsibility for the inculcation of basic values. Nevertheless, a primary objective of instruction must be the development of a better understanding of our value system. At all grade levels, instruction in the social studies should concern itself with the attainment of this objective. To the extent that Americans have a thorough understanding of the values underlying their way of life, and accept this code as their own, they will be able to do their part in achieving the great goals which they have set for themselves.

Among the values which instruction in the social studies should seek to engender in youth are:
1. Belief in the inherent worth of every individual—that each person should be judged on his merit.

2. Belief that all persons should possess equal rights and liberties which are, however, accompanied by responsibilities.
3. Belief that all persons should have maximum freedom and equality of opportunity to develop as they desire, consistent with their capacities and with the general welfare.
4. Belief that individual and group rights must be exercised in such a way that they do not interfere with the rights of others, endanger the general welfare, or threaten the national security.
5. Belief that citizens should place the common good before self-interest or group or class loyalty, when these are in conflict.
6. Belief that freedom of inquiry, expression, and discussion provide the best way for resolving issues; that the will of the majority should govern; that the rights and opinions of the minority should be respected and protected.
7. Belief that citizens should be willing to act on the basis of reasoned conclusions and judgments, even though personal sacrifice is involved.
8. Belief that government must be based on properly enacted law, not on the caprice of men holding office; that government has a responsibility for promoting the common welfare.
9. Belief that people are capable of governing themselves better than any self-appointed individual or group can govern them, that political power belongs to and comes from the people; and that the people have the right, by lawful means, to change their government.
10. Belief that the freest possible economic competition consistent with the general welfare is desirable; that government has the obligation to stabilize economic growth and reduce gross economic inequalities.
11. Belief that both competition and cooperation are essential to the democratic process and to our national well-being.
12. Belief that the separation of church and state is essential.
13. Belief that maximum individual freedom, under law, throughout the world is the best guarantee of world peace.
14. Belief that change in relations between nation states should be accomplished by peaceful means, and that collective security can best be achieved within an organization of nation states.
15. Belief that Americans should work to achieve a world in which justice and peace are assured to all mankind.
16. Belief that Americans should have reasoned devotion to the heritage of the past, and a commitment to perpetuate the ideals of American life.

The foregoing beliefs and values have been subjectively derived. Quite possibly other lists would provide a different sequence and use different language. But the important point is that there would be a high degree of agreement on the basic beliefs included in such lists. A major purpose of instruction in the social studies is to help children and youth understand basic American values and develop loyalties to them. To attain this goal it is necessary to take values into account in the selection of content for social studies courses.

THE ROLE OF KNOWLEDGE

The attainment of goals in the social studies depends upon the acquisition and utilization of information, facts, data. Each of the social sciences, in effect, is a reservoir of knowledge to be used. But the kind and amount of knowledge which can be used from one or more disciplines is necessarily determined by curriculum requirements associated with a particular stage in the educational process. In any event, one cannot be concerned with the goals of social studies instruction without being drawn immediately into considerations of content. The National Council for the Social Studies, consequently, has made frequent examinations of content areas, notably in its Yearbooks to which distinguished social scientists have contributed.

In the last few years the National Council for the Social Studies has recognized the necessity for making a more comprehensive study of the social studies curriculum. One report, issued in 1957, carries the title: *A Guide to Content in the Social Studies.* This report listed 14 themes which were proposed as guidelines for the selection of content. A second report, published in 1958, is called *Curriculum Planning in American Schools: The Social Studies.* The group which prepared this report showed special interest in the advances made by social science research in recent decades and was concerned that these findings be reflected in school programs in the social studies. Beyond noting some limited illustrations of these advances, the report underscored the need for cooperative effort among social scientists, educators, and teachers in the planning of the social studies curriculum. In such planning a fundamental problem would be the development of agreement on principles to be used in the selection and grade placement of content. Teachers have long recognized that the reservoirs of social science knowledge hold an embarrassment of riches. Indeed, the study of any one of the social sciences alone might well require all the time available in grades one through 12.

THE ROLE OF ABILITIES AND SKILLS

If young people are to command the knowledge and develop the behavior and beliefs enumerated above, they must develop a variety of skills for locating, gathering, interpreting, and applying social studies information. Stated in another way, the purpose of teaching skills in social studies is to enable the individual to gain knowledge concerning his society, to think reflectively about problems and issues, and to apply this thinking in constructive action.

The need for the systematic teaching of social studies has become increasingly urgent for a number of reasons. With the development of modern media of mass communications and the expansion in the amount of scholarly material, there has been an enormous increase in the quantity and variety of social data that the citizens must deal with in locating and selecting information that is pertinent to a given issue. With the refinement and increasingly pervasive use of persuasion techniques in many areas of daily living, there is a correspondingly greater need for skill in appraising information and evidence and the sources from which they come. With the complicated forms of social organization which develop in an urbanized society, new skills of group participation are essential for effective action.

The development of some of these skills is the special responsibility of the social studies, such as those involved in understanding time and chronology, Others are shared with other parts of the school program, but have special application in social studies. The list of proposed objectives centering on abilities and skills includes both types, for students need both to deal with social studies materials.

The acquisition of abilities and skills is a form of learning. Consequently, some principles to guide instruction in them are essential to their development. These abilities and skills must be identified with sufficient concreteness so that the description helps in planning instruction and in evaluating various degrees of mastery. It seems clear that these abilities and skills cannot be developed in a vacuum but must be acquired by pupils as they study content derived from the social sciences. The nature of these abilities and skills is such that they will not be learned—nor should they be taught—incidentally, but rather through planned and systematic treatment. Effective instruction will recognize that the maturity of the students will largely determine at what grade level given abilities and skills can be developed most effectively. Teachers must also take into account that these abilities and skills should be developed in situations as nearly like those in which they will be used as possible, and that repeated practice will be needed if students are to become skillful in their use. Even so, there will be large differences in the facility with which students use skills at any grade level, as well as in the competence achieved by the end of the secondary school. The nature of these abilities and the individual differences exhibited by students indicate that complete mastery of most of them is never achieved. But the goal is to help each student achieve the highest level of performance each year that his own potential will permit.

The objectives listed in this statement involve abilities and skills needed for effective behavior; the abilities peculiar to the social science disciplines must be developed further as the college student pursues his specialized studies.

I. Skills centering on *ways and means of handling social studies materials*
   A. Skills of locating and gathering information from a variety of sources, such as:
      using books and libraries effectively, taking notes, using the mechanics of footnoting and compiling bibliographies
      listening reflectively to oral presentations
      interviewing appropriate resource persons and observing and describing contemporary occurrences in school and community
   B. Skills of interpreting graphic materials, such as:
      using and interpreting maps, globes, atlases
      using and interpreting charts, graphs, cartoons, numerical data, and converting "raw data" into these graphic forms
   C. Skills needed to develop a sense of time and chronology, such as:
      developing a time vocabulary and understanding time systems
      tracing sequences of events
      perceiving time relationships, between periods or eras and between contemporaneous developments in various countries or parts of the world
   D. Skills of presenting social studies materials, such as:
      organizing material around an outline
      writing a defensible paper and presenting an effective speech
      participating in a discussion involving social problems
II. Skills of *reflective thinking as applied to social studies problems*
   A. Skills of *comprehension,* such as:
      identifying the central issues in a problem or argument
      arriving at warranted conclusions and drawing valid inferences
      providing specific illustrations of social studies generalizations dealing with increasingly difficult and advanced materials
   B. Skills of *analysis and evaluation* of social studies materials, such as:
      applying given criteria, such as distinguishing between primary and secondary sources, in judging social studies studies materials
      recognizing underlying and unstated assumptions or premises, attitudes, outlooks, motives, points of view, or bias
      distinguishing facts from hypotheses, judgments, or opinions, and checking the consistency of hypotheses with given information and assumptions

distinguishing a conclusion from the evidence which supports it

separating relevant from irrelevant, essential from incidental information used to form a conclusion, judgment, or thesis

recognizing the techniques used in persuasive materials such as advertising, propaganda

assessing the adequacy of data used to support a given conclusion

weighing values and judgments involved in alternative courses of action, and in choosing alternative coures of action

C. Skills of *synthesis and application* of social studies materials, such as:

formulating valid hypotheses and generalizations, and marshalling main points, arguments, central issues

comparing and contrasting points of view, theories, generalizations, and facts

distinguishing cause-and-effect relationships from other types of relationships, such as means and ends

combining elements, drawing inferences and conclusions, and comparing with previous conclusions and inferences

identifying possible courses of action

making tentative judgments as a basis for action, subject to revision as new information or evidence becomes available

supplying and relating knowledge from the social studies as background for understanding contemporary affairs

III. Skills of *effective group participation*

A. Assuming different roles in the group, such as gadfly or summarizer, as these roles are needed for the group to progress

B. Using parliamentary procedures effectively

C. Helping resolve differences within the group

D. Suggesting and using means of evaluating group progress

Certainly a major purpose of social studies instruction is to place emphasis on the development of those abilities which encourage the accurate and intelligent utilization of social science data and which make habitual the orderly processes of mind necessary to carrying on reflective thought and to taking action based on such thinking.

LOOKING AHEAD

This preliminary statement of goals for the social studies is but a first step in a process that looks forward to making recommendations for the social studies curriculum in our schools. There remains for the future the major task of working out a logical sequence of grade placement that will present a systematic overview for the social studies curriculum. Here, there must be concern for a sequential development of the essential knowledge, skills, and attitudes that should be acquired by pupils going through the school program. Also consideration must be given to programs for pupils of widely varying abilities. Some experimentation with programs seeking to achieve all the objectives set forth will in all probability be called for in order to evaluate their effectiveness. Finally, it should be recognized that there is no single way in which the materials can be best organized in arriving at the goals, but that several alternative patterns might well be suggested.

DANIEL ROSELLE

Professor of History, State University of New York, at Fredonia

19. Citizenship Goals for a New Age*

Each generation of Americans must redefine the meaning of the term "good citizen" for itself, drawing on the past for wisdom, on the present for challenge, and on the future for promise. It may be true that a good citizen—like a good poem—"should not *mean* but *be*"; yet meaning can lead to being in the crucible of time.

In 1965 the Civic Education Project, sponsored by the National Council for the Social Studies and financed by the Danforth Foundation,[1] was asked to visit public, private, and parochial secondary schools throughout the nation to identify "the most promising practices in the making of citizens." A major part of its report (to be published by the NCSS in the latter part of this year) is structured on the Project teams response to the key question: "What is a good citizen?" Here, in modified form, is the team's position on the nature of good citizenship and citizenship goals for new age.

WHAT IS A GOOD CITIZEN?

Goal 1

A citizen who believes in BOTH liberty of the individual and equality of rights for all, as provided by the Constitution of the United States: it may have seemed logical for John Randolph of Roanoke to exclaim in his day: "I love liberty, and hate equality." Today this schism in the democratic ideal is archaic. In the new social mathematics of our times, the simple division between liberty and equality has been replaced by the more advanced equation: "Democracy = Liberty × Equality."[2]

Social Education, XXX:415–20, October 1966. Used by permission.
[1]Members of the Civic Education Project team are: Dr. Donald Robinson, *Chairman,* Associate Editor *Phi Delta Kappan;* Dr. Elmer Pfleiger, Director of Social Studies, Detroit Public Schools; Dr. Harold Oyer, Assistant Superintendent of Schools, Elkhart, Indiana; and Dr. Daniel Roselle, State University of New York at Fredonia.
[2]Leslie Lipson, *The Democratic Civilization* (New York: Oxford University Press, 1964), p. 543.

Goal 2

A citizen who recognizes that we live in an "open-end" world, and is receptive to new facts, new ideas, and new processes of living: It is difficult for men to forgo what Crane Brinton[3] has called "the delights of certitude"; yet our age demands flexibility. Jacques Barzun puts the matter this way:

> . . . no one idea, no one explanation, is omnicompetent. Contradiction, or at least nonuniformity, is a fact of experience. Even in the world of matter, physicists have found it expedient to regard light now as waves, now as corpuscles, for it acts by turns as if it were each of these things. Men in society act in more diverse ways than matter, and the arts are pragmatic techniques for recording these diversities.[4]

The good citizen may believe that "nothing is very new that is not at the same time very old,"[5] but he does not permit the past to blind him to the present. On the contrary, he is always open to the endless currents and crosscurrents of new ideas. Even his priceless possession of democracy he views as still in the *process of becoming,* rather than as rigidly fixed for all time. "Democracy is not an abstract concept of the kind that can be set forth mathematically in terms of pure ratiocination," writes Pierre Teilhard de Chardin. "Like so many of the notions on which modern ideologies are based . . . it was originally, and to a great extent still is, no more than the approximate expression of a profound but confused aspiration *striving to take place."*[6] The good American citizen, living in an "open-end" world, would agree.

Goal 3

A citizen who makes value judgments that enable him to function constructively in a changing world: Values, as Robin M. Williams, Jr. makes clear, "are not the concrete goals of action, but rather the criteria by which goals are chosen."[7] A major dilemma of Americans is how to construct values in an age when new explosions of knowledge disrupt —or overwhelm—the foundations of their society. At a time when astronaut John Glenn's space capsule is already considered dated enough to be placed in the Smithsonian Institution, the mere memorization of a body of facts is no longer a guarantee of an "informed citizenry possessing sound values."

[3]*Ideas and Men* (Englewood Cliffs, N.J.: Prentice-Hall, 1950), p. 423.
[4]*Of Human Freedom* (Philadelphia, Pa.: J. B. Lippincott, 1964), p. 183.
[5]Lin Yutang, *The Secret Name* (New York: Farrar, Straus, 1958). p.
[6]*The Fugure of Man* (New York: Harper and Row, 1964), p. 238 (italics mine).
[7]*American Society; a Sociological Interpretation* (New York: Afred A. Knopf, 1960), p.400.

Thus an American educator declares:

> Change in our own time has had a profound effect on the social character of people. This effect has been widely noted and studied, but its implications for responsible citizenship in a free society have not been appraised adequately or taken into sufficient account in making policy for our schools. Change, among other effects, has made it increasingly difficult for the individual to gain an adequate inner sense of *self*. Some of the most evident social facts of our time are impermanence, diversity, and movement. In consequence, stable values and a sense that one's life is coherent and meaningful are harder to come by than they were even a generation ago.
>
> The search for self is a central task of adolescence. The questions of adolescence are those of identity: "Who am I? Where am I heading? What do I believe in?" To the degree that firm personal values and agreement between one's values and actions are not achieved, the search for self fails. The result is a modern phenomenon: the adult adolescent— the chronically uncertain, restless, and often irresponsible adult.[8]

Recognizing the seriousness of the problem, a good citizen does not settle for philosophic nihilism. Instead, he conscientiously develops "a spirit of critical inquiry"[9] in a persistent effort to form sound value judgments. Such citizens ask themselves: "What *quality* of life [do] we want, both public and private, as citizens of this great republic?"[10] And they make full use of their critical intelligence in their search for answers.

Goal 4

A citizen who accepts the responsibility to participate in decision making by informing his representatives, experts, and specialists of his reactions to alternative public policies: No American citizen is expected to be an automated cornucopia of facts and figures on every matter handled by society. As Evron and Jeane Kirkpatrick point out: "Fortunately, democracy does not require that all men be equally expert in their knowledge of politics or public policy. Fortunately—because if democracy required every citizen, or every voting citizen, or even most voting citizens to understand and judge the myriad of complex issues which confront the nation in this age of technical specialization, international involvement, and interdepend-

[8] Franklin Patterson, *High Schools for a Free Society* (New York: The Free Press of Glencoe, 1960), p. 66.

[9] *The Statement on Academic Freedom,* jointly sponsored by the American Historical Association and the National Council for the Social Studies, takes the position that "the development in students of a scientific temper in history and the related social studies, of a spirit of critical inquiry accompanied by a necessity of confronting unpleasant facts, are far more important objectives than the teaching of special interpretations of particular events."

[10] Question posed by Adlai Stevenson in *Life,* May 30, 1960, p. 99.

ence, democracy would be impossible."[11] Further, "It is important to recognize our dependence on experts, and to disabuse ourselves and our students of the notion that good citizenship requires omnicompetence concerning public policy and the institutions by which it is made."[12]

What *is* required of the good citizen is that in major issues of public policy—where alternative plans of action are proposed to the American electorate—he make every effort to participate in the process of inquiry, discussion, and debate leading to a decision. Thus, E. E. Schattschneider, who believes that the power of the people in a democracy depends on the *importance* of the decisions made by the electorate, not on the *number* of decisions they make, defines democracy in this way:

> Democracy is a competitive political system in which competing leaders and organizations define the alternatives of public policy in such a way that the public can participate in the decision-making process.[13]

Such participation is a basic responsibility of a good American citizen. Rousseau's statement, "As soon as any man says of the affairs of the State, 'What does it matter to me?' the State may be given up for lost,"[14] seems unnecessarily dramatic in today's Age of the Expert. But the implications behind his remark still hold.

Goal 5

A citizen who develops skills and acquires knowledge to assist in the solution of political, economic, social, and cultural problems of his time: Critical thinking skills are among the most important for the American citizen to develop. These have been described in this way: The citizen

> (a) locates and evaluates evidence relevant to the issues at hand, (b) analyzes the elements of a controversial issue and weighs the motives of interested parties, (c) understands the methods and devices of the propagandist, (d) reserves his reasoned decision until considerable evidence has been weighed, then takes a working hypothesis which he acts upon if action is necessary, (e) subjects this working hypothesis to future modification if new evidence warrants it.[15]

Related skills invaluable to the American citizen in decision making are "those of *gathering information* through reading and listening; of *in-*

[11]Evron M. Kirkpatrick and Jeane J. Kirkpatrick, "Political Science," in Erling M. Hunt, *et al., High School Studies Perspectives* (Boston: Houghton Mifflin Co., 1962), p..101.
[12]*Ibid.*, p. 102.
[13]E. E. Schattschneider. *The Semisovereign People* (New York: Holt Rinehart and Winston, 1960), p. 141.
[14]*The Social Contract,* book III, chap. 15.
[15]Ryland W. Crary, ed., *Education for Democratic Citizenship,* National Council for the Social Studies, 22nd Yearbook (Washington, D. C., 1951), p. 157.

terpreting information by organizing logically and evaluating accurately; and of *communicating information* through speaking effectively and writing lucidly."[16]

A third group of skills involves the effective use of *techniques of group participation.* The importance of these skills was stressed by Hubert H. Humphrey in a letter written in 1958: ". . . Luckily, in the last few years, a number of fine books have been written by people with experience in government at many levels. The great improvement, in my mind, has been that they deal with government as a *process* rather than merely as a *structure.* Students now are able to get a much more realistic view of government and an appreciation of its dynamic, human component. Specifically, some of the concepts that are now put across are the tremendous role of *group action* in politics, without the connotation that somehow such activity is evil. . . ."[17]

Goal 6

A citizen who takes pride in the achievements of the United States, and at the same time appreciates the contributions to civilization of other peoples throughout the world: A citizen does not idolize every aspect of the American past, but he is proud that he is unalterably linked to it. He can visualize himself in the current of time, and find identification and purpose in this statement by John F. Kennedy: ". . . The torch has been passed to a new generation of Americans—born in this century, tempered by war, disciplined by a hard and bitter peace, proud of our ancient heritage—and unwilling to witness or permit the slow undoing of those human rights to which the nation has always been committed. . . ."[18] A citizen demonstrates his pride in his American heritage by gladly meeting his responsibilities: he votes, obeys the laws; educates his children to understand his country's traditions; and, in time of peril, defends his nation.

At the same time, a good citizen makes a conscientious effort to understand how *other* human beings in *other* lands view the world and its development. He recognizes and appreciates the contributions to civilization of other peoples. As early as 1916, the famous *Report* of the Committee on the Social Studies urged "the cultivation of a sympathetic understanding of . . . [other] nations and their peoples, of an intelligent appreciation of their contributions to civilization, and of a just attitude toward them. . . ."[19] Such an attitude on the part of the American citizen has never been more important than it is today.

[16]Helen McCracken Carpenter, "Skills for Democratic Citizenship in the 1960's," in Carpenter, ed., *Skill Development in Social Studies,* National Council for the Social Studies, 33rd Yearbook (Washington, D. C., 1963), p. 15 (italics mine).

[17]Humphrey to Daniel Roselle, May 23, 1958 (final italics mine).

[18]Extract from Inaugural Address, January 20, 1961.

[19]Cited in Henry Johnson, *Teaching of History* (New York: Macmillan Co., 1940), p. 113-14.

Goal 7

A citizen who remains constantly-aware of the tremendous effects of scientific discoveries on American and world civilizations, and works for their use in the quest for improved living for all mankind: Ours is an age in which modern scientists investigate the number of atoms (not angels) that can dance on the point of a needle, and other more complicated problems.[20] As each discovery is disclosed, it may bring with it new and profound political, economic, social, or cultural problems for society to solve.

Thus, in the early 1960's, molecular biologists reported that they were on the verge of discovering the specific relationship between the geometric shape of the molecules present in the cell chromosomes and the specific genetic characteristics of a living organism. Such knowledge would make it possible for the organic chemist to modify, in a predetermined way, the shape of certain chromosome molecules. This step in turn would modify the basic hereditary characteristics of the organism—human or otherwise —developed from these cells. According to scientist Oscar E. Lanford:

> This discovery, which in the scientific circles is knows an "breaking the genetic code," will mean that man is close to the point at which he can by laboratory procedures vary, in a predetermined way, the heredity characteristics of his offspring.[21]

A good citizen recognizes the vital moral problem that arises from this discovery: *Does man dare to alter the pattern of human life itself?* The importance of being aware of this and other problems created by major scientific breakthroughs can no longer be minimized by stating that "the chief duty of the American citizen is to vote." Vote he must for *national* survival—but for *human* survival, he must come to terms with science.

Goal 8

A citizen who realizes the importance of economic security and economic opportunity in the lives of all men, and concerns himself with strengthening both: The sum total of human knowledge has increased tremendously in the last two decades. This development has confronted the American citizen with economic problems of great complexity. New knowledge about production is a case in point. Hubert H. Humphrey reports:

> Between 1960 and 1970, estimates are that 22 million jobs will be eliminated [in the United States] by automation and more efficient pro-

[20] In June 1962, a microscope that can show the number of atoms dancing on the point of a needle was installed in the Henry Krumb School of Mines at Columbia University.

[21] Address by Dr. O. E. Lanford delivered at his installation as President, State University of New York College at Fredonia, May 1963.

duction techniques. At the same time an additional twelve-and-a-half million new persons will have moved out of classrooms and into the labor force for the first time. We shall have to provide close to 300,000 jobs per month just to keep up with the current effects of automation and new labor force alone.

Three hundred thousand jobs a month, just to stay even, is equivalent to a whole new industry the size of the entire meat-processing industry or all of the General Motors production complex per month. Put another way this means we shall have to find new jobs every single month for a group of workers the size of the population of Miami or Akron or Omaha.[22]

In 1964 President Lyndon Johnson summed up the situation when he said: "In this political democracy, what you have and what you own and what you hope to acquire is not secure when there are men that are idle in their homes and there are young people adrift in the streets, and when there are thousands that are out of school and millions that are out of work, and the aged lying embittered in their beds."[23]

A good citizen faces up to this fact. He realizes that economic security and economic opportunity—like political and social democracy—are vital factors in the health of his country.

Goal 9

A citizen who uses the creative arts to sensitize himself to human experience and to develop the uniqueness of his personality: "America may end in spontaneous combustion, but never in apathy, inertia, or uninventiveness," wrote Alistair Cooke in 1952.[24] The good citizen contributes to the spontaneity, energy, and creativeness of American society by developing his individual potentialities fully.

In his search for what John W. Gardner called "perpetual self-discovery, perpetual reshaping to realize one's best self, to be the person one could be,"[25] the good citizen turns to the creative arts—music, art, literature, and related fields. These multicolored fountainheads of thought and feeling enable him to develop the uniqueness of his personality by *sensitizing* him to a variety of human experience. Harold Taylor describes the importance of this function in these words:

> Until the individual becomes sensitive to experience and to ideas, until they mean something to him personally, or, to put it differently, until he becomes conscious of the world around him and wishes to understand it, he is not able to think creatively either about himself or about

[22] *War on Poverty* (New York: McGraw-Hill Book Co., 1964), p. 152.
[23] Cited in *ibid.*, p. 31.
[24] Quoted in John W. Gardner, *Excellence* (New York: Harper and Bros., 1961), p. 17.
[25] *Ibid.*, p. 136.

his world. His sensibility, his values, his attitudes are the key to his intellect. It is for this reason that the arts, *since they have most directly to do with the development of sensibility,* are an essential component of all learning, including scientific learning.[26]

The good citizen views mankind in the mirror of the arts, and in the process discovers the unique features of his own image.

Goal 10

A citizen who has compassion for other human beings, and is sensitive to their needs, feelings, and aspirations: As the philosopher Martin Buber points out, each person has a responsibility to treat every other person as a "Thou," not as an "It"—that is, as a fellow human being, not as an object of political, economic, or social exploitation.[27] In an age of increasing "depersonalization," compassion for and sensitivity to others are essential.

In Asia the average life expectancy is only 45 years; in Africa nine out of ten Africans are illiterate; in the Middle East thousands of children waste away from brutal diseases; and in the rich and powerful United States over 35 million persons live in poverty. A good American citizen does not ignore these and similar facts, nor does he assume that intellect without compassion can solve the world's problems. He realizes that sensitivity to the conditions of others is a necessary first step leading to intelligent civic behavior.

Lyndon B. Johnson identifies the humanistic task of the American citizen in these words: "The task before us is truly for the educated mind because the educated mind sees things not only clearly but *compassionately.* Otherwise, that mind is merely trained. We are dealing with humanity and if we do not treat people as human beings the educated mind is a sham and a fraud."[28]

Goal 11

A citizen who understands that the continuation of human existence depends upon the reduction of national rivalries, and works for international cooperation and order.

The good citizen is deeply disturbed by the magnitude of war, and equally concerned by the useless death of even one human being. He realizes that man *can* alter archaic ideas from the past; and that if he remains a prisoner of a war mentality, he is his own jailer. Recognizing that human

[26]*Art and the Intellect—Moral Values and the Experience of Art* (New York: Museum of Modern Art, 1960), p. 13 (italics mine).

[27]*I and Thou*(New York: Charles Scribner's Sons, 1958).

[28]"The Century of the Educated Man," in *Vital Speeches of the Day,* August 15, 1963, p. 654–55 (italics mine).

existence depends upon peaceful relations among men, the citizen strives to reduce national hatreds and to strengthen international cooperation and order.

"It is painfully and incontrovertibly clear," writes Henry Cabot Lodge, Jr., "that without world order our ultimate destruction is only a matter of time. When we face this alternative, we know that we can, will and must create world order."[29] The good citizen agrees. He does not demand that all people fit into a single mold of life, but welcomes them with the words: "Give me your difference."[30] The good citizen works with his fellow men everywhere to build a world of law and order.

Goal 12

A citizen who develops a set of principles consistent with his democratic heritage, and applies them conscientiously in his daily life: The citizen sets up principles not as inflexible censors of his conduct, but as intelligent guides to democratic behavior. In the words of Francis Biddle, the citizen-philosopher has a responsibility "not so much to formulate a rationalized and comprehensive system as to develop what Jacques Maritain calls 'an adequate ideological formulation,' expressing the American view of civilization in new symbols and fresh language."[31]

It is of prime importance that the citizen translate his principles into action. "What Americans have done," writes historian Henry Steele Commager, ". . . is to realize, to institutionalize, to actualize, the principles and doctrines and values inherited from older civilizations, to translate them, that is, out of the realm of theory and doctrine and into the realm of practice, *to transform them from bodies of cherished opinion to bodies of felt activity and practice.*"[32]

The good citizen will continue to test his principles on the basic issues of his own times—and to strengthen his *sense of purpose* in an ever changing world.

THREE NEEDS
INFORMATION—ANALYSIS—COMMITMENT

A careful study of the 12 "Citizenship Goals for a New Age" makes clear that there are three major needs for the development of good citizens

[29]Quoted in *Pathway to Peace* (Minneapolis, Minn.: T. S. Denison and Co., 1957), p. 89.
[30]Words of Dr. Everett Clinchy, former President of the National Conference of Christians and Jews. Quoted in *ibid.*, p. 30.
[31]"Freedom and the Preservation of Human Values," in *Preserving Human Values in an Age of Technology,* Franklin Memorial Lectures, vol. 9, ed. Edgar G. Johnston (Detroit, Michigan: Wayne State University Press), p. 68.
[32]"Human Values in the American Tradition," in *ibid.*, p. 29–30.

in the United States today: The need to
1. Create an informed citizenry.
2. Develop an analytical citizenry.
3. Promote a committed and involved citizenry.

Mrs. Deborah Garfield, teacher of American history at Yorktown High School, Arlington, Virginia, stressed these three needs when she said:

> A good citizen must learn the ways of finding out facts, ideas, and values. He must develop the *ability to know:* where to find information, how to find it, how to evaluate it, and how to communicate his findings to others.
>
> But good citizenship is not just frothing at the mouth; rather, it involves making precise, *analytic judgments.*
>
> Finally, the good citizen can often be identified by his degree of *commitment and participation* in public affairs.

Most of the students interviewed by the Civic Education Project team expressed views similar to those of Mrs. Garfield. When asked, "What is a good citizen?" the students gave these responses:

Typical responses indicating a need for an informed citizenry.
Linda Ellis, Henniker High School, Henniker, New Hampshire:
"A good citizen is one who finds out information before making a decision."
Harry Greenwald, Miami Beach High School, Miami Beach, Florida:
"A good citizen is someone who tries to keep informed of what is going on. People often don't take the time to care."
Donald Schueman, West Leyden High School, Northlake, Illinois:
"A good citizen is someone who knows his country and understands the laws—not only obeys them but understands them."

Information is not a permanent collection of "facts" pinned down for all time. Facts, like butterflies, have wings. Nevertheless—and admitting the constantly changing nature of man's knowledge—it is still a prime necessity for the citizen to keep himself as well informed as possible about the facts of the past and the present.

Typical responses indicating a need for an analytical citizenry.
Scotty C., Darien High School, Darien, Connecticut:
"Lots of times things come up where the crowd is against your position, and I think you face discrimination against yourself. At that point, it is necessary for a good citizen to think and analyze for himself and to do what he thinks is right—notwithstanding the feelings of the crowd."
Annie Price, Dubose Junior High School, Alice, Texas:
"A good citizen is one who can listen intelligently, be impartial—that is, objective—and analyze. And one who has the courage to stand up for what he believes in."

Calvin Clabiorne, Oakland Technical High School, Oakland, California:

"A good citizen thinks and questions until he understands the laws of the land. And if, as a result of his questioning, he finds bad laws, he sees it as his duty to change them." [by regular legal means].

"Where is the wisdom we have lost in knowledge? Where is the knowledge we have in lost information?" asked T. S. Eliot in *The Rock*. Many of the students interviewed shared his conviction that *intelligent thought* must be added to knowledge if man is to find meaning in modern life. Meaning—and the ability to survive in an increasingly complicated world! G. K. Chesterton may have had that in mind when he was asked, "If you were cast away on a desert island, and if you could carry only one work of literature with you, what would it be?" He answered, "The Complete Manual for Shipbuilding."[33]

An analytical citizen runs the risk of reaching some unsound conclusions. (Even a scholar like Aristotle concluded that women have fewer teeth than men, and the learned Pythagoras taught that it was dangerous to let swallows rest on the roof of a house!) Yet analysis remains a key tool to assist the citizen to solve the persistent problems of the contemporary world.

Typical responses indicating a need for a committed and involved citizenry.

Marla Overby, Labette County Community High School, Altamont, Kansas:

"The most important things are to vote, and to serve on juries, and perform duties such as that—and also to help other people willingly."

John Hausner, Phoenix West High School, Phoenix Arizona:

"A good citizen is one who looks out for the other fellow as well as for himself. And who participates in things—elections, community projects, and others."

Moira Stacey, Rim of the World Junior-Senior High School, Lake Arrowhead, California:

"A good citizen is a person who is responsible—to himself, to people, to the country, to all of society."

Glenn Keife, De LaSalle High School, New Orleans, Louisiana:

"A good citizen is one who knows what his duties are and practices them, and gets others to do so too."

Mary Chris Roman, St. Scholastica High School, Chicago, Illinois:

"It should start right on the community level. If a good citizen thinks something should be changed, he contacts others—thus he plays an active role—he participates."

One need not go to the extreme of Thomas Huxley and say "the great end of life is not knowledge but action" to understand the necessity for a

---

[33]Quoted by Phyllis McGinley in her essay *Profession: Housewife.*

committed and involved citizenry. Richard W. Poston puts it more reasonably when he asks:

> Can the principle of a democratic society with its tradition of free-
> dom succeed in the modern world?. . . . The answer to that question will
> depend upon the action of people within their communities. For without
> thought, action, and participation by the people in their own community
> life no democratic society can long exist.[34]

The key word here is *participation*, and implicit is the idea that participation is a responsibility of everyone—the "haves" as well as the "have
nots." The assistant superintendent of schools in a wealthy suburban community in New England realized this. He called his well-fed, well-clothed,
well-housed students "culturally disadvantaged" because they did not have
the opportunity to participate in the experiences of millions of citizens less
fortunate than they!

Certainly, it must be reaffirmed that the making of good citizens is not
just the responsibility of the school, but depends on community participation as a whole. This key point—so often stated and so often forgotten—was
brought home again and again to members of the Civic Education Project
team. It is reflected most sharply in this comment taken from the team's
observation notebook:

> This morning we walked about the slum area that surrounds the
> school we visited yesterday. It was a different world from the shiny
> make-believe, coffee-break, excuse-me-sir Utopia of the Central Ad-
> ministration Building. There were ugly houses, and filthy streets, and
> beer cans rusting in the sun, and people rusting with them. There was
> dirt that could not be swept away by memos or by television programs
> or by speeches. It was horrible.
>
> What are we doing talking about citizenship education? How can
> the schools turn out good citizens when slum communities are there
> negating the academic niceties? Education is *not* enough—is not a uni-
> versal panacea—is not *the* solution. The attack has to be many sided:
> better education; better housing; better clothing; better jobs; better
> everything.
>
> All the sweet talk about citizenship seems to go out the window
> when you see a child sitting in the gutter playing with a rat's tail—and
> when you know that probably the child's only sin was being born in the
> wrong neighborhood. How long will it be before all communities *develop
> a conscience and act?*

[34]Richard W. Poston, *Democracy is You* (New York: Harper and Bros. 1953), p. 11.

part **II**

How?

IIA. How Shall We Organize and Manage Our Classrooms?

A sound rationale for selecting subject matter is important; but appropriately selected content is not enough. The teacher is faced next with issues surrounding the presentation of content to students so that it not only whets their intellectual appetites but even motivates them to continue learning outside the regular classroom. Many potentially exicting lessons, containing intellectually valid content, have had a practically negligible impact due to ineffectual learning procedures. Thus, teachers cannot ignore questions as to the best manner to approach a topic and the most effective techniques for their purposes.

Specific techniques by themselves, however, are not sufficient. The teacher must also concern himself with establishing a viable means of class order; developing an intellectually stimulating learning atmosphere; selecting the proper materials needed to develop the knowledge, skills, thinking processes, attitudes, and values desired; planning his lessons so that provision is made for individual differences among learners; establishing a common frame of reference within which all will work; and then devising adequate means of evaluating what his students have learned and how well he has taught. This is obviously a very tall order! But teaching is a complex, involved operation, and true success comes only with thorough attention to instructional strategies.

The articles in the following sections comprise the heart of this book. You now approach the materials which address themselves specifically to the methods of successful instruction. The first group of readings considers basic issues related to the all-important classroom atmosphere; teacher personality and pupil motivation and deployment are all treated as fundamental aspects of establishing a good environment for learning. Consider questions such as: How informal or formal should I be? What are the best ways for me to reach a specific class for a given purpose? When and why do I alter the seating or grouping in the room?

JAMES A. MICHENER

*Formerly of Colorado State College of Education, Noted author
and holder of the Pulitzer Prize for* Tales of the South Pacific.

20. Who Is Virgil T. Fry?*

I have never known a man more fascinating than Mr. Virgil T. Fry.
His fascination grows daily because I have never met him.

Mr. Fry, you see, was my predecessor in a small Indiana high
school. He was a teacher of the social studies, and he was fired for in-
competency. I was brought in to take his place.

Dr. Kelwell, the superintendent of schools in Akara, first told me
about Virgil T. Fry. "Fry," he said, "was a most impossible man to
work with. I hope you will not be like him."

"What was his trouble?" I asked.

"Never anything in on time. Very hard man to work with. Never
took advice," was the reply. Dr. Kelwell paused and leaned back in his
chair. He shook his head violently: "Very poor professional spirit." He
nodded as if to agree with himself, then repeated, "I hope you won't be
like him."

The principal, Mr. Hasbolt, was considerably more blunt.

"You have a great chance here," he said. "Mr. Fry, your predecessor, was a very poor teacher. He antagonized everyone. Constant source
of friction. I don't recall when we ever had a teacher here who created
more dissension among our faculty. Not only his own department either.
Everyone in this building hated that man, I really do believe. I certainly
hope you won't make the same mistakes." He wrung my hand vigorously
as if to welcome me as a real relief from a most pressing and unpleasant problem.

The head of the social-studies department in which I worked was
more like Dr. Kelwell than like Mr. Hasbolt. He merely hinted at Mr.
Fry's discrepancies. "Very inadequate scholar. Very unsound. Apt to
go off half-cocked," he mused.

"In what way?" I asked.

"Oh—lots of ways. You know. Crack-pot ideas. Poor tact in expressing them. You have a real opportunity here to do a good job. I certainly hope you won't make Fry's mistakes."

But if the head of my department was indirect, the head of the English department wasn't. "That man!" she sniffed. "He really was a terrible person. I'm not an old maid, and I'm not prudish, but Virgil T. Fry

*Clearing House, 16:67–70, October 1941. Used by permission.

was a most intolerable person. He not only thought he could teach social studies and made a mess of it, but he also tried to tell me how to teach English. In fact, he tried to tell everyone how to do everything."

Miss Kennedy was neither an old maid nor prudish, and she was correct when she intimated that the rest of the staff felt as she did. Mr. Fry had insulted the music department, the science department, and above all the physical-education department.

Tiff Small was head of athletics. He was a fine man with whom I subsequently played a great deal of golf and some tennis. He wouldn't discuss Fry. "That pansy!" and he would sniff his big nose into a wrinkle. "Pretty poor stuff."

Mr. Virgil T. Fry's landlady ultimately became my landlady, too, and she bore out everything the faculty had said about her former boarder: "Never cleaned his room up. Smoked cigarettes and dropped the ashes. I hope you don't smoke. You don't? Well, I'm certainly glad. But this Mr. Fry, my he was a hard man to keep house for. I even pity the poor girl that got him."

Remembering Tiff Small's insinuation, I asked my landlady if Fry ever went with girls. "Him? He courted like it was his sole occupation. Finally married a girl from Akara. She was a typist downtown. Had been to the University of Chicago. Very stuck-up girl, but not any better than she had to be, if you want my opinion. Quite a girl, and quite good enough for him."

As the year went on I learned more about Fry. He must have been a most objectionable person, indeed, for the opinion concerning him was unanimous. In a way I was glad, for I profited from his previous sins. Everyone was glad to welcome me into the school system and into the town, for, to put it baldly, I was a most happy relief from Virgil T. Fry.

Apart from his personality he was also a pretty poor teacher. I found one of his roll books once and just for fun distributed his grades along the normal curve. What a mess they were! He had 18% A's where he should have had no more than 8%! His B's were the same. And when I reached the F's, he was following no system at all. One person with a total score of 183 was flunked. The next, with a total score of 179 had received a C! And in the back of his desk I found 247 term papers he had never even opened! I laughed and congratulated myself on being at least more honest than my predecessor, even if I excelled him in no other way.

I was in this frame of mind when Doris Kelly, the sixteen-year-old daughter of a local doctor, came into my room one evening after school. "May I ask you a question?" she said.

"Of course."

"Maybe you won't like it," she replied, hesitating a moment.

I laughed. "Certainly I will. What is it?"

"Why don't you teach the way Mr. Fry did?"

I was taken aback. "How did he teach?" I asked.

"Oh," was the answer, "he made everything so interesting!"

I swallowed and asked her to elaborate.

"Well, Mr. Fry always taught as if everything he talked about was of utmost importance. You got to love America when you got through a course with Mr. Fry. He always had a joke. He wasn't afraid to skip chapters now and then.

"He could certainly teach you how to write a sentence and a term paper. Much better than the English teachers, only they didn't like it very much. And did you *read books* when Mr. Fry taught you! Ten, maybe, a year, and all in the very kinds of things you liked best. Hitler, strikes, the Constitution, and all about crime. Just anything you wanted to read.

"And class was always so interesting. Not boring." She stopped and looked at me across the desk with a bit of Irish defiance in her eye.

She was a somewhat mature girl and I concluded that she had had a crush on this remarkable Mr. Virgil T. Fry. "Did all the pupils feel that way?" I asked her.

"I know what you're thinking," she said, smiling. "But you're wrong. Everyone liked him. Almost every one of them did. And the reason I came in to see you this evening is that none of us like the way you teach. It's all so very dull!"

I blushed. Everyone had been telling me what a fine job I was doing. I stammered a bit, "Well, Mr. Fry and I teach two different ways."

"Oh, no," she insisted. "It's not that. Mr. Fry really taught. He taught us something every day. I'll bet you ask all the pupils they'll all say the same thing. He was about the only real teacher we had."

I became somewhat provoked and said a very stupid thing. "Then why was he fired?" No answer.

"You did know he was fired, didn't you?"

Doris nodded.

"Why?" I repeated.

Doris laughed. "Jealousy," she said.

I was alarmed. I wondered if the pupils really did dislike my teaching as much as Doris had implied. The next day in a class of which Doris was not a member I tried an experiment.

"Well," I said, "we've now reached the end of the first unit. I wonder if it wouldn't be a good idea to go back to a discussion of the big ideas of this unit?" I paused.

Not much response, so I added: "The way Mr. Fry used to do? Remember?"

Immediately all the pupils sat up and started to pay attention. Most of them smiled. Two of the girls giggled and some of the boys squirmed. They obviously wanted to accept my suggestion. "Tom," I asked, "will you take over?" for I had no idea what Mr. Fry's method was.

Tom nodded vigorously and came to the front of the room.

"All right," he rasped, "who will dare?"

"I will," said a girl. "I believe that Columbus came to the New World more for religious reasons than for commercial reasons."

"Oh!" groaned a group of pupils, snapping their fingers for attention. Tom called on one.

"I think that's very stupid reasoning, Lucille. Spain was only using religion as a mask for imperialism."

Lucille turned in her seat and shot back, "You wouldn't think so if you knew anything about Philip the Second."

And the debate continued until Tom issued his next dare. A pupil accepted and defiantly announced: "I think all that section about Spain's being so poor at colonizing is the malarkey. Everything south of Texas except Brazil is now Spanish. That looks pretty good to me."

I winced at the word "malarkey" and the pupils winced at the idea. The tigers of Anglo-Saxony rose to the defense of the text and the challenging pupil did his best to stand them off.

A few nights later I drove some other pupils to a basketball game in a nearby city. One of the boys observed, as we were coming home: "Class has been much better lately. I sort of like history now."

"How do you mean, better?" I asked.

"Oh, more the way Mr. Fry used to teach."

"Was Mr. Fry such a good teacher?" I asked.

"Oh, boy!" chortled the crowd, all at once. And one continued, "Was he? Boy, he could really teach you. I learned more from him than my big brother did at the university, in the same course. That's a fact! I had to read more, too, but I certainly liked it."

"I always thought he was rather—well, sissy?" I observed.

"Fry? Oh, no!" the boys replied. "It's true he didn't like the athletic department and used to make some pretty mean cracks about athletes, but we all liked it a lot. No, Mr. Fry was a very good tennis player and could swim like a fish."

The question of reading bothered me. I had always aspired to have my pupils read a great deal, and here they were all telling me that last year they had read and this year they hadn't. I went to see Miss Fisher, the librarian, about it.

"No," she said, "the books aren't going out the way they did last year."

"Could it be that maybe Mr. Fry knew how to use the library better?" I asked.

"Oh, no!" was the laughing reply. "You're twice the teacher Mr. Fry was. All the staff thinks so. He was a terrible person around a library!"

This depressed me, and I sought for an answer outside the school. I went around that night to visit Dr. Kelley, Doris' father.

"The fact is," he said, "you're in a tough spot. Virgil T. Fry was a truly great teacher. You're filling the shoes of a master. I hear the children talking at table and about the house. Fry seems to have been the only teacher who ever really got under their skins and taught them anything."

He paused, then added. "As a matter of fact, the pupils find your teaching rather empty, but I'm glad to say they think it's been picking up recently." He knocked out his pipe and smiled at me.

"Then why was Fry fired?" I asked.

"Difference of opinion, I guess," the doctor replied. "Fry thought education consisted of stirring up and creating. He made himself very unpopular. You see, education is really a complete social venture. I see that from being on the school board. Fry was excellent with pupils but he made a terrible mess of his adult relationships."

"You're also a father," I said. "Don't you think your daughter deserves to have good teachers?"

He lit his pipe again. "Of course, if you want the truth, I'd rather have Doris study under Fry than under you. In the long run she'd learn more." He smiled wryly.

"At the same time, what she learns from you may be better for her in the long run than what she would have learned from Fry."

"May I ask you one question, Doctor?" I inquired. He assented. "Did you concur in Fry's dismissal?"

Dr. Kelly looked at me a long time and drew on his pipe. Then he laughed quietly. "I cut board meeting that night. I knew ahead of time that the problem was scheduled to come up."

"I think I would always cut board meeting," he answered. "Fry was a disruptive force. He was also a very great teacher. I think the two aspects balanced precisely. I would neither hire him nor fire him. I wouldn't fight to keep him in a school and I wouldn't raise a finger to get him out of one." I frowned.

He continued: "The fine aspect of the whole thing is that you, a beginning teacher, don't have to be all Fry or all yourself. You can be both a great teacher and a fine, social individual. It's possible."

Dr. Kelley laughed again as he showed me to the door. "Don't worry about it. And you may be interested to know that your superintendent, Dr. Kelwell, feels just as I do about the whole problem. He stood out till the last minute to keep Fry. Very reluctant to have him go."

I went home badly confused.

As I said before, I have never known a man so fascinating as Mr. Virgil T. Fry. Not a member of his faculty has a good word to say for him and not a pupil in any of his classes has an unkind word to say against him.

HARTLEY KERN

Social Studies Teacher, Mann Junior High School, Los Angeles

21. Motivating the Pupil's Creativity in the Classroom*

Amid the furor that the Sputniks have aroused in our educational system today, there is the ever-present concern with pupil motivation. Teachers are worried about student apathy in their classes and many a finger has been pointed and an abundance of solutions offered. This article will be concerned with the methods the writer has found rewarding in stimulating student motivation.

The problem of getting students interested in their work has always been with us. It is a well-recognized fact that if the students are interested in their class work, many of the other problems a teacher has to face are minimized. Before any methods can be presented for stimulating motivation, it is necessary that the nature of the student himself be understood.

Secondary school teachers often make the mistake of assuming that their pupils are endowed with less intelligence than they actually possess. They are in agreement with the legal code and assume that persons below the age of eighteen are not responsible for their conduct and must be treated in a different manner than are members of the adult community. Such teachers spoon-feed the subject matter to their students and coddle them in all academic pursuits. This writer maintains that students will always measure up to their teachers' expectations. If the teacher looks upon them as immature and irresponsible infants, they will be so; if treated as young adults with important responsibilities, they will react accordingly. The fact is that secondary school students have the mental capabilities of adults and must be expected to use these abilities.

The purpose of academic work is to help the student learn about the past and to think critically and objectively about the present. One way this goal can be reached is by looking once again to the foundations of our democratic society. Our country is founded upon the ideals of freedom of the intellect and freedom of the individual. It is considered good that a man be allowed to think for himself, especially when this thinking involves value judgments, ethical norms, and rational explanations. One must not be subjected only to one ideology or one point of view. For those who are seeking a method of pupil motivation, the writer suggests a class-

California Journal of Secondary Education, 34: 263–68, May 1959. Used by permission.

room situation where every student is encouraged to express his own ideas freely and where these ideas are acknowledged as being worthwhile by his classmates and teacher. If a student realizes he will not be ridiculed or put under pressure for any original ideas or questioning of traditional ideas, he will begin using his mind more critically. If he realizes that he has something to offer to his classmates and to the teacher, then this is the necessary motivating force.

Basic to this concept of free expression within the classroom is the acknowledgment that not all ideas are good ideas. Students will be taught to discriminate between logical analysis and emotional attachments. Experts will be recognized as people who possess greater ability to interpret a situation through their better training. The opinions of the doctor, the lawyer, and the historian concerning their special fields are considered more valid than those of the layman. However in a democracy where it is believed that all men intrinsically possess the ability to think for themselves, it must be realized that no one point of view concerning any particular area is ever totally correct. Within this point lies the crux of this article. Each individual possesses the right and the ability to discover for himself and for others a new approach or answer to a heretofore noncontroversial and accepted point of view.

It might be asked how this is related to the actual classroom situation. If a teacher allows his students to think in a creative fashion without feeling threatened, if he actively promotes original work, if time is allowed for controversial discussion, if students are encouraged to disagree critically with each other, the text, and the teacher, if a teacher shows by his actions that he favors these activities, then he is on the road to motivating his students. Pupils will work hard and become interested in applying themselves if they feel that they really have something to offer to the class.

Many teachers feel it is necessary to start out the beginning of each new semester with work in the subject matter. It should be realized that it takes time to create the type of situation wanted, and that if the teacher takes a few days or a week to get to know the students first, and to explain to them what he is trying to accomplish, then the rest of the semester will flow more smoothly.

The first thing that a teacher must do in a class if he hopes to motivate all students is to explain to them his philosophy of education. He must tell them that he considers the role of education in our schools to be the development of the mind and the ability to think for oneself on one's own feet, not just for the presentation of facts accepted without question and committed to memory.

During the first few days of the term it must be stressed that the classroom will be run in a democratic manner. We have all heard about democratic atmosphere in the classroom; but here the writer means a democracy based on law, not anarchy. The teacher is to be considered the leader because of his training, not because he is a better or more intelligent person. Once the framework of rules has been established, the teacher can create a situation whereby the students and teacher become better acquainted. At this point there will be further talks on the teacher's philosophy and orientation to what will be taking place in the classroom during the term.

For some teachers, creating this type of classroom environment presents problems. When you encourage free discussion it is difficult to cover all the material and impossible to follow any pre-conceived plans, since the work will be based upon the interest and inclination of the group in problem areas. Therefore, daily lesson plans are frustrating and you will soon find yourself using well-developed unit plans covering the broad areas you want developed. In this way your time sequences will be less restricted. It is helpful to pass out unit assignment sheets to the students. These sheets should list the basic ideas behind the entire unit, followed by a list of discussion questions on the most pertinent problems in the area of study. At the bottom of each sheet should be a category of extra credit work that students can do should they finish their work before the rest of the class. All extra work should be of an original nature with the exception of a research paper done in collegiate form. Students appreciate these assignment sheets because they are enabled to work ahead of the class, or, when absent, to know just what they have missed. They also are able to see the over-all general plan of the unit through these sheets.

The mind cannot function creatively and enthusiasm will vanish if pupils are forced to conform to many specific rules. Once students become stimulated, the teacher must provide the necessary equipment to direct their enthusiasm in a thought-provoking channel. This means the students must make use of the library frequently, book lists must be developed, and interesting work projects and displays created. Pupil interest usually evolves into group and committee work, panels, and debates. This often requires double assignments, multiple texts, and, most of all, very efficient planning.

Once a class starts moving, the situation is generally as follows: The class as a whole is studying the present assignment, each student is working on one or more projects, and the class is divided up into research, audiovisual, and debate teams. This is a far cry from the "read book, answer questions, test" variety of activity. It should be realized that there is no half-way point. If your object is to teach *everyone* in the class and not just the few gifted and the problem children, then you will either have a highly motivated steamed-up group of fireballs or a lethargic watch-the-clock group of bored individuals.

Each teacher should realize that in every class there is a large group of divergent interests represented and that not all of the students will possess a fervent interest in the subject matter at hand. Therefore the teacher should attempt to cross subject lines and tie in different areas of study in order to bring as many students into the fold as possible. For example, if you are studying any historic period, attempt to tie in literature, the arts, music, science, religion, the military, clothing, foods, transportation, etc. Some students become interested in the Roman Wars simply by bringing into the classroom information concerning the type of weapons or money used. Others may be interested in the dress of the period, etc.

Creative expression and activities that tend to promote it, must be stressed, such as: individual and group projects, debates, committee work, plays, and role-playing. Silent reading, frequent tests of factual information, or discussion of specific answers to lists of questions cannot promote a process of critical thinking nor motivate the students to do any original work.

Many teachers feel it is important to start the classroom period with work on written assignments, their object being to occupy the students for the first few minutes while certain routine matters are taken care of. Such activities as writing down lists of words, or answering specific questions are methods that are often employed. However, the writer feels it is also quite important to start the class *thinking*, so that their minds will be receptive to what will follow during the period. Defining proverbs or quotations pertaining to the present unit of study, restating the point behind the last day's lesson in a paragraph, or answering some broad general question by stating an opinion rather than a fact, are examples of the types of activities that might be employed.

One thing that must be stated over and over in the classroom is that the teacher is looking for original work. This means that no type of homework, project work, or written reports should ever be copied. However, this will not be fruitful unless the student is paid for his originality by getting good grades. He must be made to realize that the primary criteria for grading are not neatness, size, nor amount of time put in, but thorough involvement. If you ask a student to turn in a term paper concerning the arguments for and against the Monroe Doctrine, and Student A turns in a definitive ten-page critical analysis with no bibliography, and Student B turns in an unoriginal, less comprehensive fifty-page report with a long bibliography consisting mostly of standard sources, then Student A must receive a higher grade than Student B. The writer is opposed to giving an A grade for any written work unless there are some well thought out, original (not copied) views contained within it.

Much has been written about the type of tests that should be given in the classroom. Actually, the most important thing is not the type of test that is given, but what the student is being tested for. It is much more important to test for understanding than for retention. If the students know that they are going to be tested on their ability to retain a series of facts, they will not be motivated toward a broad understanding of the course nor become involved in their own specific areas of interest. Therefore the questions, whether they be objective or subjective, should test for a broad comprehension of the subject matter and should include only the pertinent facts studied within the unit.

If the students are confronted with the idea that all problems have been solved for them and all they have to do is learn the answers, this is not going to motivate them to try to create anything new and original. However, if the teacher presents a problem to the class and informs the students that the solution to the problem, held true for centuries, was later disproved, then it will become apparent to the students that present-day problems and their solutions might some day in the future be also disproved. This may motivate them to use their own reasoning in relation to the facts.

Never answer a student's specific question! Never let the student come to the conclusion that the teacher is there to supply factual information as if he were a walking dictionary. If the question requires an answer of factual nature, then it is the role of the teacher to point out to the student where this information can be obtained. On the other hand, if the answer requires a logical analysis, then it is the teacher's job to aid the student in analyzing the situation, always allowing the student to arrive at his own conclusion. If a student asks whether or not the solution he reached is absolutely correct, it should again be pointed out that no answers are *absolutely* correct, but that his answer is perhaps a good one or one accepted by a recognized authority. It could be pointed out to some students that there are other interpretations that might warrant a research project on their part. If the student comes up with a weak answer, you should let him know that his is one of many answers, but that the experts in the field today are in disagreement with it.

A teacher who is interested in helping students to think for themselves will always let them disagree with him and with each other. In any area of study you will find among learned people different evaluations and contradictory ideas. One is forced to conclude that in almost any discussion there is no one final interpretation. In the classroom the textbooks and the teacher will usually accept one system of thought. If the teacher wants to motivate student thinking, however, he must never reject a *logical* deviation from the "accepted" point of view. He must let the students know that even mathematics and history are explained in terms of certain assumptions which may be wrong. The student must be aware of the fact that there are other less popular interpretations. This does not mean that there are not correct answers, but simply that all answers should be accepted on their own merits because of the logical proof contained within them. Proof should never rest on the laurels of authority. This also does not mean the teacher should allow the students to express all ideas indiscriminately or that all student ideas should be given equal weight with those that come from the teacher and the book. Ideas should be considered only on the basis of thought and logical defense.

It must be remembered that the whole key to the problem of motivation lies in provoking the students to think on their own. Thinking promotes thinking, since the two are permanently interwoven.

JEAN D. GRAMBS

Department of Secondary Education, University of Maryland

22. *Using Group Work in High School Classes**

The professional literature today includes more and more articles about "group process," "group dynamics," and "group work." These articles stem in large part from the ideas and techniques developed by the Reasearch Center for Group Dynamics over the last several years.[1] In addition, a number of publications of the Association for Supervision and Curriculum Development of the National Education Association on the administrative and classroom level have provoked wide interest.[2] A recent series of articles in the *NEA Journal* have also been stimulating and helpful to many in education.[3] However, for the average high school teacher these publications leave unanswered the perennial question, "But how can I do these things in my classroom?"

Group work in the high school is actually not a new idea at all. The teacher who has had committees working on various projects has, all unknowingly, been doing work with his students. The real difference between this familiar committee work and what we call "group work" is that in the latter instance the procedures used are deliberately selected for increasing student learning, for bettering individual adjustment, and for filling up some of the gaps in the social skills of our young people.

Briefly, one might summarize the reasons for utilizing group procedures in the high school class as follows:

1. Group learning of some kinds of material is more efficient than individual learning.
2. The quality of group work is often higher than the quality of individual effort, with resultant benefits for the individuals engaged in the group production.

[1]Kenneth Benne and Bozidar Muntyan, *Human Relations in Curriculum Change: Selected Readings with Special Emphasis on Group Development*, Circular Series A, no. 51, Illinois Secondary School Curriculum Program Bulletin no. 7 (Springfield: Supt. of Public Instruction, June 1949). An excellent collection of the major writings in group dynamics and related fields by those who have worked most closely with this area.

[2]*Group Processes and Supervision*, Association for Supervision and Curriculum Development, 1948 Yearbook (Washington, D.C., 1948); *Toward Better Teaching*, Association for Supervision and Curriculum Development, 1949 Yearbook (Washington, D.C., 1949), chap. 3.

[3]Leland D. Bradford *et al.*, "Group Dynamics and Education," *National Education Association Journal*, vol. 37, 1948–49 (nine articles reprinted by Division of Adult Education, [Washington, D.C., 1949]).

3. Small groups provide more opportunities for a wide sharing of leadership roles among all class members, and thus the learning of leadership skills.
4. Participation and involvement of all members of a class in the learning situation are assured through focusing of individual effort in a small group situation.
5. Group procedures help the individual learn the skills of adjusting to others that have not and cannot be learned at home due, in part to today's small and mobile families.
6. Group learning provides a serious focus for boy-girl cooperative activities, and is thus an important supplement to the glamorous party situations in which most boys and girls meet.
7. Peer recognition, accorded in the small group situation, is more apt to motivate students to increased efforts than a grade or recognition by the teacher.
8. The group situation provides the teacher with an opportunity to watch students in action and gain important insights as to individual needs and potentialities.

The classroom teacher has available two types of group activities: short-run and long-run groups. These two types differ in many respects. In this article we will discuss the classroom procedures for utilizing short-run and long-run group techniques.

I. SHORT-RUN GROUP ACTIVITIES

The short-run group is one in which the group activity lasts for only a portion of the class time and where the purpose is to maximize the involvement of the whole class. Such group discussions have been called "buzz sessions" when used, as they have been, in adult meetings and conference groups.[4] An example of how the short-run or buzz group works in a high school class shows this technique in operation:

> A teacher was called on to substitute in a Senior Problems class. The students were engaged in a vocational exploration unit. The substitute teacher, being new to them, decided to try a "buzz session." He counted them off by fives, and asked each group to list their answers to the question, "What major problems do you think you will face when you enter the world of work after graduation?" The groups were given ten minutes to make their lists, then a report was asked for from each group. A master list was put on the blackboard, and the class proceeded to a lively discussion of "Are all of these problems of equal importance?" "Which problems can I solve myself?" "Which problems can I solve now in school?"

[4]Leland D. Bradford, "Leading the Large Meeting," *Adult Education Bulletin*, 14:2, December 1949.

Every student in the example given above was drawn into the thinking of the class. For such a purpose the small, short-run group is unexcelled as a teaching technique. After all, when a class really gets interested in a discussion the teacher fully knows that, in the typical class discussion, barely one-fourth to one-third of the students will get a chance to have their say. And often only a few stars really carry the major portion of the fireworks. However, when a class luckily chances on such intellectually stimulating areas, the use of the buzz technique will enable *all* students to become participants.

The following are the specific factors to be considered in utlilizing short-run groups in the classroom:

1. Focusing the Problem. The teacher probably will want to select a provocative topic for class discussion, particularly the first time the buzz group is going to be used. Such immediate and catchy topics as "Can you learn more from school than a job?" "Should married women work?" "Has science made life easier or more complicated for us?" are good starters. Each subject field will have its own "natural" topics that can always be counted on to get the class debaters going. After a few teacher-selected topics the class itself should be encouraged to define questions for buzz group consideration.

Whatever the source, the statement of the problem should be simple. The best pattern is a one sentence statement that suggests a listing of possible items under it. For example, the teacher may put on the blackboard, or duplicate on paper, the following:

1. What are the main things teen-agers do for recreation in our town?
   a.
   b.
   c. etc.
2. What recommendations would you make for a better recreation program for teenagers here?
   a.
   b.
   c. etc.

This outline directs the attention of the group to the immediate problem and puts them under a kind of "discipline" to organize their thinking productively.

2. Time. A clear time limit should be set for the buzz groups. This should be shorter rather than longer; it is better to put the groups under time pressure than run the risk of having some groups finish early and have nothing to do except interfere with others. Only through trial and error will the teacher learn how long a given topic will take the students, but typically a ten minute buzz session is adequate for high school students. If, however, it seems that several groups are finishing way ahead of time the teacher should announce, "I guess you could do this faster than I thought; some groups are nearly done; I'll give you all just one more minute!" Or, as the time limit approaches an end and the teacher, by walking around the class, sees that no group is anywhere near done, can say, "This is a tougher task than we thought; I'll have to give you an extra five minutes."

Time, well used, is a prime discipline factor in the buzz group technique. Even the most listless of young people will find it difficult to resist the admonition "There isn't an awful lot of time, you know; I wonder which group is going to have the best list of answers to our problem!"

3. Reporting. When buzz groups are first used, the teacher can aid the groups by arbitrarily assigning a "reporter" who thus also acts as secretary. If the assignment is mimeographed, the teacher can easily designate the reporter by merely handing him the one sheet of paper with the question on it, and indicating that he will be asked to give the report on the group's findings. The same result can be achieved, if the question has been placed on the board, through passing out a single white card or sheet of paper, again to a single student in the group, who then uses this "special form" for reporting group concensus.

In selecting these reporters, the teacher should choose at first the more efficient, competent students who can be counted on to get to work on a task; later the designation of reporter can act as an effective silencer for those who are apt to talk too much—they will have to concentrate on writing down the group's thinking and won't have a chance to chatter! The task of being reporter should be given every student eventually since it is an important opportunity to learn to speak before others.

Some teachers do not assign any one person as reporter:

> For an oral English exercise, one teacher assigned a different story from an anthology to each small group. They were to read it together, then summarize the main plot. Anyone in the group would be called on to give the group summary. This put everyone on his toes, but was a particular help to those who were most allergic to oral English; their speech was prepared with the help of four others, and they had the moral support of their classmates when going through the ordeal of a public presentation.

When the time for the group discussion is up, the teacher—and later perhaps a student chairman—can ask for a report from each group. Depending on the problem, the results of each group's thinking can be listed on the blackboard, or tallied under appropriate headings.

4. Follow-up. After all the groups have reported, a class analysis of the results will be appropriate, or the teacher may summarize the significant outcomes to be noted in the thinking of the whole class. It is also important to consider with the class how the group discussions themselves went, and to encourage suggestions for the next time a buzz group is used. A brief analysis of what helped the group thinking and what hindered it, some inquiry into which group roles are useful and which are detrimental, and a look at the function of the reporter or leader will lay the groundwork for increased group thinking skill.

Some Special Problems in Using Buzz Groups

Should any special grouping of pupils be used? The buzz group lasts such a short time that it is usually most feasible to utilize the seating arrangements already established. The more quickly groups can be formed, the better; more deliberate selection of group membership will occur with groups that last for a longer period of time, as will be considered in a later article. If the chairs are in rows, each row may be designated as a group, or, if the rows are too long, the first and last seats across the room may be made into a group. To vary the groupings, the rows from corridor wall to window can be organized into groups. Another method would be to use the squares made up of four facing seats in two adjoining rows; this would introduce new work companions to each other. The class may be divided according to point of view on the subject; or a class may be arbitrarily divided into pro and con sides, and sub-groups organized in each section.

At no time should such buzz groups contain more than five members and experience indicates that even three or four are large enough for some problems. The larger the number in the group the more time for gathering all opinion; but if there are too many small groups, then the time needed for reporting from all groups must be increased.

Can buzz groups be used in rooms with immovable seats? And when every seat in the room is filled? This makes the problem more difficult; admittedly it is easier in rooms with movable furniture. However, any teacher will have noticed the facility with which students hover over each other at the beginning of the period, and how easily they squirm around for a *sub-rosa* chat. It is possible to have all of the first row meet towards the front of the room as a group; all in the second row meet towards the back, etc., and thus overcome some of the difficulty inherent in a rigid setup. The teacher's desk or any table in the room can also be used as a center for a group, thus relieving the congestion.

Won't such groups get too noisy? When the students are intent on a problem and are under time pressure, the buzz of conversation will not be such as to bring an irate neighboring teacher down on one's neck. The teacher will want to remind the class to keep their voices down, of course. When a group gets too excited and voices rise, the teacher may walk casually over to them and remind them that others may be disturbed.

What is the function of the teacher while the groups are in session?

The teacher will find it essential to walk around the room observing the groups. But even more, he will find that some groups will have questions or problems that he can, with a word, help resolve. Or, if a group becomes bogged down, he can rescue it; some groups find it hard to get started, and the teacher can suggest a way to get going. It is rare that the role of the teacher will be disciplinary; the groups are usually too busy to notice him! It is also important for the teacher to keep an ear open to the trend of group discussion in order to be prepared for some of the problems or questions which may emerge. As is true of most group discussions, if enough people talk long enough the whole problem area will be covered; the teacher can be assured that via the buzz groups the alert adolescent mind will usually touch on every important phase. A check on the groups in action may reveal what gaps, if any, are likely to occur.

Can group consensus always be reached? The teacher will want to discourage vote-taking in groups that last only ten minutes and have only five members. The concept of consensus can be discussed with the class, with a reminder that a minority position should be respected if such opinion resists the analysis of the rest of the group members.

What discipline problems are liable to arise? Surprisingly enough, this kind of group activity is almost irresistible. Even the most sullen, obdurate, antisocial adolescent finds it hard to sabotage this kind of small group in which he is inextricably plunged. Under the pressure of time "to produce," the other members of a group can usually be counted on to discipline anyone who tries to disrupt what is going on. When the time comes for the group reports, the students will almost invariably come to very acute attention not only in order to see that "their" group report is heard, but to see how the efforts of others compare to their own.

Other Ways of Using Short-Run Groups

The discussion so far has emphasized the use of the short-run group technique for controversial topics primarily. However, teachers have found it highly useful for other purposes also. These are:

1. *Group reading of material.* When there is a limited supply of some item, the teacher can give each group one or two copies of the material, ask them to read it together, summarize the main points, and report to the class. Group reading of text material can also be a great aid to slower students when others in the group aid in summarizing important points; this also insures reading of the assignment by everyone!

2. *Group evaluation.* Written material prepared by students, such as compositions, essay examinations, and the like, can be graded by sub-groups. Major errors in punctation, spelling, etc., may be dis-

covered and reported to the class as the basis for further work. Or each group can select the best item for posting on the bulletin board or presentation to the class.

3. *Group problem solving.* Where new material has been presented in class the teacher may assign a few practice problems to groups to see if the principles have been understood; end-of-chapter questions may be answered by small groups working together; test for review may be made up by groups, etc.

4. *Participation in course planning.* Teachers will find it helpful to call on small short-run groups to provide suggestions and evaluate plans for the next unit of work.

The short lived group activity has many potentialities in the high school classroom. It is unusually valuable where maximum participation by all students is desired; after one or two tries, the teacher will find buzz groups are easy to use and highly rewarding in terms of student response and productivity.

II. LONG-RUN GROUPS

In the long-run activity, groups attack extended problems and work together until the completion of the project. When students are in such groups for several days, weeks, or even months, new problems of social relationships appear. What kinds of projects can be undertaken? How should the groups be organized? How can the teacher and the groups evaluate the efforts of group members? These are vital questions in using long-term groups work in the classroom.

What kinds of projects are suitable to long-term group activity? To answer this question we need to see how the class can be grouped. There are many ways of dividing a class. For instance, some projects depend on differences in *interests* on the part of students. Some projects need *special skills.* Writing a radio script might be a group project in which some students would do the writing because of superior ability, others would do the sound effects, others would check the factual information needed, others would take care of the electrical equipment for recording. Groups may be arranged *in different ability levels.* In mathematics the class may be divided according to different levels of skill or achievement. Students may be separated according to reading ability in a social studies class and given different textbooks accordingly. Under the fourth category would come groups where some *common factor* such as vocational choice would reveal important differences. Each sub-group may be challenged to relate current learning to their future goals. *All-boy* and *all-girl* groups, where different points of view might be expected, are very interesting to young adolescents.

Sociometric tests provide a fifth way of dividing a class.[5] It gives the teacher important clues about who already belong to a natural group, who is outside the central groups, and who is rejected by the class in general. The teacher can then arrange groupings for guidance purposes to help those outside the group to learn group skills, to reduce clique exclusiveness, and provide leadership opportunities for natural class leaders.

Arbitrary groupings make it possible for the teacher to rearrange the usual working groups in the classroom. Thus, if the same students seem always to be together, are not developing a wider range of acquaintance, some mechanical device for grouping may help to lead them out of their own tight circle. Arranging groups alphabetically or by rows may help to widen the student's range of friends without seeming to be directed at any one person or group.

This analysis of the many ways to "slice" a class demonstrates one of the most important functions of group activity. Used imaginatively, for different kinds of projects, these groupings make it possible for a student to achieve recognition for some particular skill or attribute or idea, allow individual differences to be met, and finally, make it possible for all members of the class to learn to work together with every other member of the class on some common basis.

The kind of project that the group will work on will, to a large extent, determine the composition of the group. Not all subject matter can be dealt with through the group process. Not all students are capable of their best work in a group, just as some individuals are unable to work alone. In any subject, however, several *different* kinds of long-run groups should be utilized each semester or year. Keeping a record of who works in what group will aid the teacher in shifting groups personnel so that the benefits of an extended circle of work companions can be realized.

Hazards to Avoid

It must be remembered that for every report of success, there will be many trials and mistakes and failures. Some of the typical mistakes that are made are:

1. Rushing into group or committee work without careful preparation on the part of students or teacher.
2. Failure to provide needed materials. If groups are to do research, the materials of research must be available.
3. Inability of the teacher to guide the groups due to individualization of previous training. To develop group spirit it is necessary to treat the group as a whole, but often we see only individuals, rather than group relations.

[5]"Dynamics of the Discussion Group," *Journal of Social Issues,* vol. 4, no. 2, Spring 1948.

4. Projects too complicated, or too simple. If timing is wrong on the group project, the group is liable to disintegrate rather quickly.
5. Putting the wrong people together. Often a teacher needs to experiment with various ways of grouping the class before he will find out which grouping will click in his class.
6. Overdoing group work—allowing insufficient opportunity for individual achievement.
7. Confusion and lack of definiteness as to group product. A specific and clear and preferably *concrete* outcome should result from group effort.
8. Over-emphasis on inter-group competition. This will transfer focus from real learning to attempts to out-do others at any cost, and thus the value of cooperative effort will be lost.

Evaluating Group Techniques

Since this approach to learning is relatively new, it is important for the teacher to know if it is working satisfactorily. One of the more obvious ways of evaluating the success of group methods is by a subject matter test. Do the students know as much as one expects them to know from use of other classroom methods? If the subject matter seems to be acquired to the same extent, then one is assured of one measure of success of the group approach. There are other ways of evaluation. Studies of groups indicate that one important measure of success may be the extent to which the group itself can appraise its progress. If a group of youngsters stop and look at themselves as a group and report objectively about their progress, then one important new outcome has been achieved—a new growth toward adult behavior has occurred. From an objective view then comes the prescription for what might be done to make the group, and the individual in it, function at a more adequate and mature level next time.

By observing student behavior the teacher can often tell whether the group work is affecting them. If those students who previously had no friends now appear to have someone to talk with when class is over, then the groups have had an important socializing effect. The use of sociometric questionnaires as a basis for short or long-run groupings is extremely useful in indicating to what extent group experiences have or have not actually affected the social relationships of youngsters in a positive direction.

Preliminary to all evaluation, however, is some basic understanding between teacher and student about what constitutes good work. When using group techniques, the teacher might well pause, after the first classroom experience with this method, and discuss with the class whether they enjoyed the experience, what things made it good, what things made it less than good. The basic question of: what makes a good group? then becomes important to everyone. Periodic re-evaluations help the class to grow in skill and insight. How are we doing now? and, What can we do to improve?

are important follow-up questions that the class could help the teacher answer.

Planning with the Class as to what Constitutes a Good Group

How does one grade a group product? Here again some pupil-teacher agreement is very useful, in fact it is mandatory. Since not everyone contributes alike to any group project, there must be room for both individual and group recognition. This can be accomplished by having a group grade on one end product—say a report or an oral presentation, while also having an individual grade on some common assignment, such as a quiz of subject matter that the group is covering, a written report of individual reading or interviewing, and so forth. Students will be very intent on knowing how the grades will be weighted; it is important to give the group product sufficient weight in the total grading to encourage the best effort of everyone. But in order to account for individual differences and other imponderables, some provision is needed for an individual assessment of growth.[6]

One interesting method of evaluating the "attractiveness" of a given group is to ask the members of the class, individually, to report how much weight they feel should be given to their group as against their individual projects. Where the groups are successful in doing a good job, the students will tend to assign more weight in the final grading; where the groups are not functioning so well, the students will wish their own individual work to get the greatest share in the total grading.

In evaluating the success of the group approach, the teacher might well utilize some of the following specific aids.

1. Meeting evaluation form. At the end of a class period, after the groups have been meeting for some time, the teacher might use a very simple form in order to get a quick check on the level of satisfaction with their meeting.

HOW GOOD WAS OUR MEETING?

Name_____ (or group no. or group topic)_____

Check in the square below at the point which best indicates your feeling about your group meeting:

□ Swell   □ Not Very Good
□ Good   □ Terrible
□ All Right

What was the best thing about the meeting? What was the main weakness of the meeting? Comments and suggestions.

[6]Donald Bergh, "Planning in the Core Class," *Educational Leadership,* 8:208-14, January 1951; Helen Jennings, *Sociometry in Group Relations* (Washington, D.C.: American Council on Education, 1948); Norman Naas, "Group Work: Popular Feature of Social Living Course," *Clearing House,* 25:147–48, November 1950.

These may need to be anonymous, using only group number or project in order to protect individual respondents. After the teacher has looked them over, it might be useful to give the reports to each group to review. A summary of the feelings of all the members of the group could be reported to the individual groups for their own use, or to the whole class, in order to increase group morale and arouse some moderate inter-group competition to be "the best group."

2. Group participation records. These may be filled out either by the teacher as he observes the groups, or may be done by a member of the group with that special assignment. This will help the teacher as well as the group see to what extent certain individuals are doing either too much or too little in the group's life. Various kinds of observational forms may be devised by the class itself for special purposes.

    A. Quantity participation record: A tally mark is recorded after each person's name every time he makes a contribution. This gives a sum of contributions.

    B. Quality participation record: As each person makes his contribution, an evaluative mark is put after his name. These marks are:

+ plus	— a contribution that aids the group thinking.
— minus	— a contribution that delayed or interfered with group progress in thinking.
0 zero	— a remark that neither aided nor hindered—a "blah" remark.
?	— individual asks a question.

In using this scoring method, it is often difficult for observers to put down many minus marks as it is apt to hurt the feelings of those so evaluated. However, if the discussion about the scoring is objective and everyone sees that a minus score might mean just lack of skill in group participation, then the negative factors may be recorded without damage to morale.

    C. Group interaction record: An arrow is used to join the names of individuals whenever they talk to anyone else. When an individual addresses a remark to the group as a whole, the arrow should point out towards the edge of the paper. The pattern recorded here is one of the most interesting, since it is possible to note whether the leader or chairman is dominating the discussion, or if two people are carrying on a personal argument to the exclusion of everyone else.

3. Use of group observers. It may be helpful to assign one student to each group as an observer for one class period. These observers then can report to the whole class on how well the group was able to work together, the things that helped the group move towards its goal, the things that interfered, and some observation of the roles different people play in group endeavor.[7] The role of the observer provides excellent training. As soon as an individual is outside the group, watching only for group interaction and evidences of progress toward the goal, he learns a great deal about how to be a good group member. The task of observer is often useful with students who have particular difficulty in working with a group.

4. *Uses of group recorders.* The group recorder can report both to the group and to the teacher or class about the group's progress. This recorder is more than just a secretary—and should be an assignment for boys as well as girls. The recorder helps the group to think towards its goal. The leader of the group, either elected or spontaneous, can help balance the discussion and include those who are least verbal. But besides the leader one person is often needed to help keep group thinking focussed. The recorder asks such questions as: "Now what is the issue we are discussing?" "Is this an accurate statement of what we decided to do?" "I am not sure that we covered the point raised by John a while back regarding . . . " Thus, he or she helps keep the group moving forward. From the record made in this fashion, the teacher as well as the group has a sense of where it is going, and how. A progress report can then be made from time to time to the whole class and then a general evaluation of progress will be in order.

5. *Individual participation—appraisal methods.* Often the class as well as the teacher may be dissatisfied with giving a whole group the same grade for the group report or group product, whatever that may be. It is obvious that some students will do better work and more work than others. As a method of helping equalize the work that is done in the groups, as well as getting individual efforts appraised, teachers may ask the members of the group to evaluate each other. Each may also evaluate his own progress.

The teacher will find it more useful to develop a rating form with the assistance of the total class. When the class aids in building such evaluative tools, they are learning some very important lessons in social skills. In addition, they are learning to discriminate among ideas, to establish sound values, and to view behavior—their own and others—objectively. It is easier for students in the class to fill in such a rating form intelligently if the items and the form itself have been phrased and designed by them. The words are their words—the ideas are phrased in terms understandable to the class members and it is clear to them just what it is they will do with the rating form. This class procedure also aids in discipline since all members together have agreed on what is desirable. The knowledge of later peer appraisal serves as a powerful goal towards conformity with moderate classroom control needs.

Discipline problems that may arise in connection with group work are best dealt with through class and group discussion, thereby using group

---

[7]Bradford *et al.,* "Group Dynamics"; "Symposium on Group Dynamics," *National Association Deans of Women Journal,* 12:99–113, March 1949.

pressure to aid individuals in their obligation to meet social responsibilities. Where group problems are intrinsically interesting and students are successful in doing a good job, discipline disturbances will be rare, as experiences of a number of teachers have shown.

Reporting on the Group Project

While some long-term groups suggested here will not have anything to report to the rest of the class (for instance, problem-solving in a mathematics class), others need to share with their classmates the results of their research. Experience with group reports has been gratifying wherever the groups have been encouraged to try new ways of educating their classmates. The steps to be taken with the class prior to group reporting are:

1. Set a deadline when groups will report.
2. Agree on the function of the group report. If the report is to inform, then the group must emphasize facts, must seek ways of discriminating between important and unimportant facts, should find media for presenting factual material so all can see it at once, such as graphs, charts, slides. If the report is to stimulate discussion, then a panel, debate, dramatic introduction of some sort is called for.
3. Discuss what it means to educate others. The class will need very often to analyze the difference between that which is educational, and that which is merely novel, entertaining, or startling. Turn the thinking of the class upon what their classmates *need* and *want* to know.
4. Encourage originality. Suggest some things that groups can do to enliven their report and attract the interest of the class.
5. Review the material on good oral reporting. Since the success of many group reports will depend on the skill of the members in oral presentation, some class discussion of oral reports skills is very useful.
6. Arrange for responsibility for evaluation of information contained in the report. It should be clear just what the class audience will be asked to recall as a result of the presentation.
7. Designate clearly the teacher's role during the group report. Sometimes the teacher may request a few moments at the end of the report to add or summarize or point up some item the group may have overlooked. Or the teacher may want to do a brief evaluation of the report. Once in a while a discussion gets so lively or a report is so amusing the class gets somewhat out of hand; then the teacher should step in. Also, if a group member ties up completely with stage fright the teacher may want to come to his rescue rather than leaving it up to a chairman. But the teacher's role primarily is in a back seat; the report belongs to the group.

Remember that it is not always necessary for a group to report to the class. Sometimes a great deal of time is wasted in listening to other students report. The use of the group report should be a significant activity. Each report must be carefully worked out. Sometimes using bulletin board displays or circulating a written report can be used as a substitute for the oral report. Too frequent group reports can be just as monotonous and inefficient as too few.

CONCLUSION

Group procedures, as outlined here, are similar in many ways to the committee work that is often used in high school classes. The basic difference is that, in addition to learning outcomes, the teacher uses the group deliberately to increase the development of human relations skills on the part of young people. The group *process* is a focus of attention as well as the group *product*.

Group procedures, both short and long-run, have much to offer the high school teacher in terms of increasing the range of student participation, increased interest, and overall classroom morale. Used with discrimination group teaching can overcome some of the lacks of today's mass schooling.

JACK R. FRAENKEL

Associate Professor of Interdisciplinary
Studies in Education, San Francisco
State College

RICHARD E. GROSS

Professor of Education, Stanford
University

23. Team Teaching: Let's Look Before We Leap!*

During the 1950's and 1960's, the quality of education offered in the secondary schools has become of increasing concern to both professional educators and the lay public alike. As a result, many traditional approaches to learning, once secure in their acceptance by the educational profession, have been thrown open to question. Perhaps non-instructional tasks might be removed from the teacher's back. Possibly all learning does not have to be directed by teachers. Conceivably, greater emphasis on individual study might be fruitful in some situations. Maybe programed instruction holds considerable implications for education in the future.

A particular irritation has been the limiting effect which many traditionally organized school systems have placed upon the teacher's time. The staggering load of a five-period day and 50-minute classes, topped not infrequently by three different subject-matter preparations and extracurricular duties, leave most teachers little time for improvement of their individual capabilities. Accordingly, structural variations which offered relief from these traditional limitations were eagerly welcomed.

In addition to an emphasis upon the structural reorganization of the activities of the teacher and students within the school, a considerable ferment has been developing within the social studies.[1] Not only have new approaches and organizations been urged for the course content of the disciplines traditionally offered in the schools (i.e., history, geography, political science, and economics), but also advocates have appeared urging inclusion of the behavioral sciences in the secondary school curriculum.[2]

The publications which probably most encouraged consideration of team teaching, large and small group instruction, teacher aides, inde-

---

*Social Education, XXX:335–37, May 1966. Used by permission.

[1] See James M. Becker, "Prospect for Change in the Social Studies," Social Education, pp. 20–23; January 1965; Richard E. Gross, "Emerging Horizons for the Social Studies," Social Education pp. 21–24, January 1960; Leonard Kenworthy, "Ferment in the Social Studies," Phi Delta Kappan (12–16) October 1962; Franklin Patterson, "Social Science and the New Curriculum," American Behavioral Scientist 28–31; November 1962.

[2] See The Social Studies and the Social Sciences, American Council of Learned Societies and the National Council for the Social Studies (New York: Harcourt, Brace and World, 1962); also Eldon E. Snyder, "The Behavioral Sciences and the Social Science Curriculum of the American High School," Social Studies 5–9; January 1965.

pendent study, and flexible scheduling as a means of structural reorganization were the three pamphlets prepared by J. Lloyd Trump: *Images of the Future, New Directions to Quality Education* and *New Horizons for Secondary School Teachers.*[3] Shortly after these appeared, a flood of other articles began to appear in the professional journals. Since 1957, over 200 articles and books have been published on team teaching.[4] By way of contrast, not a single article concerning the subject was listed in *Education Index* between 1955 and 1957.

It must be admitted that team teaching seems to mean various things in various places. Considerable diversity exists in terms of both methodological organization and aims of instruction. It probably would not be an exaggeration to state that there are as many different types of team teaching as there are different school systems which utilize such teams. As observed in some situations, for example, it is merely take-turn teaching; here the true concept of teamed instruction seems completely lost.

Some characteristics are more commonly cited than others, however. Often flexibly grouped by ability, students are divided for various types of instruction into large classes for oral and visual presentations, and into smaller groups for discussion and debate. Frequently sessions are provided where students may study individually by themselves. The large classes usually number around 90 or more students; the smaller ones, 30 or less.[5] Team members determine staff competencies and make assignments accordingly; they also determine the sequence and manner of the subject to be presented and, using their combined professional judgment, whether large groups, small groups, or individual study, will prevail during the time allotted to them.

What are the advantages of team teaching? Many have been suggested: Teachers will be able to pool their talents, thereby giving the student a far richer educational offering than they would otherwise experience. Unnecessary duplication can be minimized. Through combined teacher planning, and the variety of instructional situations provided, individual differences among students can be more adequately considered. The type of instructional presentation needed can be more closely matched to student interests, needs, and abilities. Differentiated instruction geared to differing student abilities can be more easily arranged. During individual

[3] National Association of Secondary-School Principals, Commission on the Experimental Study of the Utilization of the Staff in the Secondary School, Washington, D. C., N.E.A., 1959.

[4] See David Beggs, *Team Teaching: Bold New Venture* (Indianapolis: McGraw-Hill, 1964); Judson T. Shaplin and Henry F. Olds, eds, *Team Teaching* (Evanston, Harper and Row, 1964); Nicholas Polos, *The Dynamics of Team Teaching.* (Dubuque: William C. Brown Co. 1965); to mention but three of these volumes.

[5] Team advocates emphasize, however, that the maximum number of students allowable in such small group sessions should be 15. More than this makes them ineffective for the discussion purposes for which they were designed.

study periods, able students or those students with special interests, can pursue their bent at their own pace and in greater depth than an ordinary classroom situation might allow. Teachers will be more free to plan, study, prepare, relax, and be creative.[6]

On the other hand, a number of arguments—both logical and psychological—seem to offer themselves against such instructional arrangements:

First, the teachers as individuals. Are all teachers suited for team operations? Many prefer and, in fact, are more effective, when working alone. What about the unimaginative, the less flexible, those not willing or able to compromise? How about the timid and the insecure? Not every teacher is prepared, either academically or psychologically, to emerge from the isolated cave he has known for so long into more open cooperation with and comparison by colleagues and students which teams afford.

Secondly, the curriculum. Some subjects may lend themselves more readily than others to team organizations. Economics, for example, may need more tutorial assistance from the individual teacher than team situations may allow. It may be difficult to organize in large groups the less formally structured presentations, such as a problems course or the emphases that "inquiry" or "discovery" approaches might entail.

Thirdly, the facilities. Not all plants can handle team arrangements. Are there rooms sufficiently big for large group presentations? Is there sufficient space for individual study? Will enough rooms for small group discussions be available? Does the school schedule permit modification, considerable student movement, and frequent changes in room assignment and usage? Can team operations take place without disturbing other more traditionally arranged classes?

Fourthly, the administration. Is it one geared to change and susceptible to new ideas? Can it permit, even welcome, a less than permanently arranged staff and facility utilization? Is it one willing to experiment— to revise and revamp, to tolerate ambiguity and open-endedness? Is it flexible?

Lastly, the students. Can all types of students benefit from the various types of instructional arrangements inherent in team instruction? Certainly many things we have observed make us suspicious as to whether or not teams are maximally effective with all ability levels. Large amounts of factual material presented without any chance for immediate feedback (as in large group lectures, for example) may be less effective with students of

---

[6]Some school districts have been able to hire departmental secretaries who type dittoes, prepare audio-visual aids, and correct objective tests; sometimes professional graders (house-wives or other personnel able to work in the schools on a part-time basis) have been hired whose sole responsibility has been to relieve the pressures of grading which limited the time of many teachers.

lesser ability than more conventional arrangements. Group cohesiveness may be minimal—a large number of students may have difficulty identifying with the large lecture groups and it seems quite likely that the small discussion groups may not meet frequently enough for any cohesion to take place.

Students of lesser ability may have trouble adjusting to the flexibility of schedule around which the team revolves—indeed, may, in fact, need more regularly spaced presentation and a more steady instructional situation. Such students may not be prepared to make effective use of the individual study periods so often programmed into team operations. It might well be questioned whether or not non-verbal students will benefit from the smaller discussion groups which are especially provided for in the team design.

It should be noted that team teaching, as presently described and designed, seems especially geared to middle-class students. What about those described as "culturally disadvantaged"? Their weakness in formal expression, and "paying attention;" their utilitarian orientation; their emphasis upon immediate satisfaction of needs; their more ready response to visual and kinesthetic signals rather than oral and written stimuli; their basic anti-intellectualism; their proficiency in physical and motoric skills rather than mental problem solving; their lack of "test-taking skills;" their lack of reading material in the home, and their resultant reading weaknesses; their preference for spontaneous over structured situations; all these seem to prepare them for failure rather than success under current team teaching practices.

Whether this necessarily must be so is something else. If maximum provision for individual differences can be provided for within the team structure; if teams can be organized which are committed to experimentation and flexibility; if a variety of activities—not only intellectual, but physical as well—can be provided; if presentations can be prepared which consider the cultural backgrounds of the students involved; if imaginative teachers can be employed to plan programs to involve *all* the students within their charge; if less emphasis can be placed upon the traditional chronological content and more innovational programs offered instead; then perhaps team teaching can be all that its advocates urge that it is. One observes, however, too many situations in which numerous of the aims of the social studies are being neglected. What essential skills, for example, are being developed where pupils meet in large groups every day, have little or no library research assignments related to the continual lectures, and seldom, if ever, are given the opportunity to discuss?

The essential question is this: Is team teaching more effective in producing learning than the traditional classroom arrangement of one teacher operating independently within an individual classroom? The only way we can answer this question is through research! What empirical evidence exists which supports team teaching as being more effective? Sad to say, such evidence is extremely slight.

The research journals, to say the least, are disappointing. Only one article on team teaching appears in *The Journal of Educational Research* between January, 1960 and May, 1965.[7] No reports appear in the Cooperative Research Project Bulletin of the United States Office of Education.[8] The vast majority of articles on team teaching have been collected in the January 1958, 1959, 1960, 1961, 1962, and May 1963 issues of *The Bulletin of the National Association of Secondary-School Principals*.[9] Each issue contains summaries of the experimentation undertaken by various school systems. Only some data on learning is given, however.

The Research Division of the National Education Association has published abstracts on team teaching, but only one of these is not a previous article taken from the *Bulletin*. The *Review of Educational Research* briefly deals with the topic in but a part of one issue, entitled "Curriculum Planning and Development."[10] The two issues of *Social Education* which have carried a review of research in social studies education contained no reference to experimentation with teaching teams.[11] We were able to locate only two dissertations and one master's thesis.[12]

With few exceptions, the following quotation is typical of the subjective evaluations which appear:

1. Teachers who have worked on a team favor its retention and extension.

2. Students comment favorably on the flexibility and variety of method and materials used.[13]

[7]Ken Giffin and John Waite Bowers, "An Experimental Study of the Use of Lectures to Large Groups of Students in Teaching the Fundamentals of Speech," *The Journal of Educational Research*, pp. 383–386, May 1962.

[8]U.S. Office of Education. *Cooperative Research Projects, Bulletin 1961.*

[9]"New Horizons in Staff Utilization," *The Bulletin of the National Association of Secondary-School Principals*, vols. 42–47.

[10]David R. Krathwohl, ed., "Curriculum Planning and Development," *Review of Educational Research*, vol. 30, no. 3 (Washington, D.C.: American Educational Research Association, 1960).

[11]*Social Education* 28:277–92, May 1964; 29:15–20, January 1965.

[12]Jack R. Fraenkel, "A Comparison of Achievement Between Students Taught by a Teaching Team and Students Taught in Traditional Classes on a Standardized Examination in United States History" (Master's thesis, San Francisco State College, 1965); William Nesbitt, "An Experimental Study of the Relative Effectiveness on Learning in Selected High School Subjects of the Conventional Methods and A Composite of Procedures Involving Modern Educational Media in Addition to Classes of Varying Sizes, Team Teaching, and Teacher Aides" Ph.D. diss. University of Texas, 1960); and Scott Thomson, "An Analysis of Achievement Outcomes: Team Teaching and Traditional Classes," (Ed.D. diss. Stanford University, 1963).

[13]Lloyd S. Michael, "Team Teaching," *The Bulletin of the National Association of Secondary-School Principals*, 47:36–63, May 1963.

Articles on team teaching which appear in the professional journals seem to be almost unanimously descriptions of: (1) how teachers and students who experienced a team teaching venture liked it, or (2) descriptions of pitfalls to avoid before embarking on such a venture. In the main, the reports center on a description of structural arrangements or methodological arguments. None specifically describe any attempts to evaluate empirically a difference in content mastery by students when team taught as compared with more traditional approaches.

Before wholesale acceptance of team superiority occurs, therefore, more carefully structured and controlled research on the learning achievement of pupils instructed by teaching teams as compared with more traditional approaches should take place. According to one definition, team teaching is "a type of instructional organization, involving teaching personnel and the students assigned to them, in which two or more teachers are given responsibility, working together, for all or a significant part of the instruction of the same group of students."[14] It should be noted that according to this definition, organization can differ as can the statement of objectives which the team proposes to accomplish. No one particular organizational structure is at present mandatory. What is essential is that one's aims are clear, that researchers carefully describe the particular structure under investigation, and that any extrapolation of research findings be applied only to team operation in the same manner. We have raised many queries about team instruction that demand investigation.

In short, let's look before we leap!

[14]Judson T. Shaplin, "Description and Definition of Team Teaching," Shaplin and Olds, eds., *Team Teaching*, p. 6.

IIB. How Do I Plan for Instruction?

Once the teacher has made the overall decisions about course organization and classroom management, he turns next to more specific tactics. With continuing attention to purposes, to the kinds of pupils he will have, to the principles of learning, and to the instructional materials available, he moves into two kinds of complementary planning. Initial planning concerns unit or longer-term arrangements and is followed by attention to daily lessons. The editors believe strongly in the value of rigorous planning, both long and short term. Such preparation does not preclude considerable involvement of the pupils in many aspects of the direction of their own learning. Nor does it imply that a degree of flexibility should not be built into unit calendars to allow for emerging developments. Operating in a social studies laboratory situation with well-conceived unit plans, the teacher will usually find the combination of elements most conducive to learning for the largest number of students.

While the experienced teacher tends to have to give less time to both long and short term preparation than the beginner, there are very few teachers who can regularly bring off a truly fine lesson without careful thought and adequate plans. Well prepared, daily lessons that also link yesterday with tomorrow are basic to continuing instructional success. One of the inexcusable reasons for unhappy students rejecting studies is the too frequently experienced "off-the-cuff" attempts to teach.

In reading the following articles, review the arguments for planning in terms of larger blocks of time. What contributions will unit organization bring to your instructional program? How can you incorporate student involvement into the development of a weekly calendar? What are the essences of an effective daily lesson plan? How will planning be affected if you are moving into a team teaching or flexible schedule situation?

JOHN JAROLIMEK

Professor of Education, University of
Washington, Seattle

24. The Taxonomy: Guide to Differentiated Instruction *

Discussions of differential instruction in the social studies ordinarily focus upon variations to be made in learning activities which the pupil is expected to perform. Most frequently the recommendations have to do with variations in reading requirements or variations in work-study activities. The teacher is advised to use more difficult reading material with the more capable pupil than with the less able one. Similarly in the case of work-study activities, the suggestion is made that the able pupil be directed toward activities which involve more independent research, more reading and elaborative thinking than his slower-learning classmate. In general, these recommendations are sound ones; but they are apt to be something less than adequate unless, in addition, careful consideration is given to the complexity of the intellectual tasks with which each of the pupils is going to concern himself.

Varying the difficulty of intellectual tasks relating to a social studies unit is a procedure which seems to have received less attention from teachers than it deserves. The hope is that if pupils are placed in reading materials of varying difficulty and are involved in varying types of instructional activities, this will, in itself, result in some differentiation of instruction with respect to complexity of learnings. No doubt this occurs to some extent. However, variations in complexity should be a deliberate and planned part of the teaching plan rather than be allowed to come about by a happy accident. In order to build such diversity in conceptual complexity into the program, one needs to begin with instructional objectives. The procedure under consideration here would hold general objectives constant, but would vary specific objectives in terms of the capabilities of individual pupils.

In an effort to plan deliberately for differentiated instruction in terms of the complexity of intellectual operations, the teacher may find Bloom's *Taxonomy of Educational Objectives*[1] to be a helpful model. The *Taxonomy* classifies various types of educational objectives into six groups or

Social Education, XXVI:445–47, December 1962. Used by permission.
[1]Benjamin S. Bloom *et al. Taxonomy of Educational Objectives, Handbook I: Cognitive Domain.*(New York: Longmans, Green and Co. 1956)

categories as follows:
1. Knowledge
2. Comprehension
3. Application
4. Analysis
5. Synthesis
6. Evaluation

These are ordered in terms of an hierarchy representing an increasingly complex set of cognitive relationships as one moves from category one to category six. Behaviors in each succeeding category are to some extent dependent upon an understanding of related objectives in a prior category. Sub-heads of each of the six categories indicate that they, too, are ordered from simple relationships to complex ones. Hence, children in the primary grades need not concern themselves solely with objectives in the *Knowledge* category but may make applications, analyses, and evaluations providing these are kept simple and clearly within the realm of direct experience.

It is perhaps true that the bulk of elementary social studies instruction concerns itself with objectives represented in category one—*Knowledge.* This includes knowledge of specifics, facts, terminology, events, etc. To a degree, an emphasis on knowledge is inevitable at early levels since pupils are rapidly building their cognitive structure. However, the *Knowledge* category is itself spread along a continuum ranging from a knowledge of specifics to a knowledge of universals and abstractions in a field. Pupils of varying abilities might be expected to deal with different specific objectives in the *Knowledge* category. Instruction is limiting and narrow when all pupils deal with *Knowledge* objectives pertaining only to specifics, facts, terminology, and events.

The teacher must, of course, be concerned with objectives in category one—*Knowledge*— because it is fundamental to all of the others. Particularly important would be the development of a knowledge of the terminology of the social studies. Without a grasp of the vocabulary, the pupil is unable to consider problems in the social studies thoughtfully. Knowledge of specific facts is important, too, not as an end in itself but because such specifics are prerequisite to the achievement of more complex intellectual objectives. Objectives in this category are relatively easy to teach and evaluate because they depend almost entirely upon recall of information. They have traditionally been a part of the social studies curriculum in most schools and consequently are familiar to teachers. While they are important, at the same time this does not give the teacher license to teach them in ways which are educationally and psychologically unsound.

In addition to knowledge of specifics, one finds in this category two other types of knowledge objectives. The first of these—"knowledge of

ways and means of dealing with specifics"— would seem to have especial
significance for the social studies. Included would be such knowledge of
conventions as might be called for in the understanding of procedures in
various affairs of citizenship—how a bill becomes a law, how government
officials are elected, how laws are enforced, and so on. It deals, too, with
trends and sequences such as knowledge of events which led up to more
important events, steps in the production of goods, or the chronology associated with historical developments. The third large subhead entitled
"knowledge of the universals and abstractions in a field" constitutes the
highest order of the *Knowledge* category. In the social studies it would call
for a knowledge of major generalizations relating to the social sciences as
these are forged out of the varied experiences of pupils. An example of
such a generalization would be "Man's utilization of natural resources is
related to his desires and his level of technology."

The second large category—*Comprehension*— requires somewhat
more complex intellectual activity than recall, as is the case in the *Knowledge* category. "Translation" and "Interpretation" are the two facets of
Comprehension most appropriate for elementary social studies. Data
gathering brings the pupil into contact with a great variety of source materials. He uses maps, charts, graphs, encyclopedias, atlases, and others.
Data so abstracted must be translated into usable form for the purpose of
problem solving. Literary material, when used, requires both translation
and interpretation. Much of the social studies reading material is presented
in highly condensed form and has within it many possibilities for interpretation and extrapolation. If pupils are to avoid making "bookish"
reports, for example, they need to be able to make a translation of the
material into their own everyday language. Social studies programs could
be greatly enriched, especially for the capable pupil, by directing greater
attention to objectives which fall into this category—translation, interpretation, and extrapolation.

The third category is called *Application.* It means esentially that the
pupil is able to use what he learns; that he can bring his knowledge to
bear upon the solution of problems. Numerous authors have called attention to the need for pupils to apply what they learn. Many interesting and
stimulating experiences for children have resulted in situations where imaginative teachers have provided opportunities for children to apply what
they have learned to life about them. Applications of learning may be
represented by some classroom activity such as dramatic play, a construction, or a report given to the class; or they may include a service project in conservation, school government, or community service. Applications need not manifest themselves in overt behavior; applications may
be made wholly at the intellectual level. The pupil may, for example, apply

and use knowledge previously gained in thinking creatively about new problems or situations. Perhaps most of the applications which are made are of the intellectual type.

Categories four and five—*Analysis* and *Synthesis*—represent high-order intellectual processes. In the case of *Analysis*, the pupil must delve into the subject to a sufficient depth to perceive its component elements, relationships, or organizational principles. Such procedure enhances the development of concepts in depth, for the pupil is led to ever finer discriminations in what is relevant and what is irrelevant with reference to topics under study. Problems in the social studies oftentimes seem deceptively simple because an inadequate analysis is made of factors relating to them. It is only when one explores a problem in depth and makes a careful analysis of fundamental elements, relationships, or organizational principles that he appreciates the complexity of it. Many elementary pupils are ready for the stimulation which such analyses could provide.

While *Analysis* calls for the isolation of relevant data, *Synthesis* requires the bringing together of related elements and reorganizing them into new cognitive structures. In the *Taxonomy, Synthesis* is further described as "the production of a plan or proposed set of operations," or the "derivation of a set of abstract relations." For elementary social studies, *Synthesis* can be represented by the reporting of research which a pupil has conducted over a period of time. The reporting of work done on "Pupil Specialties" would be a case in point. Bright pupils find this to be an especially challenging and interesting learning experience. A capable fifth-or sixth-grade child can, through accumulated research, present an amazingly well prepared synthesis if he has proper guidance from his teacher.

The final category—*Evaluation*— concerns itself with judgments. It assumes a considerable knowledge of the topic on the part of the pupil in order to make such judgments. To some extent it demands the use of learnings which are represented in all of the other categories. Judgments, according to the *Taxonomy*, are of two types—those based on internal evidence and those based on external criteria. Internal evidence would constitute evaluation made on the basis of clearly recognized standards with respect to internal consistency, organization, or structure. For example, a pupil looks at a map and must decide whether or not it is a correct and honest representation—rivers cannot be shown to run toward higher elevations; cities cannot be placed across rivers; colors used on the map must be consistent with those in the key, and so on. Charts, graphic material, or written reports should not contain conflicting data. A mural showing the life of the Woodland Indians should not show an Indian weaving a Navajo blanket. Judgments of this type are not especially difficult to make when one is thoroughly familiar with the material and knows what standards to apply. Judgments in terms of external criteria probably involve a level of criticism too complex and much too involved to be handled by elementary-school-age children.

It is apparent that the *Taxonomy* has much to recommend its use as a model in planning for differentiated instruction in elementary social studies. The teacher would have to become thoroughly familiar with it and with the types of objectives which might be placed in each of the categories. Perhaps the teacher would find it helpful to prepare the various categories in chart form, and in planning a unit, list possible objectives in the various categories. Use of the *Taxonomy* may also result in objectives stated more clearly in behavioral terms, as has been suggested by some authors.[2] Thus, with a knowledge of the capabilities of individual members of his class, the teacher could move pupils in the direction of those objectives which are best suited to their abilities. This would insure that all categories had been considered and that ideas would be dealt with at varying levels of difficulty.

Thus as the teacher plans his unit, he makes a careful analysis of the topic to be studied. Then he identifies specific, attainable objectives which could be classified in several categories included in the *Taxonomy*. In accordance with this knowledge and a knowledge of the pupil he teaches, he plans appropriate learning activities which make the attainment of those objectives possible. Combining this procedure with other generally accepted practices for individualizing instruction, the teacher would present his class with a highly diversified and stimulating attack on the study of problems in the elementary social studies. Certainly the *Taxonomy* deserves further investigation not only in terms of its usefulness in curriculum improvement but also as a guide to the teacher in differentiating instruction.

[2]Dale P. Scannell and Walter R Stellwagen. "Teaching and Testing for Degrees of Understanding," *California Journal for Instructional Improvement*, March 1960.

WALTER E. McPHIE

Associate Professor of Social Studies Education, University of Utah

25. The Teaching Unit: What Makes It Tick?*

Anyone who has completed a teacher preparation program at some university or teachers college has heard the word *unit*—and heard it often. It may be a teaching technique or method to some, a part of curriculum structure to others, or a combination of both to still others, but one thing is clear: the word itself is no stranger in the teaching profession.

Most of the literature on units in teaching is supportive. It is a rare methods text for either secondary or elementary school teachers that does not promote, either openly or by implication, teaching with units. It is championed as the *modern* way of teaching, the most effective method of curriculum arrangement.

Occasionally in the professional literature a questioning voice is heard which suggests that another look at the basic assumptions about unit teaching is needed. Criticism, however, is more often heard from practitioners in the field, new and experienced teachers who honestly and sincerely prefer to teach on a day-to-day basis. To some of the critics, developing units of study is "busy work," a nonsensical submission to the whimsical desires of people in ivory towers who are too far removed from reality. To others, unit teaching is still a hazy concept; these people are not really sure what a teaching unit is. In their eyes the literature seems to be contradictory, professors of education do not appear to be in full accord on the matter, and discussions with colleagues shed little additional light. For this group of teachers, unit teaching is not clearly enough defined to be seriously considered as an alternative to already established daily routine.

WHAT IS A "UNIT"?

Perhaps the easiest way to define a unit of teaching is to draw back and look at the word in other contexts. For example, a busy mother, while shopping in a local department store, sees a skirt-blouse combination on sale which would just fit her daughter. She really likes the skirt but does not care for the blouse.

"How much would it cost if I just bought the skirt?" she inquires.

Clearing House, 38:70–73, October 1963. Used by permission.

"I'm sorry," replies the clerk, "but we must sell this set as a *unit*."

Some people who become a little panic-stricken at the thought of being forced into using teaching units would not give a second thought to the explanation given by the clerk. They would immediately understand that for some reason the composite parts of the skirt-blouse set belong together as a whole entity and that to use them otherwise would be disadvantageous.

Other examples of the word *unit* could be given which would demonstrate the general use of the term (automobile mechanics speak of the various units in the complex make-up of their machines; refrigerator and radio repairmen often refer to units in their work; and so on). Certain common elements emerge from these examples, which should help to clarify the meaning of the term *unit* as it applies to teaching. First, there is a single mass or entity characteristic which is often composed of minor parts. Second, there appears to be some logical reason for the kind and/or size of the mass or entity and this reason most often is based on function or purpose. Therefore, a unit of teaching would be a single mass or quantity of subject matter (concepts, skills, symbols, and so forth) which for some logical reason appears to belong together or to form some reasonable single entity. Units of teaching involving *The American Revolutionary Period, Punctuation,* or *The Back-Stroke in Swimming* serve as good examples. In each case smaller bits and pieces of information are grouped together into a larger, meaningful mass of subject matter which can be identified easily as an entity and which can be referred to logically as a *unit.* Such a process is no more complex or confusing than seeing a skirt and blouse kept together for a given reason.

WHY TEACH WITH UNITS?

Having established that the word *unit* is neither awesome nor difficult to understand in teaching or any other context, there still remains the task of demonstrating the advisability of using such an approach. Once again, it may prove helpful if activities in life other than teaching are examined first.

For example, consider the businessman who must drive from Salt Lake City to attend a conference in San Francisco. If asked where he is going he will respond unhesitatingly, "San Francisco." This response indicates an awareness of the *ultimate* goal—just as a teacher if asked what he is teaching might respond, "United States history," "home economics," or "algebra." If it were possible, however, for the questioner to look secretly inside the businessman's mind and just as secretly accompany him on his trip, he would discover that he does not *actually* drive from Salt Lake

City to San Francisco but that he drives from Salt Lake City to *Grants-ville, from Grantsville to Wendover, from Wendover to Wells, from Wells to Elko, from Elko to Carlin,* and so on *until he reaches his ultimate goal,* San Francisco. The 800-mile trip is too distant, too remote, and too time-consuming to represent a realistic, workable goal. Therefore, the traveler breaks the trip into smaller, identifiable goals which are more satisfying because progress is more easily seen and because achievement is in the immediate foreseeable future. It is significant to note, however, that he does not carry the breakdown of the ultimate goal to the extreme. For example, he does not attempt to drive from tar-strip to tar-strip on the highway, from telephone pole to telephone pole, or from mile to mile as indicated on his speedometer. Such short, unchallenging goals would be too small, too insignificant, and too unrelated to the ultimate goal for the traveler to find them useful.

Once home from his trip, the businessman notes that he has a backlog of unfinished tasks. As he starts to take care of the unattended chores, he once again demonstrates the natural tendency to approach major tasks in terms of *units*.

While mowing his lawn he finds himself cutting a swath across the middle of a particularly large section, dividing it into two or three smaller areas rather than working his way tediously toward the center of the apparently never-ending larger section. He does not, however, pluck the grass blade by blade, nor does he cut his lawn in square foot or square yard sections.

While other examples are plentiful, the foregoing clearly illustrate several obvious facts: (1) when man is faced with a large task, he naturally—almost automatically—divides the task into smaller segments which are more easily handled and are psychologically more motivating; (2) the smaller segments are not just selected at random, but represent logical, meaningful portions of the larger goal; (3) if the smaller segments of the large task become too small, they lose appeal, challenge, and identity with the larger task.

Teaching with the unit approach offers no exceptions to the generalizations given above. In teaching, the larger goal is represented by the basic knowledge which the students should acquire from a given course. Since this task of teaching is so large it is unmanageable and too distant to be challenging. Therefore, the teacher divides the basic understandings of the course into smaller segments. These smaller segments (or units) are chosen on the basis of their logical cohesiveness and their ability to stand alone as subject matter entities. Teaching on a day-to-day basis rather than from within the framework of a unit is the equivalent of breaking the large goal into areas that are too small to be challenging and that are not easily related to the larger task.

HOW IS A UNIT PLANNED?

Once a person has convinced himself that the unit approach to teaching is not mysterious and that it is the natural way to attack any large task, he is ready to start with actual unit planning. This will involve four basic steps: (1) selection of objectives, (2) determination of teaching procedures, (3) identification of teaching materials, and (4) justification of the three previous steps.

The teacher's first step, within the confines of the unit chosen is to *select* the basic understandings (concepts), skills, or new vocabulary which need to be developed. This suggests that the teacher will analyze the subject matter contained within the unit very carefully and will decide on certain things to be emphasized, learned, and remembered. Some authorities disagree with such a suggestion; they maintain that such an authoritarian approach kills the incentive and initiative of the students. Such opposition is based on a minunderstanding of the proposal. The suggestion that the teacher should select the fundamental objectives to be achieved in advance *does not* imply a lack of flexibility. It simply suggests that it is necessary for the teacher to be prepared to give focus and direction in his teaching. It allows for deviation from the advance plan, *but offers something from which to deviate.*

The second consideration for the teacher is the procedures necessary to achieve the objectives. Most literature on unit planning speaks of multitudinous lists of activities which could conceivably fit within the framework of a given unit, but it seems advisable to seek out methods, techniques, and procedures which apply *specifically* to the individual objectives. Whether the teacher includes many or just a few procedures for teaching each objective depends upon whether the teacher wants the unit to be a resource unit or a unit plan from which to teach directly. In either case, however, there should be a specific relationship between the stated objectives and the procedure proposed. Then nothing is left to chance; each objective has its corresponding procedures which have been planned to insure that the desired learning takes place. Again, this does not suggest rigidity. Rather, it insists on basic preparation with the clear understanding that the teacher has the right and obligation to deviate and make adjustments whenever the current situation demands.

Identifying materials which will aid in the achievement of the objectives is in reality part of the responsibility in determining procedures. It is given separate space here since many teachers feel that it is important to list the materials in a special place on the unit plan where the list can be quickly checked prior to commencing a lesson. This helps to prevent an often-heard statement: "I had meant to bring such-and-such today to demonstrate this point, but I seem to have forgotten." The advisability of using materials such as films, slides, realia, charts, graphs, pictures, the chalkboard, and other audio-visual aids is generally conceded by most teachers. The most important thing to be remembered is that these materials are only *means*—not ends.

The fourth task in unit planning is one which rightfully encompasses the other three. What is the justification for the objectives selected? For the procedures chosen? For the materials to be used? The teacher should ask: "Am I attempting to teach this basic concept because I have thought it over carefully and believe it is important for the students to understand *in the light of some purpose*—or am I attempting to teach something simply because it is today and I taught something yesterday which seemed to precede this? Am I going to show this film because it will really help to clarify a justifiable concept or skill—or is it because film-showing takes up most of the period and requires relatively little of me?" Unit planning which is scrutinized with such introspection cannot help but yield superior results.

In summary, the unit approach to teaching is a simple, natural one. It has been demonstrated that man uses this approach in nearly every large task. Unit planning involves the segmenting of large teaching goals into smaller, cohesive, and meaningful entities of subject matter. It also involves the selection of basic objectives within the smaller segments (units) which are important for the students to learn and retain. Once the latter has been done, it is then necessary for the teacher to determine the proper procedures to be employed in achieving the objectives, to identify appropriate materials to be used in the learning process, and to justify the objectives, procedures, and materials. With all of this clearly in mind, and with a determination to teach well, teachers should be able to look forward to the security and satisfaction which comes from knowing what needs to be done and how to do it.

JOHN J. HOSMANEK

Principal, Tremper High School, Kenosha, Wisconsin

26. Planning for Good Learning*

Perhaps one of the most neglected aspects in the pre-service training of teachers is day-to-day lesson planning. The cadet teacher usually goes to great lengths to prepare a lesson, but infrequently learns to use a practical, professional means for promoting multiple good-learning situations. Lesson planning is one of the most difficult and necessary tasks of a teacher. And no matter how experienced or creative a teacher may be, a better job of teaching can be done through planned lessons. Of course, the fact that a teacher is experienced or a beginner may make a difference in the kind and amount of planning necessary. The reasons for having every teacher carefully structure lessons, however, are so impelling that they cannot be discounted. Through planning, the following things are accomplished:

1. A continuity in the material being learned is ensured.
2. Materials are organized so that they are available when the teacher needs them.
3. The teacher gains confidence, and continuity, knowing what is next.
4. An adequate distribution of time during a period is provided.
5. Intelligent pacing of the work, provision for motivation and initiation, development, supervised study time, culmination, and evaluation are planned.
6. Worth-while and appropriate activities, procedures, and aids to learning are selected.
7. More effective teaching in harmony with objectives and philosophy is possible.
8. A continuity of learning, in the event it is necessary for a teacher to be absent, is possible.
9. One of the commonest invitations to disciplinary difficulties—poor planning or a lack of planning—is avoided.

Lesson planning is actually thinking through and setting the stage for good learning-teaching situations. Such planning is written down to permit necessary reorganization and to facilitate placing the plans into action.

Planning should most always proceed from the general or long-range

*Bulletin of the National Association of Secondary-School Principals, 43:28–30, December 1959. Used by permission.

plan to the specific or daily plans. It would seem logical that an outline or course of study for the usual type of subject would serve as the long-range plan. Units of study within such a course of study would provide a basis for shorter range plans, and daily plans can be concerned with the detailed content and learning-teaching activities to be used in a class period.

Plans, of course, need to be used flexibly and need not serve as unalterable procedure schedules. The resourceful, imaginative teacher will undoubtedly frequently depart from plans written out earlier as he senses student interest or disinterest, need for repetition, or good understanding.

Teachers who still use the old page-by-page approach or assignment-regurgitation sequence possibly find it an easy way to teach. In some exceptional circumstances, where the teacher skillfully supplements the "regurgitation" portion of the sequence, this can still serve as a basis for day-to-day classroom activities. However, because it seldom meets the students' interests or needs, particularly on the junior high-school level, it is seldom as satisfactory as some other framework.

A suggested framework or outline on which to structure worth-while and educationally sound plans could be similar to this one based on a unit approach:

    I. Teacher-Student Planning
       A. Goals—objectives
       B. Approach
   II. Organization of Available Materials
 III. Student Research, Experimentation, or Reading
 IV. Organization of Research or Reading
    V. Study (including supervised study and assignments)
 VI. Presentation of Findings
      (Selection of appropriate vehicle; *i.e.,* skit, playlet, booklet, theme, mural, *etc.*, utilizing language and fine arts)
 VII. Summarization of Unit
VIII. Evaluation and Testing

Another structured approach could be similar to this:

    I. Initiation and Motivation of Lesson
       A. Basing motivation on students' interests, needs
       B. Beginning with what students know, working toward what they can discover.
       C. Employing appropriate devices to focalize student attention at beginning of period
          1. Anecdote
          2. Bulletin board display
          3. Question
          4. Refer to text, newspaper, comment

      5. Synopsize and lead into day's work
      6. Audio-visual aids

II. Development and Application of Lesson
  A. Requiring students to know what to do and how to do it
  B. Providing adequate supervised study or work time
  C. Varying appropriate techniques
     1. Group or committee work
     2. Text and supplementary materials
     3. Organize committees for work
     4. Discussion
     5. Planned field trip
     6. Utilize resource person
     7. Audio-visual aids to learning
       a. Blackboard
       b. Bulletin board
       c. Films, filmstrips, slides
       d. Recordings
       e. Demonstration with model or actual material
     8. Controlled experiment or demonstration
     9. Study guide questions
    10. Report, dramatization, *etc.*
    11. Symposium, panel discussion, debate
    12. Review, drill, remedial teaching

III. Conclusion—As appropriate, this can lead to:
     1. Summarization
     2. Assignment and supervised study
     3. Evaluation
     4. Further planning—as a "bridge" to the next unit

An imperative aspect of good lesson planning, implied in the above outlines is resourcefulness, initiative, and judgment based on a knowledge of one's self and his students, as well as appropriate teaching methods. Some of the more common "pitfalls" teachers need to guard against and to keep in mind as they plan lessons are these:

1. Just because the teacher considers something important, doesn't make it so to students.
2. Too much "straight" talking and lecturing can be boring even if the subject is important and interesting.
3. Confusing democracy with chaos is inexcusable and may be due to inadequate planning.
4. Over-estimating the attention span of students can lead to poor results.

5. Expecting all thirty or more students to react with equal interest, attention, and enthusiasm is impractical.
6. Overdoing "reports," "projects," or any other technique leads to the "Here we go again" sterotyped routine.
7. Using a textbook as "the one and only" resource calls for a "book-keeper" or "class manager" instead of a professional teacher, and implies to the public that anyone can "teach."

SIDNEY L. BESVINICK

Vice-President, University of Pennsylvania

27. An Effective Daily Lesson Plan*

Teachers are constantly planning. They plan the scope and sequence of courses, the content within the course, the topics or units to be covered, the activities to be used, and the tests to be given. They familiarize themselves with resource units, textbooks, and available materials. But the biggest single stumbling block to effective teaching is still a good lesson plan.

What's wrong with the lesson plans most teachers use? For one thing, the usual plan is too brief. A good lesson plan is quite lengthy and time-consuming to prepare. Second, most teachers don't use a systematic form for their plans and omit things that should be included. Third, the teacher may know from his plan what he is going to teach today but pity the poor substitute if the regular teacher is absent at the last minute!

Lesson plans should be simply stated, clearly written, and flexible, but the following rules form a better set of criteria against which to judge a lesson plan:

1. The teacher should be able to teach from it.

2. Someone else who is qualified in that subject area should be able to teach from it.

3. It should be useful as a basis for planning the lesson if it is taught again sometime in the future.

Many so-called lesson plans are really "layout sheets." They merely list what is to be covered day by day in cryptic form. For example:

Monday—Introduce *Macbeth.*

Tuesday—Biographical sketch of Shakespeare's life.

Wednesday—See film on *Macbeth.*

Thursday—Discuss major scenes.

Friday—Begin reading the play.

And so on, until the last lesson in the unit states:

Wednesday—Test on *Macbeth.*

The accompanying lesson plan form was designed for secondary school teachers with the criteria previously mentioned in mind. Mechanically, the form is more useful if the plans are kept in a loose-leaf notebook with page one of the plan on the left facing page two on the right.

Clearing House, 39:425–27, March 1965. Used by permission.

DAILY LESSON PLAN FORM

Date (3) _ _ _ _ _ _ _ _ _ _ Subject (2) _ _ _ _ _ _ _ _ _ _ Teacher (1)_ _ _ _ _ _ _ _ _ _

Unit problem: (4)

Purposes or objectives for today: (5)

Content to be considered: (6)	Notes (11)
Procedures: (7)	
Evaluation techniques and/or questions: (8)	

Assignments: (9)
  Class
  Individuals	

Pupils to see, things to do: (10)

FIGURE 27-1

Here are descriptions of the various sections, why they are included, and how they may be used effectively.

(1) The name blank is included so that you may have your plan returned if a supervisor or a department head checks it or another teacher wishes to borrow it.

(2) The subject is recorded in case one has to make lesson plans for more than one subject each day. A different plan sheet is obviously needed for every course.

(3) The date blank is used to provide a thread of continuity so that the plans may be linked together in a chronological order.

(4) The title of the unit or topic is listed on every plan sheet so that the planner will never forget what is under consideration. If some idea finds its way into the lesson and has no bearing on the unit, it should be stricken from the record and omitted.

(5) Forget about major and minor, specific and gross objectives. Determine the major concepts or skills learners are to acquire from this unit or topic and place them in the general unit plan. Limit yourself to six or eight and concentrate your efforts on them. List the one or two objectives which the class will examine today in the space provided.

(6) List in outline or brief form the content to be discussed and emphasized today. Don't be long winded, but don't be too brief. "Lecture on the causes of World War I" or "Demonstrate how to derive the quadratic equation" are hardly ample descriptions of content. Remember, someone else in your teaching field ought to be able to teach from this plan too.

(7) Procedures should also be listed in some detail. When this form is first used, it is surprising and embarrassing to see how many times "lecture," "discuss," and "question" are used to describe the activities to be undertaken. Gradually teachers find and utilize other teaching techniques to vary their classroom activities.

Sometimes the content is lengthy and the procedure simple. For example, the content may be a detailed development of the use of per cent in a seventh-grade arithmetic class and the procedure might be a chalkboard lecture. On the other hand, at times the content may be expressed as a single concept and the procedure for developing it might be quite elaborate, such as a scientific principle and a laboratory demonstration for presenting it to the students. Since it is impossible to tell in advance which of the two sections will require the greatest description, considerable space should be allocated to both of these parts on the form.

(Because of space restrictions, items 6 and 7 have been shortened in the form shown. On the actual lesson plan at least half of a page is set aside for each of these sections.)

(8) Every plan needs to be evaluated. Each day the teacher should seek to determine, either orally or in writing, whether the learners have grown more sensitive to the concepts and skills that are being investigated. A key question, if not overused, is: "What did you learn today?" One or two objective-type test questions made up each day also provide an excellent set of items for use at the end of a unit or a reporting period as a test instrument.

Don't forget to evaluate occasionally the students' attitudes toward how they are learning; that is, the procedures being used.

(9) List the assignments, if any, for the class or for individuals.

(10) Make a note if a resource speaker needs to be contacted, a film ordered, library books obtained, or if a parent conference is due. This would be inserted in the last section on the second page.

(11) The portion of the page headed "Notes" is very important. If a certain technique goes over well or misses, or if a point of content has been omitted which should have been included, a phrase or two that will focus your attention on it in future plans should be noted in this space. Thus you can continually revise and up-date the plan, making it more interesting and worth while.

There are many teachers who will feel that this type of lesson plan asks too much of them. To do something like this would require at least an hour of preparation each day. This is true, but a perfect, complete lesson each day is not expected during the first year the form is used. In the span of two or three years, however, by building on the previous plans a teacher can develop a fairly satisfactory set of daily lessons. Naturally, some changes and variations are needed each year to tailor the plans to the needs of individual classes. Basically, though, the major concepts and procedures are still there.

Plans worked out in this fashion are thorough and complete, and give the teacher a feeling of security. Many problems of classroom disorder are averted because the students are busy with planned activities. The teacher sees direction in what he is doing; the substitute's task is simplified; the learners are more content; and the supervisor has a meaningful base for offering constructive criticism.

Helping people learn is hard work and a big responsibility. It demands a great deal of time-consuming planning, but the results are worth it.

IIC. How Do I Instruct?

Knowledge is gained in many ways. Recognizing the diversity of youth in any class, it is surprising that teachers tend to employ a most limited scope of methods. Variety in instructional procedure is also suggested by the content being studied and by the media and materials available, as well as by our purposes. A host of resources, from excursions in the community to expert teachers of other subjects in the school, is available to be tapped in numerous ways.

Teachers should also give serious attention to the specific skills essential to the subject matter. It is unfortunate that skill development is frequently taken for granted. Competencies do not spring automatically from learning content; rather, a discipline is understood through practice in the use of its processes. Many skills, of course, are transferable and the value of their inculcation reaches far beyond the learning of one subject.

Prime among the skills of democracy is competent inquiry. An entire subsection which follows is devoted to the manner in which students may be helped to become effective thinkers. The problems of developing responsible citizens are the focus of another subsection. The social studies teacher will most likely attain his citizenship purposes if into the bulk of his instruction he regularly links the teaching of attitudes and values to the building of skills, particularly the problem-resolution skills.

Ultimately the degree of success in instruction comes down to the number of pupils the teacher is able to reach individually. We may group pupils in different ways for good reason, and companionship in learning often serves an important purpose; but eventually all education occurs within the single student. He must be understood. He must be motivated. He must be guided. He must be helped to learn in a somewhat personalized pattern, and he and the teacher together should assess his progress. The sooner teachers will move from the usual common group instruction to more individually patterned programs, the sooner the efficacy of our instruction will materially increase.

Even when we hold similar goals for individual pupils, the roads to learning must frequently vary. Teachers should attempt to use the approach or medium that best promises success for the largest number of pupils; even then, however, specialized assignments are often in order for some small groups or individuals. The final section of this part of the book suggests but several of the means which can be employed in making your social studies classroom a learning laboratory.

As you review these suggestions for instructional success, ask yourself: with which of these avenues do I need to become more familiar? How do I decide which approaches or which media to employ in any particular circumstance? How can I avoid possible pitfalls and how can I be prepared to involve unmotivated pupils?

IIC-1.
The Teaching of Thinking

HELEN SAGL

Professor of Education, Indiana University

28. Problem Solving, Inquiry, Discovery?*

What's in a name? Today, hundreds of years after Shakespeare wrote these words, this question continues to absorb man's attention. Educational writers' current preoccupation is with three terms associated with children's learning—*problem solving, inquiry,* and *discovery.* Are these names for truly different phenomena? Or are they names for basically the same phenomenon? Do these names identify unique phenomena or are they "roses by any other name"?

These are no mere academic questions. On the contrary, they reflect a real need to find ways and means for improving the effectiveness of children's learning, particularly in the content areas of the curriculum; for example, in social studies. Created largely by the knowledge explosion, this concern for children's learning is taking many directions, one of which is the search for strategies that will produce an optimum mode of learning for children; hence the current anatomizing of the terms *problem solving, inquiry,* and *discovery* by educators and writers.

Certainly a consensus of the meaning of these terms would go a long way toward dispelling the confusion that now exists about them. But, if anything, the microscopic scrutiny to which some writers are subjecting these terms is producing a divergence of interpretations rather than a consensus about their meaning.

RELATIONSHIP OF TERMS

What is happening as a result of attempts to anatomize the terms is that some writers are attributing singular properties to *problem solving,*

Childhood Education, 43:137–41, November 1966. Used by permission.

to *inquiry*, and to *discovery,*, describing each as a more or less desirable mode of learning. Thus *problem solving*, according to some writers, is a formalized process that suffers from the dangers of stereotyping, while *inquiry*, by being open-ended in nature, avoids this pitfall. Others eulogize *discovery*, contending that it puts the emphasis in the learning spectrum where it belongs—on insight. Still other writers have, indeed, called a "rose by any other name," for they use the terms interchangeably to identify essentially the same process. And this confusion is further compounded by writers who define each term—*problem solving, inquiry*, and *discovery*—as a process of search.

Undoubtedly much of the confusion about the definitions of these terms is a matter of semantics rather than a dilemma that only scientific study can resolve. At least the interchangeable use of the terms by writers suggests that this may be the case. What few, if any, writers are doing, however, is defining the meaning of these terms in relation to each other. Why writers have not pursued this relationship, why they have not explored it more fully, is a moot question. To be sure, a few writers—Bruner, for one—seem to suggest that a significant relationship among them exists.

> It is evident then that if children are to learn the working techniques of discovery, they must be afforded the opportunities of problem solving. The more they practice problem solving, the more likely they are to generalize what they learn into a style of inquiry that serves for any kind of task they may encounter. It is doubtful that anyone ever improves in the art and technique of inquiry by any other means than engaging in inquiry or problem solving.[1]

Opportunities for problem solving facilitate the task of developing techniques of discovery and a style of inquiry. One approach to the meaning of the meaning of these terms, then, is to consider them in relation to each other.

Using this premise as a base, a logical point of departure in exploring the nature of the relationship among *problem solving, inquiry, and discovery* is to define the problem-solving setting. Here there is a general consensus, for most writers describe a problem-solving setting as one in which there is a blocked goal, a new or novel element that impedes progress toward the goal, inadequate or ineffective habitual or known responses with which to resolve the new element, and a resultant problem to be solved.

Problem Solving Not Sequential

The task of resolving problems is often defined in relation to Dewey's five steps to complete thought or Thorndike's more specific analysis

[1] Jerome S. Bruner, "Structures in Learning," *National Education Association Journal,* 52:27, March 1963.

of the steps in problem solving; namely: becoming aware of the problem, clarifying it, proposing hypotheses and testing hypotheses against experiences. *But there is no mass of evidence that children always solve problems in this logical order.* In fact, *there is a growing belief that problem solving may not occur as a sequential process.*

Currently, at any rate, the sequence of learners' problem-solving activities receives little attention from those seeking to shed light on these activities. Rather, the focus seems to center on data-gathering and data-organizing processes involved in problem solving; on inquiry activities such as theorizing and hypothesizing; and. on conditions that enable learners to discover and formulate generalizations that illumine their problems.

More specifically, problem solving is conceived by many to be a searching process in which learners engage in inquiry into possible solutions to their problems and gather data which they construct into conceptual schemes that facilitate discovery of organizing principles imbedded in the data. In this concept of problem solving, learners are guided to discover relationships among data by engaging in problem-solving experiences that facilitate this discovery. In short, by structuring data-producing experiences that lead to almost inescapable conclusions, teachers guide learners in their efforts to formulate generalizations that illumine their problems.

Discovering Relationships

What is most important here, of course, is the fact that the learner is the discoverer of the relationships; that, even though the results of his search were predecided, he *discovers* them as he perceives the relationships among the data he gathers. Pieces fall into place at this point; the learner discovers the meaning of the relationships among the data. This is the act of discovery or, as it is sometimes referred to, the *moment of insight.* Subsequently, having made his discovery, the learner verbalizes his conclusion about the data as a principle or generalization that sheds light on the problem he sought to solve. And, most important, he can verify the generalization he has formulated.

Not all problem-solving activities result in this kind of closure, however, for to confine problem solving to controlled experiences that lead to verifiable generalizations is to limit the learner's understanding of his environment. As Suchman points out, "The pursuit of greater meaning or of new understandings is the larger purpose of education." [2] Developing a style of inquiry that adds new dimensions to the child's learning is, therefore, also a significant aspect of the problem-solving process.

[2] J. Richard Suchman, "Inquiry." *The Instructor (January 1966).* pp. 24, 61.

Prediction of What Will Happen

Some problems have no certain answers. But inquiry into such problems produces insight into their causes and opens new channels of thought about them. Inquiry, in essence, is a process in which children zero in on a problem and hypothesize and formulate theories that get at the areas of why and how. The focus is not on established generalizations but on theories that predict what would happen when put to the test.

In the process of formulating their theories, learners draw on their own storehouses of conceptual ideas, speculate and experiment, as well as look for data that are appropriate to their theories. And, although the teacher guides learners in this inquiry, he does not direct it toward a specific conclusion. For those teachers who consider closure essential, time spent in inquiry, in theorizing and hypothesizing may be time wasted. By the same token, however, the thinking in this aspect of problem solving must surely contribute to the development of the power of rational thought, to say nothing of adding to the dimension and meaning of learning.

How problem solving embraces controlled search, open-ended inquiry and discovery may be clarified by following a group of pupils in their pursuit of a social studies concern.

A teacher considers it important that his children acquire the generalization: *People everywhere have certain basic needs and wants; how they meet these needs depends upon their environment and cultural level.* To accomplish his purpose, he plans for and executes a series of strategic operations. He provides an opportunity for his pupils to raise significant problems bearing on this generalization. He structures a pattern of experiences that yield data that shed light on these problems, and he involves the pupils in these experiences. He engages them in frequent periods of open-ended inquiry during which they theorize about possible solutions to the problems. He helps the pupils organize the data they accumulate and leads them to discover relationships. Finally, he helps them verbalize their discovery as a generalized statement or a principle. Later he arranges new opportunities and new experiences by which the pupils test the conclusion they have verbalized.

To illustrate, the teacher regulates the classroom environment to stimulate his pupils' interest in and curiosity about man's needs for food. Among the problems that this situation generates are the following:

Why are some kinds of foods grown in some areas of the world but not in others?

Why are farms in the United States employing fewer workers than in the past?

How is science changing people's eating habits?

How can food growers meet labor shortages?

Why are supermarkets an important community business?

As the focus of their initial data-searching activities the pupils select the problem: Why are some kinds of food grown in some areas of the world but not in others? Under teacher guidance they gather pertinent data from geography books, reference books, newspapers and periodicals; they view films and slides that provide information about food production in various parts of the world; they make study trips to observe irrigation practices and similar operations. The result of these endeavors is a body of facts—types of food grown throughout the world, rainfall, growing seasons and temperature needed to grow each type, man's efforts to modify these conditions.

Having guided the pupils to accumulate this body of facts, the teacher helps them organize the facts to find relationships among them. He asks, for example: "How does the length of a growing season influence the type of food grown in an area? Do some foods grow in tropical areas only? How does irrigation change the kind of food grown in an area?" With these and similar questions the teacher guides the pupils to find relationships among the data and to *discover* this generalization: that the food produced in an area and the geography of an area are directly related but that the relationship is not an absolute one, since man is increasingly modifying conditions by which food is produced.

Working in this pattern, the pupils pursue many avenues of search for data that illumine the problems they identified earlier. But not all of their problem-solving activities result in discovery of pre-established generalizations. Some take the form of open-ended inquiry that produces theories rather than known answers. For example, as a result of their data-gathering experiences, the pupils *discover* that farmers who use mechanical devices to harvest their crops employ fewer people than those who do not. "What of fruit and vegetable growers?" they ask. Since Congress has passed a law prohibiting employment of migrant workers who are not United States citizens, such growers are having harvesting troubles. "Could they also solve their labor shortage with mechanical devices?"

The pupils review the situations in which farmers use mechanical devices and note that, although vegetables and fruit might be more difficult to harvest than corn or wheat, soybeans or alfalfa, using mechanical devices does not seem impossible.

Drawing on their individual storehouses for conceptual ideas about the use of machines in performing tasks, about harvesting and related phenomena, they inquire into the problem and formulate theories about its solution. The following is a sample.

"In the same way that airplanes are used to spray crops, balls could be dropped from them to knock off fruit like hail knocks it off. . . ."

"But hail bruises fruit, doesn't it? . . ."

"Big nets are dropped from airplanes to capture animals. A net dropped over a tree and tied around the trunk like a laundry bag would catch the fruit. . . ."

"Instead of a net tied *around* the trunk, spread it out on stilts *under* the tree. . . ."

"Or instead of dropping something from an airplane to knock the fruit off the tree, use a machine that shakes the trunk. . . ."

"A corn picking machine must work something like ice tongs. Use the same idea for picking fruit. . . ."

"But what about the many different sizes of fruits and vegetables there are? Could a machine work on all? . . ."

"Try experimenting with seeds to grow more of the fruit and vegetables the same size and shape. . . ."

"Would using mechanical devices decrease or increase how much it would cost to harvest fruits or vegetables? . . ."

"Such a machine would be very expensive. A little thing like a lawn mower costs a lot of money. . . ."

"But many farmers use the same wheat cutting machine. A big orchard owner could rent the machine to many others. . . ."

"Not if the fruit all ripens at the same time. . . ."

(These pupils did not follow through on their theories and attempt to find data to substantiate them. However, they might have decided to do so. In this event, their efforts would have led them to validate their theories, or refute them, or to conclude that there were not enough available data to test them.)

GENERALIZATION RESULTS IN BROADENED CONCEPTS

Thus, weaving in and out of problem-solving activities that generally produced the desired discovery and closure but in other instances resulted in open-ended solutions, the pupils formulated a generalization about people's need for food and the factors that control the way this need is met.

Other problem-solving activities focused on other needs such as clothing, shelter and need to express esthetic impulses, carried on in less depth and over a shorter period of time, served to verify the basic generalization and resulted in a broadened concept of man's needs.

The answer to the meaning of the terms *problem solving, inquiry,* and *discovery* lies not so much in defining the discreteness of the terms as in exploring the relationship among them. In short, to know the meaning of one is first to know the relation of one to the other.

RICHARD E. GROSS

FREDERICK J. McDONALD

Professor of Education, Stanford
University

Associate Professor of Education and
Psychology, Stanford University

29. The Problem-Solving Approach

Down through the centuries master teachers have liberally interspersed the learning experiences of their students with problem resolution. Despite the virtues claimed for this educational approach, there has been comparatively little application of the process in the schools of the nation. This holds true even in lessons and courses in mathematics and science where one would expect to find the most meaningful use of effective thinking procedures. Forward-looking science educators have decried the mistaken notion held by so many teachers in all curricular fields that problem-solving abilities are merely by-products of the memorization of the lesson or result almost automatically from learning a set of facts. Such conditions have continued to plague science instruction in spite of the fact that every "major report in the field of science education for the past quarter of a century has emphasized the importance of the problem-solving objective."[1]

What accounts for the continuing sparsity of problem-centered teaching? In addition to nine reasons for these conditions which have been outlined recently,[2] two basic causes may be cited. In the first place, no psychological area has been subjected to less diligent and thorough research and, while considerable research at the laboratory level has been conducted, many studies have limited application in the schoolroom. In 1941 when Glaser was preparing his own research on critical thinking, out of some 340 studies which he reviewed he found fewer than thirty holding any practical application for teacher use in the classroom.[3] A review of experimental findings in the decade following Glaser's study reveals much the same situation.[4] A prime, continuing need is for more controlled experimentation and well-planned action research in school situations which may help develop proof for the theoretical claims made for the problems approach.

*Phi Delta Kappan, XXXIX:259–65, March 1958. Used by permission.

[1] E. Obourn and G. Montgomery, "Classroom Procedures for Developing the Elements of Problem Solving," *Science Education,* pp. 72–80, February 1941.

[2] R. E. Gross, "Problem Solving: Why It Isn't and What It Is," *California Journal of Secondary Education,* pp. 108–12, February 1956. This article is one of a symposium in this issue devoted to problem solving.

[3] E. M. Glaser, *An Experiment in the Development of Critical Thinking,* Contributions to Education no. 854 (New York: Columbia University, Teachers College, 1942).

Secondly, much of the psychological research which does hold implication and meaning at the instructional level has not been made readily available or understandable for the practitioner. [5] The average teacher can gain little from the intricate, specialized reports, and few psychologists or educators have attempted to state results in forms useful for the teacher in the lower schools. Two yearbooks of the National Society for the Study of Education have devoted a number of chapters to problem solving wherein some of the contributing authors did attempt to translate some of the technical research into useful terms. Much more of this is needed. [6]

Another difficulty in this area is the differing conceptions as to just what is involved in and meant by problem solving, and this is true among both psychologists and educators. Some teachers, for example, hold to the belief that studying *about* a problem, generally as a topic, is problem solving. Others are satisfied with the student analysis of a remote problem drawn from some aspect of subject matter. A third group of teachers feels that pupil consideration of problems which are essentially adult and of a social nature fulfills the process. Still other teachers will only accept direct pupil involvement and action concerning immediate personal and social problems of real moment for the students as providing a full experience in problem solving. Just what is problem solving?

FROM FINDING RULES TO FORMAL REASONING

One of the major difficulties in psychological research on problem solving has been to clarify the characteristics of the phenomenon under study. There is at present no common agreement on what is meant by "problem-solving behavior," and, as a consequence, there is considerable diversity in the kinds of behavior that have been investigated as well as in the methods of investigation. In terms of the operations used in research, problem solving has been described on some kind of a continuum which includes behavior varying from finding exceptions to rules to formal reasoning of a complex nature. Included among these definitions are descriptions of problem solving as reorganization, as integration, and as "insight." This diversity of meaning should alert the reader of research in this area to the intimate connection between what has been found about problem solving and how the process is defined. The diversity further suggests that it is probably

[4] O. H. Mowrer, "Learning as Problem Solving," *Review of Educational Research,* pp. 478–81, December 1952.

[5] D. M. Johnson, "A Modern Account of Problem Solving," *Psychological Bulletin,* pp. 201–29, April 1944.

[6] National Society for the Study of Education, *Learning and Instruction,* 41st Yearbook, pt. 2 (Chicago: University of Chicago Press, 1942); *idem, Learning and Instruction,* 49th Yearbook, pt. 1 (Chicago: University of Chicago Press, 1950).

more meaningful to think of problem solving as a complex of many functions rather than as some single unitary function.

DEWEY GAVE US LOGICAL ANALYSIS

Essentially, psychological research is oriented to determining how
people go about solving problems. Dewey's conception of the stages in the
problem-solving process[7] has dominated thinking about this process, but
what is too frequently overlooked is that Dewey's description is a logical
analysis rather than a description of how people in fact do go about solving
problems. A number of investigations have been concerned specifically
with this problem: that is, given a problem, what is the method of attack
used by the problem solver?[8] The results of these investigations suggest
that any problem-solving process involves three essential functions: (a)
an orienting function; (b) an elaborative and analytical function; (c) a
critical function. The first of these aspects is an information-gathering function, the second, a hypothesis-formation function, and the third, a hypothesis-testing function. These processes, while they can be identified in
problem-solving situations, are not necessarily sequential in character in
each individual, nor is there any reason to believe at the present that they
necessarily depend on each other. The problem of psychological investigation is to determine how these aspects of the process vary with the problem to be solved and in relation to the characteristics of the solver. While
investigation of these problems is far from complete, a considerably body
of evidence has been developed that gives us some insight into the factors
involved in problem solving.

The influence of the problem on the process has been investigated in
terms of the kind and complexity of the problem. The more complex
the problem, the more apparent the differences in the problem-solving
processes utilized by problem solvers. Subjects who solve easy problems
seem to depend largely upon immediate and obvious cues, whereas subjects who are capable of solving more complex problems appear to be capable of formulating a variety of hypotheses and to be able to ferret out less
obvious cues.

Of particular interest to the educator are investigations dealing with
the life-likeness of the problem. A common assumption is that problems
solved by students must be as "life-like" as possible. Do "life-like" problems in effect lead to "better" problem-solving? At least one series of inves-

---

[7] John Dewey, *How We Think* (Boston: D. C. Heath, 1933). Originally written in
1910, this germinal statement remains most pertinent reading today.
[8] Karl Duncker, "On Problem Solving," *Psychological Monograph,* no. 270, vol. 58;
Max Wertheimer, *Productive Thinking* (New York: Harper and Bros., 1945).

tigations suggests that the realism of the problem does not necessarily produce qualitatively superior solutions to problems.[9] When problems are presented to subjects on a realistic to unrealistic dimension, that is, when the problem versus the situation in which the problem solver merely thinks about the problem, expected differences in the kinds of solutions evoked do not appear. As a matter of fact, when laboratory problems with varying degrees of realism are used, or when field problems with varying degrees of realism are used, or when laboratory problems and field problems are compared, subjects in general generate the same kinds of solutions, and do not appear to benefit from the greater reality of some problems than of others. In solving field problems as against solving laboratory problems, new elements do appear in the solutions but these do not apparently change the general character of the solution. One difference that does emerge is that a greater amount of time appears to be necessary for the solution of laboratory problems than for field problems. This may suggest a greater degree of involvement in a field type problem which motivates quicker solutions, or it may suggest that clues which are available are more quickly grasped in the field situation than they are in the laboratory situation.

'LIFE-LIKE' PROBLEMS?

It should be noted that this research does not suggest that "life-like" problems should not be used, but that their use does not appear to evoke superior solutions. This kind of a problem may in fact have other values, such as transfer values, potentiality for arousing interest, task involvement, and changing attitudes that would recommend their inclusion in curricular experiences, though these questions themselves should be investigated.

A major theoretical question and one that is of great practical importance to the educator concerns the amount of information and guidance that is necessary in the problem-solving process. The question has been fomulated most frequently in the form, "Should the method or principle be taught?" A recent investigation has provided some answers to this particularly vexing question. The general conclusions in this respect are: (a) that the amount of information used in guiding problem-solving activities must be appropriate to the task set for the student; (b) that some appropriate guidance is beneficial, but that failure to provide it will delay rather than prevent the solution; (c) that the effectiveness of guidance does not

---

[9] I. Lorge *et al.*, "Solutions by Teams and by Individuals to a Field Problem at Different Levels of Reality," *Journal of Educational Psychology*, 46:17–24, January 1955; *idem*, "Problem-Solving by Teams and by Individuals in a Field Setting," *Journal of Educational Psychology*, 46:160–66, March 1955.

depend solely on the amount of information imparted; (d) that more explicit instruction may be just as effective as more directive guidance for the less able students. The less able students appear to profit little from knowledge of the principle of solution and tend to be more effective when a method is available. [10]

PROBLEM-SOLVERS USE MANY METHODS

When the focus of interest in investigation has been on the general methodology of the problem-solver, it has been consistently found that subjects tend to use a variety of general methodologies. These can be roughly grouped into three categories: (a) trial and error behavior; (b) sudden insights; and (c) gradual analysis. These three methods are not necessarily qualitatively different but may be arranged on a continuum, and subjects in investigations shift from one general method to another during the problem-solving process. It is probably unduly confusing to refer to these approaches as methods, particularly since it is not known under what conditions these various kinds of approaches are evoked or can be evoked.

Considerable research has been done on the characteristics of problem solvers and the relationship of these characteristics to the correctness, the quality, and the speed of solution of problems. More recent investigations have concentrated on the anxiety level of learners, and the general conclusion of these investigations has been that high anxiety tends to produce a rigidity of set which interferes with learning and with problem solving.

The problem of "set" in problem solving has been one of the more fruitful areas of investigation. It has been demonstrated repeatedly that inflexibility of set interferes with problem solving. [11] The theoretical problem is to determine what personality characteristics of the solver tend to produce inflexible sets and what elements in the problem-solving situation are likely to evoke "sets." Luchins has outlined the factors which appear to maximize and reduce sets. Among the factors maximizing set are: (a) an increase in the number of set-inducing problems; (b) creation of a "stress" atmosphere; (c) giving instructions to generalize a method of solution; (d) presenting tasks as "isolated drill." Among factors tending to reduce set are: (a) increasing the number of problems requiring a direct solution as distinct from problems for which a method is available; (b) interspersing problems solvable by a method and those solvable by a direct

[10]B. Gorman, "The Effect of Varying Amounts and Kinds of Information as Guidance in Problem-Solving," *Psychological Monography*, no. 431, vol. 71.

[11]N. R. F. Maier, "An Aspect of Human Reasoning," *British Journal of Psychology*, 24:144–55, October 1933.

attack; (c) increasing the complexity of detail in the problems; (d) offering clarification of the nature of sets and their possible deleterious effects.[12] Other research suggests that set varies with the complexity of the task, and that there is some tendency for set to persist the more complex the task.[13]

A persistent problem and one of concern to educators is the relationship between group and individual problem-solving processes. Studies in this area have suggested that group solutions of problems tend to be superior on many dimensions to individual solutions.[14] However, this conclusion is somewhat suspect because the studies in this area have not been rigorously controlled. One explanation for the differences that have been found is that group activity maximizes the amount of information available for the solution of a problem, introduces more hypotheses for solution, and permits the greater exercise of the critical function. However, what is not known is whether in establishing groups for problem solving the process of building groups automatically insures in some way finding a problem solver in each group who is essentially responsible for the group's superior success in this respect. While a wide variety of problems has been used in these studies, it is still not known whether group problem solving is uniformly better than individual problem solving for all kinds of problems. Most studies have also shown that while the group is superior there are frequently individuals within the groups who have solutions which in effect are better than the groups' solution, either qualitatively or in terms of such factors as the speed of solution and the like. Again it should be noted that group approaches to problems may have other values which recommend this approach to educators. But present evidence certainly does not permit the conclusion that a group is superior to individuals simply because it is a group, and it is important therefore for educators to clarify what they expect to be achieved by using group methods.

Surveying the diversity of literature in this field shows that there is general agreement on what is involved in the problem-solving process. The process appears to involve the following elements: (a) an awareness of a problem which is personal in character; that is, the problem solver is disturbed by a given situation; (b) a data-gathering phase, in which the solver familiarizes himself with the task and the materials available for solution; (c) a hypothesis-formation stage in which the solver formulates solutions; and (d) a hypothesis-testing phase in which solutions are tested. The educa-

---

[12]A. S. Luchins, "Mechanization in Problem-Solving: The Effect of 'Einstellung'," *Psychological Monograph,* no. 6, vol. 54.

[13]"Symposium: Problem-Solving," *Acta Psychology,* 11:213–17, June 1955.

[14]M. E. Shaw, "A Comparison of Individuals and Small Groups in the Rational Solution of Complex Problems," *American Journal of Psychology,* 44:490–504, July 1932. For a critical analysis of this study see I. Lorge and H. Solomon, "Two Models of Group Behavior in the Solution of Eureka-Type Problems," Psychometrika, 20:139–48, June 1955.

tional process can contribute to the development of competence in several aspects of this total process. Thus it is the curriculum which can provide problems which evoke the problem-solving behavior. Furthermore, curricular experiences can develop competency in data-gathering techniques and methods for hypothesis-testing.

What are the implications for educators in this research on problem-solving? The present state of the research does not provide immediate, usable answers to many particular questions. The research does suggest certain lines of inquiry that educators can fruitfully pursue. The major problem for the educational process is to determine the character of problems to which students will be exposed in the course of their educational experience. What range and kinds of problems will have maximum utility in developing problem-solving abilities and at the same time will have the greatest transfer value for out-of-school activities? Probably the curriculum should contain a wide variety of problems so that students will be exposed to as many different kinds of problems as possible. In any event, it seems necessary to keep distinct, when planning curricular activities, two aspects of the function of problems in the curriculum, namely, their utility in developing problem-solving ability and their utility for transfer to out-of-school activities.

HOW CAN CURRICULUM HELP?

A second implication from psychological research would be that problem solving should not be thought of as a single, simple unitary process, but as an extraordinarily complex process which has many different aspects. The problem for the school is to determine what aspects of the problem-solving process can be effected by curricular experiences. It seems obvious that the school can improve the information-gathering abilities of students and likely influence the hypothesis-forming abilities of students, though the range of individual differences in this respect will probably affect what the schools can do. Finally, the schools can certainly develop methods of testing hypotheses which can be communicated to students.

The question of group versus individual problem solving needs to be pursued in educational settings. A considerable emphasis on group methods may be wasteful in terms of developing competent problem solvers. On the other hand, the group method may have values which strongly recommend it. In any case, this question of appropriate methodology needs to be more thoroughly explored than it has to date.

WE MUST APPLY PSYCHOLOGICAL RESEARCH

What seems most important for the practical application of psychological research to education is that educators themselves become concerned with experimentation in this area. Such factors as the influence of set upon problem solving are important factors that must be analyzed in terms of what it is in the learning situation which tends to produce inflexible kinds of sets. Variables such as the method of instruction, the mode of presentation, previous experiences in problem solving, and so on, are undoubtedly all important factors. Bloom, for example, found lack of reading ability to be a key factor in failures to solve problems at the college level.[15] What are other sources of inadequacy? Is certain content or are particular courses more efficacious for the process? Furthermore, problems such as the developmental characteristics of problem-solving abilities need to be investigated. For example, do younger children approach problems differently from adolescents or adults? Are there significant sex differences in problem-solving competency? Still another important unknown is the relationship between concept formation and problem solving.

Williams, in his recent survey of problem solving, concludes that educators need: (a) to identify the types of problem situations which offer the best opportunities to develop effective thinkers; (b) to build awareness in the students of multi-factored, non-academic problem situations and just what they demand; (c) to help students understand the factors which affect problems and problem solving such as personal attitudes, physical and environmental conditions, and motivation; and (d) to provide deliberate and repeated problem-solving situations and practice.[16]

It is impossible in a brief article to review school level research on the problems approach in all curricular areas. Selections from the field research in the area of social education will now be cited to reveal what has been done and to point out gaps and opportunities open to interested investigators.[17]

Many stimulating reports on problem-solving experiences at all grade levels are available, but commonly these represent a teacher's after-view of a new but essentially uncontrolled situation. While such expositions may lead readers to launch their own trials with effective thinking procedures, they provide very limited evidence as to the value of the problems approach as measured against other means of instruction and curricular organization.[18]

[15]Benjamin Bloom, "Implications of Problem-Solving Difficulties for Instruction and Remediation," *School Review*, pp. 45–49, January 1947.

[16] F. E. Williams, Jr., *Factors, Methods, and Procedures of Problem-Solving*, Educational Specialist Paper, School of Education Stanford University, 1956).

[17] A number of the studies hereinafter reported are adapted from "Trends in the Use of the Problems Approach," chap. 7 in G. L. Fersh, ed., *The Problems Approach and the Social Studies*, National Council for the Social Studies (Washington, D.C., 1955). This bulletin has the most complete coverage on this topic now available. An extensive bibliography is included.

[18] Typical, for example, are Florence Cleary *et al.*, "Project in Problem Solving," *Clearing House*, pp. 82–86, October 1951; and J. W. Hanson, "A High School Experiment," *Educational Leadership*, pp. 220–27, January 1949.

Cook and Koeninger experimented with different methods and varying course organization for college sociology classes. They attempted to measure increases in factual knowledge, in the skills of critical thinking, and in changed attitudes. Students working in groups via the problems approach gained as much in knowledge of content as those in classes otherwise organized and at the same time improved much more in attitudinal tendencies and critical-thinking ability.[19] Glaser in the study mentioned earlier pitted four control classes against four classes given guidance in the principles and processes of problem solving via special units. After evaluation with instruments he himself developed he concluded that the four experimental classes had made significantly greater progress in developing critical-thinking ability and that pupils' attitudes toward rational problem-solving procedure are susceptible to educational improvement. He pointed up the fact that group problem-solving experiences are especially valuable because children learn thereby the essential democratic means of cooperating with their fellows.

HOW TEACH SOCIAL STUDIES?

A significant experiment in this area was the Stanford Social Education Investigation. Most of the important findings of this five-year study, which involved ten teachers in five school systems, have been reported in *Education for Social Competence*.[20] The staff attempted to contrast the relative effectiveness of the chronological, topical, and problems methods in social studies classes at the senior high-school level. Although many results, such as improved skills and attitudes, favored the problems groups, Quillen and Hanna were restrained in their concluding recommendations. Differences between classes often were very narrow and students in the chronologically-organized classes did make the most significant gains in the amount of information learned about American history and, perhaps surprisingly, in research techniques. These results are not compatible with certain statements of other investigators who claim students always learn more facts as well as varied social studies skills when using the problems method, no matter what the course may be. Students in topically-organized classes generally made the least significant progress in a number of areas. This is important to note, since so many texts are organized in this fashion, at least in part, and especially since the type of "problems approach" applied by many instructors is merely a topical study of problems stated in the form of a question. The all-important role of the teacher, regardless of the form of curri-

[19] L. A. Cook and Elaine Cook, *A Sociological Approach to Education* (New York: McGraw-Hill Book Co., 1950), pp. 33–34.
[20] I. J. Quillen and Lavone Hanna, *Education for Social Competence* (Chicago: Scott, Foresman and Co., 1948), chaps. 5–7.

cular organization, was clearly evidenced in the results of this investigation.

CURRICULUM, PRESENTATION RECOMMENDATIONS

A more recent study by Kight and Mickelson attempted to investigate the related effects of problem- and subject-centered types of presentation upon learning facts, learning rules of action, the ratio of rules of action learned to factual information, and the connecting of specific facts with their corresponding rules of action. In attempting to circumvent one of the difficulties related to the influence of teaching personnel revealed in the Stanford study, twenty-nine teachers taught problem- and subject-centered units in rotation to 1,450 students in English, science, and social studies classes. In terms of total combined results, pupils learned more factual information in problem-centered units; however, differences were not great in a number of cases and social studies groups gained fewer facts than rules of action as a result of their problem-centered units. The problem presentation showed marked superiority in helping pupils learn rules of action in all areas. There was a high positive correlation between learning facts and rules of action by problem solving, as compared with a low correlation in the subject-matter approach units. Four recommendations for curriculum organization made by the investigators are:

1. Organize each instructional unit around a clearly stated, genuine pupil problem.
2. Elaborate the major pupil problem into its sub-problems.
3. State and present the problem and sub-problems in each instructional unit as something to do rather than something to know.
4. Focus all factual information presented directly on the solution of the pupils' problems.

Five further recommendations for classroom presentation follow:

1. Make every effort to show the pupils that the problems stated in the instructional units are their own personal problems.
2. Make doing rather than knowing primary in the presentation of all pupils' problems.
3. Focus all factual information presented indirectly on the solution of the pupils' problems.
4. State clearly and teach specifically the rules of action necessary to the solution of the problems.
5. Point out the factual information which serves as reasons for rules of action taught. [21]

[21] S. S. Kight and J. M. Mickelson, "Problem vs. Subject," *Clearing House,* pp. 3–7, September 1949.

Kight and Mickelson found the problems method superior for children of both low and high I.Q. Two other teachers working with slow learners have likewise claimed that the problems approach and group planning and discussion increase the ability of students to distinguish between fact and opinion and enable them to recognize various sources of information as holding effective solutions for the problems under consideration. They maintain that generally the skills of critical thinking are much better learned in the pursuit of meaningful problems than when taught as abstract exercises. [22]

In the Philadelphia Open-Mindedness Study, an attempt was made to find out what problems are important to elementary school children and to help them deal with complex problems by checking on availability of facts and opportunity for solution. These simple steps were formulated to guide them: (1) know the problem, (2) get the facts, (3) put the facts in order, and (4) reach a conclusion. Results indicated that pupils recognized the importance of facts in relation to the problem concerned; that they were stimulated to acquire information by the problems approach. [23] Russell has recently gathered much of the research concerning problem-solving abilities and applications appropriate for elementary school children. [24]

SKILL WITH TECHNIQUE SLOW TO DEVELOP

Bayles has reported on six studies with "reflective thinking" which he directed. [25] Basically all were concerned with how well do members of classes taught in a problem-solving manner compare with those taught conventionally in regard to what is covered in typical, standardized examinations. He reports that without qualification, even where the conventionally taught students were coached for the tests, the pupils in the experimental classes did significantly better. An important observation coming from these studies concerns the point that improvement in problem-solving teaching is slow. Gains grow considerably after a teacher has had several years with the approach.

At the secondary school level, problem-centered teaching has found its strongest support in recent years from those educators who have been promoting the core movement. Much more research, however, is needed with core courses. These classes, which cut across subject-centered divisions and

---

[22] Jemina Miller and Grace Weston, "Slow Learners Improve in Critical Thinking," *Social Education,* pp. 315–16, November 1949.

[23] Joseph Goldstein et al., "Thinking Can Be Learned," *Educational Leadership,* pp. 235–39, January 1949.

[24] David Russell, *Children's Thinking* (Boston: Ginn and Co., 1956).

[25] E. E. Bayles, "Experiments with Reflective Teaching," *Kansas Studies in Education,* vol. 6, no. 3, April 1956.

wherein teachers and pupils plan out units based upon problems of real concern to the young people, need to be compared in many ways with more conventionally organized courses.[26] Teachers and administrators who favor the "guidance approach" in educational programs have also done much to promote problem solving in the schools. Writers in this area have uncovered some amazing opinions about the true problems of normal adolescents[27] as well as those of delinquents;[28] these pose provoking challenges to those who seek a functional, general education for youth.

Peterson's study of the historical development of the problem-solving method in education isolated ten basic postulates which form the philosophical basis of the problem-solving approach.[29] His conclusions underscore the points and recommendations made in this article. Research to date on problem solving and on the problems approach indicates primarily the need for much more and more carefully planned and integrated research in this area which is indigenous to and so important in American education.

[26] Dale Williamson, "A List of Problem Areas Used in Core Programs by Various Schools in the United States," mimeographed (Columbus: Ohio State University, 1956). This report is drawn from a master's thesis and includes a valuable and comprehensive list of problems now being studied, grades 7–12.

[27] H. H. Remmers, *The American Teen-Ager* (Indianapolis: Bobbs-Merrill Co., 1957).

[28] G. B. Hunt, *These Are Our Children* (Barrow, Fla.: "These Are Our Children" Publishing Co., 1950).

[29] L. I. Peterson, "The Historical Development of the Problem-Solving Method in Education," (Ph.D. diss., University of Southern California, 1951).

LAWRENCE E. METCALF

Professor of Education, University of Illinois

30. The Reflective Teacher*

It is easy for a modern educator to conclude that there are no horizons in the social studies today, except those that have been lost since the Eight Year Study. There are no large and exciting projects in social studies education such as are believed to be taking place in science and mathematics. With the assistance of Sputnik and the Cold War, science and mathematics have stolen all the headlines. Yet there are unrecognized horizons for the social studies in certain quiet developments now occurring at the level of basic research into the nature of teaching and subject matter. These developments are producing certain refinements in the theory and practice of reflective teaching.

The classical theory of reflective thinking as a method for teaching concepts and generalizations has been put by John Dewey.[1] Recent research on the logic and linguistics of teaching point toward certain refinements in Dewey's basic theory, although some of the investigators perceive themselves as anti-Dewey, or at least as having gone beyond Dewey. The import of these studies for teaching the social studies is not entirely clear, but at least two broad lines of development are beginning to suggest themselves. First, it is already clear that the traditional course in methods of teaching will have to give more attention than it has to the logical foundations of method. The methods course will become less technical and more theoretical in its content, a development that could silence those superficial critics of education who have claimed that all we need do to save the public schools is to eliminate courses in methods of teaching in favor of additional courses in "solid liberal arts content." The second development that is beginning to emerge is a preference for conceptual over factual content in both the elementary and secondary schools. No one has yet dared to suggest a similar reform at the college level.

The movement toward an emphasis upon the logical as well as the psychological aspects of teaching method, recent though it is, has already resulted in the publication of a methods textbook by Hullfish and Smith which assumes that reflective thinking is the only educational method.[2] This book is largely concerned with the problem of warranted belief, and how teachers may help students determine whether there is any warrant for holding cer-

*Phi Delta Kappan, XLIV:17–21, October 1962. Used by permission.
[1] How We Think (Boston: D. C. Heath, 1910, 1933).
[2] H. Gordon Hullfish and Philip G. Smith, Reflective Thinking: The Method of Education (New York: Dodd Mead, 1961).

tain beliefs. The authors of this book classify beliefs into three kinds, the analytic, synthetic, and evaluative. The procedures for verification of a belief vary with each type. In fact, verification has three different meanings. It is significant, particularly for the social studies, that the authors believe that all three kinds of belief can be verified, and they discuss the logical problems involved in each kind of verification.

Their discussion of the difference between the form and the function of a belief is also significant for the social studies teacher who favors reflection as a method of teaching. How is it possible for a statement that is synthetic in form to function as if its form were analytic? This possibility becomes a reality for the person who holds a synthetic belief not only without any evidential ground but also without any notion of the kind of factual knowledge that would make it necessary for him to give up his belief. A defining attribute of any belief that functions as analytic is that its possessor will not modify or reject it in the light of his experience with it. In Hullfish and Smith's terms, it is held in such a way that it is treated as true "come what may in experience." To illustrate the matter further, the principle of identity or non-contradiction as we find it stated in logic is analytic in both form and function. But a statement that is obviously synthetic in form, such as, "Negroes are intellectually inferior to Whites," is held analytically by any person who lacks a concept of evidence. Many high-school students lack this concept, and a social studies teacher who would have students reflect upon their prejudices may first find it necessary to teach the nature of evidence.

In his essay on the uses of subject matter, Henderson has suggested a taxonomy of belief that is more complete than Hullfish and Smith's.[3] He has defined eight kinds of statements, and has labeled them as follows:

1. Statements
  1.1 Analytic
    1.11 Singular
    1.12 General
  1.2 Contingent
    1.21 Singular
    1.22 General
2. Prescriptions
  2.1 Singular
  2.2 General
3. Value Statements
  3.1 Singular
  3.2 General

Since he refers to these as statements of knowledge, he evidently shares with Hullfish and Smith the idea that value judgments and definitions, as

[3] Kenneth Henderson "Uses of Subject Matter," in B. O. Smith and R. H. Ennis, eds., *Language and Concepts in Education* (Chicago: Rand McNally, 1961).

well as propositions, may be verified in some way. He does not discuss the problems of verification where values and definitions are concerned, matters which receive considerable attention from Hullfish and Smith. It should be noted that Henderson uses the term *contingent* for those statements that Hullfish and Smith have called synthetic. Whether they are called contingent or synthetic, they amount to what logical positivists mean by testable propositions. Henderson also differs from Hullfish and Smith in making a distinction between prescriptions and evaluations, and between statements that are singular or general in their subject.

THE VALUE OF CLASSIFYING STATEMENTS

The classification of statements, whether the statements represent knowledge, belief, or opinion, is useful in at least one regard to all teachers of social studies who seek reflection. It would be a mistake for a teacher to ask a student to present evidence in support of his analytic statements. An analytic statement usually takes the form of a definition, and for such a statement it would be more appropriate to ask for an example or an illustration. Bruner's work on concept attainment also suggests the appropriateness of asking for defining attributes, and to note whether the student can distinguish between the defining attributes of a concept and its non-defining or noisy attributes.[4] If a teacher wants a student to reflect upon a contingent statement, he will ask the student what else must be true if the statement is true. Hullfish and Smith make the same point when they say that every synthetic statement implies a prediction. The simple statement that "it is raining" implies that other things will be true if, indeed, it is raining. Ennis has defined critical thinking as the correct assessing of statements, and has identified 12 different kinds of judgment to be made by those who think critically about the statements they encounter.[5] The point must be well taken that a teacher who seeks reflection in his students cannot succeed if he treats all statements as if they were of the same kind.

Henderson's concept of a contingent general statement is especially significant for those teachers of history who claim that a reflective study of the past increases students' understanding of the present. A contingent general statement, *if it is expressed in the present tense,* is the only kind of statement in history that arches through time, and breaks down the wall of separation between past and present. The statement that, "Unless American soldiers fought like Indians, the redmen usually defeated them," is contingent general in form, but its subject matter is in the past. But a statement

[4] J. S. Bruner, Jacqueline J. Goodnow, and G. A. Austin, *A Study of Thinking* (New York: Wiley, 1956).
[5] R. H. Ennis, "A Concept of Critical Thinking," *Harvard Educational Review,* 32:1, Winter 1962.

that "Roman Catholic loyalty helps a presidential candidate of the Roman Catholic faith more than Protestant prejudice hurts him" (a statement that has received some confirmation from Louis Bean's study of the election returns of 1928 and 1960), in addition to having a contingent general form is cast in the present tense, and thus has a subject matter that is not limited to the past. Courses in history that fail to emphasize the study of such statements, what they mean and whether they are true, cannot back up the teacher's claim that an understanding of history clarifies present-day problems.

One can infer from the textbooks that are popular with teachers of social studies that the teachers of these courses prefer contingent singular to contingent general content. These are the "facts" that teachers believe students must learn in order to acquire enough background to think about current problems. Typical content in high-school American history courses is illustrated by statements such as the following, each of which is taken from one of the leading textbooks in the field:

> After the capture of Mexico City it was some months before a Mexican government could be found to sign a peace.
> The most famous of the railroad consolidators was Cornelius Vanderbilt (1794–1877), who built up the New York Central system.
> The Roosevelt Corollary was first put into effect in Santo Domingo.
> The advance of labor unions was aided by the National Labor Relations Act (also called the Wagner Act) passed by Congress in 1935.
> World War II did not inspire the enthusiasm and idealism of either the War Between the States or World War I.

The usefulness of this kind of content is reduced to a minimum when teachers require that it be learned apart from and prior to reflection. Hullfish and Smith put the issue clearly and succinctly:

> . . . Some critics say, for instance, that, since thinking cannot go on in a vacuum, students must first be given the facts they may later use in thinking. Now, of course, the alternatives are not gaining facts apart from thought or thinking apart from facts. The question is how facts are to be best gained. This introduces a third alternative, using facts within a reflective process (p. 213).

The use of facts within a process of reflection gives the facts some kind of order. There are two kinds of order suggested by Henderson, Hullfish, and Smith in their taxonomies. One kind results in concepts, the other in generalizations. Much of the literature on teaching the social studies has not distinguished between these two kinds of order. In fact, it is not unusual to find in a textbook on teaching the social studies that the teaching of concepts and generalizations is treated as a single topic. Bruner has defined a concept as a category, which suggests that the teaching of concepts would require students to engage in acts of classification. Students, for instance, would use their information about events as part of the basis for grouping them according to their common attributes. If imperialism is defined by attributes *a, b,* and *c,* then any event which possesses these attributes would be classified as an instance of imperialism. The author of this article has suggested that the sorting of events is one of the processes with which a teacher is concerned when he teaches a concept.[6] The kind of order which results from classification is basic to all thinking and cognition, and it focuses instruction upon the study of analytic statements. Such statements are never true in the sense that they have evidence to back them up, but rather they are what Hullfish and Smith have described as formal truths. Such statements are *necessarily* true because of the way in which terms are defined, and because of the way in which we have *chosen* to structure experience. Bruner puts the point well when he says that concepts are not discovered; instead, they are created.

BACKING UP CONTINGENT GENERAL STATEMENTS

A second kind of order is obtained when contingent singular content is organized and presented according to the generalizations (contingent general statements) toward which they point. The statement that government deficits foster inflation under the conditions of full employment or imperfect competition is an example of contingent general content. This kind of statement may be tested empirically and found to be probably true or false. Sometimes evidence is unavailable, and in this case we reserve judgment. The teaching of generalizations includes two aspects. One aspect is concerned with what the statement says. This requires the learning of analytic statements (concepts). In the example above, students must define deficit financing, full employment, and imperfect competition. From the subject matter of economics students can learn the correct meanings of these terms. Bruner calls these correct meanings official definitions, to set them apart from the opinions students may have about the meaning of full employment, etc. But the teaching of generalizations, unlike the teaching of concepts, does not stop with definitions. The second and crucial aspect is empirical. It seeks to answer the question: Is it true that deficit-financing has certain consequences under certain conditions? At this stage of instruction the reflective teacher wants to know whether students have evidence to back up their contingent general statements.

[6] L. E. Metcalf, "Teaching Economic Concepts in the Social Studies," *The Illinois Councilor,* 21:1, March 1960.

THE 'WHAT' BUT NEVER THE 'WHY'

If teachers of social studies insist upon teaching the facts out of all relationship to concepts or generalizations, they cannot expect students to grow in their understanding of social phenomena regardless of whether the phenomena are in the past or the present. If this kind of instruction occurs in a history course devoted to the pleasures of chronological narrative, the teachers may be entertaining, interesting, metaphorical, and even poetic but their students will not develop any capacity to generalize their learning. They may at best learn a great deal about *what* happened, although this can hardly happen if terms are never defined, but they can never learn *why* anything happened, because their content has no power to explain or predict events. The reason why this is so is suggested clearly by Swift's study of the teaching of explanations.[7]

High-school social studies are so much devoted to contingent singular content that they seldom try to explain why events have occurred except in a descriptive sense, and Swift has observed that many teachers and textbook writers cannot tell the difference between an explanation and a description. In order to tell the difference, and also in order to assess the correctness and adequacy of any explanation, one needs a model from which to work. Swift has borrowed his model from Hempel, and has studied the problem of teaching historical explanations as an aspect of instruction in critical thinking.

Hempel's model, which he borrowed from the physical sciences, and which he suggests as a research tool for professional historians, casts explanations into the form of a syllogism, the major premise of which is a contingent general statement. For reasons already offered, the author of this article believes that this contingent general statement should be expressed in the present tense. Other criteria are implicit in Hempel's model. The major premise should be testable and true (Hempel refers to explanations that rest upon an untestable premise as a pseudo-explanation). The minor premise, which describes the existence of the antecedent conditions for the occurrence of the event to be explained, should also be historically true. Finally, a description of the event to be explained should follow logically from the truth of the major and minor premises. Swift has summarized the meaning of this kind of explanation as "a deductive argument possessed of empirical content."

The explanations offered by high-school social studies textbooks are

[7] L. F. Swift, "Explanation as an Aspect of Critical Thinking in Secondary School Social Studies" (Ph.D. diss., University of Illinois, 1959); *idem*, "Explanation," in B. O. Smith and R. H. Ennis, eds., *Language and Concepts in Education* (Chicago: Rand McNally, 1961); *idem*, "The Teaching of Explanation in History," (unpublished, 1958).

usually incomplete by Hempel's standards, and require "filling in." These incomplete explanations usually imply, but do not state openly, a general law. Such explanations may abound even in the writings of historians who deny that there are any laws in history. A typical example of an incomplete explanation is the statement, "The Pilgrims came to the New World to escape religious persecution." This sentence standing as it is will make sense to most high-school students. They will believe it in the sense of not doubting it, and may even commit it to memory as an item of information. If this incomplete explanation is cast as a syllogism, doubt flows in from all directions.

> Major Premise: If a group of people is persecuted for its religious be-
>   liefs, it will migrate to a new territory where it will be
>   free to practice its religion.
> Minor Premise: In 17th century England a group of people called the
>   Puritans were persecuted for their religion.
> Conclusion: The Puritans migrated to the New World.

The teacher needs to raise only a few questions about this syllogism before the students sense its inadequacy. Many people who have been persecuted for their religious and other beliefs have not migrated. In fact, many of the Puritans did not, and hence we reserve the term *Pilgrim* for those who did.

The discovery of negative cases always calls for the rejection or modification of a proposition. It is not easy in the social studies to find propositions for which there are no negative cases. It is even difficult to frame propositions precisely enough to distinguish between negative and positive cases. We often settle for propositions that are grossly probable in their truth. Sometimes we are no more precise than to distinguish between the possible and the impossible, or the probable and the improbable, without specifying except in a very rough form the probability that a certain kind of event will occur under certain conditions. If the major premise in the above syllogism is modified so that it becomes a probabilistic rather than a certain truth, it might read as follows: If a group of people is persecuted for its religious beliefs, it *usually* migrates to a new territory.

The term *usually* gives us trouble, for it leaves unanswered the question, "How many negative cases would make it necessary for us to reject the probable truth of our premise?" Clearly, we would have to reject the premise if the number of negative cases exceeds the number of positive cases. But this observation raises the further question, "What constitutes a representative and adequate sample of cases?" What history, and how much history, would students have to study in order to test fairly the truth of a premise? Teachers of social studies are not yet well trained in logic or sampling and probability theory, and this is the kind of content that belongs in the methods course of the future.

The use of a qualifying term gives us another kind of trouble. It destroys the logical tightness of a syllogism. A description of the event to be explained cannot be deduced from premises that are merely probable in their truth. At best we can conclude that a certain kind of event is likely to occur under certain conditions. Unless we can identify conditions that account for negative cases we are forced to treat the major premise as a plausible hypothesis rather than a principle or general law. This may be the only kind of truth commonly available from the subject matter of the social studies. Nagel's analysis of explanation in the social sciences has explored thoroughly the limits of knowledge in history.[8] Given this state of affairs, the use of Hempel's model helps students to learn the extent to which their social studies content is a reliable guide for conduct, and better grounded than "common sense," if not as well established as physics or chemistry content.

There are many other considerations to be faced by a reflective teacher of the social studies, and basic research has begun to explore their dimensions. Unfortunately, limitations of space do not permit their treatment in this article. But it should be clear from what has been reported here that the new horizons for the social studies are in methods of teaching. The suggested reforms in method also call for revisions in social studies content, and the teacher of the future, in addition to knowing a lot of history, will also need to know more social science than has been required of him in the past. It goes without saying that he will have to be well trained in logic, linguistics, and the philosophy of science. As long as the social studies curriculum devotes most of its instructional time to history he will need to be a student of theories of history, and what history is, and what kinds of history there are, and how history is different from such social sciences as sociology and economics.

[8] Ernest Nagel, *The Structure of Science* (New York: Harcourt Brace, 1962).

GERALD LEINWAND

Assistant Dean, School of Education, City College of the City University of New York

31. Queries on Inquiry in the Social Studies*

The "in" group is reading Bruner these days, and he has much to say to teachers of the social studies (or to teachers of history and the social sciences, if you prefer) who are interested in curriculum innovation. His idea of spiral curriculum development, of learning and understanding structure, of curriculum as process rather than revealed truth, his emphasis on inquiry and discovery, are all appropriate and pertinent to the so-called "revolution" in the social studies. Bruner's ideas surely offer desirable alternatives to some of the curriculum designs and teaching strategies which we have perhaps for too long been using.

But abroad in the land of curriculum today is a school of thought that would take Bruner's germinal ideas and make them into a cult, an orthodoxy, and give them an acceptability that perhaps even Bruner himself does not intend they should yet have. This has led to the hasty abandonment of the teaching theories and curriculum designs of the recent past and to substitute far too quickly the idea of curriculum as "discovery and inquiry." It is not that discovery and inquiry are bad in themselves; effective teachers from Socrates onward have taught by inquiry and have urged their students to inquire and discover for themselves. But to substitute process, discovery, and inquiry for the sum total of social studies teaching and curriculum making is to misplace the emphasis, to distort the place inquiry can really have, and to distract from effective social studies teaching.

Essentially three aspects of the new approach to social studies teaching may be identified. These have to do with the following:

1. The curriculum of the social studies as process and structure.
2. The student of the social studies as a social scientist.
3. The social studies as behavioral science.

THE SOCIAL STUDIES AS STRUCTURE AND PROCESS

In examining new curriculum proposals for a sequential K-12 spiral curriculum, one is reminded of the Queen's statement in *Alice in Wonderland*: "Now, here, you see, it takes all the running you can do to keep in

Social Education, XXX:412-14, October 1966. Used by permission.

the same place. If you want to get somewhere you must run at least twice as fast." Most of the curriculum bulletins, though using the vocabulary of the new social studies, are running twice as fast but are essentially staying in the same place. A sequential structure that can be supported by evidence from the social sciences has yet to emerge, and, as a result, much of what has emerged from the hands of those eager to board the bandwagon of structure is a mere excuse for a spiral curriculum hastily pasted together and providing but a veneer of the allegedly new on a base of the genuinely old.

Current curriculum proposals might be accorded a greater measure of respect if they made a radical departure from the old and were solidly, daringly based on the concepts of Bruner and some of the proposals of E.S.I. Instead, because they hedge, because they are equally unprepared to discard the old or adopt the new, current curriculum designs represent for the most part some not very skillful juggling of units, topics, and subjects, and the more they change, the more they appear to remain essentially the same. Curriculum tinkering at best yields a niggardly harvest, at worst is educationally barren. Some wild oats of curriculum innovation have been sown and we may well reap a bitter harvest of social science illiterates.

Aggravating matters is the fact that materials for implementation for whatever is new in the curriculum remain to be provided, and the so-called creative teacher is still relied on to find the sources, edit and reproduce them, and make them available for classroom use. This overused dodge of responsibility has often resulted in an undue shift of the burden from the shoulders of curriculum makers, who logically should be able to provide appropriate materials to carry out their plans, to the shoulders of teachers who, with classes still too large and a myriad of other responsibilities, are unable to do so. Moreover, because of the highly sophisticated nature of the concepts with which the new curriculum designs attempt to deal, it is doubtful whether the great majority of teachers, whose professional preparation remains unfortunately still too limited, have the talent required to improvise in the future as they have in the past. It appears that we have already moved too far and too fast—faster in curriculum design than classroom materials actually permit—and some retrenchment is indeed in order lest teachers feel left so far behind that the race seems hardly worth running. The curriculum bulletins need but be scratched and we are down to what has traditionally been done—and, because the materials are not widely available, heralding the birth of a brave new world of social science teaching seems premature.

THE SOCIAL STUDIES AND THE SOCIAL SCIENTIST

Today the thought on the frontiers of social studies teaching is that students should be taught to think as historians, economists, or sociologists.

Teachers are asked to organize their instruction so that they show students how to use raw data to reconstruct the past, to make up models of economic activity, and to order social and behavioral patterns. One cannot help but wonder whether curriculum innovators want the student to prepare to learn the processes of the historian, the economist, and the sociologist, plus those of the geographer, the anthropologist, the political scientists, or whether they would be satisfied if the student learned one? And would they ignore the auxiliary professions upon which the social scientist depends, such as those of the archeologist, philologist, linguist, paleographer, chronologist, numismatist, and statistician?

The alternatives that Bruner and others have suggested certainly do provide an opportunity for students to acquire an *appreciation* of the work of the social scientist—but it is doubtful that we can make social scientists of many of them, and it is even more doubtful that a mode of inquiry common to history and the social and behavioral sciences can indeed be identified. Moreover, to have the student perennially assume the role of the social scientist and discover what the historian or economist already knows is artificial. At its best it is play acting and, if what the student discovers is quite contrary to what he should discover, the entire procedure becomes wasteful—if not downright ludicrous.

Essentially, before one can discover for himself he needs background, knowledge, information—as well as the process by which that knowledge has been acquired. What does it profit a pupil if he learns the process but loses the cultural perspective common to the human society? What does it profit a pupil if he learns process but cannot understand the place of men in the sweep of events that made this country what it is? What does it profit a pupil to discover—only to find that what he discovered does not even come close to what scholars believe actually took place? "Promoting the concept of discovery alone as a method of instruction is likely to be deceptive and a vain pursuit because it is incomplete. We should pay as much attention to the question of consolidating the student's new insights as to the methods for eliciting these insights." [1]

All this, and few dare mention the hard core reading disabilities found among students the nation over. I am not talking here about urban and rural disadvantages groups alone. Can one seriously believe that it is appropiate to talk of preparing students to think as social scientists think when too many pupils cannot read on or near the grade levels? Can we use the documents such as the Mayflower Compact, the diaries of John Adams, the essays of de Tocqueville, the log of Magellan, the letters of Cortez, that are urged upon us, with non-readers? There is much that can be done with pictures, models, artifacts and simplified reading sources;

[1] Bernard Z. Friedlander, "A Psychologist's Second Thoughts on Concepts, Curiosity, and Discovery in Teaching and Learning," *Harvard Educational Review, 35:30,* Winter 1965.

such has always been the case, but our success has not been spectacular. Whatever else we may do or wish to do, in the last analysis to be a student of the social studies, much less a social scientist, one must read.

And even if these obstacles did not stand in our way, the question would remain. Should we make social scientists of our students? If in the process of making social scientists we sacrifice the common heritage of mankind as a body of accumulated wisdom and knowledge which can and should be understood and appreciated, although admittedly not unquestioned or un-critically accepted, then the answer is a decided no. There is a store of human experience, as yet unfinished but worth studying; to that store some students may indeed consciously add, and all will, as adults, unconsciously contribute through their participation in the economic and political life of the human community. Among these experiences is the history of one's na-tion—a history, not to be examined either uncritically or chauvinistically, but to be discovered as a moving story of one people's struggle from sub-ject to citizen in a great society.

I, for one, am doubtful that this can be accomplished through induction alone, and I am skeptical of the possibilities of having students see the great overriding concept or generalization by giving them a worm's eye view of the experiences of one man, one explorer, one city, or what have you. It may be appropriate for biological scientists to study the life cycle of the amoeba and to glean from it insights into the life cycle of man. But it has yet to be demonstrated that the same procedure is appropriate for the student of the social studies. Can we in a limited period of time realistically build up an adequate reservoir of inductive experiences so that students can discover for themselves the theories of government upon which the Declaration of Independence depends, the nature and meaning of revolu-tion, the implications of nationalism and imperialism, the causes of war, the ways of peace, the structure of the Constitution, or the change in status that home rule brought when the revolution was won? Some alternatives to the procedures heretofore believed to be the sole arsenal of a teacher's strategy are indeed desirable, and inductive case studies are useful addi-tions to that arsenal and are surely appropriate. But to so structure an en-tire curriculum from K-12 is to fragmentize rather than unify the learning experience of the student.

HISTORY AND THE SOCIAL SCIENCES

Increasingly the shift has been away from history and to the behavioral sciences. Indeed, there are those who would have us believe that history is dead and that instead the social studies K-12 sequence should be ordered around anthropology. That anthropological and indeed sociological insights have for too long been neglected, one cannot deny. But to suggest that anthropology rather than history should be central to the structure around which the discipline of the social studies is to be built (if there is one) is to overlook the integrative possibilities inherent in the study of history.

To be sure, history for today's student must be very different from that which his teachers have studied. "It should not only record the achievement of the past, but also try to find analogies applicable to the confused present."[2] And surely in its study we must find "devices for stimulating insight and imagination, for shaking the mind loose from the tyranny of conventional words, unexamined clichés, and pleasantly familiar paths of thought."[3]

Although the social sciences can contribute enormously to its study, history remains the integrating discipline *par excellence*. It seeks to order man's experience in some intelligible pattern so that both the past and the present can be more appropriately and pertinently interpreted. "A people who cannot look back to their ancestors cannot look ahead to posterity," and to destroy the historical perspective of our students is to deny them an understanding of their heritage. Part of that heritage is anthropological and sociological to be sure—but to sever the trunk of the social studies curriculum and to expect its branches to flourish is to render a disservice to those we teach.

One cannot be unmindful of the outstanding work of Bruner and of some of those working in curriculum who are attempting to adapt his ideas to the needs of the social studies for today's schools—but it is the element of cultism, of the neo-orthodoxy which is already apparent, to which one must strenuously object.

There may be need for curriculum modification, but there is a greater need for more effective teachers. There may be need for a unified curriculum, but there is a greater need for first understanding the principles around which such a curriculum may be organized. There may be need for students to appreciate the mode of thought and the procedures of the historian and the social scientist, but there is a greater need to examine critically the accumulated store of experiences of the human community. There may be need for the inductive approach, yet the deductive cannot be summarily abandoned.

The changes inherent in the incipient revolution in the social studies are welcome, but only to the extent that they encourage teachers to go on with the job of teaching, in the best way they can, man's message to man.

[2]Thomas C. Cochran, *The Inner Revolution,* The Academy Library (New York: Harper and Row, 1964), p. 185.
[3]*Ibid.*

IIC-2.
The Teaching of Skills

JOHN R. O'CONNOR

Principal, Francis Scott Key Junior High School, Brooklyn, New York

32. Reading Skills in the Social Studies*

Generally, one is considered to be skilled if he possesses a high degree of competence in a trade, profession, a sport, or, in school, in a subject area. The student with skills is the one who is bright, superior, able to grasp information and insights with little apparent effort. On the other hand, we label as a "slow learner" the student who has few skills—and often consider it impossible for him to achieve proficiency in the use of the skills in the subject area. If this is so, we may as well surrender our efforts to teach the "slow learner," for truthfully, without skills, no one can succeed in the social studies.

"Slow learner" has become that convenient term by which educators describe any child who seems yearly to fall further behind in his efforts to master conventional subject matter. Most often, however, when a pupil is categorized as a slow learner, what is really meant is that he is a *slow reader*. There is nothing startling about the fact that some children read less capably than others. This has always been so, and as long as we continue to establish a norm that purports to represent the "average" reader, we will always have pupils who surpass the norm or lag behind it. Although there is considerable hesitation in admitting that we will inevitably have slower readers, no matter what we do in our schools, the truth is that a "norm" decrees by its nature that some must be slower than others.

The task of the teacher, therefore, is one of *raising the norm*, so that the slower reader of today is the equal of the better reader of yesterday. And this is not an unlikely promise, for studies in both the reading and

Social Education, XXXI:104–107, February 1967. Used by permission.

social studies abilities of present-day pupils reveal that slower readers of this age, in great part, achieve and surpass the norms established by standard measuring instruments of 30 years ago. [1]

In the social studies, the slow reader suffers because of the all-too-prevalent concept that a class must "cover" a certain amount of subject matter in an established number of weeks or months. The object of this article is not, however, to enter into a discussion of the nature of syllabi or the approaches to time allotments or emphasis upon the varied social studies disciplines. It is, rather, the censure of any orientation that provides lip service to social studies instruction without an emphasis upon social studies skills and the methods of instruction in those skills.

Let us admit, first, that the *basic social studies skills are reading skills.* Social studies teachers pride themselves on the fact that in their classes, if in few others, their pupils do read. After all, the textbook must be consumed and research must be carried out by means of a variety of reference materials. Assignments are made for out-of-class reading from library sources as well as the textbook. Often the daily homework assignment is, "Read pages 41 to 44 and answer these questions. . . ." Yes, the social studies student reads, or at least tries to read and to understand what is expected of him. But how does the slow learner—the slow reader—fare under this kind of reading program? Is he being taught to read within the framework of the social studies?

More often than not, the reading difficulty that plagues the majority of slow learners has caused them to fall behind in their social studies, and it has convinced them that they *cannot* read better than they do—and that failure awaits them again each time they renew the attempt. What is more, it probably does, unless there is a structure in social studies teaching that combines improvement in reading skills with the development of specific social studies skills, knowledges, and concepts. If there are certain skills whose development is an obligation shared by the social studies, we must *consciously* plan for their development. Students do not learn skills by chance. Inherent in any skills program is a fundamental concept: a skill must be taught, and it must be practiced, consciously and with effort.

In the 1963 NCSS Yearbook, *Skill Development in the Social Studies*, skills in which the social studies at least share responsibility for development are listed: locating and gathering information; organizing and evaluating information; reading, speaking, and listening; interpreting pictures,

[1] J. R. O'Connor, "Social Studies Achievement, 1932–1962." *High Points,* 46: 46–50; March 1964. Scores achieved by 207 seventh- and eighth-grade children on the Metropolitan Advanced Reading Test, Form A, administered in January 1964, were compared with scores attained by the same children on the Metropolitan Advanced Reading Test, Form A, 1932. Whereas 142 pupils were "below grade" in reading based on the 1962 norms, 84 were below grade on the 1932 test. No children in either grade were more than one year below grade based on the 1932 standard.

graphs, charts, and tables. Going further, Eunice Johns and Dorothy Fraser emphasize that these skills must be taught *functionally* and in the *context of study;* there should be repeated opportunity to *practice* the skill; and that skills instruction must move from the simple to the complex.[2]

We can heartily subscribe to all these suggestions and recognize the service they render in the development of social studies skills.

But let us be specific. The basic skill that leads to most others in the "shared" skills category is the ability of the student to find the *main idea* of a paragraph or section (or even a sentence). Without this ability, we can forget about our students being able to outline, summarize, or take notes effectively. Going further, all the skills involving critical thinking, substantiating opinions with proof, and supporting generalizations are based upon the ability of the youngster to determine the main, the important, the central thought of the spoken and written word. The ability to recognize the main idea and its supporting details is related to the ability to separate the relevant from the irrelevant.

But how often have we asked pupils to utilize these skills without having taught them, given opportunity for practice and reinforced them continually? Normally, a social studies teacher expects that the skills have been taught—by someone else in some other class. Even if they have been, a skill is not just taught; it must be practiced. This practice is necessary even for the student with a high intellectual capacity if he is to acquire the competence of which he is capable. The skilled carpenter and surgeon have practiced their arts after first having been taught them.

Do not think that the recognition of the main idea of a selection is too difficult for the slower reader. The frequency of error of our slower readers of junior high school age on standardized reading tests has been analyzed and has revealed that questions requiring pupils to determine the main thought of a paragraph are answered correctly *most* often. There have been more correct responses for questions involving the selection of the main thought than for questions that test the ability to note significant details or the meaning of words in context. This is true whether the pupils were reading at a fifth- or tenth-grade level. The task of the social studies is to apply this skill as emphasized in the 1963 Yearbook, functionally and in the context of study.

I am not suggesting that the social studies teachers become teachers of reading exclusively. I am suggesting that in the social studies we should know the skills our students possess and ought to possess—reading skills, let's call them—and that the ability to use these skills is fundamental to

[2]Eunice Johns and Dorothy McClure Fraser. "Social Studies Skills: A Guide to Analysis and Grade Placement," in Helen McCracken Carpenter, ed., *Skill Development in Social Studies*, National Council for the Social Studies, 33rd Yearbook (Washington, D. C., 1963), pp. 310 ff.

their success in their studies. Let us examine a few practical applications of reading skills to the social studies.

The teacher begins by selecting a textbook passage about three paragraphs in length. He asks the students to read silently each paragraph in turn and to select the main thought of the paragraph. (What is the paragraph about?) Inquiry is then made as to the reason for the selection. Members of the class are encouraged to comment on the choices of their classmates. (This kind of discussion will prove invaluable as students progress in ability and become concerned with the author's purpose in writing.) As a result of this procedure, the class will have selected three main ideas—three headings for a basic outline. Now the *reasons* for the selections of these important ideas are recalled; these are the details that support each of the headings. Thus, a simple outline has been developed, while subject matter has been learned. This kind of developmental process can be used again and again until it becomes part of the student's equipment whenever he is called upon to outline and summarize. Furthermore, how much better he can study and digest a new lesson on his own with this aid to learning available to him!

In performing a basic research assignment, students will build upon the process of making an outline. The shopworn project that requires a student to look for information in the library from some nebulous source and make a report with pictures and charts (to be finished in two weeks) must go! This kind of project is best entitled, "Frustrating the Slow Reader."

Rather specific materials must be known to the teacher and the students must be directed to them and instructed in their use. For example, students may read a specific article from a magazine, preferably one that the teacher has read, and submit five important ideas from the article. Then, in conference with the teacher or in a class situation, the reasons for the selection of these ideas may be discussed. Logically, students will follow the lessons learned in class on the method of determining the important ideas. Now the article may be reread for supporting statements. The details are filled in and the outline for the report is made before the student moves on, in due time and with sufficient planning, to the more complex outline or summary.

What would you think when you observe such a scene as this in a classroom? The class secretary is at the chalkboard prepared to record the notes of the class discussion. After a few minutes in which the class suggests problems resulting from the introduction of machinery in the eighteenth century, the teacher asks the class to suggest the *main idea* of the discussion. The secretary dutifully writes the suggestion on the board. The teacher then asks, "What have we discussed that supports this idea?" As the class responds, the secretary writes the sub-topics in proper outline form. A glance at pupil notebooks reveals that on a series of successive lessons pupils have recorded notes with the labels of "main idea" and "sub-topic" next to the statements recorded. It does not require great wisdom to discern that this class is going to use this procedure in all their work.

In the process, content has not been forsaken. In fact, the important ideas of the passage have been made more memorable. It is not idle guessing to state that the student will probably retain such information for a greater length of time as well. For the student is not only practicing a skill, he is focusing on the important ideas—and the use of the skill makes it possible.

The same emphasis prevails during the viewing of a film or in listening to a speaker. Listening is one of the "shared" skills. During the presentation, notes are recorded. Instead of an immediate discussion of the film or speech, which can become rambling in nature, it is most effective to have the students present the ideas they have selected from the notes they have just recorded. When these ideas are seen on the chalkboard, it will be obvious that there is considerable overlapping in wording; some are then condensed into a single idea, and the important ideas evolve. The message of the presentation is spotlighted through the important ideas presented, and the skill is being practiced functionally.

Stress on this technique during a talk will help to overcome a common criticism that students do not listen. Do we *direct* their listening? Do we check their listening skills by reading in short bursts and calling for a brief statement of the important idea of the selection? Do we afford the opportunity for youngsters to judge the relative importance of the speaker's words? The answer to these questions must be an affirmative, for most of us secure much of our information from the spoken word. Practice in listening is as important as practice in reading in the social studies. And, the intensity of the concentration is even greater, for there is no chance for the listener to refer to material already spoken. Just as we expect youngsters to look for clues and inferences in the written word, we hold the same expectation for them in the spoken word. Too often we have assumed that listening has taken place. We must be assured that it *has* taken place.

Hopefully, the traditional homework assignment of "Read and answer these questions" is on its way out with the slow learner. Quite honestly, this type of assignment does have for its purpose the elicitation of the important ideas of the reading assignment. But if we wish our youngsters to concentrate on the location of important ideas and facts, why don't we specifically ask them to do so. The assignment may just as easily read (and with greater value in its statement of purpose and development of skill): "Read pages 61 and 62. Select the main idea of the first paragraph; select the main idea of paragraphs 2 through 5." The approach has been altered but not the emphasis, and the skills practice may result in better understanding than the search for specific and unrelated items.

Instead of "Identify these words or terms," we can ask: "What word in the second paragraph means the same as "growing in amount"? In the following paragraph as "route or road"? In the last paragraph as "journey to a holy place"? And the student might even be asked, after instruction in the skills of determining the meanings of words in context, to name the *clues that helped him* to tell the meaning of the word or expression.

Part of the task in improving skills, and perhaps the greatest part, is proving to the student that he can learn. He must succeed, and he will succeed as the instruction in skills becomes basic, specific, and continual. Even such an advanced skill as skimming for content can be taught to the slow reader, once he is convinced that he can do it. The fascinating instrument, the controlled reader, can be so manipulated as to convince the youngster that he can read faster than he believes he can by starting him at a faster rate and then slowing the rate until he is able to read with understanding. He will find that he is reading with comprehension at a rate that he believed was beyond his grasp.

The ability to skim social studies materials can be demonstrated by this simple process. Students are asked to open their books to a page selected by the teacher (preferably one without sub-headings) and simply read the first sentence of three or four paragraphs. Then, they close their books. After the sentences have been written or paraphrased on the chalkboard (or have been previously prepared for the overhead projector) a pattern appears in these sentences. The class is asked what this page is all about. You may be surprised how well they can determine the topic being discussed and even give a tentative title for the passage. Most often, the leading sentences become headings for an outline of the passage —and this understanding has accrued *before* the selection has been fully read. The reaction of students to this demonstration is evidence that here is a stimulus to intensive effort in the improvement of skills, for they have learned quickly and dramatically that they have the abilities that are useful, and that practice will sharpen them to a keen edge.

Students are expected to reason. This reasoning may involve the ability to make inferences from the spoken word or written materials. Allied with the inferential ability are the skills of drawing conclusions, forming hypotheses, and making generalizations and judgments. All of these are skills of the social studies, and they are important components of instruments used to measure reading ability.

Our teachers have developed a group of questions that they have come to term "collateral questions." Their purpose is to develop in youngsters the ability to infer, predict, and characterize people and events. For example:

What would be a good title for this selection?
From what you have read, would you guess that . . . ?

As a result of this action, would you say that . . . ?
Reading between the lines, what do you think of the statement
that . . . ?
What will probably happen when . . . ?
What do you think the result would have been if . . . ?
What word would you use to describe . . . ?
How would you characterize this person or event?

Of course, not all of these questions are posed in a single class session,
nor are all of them adaptable for every lesson. But the possession by teachers of a fund of questions with specific purposes leads to the kind of thinking on the part of students that assists in the development of "thinking"
skills. All of these are inherent in social studies instruction, and they
would be used more often if there was an awareness of their purpose
and their contribution toward the success we seek with our slow learners—
and our rapid learners as well.

Unfortunately for our slower readers, new patterns in the social studies
do not seem to take him into account. Emphasis on research materials has
always required specific skills in the social studies. Now, there is an increasing emphasis on the ability to derive information from original
documents. Curriculum planners have not faced squarely the problem of
the slower reader in the "new emphasis." Quite honestly, new curricula
will have little effect on any student who does not possess reading competence. There is little use in changing our areas of emphasis in the social
studies without concerning ourselves with the most vital of means by which
objectives are to be accomplished. It is certainly not in our interest to
omit one-third of our students from the benefits of a new focus. There is an
increasing need for the concern of *all* social studies teachers with the reading competence of *all* our students.

Herein lies a possible flaw in planning—unless adaptations are made
individually by teachers everywhere. One can foresee the barriers placed
before some of the youngsters when asked to read the Magna Carta, the
Emancipation Proclamation, or a Supreme Court decision. For what good
is familiarity with a document if it cannot be read with comprehension?
Yet, the opportunities for reading growth are more readily available to us
in the new curricula than even before. The opportunities cannot be lost.
They will not be if social studies instructional practices are a reflection of
the inherent importance of reading skills and their application within
the framework of the social studies. There is no doubt that, if reading
improvement is going to take place, social studies teachers are going to be
the primary source of the improvement.

This is not an attempt to be either comprehensive or definitive on the
subject of reading-social studies skills. I have tried to convey my deep concern at the assumption by some that what we should be doing in this field

is not our proper function. *All* our students need instruction in fundamental skills. Of particular concern is the success of our slower readers,
whose abilities can be harnessed within a structure that enables them to
grow and succeed or who can be left to flounder and fail because they do
not possess the necessary building tools. We are concerned with the need
to "reach" the slow reader. Make no mistake—such pupils can succeed,
and the development of basic skills in both social studies and reading is a
primary step in the process.

HENRY W. BRAGDON

Editor, New England Social Studies Bulletin

33. Teaching Writing Through History*

English is not a subject, like physics or geography or Latin. It is a universal skill, and every teacher of academic subjects should be in some degree a teacher of English.

One of the English teacher's strongest allies is the history teacher. There are all sorts of ways in which the history teacher can and should give training in writing. He may assign research papers, book reports, précis of documents, and formal arguments in matters of controversy. And his every test should require written answers.

Yet in hundreds of high schools the classes in history, civics, problems of democracy, and so forth, do very little writing, and in some, none at all. A recent bulletin for teachers from a state board of education lists thirty-one separate "activities" which "the modern teacher of social studies" should promote in her "classroom laboratory." There are "planning activities," "reading activities," and "storing activities." There are "reporting and reciting" and "carrying out research," but no specific mention of writing.

Part of this lack of interest stems from the change from history to social studies. A generation ago, the study of history in many schools was a meaningless round of learning dead facts and regurgitating them on paper. In justifiable rebellion against this profitless business came the idea that the study of man in society should concentrate on real problems, such as public housing or agencies for world peace, instead of the Kansas-Nebraska Act or the Tariff of 1816. Students should be trained in social skills, such as making oral reports and carrying on discussions.

Now, writing is not an obvious social skill. It is, in fact, a lonely business, and a person engaged in writing of necessity withdraws from the group. Indifference, even apathy toward writing is increasing. I have seen it argued in an educational journal that, while the ability to write may be a graceful accomplishment, in an audio-visual age it is no more necessary than playing the violin.

Another influence toward the abandonment of pen and paper is the so-called objective test, in which the candidate simply checks off the answers. There can be no question that objective tests have been refined until

Atlantic Monthly, 204:118–20, November 1959. Used by permission.

they are increasingly successful in their primary task of measuring achievement and predicting future success. The difficulty is that they have entered the classroom. Schools can purchase objective tests designed for any standard course or text. This relieves teachers of the burden of concocting their own questions and reduces correction to the purely mechanical process of checking off the right answers.

The results of the abandonment of writing have been appalling. In 1955 a College Board committee tried out simple essay questions on several hundred freshmen recently admitted to top-ranking colleges. At least 80 percent of the candidates failed, and about 40 percent failed abysmally. They did not know how to analyze a problem, or how to relate what they knew to it, or how to hitch one limping sentence to another in ordered sequence.

Objective tests have little place in a properly run history course for academically competent students. They imply that knowing history is simply a matter of guessing the right answer, and they suggest that there are simple right and wrong answers to complex problems. Above all, they encourage teachers to evade their obligation to share with English teachers the duty of teaching effective writing.

With the increasing awareness that American education has slighted the gifted, there has been a return to written tests. All the tests given, for instance, in the Advanced Placement Program of the College Entrance Examination Board are primarily written. So far, however, this program affects only the ablest students in the strongest schools. Even in this privileged area there has been too little serious thought about what written tests should do. Here is a question asked in a famous Eastern preparatory school:

Describe the four reasons for the Seven Years' War.

The first "the" gives this question away. The boy answering it has been taught that there are four official causes of the Seven Years' War and now is asked simply to hand them back. A question in history or social studies should be so designed that it encourages the candidate to write something approaching an essay. Furthermore, the answer should be judged for its quality as an essay, as well as for historical content.

Generalizations are fruitless unless supported. So essay questions should ask for facts, hard facts, but insist that they be related to the question. Students are tempted to parade what they remember, regardless of relevance. They should lose credit if they have not *aimed* the facts at the problem under discussion.

Some teachers, although agreeing that the essay question has its uses, fear that without testing on specific details students will not learn facts. Yet testing nothing but facts encourages the notion that they are important in isolation. A teacher can get across the idea that facts are vital only insofar as they have significance by the use of short written questions such as the following:

> Explain the interrelationships between FOUR of the following pairs:
> 1) Lenin: :Mensheviks
> 2) Poland: :Danzig
> 3) Five Year Plan: :Kulaks
> 4) Beer Hall Putsch: :March on Rome
> 5) Munich Conference: :Self-determination

These keep emphasis on the generalizations which tie facts together, rather than on rote knowledge. Each is designed to produce a little essay, in which skill in written expression, judgment, and ingenuity count.

Effective essay questions do not just happen. They have to be devised with many factors in mind: what the students have studied in class and outside, how far advanced they are, how much time is allowed, just how much progress toward a new juxtaposition of material can be fairly demanded, whether the directions are clear and understandable.

Phrasing is immensely important. A certain element of challenge can release the floodgates and make a student write better than he thought he could. Consider these two questions:

> Explain the effects of the Emancipation Proclamation.
> Describe what you consider to be three principal causes of the War of 1812.

There is nothing especially wrong with these, but you can nudge the pupil toward setting up an argument rather than just retelling what he knows by presenting paradoxes:

> "The Emancipation Proclamation did not free a single slave." Is this true?
> Explain why the War for Seamen's Rights was opposed in maritime Massachusetts and supported in inland Kentucky.

It is easy to go off the track. Here is a former College Board question which turned out badly:

> How did Hamilton and Jefferson disagree on economic and political questions? Show why two political parties developed out of the conflict.

The trouble with this was that most candidates wrote not one essay but two, failing to tie together the two parts of the question. It would have been an improvement to have hitched them together in the question:

> "Out of the disagreement between Hamilton and Jefferson on economic and political questions developed two political parties." Explain this quotation.

It is important to remember that the way students are tested often determines how they will study. There is almost universal testimony from teachers that pupils will study less hard for an objective than an essay test, if only because in the former there is always the hope of guessing the answer. But assume two equally conscientious students putting in equal time on the same material, one studying for an essay test and the other for an objective test. You will find that they are likely to tackle their reviewing quite differently. The objective test, with its many items—a hundred responses an hour is standard—tends to put emphasis on particular facts or concepts, so the student prepares as he might for a quiz-kid program. The essay examination emphasizes the larger picture, and to do well the student must grasp the main ideas and relate details to them.

It is often a useful practice to give out essay questions in advance. If these are chosen with care, the students will usually study with more purpose than if left to their own devices. One could fairly well take care of the period of the 1920s in American history by telling a class that it will be asked to assess one or the other of the following quotations:

"The business of America is business."

—Calvin Coolidge

"America has evaded her responsibilities as a world power, and has retreated into a sullen and selfish isolationism."

—Woodrow Wilson

Essay questions usually involve exposition, but they can also be used to stimulate the imagination. Each of the following questions has produced answers which revealed that some students could project themselves into the past and think in terms of a society alien in space, time, or culture:

Assume yourself to be an Athenian peasant at the time of Solon and explain what the introduction of money had meant to you and your family.

Assume yourself to be an Athenian gentleman of the fourth century B.C. miraculously transported by a time machine to America and endowed with the ability to speak English. Explain in a connected narrative your reactions to any THREE of the following: a dinner party, a professional wrestling match, a play, Congress.

Assume yourself to be the Spanish ambassador to the court of Queen Elizabeth. Write a letter home, giving your impressions of the Queen and of her foreign policy.

The above questions were given out in advance so that the students could think out possible answers, but all the writing was done in a single class period, with no more notes than could be put on a single three by five inch card. Put under pressure, students write better than if they had time to polish.

This "you were there" type of question is especially valuable when it can be tied in with contemporary source material. Having already studied a period in texts, a class can get the feeling of the times by browsing through magazines of the period. The following question was designed to create awareness of that grim era when the democracies seemed helpless against the rise of totalitarianism:

> Assume yourself to be someone living during the period between the Munich crisis in September, 1938, and the fall of Poland in September, 1939, and give your opinion about the future of democracy.

This produced, among other characterizations, a Nazi waiter talking to an American newspaperman in a Munich beer garden; a Polish exile in a Paris bistro; and an ex-Communist, a young man who had joined the Communist Party during the Farmers' Holiday in 1933, while at the University of Iowa, and who was now, in September, 1939, writing to a former Comrade to explain why he had just resigned from the Party and was on his way to join the Canadian R.A.F.

The illustrations of essay questions given here have nearly all come from one school with a strong academic tradition and a selected student body. It may be argued therefore, that the training in writing and analysis suggested is beyond the reach of the general run of students. But surely we are increasingly aware that those able to profit by rigorous academic training need special attention just as much as slow and "exceptional" children. There are many high school teachers, too, who believe that the essay test can be used with great benefit for all students within the normal range of ability. In a number of high schools, essay tests are graded by the English department as well as the social studies department.

Practical objection to the use of essay tests may come from those who point out that essay testing will impose further duties on already burdened teachers. It cannot be done, at least not well, by a teacher with a pupil load of 180 to 200, meeting twenty-five classes each week and patrolling study periods, a home room, and the school cafeteria between times. The answer is to lighten the burden, even if it costs money. In *The American High School Today*, James B. Conant recommends that the pupil load of English teachers be limited to 100 pupils in order to allow for the correcting of weekly themes. If the social studies teacher should also require constant writing, his teaching load should also be limited.

The essay test is a major means, and a far too neglected one, of teaching a pupil "to learn to argue a case and weigh evidence, to seize the point at issue, to arrange his thoughts and marshal facts to support a theory, to discover when a statement is proved and when it is not, to reason logically and express himself clearly—in fact, to play the great game of the intellect."

WALTER E. McPHIE

Associate Professor of Social Studies Education, University of Utah

34. Student Reports and the Social Studies*

"In our study of this unit," the social studies teacher explained to the students in his United States history class, "I want two volunteers to prepare reports on Alexander Hamilton and Thomas Jefferson. Unfortunately, you won't have very much time because we will need the reports tomorrow, but they need not be very long—and I don't think it will require too much effort. Of course, I will give extra credit to the two students who volunteer."

Following the usual period of hesitation which inevitably accompanies requests of this nature, two volunteers were "obtained" and the class resumed its normal routine. Apparently the only ones still giving any thought to the reports at this point were the two students who were wondering uncomfortably if they had made a mistake in letting themselves get "roped" into this assignment.

The next day, at the appointed hour, the teacher asked, somewhat doubtfully, if the assigned reports were ready. Receiving an affirmative reply, he instructed the student whose report dealt with Alexander Hamilton to speak first; the report on Thomas Jefferson would follow. Accordingly, the two student "volunteers" stood before the class and, each in his turn, read monotonously sterile, but factual, accounts of the lives of the two men. It was difficult to question the accuracy of the reports since both had been taken nearly verbatim from widely accepted and highly sophisticated sets of encyclopedia. Of course, each student had changed a word or two in various places to avoid absolute plagiarism—and one boy had even deleted several sentences which contained words which he could neither understand nor pronounce—but basically it was a "copy job" exactly like almost every other student report presented in class that year. The fact that the students in the class were bored, the teacher was bored, and even the students presenting the reports were bored didn't appear to surprise or bother anyone. Following the reports, the teacher asked if there were any questions, but since no one cared or knew enough about the topics to ask intelligent questions, there were none. The teacher then thanked the boys politely for their efforts, quickly glossed over the fact

*Social Education, XXX:96–98, February 1966. Used by permission.

that perhaps it might have been better if the reports had not been read —and then everyone appeared to be relieved that the whole thing was over.

If the above account appears to be a bit "overdone" in its portrayal of a poor teaching situation, the reader is indeed fortunate. Many readers will recognize, all too painfully, that it represents a fairly realistic scene which is repeated daily in schools throughout the nation. In a few cases the fault lies with teachers who are either lazy or just do not care. This article is expected to have little or no effect upon them. However, in many instances, failure is due to an honest lack of understanding of how to implement student reports effectively. It is hoped that this paper will assist teachers who may have such a problem.

What is a student report? First and foremost, if a teacher is going to use student reports effectively, he must know what they are. To say that student reports constitute a *method of teaching* sounds so simple as to be utterly ridiculous. However, if it is thoroughly understood that when a teacher assigns a student to give a report, he is in fact using a teaching method, this understanding might supply the key to the problem. Student reports are *not* something which must be done periodically to break monotony. They are *not* something which, when absent, necessarily indicate poor teaching. They are *not* something all teachers must demand, and, certainly, they are *not* something Mr. Smith must call for if he wishes to keep pace with Mr. Brown. Student reports constitute *a method of achieving an educational goal*—just as assigning students passages to read in textbooks, giving a lecture, holding a question-answer session, etc., are methods of achieving educational goals.

When should student reports be used? If it is correct to conclude that student reports can be described as a teaching method and that teaching methods are used to achieve educational goals, it follows that whenever a teacher uses a student report he should do so with a particular goal in mind. If a teacher accepts his responsibility for selecting the most important concepts from any course of study and teaching them to the best of his ability, then, whenever he decides to use a student report, it will be because that particular method is suited to the teaching of a given concept better than any other method. Of course, the teacher may have goals in mind other than the acquisition of subject matter understanding. For example, he may want to teach his students how to do elementary research, how to organize the results of such research, and how to report research findings to a group in the most effective manner. The fact that student report method can be used to develop both subject matter understanding *and* skills at the same time is an indication of the importance of such a method. However, the critically important thing to be remembered when contemplating the use of a student report is that it must never be used in a "vacuum," in a manner unrelated to specific goals. Whenever a student report is used in a classroom, specific results in terms of the achievement of some goal or goals should not only be anticipated but strictly required.

How can student reports be used most effectively? Perhaps another look at the example given at the outset of this article will be helpful in discussing the effective use of student reports. Undoubtedly the unit on United States history which the class was studying embodied events which included such important personalities as Alexander Hamilton and Thomas Jefferson. Again undoubtedly, the teacher thought the students ought to know *something* about the lives of these two men, and therefore felt justified in assigning reports. However, it is at this point that a rather serious weakness in the thinking and planning of the teacher becomes apparent. If the entire course of United States history were approached on a *students-should-know-something* basis, very few positive results could be anticipated. If a method needs to be preceded by a goal, certainly a more definite goal than "something" is needed to merit a student report. If, however, the teacher in this example had a more specific goal in mind, his manner of presenting the assignment did not indicate it.

A teacher's work and responsibility do not diminish when using student reports. Far from it. They are as important and demanding as ever. The teacher who assumes that he can "take it easy" while the students give the reports hasn't understood the first principle of using this method. What *should* the students know and understand about Hamilton and Jefferson? This is the key question which the teacher needed to answer for himself *before* assigning the reports to the students. He needed to determine in a rather specific way what his teaching goals were *before* he chose the method to be employed. He may have decided that it would be in the best interests of his students to give them a brief overview of the early childhood and growing-up period of each of these two men, including some of the major influences which shaped their lives. He may have wished to present a selected few of the major contributions each man made to his country. Perhaps he may have decided that a comparison of the political and economic views held by each of these patriots was in order. Or, perhaps, he may have chosen emphases which differ totally from those already suggested. Probably no one can say what precise information *should* have been selected for such a report, but the teacher's maturity, background, and training had prepared him to accept the professional responsibility to give direction and assistance in this regard. In this he failed.

Once the teacher made the decision as to the most important concepts to be learned about Hamilton and Jefferson, the most effective method needed to be determined. Once again, there were many alternatives. He might have decided to assign specific materials to be read by all the students with the intent of using the newly acquired information as a basis for discussion. He might have used a movie or a slide film which emphasized the points he desired to drive home. Role-playing might have been effective if the two students chosen to play the parts were helped sufficiently to acquire adequate background. The methods and approaches which might have been used in achieving this particular educational goal were almost limitless, but in the case of our example the use of student reports was the teaching method selected—a defensible choice, if handled effectively.

Perhaps there are certain steps which, if followed, would permit teachers to get the best results from the use of student reports. While not everyone may agree completely with the steps suggested below, the basic elements are represented. It is not difficult to see that, had the teacher in the example used such a procedure, certainly he would have accomplished much more than he did.

1. As was pointed out above, the first step is for the teacher to decide that the use of student reports is the best method for achieving some specific educational goal or goals which have been selected on the basis of careful consideration. If another method will do the job more effectively, all things being equal, student reports as a method should be set aside until they will serve best.

2. When the assignment is made, sufficient time should be allowed for the students to prepare themselves adequately for the reports. The teacher has the right and the responsibility to demand quality work from the students who are developing the reports—but not if the students have been forced to do a superficial job due to a lack of time.

3. In consultation with the students, who have either been selected by the teacher or who have volunteered, the teacher should designate rather specifically the kinds of information which are to be expected in the reports. Since the teacher should have already given serious thought to the selection of important facts and concepts relative to the topic being taught, he should experience little difficulty in pointing the students in the right direction. Obviously, this does not mean preparing the reports for the students, putting words in their mouths, or drawing conclusions for them; there should be ample room for the talents of the students to be demonstrated. It does mean, however, that the efforts of the students will be focused in some direction, in order that some logical, orderly, and, meaningful information can be anticipated.

4. The students may need some assistance in locating sources of information. Again, the teacher should not do the work for the students; this should be a valuable research experience for them. But students must learn *how* to do proper and meaningful research and, therefore, they very likely will need teacher assistance.

5. Teachers should expect to help students synthesize information obtained from their research into a concise and well-organized report. Further assistance may be needed in the preparation of notes from which the students may present their reports without resorting to "reading every word."

6. The presentation of the report will also need teacher criticism and suggestions. Students need to learn how to make their reports interesting as well as informational by using vocal emphases, by avoiding pacing back-and-forth or statue-like rigidity, by using chalkboards, maps, diagrams, graphs, charts, globes, pictures, etc., to illustrate, and by pacing the presentation so that it neither drags nor races.

7. At the conclusion of the report, members of the class should be permitted and encouraged to ask pertinent questions. The students who give the reports should probably be given the opportunity to answer the queries first, but the teacher and other students may be brought into the discussion with considerable profit. Much clarification is gained by so doing.

8. After the question session, the teacher should be prepared to add to the presentation or make corrections if necessary. Though the students have received guidelines from the teacher, it is probable that some significant ideas have been glossed over superficially or neglected completely. If that is the case, the teacher should recognize that his teaching method (student reports) has not been completely successful and, just as with any other method which fails to achieve the objective completely, compensatory action must be taken.

9. Unless the teacher takes special care, there is danger that only the students who prepare the reports will derive benefit from them. Members of the class need to be made aware of the fact that they are expected to pay just as close attention to the students who are giving the reports as they would to the teacher. Valuable class and preparation time has been expended in order that reports will provide profitable learning experiences. Therefore, it would appear to be logical and altogether proper for the teacher to include test questions which have been drawn from the material presented in the reports in regular examinations.

By way of summary, if teachers will plan carefully where they are going and then choose the method, or methods, which appear most likely to accomplish the task, they will establish a solid foundation for successful teaching. And, when student reports are judged to be the most appropriate method for achieving a given educational goal, if teachers will allow sufficient time for adequate preparation, demand quality performance, assist the student in seeing what needs to be emphasized, in finding information, in organizing and synthesizing their material, and in learning how to present their reports most effectively, they can justifiably expect pleasant educational experiences and positive, rewarding results.

RALPH ADAMS BROWN

*Professor of History, State University, College of Education,
Cortland, New York*

35. The Use of Outline Maps*

Quality and excellence are key words in our time. We hear less about personality development and more about solid work in mathematics, less about social adjustment and more about home work, less about automatic promotion and more about honest grades, less about protecting the inferior student and more about challenging the superior boy and girl.

Starting with a new emphasis upon mathematics and science, just after the Russians placed Sputnik I in orbit, this emphasis upon excellence, upon academic ability, has spread throughout our public school system. Rightly so, for in the final battle for the minds and hearts of mankind, excellence in English or art or social studies is just as important as in mathematics or science.

In accepting the challenge of our time, the demand that students be required to work, to learn, to think at higher levels and increased tempo, teachers are turning to new materials and new techniques. We hear much about teaching machines, E.T.V., programmed learning. It would be barely short of tragic if, in the process of adopting and adapting these newer aids, we forgot or ignored those tools that have served us well in the past.

One of the most effective tools that the social studies teacher can use—and it can also be used by teachers of languages, music, art, science and literature—is the *outline map*.

In general, an *outline map* is considered to be a flat map on which only the minimum of boundaries is shown. Occasionally such maps also show principal rivers and mountains. Most frequently used are the desk maps. Each student is provided with a map, either for the purpose of following instruction in class, or for a work assignment. Larger outline maps, known as wall outline maps, are also useful. This is especially true when the teacher is lecturing or introducing a unit of work.

One of the real advantages of the outline map is its inexpensiveness. No school system at all familiar with the terrific expense of the newer techniques and materials should hesitate to purchase outline maps in generous quantity.

Two of the most difficult relationships for children in the lower ele-

Social Studies, 52:167–70, October 1961. Used by permission.

mentary grades are the problems of time and place. Perhaps nothing is so valuable in overcoming the latter problem as the outline map. This may be a simple, hand-drawn map of the school grounds and the neighboring streets, prepared by the teacher and used by the smaller children. Such maps can be completed by the youngsters—naming of streets, locating houses and street crossings and stop-lights, and even showing compass directions.

Outline maps can be used by any alert teacher to promote a feeling of place security and place sense. The teacher may start with outline maps of his state and then progress to larger political units.

This matter of simple location is important. Skill in place location and the development of real place sense come with frequent practice. This writer doubts that any device or method can be used to develop in pupils a real understanding of place location and place relationship as effectively as can be done with individual outline maps.

Feature identification is also important. The fifth-grade youngster, studying American history, is at a real disadvantage if he cannot look at a map and identify the Missouri and the Mississippi Rivers correctly. This identification, like place location, needs to be repeated often and continued through the intermediate grades.

In both review and testing, the social studies teacher in the elementary grades can make frequent and effective use of outline maps. The large wall-type outline is wonderful for review sessions. Individual desk maps are often used for part of an examination.

This use of outline maps for both review and testing can be extended into the junior and senior high school. It is important that social studies teachers in grades seven through twelve continue some of the exercises in geographical appreciation and understanding that were initiated in the middle grades. High school and college teachers of history, for example, frequently complain because their students are, they claim, geographically illiterate. They thus overlook the fact that they themselves are in part at fault; that history and geography are inexorably linked, and therefore that no teacher of one can afford to ignore the other.

From time to time exercises in place location and in identification should be assigned, all through the junior and senior high school years. For ease of both assignment and checking, the use of commercially prepared outline maps is superior to any other method. Such exercises assist the student in retaining knowledge of place, distance and direction that he first acquired in the middle grades.

All map assignments in the secondary school should be made in recognition of the value of progression from the simple to the complex, from the easy to the more difficult. While many teachers in the intermediate grades may use this principle in planning their work, there should be conscious acceptance of it in grades seven through twelve. Individual differences can be accommodated in this way, but every high school student should realize that his map work is becoming more difficult. For one example, the simple location of the Missouri River has value in a class of fifth graders learning about Lewis and Clark for the first time. An eighth or eleventh grade class, however, should be able to relate the Missouri to such other features as the Continental Divide, the Columbia River, the problem of flood control on the lower Mississippi.

The major use of outline maps in secondary school social studies classes is related to learning or at least to demonstrating relationships. When we think in terms of challenging gifted students, of encouraging sound thinking and critical analysis, or even of the task of developing an intelligent awareness of problems and conditions among all citizens, this matter of relationships becomes a factor of major importance.

In discussing the use of outline maps, numerous writers have argued that an outline map, especially the individual desk map, should be used to locate or show only a single feature. The basic reasoning here is good; it hangs upon the easily established fact that a map which is cluttered by too much detail becomes meaningless to the student.

In the elementary grades no one would argue with the above point of view. A sixth-grade class, busy with the location of European capitals, should not be asked to include pre-Versailles national boundaries on the same map. A fifth-grade class at work establishing the principal routes of travel to the Far West, should not be asked to inlude the dates, names and boundaries of our territorial acquisitions.

As we reach more advanced work on the secondary level, however, there is a real justification for the use of an outline map to include two or more features. This should never be the attempt of a teacher to economize—these maps are so inexpensive anyway—but rather should be done to show relationships. Recognizing and really understanding relationships can often be among the most important values derived from work in the social sciences.

Such a relationship sometimes involves two geographic features. A high school teacher of American history, in connection with a unit on the American Revolution, might give each of his students an outline map and then make the following assignment: "On this outline map of the southeastern United States, I want you to locate two sets of data. First, the principal rivers in Virginia and the two Carolinas. Second, the principal centers of population during the last half of the eighteenth century. On the classroom shelves you will find several books to help you. Among these are the large historical atlas of the United States that we were using last week, Lossing's *Pictorial Field Book of the American Revolution,* and the *West Point Atlas of American Wars.* Other books, including our own textbook, will be of help. This map will be due a week from next Wednesday."

On the day the above assigned maps became due, the teacher might display a wall map showing the routes of Cornwallis, Campbell and Green, as well as the principal "hideouts" of Marion and Sumter, during the Revolution. He might then conduct a discussion that would revolve around (a) the reasons for the British campaigns in the Southern states, (b) the importance of rivers to both civilian living and military occupation, and finally (c) the relationship between transportation, communication and population growth.

Some teachers will at once protest that their school libraries do not contain the books and materials necessary for such an assignment. Many of the same final objectives, though not all of the work experiences, can be obtained if the teacher will display several wall maps showing principal geographical features and population centers. Then the students can transfer the appropriate information to their own outline maps.

Another example of the use of outline maps to show the relationship between two geographic factors would be to take an outline map of the eastern United States and show, in one color, the principal routes to the western settlements between 1750 and 1815. Then, with another color, show the principal settlements west of the mountains between 1775 and 1815. Students preparing and discussing such a map would gain new and perhaps lasting appreciation of the role of rivers and mountain passes in establishing the pattern of our Westward movement.

A different type of relationship that can be shown by the use of outline maps involves a geographic and an economic factor. For instance, a class in world history, studying the expansion of Europe in the 16th century, might be given this double assignment. On an outline map of the world, students could be asked to show the principal seaports and trade routes known to exist at some period such as 1650 to 1700. Then on the same map, with different shading or color, the students could show the territorial claims and principal settlements of Spain, Portugal, Holland and Great Britain.

Another comparable assignment, involving geographic and economic factors, could be used in either the eighth or eleventh grades. A class studying the Civil War and its background, might be given an outline map. The class could be asked to locate the areas where cotton, corn and wheat were produced in the decade of the 1850's. On the reverse of the map they might prepare graphs to show changes in annual production of each of the three commodities. The final step would be to locate all railroads existing in 1850, and then to show new railroad construction between 1850 and 1860. Students with such information on their desks are in a position to understand the roles of agricultural production and railroad building in such events or conditions as the vote of the Northwest for Lincoln in 1860, the decision of the South to secede, and the neutrality of Great Britain.

Yet a third way of using outline maps to combine two types of information deals with cultural and economic data. A class in senior high school American history might show, on desk outline maps, those areas of the nation where the quantity and the value of manufacturing increased between 1890 and 1910. Using a different color or shading, the students could then show on the same map the percentage increase in foreign born residents during the same period.

A somewhat similar exercise would be to show the extent of a certain industry, at intervals of ten, twenty or fifty years. Four maps might show the location of the textile industry in 1850, 1875, 1900 and 1925. The percentage of inhabitants of different national groups might be shown for each major manufacturing area, on each of the four maps. Thus a teacher could illustrate such facts as: (1) the new immigrant usually did the most unpleasant or poorest-paid work, and (2) certain national groups seemed to work in sequence. (For example, in the New England textile mills the Irish were followed by the Polish and they, in turn, by the French-Canadians.)

The above illustrations can be multiplied, a hundred times, by any imaginative social studies teacher. There is a real need for more vital, dynamic and imaginative instruction in the social studies. One way to move in that direction is through the expanded use of desk and wall outline maps.

LESLIE P. CUMMINGS

Department of Geography, University of Iowa

36. Using Maps and Diagrams More Effectively*

Despite the attention which has been given to map reading and map-making skills by professional geographers, curriculum study groups, textbook writers, and others, maps and graphs are often inadequately used in the teaching of geography. As Kohn has reported, ". . . tests given to freshmen entering our colleges and universities demonstrate over and over that map making and map-reading skills are not being well developed in most elementary and secondary schools."[1]

One of the reasons for the inadequate grounding in mapwork is the lack of interest-creating factors in many geography classes. There are at least two possible ways to improve this situation:

1. Prepare more lessons in which the mapping of spatial distributions is a central part of the classwork.
2. Introduce some of the ideas now used only at the college level.

To illustrate, two recent articles on population pyramids[2] discuss pyramids as graphic methods useful in portraying population structure. Such diagrams might be introduced in a lesson dealing with the development of generalizations relating to the age structure of a country's population. Similar graphs can be used to depict employment structure, as well as age-sex relationship, as in Figure 36-1.

At the junior high school level pyramids similar to these might be constructed on graph paper by different members of the class, then colored and displayed on a wall map of the world so that differences and similarities in the population structure of the world's political units might be visualized more readily. Data for the construction of these diagrams are readily available in the *United Nations Demographic Yearbook*.

Social Education, XXX:623–26, December 1966. Used by permission.
[1] C. F. Kohn, in James D. Koerner, ed., *Case for Basic Education* (Boston: Atlantic–Little, Brown and Co., 1959), p. 67.
[2] Frank Seawell and Jerome Clemens, "A Population Profile," *The Professional Geographer,* 16:20, March 1964; L. D. B. Heenan, "The Population Pyramid: A Versatile Research Technique," *The Professional Geographer,* 17:18–21, March 1965.

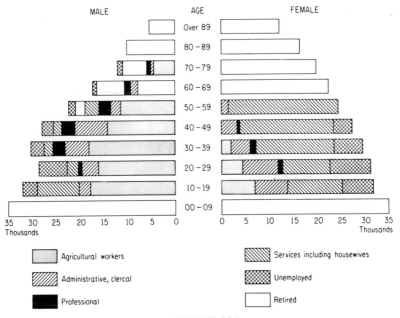

MALE   AGE   FEMALE

Over 89
80 – 89
70 – 79
60 – 69
50 – 59
40 – 49
30 – 39
20 – 29
10 – 19
00 – 09

35 30 25 20 15 10 5 0   0 5 10 15 20 25 30 35
Thousands   Thousands

Agricultural workers   Services including housewives

Administrative, clercal   Unemployed

Professional   Retired

FIGURE 36-1

PORTRAYING SURFACES ON MAPS

Ninth and tenth graders can be introduced to many of the more abstract concepts underlying spatial distributions. One of these concepts is that of "surface." Most high school students are familiar with the notion of viewing land areas as surfaces, with their hills, valleys, rivers, or plateaus. They are not, however, aware that such phenomena as population density, migration from "depressed areas," transport costs, and the like, can also be viewed as surfaces with "pits" and "peaks" and "valleys of movement." Like contours on a topographic map, lines of equal population density can be constructed and viewed as demographic contours. Where the "contours" are close together, a sharp fall-off in density may be visualized; or on such a "surface" there might be "plateaus" where population density varies very little over wide areas. To make these lines more realistic, John Q. Stewart[3] has introduced the analogy of the Sand Pile Citizen, quoted by Warntz.[4] Instead of depicting population by dots or as densities over areas, Stewart would have us imagine a person surrounded by a sand-

[3]*Coasts, Waves and Weather for Navigators* (Boston: Ginn and Co., 1945), pp. 164–65.
[4]William Warntz, "A New Map of the Surface of Population Potentials for The United States, 1960," *Geographical Review,* 54:170–84, April 1964.

pile built up to some arbitrary height. The heights of the sand would decrease proportionally as distance from the person increases. If this is done for each person, the three-dimensional model so obtained can be said to represent the density of that population, and isoline maps can be drawn to show "terrain." Instead of representing densities by chorochromatic, chorpleth, or dot maps, the variation in spatial distribution can be depicted graphically by isolines, and these isolines converted to "surfaces" using techniques suggested by Robinson and Thrower[5] or Kitiro.[6]

Mapping of surfaces could also introduce and utilize isarithmic, isopleth, or isoline[7] techniques along with layer tinting, illuminated contours or plastic shading. For example, Amedo[8] has used this idea in a paper prepared for a class lecture. In his work, economically depressed areas and areas of high unemployment stand out as "peaks," while prosperous areas become "pits." One can see the movement of people "down-hill" to the pits, a movement which one can equate with the down-slope movement of water. In addition, the intensity of movement bears a visual relationship to the degree of steepness of the "slopes." The idea here is to translate data into some visual form which will convey to the class much more quickly the relevant relationships.

Since the effectiveness of the portrayal of equal intensity areas by isolines depends very much on the frequency and/or density of observation, one should always choose those distributions for which numerical observations exist at a large number of points. For example, records at climatic stations could serve as the basis of a class exercise geared to the construction of a "surface" of rainfall or temperature distribution. Even here, however, the fit of the isolines is partly a matter of judgment, as Blumenstock[9] has pointed out. In portions of a map where control points are sparse, isolines must be subjectively drawn. When introducing isoline maps, a teacher should choose an area of the country for which sufficient information is available, and use this knowledge in making decisions about the location and trends of isolines. For example, because of the probability of greater rainfall on

[5] Arthur H. Robinson and N. J. W. Thrower, "A New Method of Terrain Representation," *Geographical Review*, 47:507–20, October 1957.

[6] Tanaka Kitiro, "The Relief Contour Method of Representing Topography on Maps," *Geographical Review*, 40:444–56, July 1950.

[7] There has been no agreement on the use of these terms. See E. Raisz, *General Cartography* (New York: McGraw-Hill Book Co., 1948), pp. 246–49; J. K. Wright, "The Terminology of Certain Map Symbols," *Geographical Review*, 24:653–54, 1944; E. A. Robinson, *Elements of Cartography* (New York: John Wiley and Sons, 1953).

[8] D. Amedeo, "Potential Migration," (New York: unpublished paper, Department of Geography, University of Iowa, 1965).

[9] D. Blumenstock, "The Reliability Factor in the Drawing of Isarithms," *Annals of the Association of American Geographers*, 43:289–304, 1953.

the windward slopes of a mountain, one would place the isolines closer together than one would if he were drawing a rainfall map for a lowland area.

Adequate information concerning the making and reading of isoline maps is found in Robinson[10] while the notion of "surfaces" and suggestions for its classroom use will be discussed in a forthcoming publication.[11]

SAMPLING PROCEDURES IN MAP MAKING
AND MAP READING

The need for sampling in map making arises from the impossibility of obtaining observations for every conceivable location on the "surface" of a distribution. Some points have to be selected in a random manner (the sample), and inferences made about the total study area (the "population," statistically speaking) from the sample values. Before using any of the usual sampling plans (random, systematic, stratified, and cluster sampling),[12] the teacher must stress:

1. The need for sampling in geography.
2. The necessity for random selection.
3. The procedures for making random samples.

Mundane examples of sampling can be used:

A. A doctor makes inferences about a patient's blood stream by examining a single drop.
B. One soil sample tells us something about a large area.
C. Public opinion polls, election predictions, and TV ratings are based on samples.
D. Examining a few rats may disclose facts about the un-examined millions.

In the classroom many devices can be used to make a random selection:

1. Shuffled deck of cards.
2. Numbers from a hat.
3. Numbered balls as in bingo.
4. Random number tables.[13]

[10] E. A. Robinson, pp. 178–94.
[11] K. W. Rumage and L. P. Cummings, "Introduction to Geography—A Conceptual Approach," a one-semester course outline for the A.A.G. Commission on College Geography.
[12] H. M. Blalock, *Social Statistics* (New York: McGraw-Hill Book Co., 1960). Explains also the use of the Random Numbers Table.
[13] *Ibid.*, pp. 437–49, can be put on the overhead projector for use by the class.

The use of Random Number Tables is again a relevant interest-creating device, especially for the upper grades of the high school. Certain elementary computations (mean, standard deviation of the sample values)[14] can accompany the lessons on sampling. If the teacher selects the sample size carefully and sees that no two students use the Random Number Tables the same way, much interest can be generated when they see how small the difference is for the class as a whole. Sampling can be introduced, for example, when studying the average size of farms in an area, or the dominant types of slopes on a topographic map, and so on. The procedure is relatively simple. First, the study area should be gridded; then numbers assigned to the small squares; and finally, the sample should be drawn randomly by any of the methods mentioned above (see Figure 36-2).

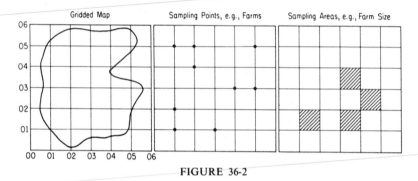

FIGURE 36-2

COMPARING MAPPED RELATIONSHIPS

In a classroom situation the teacher has to use visual methods when comparing pyramids, surfaces, and the like. The shortcomings of this method have been investigated by McCarty and Salisbury.[15] After tests on selected groups, they concluded that "only in cases in which the degree of association is very high does the process (visual comparison) produce results which approach the standards of accuracy generally demanded in present day research and teaching."[16] The teacher might circumvent this difficulty by choosing data in which the range is sufficiently large to bring out contrasts. Colors can also be utilized. For example, a rainfall "surface" can be drawn on transparent

[14]H. E. Yuker, *A Guide to Statistical Calculations* (New York: G. P. Putnam's Sons, 1958). An excellent step-by-step method for computation is given.
[15]H. H. McCarty and Neil Salisbury, *Visual Comparison of Isopleth Maps as a Means of Determining Correlations Between Spatially Distributed Phenomena.* Department of Geography, University of Iowa, 1961.
[16]*Ibid.,* p. 78.

paper and shaded yellow, while the crop distribution for the same area can be colored blue. Superimposition of the maps will show the area of correspondence as green.

Map making and map reading are important interest-creating factors. The high school teacher should not only plan his lessons so that they will culminate in some map exercises, but should try to introduce some ideas not yet included in geography texts. A well-prepared series of exercises will repay the effort in the great amount of class interest generated.

JAMES B. LINDBERG

University of Iowa

37. Developing Problem-Solving Skills*

Among the several alternative teaching strategies that are available for organizing a course or a program of instruction, the "problem-solving" approach has proven quite popular in many fields, including geography. Problem solving involves the student in the conduct of scholarly inquiry. He learns by doing. He obtains a knowledge of the best of the wisdom of the past, and at the same time acquires abilities to solve problems that may confront him in the future.

There are some ever-present dangers in adopting the problem-solving approach, however. It may develop into little more than a series of case studies that leave the student with little in the way of an integrated view of the subject matter. It may also lead to an over-emphasis on techniques of analysis without a paralleling development of concepts, ideas, and theories.

This paper attempts to provide some guidelines for a sound teaching program in geography that emphasizes the problem-solving approach. A philosophy of problem solving is presented that is consistent with modern methods of scientific inquiry, and illustrations are provided that show how this philosophy and the skills to implement it may be presented effectively to students. Although the exercises that are provided were originally designed for beginning college students, they can be made appropriate for other levels of instruction.

WHAT PROBLEM SOLVING IN GEOGRAPHY IS

In the sense that the term is used here, a geographical problem is simply a situation in which the *locational* features of some phenomenon are poorly understood. Problems in geography, therefore, are not to be confused with social problems such as "The Problem of Democracy," or the "Smog Problem." Such titles suggest that the inquiry has important value connotations and usually calls for some form of corrective action. Someone has said that "almost any intellectual itch" can be viewed as a problem. Although we would not like to carry such a definition that far, it does convey the sense of the usage intended in this paper.

Social Education, XXX:645–48, December 1966. Used by permission.

Problem solving in geography can be viewed as a series of steps, each dependent on the other, but not necessarily following a prescribed order. The sum total of these steps results in usable answers to research questions.

We have come to view such a procedure as falling into three segments:

1. The identification of the problem situation (including specification of the phenomenon of the problem), a knowledge and appreciation of the precise measurements involved, and an awareness of the scale at which the problem is to be attacked.
2. The formulation of tentative explanations or hypotheses, either from theory, or from similiar situations in the past, or simply from intuition.
3. The verification of the correctness of the tentative explanations through laboratory experiments, or as is becoming more common in geography, through statistical analysis.

The question of location is at the heart of every geographical problem. For that reason most problems in geography involve constructing or using maps at quite early stages in the inquiry. In fact, a map is the most convenient way of stating a geographic problem, and the source of important hypotheses.

STATING GEOGRAPHICAL PROBLEMS

Each of the major fields of learning has a class of problems to which that field directs its major emphasis, and persons trained in that field are expected to have a measure of competence to solve those kinds of problems. The problems to which geography directs its attention are problems of location and spatial arrangements of phenomena. Students, however, frequently experience difficulty in seeing the particular nature of geographical problems. A useful exercise for helping students grasp the meaning of problems involving location is to ask them to prepare a map of the location of students in a classroom. Each student is given an "outline map" of the classroom (technically, a blue print) with desks, doors, and other features indicated. They are then asked to mark those desks that are occupied by students. The resulting "map" becomes the geographical problem to be solved; that is, "Why are the students distributed as they are?" or, "Why have students located themselves as they have in this classroom?" The map itself, it will be noted, is not the solution to the problem; it is only a necessary first step in defining the problem.

It should be made clear that geographers are expected to deal with a particular class of the several problems that might be present in such a situation. The location problem, for example, does not consider why the students enrolled for that particular class, or why they meet at 9:00 A.M. rather than at 11:00 A.M. Such a knowledge may be tangentially useful to a complete solution of the location problem, but it is not the problem to be solved.

FORMING TENTATIVE EXPLANATIONS

Completed maps (see Figure 37-1) can be used to initiate a discussion of the nature of geographical knowledge and of the methods of geo-

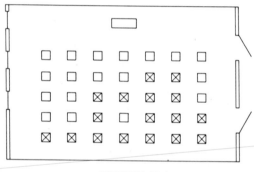

FIGURE 37-1

graphical inquiry. Explanations for the pattern of student locations involve the fact that students must sit at desks, and that locations in the room without desks are not occupied. Frequently, the arrangement of students is skewed toward the side of the room from which they enter (at least in a room not fully occupied). Usually, too, the pattern exhibits some orientation with respect to the front of the room: in some cases front seats are left vacant; in others the arrangement is "cone-shaped" so that students might better view a demonstration at the front of the room. In some cases a "planning authority" may have asked students to occupy alternate seats, or some similarly prearranged pattern.

Analogies to the more traditional problems of geography are immediately apparent. Consider a map of the location of manufacturing plants in a large region. Desks become the local site resources of a water supply, a labor force, or industrial buildings. Locations without such facilities do not have manufacturing plants. In a country that is not fully developed, plant locations may exhibit a skewness toward one side of the area, perhaps toward the seacoast or railroad lines. Orientation with respect to market concentrations or material sources may also be evident.

As we have seen the completed map, whether it be of student locations in a classroom, or of manufacturing plants in a large region, or of rainfall amounts across a continent, brings forth many possible answers to the question of "why?" To the geographically inquisitive, the map itself is never completely satisfactory; it literally begs for explanation. Thus, the heart of geographical inquiry has always been the explanation and interpretation of locations and location patterns, usually as they are seen on maps. The mark of a well-prepared student of geography is his ability to come quickly to explanations that will prove valid—i.e., explanations that will stand the test of time and repeated verification.

How does one arrive at satisfactory explanations for location patterns? In the classroom example, explanations were based on an intimate knowledge of the motivations of students under different conditions. For example, from experience it is known that many students prefer to sit near the rear of the room so they will not be called upon to recite, or on warm days they prefer to sit near a window. Out of these types of understandings, tentative explanations for observed location patterns may be developed. Normally, such explanations will involve several different factors operating simultaneously, and the resultant hypothesis will be "multi-variant" in nature.

For most location problems in geography, however, the motivation and forces at work are not so familiar as are those related to the seating of students in a classroom. Under such situations, a variety of strategies and aids are available to the geographer to assist him in arriving at valid solutions to his problem.

Frequently, the particular problem at hand belongs to a class of problems toward which a good deal of prior investigation and thought has been directed. The results of this prior work are brought together in the form of a body of generalizations, laws, and theories stating the relationships involved. By reference to this body of theory, students can arrive more readily at those types of explanations that others have found to be valid or have thought to be valid. For a problem in the location of manufacturing plants, for example, valid explanations quite often are obtained by forming hypotheses appropriate to the problem out of the general relationships embodied in what is termed "industrial location theory." Such theory postulates, for example, that those types of manufacturing plants in which the production process involves a large reduction in weight in converting materials into finished products will likely locate near the material sources so as to minimize transport costs. Applying this generalization to the particular facts of the problem at hand leads the student quickly and surely to appropriate solutions.

This close link between finding solutions to problems and applicable location theory means that much of the instructional effort in geography should involve teaching students the nature and use of theory. However, teaching existing theory is never by itself sufficient. It is only in the application to problems, that is, to the facts of the "real world," that our body of theory is altered and sharpened and made more applicable.

In some cases, a suitable body of theory may not be available for solving the problem at hand, or it may be so poorly developed as not to be applicable. In such a situation, alternative procedures must be adopted. One such procedure might be termed "trial and error." Returning to our location of students in the classroom problem, let us assume that our knowledge of student motivation is poor and that there exists no suitable body of theory from which we can deduce likely student locations, nor are there solutions to prior problems of a similar nature from which we can draw our hypotheses. In such a seemingly hopeless situation we might likely do some "field work."

Ask students to make maps of the occupied seats in each of their other classrooms. Some will have no windows; others will be classrooms with maps hung on the front wall for students to read; still others will be rooms with doors at the front rather than at one side. Assemble and compare all of the completed maps. If it happens that, regardless of the configuration of the room or the nature of the class, each map shows rear seats occupied and front seats empty, then one can be reasonably certain that the explanation of the original problem map has "preference for seats towards the back of a classroom" as its dominant factor.

VERIFYING TENTATIVE EXPLANATIONS

It may have occurred to some that the procedure just described constitutes quite a good test of an original hypothesis about the tendency of students to sit towards the rear of classrooms. And, in fact, that is just what it does.

In many fields of learning, the verification of theoretical deductions involves controlled experimentation. Proposed solutions to problems are evaluated in the laboratory under ideal circumstances so that the operation of individual forces can be observed and their relative strengths evaluated. In geography, however, it is rarely possible to subject the phenomena of the problem to laboratory testing, and rarely is it possible to find repeated situations in which common elements might be expected to operate so neatly and simply. Verifying solutions to problems in geography, therefore, almost always takes place on paper, and the isolation of relevant variables is accomplished statistically.

Using our classroom example one more time, we can illustrate the procedure. Suppose our knowledge of student behavior leads us to hypothesize or predict in advance that students will occupy rear seats and seats near the door with the strengths of these two desires exactly equal. This two-variable hypothesis then can be used to prepare a hypothetical map of occupied seats. If the hypothetical map compares reasonably well with the actual map of occupied seats, we can state with some certainty that we have a solution to our problem. The comparison procedure in this case can probably be done visually. In more complex problems some form of statistical comparison is necessary, but the idea is essentially the same.

It should be pointed out that our simple two-variable hypothesis would probably not achieve complete agreement with the problem. We have not, for example, taken account of the student with poor eyesight who must sit in the front of the room. If complete solutions are desired we would need to include, not only special circumstances of this kind, but additional general forces as well.

Thus, it is seen that problem solving becomes a continual interplay between fact and theory. Clues to problems are provided by the deductions of theory, and valid solutions to problems are the means by which generalizations and theory are made more "real" and more applicable.

The problem presented in some detail below is intended to illustrate the above procedures as they might apply to a somewhat more typical geographical problem. It involves the location pattern of retail gasoline service stations in a state utilizing data from the U.S. Census Bureau.

SAMPLE PROBLEM:

Location Pattern of Gasoline Service Stations

The purpose of this exercise is to introduce the student to a relatively simple, but nonetheless real problem in geography. It employs common cartographic and graphic methods to test a simple one-variable locational hypothesis.

The problem: From the U.S. Census of Business, Retail Sales Volume, obtain data which specifies the number of gasoline service stations in each county in a state. Prepare a map of the location pattern of gasoline stations. Utilize any mapping technique that appears appropriate; i.e., dot patterns, graduated circles, shading. Remember, you only know that there are so many service stations; you do not know where within the county these stations are located. This fact defines the scale of research at which this particular problem is stated, and your solution must be appropriate to that scale. Your completed map constitutes the problem to be solved.

The hypothesis: Available theory and our knowledge of gasoline retailing leads us to hypothesize that *the number of stations in a county will be proportional to the population of that county.* Thus, we can state as a hypothesis that we expect the map of service stations to exhibit similar patterns of variation as that of population. More complex hypotheses could no doubt be formulated, but for the present, we shall be satisfied with this rather simple, yet illustrative, statement.

The verification procedures: Our hypothesis states that a map of population should look like our map of service stations. Therefore, prepare a map of population by counties for the same study area. The symbols used should be similar to those employed on the service station map so as to facilitate visual comparison.

Do the maps compare? Are the counties containing large numbers of service stations the same as those with large populations? Do the low values coincide? Is correspondence obtained in counties of intermediate values?

It may prove difficult to compare satisfactorily two location patterns by means of "map comparison," especially at the intermediate values. If such is the case, an alternative procedure employing a simple graph might be employed.

Construct a two-axis graph as is shown in Figure 37-2. Scale one

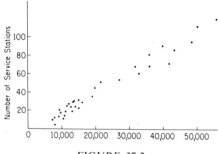

FIGURE 37-2

axis so as to accommodate the range of values of your problem variable; i.e., service stations. Scale the other axis to accommodate values of your hypothesis; namely, population. The two axes need not have the same intervals. Place a dot on the graph at the point representing the value of each county on both axes. Your completed graph should contain the same number of dots as there are counties in the study area.

Do the dots array themselves in a straight line? If they do, then variations in the number of service stations are exactly paralleled by variations in population at those same locations. This is our hypothesis, it will be recalled, and it has been confirmed. It is likely, however, that the pattern of dots will not form a straight line as depicted in Figure 37–2. The departures can provide, then, a basis for incorporating additional factors into the analysis.

JOHN F. OHLES

Associate Professor of Secondary Education,
Kent State University, Ohio

38. The Mechanics of Discussion*

There is a general recognition among teachers that discussion as a teaching technique has a special role, a particular value for inculcation of democratic ideals in a democratic manner. Yet, effecting this democratic procedure is shackled in misunderstanding, abuse, and, particularly, ignorance of the mechanics of the process.

To begin, it might be meaningful to suggest what classroom discussion is and is not. Discussion is a well organized, purposeful, learning experience; unique in its facilitation of understandings and attitudes; especially adapted to guiding students into structured discovery of generalizations; a tool as easily abused as used; a source as well of deep satisfaction as deeper frustration. And most certainly, discussion is not the regurgitation that is recitation, an occasional student response in that which is lecture. It is not an exchange of ignorance, a by-play on controversy, a housed version of street corner banter, an aimless verbal wandering in an academic pasture.

Discussion may lead to understandings impossible to come by in the superficiality of a textbook. It should find pupils mentally engaged in involvement in the search for answers to: What would you have done, felt, seen, believed, experienced, understood? Only in discussion technique is there opportunity to engage every individual in a group search for a worthy learning experience. It is this involvement with a particular aspect of learning that differentiates classroom discussion from the politicking of a town meeting or the aimlessness of a bull session.

But all forms of discussion have some aspects in common. Probably most important is the shared base on which discussion is structured. No discussion may proceed without a similar background of information from which the process evolves. Thus, it is difficult for most Europeans to engage in a discussion about baseball or most Americans to argue the merits of cricket. Some foundations for discussion may evolve from common experiences as earthly men or members of a nation, shares of a common social grouping, survivors of an experience. In the classroom, additional common knowledge may be extracted from a textbook, lecture, film, tele-

*Journal of Secondary Education, 40:16–17, January 1965. Used by permission.

cast, etc. Ability to engage in a discussion is directly related to wakeful presence during a movie or thoughtful reading of a text. Every individual devoid of the common base becomes a spectator, and learning by discussion is best achieved as a participant.

Participation in a discussion is not solely indicated by speaking. For the more introvertive, participation may frequently be mental and silent, although spontaneous forces in a spirited and meaningful discussion may well find the most reticent actively engaging in the process. Requiring verbal participation of all is not only unrealistic but is likely to burden the discussion with rigid formality and forced answers. To a skilled observer, vocalizing is not a worthy clue to participation in the absence of blank stares, nodding heads, sneak reading, or furtive conversation. Let it be recognized that for some individuals speaking is a means to escape from boredom.

Now if discussion requires a common base for a class, it needs, as well, a recognized objective by the teacher. A discussion ends when the learning objective is reached; its success is measured by the ease and clarity with which all participants are led to the goal. This goal is a particular learning experience.

Controversy is frequently hailed as the means to a discussion. In reality, controversy is not required, but is often a common aspect because a discussion depends on ideas and opinions for much of its momentum. Controversy is neither to be sought nor avoided; it frequently has a role to play in the evolution of a process. Like all else in a classroom discussion, disagreement should be controlled and used.

Like the pupils, a teacher has an active role to play. He initiates, directs, and concludes a discussion. On his skill rests the likelihood of the success or failure of a teaching technique. His role consists primarily of controlling mechanics of the process. Initially, he poses a question relating to the common base of information—this being his only opportunity to plan a question in advance. To engage every youngster in the process, the question should be one that all can answer. From answer to question one, the next question is posed to slowly and purposefully carry the group along toward the objective. As group interplay develops, the teacher may refrain from participating until progress comes to a temporary halt or darts off in an unsatisfactory direction.

Discussions are fraught with possibilities for tangents and it is the role of the teacher to permit pursuit of a tangent or to redirect group thinking toward the goal. Tangents are worthy objects when they reflect strong interests on the part of the youngsters, or when they are educationally as fruitful as the original goal. The teacher must make a speedy decision with reference to a tangent and, as with all snap judgment, errors are likely. It is probably equally as erroneous to stifle a worthwhile tangent as to perpetuate a worthless one.

It should be no serious problem to terminate a tangent. The exaggerated concern for individual emotionality is sometimes projected into a form of pupil-rejection by the teacher in a situation such as this. Realistically, however, most youngsters are not emotionally unstable, hanging but by a hair from insanity. It is a simple procedure to defer further discussion on a topic and to return to the basic train of thought with a question similar to that from which the tangent evolved. The vital concern here (as with much in teaching) depends less on what you do, than how you do it.

Basic to the mechanics of discussion is the phrasing of a question, extracted from the previous answer. The question should be clear, specific, and involving a step in logic small enough to enable the class to follow the discussion. Awkward pauses after a question or an interchange among just the brighter students may suggest a poor question, or too large a jump in thinking.

Development of a discussion into an interchange among just a few members of the class may suggest too rapid pacing and loss of a class through complexity of the discussion, a topic that is not of interest to the group, or failure to relate to a common basis of information. It would be preferable to terminate a discussion in which only a few participate rather than continue to ignore the larger group situation.

A broad discussion topic (e.g., The Civil War) ought to be broken down into a series of related discussions, each with a specific objective. Objectives that are too broad in scope provide too obscure a guide and are likely to result in that aimless banter that often passes for discussion.

Discussion, as any other technique, relates particularly well to specific situations, less favorably to others. In no other way may certain appreciations be gained. An appropriate question posed by a discussion might be, "Do you understand what it meant to leave a native country to emigrate to the United States? What would you have done?" This subject would be appropriate to various topics in American history: the Pilgrims, slave trade, various immigrations, displaced persons, Cuban refugees.

The skillful teacher finds in the discussion technique an essential tool. He recognizes the absolute necessity of careful preparation, of ensuring adequate background, careful shepherding of the process, need for perfection of the arts of questioning, listening, guiding, stimulating. But if the efforts are great, the rewards are greater in terms of learning as well as group and individual satisfactions.

This, then, is the discussion procedure. Although an object of confusion and misuse, it is an effective learning technique, a practical application of democratic processes, a reasonably and mechanically structured method of instruction. Neither overwhelmingly difficult nor ridiculously simple, it should be thoroughly understood by every teacher and wisely used in every classroom.

KENNETH H. HOOVER

Professor of Education, Arizona State University, Tempe

39. The Debate: Valid Teaching Method?*

Debate has long been a controversial teaching method. Its critics have contended that the technique creates an artificial black-and-white situation in which neither party, according to the rules of the game, is permitted to alter his position. They further contend that a mere "play upon words" all too often tends to divert one's attention from the reality of the proposition being studied. Some people even object to the use of a staged argument, claiming that "education must place greater stress on cooperation."

While the foregoing criticisms are indeed germane to the processes of formal debate, they suggest, at best, an imperfect understanding of the technique. In fact, a survey of general methods books over the past ten years discloses very little emphasis on debate as an instructional method.[1] This suggests some confusion of basic purposes involved, along with certain deficiencies in application of the technique. Accordingly the purpose of this paper is to make a case for classroom debate, showing how certain worthy instructional purposes may be achieved through debate procedures.

THEORETICAL FRAMEWORK

Discussion, debate, and persuasive speaking are actually elements of a continuum very commonly employed in the processes of resolving issues. The basic *discussion* attitude is *openmindedness*; the discusser avoids a two-valued orientation, seeking to find a "middle ground." The *debater*, on the other hand, has moved from an attitude of searching with others for the best solution to one of conviction that he has found the best solution. His purpose is to convince others of his views. As Gulley points out, "Where discussion is cooperative, debate is competitive. Where the discusser inquires, the debater advocates."[2] The *persuasive speaker* differs little from the debater, in that he too is convinced of the wisdom of a given position on an issue. His purpose is to *sell* the audience on a point of

---

Clearing House, 40:232–35, December 1965. Used by permission.
[1] The one exception is a book by the writer, *Learning and Teaching in the Secondary School* (Boston: Allyn and Bacon, Inc, 1964), chap. 6.
[2] Halbert E. Gulley, *Discussion, Conference and Group Processes* (New York: Holt, Rinehart and Winston, Inc., 1960), p. 120.

view. Unlike the debater, however, he does not have to cope with opposing arguments. There is no organized opposition to his views.

The processes of discussion, debate, and persuasive speaking are commonplace in our society. Indeed some elements of each are employed in all three approaches. Each technique, however, has been somewhat systematized for classroom use in order to insure fair play.

PURPOSES OF DEBATE

Debate is appropriate when a highly controversial issue must be examined. By presenting extreme positions with respect to an issue it is presumed that the listener will become less extreme with respect to the matter. Just the mere recognition that there are organized, logical arguments in opposition to one's view is sometimes sufficient to create doubts where formerly none were tolerated. In any event, the listener will be able to clarify his stand on an issue. Rather than merely knowing what he stands for, through debate he gains some objective basis for his stand.

Group discussion, of course, is ideal for assisting an individual to make up his mind. When several members of a discussion group, however, have already made up their minds on a problem, the processes of reflection are replaced by those of advocacy. When such a state of affairs develops under the guise of discussion, a state of chaos exists. At this point the teacher can himself present the pros and cons of an issue, or he can let selected students assume this responsibility.

Debate is almost unique among the instructional techniques in its emphasis on strategy to gain an advantage over the opposition. It is in this realm that much creative imagination comes into play. Bright students especially enjoy pitting their wits against others. Sometimes strategy involves leading questions; at other times it may use an opponent's argument to support one's own views; on other occasions it may even focus on the use of "loaded words" or the association of one's opponents with some "ism," e.g., Communism, socialism, traditionalism, conservatism, or the like. As "undesirable" as these points of strategy sometimes may be, they are, nevertheless, a very real part of man's existence. Thus debate can be used as a ready-made situation for preparing youngsters to cope with basic realities of our time. (This function will be discussed in more detail in the follow-through aspect of debate procedure.)

ESSENTIAL STEPS OF CLASSROOM DEBATE

1. Selection of Problem and Debate Participants

As previously indicated, debate is appropriate when the members of a class tend to hold strong and perhaps extreme views on a problem. The issue may be of a local nature, or it may be national in scope. The debate proposition "Resolved, that students should be permitted to drive their own cars to school" would represent a purely local issue. (This assumes, of course, that under existing conditions such a practice is forbidden.) A national issue might be: "Resolved, that the minimum voting age throughout the United States should be lowered to 18 years."

Debate participants should feel keenly about an issue and should be somewhat evenly matched. Since one important purpose of a debate is to render polar positions less extreme, it is highly desirable that the participants debate the side in opposition to their views. For example, an individual who feels that the minimum voting age should be lowered to 18 years might be asked to take the *con* side of the argument.

2. Organization of the Case

There are three major issues to every debate: Is there a need? Will the specific plan of the affirmative remedy the existing state of affairs? Is the plan feasible or desirable? Members of the affirmative (usually two in number) must effectively support all three of these issues. Thus they must assume the "burden of proof."

The negative team members may attempt to destroy all three issues, but they need not do so. If they can destroy any one of the three issues they have accomplished their purpose. In essence, the negative team supports the status quo—conditions as they are.

3. Preparation of the Class for Debate

It is usually desirable to ask each student to make a list of opposing arguments on the opposite sides of a sheet of paper. In doing so, he will usually desire to make a list of unanswered questions as the debate progresses. Whenever possible, the student notes aspects of strategy which tend to throw one team or the other off-balance.

4. Debate Presentation

The most common debate style consists of two parts: the constructive speeches and the refutation-rebuttal speeches.

Each speaker, in the constructive portion of a debate, speaks for an equal length of time, alternating one with the other. The first affirmative speaker defines his terms, establishes the need, and may present briefly the main steps of his plan. His partner expands the plan and shows why it is workable and desirable. The negative speakers, conversely, take the opposite stand. All speakers adhere to the rules of effective persuasive speaking.

It is in the refutation-rebuttal speeches that the actual clash may be expected. This portion of a debate provides each speaker with an equal opportunity to destroy the arguments of the opposition while repairing damages to his own case.

5. Debate Evaluation

In a classroom debate it is usually not desirable to select a winner. The instructor often evaluates each participant, however, on the merits of various aspects of the debate. Many of these points will correspond to those that are deemed essential to regular persuasive speaking.

6. Follow-through Review Analysis

This is one of the most essential aspects of the debate procedure. Usually one-half to a full class period should be given to this phase of debate procedure. This step can be divided into two parts: The review analysis and an analysis of the various techniques of persuasion employed.

The review analysis should focus upon three major questions:

a. What were the major points made?
b. How did each of the major points withstand the arguments of the opposition?
c. What are some related problems which might bear investigation?

The first two questions are primarily for purposes of recall, leading to the third question, which is designed to expand learning to other, related areas. To illustrate by using the minimum voting age problem: Should the poll tax be abolished for state and local elections? Should the residents of Washington, D.C., be granted the right to elect their own district officials? Should a man who has "paid for his crime" be permitted to vote? Who should determine a voter's qualifications? Should one be required to express his views at the polls?

The follow-through discussion should also focus on the persuasive techniques in evidence. Some or all of the following points might be considered:

a. The effects of emotional appeals.
b. Distortion of facts or evidence.
c. Use of loaded words or question-begging terms.
d. Use of questionable evidence.
e. Incidences of "glossing over."
f. Use of high-order generalizations as a technique of avoiding real issues.
g. The impact of traps, psychological devices, and the like.
h. The use of inferences.
i. The art of capitalizing on existing biases of a group.

THE ADVANTAGES

I have used classroom debate in both high school and college classes. Not only is it exciting to both participant and listener, but it provides a very practical approach to the study of controversial issues.

Among the more important advantages of classroom debate are the following:

(1) It provides a legitimate release for strong emotions.

(2) It forces a strongly biased individual to listen to the organized efforts of the opposition.

(3) Debate provides the able student, especially, with an ideal avenue for verbal finesse and development of creative imagination.

(4) The procedure provides a basis for an examination of techniques of persuasion.

(5) Debate affords a legitimate means of coping with an impasse when processes of discussion break down.

(6) The method may be used effectively to study issues which may otherwise be too "hot to handle."

JAMES H. McGOLDRICK

Administrative Assistant to the Superintendent,
Bristol Township School, Pennsylvania

*40. Teaching Research Techniques in the Social Studies**

Teaching the techniques of research is one of the major problems facing the social studies teacher. We know that skill in the research art is essential to all of our students; we know that the basic techniques must be "taught" and that the student must work at them if he is to master their use.

But this knowledge still leaves us with the problem of actually teaching the skills and techniques and this can be a problem to tax a Job.

How to teach these skills?

One effective method is to begin on the first day of school with the assigned textbook. This serves several admirable purposes, not the least of which is to familiarize the student with the text. Properly chosen textbook problems can be used to teach the basic research skills and to build in our students a habit of following correct procedures. Once these basic skills become habit we can "introduce our scholars to a world wider than the textbook."[1]

And this is a point at which all of our carefully taught research techniques can collapse like a star that has exhausted its hydrogen.

Obviously, we cannot continue to teach research techniques by posing textbook problems. Sooner or later disenchantment will set in; sooner or later the young minds will want a more challenging task. What then?

Here we must recognize that, in the order of events, toddling comes first, then walking, then running. So, also, when teaching research skills. Our textbook problems constitute the toddling stage; our goal is the running stage during which we can pose real research problems for our students with some hope that they can be successfully completed. Before then, however, we must pass through the walking stage during which we expand the research horizons of our charges. The problem, then, is to move our stu-

---

*Social Studies, 54:15–17, January 1963. Used by permission.

[1]James McGoldrick, "Research Starting With The Textbook," *Clearing House*, September 1961. The procedure outlined in the above paragraph is treated in some detail in the article in *Clearing House*.

dents from the toddling stage—the textbook problems—into the walking stage, and, ultimately, into the running stage.

One way to do this is by a series of research projects that begin with a simple nontextbook task and move by graduated steps through a fairly complicated job. Each step should develop technique a bit more; each step should also reinforce the habits ingrained in earlier steps.

Such a series can begin with a dittoed copy of The Gettysburg Address and the question: What kind of man wrote this speech? The neophyte researcher will scan the Address and answer the question by listing all of the traits usually ascribed to Lincoln. When we ask "Precisely what words in the speech show that the author was kindly, humane, etc.," the student will have learned a valuable lesson. This discussion should lead to the question of whether the written word is to be accepted as literally true and, if not, how do we determine if the written word simply says what the author thinks his audience wants to hear?

This lesson should not be a one-shot affair. It deals with the single most important technique of research and it must be learned well. A number of speeches should be dealt with in the same manner and a number of written works also.

From such assignments we can move our students, when individually appropriate, into the more complicated but still directed work:

> Using *The Dictionary of American Biography* and T. A. Bailey, *A Diplomatic History of the American People,* find out: (1) who was John Hay, and (2) what part did he play in our acquisition of the Panama Canal?

Using just the two sources we have listed, plus his textbook, the student will discover that Hay was a longtime Secretary of State around 1900 and that he negotiated the treaties that made possible the Canal; the student will also discover the provisions of the treaties. In short, he will have taken a step toward real research.

After a few such sessions, we can set our students—again when individually appropriate—a more difficult task involving the reading of two or more books and the organization of the knowledge thus gained into a coherent pattern. For example:

> Read E. S. Osgood, *The Day of the Cattleman,* and W. P. Webb, *The Great Plains.* When you finish, write a brief paper explaining why the farmers were able to drive the ranchers out of most of the plains area.

When the student applies the techniques we have been teaching him all year to the two books assigned, he can write such a paper. Since the topic is not discussed as such in either book, he will be forced to think, to select his material, to organize it in a sensible pattern, and, for him at least, discover a new truth. In sum, he will have done a piece of research that has value and is uniquely his.[2]

[2]In "Comparative Reading Helps," *English Journal,* January 1961, I have described in detail a technique somewhat similar to the one used in this paragraph and the one preceding; one of the major differences between the *English Journal* article and the assignment listed here is that the one in the *English Journal* uses novels.

The Teaching of Knowledge

JACK R. FRAENKEL

Associate Professor of Interdisciplinary Studies in Education,
San Francisco State College

41. Ask the Right Questions!*

Max Lerner once described his passing the front of a small pawn shop where a sign in the window asked: "If you're so smart, why aren't you rich?" Admittedly fascinated by the sign, he returned to it again and again. "I couldn't answer the question," he remarked, "and what's more, I didn't know why I couldn't! Then it came to me. It was the wrong question!"

Many teachers ask such "wrong questions"! Certainly every teacher needs to be able to ask the "right" questions. But what are the "right" questions? I am not speaking in an absolutist or totalitarian sense, where "right" refers to only one type of action, predetermined by some external source. Rather, I propose that there are several different types of questions which teachers may ask, depending upon what purposes they have in mind. In this sense, the "right" questions are those which assist the teacher in achieving a particular objective or set of objectives he considers important. Unfortunately, far too many teachers have *no* purpose in mind.

I am convinced that you can tell a great deal about a teacher by the answer he gives to the question: "Why are you teaching this [fact, concept, generalization, or whatever it may be]?" Teachers need to continually ask themselves: "Why am I doing this?" By asking themselves this question, and arriving at a satisfactory answer (however temporary), they can determine what questions to ask their students. Teachers who know the "why" of a particular undertaking will most likely be able to convince students of the relevance of that which takes place in the classroom. If the teachers do not know why something is important, certainly the students cannot be expected to know. And if the students are not convinced that what they are being asked to consider, think about, or deal with is important (i.e., relevant), they quite likely will not consider it at all.

Clearing House, 40:397–400, March 1966. Used by permission.

All students implicitly, at least, ask every teacher, "How is what you are talking about relevant to me as a person?" Some even do this explicitly. It is a primary responsibility of every teacher to make education relevant to the concerns of students. I call this involvement. Students must be involved in what takes place in the classroom. If they are not, the great majority of what is presented will simply be dismissed as irrelevant, or at best quickly memorized, regurgitated, and forgotten.

Teachers must also ask themselves: "Where am I going?" "What do I want to accomplish?" "Why do I want to accomplish this?" "How can I most effectively accomplish what I wish to accomplish?" Answers to such questions will help decide what questions must be asked of students.

The questioning technique reveals the type of teacher. If primary interest is in having the students acquire factual knowledge, certain types of questions will tend to be asked. If teachers are interested in students' being able to synthesize the knowledge they have acquired, questions of a different order will be asked. Should they desire their students to be able to analyze the facts they have acquired, yet another type of question will be necessary. And finally, should the goal be the exercise of creative thought, queries of still a different nature will be needed.

Let me suggest a taxonomy of questions which various purposes would require. Consider this classification in terms of the purposes which teachers might have, the actions required or desired of students, and the types of questions which teachers would accordingly ask. Such a classification would look like this:

Purpose	Type of Question	Student Action Desired
I. Knowledge acquisition	Factual	Remembering
II. Knowledge synthesis	Descriptive	Remembering
III. Knowledge analysis	Explanatory	Reasoning Exercising judgment
IV. Creative thought	Heuristic	Divergent thinking

Let us consider each of these in turn.

FACTUAL QUESTIONS

The key words involved in this type of question are "who," "what," "when," and "where." Primarily the purpose is to determine if students have acquired or obtained a desired amount of factual information; teachers are asking them to remember what they have learned beforehand. There is but one correct answer. Examples of such questions would be:

1. Who was the commander of the British forces during the Battle of Bunker Hill?
2. Who were the Grangers?
3. What territory did the United States gain by the Treaty of Guadalupe Hidalgo?
4. When did Pakistan and India become separate states?
5. What is the present population of the Soviet Union?
6. Where can we find the capital of Czechoslovakia?
7. What classes of people were guaranteed rights in the Magna Charta?
8. When was Franklin D. Roosevelt first elected to the Presidency of the United States?

It should be obvious that questions such as these are important ones. Students need information with which to work. One cannot think if one has nothing to think about! Far too often, however, teachers never go beyond this. If we want more from our students than simply the extent of factual knowledge which they have acquired, we must ask questions of a different sort.

DESCRIPTIVE QUESTIONS

The key word here is "how." Teachers are interested in helping students put together and organize into some sort of relationship the facts which they have gathered—to make some sense out of their data. It is assumed that some type of relationship exists, and that there is some continuity or sequence within the material. For example, students might be asked to describe, compare, contrast, compare and contrast, or simply synthesize. Examples of such questions are:

1. Describe the kinds of problems faced by immigrants to the United States in the 1920's.
2. Describe the characteristics of the five major vegetation zones of the Soviet Union.
3. How has African nationalism since 1945 differed from that prior to World War II?
4. How did the Whigs campaign in 1840?
5. Describe the effects of the Panic of 1837.
6. Compare peasant life in the Soviet Union under Stalin with peasant life under Khrushchev.
7. Contrast the executive branch during the administration of George Washington with the executive branch today.

8. Compare and contrast Jacksonian Democracy with Jeffersonian
democracy.

In short, one answer is still desired and students still are asked to exercise their powers of recall. However, they are asked not only to remember, but also to organize the facts which they have learned. For analysis, however, a third type of question, that of explanation, is necessary.

EXPLANATORY QUESTIONS

The focal point here is the "why" of things. Not only must students remember and organize material, but they must also exercise reason, make inferences, seek causes and effects. In short, they must tell *why* they think as they do. Questions with these purposes in mind are typified by such requests as: "Explain what you mean by that, John!" "Why did you choose what you did, Susan?" "Why did these things happen?" "Which way is best?" "What other alternatives might exist?" "How valid is this author's argument?" Hence, such questions as these appear:

1. Why do you think Jefferson was a greater President than Jackson?
2. Why do you feel the South was justly irritated with the Abolitionists?
3. Why has Russia lagged behind the West in economic development?
4. What conclusions would you draw from the author's argument?
5. What other alternatives existed for the Republican Party in 1960?

Here many answers, all equally acceptable, are possible as students reflect and analyze the data they have gathered. Teachers, however, cannot push their own ideas, for they must encourage students to present and defend *their* reasons for thinking as they do. Unfortunately, far too few ask questions that encourage these answers. Even fewer promote heuristic learning. And that brings us to the final category.

HEURISTIC QUESTIONS

It is with this last level that teachers, in effect, enter the stratosphere. Teachers who encourage students to think heuristically breathe rarefied air. They are themselves pretty rare birds. For here no answers are more acceptable than others. Heuristic questions require students to seek and determine for themselves what they consider to be acceptable answers. Guilford referred to this type of activity as divergent rather than convergent thinking.[1] In actuality, students venture out onto heretofore uncharted

[1] Cf. J. W. Getzels, "Creative Thinking, Problem-Solving, and Instruction," in *Theories of Learning and Instruction*, National Society for the Study of Education, 63rd Yearbook (Chicago: University of Chicago Press, 1964), p. 247.

seas. These include queries like:

1. What might have happened if Barry Goldwater had been elected President of the United States in 1964?
2. If you were inventing a language for Martians, where would you begin?
3. Why do some men become poets and others beatniks?
4. What kind of world might exist if there were no sound?
5. How would you describe eternity?

In essence, students are asked to venture out onto their own, to make a creative leap into the unknown, to stretch both their imaginations and their intellect. The atmosphere produced by such questioning is a difficult one for many teachers to endure, for questions of this kind ask students to seek knowledge on their own initiative rather than to passively receive it from the teacher's hallowed lips.

SUMMARY

Purpose is essential for effective teaching. Far too few teachers know where they are going. Even fewer know why they do as they do. Teachers must ask themselves: "What are my purposes?" "What do I want to accomplish?" "Why am I doing this?" One's purposes determine, in turn, the types of questions one needs to ask. Acquisition of knowledge calls for one type; synthesis a second; analysis a third; creative thinking a fourth. It is argued that teachers must both ask questions and encourage their students to ask them, for by continually seeking to move from questions of the order of Type I to those of Type IV the teacher will be more likely to prevent the development of uncritical minds which readily and quickly accept all information without question. In essence, "what we know is what we ask about"!

RICHARD E. GROSS

Professor of Education,
Stanford University

DWIGHT W. ALLEN

Dean, School of Education,
University of Massachusetts

42. Upside Down but Not Backwards: Beginning U.S. History with a Unit on Current Events*

Many ways have been proposed in regard to the grouping of historical materials for the classroom. Traditionally the presentation has been chronological. It is also not uncommon to find topical orientation particularly in more recent periods of study. In this article we wish to propose another way in which to initially present history to high school students. While the experience described and the unit included are in U. S. history, the approach could be used in any historical study. We believe it presents a key to a more vivid appreciation of history, making history for the students the real and living contribution to knowledge that it is.

How can secondary school youth find purpose in history? How can they be motivated to study history so that they come to understand the place of history in their own lives? Students need to grasp the relationship between themselves, their prime concerns, their day, the problems of the hour, and history's engendering forces. The instructor builds these conceptions in a variety of ways but he continually emphasizes in all that history helps tell his students just why they are, where they are, as they are today. Such history serves as memory, guide, and conscience. It aids individuals in assessing their present, society's progress and its mistakes, current challenges, and the chances for the morrow.

The instructor who would bridge the gap between immediate youth interest and needs and the contribution of history also regularly emphasizes the point that history is anything *but* a collection of facts about yesterday's events. He helps the student realize that history is rather an imaginative and creative search, interpretation and *use* of the past. It helps explain how and why people acted as they did; it reveals the very human and personal bases for many important events; at the same time the factors of chance are presented, yet the student realizes that today's world need not have turned out as it has. This kind of a history approach also indicates

*Social Studies, 49:180–84, October 1958. Used by permission.

the incompleteness of the record available, the lack of *a* history, the constantly altering and conflicting interpretations, and the need for critical objectivity in reading about and discussing any occurrence, past or present. The student in such a class also comes to recognize the import of one's own values as he looks for meaning and direction in *his* story of man.

These important understandings and attitudes result from a thoughtful experience *with* history *today*. Students are most familiar with and concerned about their present surroundings. Quite simply put, first of all, one "lives here, lives now, and lives in this way." The following unit seeks to exploit the adolescent's pre-occupation with himself and his immediate surroundings and groups by beginning a course in U. S. history with a three or four week period of study entitled, "The United States Today: History in the Making." In the classes in which this technique was used, it has been quite successful, though the findings were in no way tested by experimental design.

The first assignment was to select from any one newspaper three articles: first, the one which, in the student's opinion, was most significant in terms of the local community or state; secondly, the student was asked to select the article of most importance nationally; finally, the student was to pick the one of greatest international significance. No attempt was made to define "significance." The important part of the assignment was for the student to be able to justify his selection in his own way, not that he select the same articles as the teacher. As a matter of fact, illustrative of the wide variation in what was thought to be significant, one student selected a very small article cut from the neighborhood paper as her most significant local news. It was the report of rattlesnakes having been sighted in the new sub-division in which she lived. Personally, one would have to agree, this did have valid significance for this student.

We made a list on the board of all the subjects mentioned in each of the three categories and discussed the way the class felt about each one. Some of the problems were quite specialized (e.g. the rattlesnakes), some quite general, even on a local level (e.g. juvenile deliquency). The students were asked to speculate on the historical significance of these "current events" in a year—ten years—a century. It was not difficult for them to pick the items that in all probability would have continuing importance. Many students spontaneously commented that they had not realized that this was *real* history. Current affairs were something separate from history. History was something to which they were oriented by a very slim thread.

Subsequent assignments attempted to consolidate the student's new historical awareness. They were asked to list the ten most important problems on various levels; their consensus was compared with a recent poll of public opinion. They disagreed in several important instances with the results of the adult poll, correctly pointing to the relatively transient or superficial nature of problems such as "pay TV" or the proposed humane slaughtering act. For the balance of the unit they were given the option in many areas—political, social, economic, religious, scientific, etc.—in which to explore specific problems which interested them and to trace their historical development.

The students began to realize that no one could intelligently begin a debate on the merits of Social Security without knowing its origin or the alternative situations arising when there was no Social Security. The difficulties arising in a local community due to the cancellation of a shipyard contract by the government brought up the entire area of pork-barrel legislation, how it came about, why it continued, and also, surprisingly, its advantages—most specifically in the entire concept of regional, internal improvements. The picture of a white boy snarling at a Negro in the process of school integration of the races pointed out a lesson in citizenship, but, too, when forced to answer "why" he did that, there developed an understanding, more important by far than the date of a fugitive slave law. Examining the quirks of history in the making—the passage or failure of major legislation by a narrow margin, made more significant a few weeks later the discussions of such events as the adoption of the Declaration of Independence and the acceptance of the Federal Constitution on the part of the various states. [1]

Later, as these classes began discussions of each historical period, their almost automatic reaction was to relate developments to current and analogous situations. We feel that this is a major responsibility of history instruction. There is no *one* place from which to start any historical study, but the major justification for the study of history lies in its current applications, whatever they may be. Whether the lessons of ancient history begin with Herodotus or with fable or myth, our personal lessons of history begin with the remembrance of a burnt finger on a stove. The history teacher can attain his aims by organizing his course in such a pattern.

In an attempt to move to the sort of vital history experience described above and from the unhappy but typical views of history as something dead and fixed, as memorization of names, as a mere chronology of events, and as a collection of affairs largely unrelated to contemporary times, we present the following introductory unit for a course in U. S. History.

UNIT I HISTORY IN THE MAKING:
THE UNITED STATES TODAY

I. Introduction

In beginning your study of United States History it is important for you to understand WHY history is important. Every day in a democ-

[1] For a further discussion with many examples of this "present-past" approach to history, see Richard E. Gross, "Current Affairs and American History," *Social Education*, pp. 173–75, April 1956.

racy such as ours we are called upon to make decisions—or to select representatives to make decisions for us. In order to do this intelligently we must, each one of us, be aware of the background which lies behind any current situation. It is hoped that you will come to realize the necessity of knowing what has gone before—of knowing history—to successfully solve problems facing us today. History does not give us specific answers, but it gives us information upon which we can act.

II. General Instructions

Evaluation of your learning during this unit will be based on three types of work; equal credit (one-third) will be given for: the written exercises, class participation and projects, and quizzes and tests. The level of work a student selects for his written project will determine the highest possible grade for his written work, but it does not guarantee in any way that he will receive this grade. For investigational exercises a minimum of two different reference sources must be used (these references must be different types; for example, two encyclopedias may not be cited to meet this minimum requirement). For advanced learning activities a minimum of four references must be used, including one periodical source. Exceptions to the above requirements can be made with the permission of the teacher. Such permission will be given for activities as book reports in which case the only outside reference material normally cited will be background information on the author or comparisons with other volumes. In all cases be sure and check with your teacher and the librarian for suggested sources of information.

III. Requirements

A. All Students: All students will be required to complete the first two investigational exercises. They will be turned in for analysis by the teacher one week from the date assigned. Students should keep these exercises when returned and make any changes indicated by the teacher prior to handing them in along with the remainder of their work at the end of the unit.

B. Those Students who are Working for a Grade of "C": In addition to the requirements for all students, those students who are working for a grade of "C" will complete three additional exercises, two of which are to be selected from the investigational exercises, and one map exercise. A grade of at least "C" in the unit examination should be earned.

C. Those Students who are Working for a Grade of "B": In addition to the requirements for the grade of "C", those students who are working for a grade of "B" will complete two additional exercises, one of which is to be an advanced learning exercise, the other of which may be selected from any part of the unit. The quality of all work, of course, should be at the "B" level.

D. Those Students who are Working for a Grade of "A": In addition to the requirements for the grade of "B", the additional requirements will include at least two additional activities which may be selected from any part of the unit. Most important, however, the student working for an "A" grade should remember the need for depth and thoroughness of endeavor; he will be expected to demonstrate a top-flight quality of work for the entire unit.

INVESTIGATIONAL EXERCISES

1. (Required) Examine a newspaper and select the article which you feel is most important on
    a. an international level   c. a state level
    b. a national level   d. a local level
   Write a brief paragraph on each part, indicating why you think it to be important and what you think will be the result.
2. (Required) Make a list of
    a. the ten most important problems facing the United States today (in your opinion) and why you feel they are important. Be sure to list them in the order of importance.
    b. the same for the five most important problems in California.
    c. the same for the five most important local problems.
3. How have inventions affected the history of the United States?
    a. Prepare an oral or written presentation to illustrate conditions before and after the invention—this may be short or in outline form. (select any invention)
    b. Select between five and ten inventions which you feel have brought the most important changes in American life. Briefly indicate why you selected each invention you choose.
4. What are some of the important "checks and balances" in the U. S. Government? Select an issue and suggest a related law, tracing how that law would be passed and how the checks and balances of our our government would function in preparing the law and reviewing it. Make a chart.
5. Make a report on the history of Selective Service (the Draft) in the United States, and the provisions for Selective Service today. What alternatives does a young man have now?
6. What issues are involved in the Tidelands controversy? Why has that issue become more important in recent years?
7. Public opinion polls are becoming more and more common for everything from presidential elections to favorite TV programs. How do they operate? Do you think they can be accurate?
    a. What are some of the possible inaccuracies? Why?
    b. Assume you wanted to poll the public on a particular issue.
       Word the question so you think the answer might tend to be positive—negative—neutral.

8. We objected violently when Egypt nationalized the Suez Canal. Suppose you were the U. S. delegate to a conference which proposed the *internationalizing* of the Panama Canal. Other delegates point out the U. S. stand on Suez. Obviously we (the U. S.) do not favor an internationally controlled Panama Canal. What arguments could we use? The case for the U. S. policy must be prepared by you.

9. The Berlin airlift was an important foreign policy decision within the past several years. Describe how the airlift functioned; why you think we decided to do it.
   a. How effective do you think it was?
   b. What might have happened had we not chosen to provide the airlift?

10. There were many books published about the U. S. following World War II on national and international affairs. Select any book (with the approval of the teacher) and make a report on it. The teacher will discuss in class what must be included in a book report. Both fiction and non-fiction works may be appropriate.

11. Write a brief history of our current military alliances (NATO, SEATO). Why are they important? What are their weaknesses in your opinion?

12. The defense of America is a widely discussed topic today. How has the defense of America changed during the past fifty years? Why? Is our defense, in your estimation, better or weaker than fifty years ago?

13. The St. Lawrence Seaway has finally been approved. What effect will it have on the United States as a whole? On the Eastern part of the U. S.? Is it justifiable for the entire country to finance a regional project? Why?

14. Some people say juvenile delinquency is increasing; others disagree. What do you think? Why? What can be done to reduce the current delinquency rate below what it is today?

15. Select any phase of the integration-segregation issue which interests you. With the teacher's permission prepare a report which you find useful.

16. Biography
   a. Select a great man; read about him and make a report on his contributions and why you feel he was able to accomplish what he (or she) did.
   b. Select a not-yet-great man (young scientist, politician, business man, etc.) and tell why you feel he (or she) will become great—a success in his field. What are the ingredients of success?

17. Make a chart showing how means of communication have changed, showing methods of one hundred years ago, fifty years ago, and today (both domestic and international).

18. Make a chart showing comparable travel times and means of transportation one hundred years ago, fifty years ago, and today (both domestic and international).

19. Make a chart of the United Nations Organization. Discuss the relationship of the U. S. Government to the United Nations and how we are bound by UN decisions. Select a particular function of the UN and investigate it in some detail. (Example: The United Nations issues UN stamps. How is it able to do so? Who can use UN stamps; where does the revenue from such stamps go? Why were special UN stamps issued?)

20. We hear much about high taxes. You might find it interesting to make a chart showing where the "tax dollar" goes. After making the chart, pretend you are a congressman on the appropriations committee. What changes would you make in apportioning the national budget? Why? Could you reduce the budget? How?

21. Devise a way to present graphically the balance of trade for the U. S., including our major imports and exports. Prepare two such charts, one for 1900 and one for 1957 showing how such imports and exports have changed. If you are interested, you might select earlier periods for additional comparison.

22. Investigate and report on the significance of polar air routes on: travel, industry, international relations, communication, and other topics you find affected.

23. In some parts of the United States it is possible for an eighteen-year-old citizen to vote. Do you support this practice? Why or why not? What are some of the arguments which have been made on both sides. You might present your findings to the class in the form of a panel discussion. It might be interesting to make a questionnaire to distribute to the class to determine class opinion.

24. You are teaching a citizenship class for prospective U. S. citizens. The class has asked you to prepare a short summary of "election facts." Prepare such a chart or summary indicating how the president is elected, senators, congressmen; the number of senators, congressmen; how congressional representation is determined; and other information you feel all citizens should know about national elections.

ADVANCED LEARNING ACTIVITIES

1. If we suddenly had a depression, what provisions are there for relief and recovery? Select two or three typical persons of different backgrounds (e.g., farmer; school teacher; skilled workman; etc.) and indicate what they might do to provide for themselves during such a depression.

2. Make a report on the recommendations made by the Hoover Commissions for reorganization of our federal government. Which ones would you agree with? Why? Disagree? Why?

3. Select two or three important Congressional Investigations and give a brief synopsis of what investigation was made, and what the results were. Many of these investigations have been very controver-

sial. Are the investigations, in your opinion, justified? Are their methods justified? Should they be limited? How? Why?

4. Make a study of American Highways—how they were routed, financed, built, etc. What changes have occurred in thinking (e.g., freeways) in the past few years? What future changes do you anticipate? Do you think we are expanding our highways fast enough? Too fast? How do you think they should be financed?

5. Foreign aid is costing every American who pays taxes. When did we first give such aid? Did we ever receive foreign aid? Why do we give money and materials to other countries? How is the program administered? How has the program changed since 1946? What per cent of our tax dollar is spent on foreign aid?

6. Suppose you were a high school student from India and wanted to emigrate to the U. S. You would find the quota was completely filled for the next twenty years under current regulations. An English school boy would find immigration to the U. S. much easier. Why? What is the reason for such a quota system? When did it first originate? How has it changed. Do you think the system is good? Make a report to the class on your findings.

7. Prepare arguments for the following persons who would be interested in tuna tariffs and are presenting their views to a congressional committee. You might want to prepare a class presentation in skit form:
   A. Lobbyist for Japanese Tuna Exporters
   B. Lobbyist for American Tuna Fishermen
   C. Lobbyist for the Import Delicatessen Association.

8. Make a report on the history of Social Security and how it has changed since its beginning. What factors gave rise to the concept of public responsibility for the aged? Why is there a greater concern today than 50 years ago? You might consult your parents and grandparents on this activity.

9. Can you demonstrate with a collection of pictures and art forms or with a variety of records how popular American music or art has been modified through different periods of American life during the past 50 years? What do changes in these media of expression reflect about developments in American society during these years?

10. How can the atom work for us? Obviously atomic discoveries have vastly changed many things. You might be interested in looking through old encyclopedic yearbooks to find the first mention of the atom and how thinking changed so rapidly in many ways following the discovery of atomic fusion. How has this affected such things as warfare, transportation, power, etc. How would you regulate atomic testing? Would you share non-military uses with other nations? On what bases?

11. Feel free to consult your teacher for permission to conduct any other advanced learning activity that seems appropriate and which interests you.

MAP EXERCISES

1. On a map of the world show the places where U. S. troops are stationed.
2. On a map of the U. S. shade areas (states) which voted Republican and Democratic by using different color pencil or ink, in each election from 1936 to 1968 (presidential electoral only). What does such a map suggest about political forecasts?
3. Using two maps of the U. S. show how the population density has shifted from east to west by showing a comparison of 1960 and either 1850 or 1900.
4. Using per capita income as a basis for shading, show how different areas of the U. S. differ. What generalizations can be made? Why? Do you think this same distribution will continue to exist in the future?
5. Taking a field in which you are interested (Art, Music, Colleges, Oil, Cotton, etc.) devise a way to show on a pictorial map of the U. S. how such activities are distributed over the country.
6. Using two maps of the world, one polar, one ocean based—show how the concept of distance has changed by illustrating comparative distances, based on routes suggested by each.
7. Using per capita income from various countries of the world, do the same as for Map No. 4.
8. Take any current problem which you think could be graphically portrayed on a map. Consult the teacher before beginning on any project.
9. On two maps of San Mateo County show the population today and that of 1900 by using a color shading system for population density in different areas. You might make a third map showing the anticipated population in 1980 or other future date.

RICHARD C. BROWN

State University of New York, Buffalo

43. The Classroom Guest*

Have you ever invited a guest to your social studies classroom? I don't mean as a silent observer, but as an active participant in the instruction. You have? Then you are aware of the value of this type of community resource. You haven't? Then read further. The young service man (or woman) back from Korea [or Vietnam] secures the respectful attention of students of any age, and he can no doubt make a unit on the Far East more real and meaningful than any text. The local postmaster or an office holder can add practicality to your civics class. Consecutive or simultaneous visits by a local labor leader and a local businessman can insure that your students get a realistic portrayal of both sides of one controversial area of modern life. Your county agricultural agent or a farmer can help explain why food costs so much. A stamp collector, the trading representative of a foreign nation if you live in a large city, a talented homemaker, a butcher, a baker —yes, even a candle-stick maker—all can contribute something of value to your class. And, a point not to be neglected, when you invite a guest to participate with you and your students, you make a firm friend for your school.

CHOOSING YOUR GUEST

A few words about selection of classroom guests. You may want to choose and invite the guests yourself, or you may wish to give your students the opportunity of planning this learning experience. The latter can be a worth while enterprise in itself, if your students are mature enough. Perhaps you are new in the community or do not know the individual whom your students wish to invite. You may have some qualms about inviting a guest, sight unseen, into your classroom, but, if your arrangements are handled properly, you can minimize the risk of an appearance that turns out to be a dud.

"Handled properly" are the key words in the preceding sentence. When you invite your guest, tell him or her *exactly* what is involved in the appearance before the class. Tell the prospective guest the size of the class, the age level of the students, where the class meets, when it meets and the length of time you would like the presentation to take. The original

Social Education, XVII:367–68, December 1953. Used by permission.

invitation should be issued either in person or over the phone. Give the prospective guest as accurate an idea as possible of just what you expect him to do. Don't say to the local postmaster merely "I would like you to talk about civil service." Give him a good idea of the exact points you would like him to cover. Explain to him that he should be prepared to answer questions, too. If it is possible for you to provide transportation, always offer to do so. I've found, however, that in most cases guests are willing to provide their own transportation even when you have offered to do so.

PREPARATION

When your guest accepts your invitation, you may breathe a sigh of relief and think "Well, that's taken care of." Don't be so sure. Your work is just beginning. The next step is to sit down within a day or two and write a letter to your guest. You should have issued your original invitation at least two weeks before the date when you wish your guest to appear, so you'll have plenty of time to get off a letter to him. You've got him on the line now, don't lose him. Write that the purpose of the letter is to confirm your arrangements made orally. Repeat in the letter the same information you gave him previously—the size and age level of the class, the place and the time it meets. If he is unfamiliar with your school building or your campus you may wish to draw him a map or make arrangements to meet him at some convenient place.

Most important, give him in the letter a written outline of the points you would like him to cover. Of course, tell him that these are only suggestions and that he may add or omit any items that he feels will improve his presentation. Suggest that he bring with him any types of material which he feels will be helpful, such as charts, pictures, graphs, pamphlets, and the like. If he can leave the materials with your class, that's fine—it will help you build up a collection of up-to-date classroom materials. You should also include in your letter your telephone number or some way in which he can reach you if he has to cancel or postpone his appearance at the last moment.

Now that you're as sure as you can be that your guest will show up at the scheduled time and place and will be properly prepared, you can turn your attention to preparing your class for the guest's appearance. If you, rather than the class, have invited the guest, his appearance should be announced at least a week before it is made. The day before his appearance the members of the class should discuss what they might reasonably expect to learn from their guest. They might wish to prepare a list of questions to ask him if the answers are not contained in his first presentation. The day after the guest's appearance, you will certainly want to discuss with the members of your class the things which they have learned. You may want them to write an evaluation of your guest's presentation in order to fix his appearance in their minds and to emphasize the points he has made.

The night before or on the day of the guest's appearance, a phone call is not out of place, the purpose being to see if any last minute appointments will prevent his coming. Even with all of this careful preparation, no teacher can ever be absolutely sure that something untoward will not take place. Once a guest asked me if it was all right to tell a joke. I answered, "Certainly" but I didn't know he was going to tell the kind of joke which he told.

When you have read this far, you may have decided that it is far easier just to keep on teaching classes by yourself with no one but you and your students in the classroom. But try it sometime—invite a guest to your classroom. It's somewhat less difficult to arrange than a field trip and can often be just as profitable. And, remember, when you invite a guest to your classroom, you are not only giving your students a profitable experience. If you treat the guest properly and give him a stimulating experience you've made a friend for your school.

JAMES H. McGOLDRICK

Administrative Assistant to the Superintendent,
Bristol Township School, Pennsylvania

44. *Using Novels in History Class* *

Someone once said that history is the study of everything. This may be an exaggeration. It is true, however, that the teacher of history is fortunate; he can draw his material from any field of human endeavor.

One particularly rich field for material is the novel. Novelists do deal with everything under the sun and the teacher who makes a modest study of the genre will be rewarded amply by a supply of good novels pertinent to any unit in his course. Parenthetically, this is true also of courses other than history.

The uses of the novel are many. They can be used to: enrich a particular unit; expand a concept only partially developed in class; provide depth to a unit; cover a topic usually omitted from the curriculum; present a different or unusual view, one that students would not normally get.

For example, Howell's *Rise of Silas Lapham* enriches a unit on the growth of business in the United States by providing insight into the life and times of an early tycoon; Koestler's *Darkness at Noon,* by portraying vividly the peculiar mentality of the professional Communist, expands the concepts only partially developed in class; the horrifying picture of the Okies in Steinbeck's *Grapes of Wrath* lends depth to a unit on the Great Depression; Orwell's *1984* poses a terrifying view of what the future could be and thereby covers a topic usually omitted from the curriculum; finally, Roberts' *Oliver Wiswell,* a sympathetic characterization of the Loyalists in the American Revolution, presents a different and unusual view for the consideration of the student.

This is not to say that all students will achieve automatically the goals indicated above. The effective use of any learning device requires forethought by the teacher, especially the use of novels. Randomly chosen novels cannot be thrown haphazardly at randomly chosen students. Nor can the student be turned free in the library with instructions to choose a suitable work. The library is, after all, like a supermarket, wonderful for consumers who have been taught brand discrimination, confusing for the unlearned.

To avoid this confusion, we must be certain that, in addition to being

Social Studies, 54: 95–97, March 1963. Used by permission.

appropriate to the unit of study, the novel is appropriate also to the student. It can not be too far beyond his reading level. The ideas therein must be within his capabilities. His attention must be directed to those points we wish mastered.

This last concerns us here. How direct attention to those points—the salient ones—we wish mastered?

One effective way is to hand the student a typed sheet containing a hundred or so word synopsis of the novel and a list of questions he should be able to answer after he has read the novel. Also, the typed sheet should contain a brief list of books for additional study if the student so desires. (An example is appended to this article).

Both the synopsis and the questions are important. The synopsis because it serves to familiarize the student with the material in advance; it is that much maligned overview. The questions are the points to be mastered. These can be varied to suit the talents of the particular student.

Since to paraphrase Gertrude Stein, a student is a student is a student, we must check up on the results of the reading. Here the old standbys seem best. If the book is read prior to the unit it illuminates, then the oral report serves best, or perhaps a panel of students who have read the same book. Naturally, the written report can be used, or a conversation about the book between the student and the teacher.

Regardless of the method of checking employed, the experience of directed reading is superior, for the high school student, to the supermarket technique.

A SAMPLE OF THE TYPED SHEET GIVEN STUDENTS BEFORE THEIR READING.

Synopsis

Darkness at Noon is the story of an old Bolshevik, Rubashov, who falls from grace and is swept up in Stalin's great purges of the mid-1930's. Rubashov is a "good Communist," that is, he is loyal to Communism, to the Party, and to the peculiar Communist theory of history. He retains this loyalty through his arrest, "questioning," trial, even to his execution.

Basically, the book is an account of Rubashov's hearings before two different Examining Magistrates: Ivanov, a contemporary of Rubashov, a man devoted to logic and opposed to torture; and Gletkin, a younger man devoted to the idea that torture is necessary to expose and eliminate "enemies of the people." Ivanov, who conducts the initial examination, is himself purged for his "failure" in the Rubashov case. Gletkin then becomes Examining Magistrate.

Ultimately, Rubashov capitulates, confesses, is tried, and executed.

QUESTIONS TO BE ANSWERED WHEN
YOU FINISH THE BOOK:

(1) Is Rubashov's theory of history valid?

(2) Rubashov thinks that "the ends justify the means." What does he mean by this? Could a democratic society be built on this basis?

(3) Describe the personality of: Gletkin, Ivanov, Rubashov, Number One. Could any of these men rise to power in a democratic society?

(4) Rubashov thinks it inevitable that The Revolution push aside the Ivanovs in favor of the Gletkins. Is he right?

(5) What incidents in the book show the basic inhumanity of Communism? (Omit the treatment of Rubashov).

(6) In his dedication, Koestler says that the "historical circumstances" of the novel are real. Are they?

ADDITIONAL READING FOR THOSE INTERESTED
IN THIS TOPIC:

D. Shub, *Lenin.*

I. R. Levine, *Main Street, USSR.*

A. Moorehead, *The Russian Revolution.*

H. L. Roberts, *Russian and America: Dangers and Prospects.*

H. Seton-Watson, *From Lenin to Malenkov.*

T. Draper, *The Roots of American Communism.*

RODNEY F. ALLEN

Social Studies Teacher, John Dickinson High School,
Wilmington, Delaware

45. Using Speeches To Enrich History Instruction*

History teachers have been increasingly concerned in recent years with the enrichment of instruction. Introducing new methods to better their students' understanding of man's past achievements, they have also invigorated traditional methods, such as the lecture and the notebook, to convey basic factual material. This current experimentation, however, has tended to overlook one resource readily available and rich in potential— the public address as delivered by orators now gone from the American scene.

As an instructional technique, the utilization of speeches has twofold merit. First, when well selected by the teacher, an orator's words can present the spirit of an age to students far removed from the time and place of their original delivery. These words are not just the material of the professional historian, and, thus, meaningless to the students. They constitute a primary source for learning about the past in an interesting manner.

Orators chose their words to develop interest in their ideas and to capture the imagination of their contemporaries. Their phrases were appeals to reason and human emotion, with each address embodying not only the sentiments of its author, but, more significantly, reflecting the spirit and milieu of its time. By realizing that the eloquent speeches were closely interwoven with the moment of their delivery and that they are indicative of the values, attitudes, and assumptions of the audience, the students today can readily determine the successes, failures, disappointments, and aspirations of people in dust-laden eras.

Secondly, public addresses from the past will aid students in developing their ability rationally to analyze contemporary problems, when learning of an age by examining its speeches. Standing as monuments to past issues, the views of opposing orators present history to the student with more zest and interest than the usually dull, uninspiring textbooks, while challenging —almost forcing—the student to react to the opinions that they express. It is difficult for him to be passive in the face of the orator's persuasion and eloquence. He must reconcile the divergent views with his conception of the period and make a judgment as to the meaning or significance of each

Social Education, XVIII:209–11, April 1964. Used by permission.

speaker's claims. He must assess the opinions with regard to their own time, and he must isolate his own prejudice. By using this historical perspective and the available evidence, an attempt to form a rational judgment on the historical issue is essential training for future application to the problems the student will face as a citizen in a free society.

Although both of these merits stem from the use of speeches to teach history, it is not a new method, nor would their use be a return to a long-forgotten device. Teachers have carried the words of silver-tongued orators into the classroom for generations, a fact attested to by the legions of students that have heard of Washington's "Farewell Address" and Lincoln's "Gettysburg Address." The reason for concern is that the students have only heard about them and did not come into contact with the statesmen's ideas in context. These speeches were drained of their eloquence, and their ideas were extracted and catalogued before the students came to grips with them. Slogans were manufactured and recited in the classroom. Unfortunately, with this approach the students were deprived of an essential part of their education; the ideas were gleaned from the chaff, but the potential of the public address as an instructional technique was diminished.

Textbooks, as well as teachers, catalogued slogans and followed a pattern of using only the tried-and-true addresses. Their repertoire consisted of an established number of "standards" that received shallow consideration each year. The "Cross of Gold" speech, delivered by William Jennings Bryan before the Democratic Party convention in 1896, is an example of a speech that is mentioned or quoted, given a significant place in the political literature of its era, and has its title explained. While this is necessary, the title is left standing superficially as an artifact for all to view. The political ramifications of Bryan's words are lost. The "Cross of Gold" is an exercise, often times one of memorization, that is soon forgotten. In place of an understanding of Bryan's anxieties, another event is added to the long succession of events known to the student as history.

To counteract this condition the teacher may easily incorporate speeches into the daily lesson plan to supplement other methods, or, with more research, he can build an entire unit of instruction based upon historic addresses, using them as the orators did—to educate. Certainly, his students would be more receptive to them and the excitement of vigorous verbal conflicts than to a textbook.

Each period of American history is rich with speeches that can readily be introduced into the classroom for instructional purposes.[1] These

[1] For example, see: William Norwood Brigance, ed., *A History and Criticism of the American Public Address*, vols. 1 and 2 (New York: McGraw-Hill Book Co., 1943); vol. 3, ed. Marie Kathryn Hochmuth. (New York: Longmans, Green and Co., 1955); Raymond F. Stearns, ed., *Pageant of Europe: Sources and Selections from the Renaissance to the Present*

speeches are easily located. Standard historical guides, such as the *Harvard Guide to American History*[2] and the Library of Congress' *Guide to the Study of the United States*[3] serve admirably in the initial search for printed sources. Biographies of historical figures will give reference to their orations. *The Reader's Guide to Periodical Literature,*[4] *Poole's Index to Periodicals,*[5] and the New York *Times Index*[6] are only a representative sample of the fine guides with which addresses can be located. A few hours' visit to a well stocked library will be sufficient indication that the burden will not be finding material, but rather the selecting and sorting of the abundant legacy.

Anthologies provide the most easily used source for addresses in printed form. They include general collections, such as Houston Peterson's *A Treasury of the World's Great Speeches,*[7] collections centered about basic issues, such as *The American Forum: Speeches on Historic Issues,*[8] and collections of speeches by a specific orator, like Herbert Hoover's *Addresses on the American Road.*[9] Volumes containing general collections of documents usually have included many speeches. Examples are Henry Steele Commanger's *Documents of American History*[10] and Harold C. Syrett's *American Historical Documents.*[11] Not to be overlooked are the published accounts of debates in legislative halls, especially those of the federal congress, which are virtual digests of the diverse opinions on important political questions. And, since 1934, a periodical entitled *Vital Speeches of the Day*[12] has printed contemporary addresses on an exhaustive array of important issues.

Newspaper and periodical files in the local library or historical society constitute a valuable printed source for the teacher desiring to promote more extensive research and creative thought on the part of his students. Using specific topics or periods as a guide, contemporary accounts of national and local addresses can be located. These local sources lead to discoveries of local orations that shed light on broader aspects of history. And, by proceeding from the specific local concerns, national issues can be

---

Day, rev. ed. (New York: Harcourt, Brace and World, 1961); and Willard Thorp, Merle Curti, and Carlos Baker, eds. *American Isues*: vol. 1, *The Social Record* rev. ed. (Philadelphia: J. B. Lippincott, 1955).

[2] Cambridge, Mass.: Belknap Press of Harvard University Press, 1954.
[3] Washington, D.C.: Government Printing Office, 1960.
[4] New York: H. W. Wilson Co., 1900 to the present.
[5] Boston: Houghton, Mifflin Co., 1802 to 1908.
[6] New York: *New York Times*, 1913 to the present.
[7] New York: Simon and Schuster, 1954.
[8] New York: Harper and Bro., 1960.
[9] New York: Charles Scribner's Sons, 1938.
[10] New York: F. S. Crofts and Co., 1941. Revised editions available.
[11] New York: Barnes and Noble, 1960.
[12] New York: 1934 to the present.

presented. For example, a speech supporting the construction of a local railroad spur line is indicative of the town's reaction to the revolutionary changes in transportation prior to the Civil War. A speech complaining of low farm prices in a period thought to be one of prosperity is important, for it demonstrates the exceptions found in historical generalizations. Thus, by supporting or offering exception to preconceived notions, the local addresses can show the aberrations in the historical process.

These printed sources have been supplemented in recent years with recorded addresses. Original speeches by the original orator are available on tapes and discs, such as *The War Speeches of Winston S. Churchill: Famous Passages Selected by the Editors of Life.*[13] Addresses from earlier eras have been professionally recorded by skilled dramatists usually giving a remarkable degree of fidelity to what is known about the original speaker's style of presentation. But, when such professional recordings are not at hand, school or local drama groups have individuals sufficiently skilled to recreate orations suitable for classroom use, when tape recorded. Of course, the possibility of letting students make their own recordings in conjunction with an English or speech class should not be forgotten. Nor should the tape recording of contemporary radio and television addresses for comparison with those of past periods be overlooked. There is no apparent reason for not finding and utilizing worthwhile speeches in the history classroom, given these abundant resources and the ease of obtaining them.

Once the topic of instruction has been selected by the teacher and the addresses gathered, there are numerous techniques that might be found to convey the desired impressions and to develop appropriate skills. For introducing a daily lesson, for example, the presentation of an address could establish the topic or gather interest. William Jennings Bryan's address, entitled "The Forces That Make for Peace or War," as delivered before the Federal Council of Churches in 1914, might be used to begin a discussion of World War I. Conversely, to summarize the day's lesson, to give supporting evidence to the conclusions arrived upon by the students, or to leave an impression for consideration at the next meeting of the class, a speech might be read aloud or played on tape.

Aside from this, a class can compare selected addresses to understand better the topic under study and to collect facts with which to arrive at their conclusions about the topic. For the War of 1812, Daniel Webster's "Speech on the Conscription Bill (1814)" would be contrasted with President James Madison's "War Message" or with John Randolph's "Speech against the War with Great Britain (1811)." For the issues just prior to the Civil War, the addresses of candidate Abraham Lincoln and those of can-

[13]New York: *Time, Inc.,* 1959.

didate Stephen A. Douglas might be compared. For the lively election at the height of the progressive era, the campaign speeches of William Howard Taft, Thomas Woodrow Wilson, and Theodore Roosevelt make enlightening reading, or interesting listening, as some were recorded as originally delivered.

In addition to contrasting addresses within the period under study, the class can readily compare speeches of different eras to see the continuity of certain basic difficulties that face mankind. While the issue of colonial subservence can be observed through the phrases of Patrick Henry's famous oration before the Virginia Convention of Delegates on the eve of the American revolution, two different aspects of this same problem can be seen by John Brown's "Last Address to the Virginia Court" where he was tried (1859) and by the more recent words of Belgium's U.N. Representative Van Langenhove, speaking before the Institute on World Organization on the benefits of colonialism. By studying the inaugural address of Jefferson Davis, several addresses by Lincoln, and earlier speeches by John C. Calhoun, the class would be able to gain an insight into the constitutional and economic problems faced on the eve of the Civil War, but the address by Henry W. Grady before the Boston Merchants Association on "The New South" heightens the students' comprehension of the meaning of the war in the South and its economic consequences.

Used intermittently with other methods, these addresses will provide the basis for whole units of study—alone—without the use of additional material, other than, perhaps, a general factual survey provided by the teacher or a textbook. Thomas Hart Benton's and Daniel Webster's speeches during the 1820's and 30's, Lincoln's addresses on the Civil War, and Wilson's speeches on the first world war convey the spirit and the aspirations of their time, lending themselves to unit study in the American history classroom.

These suggestions are not exhaustive by any means, and there are many variations of the ones mentioned here. It is up to the individual teacher to develop methods suited to his expectations and to his particular classes. Speeches offer an excellent resource for instilling the ideas of the past into the minds of today's students. The love of speaking and hearing speeches from the rostrum, pulpit, and stump—if not the soap box in Hyde Park— has been deeply engrained in the American character. This has not diminished today, but has been magnified by television and other mass media. The teacher in search of new means with which to stimulate his students can seize upon this popularity and present speeches in a manner to foster a deeper understanding of history than is possible with more traditional methods. Perhaps the two following sample units will be helpful, although undoubtedly each teacher will want to develop his own unit according to the needs and facilities of his particular class.

UNIT I
The Coming of World War in Europe
And American Interests

A. Franklin Delano Roosevelt's *Quarantine Speech* at Chicago, Illinois, on October 5, 1937, and his address ("I Hate War") at Chautauqua, New York on August 14, 1936.

B. Neville Chamberlain's *Peace for Generations Speech* in the House of Commons on February 21, 1938.

C. Adolf Hitler's *Deprived Sudeten Germans Speech* at Nuremburg in the closing days of September, 1938.

D. Winston S. Churchill's *First Speech to the House of Commons as Prime Minister* ("Blood, Toil, Tears, and Sweat") on May 13, 1940.

E. Churchill's *"Give Us the Tools" Address* on February 9, 1941, over the radio.

F. Roosevelt's *Message to the 77th Congress* on January 6, 1941, and the earlier *War Message,* delivered on December 8, 1941.

G. Robert M. Hutchins' NBC radio address, *"America and the War"* on January 23, 1941.

UNIT II
Postwar Period
Promise, Prospect, and Reality

A. George C. Marshall's *Harvard Alumni Association Address* (Marshall Plan) delivered on June 5, 1947.

B. Henry Wallace's *The Price of a Free World Victory* delivered before the Free Nations Association on May 8, 1942.

C. Roosevelt's *Four Freedoms Address* on May 8, 1942.

D. Churchill's *Iron Curtain Address* at Westminster College, Fulton, Missouri, on March 5, 1946.

E. Harry S. Truman's *Truman Doctrine Speech* before Congress on March 12, 1947.

F. Truman's *Inaugural Address* (Point Four Program) at Washington on January 20, 1949

G. Walter Lippmann's *Phi Beta Kappa Address* delivered at William and Mary College on December 5, 1947.

RODNEY F. ALLEN

Social Studies Teacher,
John Dickerson High School,
Wilmington, Delaware

JOSEPH L. FITZPATRICK

English Teacher,
Stanton Junior High School,
Stanton, Delaware

46. Using Poetry to Vitalize History*

The tremendous scope of history with all of its exasperating details tends to overwhelm even the most dedicated student. The seemingly endless succession of dates, events, places, and persons is not only burdensome, but it is a record of eras remote from the student's time and place in the millennia of human existence. A teenager in the secondary school finds the past foreign to his limited experience. Even the sources of history are tedious for they speak of their time, and it is most difficult to get them to speak to the student without prodigious scholarship and industry.

For the classroom teacher, who consciously attempts to prevent his students from becoming orphaned from the past, the dilemma is twofold. He must motivate his students to learn, and he must make history meaningful by linking it to the students' experience. Otherwise, the past is mere necrology, and history is only a record of remote events.

When distilled to an essence, this dilemma is just what vehicle to use in order to bridge the gap between the historical era and the students' world. Jacob Burckhardt, the masterful Swiss historian, saw poetry as history's finest source. He maintained that there is a reciprocal relationship between poetry and written history due to their similarity in outlook and content.[1] Because the warp and woof of history intertwines with poetry,[2] it seems only logical that the serious teacher consider the merits of poetry in closing the "gap."

To the most casual observer these merits, or better the similarities, are clear:

1. History and poetry are literature written for an audience and hopefully for its pleasure and edification, as well as to personally satisfy

*Social Education, XXIX,529–33, December 1965. Used by permission.

[1] Jacob Burckhardt, Force and Freedom: Reflections on History (New York: Pantheon Books, 1943), pp. 67, 144. This view is amplified in his chapter "On the Historical Consideration of Poetry." Also of interest are The Letters of Jacob Burckhardt, Alexander Dru, trans. (London: Routledge and Kegan Paul, 1955); and Judgments on History and Historians, Harry Zohn, trans. (Boston: Beacon Press, 1958).

[2] While the French histor is translated to the English "knowing," the Greek histos means "web," "loom," or "warp." The poet also deals with this "knowing" and the "web" of human experience.

the author. But the intended audience must carry knowledge and experience to the literature to develop empathy with the ideas expressed. Without these, there is little comprehension, and the recorded impressions cannot expand the reader's perspective.

2. Both poetry and history are written upon the basic assumption or premise that all men want to know where they have been, where they are for the present, and where they are going. And further, it is assumed that the authors have found some answers for their readers.

3. They represent an art form which finds beauty in its style and form. While this art is to be admired, appreciated, and encouraged, it is essentially a means to convey an idea and to arouse thought.

4. In their search for the Good, the True, and the Beautiful, poets and historians depend upon an amalgamation of creativity and imagination, as a vital core.

5. Selectivity is required, and the poet and historian have a relatively free choice of subject and material for presentation. Their decisions reflect the spirit, or *Zeitgeist,* of their era as well as their personal engagement with the vital issues of the day.[3]

6. Both clear the debris from human experience and discover that which is worth preserving. They offer a framework without excessive detail, and present the significant, the tragic, the great, and beautiful in a meaningful pattern.

7. Finally, both poet and historian take the vast and diverse legacy of human experience and distill an idea or series of concepts which add meaning to existence. They appreciate the continuity between men and periods of time. They glean the fundamental motives of men from their actions and search for underlying values. In all cases, the poet and historian stand to interpret for the reader, to present a view of a longer past and a longer future.

In this context the teacher may quickly dismiss poetry dealing with nostalgic or heroic themes. They have an obvious connection to the study of the past, whether written by contemporary poets trying to construct an image for their fellows or by later generations of poets searching for golden ages and great men. Henry Wadsworth Longfellow's "The Midnight Ride of Paul Revere" and poems extolling the virtues and wisdom of Washington, Lincoln, Napoleon, and Alexander the Great fall into this category. Teachers have used their lines to heighten an interest in histori-

[3]In the writing of history and history textbooks, there is a current trend to show detachment from vital and controversial issues, justified in part by a plea for objectivity. Arthur M. Schlesinger, Jr., urges a direct confrontation with crucial issues and a commitment to enduring values. *The Politics of Hope* (Boston: Houghton Mifflin Co., 1963), pp. ix–xii, 127. There is also a tendency to see history and poetry as escape devices for withdrawing from the pressing issues and dilemmas of life in the twentieth century. Secondary school students might be made aware of this through the basic concepts of Arnold Toynbee. See his *Study of History,* abridged in two vols. by D. S. Somerville (London: Oxford University Press, 1957). Archibald MacLeish comments on this subject in his *A Time to Act* (Boston: Houghton Mifflin Co., 1943).

cal inquiry, but for senior high school students their contribution is mundane and far from sophisticated intellectual fare.

Epic poetry, while it, too, carries an obvious connection to the study of history, is of considerably greater importance. It is dramatic in its form and popular in its appeal. For the scholar, teacher, and student, epic poetry, like the sagas of the Teutons, the lore of the Charlemagne cycle, and the folk myths or "fairy tales" of the Grimm Brothers, are useful in the study of nationalism. These works were not possessed with a need for historical accuracy and objectivity. They generally present a romanticized version of national origins of a people for their own consumption. The idealized epics were vehicles to convey a sense of a common past, a national character, and even a united feeling of exclusiveness. For students examining the phenomenon of nationalism in South and Southeast Asia, the *Ramayana* and the *Mahabharata* must be understood; for ancient Rome it might well be *The Aeneid* of Virgil or the recorded legend of Romulus and Remus; for America in the years after independence, they could read Joel Barlow's *The Columbiad*.

But the advantage of utilizing poetry in history instruction lies mainly with the work of the lyric poets. Their qualities serve the teacher in a two-fold manner: first, a source for insights into a specific period of history; and then, a source for history as a continuum with universal or constant elements in the deeds of men in the flux of time.

The lyric poem is a cultural artifact for the period of its conception, and, as such, it can tell the history student a great deal about its period in a perceptive manner. There is the brevity of the poem and its fresh approach. The reader is forced to react quickly or to contemplate. With a stroke of brilliant insight, the poem can kindle with a line what hours of research in other sources might miss. The poet offers by reflection what a mere collection of facts derived from the dry, factual completeness of a textbook does not provide. And, in any case, there is little time in the high school course to allow for an exhaustive or extensive study of many primary—or even secondary—sources. The poet simply provides an opportunity to examine one source intensively to capture the flavor of his time.

What the poet elects to write about and what he says about his subject reflect the spirit of his era, or its *Zeitgeist*. There is a process of reduction as the lyric poet explores the relationship between the man and his time. This contrasts with the usual approach of history which relies on a categorization of eras and events into their component parts: causes, effects, and personalities. In the subsequent generalizations, there is a danger that the student will be left without a grasp of the totality. Here the poet does not assume that the whole is the sum of its parts. With an intuitive sense he constructs an understanding of the whole fabric, while maintaining its fundamental unity. He deals with hopes and fears and never forgets the human concerns. He deals with one mundane aspect, but lifts it to the general or abstract to give evidence as to the spirit of the time, or general outlook of the era.

In this connection, Frost's "The Gift Outright" comes to mind immediately. The maturing of English colonists into an American nation is reduced to the popular outlook forged by the omnipresence of abundant land and willing soil.[4] Wilfred Owen's "Anthem for Doomed Youth"[5] and Karl J. Shapiro's "Elegy for a Dead Soldier"[6] express the decaying futility of war and its bitterness and waste without charting each battle. With a view of one dead soldier in the mud, an impression is made which a statistical analysis of the First World War would lose.

This process of reduction is the poet's device as he uses the familiar to explain the complex facts of an historical era. John Gay offers a vivid impression of London life in his "Trivia; or the Art of Walking the Street,"[7] and other poets used their art in social criticism which is often far from subtle.[8] The plight of the traditional ethic was reduced to the plight of "The Scholar Gypsy" by Matthew Arnold, and he supplemented this with a sonnet entitled "Quiet Work,"[9] contrasting the "fitful uproar" of man's activity with the enduring, tranquil labor of nature.

Arnold with his pensive melancholy reflects the pain of transition—forced upon his era by the reorganization of life in a new industrial civilization. The old values were isolated as he wrote in "Dover Beach (1867)" that

> . . . we are here on a darkling plain
> Swept with confused alarms of struggle and flight,
> Where ignorant armies clash by night.[10]

Once the student is trained to read with perception and to appreciate metaphor, the mood of the poem becomes the focal point for his study of the transition in England during the nineteenth century. The commonplace experience of the student looking out over the ocean becomes a vehicle to comprehend the greater concern of Arnold's work.

[4]*The Poems of Robert Frost* (New York: Random House, 1946), p. 399.

[5]*The Poems of Wilfred Owen* (London: Chatto and Windus, 1921), p. 669.

[6]*V-Letter and Other Poems* (New York: Reynal and Hitchcock, 1944), pp. 42–46. This poem is available in a series by the Division of Music, Library of Congress, entitled "Poets Reading Their Own Poems." See Record PL7 (12", 33-1/3 rpm), recorded in 1947 and published in 1945.

[7]*The Poetical Works of John Gay* (London: Oxford University Press, 1926), pp. 113–19.

[8]For social criticism in American history, the teacher might use Robinson Jeffers, "The Purse Seine," E. E. Cummings' "plato told," William Vaughn Moody's "On a Soldier Fallen in the Philippines," or "America Was Promises" by Archibald MacLeish. For an excellent discourse on diverse poetry, the student might read Cleanth Brooks and Robert Penn Warren, *Understanding Poetry* (New York: Holt, Rinehart and Winston, 1960).

[9]*Matthew Arnold: Selected Poems* New York; Appleton-Century-Crofts, 1951), pp. 1, 67.

[10]*Ibid.*, pp. 53–54.

This is the magic of the poet for the history student. The poet presents a specific incident to elicit the involvement of the student, emotionally and intellectually, and to get him to bring his own experience to bear on the subject. The poem's concern and the student's experience become one.

Robert Frost once wrote that his initial response as a reader of poetry was in suddenly realizing that he already knew what the poet was presenting. The poet merely gave vital meaning to a fact of Frost's life by bringing his dormant past experience to consciousness. Here the poet was a catalytic agent, quickening the response and enabling the reader to associate with the concern of his work.

With well selected poems, the skillful history teacher can tie his students to the historical era or event under examination in the classroom. For example, he may need to impress the students with the plight of a leader who has outlived his time or even the loneliness of the elderly. Although the students are only teenagers, they can find empathy with these persons by reading Edward Arlington Robinson's "Mr. Flood's Party,"[11] A. E. Houseman's "With Rue My Heart Is Laden," [12] or Wordsworth's "Michael."[13] Eben Flood's plight becomes the students' possession, and it means something personal to see the old shepherd Michael's shattered hopes. [14]

While poetry is an excellent source for learning about its time in history, there is a fundamental distinction to be made between this use of poetry and the use of lyric poetry which speaks for all times. [15] By its employment of the universal analogy, this latter poetry transcends from the period of its conception to serve the history student in his examination of the continuum of human existence. [16]

The value of poetry is enhanced because of this projection of the particular into the realm of the general or universal. With introspection the poet uses one moment to convey the essence of all such moments. As with all art, the poem is the intensification of emotion and experience. The creator might attempt to capture the significance of the specific moment, as did Myron in sculpting the Discobolus, or in the manner of Eastern art, he

[11] *The Collected Poems of Edward Arlington Robinson* (New York: Macmillan Co., 1921) pp. 573–75.

[12] *Shropshire Lad* (New York: Avon Publications, 1950), p. 85.

[13] *The Poetical Works of William Wordsworth* (London: Oxford University Press, 1944), 2:80–94.

[14] "The Last Leaf" by Oliver Wendell Holmes is valuable here. *The Poems of Oliver Wendell Holmes* (New York: Houghton Mifflin, 1887), 1:1–2.

[15] Burckhardt, p. 143.

[16] This results from the poet's choice of an enduring idiom, theme, or reference. The poet of lasting worth ultimately comes to the concerns of all men in all periods of time. His work shows the issues which his era faced—or should have faced—and then, it transcends to the problems of later generations. Hence, the poet's concern is really the lasting concern of mankind. See Archibald MacLeish, *Poetry and Experience* (Cambridge, Mass.: The Riverside Press, 1961), pp. 23, 75. Also C. Alphonso Smith, *What Can Literature Do For Me?* (New York: Doubleday, Page, 1919), p. 125.

might show the universal aspect with a portrayal of a tiger as all tigers or a battle scene as all battles for all time.

With this in mind, Edwin Markham's "Man with the Hoe" [17] soon becomes all men with hoes in the traditional agrarian villages where the balance between man and land is tenacious and life difficult. Dylan Thomas' vision of five sovereign fingers in "The Hand That Signed a Paper, Felled a City"[18] is a conceptual framework with which to study the dynastic-state system, any of the several partitions of Poland, the despotism of Aaronzeb in Mughal India, or the sheer might of the autocrat who rules by personal whim. Its quintessence is the totality of despotism and nothing less.

While the writing of history stresses flux and history teaching delineates the evolution of the contemporary situation, poetry has an eye to the enduring qualities of man and the ever present conflicts. Hart Crane attempted to break through the barrier of time, or the "world diamentional," to show the enduring absolute values of all men. His poem entitled "The Bridge"[19] offers the reader a view of the spiritual forces in man's motivation.

With the material metaphor of a bridge, Crane related the transitions from one historical period to the next. The enduring quality was always the ideals of man. But Crane wrote in the years of the Great Depression, after the frustrating years of World War I and the shallow 1920's. While these years had seen the destruction of the old order, the poet showed that idealism was still possible in a world stressing the material aspects of life.

In the new industrial structure of life, man could find personal satisfaction, and his spiritual values still were relevant to his situation. Crane related eight phases of American existence, and saw the spiritual consciousness of the individual in each. Between these, the bridge was one of moral fibre and spiritual goals.

"The Deserted Village" by Oliver Goldsmith is another poem which speaks for its time, and then lends meaning to the eras in which all nations undergo the transition precipitated by the Industrial Revolution. In England the agrarian workers were driven off the land to huddle in burgeoning cities, and Goldsmith says:

Far, far away thy children leave the land,
Ill fares the land, to hastening ill a prey,

[17] *The Man With the Hoe and Other Poems* (Garden City, N.J.: Doubleday, Page, 1926), pp. 15–18.
[18] *The Selected Writings of Dylan Thomas* (New York: New Directions, 1946), p. 37. Thomas' poems are presented on phonodiscs: Record TC 2014 (12" 33-1/3 rpm 4 sides), published by Caedmon in 1953.
[19] *The Collected Poems of Hart Crane* (New York: Liveright Publishing Corp., 1933), pp. 1–58.

> Where wealth accumulates, and men decay;
> . . . a bold peasantry, their country's pride,
> When once destroyed, can never be supplied. [20]

In other nations industrialization siphoned the peasantry off the land, and in colonial territories urban artisans were pushed back upon the countryside. But all cases were similar. The lives of people were turned upside down and suffering was the price for industrial progress. A sense of social conscience did not develop in keeping with technology, so Goldsmith continued with greater intensity and heightened indignation, writing that

> . . . the long pomp, the midnight masquerade,
> With all the freaks of wanton wealth arrayed,
> In these, ere trifflers half their wish obtain,
> And telling treasure sickens into pain. [21]

Through this poetry, the history student can see a more pertinent meaning in his labor. The poet will put a lasting mark on the student's mind which the ordinary sequence of historical facts cannot achieve, for through the poet, values as well as facts and skills are essential. What was clear to Jacob Burckhardt will be clear to the student—that once true to the spirit of his age, the poet is part of the legacy of all men for all times. [22]

The good lyric poem's concern is simply impervious to the passing of time. It stands ready for use by the history teacher today, as both a source for its time and for comprehending universal elements in the flux of recorded history. Through the universal analogy, the gap between the student's experience and the historical era can be bridged.

[20] *The Collected Poems of Oliver Goldsmith* (Philadelphia: J. B. Lippincott, 1893), p. 33. A phonodisc of Goldsmith's poems read by Robert Speaight has been published by Argo: Record RG 119 (12", 33-1/3 rpm).

[21] *Ibid.,* pp. 40–41.

[22] Burckhardt, p. 144.

JOHN KIMBALL

Social Studies Teacher, Patterson High School, Baltimore, Maryland

47. Music and the Teaching of American History*

How can history be made more meaningful?" "Are we giving as much attention to the cultural aspects of our history as we give to the political, economic, and international phases?" "Have our pupils learned how the music, art, architecture and literature, and even the philosophy of a period reflects or is influenced by the historical developments?"[1] These questions should be examined for a number of reasons, none of which needs to be recounted here, for it is not the intention of this paper to discuss course content, but rather to suggest the introduction of music as a supplementary aid in the teaching of history.

Oftentimes, students can gain a deeper understanding of a particular period and a clearer insight into the events that took place at that time from listening to the songs that have come down to us through the years than they have been able to obtain from any reading they may have done.

There is a wide variety of approaches to the use of songs in the classroom. The suggestions here presented are intended merely as a starting point from which it is hoped both teacher and student may be encouraged to explore the field further.

Either printed songs or recordings may be used. For example, a teacher could introduce a unit on the American Revolution by playing a number of recordings of songs popular at the time of the Revolution. The students might then read the words of *Columbia the Gem of the Ocean* and discuss the thoughts and feelings they believe are expressed in the song.

If a discussion of the lyrics of a song of a particular period is used to introduce a unit, it is interesting to reopen the discussion at the termination of the unit. The students will undoubtedly find new meanings in the lyrics after they have had the opportunity of studying the period in which they were written.

The founders of this country brought songs with them from their old countries. Often they modified the words of these songs to fit their new situations. It is interesting to note here that many songs have a long and varied history, cropping up in many different locations with slight modi-

---

*Social Education, XXVII:23–25, January 1963. Used by permission.
[1] *Senior High History Bulletin* (Baltimore Public Schools, January 1960).

fications in the words. A student might trace the history of a particular song and show the different ideas it has been used to portray. Negro spirituals, folk songs, work songs, and early church music all reveal insights into the thinking and feelings of the people and the times. Music of this kind will do much to make students aware of what went into the making of America.

Correlation between the teaching of history and music may be accomplished in a number of ways and to varying degrees. The following suggestions, although obvious, may be helpful in pointing the way to further applications.

Songs can be used:

> to introduce a unit or the study of a given time period
> to increase the appeal of the study of history
> to provide more associations with an event or period
> to exemplify given events in a time period
> to illustrate what people were doing and thinking in a particular time in our history
> to emphasize an event—Bunker Hill, Independence Day, etc.
> to point up similarities and differences in modes of living, occupations, thoughts, etc.
> to provide a meaningful feeling for people of the past by developing an understanding of the hopes and fears common to mankind (particularly in folk songs)
> to provide a setting or background (e.g., Puritan life, the War Between the States, etc.)
> to indicate our relationship with other nations and cultures

Coordinated activities might be worked out between the history and the music departments of the school. For example, students might create a musical setting for a unit or lesson in history under the guidance of the music department.

Although many of the suggestions here listed will be the basis of student work, it may be helpful to list a few activities that may be carried on entirely by the students themselves.

> Research projects—tracing thoughts, as they have been expressed in songs, on freedom, justice, the Constitution, national heroes; tracing the history of slavery in song; following through songs the westward expansion and migration; portraying through songs conditions on the frontier; tracing the history of transportation through song (railroads, riverboats, etc.)
> Compositions—e.g., The Growth of Industry, from ideas found in songs.
> Panel discussions—e.g., The War Between the States in song
> Singing—Pupils singing for the class (folk songs, songs of nations, etc.)

These suggestions are of a general nature and allow wide latitude in application. The field of music and song is of such great and diverse dimensions that it is unnecessary to put each suggestion in a specific framework. Each person working with these ideas will wish to fit the suggestions into his own situation according to his needs and available resources.

A great wealth of songs, books, and recordings are available for use by teachers and students. We list here some of the more readily available materials. The first listing suggests songs appropriate to a particular time period, the second, songs appropriate for use during the study of a particular topic. There is some duplication of song titles in these two lists, but this is intentional, for the lists are meant to suggest the many ways the same song may be found useful in different situations. Following the lists is a bibliography of books in which these songs may be found. They may also be found in two inexpensive paperbacks: W. Hille, *The Peoples Song Book* (New York: Boni and Gaer); B. Ives, *The Burl Ives Song Book* (New York: Ballantine).

SONGS APPROPRIATE TO VARIOUS TIME PERIODS IN AMERICAN HISTORY

Time Period	Song Titles
1607-1789	Tobacco's But an Indian Weed
	Confess Jehovah
	The Escape of John Webb
	Old Hundred
	The Dying British Sergeant
	Why Soldier Why
	Free America
	Chester
	Yankee Doodle
1789-1815	Ye Parliaments of England
	The Star Spangled Banner
	Columbia the Gem of the Ocean
	Perry's Victory
1815-1860	America
	Home! Sweet Home
	A Yankee Ship and a Yankee Crew
	Rocked in the Cradle of the Deep
	Erie Canal
	Green Grow the Lilacs
	The Sioux Indians
	The Little Sod Shanty
	Old Folks at Home
	Sweet Betsy from Pike

Time Period	*Song Titles*
1860–1877	John Brown's Body
	The Battle Hymn of the Republic
	Tenting Tonight
	Go Down Moses
	Maryland, My Maryland
	Sour Apple Tree
	John Henry
	The Utah Iron Horse
	Acres of Clams
1877–1890	The Farmer Is the Man
	Red River Valley
1900–Present	Goin' Down the Road
	Soup Song
	Oh, Freedom
	We Shall Not Be Moved
	We Shall Overcome

SONGS APPROPRIATE TO VARIOUS TOPICS IN AMERICAN HISTORY

Topic	*Song Title*
Freedom	The Star Spangled Banner
	We Shall Not Be Moved
American Revolution	The Old Lady Who Lived Over the Sea
	What a Court Hath Old England
	The Battle of Trenton
	The Fate of John Burgoyne
	Come Out Ye Continentalers
	To the Commons
	Riflemen of Bennington
Work	Take This Hammer
	Joe Hill
	Tarrier's Song
Railroads	Paddy Works on the Railway
	Track Laying Holler
	Track Calling
	Wake Up Call
	Casey Jones
Machines	Wanderin'
Depression	Beans, Bacon and Gravy
	Goin' Down the Road

SONGS APPROPRIATE TO VARIOUS TOPICS
IN AMERICAN HISTORY (continued)

Topic	Song Title
Unions	Joe Hill
	Solidarity
Morality-Justice	Jesse James
(Badmen and	Pretty Boy Floyd
Heroes)	Captain Kidd
	Quantrell
	Jim Fisk
	Bold Turpin
Coal Mines	Down, Down, Down
	The Miner's Doom
The Sea	A Roving
	Heave Away
	Johnny Boker
	Blow the Man Down
	Rollin' Home
Immigrants	Danny Boy
Cotton	Boll Weevil
Chain Gang	Rock Me Momma
	Cornbread, Meat and Molasses
	Pick a Bale of Cotton
The West	Saddle Song
	Home on the Range
	Dreary Black Hills
	Sioux Indians
	Bury Me Not On the Lone Prairie
	Chisholm Trail
	Arkansas Traveler
	Kansas Boys

BIBLIOGRAPHY

High School Library Books on Music and Songs

The following books are from the standard high school library catalog. Each book listed has certain features to recommend its use in American history classes. Some are straight histories with relatively few songs;

others are just the opposite with the proportion of songs greater and commentary at a minimum.

Barzun, J. *Music in American Life.* Garden City, N.Y.: Doubleday and Co., 1956.

Bauer, M. *How Music Grew.* New York: G. P. Putnam's Sons, 1939.

Bauer, M. *Music Through the Ages.* New York: G. P. Putnam's Sons, 1946.

Britten, B. *Wonderful World of Music.* Garden City, N.Y.: Garden City Books, 1958.

Carmer, C. *America Sings.* New York: Alfred A. Knopf, 1942.

Ewen, D. *Homebook of Musical Knowledge.* New York: Prentice-Hall, 1954.

Ewen, D. *Panorama of American Popular Music.* New York: Prentice-Hall, 1957.

Felton, H. *Cowboy Jamboree.* New York: Alfred A. Knopf, 1951.

Howard, J. T. *Our American Music.* New York: Thomas Y. Crowell, 1954.

Howard, J. T. *Short History of American Music.* New York: Thomas Y. Crowell, 1957.

Lomax, J. *American Ballads and Folksongs.* New York: Macmillan Co., 1934.

Sandburg, C. *American Songbag.* New York: Harcourt, Brace and Co., 1927.

Spaeth, S. *History of Popular Music in America.* New York: Random House, 1948.

Wheeler, O. *Sing for America.* New York: E. P. Dutton, 1944.

Books Available from Enoch Pratt Free Library

The Enoch Pratt Free Library (400 Cathedral St., Baltimore 1, Maryland) has an extensive collection of books which will be found useful in studying the role of the song in the history of the United States. The titles listed here are those thought to be most useful to both teacher and pupil.

Andres, E. *The Gift To Be Simple.* Locust Valley, N.Y.: J. J. Augustin, 1940.

Barnes, E. *American Music From Plymouth Rock to Tin Pan Alley.* Washington, D.C.: Brookland, 1936.

Brand, O. *Singing Holidays.* New York: Alfred A. Knopf, 1957.

Carmer, C. *Songs of the Rivers of America.* New York: Rinehart and Company, 1942.

Downs, O. and Siegmeister, E. *A Treasury of American Song.* New York: Howell, 1940.

Flanders, H. *Ballads Migrant in New England.* New York: Farrar, Strauss and Young, 1953.

Greenway, J. *American Folk Songs of Protest.* Philadelphia, Pa.: University of Pennsylvania Press, 1953.

Haywood, C. *Bibliography of American Folklore and Folksongs.* New York: Greenberg, 1951.

Ives, B. *The Burl Ives Song Book.* New York: Ballantine Books, 1953.

Jackson, G. *Early Songs of Uncle Sam.* Boston: Humphries, 1933.

Lawless, R. *Folksingers and Folksongs in America.* New York: Duell, Sloan and Pierce, 1960.

Lomax, A. *Cowboy Songs and Other Frontier Ballads.* New York: The Macmillan Co., 1938.

Niles, J. *Singing Soldiers.* New York: Charles Scribner's Sons, 1927.

Sonneck and Upton. *Bibliography of Early American Secular Music.* Washington, D.C.: McQueen, 1905.

RECORDS

Pupils and teachers alike will undoubtedly have many fine suggestions for records to be used in teaching history through song. Many schools have record collections in their music departments which could be borrowed for use in history classes. One of the most comprehensive guides to collections of folksong records, readily available, can be found in *Folksingers and Folksongs in America* by R. Lawless (New York: Duell, Sloan and Pierce, 1960).

A fine student project with a high interest rating could be the listing of all the suitable titles of records about a given topic available locally, such as those owned by class members, records in the school collection, items in the local library, or those available in stores.

JOHN C. ATTIG

Social Studies Teacher, Henry Gunn High School,
Palo Alto, California

48. The Use of Games as a Teaching Technique*

Inspired by the work of Professor Glenn E. Brooks, a sequence of "war games" was played in the Contemporary Thought classes at Lyons Township High School, LaGrange, Illinois. In an attempt to simulate real-life conditions of international diplomacy and to give the students an idea of the decision-making problems faced by national leaders, the two sections of the course, meeting on alternate days, assumed the roles and functions of the two major power blocs in the world. One group assumed the roles of Soviet Union leaders; the other assumed comparable roles for the United States. In each section there were a few students representing neutral blocs and key allies, who functioned in the game as independent actors.

Each student was assigned a real-life role, i.e., President of the United States, United Nations Secretary-General, etc., and assumed the full powers and responsibilities of the role. The students were responsible for acquiring knowledge concerning 1) the powers and responsibilities of the role, and 2) the military, economic, and diplomatic characteristics and interests of the two power blocs. Each side was instructed to gain from the other actors as much as possible in the form of military, economic, territorial, and diplomatic concessions. Beginning with a crisis situation, the accidental bombing of Hanoi by an American plane, each team made a daily series of military, economic, and diplomatic moves in order to achieve the objective. Moves were made in writing and were required to be actually conceivable in real life using only real life capabilities in existence at the time of the problem. Moves were designated as public, private for designated actors in the game, or secret.

The teacher functioned in the game as observer, advisor, and umpire. In the role of umpire, the instructor reviewed each move made by the two sections in order to evaluate its realism. Less than five percent of the moves were disallowed for this reason. In the role of advisor, the instructor gave advice if called upon to do so. All questions seeking advice concerned either a clarification of the powers and capabilities of the various roles or a desired insight as to what to do in a given situation.

Social Studies, 58:25–29, January 1967. Used by permission.

The former queries were answered directly and the latter were answered in the form of suggesting possible alternative moves. All moves made in the game, including the assignment of roles and tasks, were student-made decisions. The role of observer was the most enjoyable of all. It was a fascinating experience to watch the students discuss alternative moves and the problems created for them by their opposition. The teacher made no attempt to supervise the decision-making process.

The game was played with a high degree of enthusiasm and realism. It was apparent that most of the students were emotionally involved in their roles. For example, on one occasion the Soviet Union considered painting American markings on some of their North Vietnam-based planes. These planes would attack Thailand in hopes that the United States would receive the blame. The Soviet Ambassador to the United States reacted to the proposal by threatening to defect to the United States on grounds that the leader of the Soviet government was a warmonger. The ambassador's reaction resulted in the dropping of the proposal. On another occasion a Soviet note which originally demanded removal by the United States of all armed forces from Southeast Asia in the interests of preserving peace was changed from the form of a demand to that of an urgent request on grounds that the word demand was provocative and could lead to war.

An indication of student enthusiasm for the game was the number of students who desired to attend class for purposes of conferences and negotiations on days when the other section was meeting. Eleven of the thirty-nine students in the course received passes allowing them to leave study hall and attend class meetings. An additional nine students requested passes, but they were turned down because they were in other courses and not in study hall. The willingness of over half the course-members to give up their own free study time in order to involve themselves in additional game activity was unanticipated and indicated a high level of interest. At the end of the game a vote was taken on the question, "Should the game technique be used in subsequent course offerings?" The opinion of the students was unanimously affirmative.

The game technique appears to have considerable value as a teaching tool. The enthusiasm of the students for the game would indicate that it is an excellent motivation device. During the course of the game it was never necessary to prod or threaten a student into action. Because all game activities were products of the students' own creation, initiative and originality of thought were encouraged. The students were required to think realistically about the nature of the problems confronting them and were given the chance to apply theory in a simulated real-life situation. As a tool for gaining factual knowledge, the game depended on the initiative and background of the individual student. It is probably safe to say that, in general, the greater the degree of personal involvement in the role and the game, the greater the degree of knowledge gained. No definite assignments were given in conjunction with the game, but a suggested list of readings was given to all students. A student's ability to make an effective contribution to the class was influenced by the degree of factual knowledge he possessed. Because realism was a requirement of all moves and because it was necessary for most of the players to do research in order to acquire the knowledge necessary for realism, the technique probably aided the development of research skills, though not on a systematic basis. The success of the game technique is probably limited by the personalities and group dynamics of the particular class. For example, on the day that the "President of the United States" was absent, the class suffered a noticeable decline in working efficiency, which is an indication of the dependence of the class on his personal leadership.

A unique aspect of the game was the classroom-discipline situation. The law and order variety of discipline was definitely not present during most of the game. Many times the class was very noisy. If we interpret discipline to mean that the students on their own initiative set for themselves tasks which they must and do carry out on their own free will, then the game technique was outstanding. It should be pointed out that during the course of the game not once were students either prodded into action or punished for negative social behavior. The self-discipline was one of the game's most outstanding features.

Perhaps the greatest problem connected with the game technique is evaluation. A test emphasizing the subject matter involved in the game would be hard to devise. This is due to the subjective nature of the knowledge required by the various roles. The game, however, appears to offer an excellent opportunity to measure attitudes and attitude changes. Although no examination of pupil attitudes was given during this particular game experience, the remarks of the students in their own evaluations of the game indicate that certain changes of attitude did take place as a result of their participation in it. If one were to attempt to test for factual knowledge acquired during the game, one type of test would be an essay examination emphasizing the student's knowledge of his own role, its real life functions and the knowledge necessary to make the role an effective one. Another alternative would be to give separate examinations specifically tailored for each role in the game.

How did the students regard their game experience? What did they believe they learned about the subject matter of their game, international relations? At the end of the game the students were asked to evaluate their experiences. They were unanimous in their praise of the technique. In regard to international relations, most of them said that they gained a realization that the complexities of international diplomacy were much

greater than they had believed prior to the game. Most students said they
gained an awareness of the dangers implicit in every action of the cold
war which was, in their opinion, very close to a hot war. The importance
of cooperation and coordination of efforts in order to accomplish anything
was another realization. Typical of student comments are the following
excerpts taken from their evaluations:

> I have learned from these war games that a seemingly small incident or
> a word in a sentence can have far reaching effects. I see now the care
> which must be used in diplomacy.
> I was reminded that a dictatorship is resented by strong individualists.
> In the cold war no one can remain truly neutral.
> Being American, I used to think of all Communists as the bad guys, but
> now I can see the North Vietnam point of view and why they are close to
> both the Soviet Union and Red China.
> I never realized how careful one must be when dealing with other
> countries. I also never realized the knowledge and planning that must go
> into one move.
> I learned that diplomacy is a language and culture all its own. . . . I also
> learned that cold war is really quite hot! It can be blown into a full-
> fledged nuclear war proposition in a matter of hours.
> I blandly assumed that the United States and France were good and true
> allies who felt exactly the same in respect to all sorts of things, especially
> the USSR. I know now that I wasn't even "hot."
> I learned that the Cold War can not be won, only fought. It is a continu-
> ous series of battles, mostly, which go on and on.
> I learned that the Cold War is a much more complicated matter than it
> would seem to be on the surface.
> Cooperation is the only way to gain peace with, or advantage over, the
> opponent.
> I realized the difficulty in coordinating the various departments of the
> government in diplomatic strategy.
> I learned that it isn't as easy to wage a cold war as it appears—even on
> this level.
> The significance of adequate communications was brought out by this
> problem.

In considering the events and actions that took place during the game,
including the student suggestions as to how the game could be improved,
the following recommendations should be kept in mind by anyone desiring
to use the game technique. Before commencing the game itself a short
period of preparation (two to five days) is advisable. The period of preparation would include reading assignments designed to give all participants
a desired general background of information. During this time students
would have an opportunity to familiarize themselves with their respective
roles and to organize themselves into effective groups. Students should be

supplied with a list of short job descriptions which would give them some idea of the duties involved in each role, thus aiding their choice of roles. It is probably a good idea to post on the bulletin board all moves of a public nature made during the game and all announcements made by the various actors. This would help to keep all players adequately informed of the actions of the game.

The game technique has a great use potential in courses of social studies. Mock United Nations Assemblies, Presidential Conventions, and United States Congresses are but some of the areas in which the technique could be outstanding. The game technique appears to be of highest value in a course in which there is a concentration of students possessing above average ability, but further experimentation with groups possessing all types of abilities is necessary before this opinion can be considered to be of considerable validity. Those who have a negative attitude toward their studies might be stirred into good motivation by the game situation, but, if not, they would create serious problems for those who are more enthusiastic about both school in general and the game in particular.

In summary, the outstanding qualities of the game included the enthusiasm of the overwhelming majority of the members of the class and their involvement in their roles. Their self-generating efforts and discipline, particularly in setting and carrying out tasks for themselves, were the keys to success. Cooperation among the members of the class was excellent. This, too, was self-generated. Positive aspects of the game would include the understandings of international relations which were gained by the participating students.

One of the negative aspects of the game was the fact that some of the roles were not clearly defined and others, important in real life, turned out to be relatively unimportant in the game situation. There is no way of determining in advance which roles will not be important and which ones will need greater clarification in order to be effective. Only actual experience in a game situation will indicate to what extent this is true. Corrective action could then be taken for future games. It should be pointed out that those students who lack a significant degree of self-motivation or who possess little initiative are going to have problems making their roles active and effective. These people probably would handicap the class as a whole.

FRED M. NEWMANN

Assistant Professor of Education,
Harvard University

DONALD W. OLIVER

Professor of Education, Harvard
University

*49. Case Study Approaches in Social Studies**

The "case study" approach is one of the most applauded and least analyzed methods in social studies instruction. Along with programed instruction and team teaching, the mention of "case studies" signifies innovation in the language of educational magic. Just as administrators and teachers ask for comparative evaluations of team teaching versus conventional teaching, they also ask, "Which is better, case study or conventional text?" It is the purpose of this article to demonstrate that queries into the effectiveness of *the* case-study approach are misconceived and inappropriate—mainly because there is no signle method that can rightfully be identified as *the* case-study method.

The use of "cases" for instructional purposes is nothing new. For years they have been standard equipment at the professional, graduate level, most traditionally in the fields of medicine, law, and business, and more recently in certain approaches to political science and international affairs. The attempt to broaden the application of cases to various aspects of social studies at lower levels has accentuated the need for clarification and differentiation among varied approaches. One of the major sources of confusion and ambiguity is the tendency to construe case study approaches under a single umbrella or unitary concept, depending upon objectives of instruction, styles of materials and their uses. We believe that the variety of approaches occurring within the general label will result in differences in learning. Moreover, these differences may be greater than those variations in learning accounted for by a comparison between "the" case-study technique and some other general method such as programed instruction.

This is not to suggest that case studies as a class of materials cannot be differentiated from other approaches; they do have something in common which sets them apart as distinguishable approaches to instruction. In general, case studies are investigations of *single* institutions, decisions, situations, or individuals. The object is to gather detailed information about a relatively small class of phenomena, such as the growth of a corporation, the decision to enter World War I, the living conditions

**Social Education*, XXXI:108-13, February 1967. Used by permission.

of a Negro family in an urban slum, or the behavior of a politician in an election. Although case studies focus extensively on discrete instances, rather than on sweeping sets of events, the implicit assumption is that examination of a limited incident will yield conclusions that may be validly applied to a more general class of such incidents.[1]

The Harvard Social Studies Project operates on this assumption; that is, intensive study of detailed situations will lead the student toward valid generalizations. The Project, therefore, has been considered an exponent of the case-study approach.[2] In perusing its material and materials from other curricula, we notice considerable variety in both the *style* of materials and the *uses* of pedagogical application of them. Because of a general failure in the field to distinguish between varieties of *style* and *use*, case-study approaches are lumped together as a single method—an over-simplification that has beclouded curriculum theory. As one attempt to resolve this problem, we shall describe below different styles and uses of case studies.[3] The illustrations quoted below are all selected from a unit on Labor in the Harvard Project.

STYLE OF CASE STUDY MATERIALS

Story. The story, written in the style of a novel, portrays concrete events, human action, dialogue and feelings. It tells of an episode, having characters and a plot. The story may represent authentic events, as in historical novels, or it may be totally fictitious.

Illustration

YELLOW-DOG AND BLACKLIST

The bell rang. Immediately the men in the pressroom turned off the machines and began preparing to go home. After the continuous throb and roar since morning, the silence was shocking.

[1]B. Berelson and G. A. Steiner, *Human Behavior: An Inventory of Scientific Findings* (New York: Harcourt, Brace and World, 1964). An instructive contrast between the *survey* and the *case-study* methods in social science research. The former, in gathering small bits of evidence from large numbers of individuals, aims to make general or nomothetic statements about groups; while the latter attempts to make individual or idiographic statements about discrete subjects. The survey technique looks for what large classes of phenomena have in common, while the case study tries to locate idiosyncratic differences among members of a general class. This attempt at definition is not adequate to allow one to differentiate clearly all materials into two mutually exclusive categories: case studies vs. something else. It is offered only as a general description of characteristics which many case studies have in common.

[2]Donald Oliver and Susan Baker, "The Case Method," *Social Education,* 23:25-28; January 1959.

[3]For an alternative scheme for categorizing curriculum materials, see Donald W. Oliver and James P. Shaver, *Teaching Public Issues in the High School* (Boston: Houghton Mifflin, 1966), pp. 143-46.

Jeff Sargent was trying to wash away the black web of ink which clung to the seams of his palms. "The mark of the printer's trade," he thought to himself. He was proud of his hands—supple, calloused, ink-webbed, they were like tools which he had molded during thirteen years as a press feeder. But today he wanted to get them cleaner than usual. It was his tenth wedding anniversary, and he was going to surprise Sally by taking her out dancing like old times. He had secretly arranged with the landlady to take care of the kids for the evening.

Whistling loudly over the clatter of the water drumming against the wooden sink, Jeff didn't hear Lou Silver whispering at his side until the small, balding compositor nudged Sargent's elbow. "Oh hi, Lou." He turned off the water. "Now I can hear you better. What's up?"

Silver looked carefully behind him, toward the printing machines which stood in grey afternoon shadows like a herd of stolid, silent animals. "Heard about Price and Williamson?"

"What do you mean?" Sargent's thick eyebrows pulled together in a frown as he looked down at Silver, whose head barely reached his shoulder. "What about them?"

"They got the heave-ho today."

"Fired? But why? They're the best typesetters in the plant."

"Sure, but they're loudmouths. Remember last week when they were bitchin' to the foreman about the paycut? And last month when Price said the lead fumes were gettin' so bad someone ought to tell the board of health to fix the air ducts? And when Williamson said he thought we should have more than ten minutes for lunch?". . .

The meeting had already begun when Sargent arrived. About 25 men were sitting in Silver's living room—on chairs, on tables, on the floor—smoking cigars or pipes, drinking beer, and listening attentively. Silver's small hands were slicing and shaping and pounding the air as he spoke in his clipped, nasal manner. ". . . and how long are we going to take it? Don't we have rights, too? Aren't we the men who do the work while Harper is the one who sits back and gets the profits? Is our only right to work ten hours a day, six days a week, until Harper decides to fire us?"[4]

[As the story continues, the men begin to organize workers in the plant. Finally, during a confrontation with the boss, both men are fired. Jeff Sargent decides to change his name when he learns that he has been black-listed.]

Stories seem to be one of the rarer forms of case studies in social studies; the style is more conventionally found in English courses. We find the story especially effective for the purpose of involving students emotionally in a situation. The suspense of a plot and a high level of concreteness focusing on "real" human beings tends to capture student attention.

[4]Harvard Social Studies. Project *Transition and Conflict in American Society: 1865–1930*. Part IV, "Labor," p. 101.

Vignette

Written generally in the same style as the story, the vignette is a short excerpt or slice of experience. It has no completed plot.

Illustration

CARRIE MEEBER

The pieces of leather came from the girl at the machine to her right and were passed on to the girl at her left. Carrie saw at once that an average speed was necessary or the work would pile up on her and all those below would be held up. She had no time to look around, so she bent anxiously to her work.

She worked continually at this job for some time. She felt strange as the minutes passed, for the room was not very light, and it had a thick smell of fresh leather. She felt the eyes of the other people upon her, and she worried for fear she was not working fast enough.

Once, when she was fumbling at the little clamp, having made a small mistake in setting in the leather, a great hand appeared before her eyes and fastened the clamp for her. It was the foreman. Her heart thumped so that she could hardly see to go on.

"Start your machine," he ordered, "start your machine! Don't keep the line waiting."

As the morning wore on, the room became hotter. She felt the need of a breath of fresh air and a drink of water, but she did not dare move. The stool she sat on was without a back or foot-rest, and she began to feel uncomfortable. She found, after a while, that her back was beginning to ache. She twisted and turned from one position to another, but it did not help her for long. She was beginning to get very tired. . . .

Her hands began to ache at the wrists and then in the fingers, and towards the last she seemed one mass of dull, complaining muscles, fixed in an unchanging position and performing a single mechanical movement which became more and more unpleasant until at last it was absolutely sickening. . . .

For this hard, tiring, disagreeable work, Carrie was paid $4.50 a week. After she had paid $4.00 for room and board, this left her with 50 cents a week with which to buy clothes and entertainment and to ride on the street-car on days when it rained or snowed.[5]

Journalistic Historical Narrative

This is told as a news story—a narrative of concrete events, with no conscious attempt to create a plot or characterization. It could be an hour-by-hour, day-by-day description, or it might be an eye-witness account of static conditions. The historical narrative often describes the actions of institutions as well as individual people.

[5]*Ibid.*, Case based on *Sister Carrie* by Theodore Dreiser, N.Y.: Modern Library, 1932.

Illustration

THE MINE

Now you go up the chamber, taking care not to stumble over the high caps, into the notches of which the wooden rails of the track are laid. On one side of you is a wall, built up with pieces of slate and bony coal and the refuse of the mine, on the other you can reach out your hand and touch the heavy wooden props that support the roof, and beyond the props there is darkness, or if the rib of coal is visible it is barely distinct. Up at the face there is a scene of great activity. Bare-armed men, without coat or vest, are working with bar and pick and shovel, moving the fallen coal from the face, breaking it, loading it into the mine car which stands near by. The miners are at the face prying down loose pieces of coal. One takes his lamp in his hand and flashes its light along the black, broken, shiny surface, deciding upon the best point to begin the next drill hole, discussing the matter with his companion, giving quick orders to the laborers, acting with energy and a will. He takes up his drill, runs his fingers across the edge of it professionally, balances it in his hands, and strikes a certain point on the face with it, turning it slightly at each stroke. He has taken his position, lying on his side perhaps, and then begins the regular tap, tap of the drill into the coal. The laborers have loaded the mine car, removed the block from the wheel, and now, grasping the end of it firmly, hold back on it as it moves by gravity down the chamber to the gangway. You may follow it out, watch the driver boy as he attaches it to his trip, and go with him back to the foot of the shaft . . .[6]

THE HAYMARKET RIOT

People in Chicago had feared violence, bloodshed, full-scale revolution on Saturday, May 1. That is what they had been told to expect by alarmed newspapers, apprehensive employers and a few radical labor leaders. Chicago, the site of numerous strikes already in progress, was to be the spearhead of the eight-hour movement's general strike. When both Saturday and Sunday passed peacefully, however, the citizens, the police and the newspaper editorials relaxed. But it was an uneasy peace, one which smoldered with passions. . . .

On May 3, two days after the demonstration by the eight-hour movement, the Lumber Shovers' Union held a mass meeting of about 6,000 people at the corner of Wood Street and Blue Island to demand shorter hours from their various employers. A half-mile away, across a stretch of open field, was the McCormick factory, many of whose striking workers attended the Lumber Shovers' meeting. As

[6]*Ibid.,* Taken from Homer Greene, *Coal and the Coal Mines* (Boston: Houghton Mifflin, 1894).

August Spies, one of Chicago's most out spoken leaders of social protest, was addressing the crowd, the bell of the McCormick plant
rang to signal the end of a shift. Against the warning of Spies,
about 500 of the McCormick strikers advanced toward the factory
and began to attack the "scabs" who were leaving for home. As
the "scabs" retreated back into the plant, a few guns blazed between
the aroused strikers and the police guards. Soon about 200 additional
policemen arrived, charged the strikers with clubs and revolvers and
drove them away after killing at least one striker (exact fatalities are
unknown) and seriously wounding several others. Some police were
injured, but none was killed.

The incident outside the McCormick factory snapped the
patience of August Spies, who had hurried to the scene after finishing
his speech. Low wages and "scabs" were one thing; killing was quite
another. Within a few hours he published the following handbill and
distributed about 1300 copies among the workers:

REVENGE! WORKINGMEN! TO ARMS!

Your masters sent out their bloodhounds—the police—they killed
six of your brothers at McCormick's this afternoon. They killed the
poor wretches, because they, like you, had courage to disobey the
supreme will of your bosses. They killed them because they dared
ask for the shortening of the hours of toil. They killed them to show
you "free American citizens" that you must be satisfied and contented
with what ever your bosses condescend to allow you, or you will get
killed! ...[7]

"The Mine" is an eye witness description of conditions, while "The
Haymarket Riot" narrates action of people and institutions. Eye-witness accounts are often included as "source" materials in books of readings designed for history courses. Narratives (written long after the
events take place) begin to appear more frequently in instruction in
history, political science (accounts of the making of political decisions,
the paths of legislation, election campaigns, etc.), business and economics (tales of the growth and problems of particular enterprises and
companies).

Documents

These include court opinions, speeches, letters, diaries, transcripts
of trials and hearings, laws, charters, contracts, commission reports.
Public documents have the status of formal and legally valid records.

[7]*Ibid.,* p. 115. Based on Henry David, *The History of the Haymarket Affair.* (New
York: Russell and Russell, 1958).

Illustration

AN UNEMPLOYED TEXTILE WORKER

Q. What is your business? A. I am a mule-skinner by trade. I have worked at it since I have been in this country—eleven years.

Q. Are you a married man? A. Yes, sir; I am a married man; have a wife and two children. I am not very well educated. I went to work when I was about eight or nine years old. I was going to state how I live. My children get along very well in summertime, on account of not having to buy fuel or shoes or one thing and another. I earn $1.50 a day and can't afford to pay a very big house rent. I pay $1.50 a week for rent, which comes to about $6 a month.

Q. That is, you pay this where you are at Fall River? A. Yes, sir.

Q. Do you have work right along? A. No, sir, since that strike we had down in Fall River about three years ago I have not worked much more than half the time, and that has brought my circumstances down very much. . . . And another thing that helped to keep me down: A year ago this month I buried the oldest boy we had, and that brings things very expensive on a poor man. For instance, it will cost there, to bury a body, about $100 . . . Doctors' bills are very heavy—about $2 a visit; and if a doctor comes once a day for two or three weeks it is quite a pile for a poor man to pay.[8]

MULLER V. OREGON

Excerpts from Supreme Court Opinion

. . . The single question is the constitutionality of the statute under which the defendant was convicted, so far as affects the work of a female in a laundry. . . .

It is the law of Oregon that women, whether married or single, have equal contractual and personal rights with men. . . .

That woman's physical structure and the performance of maternal functions place her at a disadvantage in the struggle for subsistence is obvious. This is especially true when the burdens of motherhood are upon her. Even when they are not, by abundant testimony of the medical fraternity continuance for a long time on her feet at work, repeating this from day to day, tends to injurious effects upon the body, and, as healthy mothers are essential to vigorous offspring, the physical well-being of woman becomes an object of public interest and care in order to preserve the strength and vigor of the race. . . .[9]

[8]*Ibid.*, p. 91. Testimony before the Senate Committee on Education and Labor, October 18, 1883.
[9]*Ibid.*, p. 183.

Court opinions, briefs, and official testimony are most typically used in the teaching of law, the area which provides, perhaps, the most widely understood referent for the term "case."

Research Data

Reports of experimental and survey studies, with statistical data that can be used as empirical evidence in the testing of factual claims.

Illustration

THE ECONOMIC SCENE, 1890

The Census of 1890 revealed a total population in the United States of just under 63 million people, of whom 23 million belonged to the labor force. The distribution of these workers among the sectors of the economy was (in round figures) as follows:

Agriculture . . . . 10,000,000 (until recently farm workers had constituted over 50 percent of the labor force.)

Manufacturing 5,000,000
Trade and finance 2,000,000
Transportation 1,500,000
Construction 1,500,000
Domestic Service 1,500,000
Professional and governmental service 1,000,000
Mines, forestry, fishing   700,000
Miscellaneous   700,000

The labor force can also be divided by sex and age. Of the 23 million workers, roughly 83 percent were males, 17 percent females. About 1.5 million of all the workers were between the ages of 10 and 15 (although these figures do not count many children working part-time on farms or in tenements). Approximately one out of every 16 workers was a child, and about one out of every six persons between the ages of 10 and 15 was working. [10]

Such data can be used to train for skills in the analysis of statistics in tabular and graph form for reaching generalizations "inductively" from raw data rather than secondary sources.

Text

The text describes general phenomena and institutional trends; detail and specifics about individual humans are included mainly to illustrate generalizations. The text also *explains,* by giving definitions, causal

[10]*Ibid.,* p. 99. Statistics taken from several sources.

theories and explicit "reasons" for the occurence of the events it describes. It presumably offers objective knowledge—information which
the reader accepts at face value, because he assumes it to be unbiased
truth.

Illustration

KNIGHTS OF LABOR

In seeking better wages and hours, the American worker depended
upon the willingness of his employer to grant them. Clearly the employer had the advantage in this relationship, for he was under little
direct pressure to improve his employees' economic conditions. If
a worker threatened to quit the job, the employer probably would have
little trouble finding a new man to take his place. This was especially
true at a time when jobs were scarce.

A worker alone dealing with an employer was at a disadvantage;
but many workers acting together could exert greater pressure. If all
the employees of a factory joined together (formed a *union*) and demanded more pay or less hours, their employer would hesitate to
ignore them. For they might simultaneously stop work (*strike*), thus
halting all production and attempting (by a *picket line* in front of the
factory) to prevent other workers from taking the jobs just vacated. An
employer could try to hire a whole new work force despite the pickets,
but that would take time, and meanwhile his factory would be idle,
producing nothing and therefore earning nothing for him. So rather
than ignore the workers or fire them, he probably would negotiate with
them as a group (engage in *collective bargaining*).

During the first three-quarters of the 19th century, American
workers tried in various ways and at various times to form labor
unions, usually on a local level and occasionally on a national level.
By the year 1877, most of these efforts had collapsed. One of them
had not, however. The Order of the Knights of Labor had been formed
in 1869 by nine inconspicuous tailors meeting in the hall of the American Hose Company in Philadelphia. Their leader was Uriah S.
Stephens, who had become a tailor after the Panic of 1837 had forced
him to abandon his studies for the Baptist ministry. Stephens gave to
the Order of the Knights its essential principles and character. It was
a secret society (to be referred to in public documents only as "*****")
in order to protect it from retaliation by employers. Moreover, its
activities centered around elaborate rituals of almost religious character. In the initiation vow, for example, a new member had to declare:

I . . . do truly and solemnly swear that I will never reveal by word,
act, or implication, positive or negative, to any person or persons what-
soever, the name or object of this Order, the name or person of any one
a member thereof, its signs, mysteries, arts, privileges or benefits, now

or hereafter given to or conferred on me, any words spoken, acts done or objects intended; except in a legal and authorized manner or by special permission of the Order granted to me . . .

Although this selection relates to a single organization, and in that sense may be considered a "case," it is written in the style of a text and differs from a conventional textbook for a course only in the sense that it focuses on a narrower range of events. We have noticed a number of published "cases" written at a highly abstract level, providing not just description, but explicit explanation.

Interpretive Essay

Clearly intended as explanation and *evaluation,* the essay reaches interpretive conclusions on abstract issues such as "What were the causes of the Civil War?" "Was Rockefeller a responsible businessman?" or "Is the welfare state inevitable?" As opposed to the text, the essay attempts to construe objective reality, rather than simply report it. The essay attempts to *persuade* the reader to accept its evaluation or explanation; that is, the reader is assumed to be critical. Essays attempt to judge the present and past in terms of ethics, aesthetics and prudence; they offer definitions of concepts; they attempt to predict the future.

Illustration

DOLDRUMS DECADE

In June, 1927, *The New Republic* published an editorial entitled "A Motionless Labor Movement?":

More and more observers of the American trade-union movement, both without and within, are asking the question, Why does not the movement get ahead? In numbers it is almost stationary. In ability to organize the basic, heavily capitalized industries such as steel, automobiles, electrical equipment and power, it shows little progress. In other industries hitherto strongly organized, such as bituminous coal, it is fast losing ground. In ideas it often appears to be sterile. Against the vivid background of hope for social regeneration from labor, which prevailed during the War and after, the existing prospect seems especially stale.

An observer noting these facts must admit as a preliminary to any further discussion that the unions have been beset with unprecedented obstacles. Their war increase in membership, gained through temporary and superficial pressures, represented in large part a hothouse growth which could not withstand the chill winds of deflation.

[11]*Ibid.,* p. 107.

Labor is traditionally slow-moving and is stirred by confused, deep currents; its process of reaction and of recovery is necessarily longer than that of a trim, executive-driven capitalist organization. In addition, it has to face the determined hostility of employing and financial groups who have laid aside none of their ancient hatred for the unions, and have gained immensely both in power and in wile. . . .

Pending the germination of leadership, labor marks time. Perhaps it is fallacious at present to speak of a labor movement in this country. A real movement would attempt not merely to get more of the same things which owners and investors already possess, it would tend to transform industry and in doing so would create important issues for public life. At present, the economic drift of the profitmaker dictates the sanctions of civilization within and without our borders; we are overborne by the brute power of accumulated things. Many are capable of seeing the danger; labor has a peculiar opportunity of doing something to avert it. Alone, it cannot save us, but it stands at the intersection of the conflict and occupies a position where strategy might count for something. Yet it finds necessary merely a defensive battle, because it is incapable of giving an aggressive lead. Its old men have apparently ceased dreaming fine dreams, and its young men are discouraged from testing their visions.

Some of the most famous "source materials" included in "readings books" are essays by political philosophers (Locke, Rousseau, the Federalist papers), economic thinkers (Marx, Keynes), or behavioral scientists (Weber, Freud).

The above categories of style represent in a sense a continuum from specific concrete portrayals of individual human action to general, abstract interpretation of institutional trends. The categories are obviously not mutually exclusive; that is, any given message may contain within itself *several* levels of style. Gathering information about the style or format of materials, however, is only a first step in the assessment of any set of "cases." In addition, one must deliberate about how the materials may be used.

USES OF CASE-STUDY MATERIALS

Case studies are employed for at least two general purposes, either: (1) to illustrate foregone conclusions, or (2) to provoke controversy and debate on issues for which "true" conclusions do not yet exist. The distinction between 1 and 2 is merely the extent to which the issue at hand has been previously decided or remains open-ended. Both categories allow for the study of descriptive issues (what the world was, is, and will be like) *and* prescriptive issues (what people should have done or ought to do). Let us consider each use separately.

Illustrating Foregone Conclusions

It is often argued that the most effective way to teach important factual information is to embed the facts in an exciting or dramatic narrative. Using the suspense or value-conflict of a well-told story tends to involve students emotionally, which renders facts intrinsically relevant, resulting in more permanent retention of the lesson to be learned. Cases quoted above contain extensive background material about the problems and institutions related to the growth of organized labor in the United States. In addition to specific facts, the teacher may wish to convey definitions of key concepts or technical terms such as boycott, public hearings, supply and demand, self-interest or free enterprise. Historical narratives, stories and hearings provide concrete examples of behavior illustrating such concepts. Similarly, the teacher may wish the students to "discover" a set of basic generalizations; for example, "employers used tactics that discouraged workers from organizing"; "wage level is partly a function of the available labor supply"; "rulings of the Supreme Court have an important effect on labor's relations to management." Cases may be used to illustrate and verify the validity of such generalizations. Finally, the cases can be used to support certain prescriptive conclusions or moral lessons: "Businessmen wrongfully exploited innocent women and children"; "Workers should use only peaceful protest and should be harshly punished for violence against the state." From these examples, it should be clear that the use of case materials does not necessarily protect the student from didactic teaching. One may use cases to support predetermined "answers," dogmatic positions, and rigid indoctrination. However, one may also use them to foster intellectual autonomy, as in the following category.

Provoking Thought On Unresolved Issues

Cases may be used in an open-ended fashion to stimulate inquiry and debate on unresolved questions of fact, definition, and policy judgments. The cases provide data relevant to controversial historical and factual issues: Did nineteenth century workers have reasonably decent standards of living compared to what they left in the old country? What was the major cause of labor riots? Answering these questions raises thorny definitional issues: the meaning of "reasonably decent," or "major cause." The cases also raise important *policy* issues on both the general and specific levels: What responsibility should an employer bear for the welfare of his employees? Should workers use violence as a threat? Should Jeff Sargent have joined the strike? Should August Spies be hanged?

The object of inquiry into issues of this kind is not to have the student learn or discover the correct answer. Rather it is to have the student ana-

lyze various positions or take a position and justify it rationally. Performance is evaluated, not on the basis of the student's mastery of substantive
truth, but on the student's performance in constructing reasonable justifica-
tions of whatever position he reaches. Using cases in this way requires that
the teacher be willing to accept from students conclusions that may be contrary to the teacher's beliefs; conversely it implies that students should not
accept a teacher's opinion at face value, but only if supported by rational
justification.

Having outlined alternative styles and uses of case materials, what can
we say about the relationship between style and use. Intuitively, we might
feel that some styles lend themselves more appropriately to certain uses;
for example, texts usually convey unquestioned conclusions, thus they
would be conducive to less provocative discussion perhaps than short
stories. Comparison of sharply opposing interpretive essays would probably
lead to open-ended debate, whereas a single research report or a single historical narrative may tend to answer more questions than it raises. In the
final analysis, however, the teacher's objectives and attitudes toward inquiry are the most crucial determinants of how cases will be used. Never-
thless, a taxonomy on style and uses, such as the one offered above, may
help to initiate greater clarification to the all-too-ambiguous notion, "case
study."

LESLIE D. ZELENY

Retired Chairman, Division of the Social
Studies, Colorado State College, Greeley

RICHARD E. GROSS

Professor of Education, Stanford
University

50. Dyadic Role-Playing of Controversial Issues*

Too often students of the social studies, to paraphrase Herbert J. Muller, are taught to go forward into the future while looking backward. In other words, the curriculum in the social studies too frequently emphasizes the past rather than the problems of the present; it often concentrates upon relatively isolated facts rather than interrelationships and meanings. Many teachers of the social studies, realizing the relative sterility of certain traditional content and approaches, have become interested in introducing their students to the insistent problems of our times, such as the problem of moral irresponsibility, the problem of national survival, the capital-labor issue, and many others. But many of these same teachers, after trying to introduce the study of vital issues, have found them too "hot" to handle and have retreated into "safe" but relatively sterile practices. This withdrawal of social studies teachers from the realities and issues of our adventurous civilization, in the opinion of the authors, represents a pitiful shirking of responsibility. More than one survey points out the overriding concern for ease and security that now characterizes so many modern youth. If the next generation is being taught (or allowed) to retreat from vital issues rather than face them with intelligent understanding, the survival of our nation may indeed be threatened. Social studies instruction should not, by omission or commission, contribute to such conditions!

DYADIC ROLE-PLAYING—A SUGGESTION

We have a serious problem in social studies education when, through tradition, insecurity, or fear, the insistent social problems and issues of our times tend to be bypassed in the classroom. Perhaps one cause of this serious neglect—that has characterized throughout history the schools of nations and civilizations who failed to help meet the challenges in their declining cultures—is the lack of a successful procedure for the study and discussion of contemporary issues. For those who retreat for this

---

*Social Education. XXIV:354–58, December 1960. Used by permission.

reason we would like to suggest a modification of role-playing as one method of teaching an understanding of social issues.

The Dyad or Pair Group

Many years ago George Simmel pointed out that the dyad, or pair group, contained the "germ" of more complex human relations. In the small pair groups, Simmel pointed out, general forms of association may go on in a relatively "pure" fashion. Thus, conflict and cooperation, two "universal" social processes, often too complicated to understand, may go on in relatively simple and intelligible form in the dyad. Wolfe states that "these forms exist as much between two groups—families, states and groups of various kinds—as between two individuals." In their teaching experience the writers have noted the relative efficiency of committees of two (or three) individuals as contrasted with the more negative results of larger sub-groups of students or teachers with whom they have worked.

Role-Playing in the Dyad

Recognizing that two human beings in a dyad may initiate fundamental patterns of human relations and resolve them most effectively, the next problem is: How may real life situations or interactions be simulated in dyads in the classroom? Furthermore, how may these pair-groups be set up in a manner to achieve a desirable learning situation while, at the same time, making the teacher a "consultant" rather than an "indoctrinator"?

The significant thing about role-playing is that it provides an opportunity for students to *simulate* the real roles of representatives of groups between which there are issues, including the defense of the opposed positions, processes of accommodation, and insight into the deeper meanings of specific controversies. One who participates in the role-playing of vital issues will not only know life but he will *feel* it too. Thus, he may become a more intelligent and understanding member of a neighborhood, community, state, or nation; and the expanded self who has "role-played" international issues could be much better prepared to understand the world scene. One who has sincerely "role-played" the issues of the day in school should find the transition from school life to real life and *role-taking* much easier than when the student has merely recited upon a social studies text.

PROCEDURE FOR DYADIC ROLE-PLAYING

Our suggested procedure for initiating role-playing in the social studies may be outlined somewhat as follows.

Student Interest in a Vital Issue

Student interest is the vital, preliminary step in role-playing. This may be developed in a regular social studies lesson. Suppose, for example, the social studies teacher wished to develop knowledge and understanding of the Berlin dispute by means of role-playing. What *not* to do is to say, "Tomorow we shall study the West-East dispute over Berlin. Please read up on the subject so we can discuss it." There are several faults with this approach, as all good teachers know; but the point to be stressed here is that a teacher-decision with respect to a vital topic has been made and assigned in an arbitrary manner. Very likely, in connection with a review of key international problems, the Berlin issue will be identified by many in a class as one of significance. At this point the teacher may assist the class in deciding upon and planning their exploration of the problem by suggesting numerous, available references, by a short lecture on the history of the Berlin situation since 1944, by displaying a map or diagram of divided Berlin, or by helping the group identify the basic, divergent positions in the West and in the East with respect to the issue. Such action promotes pupil understanding of the nature of the stalemate and of the vital importance of a solution. If such procedures develop a deep interest in the issue, then the class may be ready to proceed in dyadic role-playing.

Teacher-Class Preparation

As the foregoing suggests, role-playing, except with respect to issues with which youth are informed because of their life experience or previous preparation, must be carefully prepared for by the teacher and the class. This is also why student interest is important; incidentally, an issue in which there is interest but which is too difficult to grasp at a certain grade level had better be postponed.

Since the teacher is to be a director-consultant in a sociodrama rather than an indoctrinator, he or she must thoroughly understand the subject and "lead" the students to a most complete study of the "facts" and "issues" related to the problem.

Another consideration of importance in the preparation is the climate of opinion in the community with respect to the issue. If the subject is too "hot" to handle in the community, it probably is too "hot" to handle in the classroom; "temperature" 98.6° F in the community is a better climate than 212° F for the classroom discussion of a vital issue.

Having decided to proceed toward the roleplaying of the issue, the director-consultant and the class should study with great care the *history* of the issue. In the French-Algerian issue, for example, the problems mentioned by the class in the initial discussion should be reviewed and organized so that the full historical setting as seen by all sides is understood. This work may involve reading in books, newspapers, and magazines published during the last 25 years. But this reading must be *critical* reading for the purpose of distilling "truth" from "propaganda." Students need to be helped to see the "why" of certain positions, including their own, and the limited orientation of certain opinions, and that most issues, if studied carefully, prove to be just as complex as the many-sided Algerian crisis.

Dyadic Role-Playing

When a class has properly prepared itself for dyadic role-playing, using many of the customary ways of stimulating learnings, it may proceed with hope of success—that is, there may be set up dyads which simulate the real issue. To participate in a discussion of a controversial issue in a dyad requires thorough knowledge; and, in addition, the participation may be expected to promote further *insight* into the reasons for the position of two or more groups facing the issue and, possibly, in "inventing" some new and more promising "solutions" to be taken with respect to the issue, thus extending *wisdom* in a limited area.

Recognition of Two Positions or Statuses

Role-playing begins with the recognition of two (or more) positions, statuses, or units of behavior expectancies related to the issue at hand. In the case of the Berlin issue one might say that the West (French, English, American) is expected by the situation to want to remain in Berlin in accordance with the protocol of September 12, 1944, while the Soviet Union is now expected to represent the position of a power which, since November 27, 1958, considers the 1944 protocol null and void. In addition to the mere recognition, of course, should come an understanding of the seriousness of the difference when force is suggested as a means of imposing the will of one group upon the other group. It would be equally important to delineate the varying positions of the metropolitan French, the Algerian French, the "loyal" Moslems, and the FLN "rebels" in the Algerian imbroglio.

Identification of Actions (Roles) Associated with the Statuses or Positions

Class study and discussion should be able to reproduce the actions (in this case, written and spoken words) associated with the positions or statuses. Thus, according to *The New York Times,* in connection with Berlin the role or roles of the Soviet Union might be represented somewhat as follows:

1. The agreements with respect to Berlin now assume an inequitable character.
2. The Allied presence in Berlin is illegal.
3. The occupation is abnormal fourteen years after World War II.
4. Berlin should be made a demilitarized free city.

The role or roles of the West may be represented somewhat as follows:

1. Any change in the present status of Berlin would damage the West.
2. Occupation rights of the West must be continued without interruption.
3. There is no acceptable alternative to negotiation.
4. But, if the Soviet Union introduces another blockade, a nuclear war is a possibility.

Equally clear statements and lists would have to be developed about the dilemma in Algeria or for any other problem area. Of course, role-playing which merely repeats such foregoing "skeletal" phrases would be very dull, indeed. "Deep" study would bring out attitudes, values, and emotions accompanying the "official" positions.

Only after careful preparation on an issue of interest and after opposed positions (statuses) with their actions or roles have been identified can role-playing take place with hope of success. It is recommended that it begin with pair-group or dyadic interaction. As pointed out earlier, the pair-group is the most elemental social unit; and it is one which can be observed and understood most easily by the teacher-director-consultant. Consequently, it is recommended that role-playing in a class start with pair-groups, each of the two persons representing one of the two opposed positions with respect to the issue. Thus, in a class of 30 students there would be 15 pair-groups in which each of the divergent positions would be represented.

For the classroom teacher there are many advantages in the dyadic interactions approach to role-playing. First, it involves *all* students *actively* in the learning process. Second, it encourages participation in and the development of confidence in oral discussion for the more timid members as it also prepares them for general class participation. Third, by putting the timid, the lazy, or the unprepared "on the spot" (something which general class discussion often passes by), the "natural" social pressures may motivate many not otherwise motivated. And, fourth, the teacher-consultant is more readily able to observe the work of individuals in a group of two than in a larger group. Finally, the active small-group participation provides many opportunities for the research-minded teachers to carry on objective experiments in social psychology while teaching. For example, students with varying degrees of leadership and self-confidence can be identified and by means of individual instruction made possible by the temporary release of the teacher from her customary dominant position, may be guided toward more successful role-playing and, consequently, the development of more effective personalities.

In role-playing, as outlined in this article, the authors see many possibilities for constructive guidance of individual students within a *social situation*. This should be much better in many ways than guidance in isolation in an office down the hall where the situation is unreal. As the article develops, the reader is urged to look for other opportunities for the development of personality by means of role-playing.

Before the pair-group role-playing is completed, the teacher-director should ask for a reversal of roles or positions; that is, the teacher should ask for each student to represent the opposite position. This work should be done thoroughly, for social insight comes from seeing one's position as others see it. This reverse of positions can be expected to have an important educational result—it requires more knowledge, more social insight, more patience, and more critical thinking, too.

When an important third position exists, as in the Algerian situation, it may be necessary to have three persons and rotate roles. Or two students can first thrash out the differences between French attitudes and then move to attempt to test a composite or compromise French position against the unresilient rebel view. Here the students are helped to personally experience many-sided, emotionally-impacted issues and to grasp the great difficulties in their resolution.

The final exercise may be for the pair-group participants to "look at" the work they have just done to consider how well each position was represented, to ask the teacher for more information, to consult other sources of information, and to replay certain parts of their work for more accuracy.

Role-Playing Before and with the Group

If the teacher-consultant believes the class is now ready for "more advanced" role-playing and analysis; and if he or she has identified a "successful" pair-group (or two other students who can make a good pair-group), the class can move ahead.

After a brief consultation, the selected pair-group may appear before the class. Then, while the class listens to determine the effectiveness of their role-playing, the pair-group presents as representative a discussion of the issue as is possible.

When the selected pair-group has finished, or even before it has finished the teacher-director may call for comment and evaluation with respect to the authenticity of the role-playing. This may involve an extended discussion, including suggestions for better representation of roles. The whole or part of the activity may be repeated. Also, volunteers may be invited to "show" some possible better ways.

The teacher-director, by means of the process just outlined, has set up a second procedure which is dynamic rather than static; it has required the use of information and temporary identification with the attitudes, values, and feelings of the two groups in the conflict.

In our illustration of the Soviet Union vs. the West over Berlin, it is intended, of course, that Americans will study the Soviet position to learn how to deal more intelligently with it in terms of our national interest and the realities of the situation that also involves varying British, French, West German, and East German outlooks.

The "Invention" of "Solutions"

Classroom role-playing makes it possible to try out several alternative solutions to an issue and to have them considered by all pair-groups in the class and by a representative pair-group before the class, too. In the case of the Berlin issue such "solutions" as the following may be considered. Is the status quo the answer? Is war the answer? Is a free city the answer? Or what other "solutions" are within the range of possibility? Where *should* the U.S.A. stand with respect to the Berlin crisis; and what are the possibilities for negotiation? All ideas should be "tried out" and the probable arguments of representatives of each position presented. Some "correlation" of ideas might be seen to be possible to "save the face" of both groups and a "solution" no one has thought of before may be shown to have some merit. This is true creative thinking in the area of the social studies.

All of this work should challenge the best brains in a high school class and stimulate *all* of the students. Often the weak students will not be very successful; but, on the other hand, one can expect that they will do no more poorly than otherwise. Some may do much better, and they may learn considerably from observing the dramatic role-playing situation.

The Group Decision

The studies of Kurt Lewin and others have shown that people are more likely to act in accord with a belief *they* have decided is sound than upon a belief someone (no matter how enticingly) has presented in a lecture. Though the representation of various positions and roles in itself can be expected to have influence, Sheriff's studies imply that a *group decision*, perhaps made by a secret ballot, will determine where the majority stand with respect to a possible solution and influence those who are in the minority group too.

USES OF DYADIC ROLE-PLAYING

So much for a brief outline of a procedure which may be used in dyadic role-playing. These techniques could vitalize history classes, for many of the issues of earlier days can be brought to life by these methods. In world history the possibilities of role-playing controversial issues are legion; and the issues are warm enough to be interesting, but they are not too hot. Take, for example, the land reform issue in Rome at the time of the Gracchi, or John Huss and the Reformation, King John and the Magna Carta, the nobility versus the peasants at the time of the French Revolution, the issues over the League of Nations at the time of Wilson, etc. Histo-dramas bringing these important conflict situations to life could make world history much more interesting and exciting.

The same procedures can be applied to make some of the issues in United States history more deeply understood. For example, the issues related to the Revolutionary War, or those facing Jefferson and Hamilton at a cabinet meeting, Lincoln and McClellan at Antietam, or the rise of the New Deal, and many others are most appropriate. The authors suggest that such issues with all their facets could be "role-played" in pair-groups (dyads) to involve the active thinking of as many in the class as possible followed by a general sociodramatic presentation, analysis, and consideration of the implications of "solutions."

Contemporary issues are probably the best medium for dyadic role-playing. Local, national and international issues are appropriate in this connection. Locally, taxation problems, urban development problems, school segregation problems, management-labor problems—when submitted to dyadic interaction—can stimulate a great deal of interest and worthwhile study. These also serve to promote the development of insight with respect to community issues now too frequently slighted in social classes.

Issues are legion on the national scene. Here labor-capital relations become national issues; similarly taxation problems, civil rights problems, farm problems, conservation problems, problems of family policy, population policy, and many others can be treated by means of dyadic-interaction.

Finally, on the international scene, pertinent problems seem to mount. The crises touched upon in this article indicate the possible scope. Often these issues are extremely complex and they can prove difficult to handle. But these, too, can be treated by means of dyadic role-playing. Local, national, and international problems are now increasingly enmeshed. An issue of relatively local concern (a tariff on Fuller's earth) can produce national action and have international reverberation. On the other hand, the divisive question of the entrance of Red China to the United Nations can become a hot, community, election issue in a Congressional district in Illinois. Thus, related aspects of such contemporary affairs at different levels —local to international—provide excellent learning opportunities useful in several different phases of a unit. The writers would encourage teachers to explore the varying uses of role-playing in introducing a topic, for clarifying opposing viewpoints, as a part of group hypothesizing, in summarizing a lesson, and evaluating the outcomes of instruction.

One of the alarming tendencies in education in our time is the timidity and even failure of many teachers of the social studies to face squarely social issues past and present. *One* reason for this failure has been the difficulty the teacher has had in separating himself or herself from one side or other of an issue. Another may be the lack of enough good techniques for the "fair" and "just" treatment of issues. The authors suggest dyadic role-playing, alone or in combination with socio-drama, as *one* answer to a very important problem in teaching for citizenship.

According to Simmel, the dyad or pair-group is the "social-germ" in which fundamental or elemental social relationships take place. Since local, national, and international relationships over social issues are often too complicated or vast to be readily comprehended, especially by the young student, the "compression" of the essentials into a dyadic relationship may be expected to be comprehensible. Simulated interaction in the dyad with respect to an issue, frequently in conjunction with the sociodrama, is outlined here as a means that helps make social issues both real and, at the same time, "approachable" in the classroom.

ARTHUR A. DELANEY

Geography Teacher and Curriculum Materials Coordinator, New Hyde Park Memorial High School, New York

51. Guidelines for Selecting, Planning, Conducting, and Evaluating Field Trips*

The use of field trips as a device for teaching is not new. Teachers commonly accept the field trip to be a means by which local or community resources outside of the school and classroom are made available by means of first-hand experience.

The field trip is an escape from classroom routine; too often, unfortunately, this escape is considered to be the paramount purpose for embarking upon a safari from the confining walls of cloistered learning. Every experienced teacher is well-aware that many students eagerly anticipate a field trip as a convenient vehicle by which they can take an excursion *from* learning. We must also admit that some teachers view the field trip as a "day off from teaching," if not an outright, but temporary abdication of remunerated duties. But, yet, professionals and students alike will quickly reiterate that field trips have a definite place in the scheme of teaching and of learning. The field trip can be a dynamic and vital medium for learning *only* if it is well-planned.

It is commonly-accepted canon of the teaching profession that teachers will plan in advance for all class-room sessions. Indeed, numerous articles have been published in the educational journals about the teacher's need to develop a sound set of lesson plans. The most basic of texts used in the preparatory teacher-education courses indoctrinates the prospective teacher to the principle of developing a set of daily lesson plans which are both practical and workable. As soon as the new teacher acquires his first teaching assignment, he will find that his principal, coordinator, or department chairman will place emphasis on the teacher's ability to develop instructional plans.

If the lesson plan is to be regarded as a fundamental aspect of the teacher's professional duties, and if the field trip is to be viewed as a teaching session which has been removed from the stereotyped confines of learning, is it not equally desirable for the teacher to develop a sound and meaningful

Teacher's College Journal, XXXVI:102–104, December 1964. Used by permission.

end that is common to all good instruction? The answer is obvious. This writer, however, has observed numerous situations where teachers of all levels of experience have utterly neglected the basic principles which guide field trips to the successful outcomes commensurate with sound education.

The following guidelines generally applicable to most grade levels and teaching situations, are offered to help both the novice and experienced teacher to do a better job in selecting, planning, conducting, and evaluating field trips:

I. SELECTING THE FIELD TRIP

The following considerations should be noted in advance by the teacher:

A. Be alert to possible field trip opportunities which will broaden a course of instruction. Very often, the obvious is overlooked in favor of the spectacular.

B. Define your purpose. Why go on a field trip? The teacher *must* ask himself: "Is there anything to see on this field trip which could not be seen as well, and sometimes better, from carefully selected pictures, slides, and motion picture film?" Does the field trip include materials that can not be covered as well in the classroom or are unobtainable from other sources?

C. What materials, experiences, or concepts may be developed as a result of using a particular field trip to supplement a method or style of classroom instruction?

D. Will the resources seen and the phenomena observed be appropriate for the age and maturity levels of the group? Will it be a resource that will arouse interest?

E. Will the use of a field trip justify the time students and teachers must spend away from the classroom environment?

F. Every field trip experience should be unique in at least one respect. Is there enough original experience to be gained from the proposed trip? Will the experience gained alter or add desired attitudes and behavior patterns exhibited by your students?

G. Will the field trip develop within the student skills for observing critically and with comprehension? Will the experience of the particular trip challenge thinking of your students?

H. Will the objectives of the field trip be achieved in the amount of time available?

I. Can you make use of the resource as a general application in more than one area? How can this trip aid in the strengthening of learnings in other curriculum areas?

II. PLANNING THE FIELD TRIP

The success of the field trip depends largely upon advanced planning.

A. Arrange far in advance for suitable and appropriate transportation.

B. If possible, the teacher should go over the route ahead of time, while conditions are about the same as those expected to prevail at the time of the proposed trip.

C. Communicate with persons in charge of the site to be visited. Obtain permission from park superintendents, landowners, or others responsible for the grounds on which the trip is destined.

D. Establish a definite routine for all trips so as to reduce the management factor to a minimum. Have students prepare a standard of behavior for their group. Since field trips are generally less formal than class periods, it may be necessary to impress students that a field trip "is an educational experience and not a picnic." Such discussion will be geared to the level of group maturity.

E. The teacher should explain to his students the purpose for the trip, and what is *likely* to be observed. Prepare, in conjunction with the class, a series of trip objectives, questions to be answered, and items to be noticed at the site.

F. Arrange for any special administrative clearance: check administrative regulations.

G. If necessary, obtain the consent of parents or guardians.

H. If the trip is to be of any length, it will be necessary to locate suitable lunch and rest stops.

I. The teacher should explain suitable dress and footwear for the field trip occasion.

J. Make a working estimate of costs. In general, the problems of financing the trip should be attacked by the class as a group problem, unless, of course, the class is fortunate enough to have the school "foot the bill."

K. The teacher should outline precautions to be taken against natural hazards, if any.

L. It is important that previous to taking any trip, the teacher selects and uses a variety of materials so that each student will have enough background to do selective viewing on the trip. If possible, show photographs, color slides, motion pictures, or drawings made on a previous or similar trip.

M. It would be wise to plan enough activities to fill most of the time, but not enough to try to do too much within the available time.

N. If feasible, mimeograph an advanced guide or map for distribution to each pupil.

III. CONDUCTING THE FIELD TRIP

A. Arrange for adequate supervision.
B. Develop and implement a workable plan for group movement. If time is important, the quickest route to and from the site should be taken. Plan for a constructive activity enroute; such activity goes a long way towards eliminating possible disciplinary problems caused by boredom. Encourage students to observe along the actual route leading to the destination. Arrange in advance to take a different route for the return trip to school.
C. The itinerary, as planned by the teacher or in teacher-pupil cooperation, should be strictly adhered to except in cases of emergency. Non-educative diversions should be avoided. Unless the field trip starts and stops on time, it will lose some of its effectiveness: Concentrate only on scheduled stops to keep the experience meaningful.
D. Make the most of unexpected occurrences and observations volunteered by the group. This is one time when opportunistic behavior is to be supported.
E. Endeavor to provoke opportunity for all students to see and hear.
F. Take advantage of guided tours whenever possible. The guides possess more knowledge about the "thing" or "spot" being observed than does the teacher. Be sure, however, the guide understands what you and your students want from the trip.
G. The teacher should remain in the background during the actual period of observation. He should, however, be *readily* available to act as a resource person, or more likely, as a guide.
H. Encourage students to ask questions of all available resource personnel.
I. Encourage, if feasible, students to take notes, make drawings, or record photographs of/or about items or scenes which are important or of interest to the student.

IV. EVALUATING THE FIELD TRIP

A good field trip program should include careful follow-up in the classroom, and teacher or teacher-student evaluation of the trip for present or future use.
A. Carefully interpret or analyze the trip as soon as possible after the return to school. It is because of this principle that some teachers refrain from scheduling field trips on Fridays.

B. A quiz may be developed by the teacher; however, this writer would generally *avoid* such attempts at evaluation; there are so many better methods for arriving at a valid evaluation.

C. For many trips, oral or written reports are appropriate. These reports may be sent to the school newspaper, or, if appropriate, to the trip's host. Sometimes, one evaluation should be formulated by the students, and another by the teacher for future use or for use by other teachers.

D. The results of the trip should be compared and discussed against the framework of original objectives:
1. Did the trip fulfill its purpose?
2. Did the trip fulfill other objectives?
3. Was it worth the time and effort? Could the same instruction be achieved through the use of audio-visual or textual materials in the classroom?
4. Has the field trip provided training in research techniques, in asking questions, and in interviewing adults?
5. Has the trip provided training in the etiquette of travel?
6. What new interests were developed? Has the trip provided real experiences, useful insights and new knowledge?
7. Did the students complete the answers to the questions prepared in class?
8. Should this trip be taken again next year, and can it be recommended to classes doing similar work?

E. Discuss the field trip with a view towards:
1. Paying attention to attitudes developed by the students.
2. Noting the observations made by the students.
3. Reviewing the highlights of the trip. Point out the aspects of the trip which were important to a special phase of the subject and to other aspects which were less important.
4. Encourage students to discuss methods by which future field trips may be improved.

F. Arrange for an exhibition of items collected on the field trip, if it was a trip of such a nature.

G. Share notes taken on the trip. A "Trip Experience Log" is a highly useful tool which helps to bring the field trip in clear focus.

H. Arrange for a showing of pictures taken on the trip.

I. Develop, if appropriate to the age-level, an evaluation check list or questionnaire.

J. Make sure your students realize the larger picture of which the field trip was only a part. A field trip is rarely an end in itself: usually it is a part of a larger, comprehensive activity.

The Teaching of Attitudes and Values

EUGENE McCREARY

Department of Education, University of California, Berkeley

52. American Values*

The tragic events in our country—ranging from regional massive legalized injustice and inhumanity toward our Negro people, shameful disrespect and defiance of Congressional committees by youth of a leftist orientation, insults and abuse heaped on our Chief Justice and our representative to the United Nations by older citizens of rightist convictions, widespread dissemination of hate literature, and, finally, the tragic assassination of our President—have raised doubts at home and abroad of the health of our national value system.

The clear reaffirmation by the courts that religion is not to be inculcated in public schools further emphasizes the importance for all teachers to consider the place of values in our instruction. The social studies have always accepted in principle values as a central objective. These events raise serious questions as to the effectiveness of our citizenship training and of our teaching of democratic values.

Of the objectives for the social studies expressed in various programs and guides, the one which some teachers often feel reticent to accept and work toward is that of attitudes and values. Generally, social studies objectives lie in three areas: 1) concepts, generalizations, understandings; 2) skills and abilities, especially problem solving and critical thinking; and 3) values, ideals, and appreciations. Objectives ought to guide teachers in the choice of subject matter within the general areas set forth in curricula and suggest appropriate learning activities and procedures. Some social studies teachers assume responsibility for the objectives of 1) and 2), above, more readily than for objectives of value.

California Social Science Review, 3:17–23, February 1964. Used by permission.

Teacher reticence about teaching values arises from several considerations:

1. Some teachers fear any teaching of values would be indoctrination, an authoritarian imposition of one's own values on others.
2. Some teachers doubt that there are any universally accepted values in present-day American which teachers should presume to transmit.
3. Some teachers, recognizing that values lie at the heart of all controversial issues, fear that any commitment to particular values in advance would render impossible an objective or scientific approach to problem solving.
4. Some teachers appear to feel that attitudes and values, often labeled "moral and spiritual," are so associated with religious and spiritual commitments as to be inappropriate or inadmissible in public schools.

Dangers of indoctrination lie less in the objectives of education than in the means taken to achieve them. Democratic values, by their very nature, do not lend themselves to indoctrination. As we shall see later on, the most appropriate and effective means of working toward these values are necessarily free of authoritarianism. In short, one cannot be forced to be free and democratic! Democratic values are acquired through democratic experiences in a climate of respect for human beings.

It is true that there is some confusion as to what values are basic, general, universally acceptable, and pertinent to American civilization today. Values of a society do change. The accepted values of today are not merely the accepted values of 1776 or even of 1861. Some values remain of perennial validity; others are discarded, if only reluctantly. For example, we have changed our attitudes toward women's rights, toward slavery, toward taxation and the election of leaders, toward freedom of thought and expression, toward a spirit of respect for differences and the necessity for compromise.

Dead and dying values sometimes are used as propaganda from time to time in the heat of controversy. New values are being born in the world and in the United States today. No values are universally accepted and few of us live unequivocally by any values. We live in a society of stress and change, in a time of conflict and deep anxiety. Our values are being tested. Our state social studies program provides for us a framework of values which are presently considered central to democratic institutions.

A most important vehicle for the study of values in the classroom is the problem-solving approach.[1] This should include the analysis of solved

[1]See *The Problems Approach and the Social Studies,* Richard E. Gross *et al.,* ed., National Council for the Social Studies, Curr. Bul. no. 9 (Washington, D.C., 1960).

historical problems as well as the study of current controversial issues. It is not inconsistent for the teacher, in leading students into such problem solving, to clarify value commitments at issue—in fact, this is one of the teacher's major responsibilities. In such studies of controversy, values will be in conflict, and choices will be made. For example, the under-ground-railroad assistance to fugitive slaves was a clear violation of legal and generally accepted property rights. It was an expression of human rights. In the historic resolution of this and related conflicts we chose to affirm human rights. In considering this controversy, students need to understand the value conflict and the new commitment we made as a people. There are, of course, many other ways in which a social studies teacher should work with values beyond problem solving.

The concern about the religious nature of "moral and spiritual values" is a misunderstanding. In fact, the moral and spiritual values which have been defined for the public schools are merely the meaty kernels of social studies concepts generally accepted by scholars.

Despite the concerns of some, values remain a basic objective in social studies. In fact, unless this objective is kept in mind, the next generation, like the last, may continue to consider social studies only the memorization of dates, battles, and heroic sayings. Teachers are expected to transmit our democratic heritage, and this consists essentially of values. The problem for teachers lies in the choice of values which are founded in the traditions and experience of our people and in the choice of teaching procedures which are free of indoctrination.

In 1951, the Educational Policies Commission defined for public schools certain values which could be considered a common denominator of our democracy. These values included:

Respect for human personality
Moral responsibility of the individual
Institutions are servants of men
Common consent (peaceful adjustments rather than violence)
Devotion to truth (freedom of expression)
Respect for excellence
Moral equality for all
Brotherhood (the golden rule)
The pursuit of happiness (happiness considered as the fullest expression of one's potentialities—not mere "fun")
Spiritual enrichment[2]

In 1959 the California Teachers Association chose seven of the foregoing as values we should be concerned with in schools. Many other

[2]Educational Policies Commission, *Moral and Spiritual Values in the Public Schools,* National Education Association (Washington, D.C., 1951).

values could be listed which most of us would endorse.[3] One, for example, which is central to social studies is "respect for the contributions of all peoples to our civilization."

It is doubtful if many Americans would reject any of the above values, at least verbally. They are reflected in our basic documents. They appear to be assumptions of our institutions. It would be poor education to attempt to indoctrinate young people with these values, but it is difficult to see how our institutions and ideals can be taught without developing a respect for these values. Actually, all of the values listed are the substance and meaning of many of the concepts of the social sciences defined for the California social studies curriculum by scholars from the eight disciplines in the state "Social Studies Framework." For example, "devotion to truth" is realized by the political science concepts, "The most important of all freedoms is freedom of thought and expression," and "A free society is hospitable to new ideas and to change and encourages the unfettered search for truth." "Brotherhood" is realized by history's concepts, "Brotherhood is one of man's oldest experiences," and "No man (or group of men) has ever been able to live alone," and "Interdependence is found to be a constant factor in human relationships." "Moral responsibility" is realized by the political science concepts, "The citizen has civic responsibilities as well as rights," and "A democratic society depends on citizens who are intellectually and morally fit to conduct their government. Civic responsibility and moral courage are balance wheels for a democracy." The last value, suggested by this writer, is clearly supported by history's concept, "People of all races, religions, and cultures, in all parts of the world, and in every historic period, have contributed to the development of our civilization."

Assuming that the values mentioned are part of American ideals (leaving aside possibly other related or subordinate values), and recognizing that these values are all central features of social studies concepts—how are these and other values to be taught?

The generalizations are not to be given to the students to be learned by rote as truth. Effective learning of such generalization does not take place in that way. The generalizations are really references from which suitable learning experiences may be developed. Through the learning experiences, students will acquire a deeper and deeper appreciation of the generalized principles of the social sciences. Objectives are not something to be set up as a home plate toward which students are driven or permitted to run. Objectives are something to develop. The actual experiences in the classroom ought to help students arrive, somewhat independently, at the objectives. The methods and procedures are at least as important in attaining the objectives as the subject-matter content.

[3]See, for example, R. H. Gabriel, *Traditional Values in American Life,* U.S. National Commission for UNESCO (New York: Harcourt, Brace and World, 1963).

The teaching of values depends partly upon the presentation of purely factual material. Students need to know the facts about race, which refute the prejudices and distortions of the racists. They deserve to learn the faults and achievements of other cultures. They ought to be able to recognize the attainments of cultures we dislike—such as Russia and Red China—as well as to catalog the crimes. They need to know about the errors we have made in our own history as well as the accomplishments. However, facts alone are not the sole basis for values.

Psychology and sociology explain how attitudes and values are acquired by us. Central to the adoption of values in adolescence is the process of identification. Hero worship, or the identification with admired or significant others, is a very important process in adolescence. The search for ego ideals outside the family is part of growing up. It occurs in the development of every individual. The heroes who are worshiped may exist in the environment as actual living persons, or they may be the folk heroes and folk virtues that form the traditional heritage of a society. By admiring and striving to be like others, youth adopts, and adapts, their values. Teachers use the adolescent need for heroes to inculcate the virtues of historical figures. By encouraging students to identify with heroes or with ordinary individuals, past and present, real or fictional, we can encourage appreciations and values which appear to be basic to our culture and to our present institutions.

However, emphasis on some of the traditional heroes and their fabulous virtues will not automatically provide youth with ideals appropriate to our modern society. The individualism, the self-reliance, the assertiveness, and the violence of Thomas Paine, Daniel Boone, Ethan Allen, or Davy Crockett, mythological virtues of a revolutionary frontier epoch, would be somewhat out of place in modern America. George Washington idealized as an individualistic rebel against intolerable tyranny is a questionable ideal for modern adolescence. "The traditional—not the real—George Washington would today be regarded as a delinquent; and the adolescent who took over completely the ideal of the traditional George Washington would find himself in Juvenile Court before long."[4] According to Gerald Pearson, some of the discontent among adolescents today is the result of our continuing to present them with ego ideals taken from the Revolution, the frontier, and the period of rugged individualism, which are inappropriate and unrealizable in our modern highly organized and interdependent nation.

How are we to teach basic American values which are vital and valid for today?

1) The real qualities of men and women who have contributed to civilization may be offered as ideals for youth. Many of these qualities are still

[4]Gerald H. J. Pearson, *Adolescence and the Conflict of Generation* (New York: W. W. Norton, 1958), p. 74.

needed today. Such qualities relate easily to the values we have mentioned. For example, "respect for human personality" may be furthered through an appreciation of the many-sided genius of a Schweitzer, as it can be taught through stories of the suffering of runaways on the Underground Railroad. "Moral responsibility of the individual" may be furthered through the story of Socrates' obedience to the judgment of his city, though unjust, as it can be taught through the speeches of Abraham Lincoln. That "institutions should be servants of men" can be taught through the text and story of the Declaration of Independence, as it can be furthered by a consideration of the reasons the Supreme Court of 1954 reversed the philosophy of a previous generation in regard to "separate but equal" education for different races. Adolescents may identify with James Otis in his resentment against Writs of Assistance, as they may identify with Negroes segregated into inferior schools.

2) Values may be taught through providing opportunities for students to identify with men and women who have suffered in history—those who suffered for human faults and those who suffered because of injustice. Students can empathize with a Marat or a Robespierre, and through their tragic deaths learn respect for "peaceful adjustments rather than violence." Students will not fail to empathize with a Huss, a Galileo, or a Bruno, and acquire a soul-deep respect for "freedom of expression." Gene Debs at Atlanta Penitentiary is part of our American heritage, too. And values will be acquired through an understanding of tragic sufferers in history—destroyed by personal value conflicts—a Brutus or a Benedict Arnold.

3) Values may be taught by a study of the sources of our industrial civilization and in the achievements of many men in many fields. "Respect for excellence" more appropriately derives from students' identifying with a Shakespeare, a da Vinci, an Edison, or an Oppenheimer than from students' reveling in the exploits of a Napoleon or a Caesar.

4) Values may be taught through controversy—whether analysis of past historical problems "solved" by events or a study of current controversial issues.[5] Students, identifying with those involved in the struggles of the frontier, weighing the issues in our treatment of Indians, will acquire a deeper understanding of "moral equality." A study of the problems of immigration, including a sufficiently penetrating investigation to give insight and appreciation of the hardy, impulsive Irish laborers and the hardworking Chinese coolies who helped open our West, would deepen an appreciation of "brotherhood." Current controversial issues, such as the rising demand of minorities for equal rights and opportunities in schools, jobs, and housing, can develop values, too. The "pursuit of hap-

[5]For an exposition on techniques and a bibliography on these approaches, see Richard E. Gross, *How to Handle Controversial Issues,* National Council for the Social Studies, Pamphlet no. 14, rev. (Washington, D.C., 1961), p. 8.

piness," in its broad sense of self-realization, is deeply involved in all the concerns we have for a better education more freely available for all.

5) Exploration of other ways of life, of other faiths and cultures, deep enough to place our students in empathetic understanding of other peoples in other times and places, will broaden values. World religions, taught with real firsthand contacts (visits to other houses of worship, guest speakers, films, use of sacred texts), will deepen appreciation of the "spiritual" as well as foster "brotherhood."

6) Values may be taught by an honest exposition of the errors man has made. A fair treatment of the Mormon experience or an exposition of Lincoln's stand in the Mexican War could not but attack the seat of prejudice and encourage a deeper appreciation of the unorthodox in religion and politics. The story of the Peloponnesian War remains a storehouse of lessons for a democratic people.

7) Values may be taught through an honest appraisal of actions and viewpoints revised after experience, such as our national difficulties in establishing constitutional child labor laws, popular unfair criticism of Hoover, our relocation of Japanese-Americans during World War II. Young learners identifying with children in the factories of two generations ago or with loyal Americans interned behind barbed wire a generation ago will develop worthwhile democratic values. Likewise, an honest study of the crusades, including an analysis of motives and a comparison of cultures, would contribute to values pertinent to our world today.

To teach values by any of the means suggested depends upon the use of procedures, techniques, and learning experiences which arouse and sustain emotion as well as reason. Pupils must identify with personalities and human beings who have been or are involved in great problems and controversies if they are to see intimately, feel deeply, and understand fully. Appropriate devices for such teaching are identical with appropriate devices for any good teaching—films, pictures, songs, poetry, documents, dramatizations, parable, fiction, letters, diaries, interviews, socio-drama, cartoons, posters, field trips, guest speakers, panels, or debates. Here, of course, the reading of great literature, including our own religious literatures, has an important and appropriate place.

In social studies we must give major attention to problems and controversy because we live in a society of change and choice, in which all citizens are expected to take responsibility for meaningful decisions about international, national, and local security and welfare. At the heart of all controversy lie values—that is what the controversies are about. Values which we commonly accept today were evolved, tested, and won in great controversies of the past. We have achieved the values discussed herein to some degree, but present-day controversies often involve some aspect of these in combination or conflict with other values also important to us. Racial democracy is not quite adopted yet; economic security is still debated a little; equality of opportunity is imperfectly achieved; economic democracy is still a dangerous proposal.

Since values lie at the root of controversy, students will get close to values and an appreciation of their importance by considering "solved" issues of the past, such as "was the Constitution necessary?" or "Should we have jailed pacifists and socialists in World War I?" Students will get even closer to values when they study and attack fairly such issues as "Is public power desirable?" or "Should we now recognize Red China?" In studying the controversies, students should learn to appreciate the role of values and be more prepared to play a constructive role in future controversies from which new values will emerge.

8) Students identify not only with personalities and peoples of the past. They identify also with some of the adults with whom they work, and they are influenced by the values of those adults.

"The adolescent also attempts to reinforce his ego ideal by hero worship of adults whom he actually knows. This kind of hero worship is repeated time and again during adolescence, and with decreasing frequency during adult life. . . . The adolescent meets an adult who has abilities, capacities or points of view different from his and from those of his parents. He spends a great deal of time thinking about this adult and he tries very hard to be this person or to be as much like him as possible. He believes consciously that everything this hero-person does and thinks is inspired; and so he consciously tries to imitate him and unconsciously identifies with him. . . . After a period of such hero worship . . . the adolescent finds another hero . . . but he has changed permanently in certain respects because of his hero worship."[6]

We have reached a point in our discussion where we can talk about teacher personality, class management, subject matter, and teaching procedures in a single framework. Here we have reached the stage of application, the principle of *using* what is being learned. At this point, we may remind ourselves that democratic values cannot be indoctrinated in the sense of a dictatorial imposition. Values are best taught not by precept but by example. The surest way a good history teacher can teach the values we have been discussing is by demonstrating in all he says and does that they are his. He must live with respect for others (students and colleagues and parents and administrators), take responsibility for his own strengths and weaknesses, be willing to change classroom rules which are absurd or out-of-date, give students a meaningful part in planning learning and managing the class, demonstrate respect for truth, prize excellence, treat all people with equal respect and dignity, be friendly, and reveal a sense of spiritual value which gives depth to his purpose and faith to his work.

[6]Pearson, p. 77.

Only as we remember always that values are an essential objective in our teaching will we so choose subject matter and so conduct our classes as to fulfill a last plea of President Franklin Roosevelt in his 1945 Jefferson Day speech which he did not live to deliver:

"If civilization is to survive, we must cultivate the science of human relationships—the ability of all peoples, of all kinds, to live together and work together in the same world at peace."[7]

The science of human relationships depends upon human values.

[7]Quoted in Ashley Montagu, *Education and Human Relations* (New York: Grove Press, 1958), p. 22

PHYLLIS LIEBERMAN

Teacher, Cranford Public Schools,
New Jersey

SIDNEY B. SIMON

Professor of Education, Temple
University

53. Current Events and Values*

As consistently as failing marks are recorded in red ink, Friday in American schools is current events day. With Friday comes the ubiquitous oral reports, the dutifully written summaries, the occasional cartoon-holding-up periods and, perhaps, the faithful going over of one of the weekly magazines written expressly, and neutrally, for school children.

It seems terribly tame to carry on such weekly current events lessons in the face of a world which is shot through with rampant doubt, confusion, and contradictions; a world in which we talk of peace, but in which the arms race continues; a world in which Americans fight and die, but we are not at war. We listen to current events reports about the civil rights struggle in classrooms which are often part of blatantly *de facto* segregated schools. These are the problems we need to deal with if we are to help our students make some sense out of a world which strikes most of them as being just this side of overwhelming. If we want our students to grow to adulthood with the skills and the drive to take on some share of the responsibility for what goes on in this world, to make their voices heard on the issues of the day, something more is needed than current events Friday.

We advocate an approach to current events which puts the focus upon value-clarification. The theoretical framework for this method can be found in *Values and Teaching: Working With Values in the Classroom.*[1] This value-clarification approach puts emphasis upon the process, upon the search for an individualized value system that will help students find meaning and structure in their lives, lives which so often now merely reflect apathy, drift, conformity, or blind rebellion. Perhaps a clearer understanding of the type of approach we are recommending can be gained by examining the following three examples of current events lessons.[2]

---

*Social Education, XXIX:532–33, December 1965. Used by permission.

[1]Louis E. Raths, Merrill Harmin, and Sidney B. Simon *Values and Teaching: Working with Values in the Classroom* (Columbus, O.: Charles E. Merrill, 1965).

[2]For copies of other current events lessons, send a long, self-addressed, stamped (10 cents) envelope to Sidney B. Simon, College of Education, Temple University, Philadelphia, Pennsylvania 19122.

Let us first look at an article from the *American Civil Liberties Union Newsletter.*

SPEAK UP

In Germany they first came for the Communists, and I didn't speak up because I wasn't a Communist. Then they came for the Jews, and I didn't speak up because I wasn't a Jew. Then they came for the trade unionists, and I didn't speak up because I wasn't a trade unionist. Then they came for the Catholics, and I didn't speak up because I was a Protestant. Then they came for me—and by that time no one was left to speak up.—Pastor Martin Niemoller.

To think on and to write on:
1. In a few words, what is the gist of this statement?
2. What is the Pastor *for* and what is he *against*?
3. Which category are *you* in? When would they have come for you?
4. Do you know of any people either personally or in current affairs who were not afraid to take a stand? Tell us about them.
5. What are some things going on in our world right now about which you might need to speak up? List them here.
6. Is there something in your school, some "injustice," about which you could well speak up?
7. How do you think one goes about speaking up? What are the ways?
8. Could you pick something you listed in questions 5 or 6 and work out a strategy by which you could, indeed, speak up?
9. If you are not to speak up, who should do it?
10. We need to *value* what we do and to *do* something about what we value. Do you agree? If so, when was the last time you did?

This lesson helps to clarify the idea that we have a responsibility to speak up about the things we are for or against. Of prime importance are the questions that ask the student to describe in concrete terms how he would change or control the course of one human event.

The following article by Charles A. Wells from *Between the Lines Newsletter* was dittoed and distributed to each class member.

THE PRICE OF PEACE

Questions That Scientists Have Been Asking

Why is the total 78-nation budget for the International Atomic Energy Agency, which is responsible for the Atoms For Peace program, less than the cost of one single moon shot?

Why are there only eight engineers backing our multi-billion-dollar Agency for International Development against more than 10,000 engineers in our space agency?

Why do we spend more to produce one nuclear submarine than our total annual budget for agricultural research—in a world of hunger?

Of the more than $17 billion a year spent in the United States on research and development, why is only $4 billion spent by American industry for non-military, non-space work?

To think on and to write on:
1. Do you have an answer to these questions?
2. Which point, of any, bothers you the most? Explain.
3. Comment on: "So what? Let the scientists worry about it."
4. What questions have *you* been asking lately? (Write on some things about which you are more concerned.)

The above questions help the student to realize that the choices we make, as a nation and individually, reflect what we value. The student is asked if his values and those expressed in the article coincide, and if not, what he can do about this.

Our last example of what we consider a meaningful current events lesson was taken from the September-October 1964 issue of the *Core-lator*.

LONG ISLAND PICKETS

Long Island CORE won a precedent-setting agreement with Vigilant Associates, one of the largest real estate brokers in the area, despite counter-picketing by pro-Goldwater youths carrying placards such as: "Keep Niggers Out," "Support Your Local KKK," and "I Like Niggers—I Think Everyone Should Own One."

This group counter-picketed during the entire week of picketing by CORE. The picketing started after a CORE test proved discrimination on the part of the realtor. As many as 900 white spectators, most of them supporting the counter-pickets, were drawn to the scene where there was a heavy concentration of police. However, up to 20 white residents of Hicksville had the courage to join the CORE picket line.

To think on and to write on:
1. Do you agree with what CORE did here? Have you disagreed with anything else they have done? Explain.
2. Are you a member of CORE? Have you ever sent them any money? Have you ever attended any of their meetings? Why? Why not?
3. Would you have done what the pro-Goldwater counter-pickets did? Why? Why not?
4. Comment on what the 20 white residents of Hicksville did. What meaning did that have? Would you have done it? Why? Why not?
5. Is there anything else you want to say here?

The students are asked to examine the different viewpoints expressed in the article in an attempt to clarify their own thinking on the subject. In addition, they are confronted with an example of those that were courageous enough to act on their beliefs and are asked if they would do the same.

Such is the values approach to current events. We feel it offers the change that is so drastically needed in current events day. It is our conviction that out of such teaching will come students who are deeply disturbed about the mindlessness, the anxiety, the dangers of our world. It is our belief that these individuals will possess the determination, the knowledge, the courage to fight for the things they value, to change the things they are against. It is our hope that through the search for values we can begin to build a society where diversity is nourished, life itself is valued, and men and women live not in quiet desperation, but in full anticipation of the adventure of life. We invite you to join us in this work.

PHYLLIS LIEBERMAN

Teacher, Cranford Public Schools,
New Jersey

SIDNEY B. SIMON

Professor of Education, Temple
University

54. Vitalizing Student Research Reports*

You have been in this classroom before. You are the teacher. Your students sit before you in silent apathy. True, in one corner the three students who are "on" this morning *do* exhibit a little nervous energy. At least, as this morning's reporters, they *do* have to get up on their feet and move their mouths. But the other members of the class have little to which to look forward. They have heard reports before.

On drone the second-hand sentences until, finally, you can take little more. John declares for the whole class to hear, "The government in Brazil has alienated the people by its extreme inflationary measures." You interrupt, "John, what does that sentence mean?"

"Beats me," says John helplessly.

"How is it possible," you ask, "that you would include such a sentence in a report to our class and not know what it means?"

John stammers a moment and says, "That's what was written in the book, so I figured it must be right."

The scene is too familiar. How many reports have you as a teacher read in your lifetime which were researched and written by *Encyclopaedia Britannica* and signed by Mary Jones, grade seven? How often have you been handed a beautiful booklet that took days to complete only to find that its cutter and gluer understood little of the information it contained?

But all student reports do not have to be dull and uninspiring. Good reports, intelligently guided, can indeed foster creativity and independent study. They can widen circles of knowledge and understanding and develop the sense of accomplishment which comes from sticking to a task from beginning to end. What we need, then, is to discover ways of assuring that the reports our students prepare will be truly meaningful, reports in which "hack work" will not abound and the plagiarism won't plague us unduly.

Of the three suggestions for improving the quality of reports here presented, two have often been used successfully. The third, we think offers an interesting and rewarding alternative.

1. Reports with an emphasis upon dramatics. Instead of standing be-

*Social Education, XXVIII:24–26, January 1964. Used by permission.

fore the class and reading, or presenting from memory, or even telling in their own words *their* encyclopedia's version of a particular incident in history or conditions in a specific country, the students are asked to present the information they have gathered concerning their topic to the class in the form of a skit. Making broad use of a narrator, the skits highlight the important points the reporters choose to make, and *all* of the information that has been collected can be printed on ditto sheets and distributed to the members of the class for further study after the presentation of the skit.

The sheer fun of dramatic play is enough to justify this approach to reports. Most children have a deep sense of the dramatic and enjoy using their creative talents to work out original presentations. In order to present an exciting, dramatic play, each student must give careful consideration to all information and ideas pertaining to the report topic, with the result that a greater familiarity with and understanding of the assigned subject matter is gained.

2. Reports with an emphasis upon summaries. A second way to assure that student reports will be interesting and original is to ask for written summaries of the information the children have accumulated as a result of their research. In the process of deciding what material to include and what to omit, the students will become increasingly skilled in the art of discriminating and distinguishing between the significant and the unimportant. Moreover, this summary-type report tends to eliminate the problem of students who are apt to copy directly from the book, for each student must use his own words to prepare a précis.

3. Reports with an emphasis upon values. This, in our opinion, is the most important way to vitalize student reports. We also believe that it does much more than bring about the creation of reports that are exciting to hear, instructive to prepare, and pleasurable for teachers to read. We feel that a very real benefit from such reports is that they re-focus for the teacher the whole problem of what *is* worth including in a list of topics on which students may be asked to report. We see no great value in having a student list the mountains, rivers, and major cities of a country. We are not against mountains, rivers, and cities as such, but we want them to be studied for a larger purpose than that a student be able successfully to complete a crossword puzzle at some future date. Similarly, no important person will come to life in the mind of a student so long as we settle for merely listing his birth date, his five significant achievements, or the rate and date of his death. Such facts as these can be looked up at any time in the future and certainly cannot be considered worthy of student library research.

What then, you ask, is better? What do we advocate? We say we must lead our students into an inquiry, not of how a country looks or of what a person did, but rather of what the country or that person *is*, or *was*. The struggles and the joys of people seem important here. The happiness and the despair and the personal conflicts of a man take on significance. His shortcomings, the loyal support of the people close to him, or the treachery of his "best friends"—all enter into a report the emphasis of which is upon values. We seek to avoid the cardboard cut-out image of Simon Bolivar astride his horse. We are interested rather in learning his reactions when a peasant came to him for help. We want to know what he read, what made him laugh. We believe that an investigation of such matters spirals learning. Sheer memorization is not rewarded here. The inquiry becomes more complex than the mere copying of paragraphs from reference books. Moreover, the children gain a deeper understanding of the countries and peoples they are studying, and a sustained interest is stimulated that continues long after the report has been duly turned in and the appropriate letter of the alphabet entered in the teacher's grade book.

Perhaps most important of all, reports of this nature bring students to a consideration of alternative ways of life. The emphasis on the attitudes and behavior of a people provides meaningful insights for the youngster who is searching to find his own value system or philosophy of life. In a world in which it is becoming increasingly difficult to single out one right way to live and behave, an awareness of alternative values may well prove to be the most important thing we can give our students.

In order to illustrate the type of value-emphasis report we advocate, we here present the material which served as the basis for a successful seventh-grade unit on South America. The following paragraphs were mimeographed and distributed to each student:

> We are starting an important unit on South America. You will be asked to work on an individual as well as a group project. During the course of this unit, I hope to bring you into contact with the people of South America. You will be dealing with those people who are living, working, and struggling today as well as with those who lived and worked and struggled in the past.
>
> You will be getting information from books, pamphlets, and articles which will enable you to answer the questions raised below. This should prove an interesting and rewarding experience if you will make it so.
>
> For your individual report you will choose one of the following great men who fought to free South America from foreign rule: Jose De San Martin, Bernardo O'Higgins, Antonio Jose De Sucre, Francisco De Miranda, Simon Bolivar.
>
> Your individual reports will consider the following: What was there in the life of the man you have chosen that interested you? Are there any things in your own life which are similar to his? For what things did you admire him most? Have you known any other adults who have

these qualities? What exactly did he achieve? Were his goals or aims at all like any you have dreamed up for yourself? What difficulties did he have to undergo to achieve his goals? In what ways was he weak? How did this hurt him? How would he have made out in our world? Explain. Where did his life seem less fulfilled or satisfying? Do most great men have large areas of their life which are not fulfilled? Explain. What did his friends feel about him? How important were their feelings to him? In what ways were his friends' feelings influential upon him? Where did he display his greatest courage? Where did he display his greatest wisdom? Where did he make his greatest contribution? Who benefited from this contribution? Are there any ways he lived which would be good for people to follow today?

For your group report, you must choose one of the following countries that Bolivar helped to make free: Colombia, Venezuela, Peru, Bolivia, Equador.

You will deal with the following questions as part of your group report: What does the farmer want in the country you have chosen? What stands in his way of getting it? How does he go about getting what he wants? What help does he have? What hopes do his children have? What do they know of their own country? Of ours? What do they think and know about politics or their government? What is their day like? Where do they sleep? How many in a bed? What do they fear? When do they marry? What do they do for recreation? What part does religion play in their lives? What is their idea of a good life? How does it compare with yours? (Discuss this last question with your group and come up with some ideas.)

Answer these same questions for an industrial worker and a wealthy landowner. Are your answers the same for all of these people? If not, why not? Are any answers you have the same or similar to those of another group? Which ones? (Find this out by reading and discussing work of other groups.) If your answers are similar, why do you think this is so?

Consider the impact of these questions on a group of seventh-graders. Think of your own class and imagine how they would respond to an exploration of such problems as these. We can assure you that some students will find it too unorthodox a way for them to proceed. You must be ready to help them to learn to work with this new approach. We believe you will find the rewards worth the effort.

For one thing, you will begin to see that your students can not deal with these questions in any satisfactory manner merely by copying facts from an encyclopedia. Instead they will be drawn to a wide range of source materials: magazines, newspaper articles, materials from the various countries, as well as books which treat certain of the men or the countries in depth. The word "research" will take on real meaning and point the way to the preparation of the kind of papers which will be most apt to bring the greatest satisfaction to the authors when and if they go on to higher education.

You will find, too, that reports with an emphasis upon values force the students to analyze and interpret what they read. No longer can John merely mouth his Brazilian insights. He must now actually *have* the insight. Because the information sought after is complex and multifaceted, the students will not as readily be able to find the single right answer stated in black and white. They *must* employ their powers of reasoning and judgment to make the best use of the material they have read. We consider this an excellent way in which to open up the curriculum to a true sense of inquiry.

At this point in our discussion, many of you may be saying to yourselves, "It's all very well to handle a report in this way, but I *am* responsible for covering the rivers, mountains, etc. of Latin America, and my class must learn these facts. I can't put all of that information on ditto sheets. How will I have time to teach what my school expects me to teach?"

Fundamentally, the solution to such problems as the need to cover certain material and the desire to teach specific skills in a limited amount of time leads to the all-important question of what we are trying to bring about by our teaching. Just what is important enough to spend time on in the classroom? This is a decision each teacher must make every day of the school year. If you feel it is more important for your students to know the geography and natural resources of a country, this will be reflected in your teaching. Or if you feel it more important for your students to know a country in terms of the suffering and hopes of its people, this, too, will be reflected in the type of work going on in your classroom. We strongly urge, however, that you at least choose your position from among several alternatives and that the choice you make be based upon what you firmly believe is most essential for your students. Mere expediency is not adequate grounds for such an imperative decision.

The amazing thing about the alternative we pose; namely, the possibility of building a values emphasis into your work, is that the mandatory subject matter may still be covered, perhaps with even more satisfactory results than that obtained by standard approaches. Because of the wide reading that must be done, and due in part to the heavy involvement of the student in the content, we have found that often the necessary facts "hit" the student from a variety of sources, thus making the subject matter stick in a way which seems to last longer than the learning produced by mere rote memorization. Moreover, we believe that in the preparation of reports which emphasize values, students will better understand certain facts such as natural resources and geographical characteristics and appreciate their interrelationship with the problem of people.

Furthermore, our experience has shown that such reports contribute significantly to our teaching of important research and writing skills. Our students grow in their ability to interpret and to grasp the implications of information. Stereotyped images of—and again we use Latin America as an example—sandy beaches, warm climates, and siesta-seeking gauchos in colorful costumes disappear and are replaced by a real understanding of what such often casually dropped terms as poverty, illiteracy, hunger, passivity, and hate mean to those confronted by them every day of their lives. Thus a values emphasis takes on added significance if we feel that the kind of adults we need in the baffling and sometimes frightening world are people who have compassion for others and a true desire to devote their lives to making democracy a living creed.

RAYMOND H. MUESSIG   VINCENT R. ROGERS

Professor of Education, Ohio State
University

Professor of Education, University of
Connecticut

55. Teaching Patriotism at Higher Conceptual Levels*

As with numerous other important, all-embracing terms and concepts, "patriotism" can connote different things to various people. At a superficial level, most persons would agree with the "love of country" definition commonly found in dictionaries. Consensus dissolves quickly, however, when an effort is made to enlarge upon what love of country can and should signify operationally. "Love" is regarded generally as a word carrying positive overtones; but misdirected love—as in the case of some warped parent-child relationships—can misshape the object of affection almost beyond recognition.

It is not difficult to unveil evils conjured up under the lofty guise of patriotism. Reluctantly, Americans may recall the persecution of United Empire Loyalists during the Revolutionary War; the Federalists' creation of Alien and Sedition Acts which made it possible to fine or imprison pro-Jeffersonian foreigners; the insidious "Palmer raids" in 1919 when numerous aliens were arrested, held without trial for long periods of time, and ultimately deported; the confinement of loyal Japanese-American citizens during World War II; the insensitivities, abuses, and malpractices during the McCarthy years; ad nauseam. No one period in American history, no given political party, has enjoyed complete immunity from the infection of overzealousness in interpreting "love of country."

Perhaps some solace might be found if Americans could state with surety that chauvinism has had its day and that a balanced, mature, positive, dynamic patriotism characterizes the present and is assured for the future. Unfortunately, this is not the case. Super-patriotism is still very much with us in the form of low-level, mundane, repetitious, hortatory, inflammatory, and ecstatic pronouncements, publications, proposals, and activities of innumerable individuals and organizations claiming to be devoted to fostering patriotic attitudes and practices. Derisive epithets such as "egghead," "Ivy-Leaguer," "one-worlder," "leftist," "Comsymp," "pinko," and "Red" have been hurled freely and carelessly at dedicated persons who have served our country in war and peace; who have shared publicly their considered views on politics, economics, intergroup

*Social Education, XXVIII:266–70, May 1964. Used by permission.

and international affairs, and the like; and who have dared to suggest what they perceive as needed reforms in the United States and in the world. Reputable, responsible jurists, diplomats, public servants, theologians, professors, writers, businessmen, and others have been subjected to defamatory phone calls or an ominous silence following the answering of the telephone's ring in the middle of the night, to abusive, threatening, anonymous letters, to smear campaigns, to rough verbal and physical treatment by an angry mob, and other acts which should be unknown to a democratic society.

Public schools, among America's perennial favorites for scapegoating and the initiation of countless pet projects, have not eluded the ever-vigilant glare and occasional wrath of ultranationalistic forces. In one city several people tried to slip into a school library with the avowed purpose of ferreting out "un-American" books and periodicals. In a smaller town a group contacted the school superintendent and volunteered to "check the loyalty" of local teachers by going through all of the confidential professional credentials and probing into doubtful ingredients. Several months ago representatives of an organization for "*real* Americans" stormed into an elementary school principal's office and demanded that he produce evidence of his building's patriotic observances—carried out in the past, going on at the present time, and anticipated in the future. Even more recently a few parents "visited with" a secondary social studies teacher regarding some "suspicious" items on the United Nations that their youngsters had recorded in class lecture notes.

As a result of pressures similar to these, some systems, individual schools, and given teachers have tried to increase the tempo of what they or their more vociferous local citizens believe to be patriotic practices. Booklets and units have been produced hurriedly by school districts fearful of getting caught without "something to show" on patriotism. The names of national heroes and the dates of battles and other events long overlooked or forgotten have been exhumed so more days could be spotlighted on school calendars and underlined through the reading of stories and speeches, singing of songs, arranging of bulletin boards, and the like. In response to suggestions, appeals, and outright directives emanating from editorials, public addresses, large assemblies, and forums, etc., ·schools have held patriotic assemblies for young people during the day and programs for parents and other adults at night which have been devoted entirely to patriotism or embossed generally with patriotic elements. There are communities where the number of ceremonies centered around the flag, the national anthem, and the "Pledge of Allegiance" has been increased but where little or no thought has been given to their underlying meaning for the pupils in our nation's schools. In a few instances, some of the things being done to satisfy super-patriots have a strident, militaristic, jingoistic, totalitarian character which is inharmonious with persisting themes in the democratic symphony.

Individuals and groups clamoring more recently for increased patriotic fervor in the schools and elsewhere seem to be operating on the *a priori* assumption that patriotism is a one-sided, ever-uniform, solidly-monolithic, all-or-nothing thing. One must demonstrate his love for the United States in such and such a way, or he does not love his country at all. A limited set of ideas is clearly American; any others are un-American and, therefore, dangerous or useless. All of the writings of *this* author are acceptable, while anything penned by *that* writer should be hidden from sight or destroyed. A candidate for public office must be 101 percent faithful to a single interpretation of *the* thoughts of our founding fathers, or he is definitely a "Bolshevist." Indoctrination is the *only* safe, sure road to patriotism; and endless, repetitive exposure to the same small cluster of slogans, symbols, and ceremonies is guaranteed to achieve the desired results in time. Unquestioned acceptance, not understanding, is the goal.

There are many schools, of course, which have not been exposed to harangues from the newer, more impetuous, super-patriotic groups or which have not conceded to ill-considered insistencies. Their handling of the "patriotism problem" is more palatable to most than that of the schools which have yielded to the pressures of ultranationalists, but it is hardly more meaningful or effective. It consists of a bland diet of precooked, totally safe offerings served just often enough. No one is upset, really, but there is no flavor and little nourishment here either. The usual school day includes a quickly dispatched flag salute and pledge mumbled dutifully by the children. Once in a while one hears a brief, patriotic "thought for the day," too frequently written by some adult and commonly read breathlessly and tonelessly by a child over the intercom system. The usual patriotic holidays and events are mentioned during the year, and there are always a few nice words in February about Lincoln and Washington (always in that order—because of their birth dates, of course). Seldom is concern expressed whether these minimal gestures touch the minds and hearts and lives of youngsters.

What *should* the schools do about patriotism? Is there a way of dealing with the love of country which is neither over-saturated with indigestible chauvinism nor totally void of intellectual, moral, and emotional sustenance? Is there a respect for one's homeland which transcends frantic shouting on the one hand or apathetic ritualism on the other? Is there a substance in patriotism which can be identified and broken down into components like facts, concepts, generalizations, skills, attitudes, and appreciations? Can dimensions of patriotism be taught and caught, grasped firmly and then transferred to a multitude of situations in these anxious, troubled times? Is there a unique essence to democratic patriotism unlike the love of country conveyed in a fascistic or communistic state? If we become more and more like the powers which threaten to engulf us what will we have saved? Can we afford to ignore the need for an intelligent look at patriotism?

Perhaps the following ideas will stimulate some thought on the part of school administrators, teachers, parents, and others interested in the teaching of patriotism to our children and youth. Each of the statements below is derived from the fundamental definition of patriotism as love of country, but it is neither expected nor anticipated that each will be accepted uncritically by all individuals and groups. Each can stand alone as a basic, significant belief related to democratic behavior. Yet each is inevitably related to the other. The five points offered here are by no means exhaustive. The authors identified others at one stage in the preparation of this manuscript, but space limitations make it impossible to treat so many ingredients. Hence, representative points have been used and what space remains has been devoted to examples of methods teachers might employ to achieve these types of objectives.

A patriotic American should have a balanced love of country. In democratic patriotism there should be a degree of symmetry with respect to both cognitive and affective—or mental and emotional—elements. Americans should be both rational and capable of deep feeling, informed and devoted, sensible and sensitive. There is something in the human organism which responds emotionally to the strains of martial or laudatory music, to the sight of a flag fluttering in the breeze or dramatized by a spotlight in a darkened assembly hall, to speeches with soul-stirring phrases, to hallowed monuments, statues, and places, and to yellowed documents which have shaped the course of men's lives. Man cannot deny his sentiments, nor should he. He would be inhuman if he did not experience an occasional lump in the throat, the swelling of tears, a feeling of pride and dedication. Yet the democratic citizen's emotional impulses cannot carry him from a real world into a dreamland from which there is no return, from lucidity to blind irrationality. Although he is justifiably proud of America's strengths and achievements, he must be aware too of its weaknesses and failures. Otherwise, he cannot assume a responsible, enlightened role in improving conditions in this country. Further, while loving the United States and the noble attributes in living which it represents, he can perceive values in other cultures as well though he may not accept them as his own; identify with people in other lands as fellow human beings with at least some needs and aspirations similar to his; and understand the patriotism of others as a natural phenomenon and a potential source of positive and negative properties depending upon its interpretation and application.

> A fifth-grade teacher asked her charges to write the name of the best school in their city on a slip of paper and to hide their responses until everyone was finished. After collecting the papers and going

through them, the teacher announced that every child had chosen *his own* school. The teacher then discussed with the youngsters *why* they liked their school better than others and made a list of suggested items on the chalkboard. She then asked whether anyone had ever attended or visited another school in their city. No one had. (This school was situated in a suburban, bedroom community with low geographic mobility. A few children had attended schools in other cities, but all had remained in this school after their arrival in this area.) The class was silent for a minute. Suddenly hands went up, and several children blurted out that they only *thought* their school was better than others but that they did not *know*. A girl observed that some of the things on the board *might* even be true of *other* schools. A boy remarked gingerly that other schools could be *better* in some ways. A classmate in front of him agreed but added that other schools could be *worse* too—and that he would still like his school more than others, no matter what. Many heads nodded affirmatively after this comment. It was time for another "Why?" from the teacher, and she received several reactions. Children pointed out that they usually grew to like the close and the familiar; that they became fond of people who were good to them and of places associated with various kinds of satisfactions (such as "learning new things in school and getting to play too"); and that they were expected to be loyal to their families, friends, schools, churches, and *country*. Other things were discussed, but eventually the teacher focused the attention of her pupils upon their feeling about nations in the world. Her questions paralleled the previous ones she had asked about schools, but the children were less positive about their statements. The teacher beamed when a girl said, "Schools in one place and countries all over the place aren't quite the same thing. It's a lot harder to talk about countries."

The children slowly composed a list of several questions which the teacher wrote quickly on a fluid duplicator master. A boy left to have copies run off for everyone. Another boy offered to contact the building librarian for books that would assist the class. A girl said she was going to ask the questions of her parents, and other pupils indicated that they would follow suit. The teacher said that some class time could be made available for class study and individual help. There was agreement that further discussion should be postponed until the following Monday.

During the three days following the class discussion the teacher encouraged her pupils to try to pull their thinking together. With her help the children were able to formulate generalizations like the following:

Most people love the country where they were born or where they have lived a long time.

Every country must have good things about it. Every country has problems too. People are proud of the good things.

Sometimes they work together to solve problems.

Many nice things happen to us because we live in America. Americans get to do and have things that people in some other countries cannot do or have. (Numerous examples appeared after this statement.)

It would be hard now for any country to get along all by itself. Countries get ideas, ways of saying and doing things, and products from each other. An invention by a man in one country may be used by many other countries. America has learned things and received help from other countries. As a leader in the world, it gives different kinds of help to many nations.

The citizens of each nation believe certain things. If we know people's important beliefs sometimes we can understand better the way they live. Countries agree and disagree on beliefs. When they agree they may get along well and even work together. When they disagree they may not like each other and may even fight each other. Americans share some big ideas. (Representative ideas were listed here.) Some nations think these are good ideas. Others do not. In the past Americans have had to stick up for their beliefs. They must be strong today too so they will not lose their freedom and rights. We should understand American ideas so we can be better citizens.

A senior high school social studies teacher achieved somewhat similar results by inviting three foreign students from a neighboring university to his class on each of three separate days. On the fourth day he formed a panel with the same three resource persons. Each guest provided the class with brief, customary information on his country but was asked to focus some attention on his beliefs about his homeland. When the three foreign students met, each amplified his devotion to his country while recognizing at the same time its problems and positive and strained relationships with some other nations. The day following the panel the teacher encouraged his class to discuss "*informed* patriotism," its meaning, assets, and possible liabilities (if misinterpreted) in our society.

A patriotic American should understand the underlying meaning of national ceremonies and symbols. Every nation—whatever its social ideology—has its rituals, emblems, traditions, celebrations, folklore, and legendary personages. It is the rationale behind practices and tokens which distinguishes free people from those under the totalitarian yoke. In a democratic environment it is not enough to engage in rote observations for their own sake. There is a significant difference between the "indivisible" nation described in our stirring "Pledge of Allegiance" and the "invisible" one which so many children identify daily and cannot comprehend, between a lush "fruited *plain*" as envisioned in "America the Beautiful," and the jet *plane* festooned with grapes, bananas, apples, etc., which the little boy drew to portray these words in the song. While the "Gettysburg

Address' has *ear* appeal, especially as read by one of our great American actors, it must reach the intellect and the soul as well through discussion and contemplation. A year or so before Congress changed Armistice Day to Veterans Day in 1954, one of the authors was a spectator during the period of silence at 11:00 A.M. His thoughts had just turned to a close friend killed in World War II when he heard a loud "Shhhhh!" next to him. A mother was silencing her little boy. Naturally, the little boy asked why he was supposed to be quiet. His mother said she did not know but that he should be still anyway. This lack of understanding permeates too many patriotic observances.

Children should both know the story and grasp the philosophy in back of given patriotic actions, should delve into the meaning of words used in songs and ceremonies, and should see reasons for the reaffirmation of the democratic faith through continued observances. There is a lesson to be learned during the period just prior to a presidential election and following the inauguration of our Chief Executive. Young people can marvel at the intense rivalries that often exist before a vote is cast and the respect freely and sincerely given to the newly installed president. Children ought to discover that this regard for the head of state is not diminished by the informed criticism which citizens offer of specific executive decisions and actions.

A sixth-grade teacher wanted his pupils to understand more fully the commitment they were making each morning when they pledged allegiance to their flag and country. To establish a foundation for discussion at a higher level, he read three "pledges" aloud to the class, leaving time after the reading for questions and comments. The first was the "Boy Scout Oath" which was familiar to most of the children. Next the class listened to portions of the "Hippocratic Oath." The teacher did most of the talking this time because words like "discernment" and "regimen" were unknown to his charges. The *idea* of the oath was clear, however, and the children were intrigued by the thought that their own doctors had repeated this pledge in medical school. Finally, the oath taken by a prospective Athenian soldier-citizen was examined. The children were impressed by the fact that this pledge was administered only once and taken with real seriousness. The sentence, "I will hand on my fatherland greater and better than I found it," seemed particularly important to many children. Pledging allegiance from that time on carried both greater depth of understanding and feeling.

Having similar concerns, a senior high school teacher provided his class with selections from the letters, diaries, and speeches of selected immigrants who came to America during the second half of the nineteenth century. The feelings of these men and women upon arriving here, their gradual adjustment to a new way of life, and their joy at finally achieving full citizenship triggered other worthwhile student reactions.

A patriotic American should realize that democratic means must be used to achieve democratic ends in this society. The implications of this point should be self-evident today, for this inescapable philosophical insight has been with us for a long time. However, the consonant relationship between means and ends has still escaped many people—among them the militant chauvinists. The man who shouts, "They'll have democracy if I have to shove it down their throats!" expresses the means-ends schism that is still present in some circles. No matter how involved emotionally an individual may become in the love of his country, he cannot violate rational, moral, ethical, legal, aesthetic, and mannerly democratic canons to win others to his form of patriotism. When democratic tenets and modes of behavior are ignored in the name of patriotism, the end result is the weakening or destruction of fundamental ideals from which a love of country should have emerged.

A teacher distributed mimeographed copies of ten brief news stories to the student in her two senior problems classes. The first report discussed Adlai Stevenson's treatment in Texas from anti-United Nations, America-first hecklers and demonstrators. The second story dealt with Khrushchev's earthy pronouncements about what was acceptable Soviet art. A third item described the orderly passage of a bill by the United States Senate. Next was a story about a riot incited by a group of mothers attempting to block a court-ordered integration of an elementary school. The fifth account covered illegal voter-registration procedures—through the use of addresses for vacant lots, abandoned buildings, etc.—employed by machine politicians in a given political party. Another piece announced an open city council meeting which citizens owning property in a given area were invited to attend. The other items used were similar in import. The students in both classes were asked to rank the ten news items from "most to least democratic" in approach. A lively discussion of democratic aims and methods grew out of the reading and hierarchical arrangement of the items provided by the teacher. The students cited other illustrations with positive and negative connotations from the present and the past.

A patriotic American should grasp the import of "diversity" and "pluralism" as democratic concepts. The observation that all people are different and capable of countless patterns of living is obvious and time-worn. What one does about variations in human beings is another matter. One can choose to ignore individual and cultural diversities in the naive hope that they will "go away." Or he can acknowledge their presence and do everything possible to obscure, reduce, overrule, or eliminate multiformities in values, feelings, capabilities, wants, and actions. Still a third alternative—the one which seems most compatible in an open society— is to enjoy, prize, foster, and protect distinctness in man. Each person should be viewed as a bundle of possibilities, a one-of-a-kind character who may make the good life better through his unique insights, percep- tions, and methods of approaching or solving individual and societal problems. How many Americans would agree that there should be only one type of artist, musician, playwright, architect, engineer, teacher, doctor, or elected representative in our pluralistic country? Hopefully, no citizen of the United States seeks a monotonous uniformity. Yet too often some groups seem to operate on the postulate that there is only one kind of patriot acceptable in America. Patriotism in this wonderfully variegated homeland of ours should be a many-splendored thing. Oliver H. Perry, Walt Whitman, Susan B. Anthony, Clara Barton, Joyce Kilmer, Jane Addams, Will Rogers, Clarence Darrow, and W. K. Kellogg were all patriots—though in different ways. Our children must discover that there are many ways to love and serve America.

> A fourth-grade teacher reproduced brief excerpts dealing with the lives of four famous American patriots: Samuel Adams, Patrick Henry, Paul Revere, and Nathan Hale. The highlights of their careers were discussed and their differing roles in the movement for independence emphasized. Each biographical sketch also touched, however, on the man's background, education, vocation, interests, religion, and phy- sical appearance. The class began by discussing the love of country that served as a common bond to unite these four men. They concluded by listing and comparing the obvious differences in their backgrounds, arriving after some time at the position that "patriots" can come from many walks of life and that there is no one mold in which all must be formed.

A patriotic American should internalize a deep, abiding, and selfless respect for the rights of others. He cannot afford, nor does he want to be a religious, political, and philosophical neuter. He must have a functional, consistent, durable frame of reference, hammered out of broad and varied experience, study, consideration, and reconsideration. He possesses virile convictions, but they do not prevent him from reading and listening to the tenable positions of others. He realizes that to have intellectual and social freedom for himself he must protect fundamental rights of others. There is a kind of self-interest that leads one to do for others, to share with them, and to protect their rights and freedoms because this form of behavior protects his own integrity and contributes to a more livable life for him and others at the same time. He does not, then, disrupt a meeting of a group whose opinions he cannot accept, nor does he prevent another individual from being heard because he cannot share that man's views.

He does not maintain the naive, unrealistic stand that one man's views on general concerns are innately just as good as any others, *ipso facto*— informed or not, tested or not, moral or not, etc. But he is convinced that the roads to learning, understanding, agreement, consensus, and improvement are not paved with inquisitions, pogroms, witch hunts, fratricide, and genocide. He hopes that the truth will out with time if men seek it individually and together in an open, faithful, permissive manner. While he sometimes gets disillusioned and discouraged with mankind past and present, he never forgets his stake in humanity. He feels that some of his efforts may be a rich legacy for his children or grandchildren.

> An American history teacher divided one of his high school classes into four groups. Each group shared a different account of a problem involving the rights of others. Group 1 examined both primary and secondary materials dealing with the efforts of many men to obtain the right to vote for women. Group 2 read a story from *The New York Times* about the actions of white students in Texas who tried to help Negroes gain access to a local theater. Group 3 studied passages from *Inherit the Wind* which centered on the abuse Clarence Darrow took when he defended Scopes at the famous "Monkey Trials." Group 4 concentrated on the role played by the lawyer, Atticus, in Harper Lee's *To Kill a Mockingbird*, perceiving the problems the attorney caused for himself and his family by defending Tom Robinson. Following their reading of the materials provided by their teacher, the groups were asked to analyze and present significant dimensions of their report and their feelings about what they had studied. In each case, the concern for the rights of others, even at the expense of discomfort or risk, was apparent. Members of the class disagreed as to how far one should "stick out his neck" for others, but all, however, accepted the principle.

While years of research by skilled social and behavioral scientists have been devoted to attitude formation and change, we still know very little about this complex phenomenon. Many studies lead one to observe that it is extremely hard to deal with attitudes, let alone change them. Some pieces of research appear to indicate that the school has relatively little impact attitudinally when compared with the home, the peer group, and the media of mass communication. While the teacher is regarded by sociologists, anthropologists, social psychologists, and psychologists as a "significant other" who *may* shape some attitudes, there is evidence that the teacher is not always an ideal model for identification for a variety of reasons.

One might conclude "logically" that the schools should stick to nothing but hard and fast facts which have been around a long time and seem to be accepted with a minimum of friction from a variety of quarters. Certainly, dealing with patriotism in a more penetrating way is not an easy thing, might be a bit risky in some communities, and could be ineffectual as far as producing a change in behavior is concerned. Again, one might reach the "logical" position that concerns of this nature could be deferred. The primary teacher could pass the buck to the intermediate teacher and so on all the way up to, or beyond, the college professor. A fair question, however, is whether we can afford to lay aside this vital problem on an indefinite basis. Perhaps we will not bring about a complete, lasting renaissance in the patriotic behavior of Americans through what is said and done in public schools. On the other hand, we may surprise researchers and ourselves if we grapple systematically with democratic attitudes related to patriotism and if we try out methods tailored to those predispositions. Doing nothing or yielding to groups which make the loudest noise is certainly no solution. Why not "give it a go," as the English put it?

GRACE GRAHAM

College of Education, University of Oregon

56. *Sociodrama as a Teaching Technique* *

Not long ago a young man whom we shall call John Jones, a west coast college student, applied for a teaching position in a small eastern city. After submitting his recommendations and exchanging several letters with the superintendent of schools, he was given a contract which he signed. John and Mary, his wife, bought a trailer in which they made a leisurely trip across the United States, arriving at their destination a week before the opening of school.

The next morning John visited Mr. Brown, the superintendent.

Mr. Brown was very upset when he saw John Jones. "You did not tell me you are a Negro," he said. "We have never had a Negro on our faculty and the community would not stand for it. I don't know what we can do about you. I'll call a meeting of the School Board to discuss the matter. But I can assure you, Mr. Jones, you will not be allowed to teach here."

John Jones went home to tell his wife the bad news and to discuss with her what they should do.

A story such as this is ideal for the implementation of sociodrama as a teaching method. After telling the story, the teacher would tell her class:

"Now we shall act out possible solutions that John and Mary might find to their problem. Tim, you play the role of John, and Jane, you play the role of Mary. Remember, you decide what you are going to do and also how you think the person whose part you are playing will *feel* and talk."

The teacher then chooses one or two other casts and sends the couples out of the classroom to discuss the problem briefly. While they are outside, the rest of the class quickly list various possible solutions, such as these:

1. Sue in court for a year's salary
2. Plead with the Board for a chance, agreeing that John will leave after a trial period if he does not make good
3. Appeal to the National Association for the Advancement of Colored People for help
4. Get another job in the vicinity

Social Studies, 51:257-59. December 1960. Used by permission.

5. Settle for compensation for time and expenses of trip
6. Get a job in a Negro school

The casts return and *extemporaneously* discuss the problem and decide what they will do. Often the couples hit upon the same or a combination of the same solutions that the class suggested, but sometimes they act out an entirely different ending. The feeling that each pair puts into the dramatization usually varies from belligerency to dejection on the part of one or the other of the characters.

Following the role-playing, the class analyzes the solutions and the feelings portrayed in terms of reasoning, psychological authenticity, and possible consequences of alternate courses.

This sociodrama is an example taken from a college course in Social Foundations of Teaching where problems of minority groups are studied. The setting is present-day America, but any problem situation involving human relationships—current or historical—can be studied through sociodrama.

Classes in social studies that have learned the issues in a labor-management controversy might use a situation involving a meeting of leaders from both groups. A class might enact a scene in which the local town council discusses a problem. The mock United Nations meetings attended by high school representatives in many states are actually large-scale sociodramas. Family living courses offer innumerable problems of parent-child, brother-sister, child-peer group relationships that are natural plots for sociodramas. In sociodramas such as these, the primary purpose might be to present opposing views rather than arriving at a solution to the problem.

While stories for role-playing may come from today's headlines, they may be as old as recorded history. For example, the dilemma of Hans Van Loon, a wealthy patroon in New York who must choose sides in the American Revolution, or of Tom Smithson, a Northern States-Righter at the time of the Civil War, might be emphasized through sociodrama. In historical settings, probably imaginary characters in hypothetical situations are better material for role-playing than well known personages because the choices actually made by the latter tend to restrict creativeness.

Perhaps you are thinking, what is the advantage of this method over the usual informal class discussion beyond the fact that it adds a little variety? The chief advantage is that frequently the players and perhaps the class, too, *identify* with the roles being portrayed. In studying current affairs, their social sensitivities are developed because they learn how it feels to be in someone else's shoes. Identification with the aspirations, disappointments, troubles, and fears of others is especially important today when so much of our society is living in tight little subcultures of suburbia.

Sociodrama may help also to make everyday people who lived long ago come alive, problems seem real, and social history become more significant. They may, furthermore, add another dimension to good teaching of history: the concept of social change. Although problems of human relationships are as old as man, the solutions chosen by persons long dead might have been different had they known what we know today. Consequently, pupils must orient their thinking to that of the period being studied. Part of the evaluation of the sociodrama would entail the historical accuracy of the data cited in support of a decision. At the same time, children would be reminded that in like manner, some of the choices we make today might be unwise from the vantage point of 2500 A.D.

HOW TO TEACH USING A SOCIODRAMA

Planning

Select a problem of human relationships that fits the maturity level of your pupils. If you are lucky you may find a short story that serves the purpose which you will read to the class. You may, however, write your own story or simply describe the characters and the situation in which they are involved to your class. In any event, the number of characters should be limited, how the story ends will not be suggested, and several different endings are possible.

Procedures

1. Prepare the pupils to identify with the characters by explaining that you will choose some of them to act out the ending of the story you are about to tell or read.

2. Read or tell the story. This should not take more than fifteen or twenty minutes.

3. Choose the cast or casts. (At first, you may find it helpful to choose the actors before you tell the story.) Since you want your first sociodramas to be successful, you might choose boys and girls who would cooperate willingly and be able to talk readily. After you have used the technique a number of times, you should then choose pupils who would gain most from playing the role. For example, when you know a boy has no sympathy for unions, you would cast him in the role of a labor leader. The assumption is that he would learn something of labor's point of view from taking the role.

4. Send the actors out of the room for a three to five minutes' planning session.

5. Let the class suggest solutions. Some teachers may prefer to omit this step, but others find it useful in getting involvement from the whole class.

Perhaps with first attempts, you might prefer to spend the time in helping the class think through how they will evaluate the role-playing. At this time, you would also suggest that the class should be sympathetic with the performers and refrain from laughing.

6. Students act out the conclusion of the story. While the play is in progress, you should sit with the class and not interrupt the players unless they are obviously changing the facts of the situation as described. You should, however, recognize when a decision is reached, end the scene, and thank the performers. Sometimes the pupils themselves do not seem to realize when this point is reached.

7. Evaluate in terms of (a) emotional reactions portrayed; (b) facts cited; and (c) consequences of various courses of action. Sometimes teachers assume that they can evaluate their pupils' emotional reactions, too, on the basis of how they play roles. Thus they confuse sociodrama as a teaching method with psychodrama, a projective technique used by psychiatrists and psychologists. Since analyses derived from projective techniques are sometimes questionable even when made by expert psychologists, teachers should beware of amateur diagnosis. After all, you asked the pupil to play a role. Let's assume that he is doing just that.

A Final Word

Plan carefully so that you will establish a clear-cut problem situation that is interesting. Nevertheless, don't be discouraged if your first effort fails. Sociodrama will work on any age group from kindergarteners to adults, but older persons are more likely to laugh and be self-conscious and less likely to identify on first tries than younger children. After a little experience, the chief limitation of the technique is the lack of ingenuity of the teacher.

SAMUEL POLATNICK

Principal, Springfield Gardens High School, New York

57. A Vote for Citizenship*

Recent articles in *Social Education* and other professional journals have attested to a ferment in the social studies. Postholing; making room for sociology, social psychology, and anthropology in courses of study; team teaching; and other suggestions for curriculum revision and methodological change have attracted widespread attention. Yet, as we look to the new in social studies, there is a danger that we may neglect or slight a fundamental objective: the cultivation of intelligent, civic-minded behavior in our young people.

The dazzling advances in science, mathematics, and technology have distracted many people from an essential recognition of the need for citizenship and political intelligence of the highest order at this time. The solution of such problems as formulating correct nuclear policy, developing effective leadership, and expanding democratic values throughout the world—to name but a few—call for the fullest mobilization of our nation's wisdom, and the practice of devoted public service by all of us.

Yet it is shocking to learn from surveys that many people, particularly in the lowest eligible age brackets, do not even vote. Surely the intelligent exercise of the franchise is an essential first step in any practice of citizenship. While the exercise of the suffrage and the practice of good citizenship are functions of many institutions and factors such as the home, the church, the community, and the schools, the schools have always accepted a major share of the responsibility for preparing youth to transmit the city a little better than they found it.

As a matter of fact, our schools have developed many useful practices and procedures for developing good citizenship. Perhaps what is needed is a more systematic application of what our schools have learned of such preparation, and a careful evaluation and testing of procedures to determine which might be most effective in developing young people of different ages, backgrounds, and experiences. A survey of curricular, extracurricular, and school-community citizenship-training procedures in the high schools of New York City, conducted under the auspices of the Standing Committee in Social Studies (officers of supervisors' and teachers' professional organizations) and Acting Associate Superintendent Maurice D. Hopkins, Head of the High School Division, revealed a wide

Social Education, XXVIII:343–45, October 1964. Used by permission.

variety of valuable practices for the development of intelligent civic-minded voting and other civic behavior.

In the hope that some of the New York City experiences may be valuable to social studies teachers in other communities and that they may serve to stimulate additional thought in the area of citizenship training, we offer the following summary of practices. No one school can hope to do all these things, but surely every school can find time to carry out a few of the suggestions.

ANNUAL EFFORTS DIRECTLY RELATED
TO NOVEMBER ELECTIONS

1. Development of a series of lessons on the elections prepared by the social studies departments for social studies classes. These lessons cover such aspects of the elections as issues, candidates, the importance of voting, and the significance of the elections.

2. In some schools teachers prepare special election information sheets containing registration information, election district maps, lists of candidates, brief descriptions of election issues, sample ballots, and a few key questions such as, "In choosing your U. S. Congressman and Senator, have you determined his position on foreign aid, medical care for the aged, civil rights for minorities, aid to public and parochial schools, plans to reduce unemployment, the "Cold War," the uses of atomic energy, and atomic testing?" These materials are designed to stimulate thought and discussion about the particular election.

3. Distribution to students of election materials prepared by nonpartisan civic organizations such as the League of Women Voters, American Heritage Foundation, etc.

4. Presentation in class of "sociodramas" on the problems of voters in which students sign in registration books, inquire about particulars of the election, establish sources of information, and vote.

5. Students organize a special Student Elections Council to develop appropriate election-centered projects in which the school will participate. Some students, for example, act as baby-sitters on election day to release parents for voting.

6. Conducting of school-wide straw votes on local, state, and national elections.

7. Visits to, observation of, and participation in the activities of local political clubs.

8. Use of town meetings and panel discussions in social studies classes on issues and candidates in elections. Special attention is given to the significance of every vote by including analyses of previous close votes.

9. Judicious use of tape recordings of speeches by leading candidates to define issues and evaluate debate.

10. Arrangement for election assemblies involving the candidates for public office, and/for student speakers. Some schools center such

assemblies around dramatizations of elections, election procedures, or the significance of elections.

11. Problems of Democracy classes may arrange three- to five-day conventions involving nominations, development of platforms, and straw votes.

12. As a procedure for making elections an opportunity for joint family consideration, Parent-Teachers Associations sponsor community election meetings which are attended by parents, students, teachers, and candidates.

13. Students interview local candidates for public office.

14. Social studies clubs or discussion clubs hold meetings with local candidates present to debate election issues.

15. Provision for comprehensive bulletin board displays in classrooms and special school areas on such aspects of the elections as registration information, candidates, issues, and results.

16. Printing of features such as interviews with local candidates, and of pro and con treatment of major public issues in the school newspaper.

17. Arrangement on a broad basis—borough or city—of a student nominating convention in which students nominate candidates, debate their qualifications, formulate platforms, evaluate planks of the party platforms, and vote.

18. Demonstration of the operation of voting machines.

19. Students write letters to parents urging them to register and vote. In some schools students have prepared bilingual appeals to parents regarding elections.

20. Post-mortem analyses are made of election results in social studies classes pointing up for students how additional voting might have affected these results, the significance of outcomes for public policy, etc.

LONG-RANGE PREPARATION FOR INTELLIGENT AND CIVIC-MINDED VOTING

1. Consistent efforts are made to relate ongoing instruction in the social studies to meaningful contemporary problems. This is directed to setting issues of the day in historical perspective so that youngsters may be aided in developing intelligent positions on public issues.

2. Provision of thorough instruction on the structure and operation of national, state, and local government.

3. Careful and thorough comparisons between the practices of Communist and other totalitarian societies and the practices of democratic society with specific reference to voting, the role of political parties, and opportunities to influence public policy. The preparation and distribution of mimeographed cartoons, excerpts from public statements, and quotations from reliable secondary sources make for valuable aids in such comparison and instruction.

4. Regular and systematic instruction in current events including

current events quizzes and special assemblies. Attention is given to using tools of propaganda analysis in the examination of sources of information on current issues.

5. Provision of a problems-of-democracy course or the use of a problems-of-democracy approach which stresses voter education by affording experiences in the identification of significant and controversial problems, student research in relevant information, evaluation of sources of information, discussion of issues, and efforts to find reasonable, tentative conclusions about such problems.

6. Operation of an effective program for student participation in school government. This involves developing a statement of areas appropriate for student participation, arranging effective educational procedures for the nomination of student officers, conducting election campaigns on meaningful school issues, organizing opportunities for students to discuss the selection of leaders offering and able to carry out intelligent platforms, establishing a wide extracurricular program, providing for a regular student-developed budget and financing program for student activities, thinking through a program for encouraging good school citizenship, encouraging student-community programs, and making provision for leadership training. Essential here is the creation of an atmosphere in which student suggestions in areas appropriate to their participation are welcomed, and where feasible, put into effect.

7. Organization of a leadership class for training student leaders in problem analysis, research, and formulation of school programs.

8. Analysis of books dealing with political leaders, the operations of government, and influences upon the electorate. Thus, books such as Theodore White's *The Making of the President, 1960,* and James MacGregor Burns' *Roosevelt: The Lion and the Fox* may provide the basis for valuable discussion.

9. Organization of social studies clubs and journals to provide for discussion and research related to significant social studies problems. Such activities may include a Social Studies Forum, a Model Legislature, a Luncheon Seminar, and a Social Studies Journal.

10. Conducting of regional (borough- and city-wide) discussion conferences in which specially trained student leaders conduct afternoon or day-long student discussions of significant public issues.

11. Participation of students under local college or civic organization sponsorship in sessions of a Model Congress or a Model Legislature in which legislation is proposed and drafted under procedures similar to those followed in the Congress of the United States.

12. Stimulation of correspondence between students and legislative representatives on public issues.

13. Encouragement of projects in which students, particularly seniors, participate in political club activities.

14. Visits to legislatures and courts.

15. Preparation by teachers or students of pro and con material on current public issues which is mimeographed and distributed as a

basis for class discussion. Special background fact sheets on such issues as urban representation in state legislatures may similarly be prepared.

16. Periodic polls may be conducted to sample student attitudes on current issues.

17. Students committees prepare a weekly program guide to TV and radio programs dealing with significant issues.

18. The school and civic organizations may jointly sponsor forums on significant contemporary issues.

19. Students keep a record of votes of their legislative representatives.

EFFORTS RELATED TO DEVELOPMENT OF GOOD CITIZENSHIP BEYOND VOTING

1. Regular involvement of students in community service projects such as work with the aged and the handicapped, entertainment of hospitalized veterans, service in hospitals, construction of toys for needy children, conduct of classes in community houses, and collections for charities. Some schools have organized youth panels to speak before community groups and furnish representation on community advisory councils.

2. Preparation and discussion of case studies in problems of citizenship at a level meaningful to youngsters, e.g., whether to report a friend who has been bribed to throw a basketball game.

3. Awards to students and citizens for outstanding citizenship. This involves the development of criteria for nomination, distribution of summaries of achievements of nominees and discussion of these accomplishments, school-wide vote, and a ceremonial assembly to honor the winner.

4. Awards of certificates of citizenship and character to one student in each social studies class, unrelated to scholastic achievement. Awards for co-operation in government are made at graduation for outstanding leadership and service in student activities.

5. Provision of extensive and varied opportunities for student service to the school on squads, in offices, and for individual teachers.

6. Instructional emphasis on biographies of outstanding civic-minded men and women stressing qualities of character and citizenship.

7. Organization of special assemblies to commemorate patriotic holidays and to support American ideals such as brotherhood.

8. Organization of visits to historic and patriotic shrines such as Independence Hall and Washington, D. C.

9. Displays of documents and other appropriate materials for illustrating the American heritage.

10. Development of programs such as Big Brother assignments, orientation assemblies and booklets, and visits to home rooms by student officers to orient newcomers to citizenship opportunities in a school.

11. Encouragement of teacher participation in community affairs.

12. Development of codes for school behavior.

13. The school sponsors an annual luncheon involving student officers and members of the community's civic organizations to discuss achievements, problems, and proposals for further school-community cooperation.

PROPOSALS FOR CITIZENSHIP-TRAINING ACTIVITIES POSSIBLY NOT YET IN WIDESPREAD OR REGULAR USE

1. Creation of a regular, annual well-rounded program to give every Election Day, not only those of presidential election years, the ceremony, dignity, and respect befitting the occasion upon which the citizens of a democracy exercise their precious opportunity to affect public policy and public officialdom. This should involve the whole panoply of distinguished speakers, displays, information, and votes.

2. Expansion of contacts of the school with the political life of the community by establishing regular opportunities for students to serve as witnesses at polls and political headquarters on election evenings, etc.

3. Encouragement of programs for having foreign students visit or live with American students. This affords opportunities for young people to compare American conditions with those of other countries, and to develop a deeper appreciation of the American way of life.

4. Greater use of voting machines for teaching purposes.

5. Greater involvement of public figures in class and school-wide activities.

6. Development or restoration of courses in civics or government: local, state, and national as near to the last year of high school education as possible. "American Consitutional Problems" could be stressed with brighter students, the "Role of the Citizen" with slower children. Regular courses in the social studies should include more material on government.

7. Raising licensing requirements for teachers to require more work in local, state, and national government.

8. Greater availability of appropriate instructional materials on elections and other issues.

9. Arrangements for meetings of social studies teachers to consider voting and other citizenship matters and to develop appropriate instructional procedures and materials.

10. Greater involvement of P.T.A.'s in developing programs for student participation in school-community service and civic projects.

11. Organization of Students' Voter Leagues to undertake regular responsibility for school and community election programs.

12. Teams of students might conduct occasional polls of community attitudes on public issues.

13. Educational television stations could be of service to schools

by presenting a series of programs on issues of elections and other relevant educational emphases.

14. Provision could be made for a teacher-coordinator or group of students to maintain a file of community service opportunities for young people, and to oversee such activity.

The interest of the teachers and supervisors of social studies in the high schools of New York City in developing good citizenship has resulted in the preparation of a number of curriculum bulletins. *Developing Student Participation in School Government* (Curriculum Bulletin No. 12, 1960–61 Series) and *Problems of Democracy* (Curriculum Bulletin No. 9, 1960–61 Series) are both available from the Board of Education, New York City, and both are valuable for deeper treatment of some of the suggestions described in this article.

Certainly a further exchange of professional wisdom and experience in citizenship training accumulated in our schools will help us all to provide even more effectively for the development of our young people and for their contribution to our society. As one school reported, "The evidence of the experience here at Morris [Morris High School, Bronx, New York] is that high school youth are more ready to accept responsibility for adult-like tasks than there are opportunities for such experiences."

FRED T. WILHELMS

*Executive Secretary, Association for Supervision and
Curriculum Development*

58. Letter to a Teacher: On Handling Controversial Questions*

So, my young friend, you are resolved that in your classroom controversial questions shall get the treatment they deserve? Well then, the first thing you will need is the ability to recognize one when you see it.

A lot of teachers lack that ability. For instance, I'm willing to bet that right now a good many of them are treating the statement that margarine is substantially as good a food as butter as if it were a controversial question. It isn't. As near as I can make out, it fits precisely the definition of a "scientific truth"—to be modified if new evidence arises but valid till then. On the other hand, undoubtedly, many more teachers are thoughtlessly treating the proposals to repeal the special taxes on margarine as if there were no question about them—at most, teaching the "right side" and giving a passing nod to the "other side." Yet, regardless of what you think of the arguments either way, here is a genuine question of social policy.

How can you tell what, for school purposes, is a controversial question, and what isn't? Let's admit that the dividing line isn't easy to draw, but certainly it shouldn't be determined by the intensity of the feelings that happen to have been aroused. Take the matter of race relations as an example: Since the sovereign American people has written into its Constitution full citizenship for the Negro, I believe no American teacher has a right to treat as a legitimate controversy whether Negroes should be denied any part of a citizen's legal status. The issue is in some areas acrimonious, and I sympathize with teachers who must find a way of living with it, but the excitement about it does not make it, in the educational sense, a controversial question.

On the other hand, there are genuinely controversial questions about which little fuss is made—many more of them than we generally recognize —matters on which we have no right to teach a set view as if it were thoroughly established. Most of us have taken a position on each so long ago that—especially if there is no public debate to dramatize the issue—we

*Progressive Education, 26:8–12, October 1948. Used by permission.

have forgotten it *is* only one side of a fair question. Or, unfamiliar with a special field, we are simply ignorant of differences that are "hot as a firecracker" among a small, earnest group. Worst of all, we're pretty likely to assume that the "other side" is purely specious anyway. And so, day after day, we casually hand down certainties authorized by no known arbiter of uncertainty. If you really mean business about giving controversial questions the right treatment, you'd better learn to see deeper than the current arguments in the press. Just who gave you the right last week to rule *ex parte* that installment selling should be curbed?

Perhaps one useful, rough guide is to treat as controversial questions matters of social policy on which society has not yet made up its mind. Note that this excludes differences of opinion which simply do not require—should never be submitted to—social decision. If the schools have any business at all with a host of private and personal as well as minority group matters, it is only to teach tolerance—nay more, appreciation—of the other fellow's habits or views and a democratic zeal to protect them even if they seem "queer." Such differences are not controversial questions in the educational sense.

All in all, you are not likely to go far wrong if with sincerity you stop to ask yourself whether the set of beliefs and attitudes you should like to install with respect to some matter really are so clearly established as to be past legitimate questioning—or simply your own preferences.

That leads us directly to your second personal need: zeal to subordinate your own views to a searching, objective inquiry that will give the youngsters full opportunity to see the central problem and the issues surrounding it and to make a start toward their own, independent conclusions. Such objectivity is hard to achieve, especially since it is highly desirable that as an adult citizen you *should have* views of your own. Saying to the students, even by implication or unconscious, subtle suggestion, "Now we must look at the other side, too," simply isn't good enough. Unless your group feels that *you and they* are setting out together to get as close as you can to the heart of a fresh, vital matter, something is wrong.

Incidentally, in their attempts to be impartial, some teachers remind me of a week-kneed referee who thinks that to be "fair" he has to call as many fouls on one side as on the other. They think that a "balanced" treatment means making an equally strong case for each side. If you simply go after the truth you won't fall into that error. Another thing: It isn't your role to be the eternal compromiser. The constructive harmonization of differences is a good thing, but as Van Til points out so repetitiously that his friends eventually catch on, "The middle ground is a position, too, and the would-be impartial leader has no more right to take it than either extreme." Besides, it's often the only position of the three that's no good.

A third thing you, as a person, owe your students is *depth of percep-*

tion. Let's first put it crudely: You need to be smart enough to "know the angles." A dismaying amount of thinking is blurred by clichès like "Business wants. . . ." that ignore great and pervasive differences within the ranks of business. An awful lot of time is wasted on the beautiful arguments with which public relations men beguile the public—and never getting to the real issues which all the insiders know are the issues. It's up to you to make yourself an insider.

But cut it deeper than that: It's up to you also to make yourself a *philosopher*, to see beneath this and that passing issue the great, continuing questions that face mankind. Probably a majority of the divisive public issues of our day root down in fundamental, long-standing differences in what men expect of organized society, what they think a government is *for*. Even though a problem is important in itself, it ought somehow also to be made an *example*—this year's variant *sub specie aeternitatis*.

In all this it is not so much that it is your function to "explain" the basic questions at issue. But if *your* perception of the real nature of the problem stops at the surface, the students will hardly go deeper. And if *you* have a distorted picture of the social and political forces at work on each side of a question, you can hardly expect your students to arrive at an analysis that would be a sound basis for a program of action.

TECHNICS

In this section let's take a good bit for granted. I assume that you know that the lively, controversial questions of the day are a different kind of subject matter and simply cannot be taught out of a book or even within the four walls of a classroom. You can get plenty of guidance on teaching devices that match the subject matter—excursions, interviews, the use of many kinds of material from many interested sources, etc. If you don't have the energy and initiative for that sort of thing—if you choose to go on getting all the answers out of one book, or supplying them yourself—it's probably better to let the whole thing alone than to make an academic pretense.

I assume, too, that you are mature enough to know that a social problem worth taking up at all is worth treating soberly. Simply rule out sarcasm and every form of pettiness. If it's serious question for many people, treat it that way, and keep the treatment on a high plane. If it isn't, why not just skip it?

What I really want to get at are five mental habits and procedures I believe you and your class have got to master.

1. Focus on the Problem, not on the Fight

A controversial question arises because people have a problem on their hands, think they see a way out, and seek action. The opposition may come from groups who do not sense the problem, are not affected by it, or for some reason do not want anything done about it; or it may come from groups equally eager to solve the problem, who are sold on different ways of doing it.

Now when you come to study the resultant controversy, you have a choice: You can analyze the problem and *then* see what the various parties propose to do about it, evaluating each set of proposals in the light of the problem to be solved. Or, like irresponsible hoodlums cheering on a street fight, you can analyze tactics and titillate interest by starting a miniature replica of the struggle within your classroom, while forgetting the objectives.

I think you simply haven't any cornerstone under your thinking until you understand what the need is, what is wanted, how important it is. Maybe the problem is an old, abiding plague of the human race, suddenly accentuated under modern conditions; try to see it in its historical perspective. Maybe it is a brand new product of our new environment; try to see the forces that have shaped it. Nothing else will help you so much to the objectivity you need as to keep your eye on the fundamental objective.

2. Hunt for Common Ground

Rarely are the parties in a controversy wholly in disagreement. They may be agreed on objectives, disagreed on means; or agreed on at least *some* objectives or *some* means; they may, in fact, be agreed on just about everything—perhaps without realizing it. For democratic action whatever real common ground exists is precious. For it is the starting point toward an acceptable solution. Hunting it out bears no relation to the weak-kneed practice of compromising away essential points of either faction in order to achieve a polite harmony. In a hot controversy the school may be almost the only place where enough calm prevails so that the points of agreement can be perceived and built upon. A school is acting irresponsibly if, like some newspapers, it stirs up more conflict than actually exists by sensationalizing what does exist.

One related bit of advice: Don't be too glib in stating other people's positions for them. You've no right either to exaggerate their demands or to whittle them down to something "reasonable." If labor and management, for instance, are involved, let each of them tell you—directly or through its publications—where they stand. Let your students learn to use primary sources instead of hearsay.

3. Define the Issues

Having identified the common ground, you are in position to identify the residual points at issue. Strip them down as far as possible to the real differences. For instance, there has been quite a debate about grade labeling, with some pretty strong impugning of motives on both sides. Eventually the leaders of the two factions discovered that they were wholly agreed on the basic purpose of labeling, which is to give consumers accurate information to choose by. It became clear, furthermore, that both were agreed on "descriptive" rather than grade labeling for all products except foods—and pretty well agreed on the grade labeling of certain foods. That restricted the area of debate almost entirely to processed fruits and vegetables; and it narrowed the issue to whether a grade label or a descriptive label better informs a canned food buyer—a question that can be worked out without much rancor.

However, the purpose of defining the issues is not necessarily to moderate the debate. It is to determine exactly what the specific points of disagreement are. Once more, one should not be too cavalier in stating those issues for all parties. Find out as directly as possible from the parties themselves—and don't be taken in by the red herrings they sometimes use to keep the public from nosing out the real issues.

At this point, then, you will be able to set down what a lawyer would call the "stipulations" (the points which are not in question) and the issues (the points that are). Work out as precise a wording as you can. Keep it in view. Try to make it calm and unemotional. Your purpose is not to stir up an excited, glandular reaction.

4. Develop Criteria or Standards of Reference

The great basic premises, from which specific controversial questions are merely offshoots, all too often go unspoken, unquestioned, and unrecognized. No one can argue a specific issue soundly unless he knows what his reference criteria are. And no youngster is likely to clarify his standards of reference except as he is forced to apply them to specifics.

Given any specific issue you need to keep probing behind it: "You believe in democracy, don't you? What do you think it means in this situation? How does this proposal square up with your conception of democracy?" Such probing will enrich and realize the concept of democracy at the same time that it enlightens the issue. Religion is another good source of value standards: "How do the teachings of your religion apply? Are you going to back a proposal contrary to them?" The American codes of sportsmanship and fair play are another source: "If it's important to help an opponent up when he has been knocked down, what should you do about this social question?"

Get the reference criteria stated clearly and simply. Keep referring to them. Don't forget, either, that the differences which show up on a specific question may stem back to legitimate differences in basic premises. So don't demand unanimity on standards of reference. Work for as much agreement in standards as you can genuinely get; respect the residual differences. For instance, on some question of economic regulation, a whole class will agree on democracy as a frame of reference. But one youngster's concept of democracy may stress freedom of the strong to rise, while another is more interested in protection for all the people, even the less able. After all, one of the blessings in a democracy is the right to help define it. Help each to see just what his premises are and how they affect his conclusions.

5. Be Realistic about the Proposed Alternatives

Nothing so dismays me as to see one of the great persisting problems of mankind casually "solved" in about three days by a roomful of students. Who do they think they are, to be so much wiser than their elders—Little Orphan Annie?

There is precisely one difference between them and their elders: The grownups have to face the realities—lack of money, public apathy, politics, etc. And until school children also have to look those realities in the eye, the whole school treatment of social "problems" is a travesty.

A large number of the divisive social questions of our day hinge on the expenditure of public tax funds. "Where's the money coming from?" is a real and pressing question to responsible adults (even if often used speciously by obstructionists). It is seldom given very realistic attention in the classroom; there the unspoken assumption seems to be that if a public proposal is "good," it ought to be supported without further question, Well, a lot of things would be "good" for my family, too, but we still have to make a budget, and it never covers all of them. I do not mean that we should teach defeatism or timidity; but can't we establish the constructive attitude of a *responsible* person?

Another large share of public issues hinges around the imposition of social controls and regulation. Am I right in feeling that in the classroom situation the dice are commonly loaded a wee bit in favor of governmental action? Not because teachers are socialist or collectivist, but—I think—because the neat, orderly, blueprinted way is easier to describe and defend, to some extent compelling upon the mind. What we call loosely the "free enterprise" way (referring here not merely to business affairs) is less susceptible of charting and orderly classroom presentation. But, to put it mildly, it has turned out to be a pretty fair way of getting things done.

Again, I am not arguing for a "conservative" line or saying that we should not present forcefully the potentials of wise group action. But when we are presumably considering alternatives, let's *really* scrutinize them—on out to the ultimate commitment.

Obviously such treatment is likely to take more time than is generally given to a bit of subject matter. Well, we don't assign a geometry problem and then stop halfway through it because it takes too long. And the analogy is uncomfortably exact.

6. And, of Course, Keep Your Weight off the Decision

The teacher and the school are not arbiters of social questions. The basic assumption underlying the school's presenting controversial questions at all is that it will throw no official weight into influencing the student one way or another.

Sometimes I wonder how many schools really live up to the assumption.

Purposes

All in all, the technics of handling controversial questions in the classroom are easy enough to learn if one really believes in it. The more difficult —and the more important—thing may be to get and keep clearly in mind what we are after when we do it.

Certainly it is a good argument for classroom consideration of controversial questions that they are the *agenda of our times*—the matters of policy on which our citizenry must choose a line of action, or decide not to act. If we can create a broad basis of problem-solving intelligence on such matters, we surely cannot be wrong.

Yet I suspect the main thing we are after is a cluster of *concomitant learnings* which will apply in all future situations. If that is so, we ought to decide definitely what they are and proceed accordingly. Why not make up for yourself a statement of your long-term goals? You will likely find them mostly falling under the broad phrase, *good citizenship*. That demands many abilities and skills and attitudes, such as the desire and ability to get and evaluate relevant information, and to influence public opinion. I challenge you to find one of these to which a thoughtful consideration, in school, of the controversial problems of our day does not contribute mightily.

In closing, I should like to focus upon just one point in this matter of citizenship. In terms of the needs of our times, who is the best citizen? Is he really the rather complaisant, tender-minded conformist who always "goes along" with every new proposal (though not necessarily doing anything about it)? Much of our school procedure seems to asume that he is. Or have some of our best contributors been tough-minded people with enough vinegar in their souls to vote "no" now and then, to force an idea to prove itself before they roll up their sleeves and go to work for it?

There is an open question of values there, which every teacher must work out for himself. But, for myself, I have a hunch we have been building toward too "nice" and soft-minded a race of citizens. I feel we ought to work for a fierce love of liberty, a certain raw-boned, sturdy independence against the seeping encroachments of social conformism and bureaucratic meddling. At the time of Shays' Rebellion, Thomas Jefferson said it was a good thing for the tree of liberty to be watered now and then with the blood of patriots. Even in school it is worth an occasional bumped head.

That says it badly, but maybe you see what I mean. Totalitarianism and stateism (the democratic variety included) thrive on a love of a nice, neat order of things, of going along with the crowd. Running a lasting democracy takes more gumption than that. It takes people who can stand up on their own feet, think for themselves, and call a spade a spade. It takes people with the sense of command to be *masters* of their state, and the critical sense and nerve to blister it when it does badly. The love of democracy is a pallid, wishy-washy thing if it does not include real affection for the give-and-take, the rough-and-tumble of a society where free men stand up for their own interests and ideas.

The above is over-concentrated on the "rugged individual" angle, of course. I have done it deliberately because that angle seems to receive so little attention nowadays. Democracy also requires the largest measure of ability to work together cooperatively. It takes the ability to compromise; or, better to search out common ground and work for a constructive harmonization of differences. It takes a powerful insight into the potentialities of group action and wisdom in using those potentialities.

You see, the problem is one of achieving a nice balance: between the ability to yield and the courage to stand out alone, if necessary; between the ability to make a fight and the ability to cooperate; between a fierce insistence on essential personal liberties and genuine appreciation of social action.

And that, I think, is where the wise treatment of controversial questions can make its greatest contribution. We can teach boys and girls to reason out a position and then stand by their guns, courageously and tenaciously; in the same breath we can help them see how others have honestly and honorably arrived at *their* positions and deserve respect. We can teach them how to influence the opinion of others; and, not less important, how to be influenced open-mindedly by the contributions of others. We can teach them not weakly to compromise away essential ground; and yet, by constructive harmonization, to gain essential ground by compromise. We can educate them as the royal masters of their society; and at the same time as loyal subjects.

Perhaps in all this we have nothing greater to teach than the *art of creative discussion*. It is that rare discussion wherein everyone makes his unique contribution, yet each learns more than he contributes—where a group as a whole comes to a position better than any one member could have come to by himself. It depends more on creative listening than on clever talking. It stems, not from a sole desire to clinch one's own position by argument, but from a drive to get nearer the truth through the pooled insights of all.

Such discussion can be held only in an atmosphere of democracy. It can be maintained only by those who in some measure know the meaning of democracy, who respect themselves and others equally. In some small way, every controversy is a crisis in democratic self-management. If you can help boys and girls in your classroom frankly to face up to crisis after crisis, each time coming out on higher ground of courage, insight, and mutual good will and respect, we need have no fear for the future of our nation's democracy.

IIC-5.

Individualizing Instruction for Students of Differing Ability

RICHARD E. GROSS

Professor of Education, Stanford University

59. *Providing for Individual Differences* *

We have long known that the students in any class have more differences than likenesses. Even the age-old Hebrew *Talmud* recognized at least four types of pupils. It cleverly referred to these prototypes as the sponge, the funnel, the strainer, and the sieve. In the treatise "Abot," the rabbis explained that some students absorb all, like the sponge; others, like the funnel, take in everything at one end and let it out at the other; another group, as strainers, allow the wine to go through, retaining only the dregs; still others can be compared to the sieve, which removes the bran, retaining only the fine flour!

Today, however, we have knowledge of many more and varied differences—physical maturity, health, family pressures, interests, backgrounds of experience, mental development, socio-economic status, reading ability, special gifts, and personality are but a few of literally hundreds of very real dissimilarities that can and should be reflected in our teaching. Even in so-called homogeneous classes, as any experienced instructor will attest, individual differences still loom greater than likenesses and continue to plague the instructor who has mistakenly believed that a homogeneous class means less and easier work. In spite of these facts, the bulk of learning in the secondary school is still planned in terms of blanket aims, assignments, and assessments. Many teachers seem to refuse to admit that they do not teach a class but that they are responsible for individuals grouped together as a class.

High School Journal, 40:152–58, January, 1957. Used by permission.

This article takes for granted the reader's knowledge of the psychological findings which undergird the principle of individualized instruction, as well as the reader's familiarity with research revelations that the individual learns more, more easily, and retains longer those learnings related to his own needs and interests. The writer also assumes the reader's acceptance of the key democratic principle which highlights the import, dignity, and sovereignty of the individual. How can teachers and administrators, in a free nation such as ours, continue instructional programs which in many aspects seem better attuned to a lock-step-cog-in-a-wheel-automatist-Big Brother society?

For readers interested in developing an instructional program which is geared to the individual as a unique person, the writer wishes to point up three areas where concerted efforts will help materially in developing individualized instruction. These include: the guidance approach, real unit teaching, and the laboratory classroom. None of these is new. Semi-individualized educational programs including these factors have long been sought. The Dalton Plan, the Winnetka Plan, the Miller Unit Plan, the Morrison Plan, and the problem-project all have included attempts to adjust subject-matter and instruction to varying needs and abilities. No one has yet found *the* formula for so organizing classes; but many helpful ideas are available.

Guidance Approach. Proponents of the above plans and those forwarding more recent approaches seem to agree with the statement that, "Guidance is basically a compromise between what we actually teach in the schools and what we know full well we ought to teach!" Increasing numbers of educators, as reflected in our evolving secondary school programs, seem to be coming to recognize the instructional implications of the above viewpoint. What this means, of course, is that teachers must have as great an interest in and study their pupils as thoroughly as they have heretofore been students of their subjects. A first demand here is as complete an amount of information about the pupils and their differences as is possible. Results of previous observations, anecdotal records, test scores, peer ratings, and home visitation are examples of the efforts and kinds of information that should be amassed.

The establishment of rapport between the teacher and a new group of students is another essential. The instructor should have the time to carefully peruse the accumulative folders of each pupil before meeting with a class for the initial time. In this manner the face that goes with the name is much more of an entity. As far as names go, such a simple technique as mastering the names of all of the pupils in the first several days is a great help here. Pupils are happily surprised and respond warmly to the teacher who calls them by the right name so soon (and pronounces it correctly!);

each says to himself, "This teacher knows *me!*" A first step has been successfully taken in establishing cordial, individual relations.

Another individualizing characteristic of the guidance approach is the inclusion of personal and vocational guidance with the typical, educational guidance carried on in the schoolroom. Personal and vocational learnings and activities become educational in a class that is studying job opportunities and the necessary qualifications of employees. Such studies are being concluded in English, business, social studies, and core classes, as well as being conducted as homeroom activities.

When and where appropriate, teacher-pupil planning is one of the best ways to implement the guidance approach and individualized instruction. Some common goals will exist for all students, but even these are often reached by different means. A simple technique used by many senior high school American history teachers with poor readers, for example, is to provide junior high textbooks with which these retarded readers can attain some of the same basic knowledge that the other students gain through the senior high text. A major need, however, is for pupils to arrive at individual goals and to have individual assignments and materials whereby they can achieve. Certain students may need to emphasize work habits, others must concentrate on improving their classroom relationships, or special drill may be needed on ratio, map reading, or restrictive clauses. The pupil needs to understand the purpose of such individual goals and they are best agreed upon in private consultation with the instructor at the beginning of a unit or a grade period. These aims should be recorded on some reference form or in a notebook, and the teacher should lead the students to refer to them as the unit progresses. It can be seen that such aims serve as helpful guides for self-appraisal by the students of their personal growth. Pupils who build skills of individual evaluation and who use self-rating sheets come to view their own strengths and weaknesses so that they develop realistic levels of aspiration and have many less adjustment problems. The foregoing have been but a few examples which reflect the guidance approach attitude and reveal its help in providing for individual differences.

Real Unit Teaching. This article will not attempt to define the factors included in good unit instruction; such descriptions exist in large numbers. However, the writer is certainly not referring to a class which spends a week or two covering via recitations or total group discussions several chapters in a textbook which have been conveniently grouped under the title "unit." Unit teaching is not the only form of instruction which provides for individualization, but it is one of the best. The unit, with its long-term and varied assignments, with its diversified materials, its occasional days allotted to individual and sub-group classroom and library work pe-

riods, and with its balance of total group, committee, and individual projects, provides an excellent framework for meeting students differences.
. . . .

Units allow for teacher-pupil planning of varied aspects of the program.
Who will preside at the concluding forum? How will the welcome committee greet and introduce a guest speaker? When will the notebooks be
due? What kind of a final exam will be most satisfactory? Such planning
promotes numerous, individual decisions and actions which are most important factors in the education of young citizens in a democracy.

Even in total group discussion and recitation there can be individualization. Certainly the teacher will usually call upon some students with the
simple type of fact questions, while other pupils can be expected to answer
more difficult questions of interpretation. Incidentally, brilliant students
benefit from the Socratic type of questioning which occurs too seldom in
the secondary schools. Teachers and the students who follow such a point-
by-point defense of a statement also profit from the experience.

The importance of individualization in structuring a class discussion-
recitation was once brought home to the writer. He had asked a particularly difficult question; no one in class raised a hand or even looked in the
tell-tale ways that teachers come to recognize as signals that pupils want
to be called on. The writer went ahead and gave the answer. Later as the
young people moved out of the room to the next period's classes, one of the
brightest and most loquacious of the students muttered as he passed the
teacher—but loud enough to be overheard, "I knew the answer to that
question but I wouldn't bother to answer it." The writer stopped him and
asked why he took that attitude. He explained, "Well, I'm tired of holding up my hand; you just about never call on me!" While this student's hand
was a perennial waving tower of Pisa, the instructor, knowing the boy's
dependability, had undoubtedly been ignoring him too often. After a brief
discussion the writer and the boy came to a gentleman's agreement. He
was to stop waving his hand for every question, but when he really wanted
to make a contribution, to clarify a point, or answer a difficult query, the
writer agreed to try and recognize him. In this manner the student was
helped to better understand his own competencies, his proper, individual
role in the class group, as well as the position of the instructor. Naturally,
such schoolroom incidents aid the perceptive teacher in becoming more
adept in his individualizing procedures.

The Laboratory Classroom. The laboratory classroom, with its experiments, projects, varied instruments, wall charts, reference volumes,
and display tables, should never be limited to only the science classes. Such
facilities are essential for adequate individualization in all subject areas.
Any instructor's ability to differentiate assignments is, of course, greatly
promoted or handicapped by the amount and variety of instructional ma-

terials available. While teachers have truthfully complained that they could not teach a certain unit because reading materials do not exist or because the principal will not expend funds on pamphlets, actually too few are willing to move far enough beyond written media of learning. Thinking of boys and girls as unique individuals who learn considerably different amounts in differing ways, through varied sources of impression, underscores the truism that "sensual avenues to learning are prime sources for many nonverbal pupils, therefore, these media should not be referred to as 'merely aids.' " With universal, secondary education for numerous captive students this means that teachers must learn to do more than just supplement or reinforce booklearnings with other sources. To these pupils, the film strip, the cartoon, the object, the making of a graph, or the creation of a shop or craft product may be the major source of learning.

The laboratory classroom also extends out into the school and community. Here are further opportunities for individualization. A teacher, for example, in selecting an interview team that is going to question a clergyman must consider a number of individual needs and differences as he selects the volunteers. Which student is intelligent enough to chair the group and come back with the correct information? Who will display good manners and social understanding in this situation? Which parents might complain if their children went on such a mission? Who will benefit the most from this personal contact and trip? These and still other questions cross the mind of an instructor in such a situation; if he has not realized it before, he now sees how he must truly know each pupil. These same factors also have to be considered in setting up committee work. The sad experiences that teachers and pupils have had when committee projects misfire can usually be traced back to failures in individualization.

What is the relationship of the "group dynamics" movement in education to individualized instruction? It is commonplace to hear students and teachers attack some of the emerging practices as examples of the threat of collectivism which submerges the individual to the group. Stripped of its more faddish and overcomplex aspects, including esoteric, sociometric formulae and complicated discussion tabulation forms, what are the underlying interests of many who experiment with these processes? It is true that some want to know how to better use the group to influence the individual; but these persons commonly have the individual's welfare in mind as well as that of the group. Actually some of the prime purposes of sociograms, student reaction forms, friendship lists, role-playing and small group discussion techniques are aimed at building individual capabilities and at enabling the teacher to provide more effective learning experiences on the basis of better and more knowledge about each pupil.

In an age of ever declining numbers and influence, workers in the group process field recognize the import of retaining small, intimate, primary associations. It is in these group relationships that the individual has always taken his basic, social cues and built his personality. These workers are studying and using groups in education to find ways in which to break down the isolation of the increasingly common, large, impersonal, secondary group learning situations. This is to help the individual make contributions, feel a part, and understand his associates. The sociodrama, for instance, may allow an individual to project himself into a situation he needs to experience but never has had the opportunity before. As a student committee investigates a problem or thrashes out a report and a recommendation, key, democratic skills and attitudes are built. The use of buzz groups encourages many pupils to share opinions and to develop a feeling that a total group decision is actually the individual's own. Think how much more individualized learning is going on as thirty-five pupils discuss a problem in small groups of five or six than when thirty-four wait their turn while the teacher hears one. Those who would criticize the group dynamics movement need to be reminded that many teachers are studying groups, using groups, and altering groups for the sake of better understanding and helping their individual pupils. These instructors hope to find in these processes the means by which school and society can gain the most from each individual, as at the same time the individual builds and strengthens his knowledge, skills, and attitudes.

The reader can perceive the intimate relationship that exists between the guidance approach, the well-planned and executed unit, and the laboratory classroom. Many of the techniques that have been mentioned cut across or are employed in each of these curricular factors. It should also be clear that each of these arrangements reinforces the other. In fact, the full meaning of the term "individualized instruction" is only achieved when these three components are merged into a harmonious, educational program.

JACK ABRAMOWITZ

District Supervisor of Social Studies, Farmingdale Public Schools,
New York

60. How Much Subject Matter Content for the Slow Learner?*

Teachers of slow learners soon understand that a major shortcoming of this type of pupil is a marked inability to absorb subject matter and to use such subject matter in the development of intelligent generalizations. Nor is this too surprising since most slow learners are defeated by the existing techniques of subject matter presentation, and this, in turn, makes generalizations meaningless since they must rest upon some basis of substantive knowledge. Since the slow learner has few facts at his command he is unable to perceive the thread that ties them together or links them to other associated facts.

Awareness of these weaknesses on the part of the pupils ought to alert us to the dangers of teaching them by way of broad generalizations. Yet, the very opposite is true. Teachers seeking to devise a program for slow learners seem irresistibly drawn to the view that the subject matter must be diffused and taught through a series of generalizations. This can be explained, in part, by the inability of such students to learn and retain factual matter contained in existing texts which were designed for an entirely different sort of student. This inability frustrates teachers as well as students. At this point many teachers feel that the answer may lie in leaving specific subject-matter content and moving into the area of broad generalizations. Experience teaches us that this method, too, proves inadequate and, in turn, leads to the feeling that no method devised by man can meet this challenge.

This tendency to move into areas of generalization has its counterpart in other aspects of the slow-learner program. For instance, there are many educators who believe there is merit in a teaching program that moves *around* the stumbling block of reading retardation. For this reason they propose the most extensive use of audio-visual aids, TV programs, discussion and "buzz" sessions, and the use of comic books. When confronted by the charge that such a learning program does not permit the organized teaching of specific subject matter content they reply that it does

*Social Education, XXVII:11–12, January 1963. Used by permission.

permit the teacher to reach the pupil, in however limited a manner, at the level where he can be reached.

The proposal to employ materials that move *around* the reading problem has this much to commend it: it is an honest effort to provide some means of instruction that will not frustrate and bedevil the slow learner. It does try to provide a better climate within the classroom and it often reduces substantially the tensions that arise when such pupils are given tasks which, however simple, are beyond their abilities. But the point of weakness in this program lies precisely in the fact that it seeks to move *around* the problem of reading retardation rather than addressing itself directly to that problem.

What have we done? We have discovered that the pupil suffers from a specific deficiency. Now that we know what his problem is, we have made no effort to apply a remedy. It is as though we knew a pupil had a sight deficiency and we proposed to meet this problem by having him keep his eyes closed and relying upon his auditory senses alone. Of course this is nonsense. If a student has a sight deficiency we apply remedial measures to make it possible for him to employ his sight. Just in the same sense we must devise a program to remedy the reading deficiency which blocks the development of masses of slow learners. Teachers of slow learners must *understand* and *believe* that the problem confronting substantial numbers of their pupils is often remedial in character. Once we see this problem as a remedial one, it only remains for us to apply the appropriate remedy.

The teacher of slow learners needs to develop an unwillingness to assume that any area of specific knowledge cannot be taught to a student. No assumption of failure can be made until we have first exhausted every means of reproducing subject matter in terms that might be understandable to the pupil. The teacher of slow learners ought to keep in mind at all times that his principal function is to improve reading and comprehension skills in the social studies *and through the social studies*. In such a program the subject matter is not relegated to an unimportant position. Rather, it stands in a close relationship to the development of reading and comprehension skills. The cause of much of the pupil's difficulty is his lack of skill in reading and comprehension. The effect of improvement in these areas will be to enable him to grow in subject matter knowledge. This is especially true if our approach to the teaching of reading skills is to teach them through the use of specific subject matter in one of the regular school subjects. Growing reading skill leads to expanded subject matter knowledge and development of such knowledge motivates the pupil to work for further improvement of reading skills. The one feeds upon the other.

But does the slow learner need to know about the Congress of Vienna, the Fashoda Affair, or the results of the Renaissance? Indeed he does need to know all of this and as much more as we can teach him. He needs to know all that any other active, normal member of the community requires to make him a perceptive member of our society. It is no more difficult to teach the Congress of Vienna or the Renaissance through the medium of reading skills lessons than it is to teach "you and your family," or "what is a good citizen." It is not unreasonable to assume that there is far more likelihood of a meeting of minds and purposes in teaching factual subject matter than in trying to promote middle-class beliefs, standards, and virtues to a group that has long learned that it is rejected by the middle-class society that now seeks to teach it a *modus vivendi* upon the terms set by that very society that has rejected it.

Perhaps the major problem confronting us at this time is to impress upon teachers the meaning of a reading skills approach and to emphasize the dynamic nature of such an approach. All too often the reading skills approach, taught through the medium of an "open book lesson," has been misunderstood by teachers. The charge is often made that it is boring, lacking in stimulation, and frequently degenerates into a workbook type lesson.

Time does not permit a detailed examination of these charges. For the moment it must suffice to state that in many instances such arguments reveal a lack of understanding of the many ways in which an open book lesson can be run by a skillful teacher. Nor need such lessons be simple workbook type in organization. In any good reading skills lesson at least one third of each period will be devoted to discussion. Included in this discussion will be both the motivation at the start of the lesson and the continuing motivation throughout the lesson. The teacher will seek constantly to provide thought-provoking questions or comments which will capture and retain class interest. Discussion also enables the teacher to determine the degree to which students have grasped the meanings of the day's lesson.

Eighteen years ago when this writer began teaching his first slow-learner classes he had the good fortune to be under the guidance of a chairman whose abilities truly merited the term "master teacher." The substance of his advice was to divide the lesson into three parts composed of reading, writing, and discussion, and to make every effort to work on the improvement of basic skills. How elementary this must sound. But is it not possible that the application of elementary understandings may yet help provide us with the means for resolving the formidable problem of meeting the challenge of the slow learner?

ROBERT V. DUFFEY

Professor of Elementary Education, University of Maryland

61. *Helping the Less-Able Reader**

A question being raised increasingly often by teachers at all levels is, "What can I do to help my pupils who cannot read our social studies textbook?" This paper is directed to some suggested answers to this question. A limitation which the writer has placed upon the answers is that they must include reading; that is, they must not consist of nonreading activities.

Two basic assumptions would seem to be worth mentioning. First, social studies should not be considered a mere handmaiden to reading. "It would be quite possible," Chase has said, "to reach a high level of competence in social studies through a nonreading, nonwriting curriculum."[1] Chase does not recommend such an approach; he merely makes the point to high-light the other possible extreme of complete dependence upon text-centered instruction. Actually, success in reading and success in social studies achievement tend to go hand in hand: reading helps the pupil in social studies, and what he learns in social studies helps him to read better.[2] Our concern with reading in this present instance is its use as a means to an end in social studies.

Second, the raising of the question is an encouraging sign that many teachers are increasingly concerned with individual differences in achievement. In his "House Divided Against Itself" speech Lincoln said, "If we could first know where we are and whither we are tending, we could better judge what we do and how to do it." It would appear that many teachers have come to the place of "how to do it."

"Vagueness," Bernard de Voto said, "should not be invoked when a precise answer is possible"; but pat answers to educational questions are usually not readily found. The suggested answers to our particular problem are not advertised herewith as anything beyond possible answers, helps to be used with professional discretion.

Textbooks at lower levels of readability: This most obvious suggestion is not so easy as it may sound. For one thing, content coverage varies from

Social Education, XXV:182–84, April 1961. Used by permission.
[1] W. Linwood Chase, "Individual Differences in Classroom Learning" in National Society for the Study of Education, *Social Studies in the Elementary School,* 56th Yearbook, part 2 (Chicago, Ill.: University of Chicago Press, 1957), p. 175.
[2] Ralph C. Preston, *Teaching Social Studies in the Elementary Schools,* rev. ed. (New York: Rinehart and Co., 1958), pp. 251–52.

level to level. Further, treatment of the same content differs from author to author, albeit for good reasons, compounding the instructional task. Students in the upper grades tend to shun texts designated for lower grades. Authorities disagree on the advisability of using multiple texts at the elementary level.[3]

The suggestion is made, nevertheless, in the knowledge that it will prove workable in some instances. Its use will be greater where the possibilities of its use are better known. A master inventory of the contents— titles of chapters, stories, poems, and pictures—of all the books in a school, with grade levels indicated and arranged according to unit topics or broad topical headings (for example, "Westward Movement," "Mexican Life," "George Washington") is an excellent stimulant. Compiling and maintaining such an inventory and doing the necessary librarian work are the kinds of service projects with which gifted pupils may be entrusted.

A splendid general reference on this subject is Mary C. Wilson's pamphlet, "How to Use Multiple Books."[4]

Trade books, or children's literature: The reason for inclusion of this suggestion is best explained by Alvina Treut Burrows:

> Never before—and this is no idle superlative—has there been such a wealth of literature for children and teachers to choose from in books related to social studies. Each year since the midcentury, publishers and authors have produced approximately a thousand new titles and a respectable list of reprintings. In almost every social studies area children's literature offers some of its riches.[5]

In brief, pertinent juvenile literature is available as never before. It has always been coveted in social studies because it provides the depth and detail which textbooks cannot provide.

A service of great merit is rendered to teachers at all levels in their efforts to keep abreast of this avalanche of material by the *Bulletin* of the Center for Children's Books.[6] This publication critically reviews current juvenile books, pointing out each volume's relative importance, its strengths and weaknesses, its general content, its specific usefulness, and its reading level. Valuable information is also available from publishing houses, school and public librarians, and the curriculum offices of large city school systems.

A matter of great importance in winning over the less able reader to

---

[3]Alvina Treut Burrows, "Reading, Research, and Reporting in the Social Studies," in *Social Studies in the Elementary School,* pp. 196–197. Also Ralph C. Preston, *Social Studies in the Elementary School,* p. 263.

[4]Mary C. Wilson, *How to Use Multiple Books,* How To Do It Series, no. 16, (Washington, D.C.: National Council for the Social Studies, National Education Association, 1954). 25 cents.

[5]p. 201.

[6]University of Chicago Press, 5750 Ellis Avenue, Chicago, Illinois 60637.

the reading of a whole book is the size of the book. He must be able to see the end of the job from the time he starts. The teacher must constantly be on the prowl for shorter presentations.[7]

Junior news publications: These newspapers and news magazines[8] provide tremendous coverage. Just how true this statement is can be learned best by anyone who will take the time and trouble to clip the articles (at least two copies of each issue will be needed) of a year's subscription and file them under appropriate headings. Doing this faithfully for all the issues of all the papers at the different grade levels will result in a veritable library. Because the publishers treat the same subject sometimes on different levels, and often follow up a topic in subsequent issues, a file of clipped articles can soon become a rich repository of information on a surprising array of topics.

Special features, supplements, and tests add appeal for students. Excellent background material and suggestions for teachers can often work together to help keep the presentations informal.

Material re-written by the teacher: There is evidence to the effect that simplification of vocabulary and other structural elements aids achievement of meaning; however, this procedure has limitations.[9] Anyone using this technique must bear in mind the danger of mistaking an "easier" (shorter, less complex, more common) word or expression for an easier meaning. Seegers put it this way:

> A word is difficult or easy to a child not in proportion to the incidence
> of its general use, but according to the amount and type of association

---

[7]For example: *American Heroes Series,* by Beals and Ballard, Harr Wagner Publishing Company, 609 Mission St., San Francisco, California. Five 40-page booklets, each describing in narrative form the lives and deeds of four heroes in American history: "Discoverers of America," "Real Adventure with the Pilgrim Settlers," "American Patriots," "American Pathfinders," and "American Plainsmen." Reading level, 5. 64 cents.

Chronicles of Americans, Americana Press, 2038 Pennsylvania Ave., Madison, Wisconsin. Twelve colorful booklets: "The American Realm," "The Supreme Court," "Early Rails," "The Civil War at a Glance," "What 'Corporation' Means," "The American School," "The Great Westward Trek," "Great Presidents," "Ouisconsin," "Documents of Freedom," "America's Success Story," and "Early American Recipes." Reading level, 7+. 18 cents.

Fathers of Industry Series, Mercer Publishing Company, 16 East 52nd St., New York. Twenty-three booklets, each treating an inventor or captain of industry. Reading level, 7+. 20 cents.

Little Wonder Books, Charles E. Merrill, Inc., 1300 Alum Creek Drive, Columbus, Ohio. Sixty booklets. Reading levels, 1 through 6. 21 cents.

[8]Among the best known and most widely accepted of the classroom periodicals are the offerings of: American Education Publications, 1250 Fairwood Ave., Columbus, Ohio (issues at all levels, K-12); Civic Education Service, Inc., 1733 K. Street, N.W., Washington, D.C. (intermediate grades and upward); *Scholastic* Magazines, 33 West 42nd St., New York (intermediate grades and upward).

[9]Ernest Horn. "Language and Meaning," in The National Society for the Study of Education, *The Psychology of Learning.* 41st Yearbook, part 2 (Chicago, Ill.: University of Chicago Press, 1942), p. 399.

the child has had with the concept for which the word stands. Words
are not difficult. Ideas are.[10]

In other words, an explanation of the principle of "No taxation without representation" rewritten in words of one syllable cannot be expected to
replace the necessity of understanding the basic elements of the situation.

Social studies teachers, along with their colleagues who teach literature and with librarians and with well-intentioned but ill-informed writers
in popular magazines, sometimes raise another objection. They say—and
entirely correctly—that a teacher's re-written version of any classic—a
letter or a speech by Lincoln, for instance—loses its original quality. (We
could mention that our school editions of Shakespeare are not pure Shakespeare: certain earthy Elizabethan expressions are carefully expurgated.)
We admit that this is so; we regret the loss; but we are willing to pay this
price in order to enable perhaps another one-fourth of our pupils to get
the basic ideas *through reading*. An important part of this fourth suggestion is that all the pupils should *hear* the original so as to appreciate something of its classical beauty.

To supplement the teacher's judgment on suitability of vocabulary,
there are the usual lists of "new" words in the back of basal readers and the
normative listings like Rinsland's.[11] To help him devise interesting formats
there are works like Dunfee's and Merritt's.[12]

Material re-written by other pupils: The "other pupils" are those who
can and do read the text and are able, in addition, to summarize in their
own words their understanding of what they read. This writing, edited by
the teacher only as absolutely necessary, often communicates very nicely to
less able readers the gist of the text. The more child-like the re-writing remains, the better. Reading is facilitated when the reader's re-thinking of
the author's thoughts is made easier.

Experience charts: Taking this last-mentioned thought to its logical
conclusion leads to the writing of experience records or charts. This technique, widely used in the primary grades, has great applicability all the
way up the line. It consists very simply of the pupils dictating to the teacher

---

[10] J. Conrad Seegers, "Recent Research in Vocabulary," *Elementary English*, 23:67,
February 1946.

[11] Henry D. Rinsland, *A Basic Vocabulary of Elementary School Children* (New York:
Macmillan Co., 1945).

[12] Maxine M. Dunfee. "An Evaluation of Social Studies Source Materials by Fifth and
Sixth Grade Children" (PH.D. diss., Indiana University, Bloomington, 1949). See also by the
same author, "The Stamp of Reality." *National Education Association Journal*, 41:227, April
1952.

James W. Merritt. "A Study of Sixth Graders' Comprehension of Specially Prepared
Materials on Broad Social Conflicts"(Ph. D.) Harvard University, Cambridge, Massachusetts, 1951. See also "Children Can Understand Social Conflicts," *Educational Leadership*,
10:298, February 1953.

material that they have learned—from an excursion, a film-strip, a television program, a resource visitor, etc.—and the teacher writing it down, usually on the blackboard. After editing, it is put into permanent form on chart paper and perhaps also on mimeograph. If the products of these last three suggestions—re-writing by teacher and by pupils, and experience record—are collected, along with illustrations and comprehension checks, notebook style, each pupil will have a book of his own that he can read and understand.

The time element in this suggestion is a matter of much concern, for the content, unlike that of any of the other proposals, must be obtained in school from the pupils. One possibility is that of using members of the "Future Teachers of America" club in the local high school to take the original dictation.

When teachers make a point of re-writing just one passage a month, of guiding the better readers to summarize in writing some material each month, they are much gratified with the results in quantity of material and improvement of achievement.

Study guides: Developed by Chase at Boston University, this technique consists of series of questions matching the text paragraphs, with answers provided on the right-hand side of the paper so that they may be folded back out of sight until checking time. With each slower reader, or perhaps with two, is an achieving reader to help as a pupil-teacher. Variations on the number, kind, length, and specificity of the questions are possible, as are also the methods of using them.[13]

Pupil specialties: "Specialties" is another term for special assignments. The idea is to guide students into special assignments and to encourage them to become "experts" on these specific topics so that they will be resource persons in the classroom.[14] These specialties may be short-term (for example, an election, a trip by the President, a biography). Or they may be continuing projects (keeping a scrapbook of Queen Elizabeth, collecting stamps on a specific person, place, or event, being a radio "ham"). This technique influences reading in terms of motivation. Children sometimes read remarkably better, and more, when they are enthusiastic about the reason for it. A child's specialty can vest him with new importance. It can assure him an audience. He will know more about his topic than anyone else in his class. His peers will acknowledge his report as a genuine contribution.

The last word in educational method has not yet been written. Teachers worth their salt are always looking for new and better ways to teach.

[13] W. Linwood Chase. *op. cit.,* pp. 179–80.
[14] Donald D. Durrell and Leonard J. Savignano, "Classroom Enrichment Through Pupil Specialties," *Journal of Education,* 137:1, February 1956.

Usually the new and better has its base in something old and good. Any of the foregoing eight suggestions will be an improvement only as its classroom use is based on the fundamentally sound procedure for directing reading activities in all curricular areas with pupils at all levels of achievement.

ROBERT W. EDGAR

Professor of Education, Queens College of the City of New York

62. History, Reading, and Human Relations: An Integrated Approach*

The work that I am about to describe is an outgrowth of an effort to study the problems of beginning teachers in difficult schools with the ultimate intention of devising an improved program of teacher preparation. Since 1961 a group of us at Queens College have been concerned with bridging the gap which exists between middle-class oriented college students and the youngsters they are likely to teach in the slum ghettos of New York City. The title of our Project, BRIDGE,[1] has been a symbol of our intentions.

The total Project has had three aspects: (1) a small-school-within-a-school organized to facilitate the study of the problems of beginning teachers; (2) a program of participation of undergraduates in after-school centers; and (3) the involvement of college staff members in research and curriculum development related to educationally handicapped children. I shall describe very briefly only one, the first, of these aspects.

In this aspect we set up a center for the study of the problems of the educationally disadvantaged in an all-Negro junior high school in Queens, one of the five boroughs of New York City. Two hypotheses were used as guidelines in the organization of the center: (1) that the children in this junior high school would learn more if they remained with the same teachers in four academic subjects, including social studies, for the seventh, eighth, and ninth grades, and (2) that inexperienced teachers would have a better chance for success if they had the services of a full-time supervisor. In the three years from 1961 to June 1964, this plan was implemented. Eighty-five children were organized in three classes. Fifty-seven of them stayed in the school and in the program for the three years. The withdrawees were replaced by new entrants into the school. In a careful comparison of the intellectual growth of the children in the Project with a control group in the same class in the same school, the Project children gained on the average of five points in IQ scores as measured on the Wechsler Intelligence Scale for Children in two-and-one-half years as contrasted

Social Education, XXIX:155–63, March 1965. Used by permission.
[1] The research was performed pursuant to a contract with the U.S. Office of Education, Department of Health, Education, and Welfare, Project Number 935.

with the control group which gained less than two points. We who participated in the Project are convinced that this form of organization of the junior high schools in depressed areas merits further trial on an expanded scale.

However, I am not going to continue with an extended description of that Project. Instead, I propose to discuss a development that emerged from our initial program.

At one point in the BRIDGE Project we made a search for social studies materials to which our pupils would respond. Since they happened to be studying American history at the time, we decided to try out some simple biographical materials with them. The rather remarkable success of that initial tryout has led me to a more formal effort.

Perhaps before I begin my exposition it might be well for me to describe briefly some of the major academic characteristics of culturally deprived children as we got to know them. Our group in 1961 had a mean intelligence of 88 as measured on an individually administered intelligence test. This statistic means that at least half of the children fell below average as compared to a standard group. They ranged from 115 to 65. In reading and social studies information and skills, as they entered the seventh grade, they averaged about the middle of the fifth grade. A substantial number of them read at third and fourth grade levels. It is this lower half of the group that most of us have in mind when we speak of the culturally deprived. They represent an exceedingly difficult problem of adjustment for the teacher prepared to teach academic subjects in secondary schools.

Secondary school social studies is not often successfully taught to these children. Its teachers, untrained in the technicalities of reading instruction for example, are often unskilled in making social studies content comprehensible to such children. They forget that to understand history one must have a highly complex cognitive structure related to the who, when, and where of past events. We have only to recall our own confusions over the names of the leaders in South Vietnam, Cambodia, or the Soviet Union to remind ourselves that we, too, can be confused over who, when, and where. These children react this way to such names as John C. Calhoun, James Oglethorpe, John Winthrop, Peter Stuyvesant, and to such places as New Orleans, Kansas, West Virginia, and Idaho. A brief but critical examination of the average social studies book reveals the density of its vocabulary especially when proper nouns are seen as vocabulary. The rapid shifts in time, place, and person, typical of social studies, are bewildering to a child who has not yet developed a cognitive system which provides meaningful categories in which new data can be classified.

Too often vocabulary learning in the social studies is treated as a problem in simple repetition. Teachers forget that our functioning vocabulary is a product of meaningful repetition in an endless variety of new situations. How can James Oglethorpe be the name of a full-bodied person when one's complete exposure is a sentence or two stating that he was the proprietor and founder of Georgia and interested in the victims of an oppressive prison system in England? One of my favorite illustrations of a much more meaningful appreciation of what is involved in understanding a word is drawn from Ruth Kraus's *A Hole Is to Dig.*[2] In this brief book for preschool children she uses the word "hole" in eight delightful situations. First there is the title which is repeated in the body of the book and then: "Maybe you could hide things in a *hole*," "A *hole* is to sit in," "A *hole* is to plant a flower," "A floor is so you don't fall in the *hole* your house is in," "A *hole* is for a mouse to live in," "A *hole* is to look through," "A *hole* is when you step on it you go down." All accompanied with delightful illustrations! Even with all this I suppose we would conclude that a child's meaning for the word "hole" is based on substantial firsthand experience. In many misguided efforts to reduce the vocabulary load of social studies material, the need for extensive repetition in a variety of meaningful situations is forgotten. Mere reduction of vocabulary is considered sufficient. However, the reader with a small vocabulary needs not just content with fewer new words, but longer, not shorter, accounts with repeated use of new terms in interesting contexts.

I should like now, to turn briefly to the academic characteristics of the children. It is a cliché in educational circles to say that the study of a subject is only effective insofar as it produces student interest. Cliché or not, it is true. We as teachers have come to understand that the responses of children are valid clues to whether or not we are meeting their needs. If they respond positively to what we put in front of them, their needs are being met, even if we are not exactly sure just what those needs are and how this specific material meets them. My own contact with culturally deprived children has led me to expect them to respond when the following conditions are met.

1. They will respond when lessons are clearly and simply organized. They want to know what a teacher is trying to teach and how she proposes to teach it. In addition, her purposes must make sense to them. Such objectives as developing democratic attitudes, recognizing the rights of others, and exercising independent critical judgment, though giving larger meaning to the day-to-day efforts of the teacher, are too vague for culturally disadvantaged children to comprehend and act on. They expect to learn information and to develop skills. They recognize and approve efforts directed toward these ends. In spite of the inadequacy of these goals in the eyes of the teacher, she must at least take account of the pupils' expectations.

[2] New York: Harper and Row, 1952.

2. They understand social, political, and economic ideas or events when human beings are vividly involved in these ideas or events. An extremely interesting characteristic of culturally deprived children is their unusually well-developed insight into the unspoken and often unconscious anxieties, motivations, and feelings of others, especially teachers. Though not academically apt, they are "hep" (or is it "hip"?). They know the score and have many acute perceptions into the significance of the behavior of their elders as well as their peers. This heightened sensitivity can be used to develop their interests in people distant in time and place.

3. They respond to assurance of success. Reacting to a school system which has constantly emphasized their weaknesses, they protect themselves from failure in whatever manner is individually possible and effective. They often refuse to perform, cheat, are insubordinate, or withdraw when faced with exposure of ignorance. Close analysis of these behaviors will reveal that they have a positive, rather than a negative function. A youngster who can sustain any one of these responses avoids failure and preserves his self-respect even though he incurs the teacher's displeasure. During our Project we discovered that the very tests which we used to evaluate the growth of the children such as the Metropolitan Achievement Tests, were viewed by many of the pupils simply as efforts on our part to demonstrate once again how stupid they were. Consequently they resisted taking them.

More of their responses could and should be described, but I think that these three are the most relevant to what I have to say. If you agree with me thus far, our problem of teaching these children has become clearer. We must develop approaches to teaching the basic concepts of social studies which are consonant with the characteristics of culturally deprived children, methods which will reconcile the limitations of their responses with the demands of the subject itself.

In an effort to contribute to the understanding of this problem, Professor Carl Auria of the Queens College Department of Education and I embarked on a cooperative venture with five teachers in three New York City depressed-area schools. These teachers teach American history to eighth graders. In two of the schools all of the children are Negroes; in the other, about two-thirds are Negro and the remainder mostly Puerto Rican.

We have set out to test two hypotheses: (1) that the children in these classes will learn more, retain the learning longer, and be more interested in their studies when material on the Negro is included in their studies than they will using the customary text, and (2) that the children will learn more, retain the learning longer, and be more interested in their studies when their reading on the Negro is in fictional and biographical form rather than in a text. Each teacher is teaching American history to three classes of eighth-grade pupils. In one he is using the customary text; in a second he is using his text plus the text-like supplement that has been prepared by the Detroit Public Schools entitled *The Struggle for Freedom and Rights;* and in the third, eliminating the text entirely, he is using three biographies and two historical novels as the basis for pupil reading.

We are assuming (1) that the emphasis on Negroes will make it more possible for these predominantly Negro children to identify with the people involved in the events of American history, and (2) that reading materials combining a substantial decrease in the conceptual density with an *increase* in the amount will be more effective in developing historical knowledge, reading skill, and an understanding of human relations in these children than will a text.

This endeavor is only in an exploratory stage. We and the five teachers have had to get to know each other, to develop some security within the group, and to adjust to each others' strengths and weaknesses. In view of our limitations at this stage, we decided to confine our efforts to one historical period, selecting the period 1820 to 1880. It is a period of critical importance to the understanding of the Negro American. It also happens to be a period for which there are rich and varied materials about the Negro.

Our first cooperative task was to make our goals explicit. Since we planned to use different materials to develop an understanding of a given historical period, we had to decide just what aspect of that period we wanted the pupils to learn. We listed all the concepts which seemed relevant to the period, rated them according to their importance, and grouped them into categories: concepts of time, of place, and of people; critical vocabulary; basic social, economic, military, and political concepts; and finally, the Negro as slave and freeman. Though our categories are not of the same order and sometimes overlap, they do provide us with a framework within which we can work.

Having this framework, Professor Auria and I now proceeded to construct an instrument by which we proposed to measure the growth of the pupils. We constructed a test which we hoped would make diagnosis as well as gross measurement possible. We carried over our conceptual categories into the structure of the test. Each conceptual category is approached from several points of view. For example, we want to know how these children view time: (1) Do they think of time from a personal view, that is in relation to themselves, to their own birthdate, or to their age, or to their parents, grandparents, or other personally known figures? (2) Do they think of time in terms of familiar historical figures such as Washington, Lincoln, F.D.R., etc.? (3) Is their concept of time based on the evolutionary development of common objects such as the means of transportation (stagecoach, locomotive, automobile, airplane), of communication, of household appliances, and of dress? (4) Is their concept of time based on the classifications of history—eighteenth, nineteenth, and twentieth centures, Civil War, Reconstruction Period, 1820, 1861, etc.? Our intention is to discover some of the ways they try to build an understanding of chronology as well as to determine their levels of comprehension. The approach to place and people is similar.

This conceptual analysis also became the framework for our lesson planning. Since our five teachers were all experienced in teaching eighthgrade American history, we had little difficulty in relating the concepts to their customary text-based lessons. The teachers quickly absorbed them into the developmental unit which is their customary organization. The Detroit pamphlet was also easily integrated into their customary lesson planning. The transfer to the biography and fiction was not so easily made. Many of the concepts were not directly related to the lives and events of our books. Consequently most of our workshop time was devoted to the elaboration of our methods in using the biography and fiction.

It is now time to describe to you the biographical and fictional material which we used. I have been examining material on the Negro for several years and have occasionally experimented with various books in different junior high schools. Though the idea is not original with me, my approach relies on a classroom library designed to teach a single unit. This somewhat parallels the classroom library based on themes being exploited by Scholastic, among others. The classroom library we are using has *Frederick Douglass* by Arna Vontemps[3] as the basic book. This book is written for the fifth- or sixth-grade reading level, the level of many of the youngsters in eighth grade with whom I have been working. However, its general appearance does not make this fact too apparent to the young reader. The two other biographies are Dorothy Sterling's *Freedom Train; The Story of Harriet Tubman,*[4] and the same author's *Captain of the Planter: The Story of Robert Smalls.*[5] The selections are not capricious for they have been chosen to satisfy certain classroom needs. *Freedom Train* covers the same period at the same reading level. It is, however, about a woman, an illiterate in contrast to Douglass, who risks her life repeatedly to help others escape, another contrast with Douglass. It provides a new view of the same subject. *Captain of the Planter,* on the other hand, is somewhat more difficult and concentrates on the Civil War and the Reconstruction Period. It is suitable for those who are either somewhat advanced or for those who have become ready for more difficult reading as a result of their work in the other books. The fic-

[3] New York: Alfred A. Knopf, 1957.
[4] Garden City, N.Y.: Doubleday and Co., 1954.
[5] Garden City, N.Y.: Doubleday and Co., 1958.

tion, Meadowcroft's *By Secret Railway*[6] and Sterne's *The Long Black Schooner*,[7] add blood and thunder and excitement to the other accounts of the period. They are set in different locales and describe different but related events. The complete library consists of 30 copies of the *Douglass*, ten of the *Tubman*, 15 of the *Smalls*, ten of the *Schooner*, and five of the *Railway*—a total of 60 books.

At long last we have come to the title of this article, *History, Reading, and Human Relations: An Integrated Approach*. With this library and these books we hope to teach the basic concepts of a given historical period, a few selected reading skills, and some elementary human relation insights. I shall omit further discussion of the basic history goals, assuming that my prior discussion of the conceptual framework of the period gives you some idea of our method of achieving them. I turn briefly to the others.

The three reading skills we chose were: simple recall of factual information, the making of simple inferences, and vocabulary with political, economic, or social significance. To assist us in this endeavor, we developed a homemade workbook. As the pupils read *Frederick Douglass*, they had dittoed workbooks containing five reading exercises, each covering four chapters of the book. An exercise consisted of ten multiple-choice items and a list of ten words drawn from the relevant chapters. The first five multiple-choice questions were simple recall. For example, "What did Mrs. Auld begin to teach Fred?" The correct answer, among a choice of four, was "To read." The next five items demanded simple inferences, that is, the answer was implicit, not explicit, in the book's content. For example, "What effect do you think reading the book *The Columbian Orator* had on Fred?" Answer, "Made him determined to be free some day." The vocabulary for the same exercise included "molasses," "law," "progress," "entitled," and "estimate."

This workbook served both pupil and teacher. For the pupil it met his need for structure and for success. The task was clear. He knew what to do and was able to do it. It was usually easy. Most pupils answered most items correctly. It also individualized instruction. The pupils were able to progress at the speeds adapted to their ways of working. At one point we debated whether or not the exercises would discourage them from reading the book, breaking their rhythm and their interest. Our misgivings were unnecessary. The clear structure and the constant success developed strong motivation.

These exercises also made it possible, in fact demanded, that each teacher follow the progress of each youngster. We in the workshop agreed that teacher correction of the exercises was necessary, desirable, and not

[6]New York: Thomas Y. Crowell Co., 1958.
[7]New York: Scholastic Book Services, 1961.

onerous. As our study continued we planned to discuss the progress of individual children in our workshops. We tried to keep our attention on the child as well as on our materials and the teacher. In addition, the child's workbook contained a record of his progress with the other books. His homework consisted of extensive reading in three related books, with *The Planter* serving the function of the *Frederick Douglass* in the latter half of the unit.

Our third goal was the development of insight into human relations. We tried to achieve this goal by helping teachers to identify, create, and capitalize on opportunities to use our materials for enlarging understandings of why people think and behave as they do. We were concerned with opportunities to discuss feelings, needs, values, and moral judgments as they affected human behavior. Using a biography, the *Frederick Douglass* for example, we tried to develop the habit of asking:

> How did Fred *feel* when he arrived in Baltimore alone, without a relative or friend, to live as a slave in a strange house?
>
> How would *you feel?* Have you ever slept overnight in a strange place away from your family? How did you *feel?*
>
> *Why* did Fred work so hard to learn to read? When his lessons were forbidden, *why* didn't he just give up?
>
> *Why* did Harriet Tubman, with great danger to herself, go back south to help others escape? *Why* didn't she just try to be safe herself?
>
> *Why* didn't Frederick Douglass do the same as Harriet Tubman? What would you have done? Why?
>
> What was Fred's owner's *view of Fred?* Where did he get such ideas? Was he a *wicked* man? Did all white people agree with him? *Why* did some differ?
>
> What *kind of man* is a slave driver? *Why* do some people beat other people? What does it mean to try to break someone's spirit? When should one *obey?* When should he *disobey?*

In addition we tried to change the image of the Negro American as it is often developed from accounts of his role in history. Instead of presenting him simply as a slave, ignorant, docile, and childlike, we studied those leaders who displayed intelligence, skill, resourcefulness and courage. We portrayed Negroes as participating in the determination of their fate as well as having it determined for them. Negroes were seen as skilled workers, daring rebels, eloquent speakers, brave pilots, and responsible legislators and officeholders.

We also sought to examine the impact of status on the lives of people in the past and the present. We attempted to get at the feelings and reactions of the rejected and lowly person in any society.

> What is the effect of being poor, not just on one's food, clothing, housing, but on one's spirit?

What is the effect of being enslaved? Of being excluded? Of being ridiculed?

What price does society pay for these actions?

As we tried to think through the classroom possibilities in this area, we were sometimes blind, insensitive or overly sensitive, fearful, and distrustful of our judgments. As white teachers working with Negro youth we were sometimes afraid that we would enlarge the gap between them and us. But we were committed to an open confrontation of the problem in the faith that rational examination and study lead to better interracial understanding.

Perhaps I can summarize best for you by reiterating a few statements about the culturally deprived that were the basis of our work:

1. Culturally deprived children need a program of studies which satisfies their need for security through clear goals and simple methodology.
2. Culturally deprived children need the reassurance of repeated success experiences. The materials that are read must be well within their grasp and must be more rather than less extensive than customary text materials.
3. Culturally deprived children are person-oriented, not abstraction-oriented. They need materials which place people, not generalizations, in the center of the stage.
4. Culturally deprived children are often acutely aware of the feelings, motivations, and values of people in their environments. This sensitivity can be used in the illumination of the problems of human relations in our past and in the present.

Teachers of the culturally deprived need to develop all the skills that the above four propositions suggest: skill in analyzing their subject to identify its basic concepts, skill in the selection of materials which meet the needs of their pupils at their levels, skill in individualizing instruction in order to diagnose and meet individual pupil needs, and finally, skill in illuminating the problems of human relations. These skills are not beyond the ability of current classroom teachers and they can be learned. Let's hope that social studies teachers will set out to learn them.

RICHARD E. GROSS

Professor of Education, Stanford University

63. The Challenge of Social Education for the Gifted*

Were we to give adequate educational guidance and attention to the approximately seven percent of our youth who are endowed with superior intelligence, within a generation we would see the beginnings of almost unbelievable improvements in the social environment as well as the natural landscapes which surround us. The education of the gifted is an issue of national scope. The problem is also one of long duration; it comes to a head today because of the crisis of our times and the growing demand for able scholars, technicians, and leaders. Fortunately, in spite of recent attacks upon "eggheads" and certain other erroneous, stereotyped notions about the gifted, the American people seem to realize the import of individuality in our culture. They generally tend to accept and to expect the contributions of the brilliant regardless of our egalitarian symbols and traditions.

Now that we are fully launched into the Age of the Common Man, this becomes an especially delicate problem. The secondary schools are deeply involved because of the growing realization of their prime, general education function in developing citizens with common values, knowledges, and skills, who can and will work together in the pursuit of national goals. Educators are being called upon to develop curricula which will reserve a place for uncommon excellence while we instruct the masses. Certain writers feel this is the central educational challenge for all democracies—to build programs which will conciliate the seemingly contradictory trends of equality and individuality. There is current belief that as ever greater numbers flock into our schools, grave dangers will result as we sacrifice quality and lose much of our potential thinking and leadership toward progress. There is a fear of an ever lower common denominator as we bow to the masses and fail to recognize and plan for the varying human abilities of our students. Although we have private schools, vocational schools, and special schools, there does not seem to be much of a chance for the full development of any sort of a two or three track system, as has evolved in a number of foreign countries, to meet differing interests and qualities of public school pupils. The great bulk of American youth will undoubtedly continue to be educated in the typical, common, public school system. Our answers need to be found within this institutional framework.

*Excerpted from *Social Studies*, 45:199–204, October 1954. Used by permission.

American educators have experimented with programs for the gifted for many years, but outside of a few famous individuals, schools, or noted school systems, we have little to show for these efforts. A recent study, for example, showed that only six state departments of education are planning and promoting programs for educating the gifted. There is no question that large numbers of our potentially most able students are not reaching the levels which may be expected of them in our lower schools, in our colleges, and in their vocational labors.

To meet the needs of these students, who are particularly original, versatile, and independent, with excellent memories, superior reasoning ability, and who are speedy readers, able to master basic knowledge in half the time needed for average children, teachers have tried many approaches. Complicating the evolution of a program for the gifted is the fact that it is but one aspect of a five-pronged dilemma. We have also our slow learners, and a tour of the library card catalogue will show a real contrast, in the amount of writing and attention devoted to this important element of our school population, with that given over to handling precocious children. Then we have our handicapped children who are deserving of much attention and also those perhaps not intellectually gifted but highly skilled in certain, special abilities, manual or artistic. Lastly, the Life Adjustment Education movement has clearly reminded us of the import of the bulk of our school population, those who will be primarily followers, the average "forgotten sixty percent" of our pupils. The philosophical tendency is to recommend that all these youth, except in certain extreme cases, have a common school experience; in the heavy load of duties facing the busy teacher there is no doubt that in a number of situations she forgets more than sixty percent! Most commonly it is the gifted who by force of circumstances are left to shift for themselves.

Teachers in typical, overcrowded, short-supplied school situations have been the first to recognize that they are not able to accomplish a personally satisfactory job for all of these five types of students. Of course, a few are interested in and favor the able students, while others give special attention to the handicapped, the slow learners, or make modifications for the specially gifted. Most teachers pitch their courses to the mythical average and let the chips fall where they may. Fortunately, the intellectually gifted will often succeed in spite of what the school does or does not do for them, and it has been wisely suggested, in the light of usual classroom conditions, that one of the best things we can do for this group is to by-pass the curriculum! In traditional school programs numerous bright pupils are reacting by developing unfortunate characteristics of superficiality, glibness, restlessness, laziness, poor study habits, and even chicanery.

How have schools met and how are teachers meeting these problems of the gifted? One of the seemingly natural remedies, once the year's learnings have been assimilated, especially in the lower grades, has been to skip the pupil; we now dignify this practice by the term "acceleration." If individual and social factors have been considered and are not likely to be detrimental, moderate acceleration of a year or two often proves satisfactory. In a few ultra-modern schools where passing from grade to grade has been abolished, with students progressing at their own rates of learning, acceleration has become embodied in the curriculum. Certain ungraded groupings of gifted children, even with age spreads of four or five years, have also been acclaimed as successful. Another common approach, once the bright pupils are identified, has been to assign such boys and girls more work and, upon some occasions, more difficult work. Another method has been to use these responsible pupils as student assistants and this has meant everything from cleaning blackboards and going out on teacher errands to coaching the slower pupils or helping direct and prepare a special class activity, such as the week's assembly program. Some of these practices border upon what is known as enrichment.

In recent years there has been some controversy over the comparative value of two basic approaches—the various types of homogeneous groupings as against enrichment programs. Homogeneous grouping includes arrangements from small intra-class committees to completely separate and specialized schools for the gifted. Most common, however, are separate classes within a given school, when the school and the subject (at the secondary level) enrollment is large enough to warrant such organization. One of the most frequent arguments against so-called slow and fast groupings is the claim that we are losing the necessary democratic commonality of experience. There is worry here over the production of fragmented strata of young people with an intellectual elite at one extreme and the dullards at the other. Spokesmen for homogeneous grouping for the bright point out that realistically we cannot expect "a crow to lead a flight of eagles" and rightly claim that democratic education does not guarantee equal achievement for all but, rather, equal opportunity for each to achieve to the fullest of his ability.

Proponents of homogeneous grouping are in more vulnerable territory when they seek separate schools or separate divisions within schools to develop future leaders. Critics ask where such independently trained individuals will gain the understanding and the common touch needed to work successfully with the vast majority of the population. They also wonder how such young people will develop the characteristics whereby those who are to be led can find in the would-be leaders those necessary qualities of fellowship and trust. Certain schools have modified homogeneous grouping in various ways to meet some of the difficulties involved. Some teachers use differentiated and individualized assignments for temporary sub-groups in otherwise mixed classes. A number of administrators have written in favor of partial separation. Here the bright pupils are separated in the fundamental or academic classes while heterogeneous groups are retained in vocational, artistic, physical education classes, and in homerooms. One problem found in scheduling such an arrangement is the fact that although the pupil may be very fast in one of the basic subjects, he is not necessarily also brilliant in all of the others. Indeed, for example, such an excellent pupil in social studies may be rather slow in math. Some schools have introduced special elective seminars, honors classes, and released time for small groups from courses in which achievement is high. This free time is used in a variety of ways, from library browsing or serving as hall guards to completing correlated projects in other classes or activity in student clubs and co-curricular activities. In a few cases special classes in language, typing, or dramatics have been organized for the gifted pupils. In these situations the line between homogeneous grouping and enrichment fades considerably. Extension service courses in some states and individualized units for students to complete, along with the regular class-work, also fall into such categories.

Studies have revealed that gifted students' achievement in basic learnings in specialized classes is often not significantly greater than that of children of the same age and ability who have remained in regular classes, and that, if properly planned for, the outstanding growth occurs in the creative work accomplished, often, in heterogeneous classes. This reveals one of the fallacies of those who see grouping itself as the main panacea. The organization of ability groups in themselves is no guarantee of an improved educational program. Placing a group through the same paces but at a higher level does not automatically provide the experiences which meet the multiple needs of the precocious children enrolled therein. If we have homogeneous classes or if we have mixed groups, the teacher must still individualize instruction so that it is enriched to meet the variety of interests and talents of the youth.

Perhaps in school situations where inflexible learning and recitation of textual material remain the major purpose of the instructor, it is better for the gifted pupils to be in separate classes—providing they have a different mentor! Although the traditional college preparatory curriculum is often recommended as most fitting for the more able students, it is really only most satisfactory from the standpoint of such a school in that these boys and girls are bright enough to learn the material and work their way through the difficult requirements. That they can do this, often quite easily, is no sign that this is the best curriculum for them. The Eight Year Study long ago disproved this claim. It is possible to conclude in the light of these and more recent findings that traditional curricula and certain of their techniques are *least* helpful to many and especially to the creative needs of the brilliant.

Separate and special classes can also be attacked in that they may serve to limit needed modernization of the curriculum. Once such groups are institutionalized in our educational organization and come to serve a purpose, even if insufficiently, they will prolong the efforts to attain basic education or core arrangements and vital common learnings and other general educational aims may be lost. This is especially true at the secondary levels.

Realistically, of course, the main argument against homogeneous grouping in separate classes is that the majority of our schools do not have the enrollment, staff, or materials necessary to so organize classes. But, as stated earlier, even if a staff favors such grouping and it is possible to arrange them, the key person is still the teacher who must know each child, who is concerned for each, and who is able enough to build the units and evolve the learning experiences which will appeal to her precocious charges.

A recent study of curriculum arrangements for the gifted in high school history classes in Florida found the overwhelming majority of teachers responding in favor of enrichment techniques as the best means for reaching gifted students. Unfortunately, less than half of these teachers claimed to be doing anything for the gifted—mainly because of very large classes and the lack of materials and proper facilities. Although these are often legitimate excuses, at least in part, many teachers fail to do much for the gifted because they have not identified them and because of the lack of emphasis in their own college experience and teacher training on the import and means of handling such children.

Fortunately, we can observe other teachers, with thirty-five or forty heterogeneous pupils, organizing and succeeding in meeting not only the needs of the gifted but those of the slow pupils as well. Limiting ourselves to the area of social education, what are some of the specific enrichment experiences being planned for the fast students? Superior pupils are preparing overviews of coming units, helping teachers make pre-tests, organizing bibliographies, serving as class or assistant school librarians in charge of the vertical files, and carrying on a great variety of research followed by the writing of local history and special topics not covered in the typical class work or text. Gifted pupils are preparing social studies magazines and printing gists of articles in adult journals for use by other class members; they are conducting community surveys and service projects of infinite variety, including even the tutoring of adults for naturalization examinations. Their creativity is being challenged through activities allowing them to prepare slides, preview audio-visual aids, develop appropriate study guides, and make all sorts of displays, maps, and charts for use in the school room; creative dramas which they write on historical events or current happenings, such as a congressional hearing or a bargaining session between labor and management, are especially valuable. They conduct very mature interviews in the community, make tape recordings of events out of the classroom, and report back to the class on speeches they have heard. Some have been placed in charge of gathering realia and developing a school or departmental museum. Their ability to organize and write has been used to the extent that they keep certain texts up to date by drafting supplementary chapters.

The above sampling indicates that enrichment means, in addition to a grasp of essentials, an education that is different in kind, quantity, and levels of insight; it means wider knowledge, more complete interpretations, seeing subtle relationships, and sharing of reasoning and planning—all beyond what is necessary for the more average pupils. It calls for a wide variety of materials and experiences and responsibilities reaching to the far corners of the school and into the community. It calls for original thinking and advanced critical thinking, as well as for the nurture of the growth of special creative factors. On the other hand, enrichment means less directions, less details, less drill, less review, and calls for stressing the "whys" and "hows" rather than the "whos" and "whats."

Let us take the case of Gary, who bordered on genius, and follow the manner in which the writer dealt with him during the period of a semester in an eleventh-grade American history class. This example will serve to reveal some of the difficulties involved in handling such students and at the same time demonstrate specific enrichment arrangements. The class was of mixed ability, with four or five other very bright pupils and several equally slow. It was organized around problem-units, chronologically presented, featured a goodly amount of teacher-pupil planning, and allowed for sub-group activities, as well as a large amount of individualized projects, reading, research, and writing. Where possible, these topics were related to current aspects of the historical problem being considered and to pupils' particular interests. The bright children understood that they were to be held for the minimum learnings agreed upon for all, once we had established our class aims for the unit.

During the first unit Gary served as class secretary, completed and reported to the class his research on the Kensington Stone, and organized a theme, college style, on the historical sources of American rights and liberties. During the second unit he read the long historical novel of the Tory side of the American Revolution, *Oliver Wiswell,* by Kenneth Roberts, read revealing portions to the class, and gave the teacher a private oral review on the historical accuracy of the volume's emphases He also served as committee chariman for the group studying the Articles of Confederation, and along with several other of the artistic students started a large wall chart which was to stretch all the way across the back of the room, on American political parties and presidential elections. During the third unit he read an adult two-volume biography of John Marshall and became so involved in condensing the effect of his judicial role and court decisions upon constitutional development that he did poorly on the unit test. Here the teacher had failed to work closely enough with the student and to see that he had not grasped the unit essentials. Such students often need guidance to keep them from getting too far afield. During the fourth unit Gary's interest lagged and he failed to take part in discussions to his usual extent. One day after class he stopped by my desk and explained that he could have answered several of the questions I had put to the class which no one had ventured to try. We talked a bit and it became evident that he was discouraged because I had failed to call upon him on a number of occasions when he had his hand up. This is a natural tendency for a teacher who comes to expect a student's complete knowledge day after day and who is trying to find out more about the less dependable thoughts and understandings of the other pupils in the class. We thereupon made an agreement that he would put his hand up only when the more difficult and intricate problems were posed; I agreed to make it my business to recognize him more regularly in such situations. That same week, in discussing Gary with his Spanish teacher who said he was so far ahead of the rest of the class in his translating ability that he was running out of things for him to accomplish, an idea came to my mind. The Spanish teacher agreed to procure several Mexican textbooks and Gary was soon busy comparing our American history texts, coverage of the Mexican war with the rather different and surprising accounts in Spanish of the "Great North American Invasion." This is an example of the countless opportunities which exist for cooperative planning between the different teachers of the gifted.

One of the important factors often overlooked in working with precocious students is the need for special evaluation. Although it is fine for all students to include individual and personal goals, along with the class goals, in unit planning, this is particularly valuable for the gifted. They can carry on mature self-evaluation and should be allowed to administer certain tests to themselves and work out their own progress reports. Private, oral discussion with and quizzes by the teacher are in order. In an age of objective testing these students need written tests of the essay type to help prepare them for college. Naturally, other of their work should be planned to give experience in note taking, outlining, and the like—all of which are valuable assets for higher education. Parental conferences are very important in evaluating the total progress of the social education of the gifted and should occur regularly. At this point it is pertinent to remark on the need for informing parents in the first place of the special needs and abilities of these children. Parents most often will cooperate with the school in building the proper environment for a bright child and they can give the teacher basic, personal information, aiding him in planning with and for such a boy or girl.

Certainly the prime need in the education of the gifted is an able and ingenious teacher. Such a teacher needs adequate, instructional facilities and an abundance of rich reference materials. Bright pupils retreat or rebel, not because of lack of interest in social studies content, but because, as far as they are concerned, of impossible educational situations. Let us take the example of world history. Here the pupils who have the time and ability to read detailed, difficult accounts, telling the whole story, its inter-relations, sidelights, and color, are too commonly drilled on a bird's-eye, superficial overview of names, dates, and events which are almost as deadly to average and slow pupils. These text-centered approaches are totally unsatisfactory and time-wasting for the brilliant. They need time-consuming activities which foster new ways of thinking and raise new horizons before them.

Programs for the gifted naturally should be based upon the guidance viewpoint of discovering every pupil of exceptional ability, as well as the exceptional abilities of every pupil, and then planning for all. Ideally, we have no average pupils and even the slow can excel in some areas. The specially gifted in fields other than mental brilliance will here have their abilities fostered. Such programs provide the motivation and means through which every pupil may realize his possibilities and all can con-tribute to reaching common goals. The fundamental fact to remember is that an enrichment program as envisioned here, geared to the abilities of the gifted, includes, nevertheless, heavy emphasis upon the basic, general education essential for other students as well. The longer the writer has been involved in developing and teaching such units, the more convinced he has become that such a curriculum for superior students is also of greatest worth for the optimum growth of all other types of youth. There-fore, in building variegated programs for the able students, we are improv-ing our total plan of social education for all. And thus we hold the road open to all. The gifted come from all strata of our society; some blossom much later than others, and no man knows down which road tomorrow's hero will come.

Recently the presidents of several great universities have spoken out against the cult of mediocrity that they claim has evolved in our public schools. They feel high secondary school standards and achievement have been lost and university scholarship seriously undermined by these "day nurseries for the incompetent." Most of all they decry the resulting loss of leadership so vital in these times in most aspects of American life. Whether or not we favor potential brain trusts or happen to agree with the instruc-tional implications of the views of these particular educators, all of us can perceive the practical necessity of forwarding the full development of as many as possible of our gifted youth. We are told, for example, that this year the Soviet Union is graduating twice as many engineers as are re-ceiving their degrees in the United States. All of us have waited far too many precious hours in doctors' and dentists' offices. And how we need ever more brilliant inventors, teachers, technicians, entrepreneurs, statesmen, yes, and also the specially gifted—poets and artists, who in singing and portraying the story of America, will further strengthen us and inspire the world. This, then, is the real challenge we face.

Using Instructional Materials and Educational Media

THOMAS BELL

Director of Educational Survey Services, University of Idaho

64. *Why Not a Social Studies Laboratory?* *

Why would it not be advisable to pool all of our social studies resources into a social studies laboratory? This was done with the aid of NDEA funds in North Gem, Idaho. Locating a room for such a laboratory was no great problem. We remodeled a large classroom to suit our social studies needs. By scheduling our social studies in a particular fashion we were able to arrange for all social studies classes to meet in our laboratory through the day (American History 1st period, 7th grade social studies 2nd period, American Government 3rd period, etc.)

By moving all our present materials, globes, references, atlas, library books, film strips, etc., into the social studies laboratory we found that we had a good start.

At this point a survey was made of our present materials and our possible needs. We equipped a room as follows:

Furniture and Equipment. Furniture and equipment needs as indicated by the diagram include:

On Hand
Tape recorder
Students' desks
1 filing cabinet
Book shelving
Bulletin Board space (4 x 8)
3 globes
Storage shelves for materials

*Excerpted from *Social Studies*, 54:181–83, October 1963. Used by permission.

Film strip material moved from audio-visual room to laboratory
World History map set
2 American History map sets
Projector screen
1 conference table

To Be Purchased
1 record player
1 filing cabinet
Added bulletin board space
1 large globe mounted on a rod from the blackboard railing
1 set of sectional 30" globes mounted on peg board. Poster colors or
china marking crayons all easily applied and removed. (Includes 6 raised
relief globes)
Film strip projector—exclusively for laboratory
Magazine rack for current periodicals
Overhead projector (to be used in all departments)
Added shelving space for library and reference books
1 globe (table model)
Tape and record cabinet

Reference Material Included in the Laboratory. The accompanying chart illustrates the type of materials that were included as the program was begun. The listings include examples of the type of material that were used but are of course incomplete.

As we were developing this phase of the program an important problem entered the picture. We were actually developing a resource center and library within our laboratory. We therefore concluded that it would be advisable to employ a professional librarian to work in the laboratory. With this in mind plans were made to schedule the high school librarian in the laboratory for one period a day. Our librarian also became a member of our social studies committee.

In summary we feel the values of a concentrated social studies laboratory are many. All equipment, materials, references and globes are available when and where the teacher feels they should be used. Secondly, the laboratory helps create a social studies atmosphere that renews interest in this area in both students and teachers. Thirdly, the creation of a laboratory is a stimulation to inservice training in the social studies area. Teachers plan together, share materials, and cooperatively secure and file material to be used by all.

Lastly, this program made those concerned more aware of the importance of social studies in our schools and helped to improve our efforts in developing well educated citizens at North Gem.

CLASSIFICATION OF MATERIALS TO BE INCLUDED IN A SOCIAL STUDIES LABORATORY

Reference Books	Periodicals and Newspapers	Filing Materials on Various Subjects	Tape Recordings	Musical Records
Hoover, J. Edgar *Masters of Deceit*	*Wall Street Journal*	Famous Headlines from *New York Times*	Tape recordings of the Television Series "Twentieth Century"	Records that will supplement subject matter in all fields of social studies.
Hicks, John D. *American Nation*	*Time*	Materials that may be obtained from the following:		
Hicks, John D. *Federal Union*	*U.S. News and World Report*		Khrushchev's Address to the United Nations 1959	*Around the World In Music* by Ethnic Folkways
Shotwell, James *Facts About Presidents*	*The New Republic*	Arab Information Center American Association for United Nations		
Wish, Harvey *Contemporary America*	*American Observer*	American Committee on Africa	President Kennedy's Address on Berlin July 1961	*Folk Music of the Middle East* by Ethnic Folkways
	Current History	Asia Foundation China Institute		
Eberstein, William *Today's Isms*	*New York Times*	American-Korea Foundation		*Music of the World's Peoples* by Ethnic Folkways
Commager, Henry *Documents of American History*	*Senior Scholastic*	Pan-American Union American Friends of the Middle East		*Nutcracker Suite* by Tchaikovsky
Hopkins, Joseph G. and Robinson, Florett *Album of American History*		Anti-Defamation League Japan Society India League of America		

Tebbel, John and
Jennison, Keith
The American
Indian Wars

Howard, Robert
This is the South

Gunther, John
Julius Caesar

Constain, Thomas
William The Conqueror

Smith, Goldwin
The Heritage of Man

(This is just a sampling of books that could be included. All books that will be a benefit to the program will be moved from the central library to the Laboratory.)

Variety of Materials:

Famous pictures from magazines such as *Life*. Information from various embassies.

File Material on general subjects such as:

A F of L—CIO
Alaska
Algeria
Berlin
Civil War
Feudal System
Hitler

WALTER E. McPHIE

*Associate Professor of Social Studies Education,
University of Utah*

65. The Textbook: Tool or Taskmaster?*

Whether one observes professional people, skilled craftsmen, or unskilled laborers, one common fact seems to emerge: They all have "tools of their trade." The surgeon has his scalpel, sutures, and a host of other tools necessary for a sucessful operation. The clergyman has his books of Holy Writ, prayers, and doctrines. The carpenter has his hammer, square, level, and saw. The laborer on the road crew has his shovel, pick, and perhaps some pneumatic device for breaking up solidly packed earth or concrete. A more extensive list of people engaged in other kinds of work would serve only to lend further support to the premise that man uses tools *to help him* perform his task more easily and/or more effectively.

Teachers of the social studies also have "tools of their trade." They have chalkboards and chalk, pencils and paper, maps, globes, atlases, charts, graphs, reference books, and *textbooks*—to mention a few. For the most part the social studies teacher uses these tools in much the same manner as do people engaged in other tasks. If he wants his students to "see" something near the front of the room, he writes with a piece of chalk on the chalkboard, he points with a pointer to a map or chart, or he locates a position on the globe. If he wants to disseminate some information or give an examination, he frequently uses some form of duplicating machine. If he wants the students to give reports, enter into a debate, or engage in some problem-solving activity, he often directs them to the encyclopedia or some other set of reference volumes. In other words, as with most people faced with a task, he uses his tools *to help him* accomplish his objectives.

However, when social studies teachers use the textbook—a very important tool in the teaching profession—a rather mysterious transformation often occurs. Whereas the teacher normally uses other tools to assist him, when using the textbook *the teacher too often becomes the assistant!* In far too many classrooms the social studies text becomes the curriculum; it becomes the objective of the course; it becomes the end rather then *a* means to the end. Witness the students who have had insignificant test items "justified" by the teacher's remark, "It was in your text"—as if

---

*Social Education, XXVIII:450–52, December 1964. Used by permission.

this were the ultimate in reasons for the selection of test items, a rationale capable of satisfying the most discriminating inquiry. Witness, also, how fortunate social studies students are who do not have to play "racehorse" with their teachers as their courses go "into the stretch" near the end of March. At this time real learning becomes comparatively less important than the "obviously " significant task of *finishing the textbook*.

The seriousness of letting a textbook (a tool) assume the teacher's role in the classroom while he acts in the subordinate role of an assistant can be most clearly illustrated, perhaps, by once again looking at people other than teachers who work with tools. The surgeon would be lost without his scalpel. It, like the textbook to the teacher, is extremely important to him. However, he does not permit his scalpel to indicate the purpose, location, depth, or length of the incision. He is the master of his task; he is in control; his tools must *assist him*. The carpenter would feel only half-dressed without his hammer, square, and saw. Indeed, he could not succeed without them. But it is the *carpenter* who decides where the nail is to be driven, on what angle the board will be cut, and where the line will be drawn. Clergymen, like teachers, use books as one of their most important tools. Yet, *they* select their sermons; they use the written words to *help them* develop and emphasize the concepts which *they* have selected on the basis of their training and experience. How effective would the clergyman be who restricted himself to using the scriptures on a first-page-through-last-page basis and who, upon finding himself short of time, read wildly through the remaining sacred passages?

Unlike these other practitioners, many social studies teachers abdicate their position. They neglect their opportunity and responsibility to organize and plan their course, to select major emphases, and to determine how, when, and where the subject matter of their course should unfold in terms of the best interests of the students they face. They are content to begin with page 1 of the sacrosanct textbook and *cover* it and all the succeeding pages until the job is "done." True, they will embellish certain parts of the text—just as any good assistant would who serves his master well—but in the final analysis it is the textbook that commands.

When a teacher of the social studies is asked to teach a given course—say, American history—and is supplied with a course of study, he is in a position similar to that of a carpenter who has been given the task of building a house and who has received a set of blueprints. Just as the carpenter surveys the plot of ground on which the house is to be erected, so must the teacher survey the "plot of ground" where an understanding of American history is to be developed. Just as the carpenter studies his blueprint, deciding where he should start, when each successive part should be brought into the whole, etc., so must the teacher look carefully at the panorama of American history, deciding where he should start, when he should bring in the various segments which, when woven together, make up the fabric of this nation's past. The carpenter's training and apprenticeship experience have prepared him to make his decisions. The teacher's academic background and professional education have prepared him to make his decisions.

Having made such essential preparation, both the carpenter and the teacher are ready to determine which tools will be needed to help them accomplish their objectives. The carpenter decides that many of the things to be done can be accomplished best with his hammer and saw; other tasks will require different tools. The more experienced he is, the less thought he must give to the selection of appropriate tools; he almost automatically reaches for the "right" one. The teacher decides that in order to teach many of the concepts he has chosen to emphasize, his textbook will serve him best. He knows what he wants to accomplish and *he uses the tool* to help him do the job. Some of his other objectives will require the use of different tools. As the teacher becomes more experienced and becomes better acquainted with his tools, he, too, will reach almost automatically for a map, a globe, the text (or texts), etc., which he knows will help him do a particular task most effectively. However, even though the process of selecting appropriate tools becomes more and more automatic with experience, both the teacher and the carpenter—if they are serious in their desire to do a good job—will constantly be on the alert for newly developed, more effective tools than the ones they now possess.

One of the more prominent dangers involved in letting the textbook rule the class is that the students themselves are deprived of learning the proper use of the tool. From the very outset, students should learn that the textbook is indeed a tool, nothing more and nothing less. Obviously, the example set by the teacher is very important. The students should learn also that in order to use any tool effectively there are certain things which must be understood by the user. For example, if we may turn to the carpenter again, a novice, when driving nails, may work himself unnecessarily hard and accomplish comparatively little until he is shown *where to hold the hammer*. Since using a hammer appears to be so obviously simple, seldom does the beginner receive instruction. Therefore, he tends to hold the hammer too near the center of the handle because it provides better control and it appears to be easier. However, once the novice has been properly informed and has acquired some experience, he discovers that holding the hammer in the middle of the handle deprives him of the advantage of leverage and momentum which, in turn, requires him to expend unnecessary energy. In other words, he discovers that by using his tool improperly he works harder and accomplishes less. In like manner, many students who do not know how to use a textbook properly work diligently with the tool with only meager results. Since using a textbook appears to be so obviously simple, students frequently are left "holding the hammer in the middle of the handle." Therefore, as a bare minimum, teachers of the social studies should check their students *at all grade levels* to ascertain whether or not they possess at least the essential understandings listed below. If they do not, they should be taught them immediately.

1. *A textbook is only as reliable and authoritative as the people who produce it.* Too often students misuse this basic tool because they have never been taught to look critically at ideas which have become sanctified in print. If the author of the textbook were to enter the classroom anonymously and teach the material he has written in the text, undoubtedly there would be students who would challenge some of his ideas since they would immediately recognize him as being a mortal being and, therefore, subject to error. When the author's ideas and interpretations appear in print, however, many students fail to see the necessity of critically analyzing what is presented to them. Such habits carry over into the use of other reading tools, such as periodicals and newspapers, where the need for critical appraisal is even more pronounced than with the normally carefully edited school textbooks. Students must be taught to ask: Who wrote this material I am reading? Does the preparation and experience of the author (and others responsible for its publication) merit my confidence? Do other authorities agree with this author? Do I?

2. *Frequently social studies textbooks are useful only to the degree that they are current.* A good student knows the importance of looking at the date of publication of a book. He is also able to distinguish between a copyright date (the date when the work was first published or the date when some substantial revision has taken place) and the dates of subsequent printings (the dates when the publisher's supply has become exhausted and a new supply has been printed from the plates used in the *original* or subsequently copyrighted editions). A student who can use his text as a tool effectively also knows that the production of a textbook is an extremely time-consuming task and that the period of time between the writing of a manuscript and the final release of the textbook for sale often encompasses months and years. Therefore, even a so-called "new" book is sometimes a year or more old by the time it reaches the booksellers' shelves. A political geography text on Africa, for example, whose copyright date shows it to be several years old, is more political history than it is current political geography! A properly informed student understands these things and will ask himself: Is the information I am reading affected by time and world changes? If so, is the information I am reading up to date?

3. *A summary of the textbook is found in outline form in the Table of Contents.* The writer has frequently asked his students to write a

brief summary of the contents of their social studies textbooks only minutes after they have first acquired them. Even in senior high school, many
of the students are totally bewildered by such an assignment—particularly when they learn that they have only ten or fifteen minutes in which to
do it! Many frantically thumb through the pages in a vain effort to complete
the assignment. Tables of contents are so common that teachers sometimes
fail to recognize that students are not born knowing how to use them effectively; someone must teach them.

   4. *Information about specific items in the textbook can be found most
easily by consulting the Index.* Using the index is, again, an example of a
skill which needs to be taught if the textbook is ever going to be used effectively. A few moments of the teacher's time devoted to even such an
apparently simple skill as this may pay huge dividends.

   5. *The Preface and Foreword often contain information which is essential if students are going to understand their textbook tool.* Students and
teachers alike are guilty of passing up this information which the author
directs specifically to the reader. Few teachers or students would think of
operating a new electric drill or sewing machine until they had read the
attached cautions and instructions. These same students and teachers, however, are prone to turn directly to the "meat" of the textbook without
knowing what precautions and instructions the "builder of the tool" has
given. Students would learn quickly the advantage of reading the foreword
and the preface if the teacher would stress their importance.

   6. *Headings and sub-headings help to organize content in the reader's
mind and are helpful as comprehension check-points.* Any given chapter in
a social studies textbook is filled to overflowing with facts, figures, dates,
and complex, interdependent understandings. Students need to be taught
that headings and sub-headings are not put there just for appearance alone
but that they constitute significant aids in the use of the textbook. If a student will try to remember how the headings unfold, he will help himself to
keep the general organization of the reading in mind. Remembering the
general organization gives a framework on which to assemble facts, figures,
and data. If, while reading, the student will learn to stop momentarily at
the end of each major section and return to the heading of that section to
check his comprehension of what the heading indicates he should have
understood, he will soon learn to put the complex and interdependent concepts in their proper relationships and will increase the thoroughness of his
comprehension. As he does this, he should ask himself: What are the major
points emphasized in this section? Do these points synthesize into a larger
generalization? Does my understanding coincide with the overview provided by the headings and sub-headings?

   7. *Reading the questions which appear at the end of each chapter before actually reading the chapter helps focus attention on what the author*

has judged to be of most importance. Such a suggestion assumes that the questions are not merely fact-finding inquiries which promote an "easter egg hunt," but that they are thought-provoking in nature. By looking carefully at good questions before reading the content of the chapter, the student can avoid "covering" everything—but seeing nothing!

In conclusion, and by way of a brief summary, it has been suggested that a social studies teacher needs to remember that he *is* the teacher, that he is a person prepared and trained to present lessons in such a way that significant social understandings will take place in the minds of his students. He should remember that after careful planning he can, and probably should, use one of his most effective tools, the textbook, to *help him* in the achievement of his objectives. He should be very careful, however, that he does not permit himself to change positions with his tool, that he does not become a *textbook assistant.* It has also been suggested that if students are to be expected to use the textbook tool to full advantage, they must see proper examples and they must receive proper instructions in its use. Otherwise, they may work diligently at their tasks, expending considerable effort, and never really get the help from this tool which they could and should get if they use it properly.

RAYMOND H. MUESSIG

Professor of Education, Ohio State University

66. Using Projective Pictures*

As a (former) secondary social studies teacher I have been an enthusiastic user of a wide variety of audio-visual teaching materials. Believing with the ancient Chinese that a picture can often supplement or take the place of words, I have relied on the use of various films, filmstrips, slides, maps, charts, globes, graphs, pictorial displays, models, and murals.

It wasn't until a little over two years ago, however, that I began using carefully selected pictures dealing with social situations and dilemmas to bring out feelings and attitudes of students in my classes. A principal, a supervisor, and an art teacher in my system knew that I was using role-playing and open-ended stories to act as vehicles for the feelings of adolescents; and they showed me several simple but carefully planned drawings which were designed to stimulate discussion in classes. The interest which my students displayed as I used these drawings, the meaningful discussions connected with their use, and the simple way these pictures brought out convictions, prejudices, ideas, biases, problems, motivations, and moral and spiritual values convinced me that I should do more experimenting in this area.

My next step was to purchase *Focus on Choices Challenging Youth*, a kit of projective pictures available through the National Conference of Christians and Jews. Perhaps a brief discussion of how I used one of the pictures in this inexpensive packet will clarify this teaching approach.

The picture to which I refer shows an adolescent boy facing a judge in a courtroom. A woman is standing by the boy. A man in a business suit is observing the scene, and a policeman is engaged in writing notes on the proceedings. The producers of this kit on projective pictures provide five copies of each picture, and they suggest that the group be divided into five small groups to facilitate discussion. Although this has its advantages I have had more successful results by using only one picture projected on a screen through an opaque projector. Darkening the room and projecting the one picture seems to focus all attention on the scene and also seems to free students as they express their reactions.

While the room is being darkened and final adjustments made by our class projection crew I try to put the group at ease by chatting informally

---

*Social Education, XXII:250–52, May 1958. Used by permission.

with them about some current topic of interest in our school. I then set the stage for our discussion of the picture by saying something like this:

"All of us have problems in our daily lives. They may sometimes be discouraging problems and at other times exciting or challenging. Through experience we learn that there are sometimes many different ways of reacting to the same problem. There may be many possible approaches or solutions to a given problem, depending on circumstances related to it. Some solutions may lead to satisfying consequences; others may not. Some solutions are accepted in our culture; others are not. We may also encounter problems that we cannot solve by ourselves, problems which require us to gather more information before we can deal with them, and some problems which may appear beyond our ability to solve.

"Today we are going to view and discuss a picture which shows a boy with a problem. You are encouraged to examine his problem and his feelings and those of others who share it with him. You are also encouraged to 'put yourself into his shoes' and to ask yourself how you might react in this situation.

"Now let's look at the picture for a few moments, shall we?"

I usually allow about a minute for the students to examine the picture, and then I begin by asking them to describe what they see. A number of students generally raise their hands, but there is usually rather common agreement that the boy is facing some kind of serious charge for a crime he has committed. There is often universal agreement that the crime was a theft, and the majority of students generally expresses the belief that it was a car theft. This can lead into discussion of why a common offense by adolescents is car theft, and the discussion is usually quite interesting and enlightening to one who wishes to examine problems of juvenile delinquency. An intriguing aside is that students frequently express the belief that many juvenile crimes are committed for "something to do," for the sake of a thrill, because of peer group pressures, or because the juvenile feels it may help him to gain attention and status. Seldom do students feel that the stolen article is actually needed to sustain life.

After students have described the courtroom scene I ask them if they can think of what previous experiences might have led the boy to this problem. The following are just a few comments, taken from numerous tape recordings, which I have received relative to this question:

"The parents of the boy both worked and didn't have any time for him. He finally found several boys who also had time on their hands without anyone caring what they did, and it led to a few petty thefts and finally to a bigger one."

"Nobody seemed to be interested in the boy or understood him. In fact, not many adults understand us."

"His folks put the screws on him all of the time, so he finally decided to do something big on his own for once."

"He just took the car for a joy ride and didn't plan on keeping it; but he got caught."

"Some other boys dared him to swipe something."

I then lead discussion around to a consideration of what the consequences of the boy's actions and the actions of the court may mean in the future. Here are various reactions of students:

"The boy will be mighty scared, and he'll cry. The judge will put him on probation with the warning that if he gets in trouble again it won't be easy to face."

"The judge is going to 'throw the book' at the kid because there have been too many cases like this one and he thinks making an example of the boy will serve as a warning for other teenagers."

"This is just the beginning of trouble for the boy. He'll get sent to reform school, fall in with worse kids, learn more tricks, and end up in the state prison before he's through."

"The judge will dismiss the case and work with the parents and the boy to see causes which led to his trouble. The boy knew what he did was wrong, and he'll never get in a jam again."

Eventually I question the students on the feelings of each of the people in the picture. Speaking about the feelings of the adolescent, one student said:

"He probably feels all sick inside, and he's wishin' he wasn't there. He's also wishin' about now he hadn't done nothin' wrong. When the cops picked him up he got the shakes all over. He'll regret what he done the rest of his life 'cause he'll have a black mark against him."

Asked about the feelings of the woman in the picture, whom most of the students identified as the boy's mother, students made comments like these:

"The mother isn't angry. Instead she's disappointed . . . disappointed in herself and her boy. She blames herself as much as she does her son."

"The mother may be thinking that the few extra dollars she was able to earn by working weren't worth all of the heartaches she's had because she let her kid down."

"She just can't understand what's happened or why her boy got into this trouble. Even though she's disappointed in him, she'll stick by him and help him work out his problem."

Students had numerous reactions to the judge both as a person and as a representative of the law:

"The judge looks pretty mean to me. He probably thinks all teenagers are 'going to the dogs' and that this boy is 'typical.' That makes me mad, how adults are always thinking they were so much better when they were our age."

"I don't think the judge cares where the boy goes or what happens to him. It's just a job somebody has to do."

"A judge is in a rough spot. He has to enforce and rule on laws, but he has to deal with people too. He wants to help this boy in the picture, but the boy has committed a serious crime. I wouldn't want to be in the judge's place."

My students seemed to be more interested in discussing policemen and police work in general than in the policeman pictured on the screen. Their feelings about officers of the law ran an almost complete scale from admiration and respect to dislike and distrust. Perhaps some of these statements will reveal stronger emotions:

"Policemen today are 'right guys.' They are understanding and more apt to check into the 'why' behind a crime. They want to help youth to live decent worthwhile lives."

"Policemen are important because they protect us. If we didn't have police departments it would be just like the old western days when the six gun was law, and the fastest gunman got what he wanted whether it was right or not."

"I think cops have a chip on their shoulder when it comes to us. They think kids can't do anything right. A few teenagers get into trouble and then the cops act like we're all like that. We were just riding around in a car one night and they stopped us twice to see what we were doin'. Also when a teenager gets in an accident the paper makes a big deal out of it, and lots of adults aren't such hot drivers; but the papers don't play that up as big."

"Some cops are rougher than they might have to be, but it would be a lot worse without them."

"Law enforcement is improving all of the time. Policemen need more special training and education, and they need decent salaries too."

After we have discussed the people in the picture and related issues, I direct my students to a general consideration of laws, their origin, their importance, and their place in our everyday lives. Comments like the following have come out of this discussion:

"Any time people live together they need some kind of organization, some kind of rules to live by. That's what laws are, except they have been written down and enforced by a judicial system."

"We have to have certain limits. Even though we call this a 'free country' we are talking about freedom with responsibility. That is, we're free as long as we have equal rights under law and don't interfere with the rights of others."

"If we didn't have laws our whole country would crumble . . . like Rome and places like that where respect for law and morals and family life just 'went to pot' and individual rights didn't mean a thing."

The preceding are just a few of the reactions which students had regarding one picture. Other pictures which I have used in my classroom have triggered discussions, panels, individual and class projects, and units dealing with historical events, international relations, intergroup understanding, government, moral and spiritual values, teenage problems, the school, and the home. Pictures telling a story or introducing a problem or dilemma may be found in news pictures, comic strips, editorial cartoons, advertisements, student drawings in art classes, and magazine covers. Covers on magazines like the *Saturday Evening Post* and the *N.E.A. Journal* are often quite fruitful. Carefully chosen photographs or paintings of historical events may do a great deal to bring them to life and put them within the scope of the feeling as well as thinking level of students. The assassination of Lincoln, the first landing of Columbus in the New World, General Lee's surrender to General Grant, moving war pictures such as that of the Frenchman weeping as his beloved France is being occupied by German troops in World War II, and others are examples of pictures ideal for projective use.

I have also found it worthwhile to have students write endings to projective pictures; and in some cases I have had more interest and better writing from some students than they had previously produced through reports and themes. Another valuable technique is role-playing possible solutions posed in pictures, and an excellent pamphlet explaining this technique called *Role Playing the Problem Story* and written by George and Fannie Shaftel is available through the National Conference of Christians and Jews. The October 1957 issue of *Social Education* also carried a helpful article on role-playing by Gertrude Boyd.

There are a few "do's and don'ts" connected with the use of projective pictures which I have found both through reading and experience. This is a technique which may bring forth rather deep-seated emotions at times; and it is not the purpose or function of the classroom teacher to take the role of a clinical psychologist. Another caution is that the feelings and self-concept of individual students must be respected at all times, and a skillful teacher can keep students from revealing their most intense feelings to other members of the group. I have found that when I serve as a listener who reflects feelings by repeating a statement, by rephrasing it, or by just keeping a pleasant expression on my face I get more genuine expressions. I do not pass judgment on statements or nod approval. There is adequate time after assorted feelings have come out to ask what society expects of citizens, why laws are necessary, and so forth. The important thing to put across to students is that we all have feelings of anger or confusion, that a teacher who is understanding can accept these feelings of students, and that in discussions of this nature the teacher is not seeking to mold opinions and get the students to parrot statements.

Using projective pictures can be an unusual experience both for students and teacher. It can open many new vistas and interests. Like other methods it has its place and its limitations and can be used to excess. It is, however, an approach which I feel is worthy of the consideration of teachers who deal with feelings and attitudes as well as skills, facts, and understandings.

KIERAN J. CARROLL

Supervisor of Secondary Education, Montgomery County, Maryland

67. Using Microfilms to Teach American History*

The traditional approach to the teaching of those subjects that have been long regarded as academic has been gradually undergoing significant change. Mathematics, foreign languages, science and the language arts have made notable changes in teaching techniques in keeping with the knowledge acquired through investigations into the complexities of the learning processes. Proponents of the varied theories of learning have gained wide support but none have proved conclusive enough to command general acceptance. For approximately a half century, however, the dictum that learning is acquired by doing has been considered basically sound. Generally it is this principle that serves as the foundation for the "new" approach to the teaching of those subjects in which the public seems most interested.

To suggest that the principle of "learning by doing" has been ignored until lately is, to say the least, misleading. The new approach to the teaching of mathematics, for instance, is not a denial of this principle but a reaffirmation of it. To become a mathematician, it is maintained, one must do the things a mathematician does and think as he thinks. To learn a foreign language one must learn it as a child does, first hear it spoken and then repeat what is heard. The same kind of thinking that governs the teaching of mathematics and the foreign languages is equally evident in the fields of science and the language arts. History, however, remains a reluctant devotee of tradition. It is the purpose of this article to suggest that what is being done in other areas of the curriculum can also be done in the social studies, particularly in the teaching of the history of the United States.

More students take history than understand it. This is an unfortunate but not exaggerated observation. Seniors in secondary schools frequently indicate an interest in becoming mathematicians or scientists but rarely is an interest expressed in becoming an historian. Perhaps the reason for this lack of interest in pursuing a field of vital importance in today's world is to be found in the materials used in its teaching. Students seldom use or even see the original documents on which history is based and without

Social Education, XXV:143–44, 156, March 1961. Used by permission.

which it would be little more than fable. If students are to understand the purposes of history they must be given the opportunity to do the things an historian does and be able to buttress interpretation with documentation. An original document is in itself far more exciting than anything that can be said about it. The high school student reads about history but only infrequently, if at all, comes into direct contact with its sources.[1] The teaching of the history of the United States can be vastly enlivened by approaching it from the point of view of the historian.

Until rather recently access to source materials was limited and available only in national or private depositories. The use of microfilming techniques has now put at the student's disposal a wealth of documentary materials that formerly were denied him.

The possibilities of microfilm publications as a stimulus to research were recognized years ago. A Joint Committee on Materials for Research was established in 1929 by the American Council of Learned Societies and the Social Science Research Council to "investigate thoroughly the practical significance of innovations in the field of documentary reproduction."[2] The Committee enthusiastically endorsed microphotography and saw in it an ideal way of providing scholars with a ready access to original records while at the same time preserving the documents from the damage frequent use inevitably causes. The process of microfilming had an added advantage since it enabled students to procure exact reproductions inexpensively.

As a result of the demands made for microfilms of documents within its custody the National Archives has, since its opening in 1936, expanded its original facilities and has increased its services. While the Service Records Branch of the Archives has made monumental strides in the microfilming of its holdings, much remains to be done. Some 9,000,000 pages representing about 250 series of records have been published on over 9,000 rolls of film.[3] Basic sources for research in American, European, Far Eastern, and Latin American history are now or will soon be available.

An extensive treatment of the nature and coverage of the National Archives microfilm project is not the purpose of this paper. The primary concern herein is the use to which these materials can be put in a course in American history. The potentialities are multiple. Passenger lists of ves-

---

[1] The use of primary source material in the teaching of history is not novel. It has been suggested before and has been defended and condemned. No one, however, has proposed the use of microfilms for use on the secondary level. Cf. Robert E. Keohane, "Historical Method and Primary Sources" in Richard E. Thursfield, ed., *The Study and Teaching of American History*, National Council for the Social Studies, 17th Yearbook (Washington, D.C., 1946), pp. 325 ff.

[2] Albert H. Leisinger, Jr., "The Microfilm Programs of the National Archives," in *National Microfilm Association*, Proceedings of the Eighth Annual Meeting (Washington, D.C., 1959), p. 230.

[3] *Ibid.*, p. 233.

sels putting into American ports, for example, can stimulate discussions on immigration; the territorial papers can lend excitement to the history of the settlement of the West; the treaties signed between the United States and various Indian tribes can add to an understanding of this vexing domestic problem; and the diplomatic correspondence can provide the student with first-hand information as to the complexities of international relations.

While each of the series of records has something to offer to students in increasing their awareness, understanding, and appreciation of the stones on which this nation is built, attention will here be focused on those records that deal with foreign affairs. A study of the history of the United States, and not solely its diplomatic history, can be developed through a study of its foreign relations. There is available on microfilm the entire record of our relations with such countries as England, France, Russia, China, and Japan from the time diplomatic relations were established with them until 1906. These records include despatches from our ministers and ambassadors abroad, instructions sent by the Department of State to them, consular reports, and notes exchanged between the State Department and the diplomatic representatives from those countries residing in Washington or elsewhere within our borders. The use of these documents would make it possible for the student to follow such events as those leading to the Louisiana Purchase, the War of 1812, the acquisition of Florida, the annexation of Texas, the Alabama Claims and a host of other absorbing aspects of American history. Where textbooks, of necessity, are confined to a brief and often inadequate treatment of important events relating to the history of this country, the microfilms are eloquently revealing. Take, for instance, the space allotted in a typical secondary history textbook to the Alabama Claims and the actual negotiations that took place. The textbook dismisses the claims, after a short discussion of their background, with a mere summary of the decisions of the tribunal. The microfilms, on the other hand, would permit the student to follow this celebrated case as it developed, looking, as it were, over the shoulders of the representatives of the countries involved. The composition of the tribunal of arbitration, how its members were selected, their nationality, and the votes they cast on each issue, are all disclosed.[4] The press closely followed the proceedings at Geneva and incited bitter feelings among the citizens and public officials of both the United States and Great Britain. The British member of the tribunal was so convinced of the legality of his country's position that he voted in the negative or not at all on every issue. The reading of the official

[4] In any discussion of arbitration proceedings to which the United States has been party, reference should be made to John B. Moore, *History and Digest of International Arbitrations to Which the United States Has Been a Party*, 6 vols. (Washington, D.C.: Government Printing Office, 1898).

record relating to these claims is a wonderful example of how problems between nations can be resolved even though the contending parties may not be in unanimous agreement with the final disposition of their differences.

The use of microfilms provides not only the most direct contact with our history but gives the student an opportunity to behave as an historian. It enables the teacher to introduce the fundamentals of historical criticism to the class. A document can be examined to determine both its authenticity and credibility. It is not difficult to establish the fact that the micro-filmed documents are authentic but occasionally errors appear in the contents. The skills or methods used to detect these inaccuracies are of immeasurable value in helping the student develop the ability to think critically and weigh rather than accept what is offered as evidence. For example, there is among the microfilmed documents relating to the territorial papers of Colorado a letter from Governor Cummings dated December 14, 1867, and addressed to Secretary of State Seward. The letter should have been dated December 14, 1866, as is clear from the context, the date of receipt stamped on it; and finally and most convincingly, an examination of the records of the dates of service of the Governors of Colorado reveals that Alexander Cummings was no longer Governor of that territory in December of 1867.

The use of microfilm publications in a course in United States history would have to be supplemented by a small, but selective, classroom library. It would suffice if such a library contained a basic general history of this country, perhaps Morison and Commager; a diplomatic history, either Bemis or Bailey; Billington's work on westward expansion; Handlin's writings on immigration; and similar volumes on business, labor, social and cultural history. All of these areas, excepting diplomatic history, are referred to but not developed in the microfilmed documents. The possibilities latent in the use of these materials is almost endless. Their major merit is precisely this: They can be used to introduce any aspect of our history and in so doing enable the student to participate in what goes into the writing of history. Another and not incidental advantage in the use of these materials is that they help students to read in order to learn history. [5]

While emphasizing the advantages that the use of microfilms has over the traditional textbook approach to the teaching of history no mention has been made of its practicality. Inseparable from any consideration of its merits is its cost. One of the first questions any budgetary-minded person would raise would undoubtedly relate to the expenses involved. Would, for instance, the implementation of such a program require the purchase of a

---

[5] Cf. Helen McCracken Carpenter and Marian A. Young. "Reading to Learn History: Suggestions for Methods and Materials," in *The Study and Teaching of American History*, pp. 285 ff.

microfilm reader for each student? If so, the whole idea might be dismissed as financially prohibitive.

Individual microfilm readers would not be necessary. The Remington-Rand corporation has on the market a device that permits the projecting of microfilm onto a screen. One such projector would suffice for an entire class. The cost of this device is approximately $300, slightly more than a set of textbooks but with greater life expectancy. A roll of microfilm would require an expenditure of from three to four dollars, an outlay that, assuming reasonable care of the film, would be but rarely repeated. Even the purchase of a projector, though preferable, would not be necessary. A microfilm roll usually comprising some 100 feet and containing from 3,000 to 3,500 frames or pages can be cut into individual frames and mounted. These mounts would be of the 35 mm. variety and usable in the projectors with which schools are now equipped. The cost of mounting is roughly from one to two cents per frame.

To summarize, the use of microfilm publications has many decided advantages. Too, it provides the student with the opportunity to work as an historian works, and it is relatively inexpensive.

IID. Approaches to Evaluation

Our last section in this part of the book is devoted to evaluation—an intimate aspect of instruction. The regular examination of our aims, our content, and our procedures, the appraisal of our program, is an unquestioned mandate. Continuing review through a variety of appropriate means is essential for judging curricula and instruction, as well as pupil growth and progress. Most experienced teachers admit that they are not comfortable with their system of testing and measurement. They have come to realize that a sound, comprehensive program of evaluation is the key to needed drastic renovation in much of what is now uncritically accepted, not just in the area of assessment and grading, but in many aspects of the social studies.

Evaluation needs to encompass much more than the measurement of student achievement. Evaluative-type activities, such as pre-tests, might be used before launching a new unit to help the teacher plan for incorporation of the most pertinent learnings. Evaluation should extend to include student self-evaluation and also include assessment by the instructor of his own performance. He should, for example, attempt to check on the validity and reliability of the evaluative instruments he has employed. Too often we forget that a faulty test, rather than pupil intransigence, may be the cause of apparent failure.

Indeed, an evaluative attitude should characterize most of the instructor's actions in the schoolroom. It should reflect rather than a purely judgmental attitude, a diagnostic outlook toward pupil performance. Under these circumstances the mentor will tend to teach more from a guidance viewpoint and will measure less. Commonly too much of the evaluative process tends to center upon mere pupil reproduction of the more readily ascertainable content than the admittedly more difficult assessment of progress in skills and attitude changes. Teachers, too frequently, tend to limit evaluation to paper and pencil tests. Possibly no more than 20 percent of the evaluative activities should be typical fact-centered tests. Pupil notebooks, their contributions to classroom discussion, competencies in map and chart interpretation, participation in small-group endeavors, or ability in effective thinking are but several examples of skills or efforts that should be assessed and counted toward a grade. As much as possible of what goes on in a classroom should be amenable to evaluation of a continuing nature. It should be clear that evaluation is not just what occurs on a current events quiz, a weekly test, or the unit examination.

An entire book, not just the several readings, which limit us because of space allocation, is called for in this all-important area. The editors recommend that readers review thoroughly the broad and complex area of evaluation. We suggest that many specifics and guidelines for testing and student appraisal are to be found in the excellent 35th Yearbook of the National Council for the Social Studies, entitled *Evaluation in Social Studies,* Harry D. Berg, Editor, (1965).

As you review the suggestions for student assessment, ask yourself to what extent there is truth in the adage: "If the pupil hasn't learned, the teacher hasn't taught." What elements should I incorporate into a varied and broad evaluation program that will help account for individual pupil progress? How will I know most assuredly that the course aims have been attained? How will I know when students have accomplished that which I personally set out for them to do?

RICHARD E. GROSS

*Professor of Education, Stanford
University*

DWIGHT W. ALLEN

*Dean, School of Education, University of
Massachusetts*

68. Problems and Practices in Social Studies Evaluation*

One of the great stumbling blocks to any satisfactory, large-scale implementation of the emerging "new" social studies will be the evaluational aspects. If the "new" social studies, as promised, are thoroughly updated, highly objective, inquiry-directed, individualized, and process- and skill-oriented, assessment of student progress will be much more difficult and even less effective than present evaluation of the outcomes of traditional content and instruction. The social studies of tomorrow promise much, but proof of efficacy will be sadly lacking unless serious attention is given to helping teachers and school districts strengthen their capabilities in this crucial area. New courses, units, and lessons, as well as new media and approaches, will demand much from us that is new and improved if we are adequately to ascertain pupil understanding, competency, and attitudes. The learner involved in simulation, independent study, source interpretation, an interview in the community, small group role playing, or in case analysis will, indeed, be difficult to rate—especially when we are limited by current evaluative attitudes and practices.

How can we be so pessimistic? Several years ago one of the authors conducted a national study of evaluational ideals and practices of classroom teachers of the social studies. This had not been previously reported in print and was the first such systematic survey made since 1934. The results were disquieting, and in this paper we will summarize some of the findings without delving into the details of the research. [1]

The responding sample included more than 600 members of the National Council for the Social Studies selected at random from its mailing list. The respondents then represented a group of professionally oriented individuals whose practices could be assumed to be in advance of the evaluation procedures followed by a general sampling of instructors. Teachers were asked to reply, both in terms of an ideal and of their own practices, to 60 questions related to three elements of assessment: (1) What

---

Social Education, XXXI:207–9, March 1967. Used by permission.

[1] See Dwight W. Allen, "Evaluation in Social Studies Classrooms: Ideals and Practices" (Ed.d. Diss., School of Education, Stanford University, 1959). Available from University Microfilms, Ann Arbor, Michigan.

should be covered in social studies evaluation; (2) The administrative procedures for testing; and (3) Kinds of examinations and test items.

Some of the more general conclusions are summarized here:

1. Teachers frequently fail to relate their assessment practices to the aims they claim for their offerings.

2. Teachers are often inconsistent in their conception of evaluation.

3. Teachers are reticent, even ideally, to use the full range of evaluation techniques now available.

4. The use of many evaluation devices is misunderstood and such devices are often misused.

5. Teachers place a great amount of blind faith in the indirect accomplishment of their objectives.

6. All the purposes of evaluation are not understood by many teachers.

7. Teachers indicated by their answers that in general they have a low level of statistical sophistication.

8. Teachers almost unanimously accept both essay and objective test items.

9. A disproportionate amount of time seems to be spent in the correction of English errors in social studies work.

10. The theory of sampling and test instruction is not understood by teachers.

11. More than half of the teachers ignore the value of student-constructed test items and only about half encourage pupil-grading and self-evaluation.

12. Few teachers employ item analysis or other checks upon their testing and evaluation procedures.

13. Teachers, by their practices, encourage students to regard grading as a coercive weapon to be used against them.

14. Very few teachers perceive the major implications of the evaluation program which carry beyond the grading of students.

The above conditions are not surprising to anyone who has carefully observed classroom practices in evaluation. Such findings tend to confirm some of the previous research results of one of the authors gathered a decade earlier with a smaller and narrower sampling of history teachers.[2] Here it was also revealed that instructors failed to use the wide variety of assessment opportunities available and that paper-and-pencil tests were weighted far too heavily in the total narrow process of evaluation and grading.

The major investigator of the more recent study found four basic reasons why social studies teachers have not been more concerned with examining and improving their evaluation practices. First of all, they have been satisfied with their evaluation, and with its accuracy and adequacy.

[2]Richard E. Gross, "Evaluative Practices in United States History Classes," *Social Studies*, January 1953.

The statistical neatness of objective tests and numerical averaging lends an aura of exactness to the grading process and disguises the many subjective elements which are anterior components.

A second reason is the fact that so many of the social studies objectives are vague and ambiguous and overlap other curricular areas and do not readily lend themselves to precise measurement. This obscures the fact that there are also many specific objectives which are readily measurable in skill areas, content areas, and methods of problem solving.

Thirdly, there is no doubt that many teachers are either unfamiliar with many methods or do not understand their purpose and use sufficiently well to be comfortable in their utilization. Tests have been regarded as a panacea of evaluation, and teachers have automatically turned to tests (and even then only to certain favorite types) whenever evaluation is considered necessary.

Fourth, teachers regard evaluation as an unfortunate appendage of teaching, rather than as an integral part of it. So long as teachers do not comprehend the integral relationship of the full range of evaluative techniques with teaching objectives and activities, evaluation will never be utilized in its full potential.

Allen also concluded that there was a strong indication in the replies to the questionnaire that teachers often set their goals in terms of pre-determined evaluation techniques. Instead of really considering the most effective teaching situations, it appears that many teachers adapt their teaching procedures to the most easily contained evaluation program. This practice holds many implications for teacher education, both in-service and pre-service, and warrants further investigation.

Several special problems of evaluation in the social studies merit our further consideration. These factors complicate additionally the difficulties that beset assessment in our field.

1. We are plagued by the broad and imprecise goals that are held for the social studies; add to these the future-oriented socio-civic purposes commonly expected to result from social education, and it becomes immediately apparent that improved measurement devices may become available long before we can agree upon criteria and more immediate aims that are sufficiently specific so that their attainment may be ascertained. In many ways this is perhaps the fundamental problem besetting the social studies today.

2. Unfortunately, even as we become more specific, the problems of validity rise. Experiments with the teaching process which we have conducted at Stanford University in recent years reveal the incredible complexities of any single act of instruction. For example, in a simple teacher explanation to a class about an event, more than one hundred variables in the situation may be easily identified. We need much more careful and

rigorous research so that we can know just what causes what. More precise planning may help, but to teach a typically compounded affair, such as a revolution or an election, is difficult enough in itself; to validly evaluate key factors in pupil comprehension remains, as matters now stand, largely a pious hope.

3. A related question now appears. Do the instruments we attempt to apply in evaluation really ascertain what we believe they do? We indicated previously that the "new" social studies will call for a more sophisticated program of assessment than now commonly followed. Yet even as we build the necessary measures of skill, we remain dogged by a doubt that has not been alleviated to date: Are such tests of competency actually measures of the qualities implied or are they largely indexes of ability to apply knowledge previously learned? While the social studies share this problem with judgment procedures in other disciplinary fields, adequate assessment of admittedly fundamental skill competencies in our field must wait on the evolution of largely new instruments.

4. Among the major purposes of the social studies are those reflecting desired socio-civic attitudes. To what extent does our teaching really affect attitudes? How can we best ascertain overt, let alone covert, behavior changes in these vital areas? Indeed, should such highly personal attributes be rated? Are we really trying in the best ways known to help youth build sound and worthwhile value systems? Can a purely objective social-science approach ensure progress in this domain? Until we have better answers to these queries, perhaps teachers are to be forgiven their transgressions in regard to attitudinal assessment. But if attitude growth is a desired end, we must find ways to evaluate progress—otherwise the sham of our stated purposes will shame us no end.

5. The heart of the social studies program should rest in controversy. Often in controversy there is *no* answer, or there is the possibility of a variety of hypotheses that either can't all be tested or that will not satisfy many who are involved. A social studies curriculum moving on the frontier of ferment and change calls for evaluation of a nontraditional means; but more than that, to what extent can pupil grasp of value-laden, emotionally tinted issues actually be evaluated? Certainly new conceptions of testing and rating of problems in this area are demanded or we make a mockery of our purposes and our instruction.

6. Unhappily, the great bulk of commercial and standardized tests in the field of the social studies have been found wanting by experts. Observe the reviews in the last three Mental Measurement Yearbooks; they give at best but limited hope for longtime improvement. While achievement-type tests have been scored roundly, reliable measures of skills and attitudes have been found even more lacking. Banks of tested items will eventually provide significant help for concerned teachers, but producers

of tests must now become as creative and innovational as they have not been in the past. Until we gain much improved tests of this nature, teachers must use current measures with caution and are well advised to continue to try to evolve devices that best suit their own purposes.

We have not painted a bright picture in this important area. However, unless we are continually concerned, not only over employing evaluation wisely in ascertaining pupil progress, but also in establishing realistic aims, in setting up purposeful curricula and courses, in critically reviewing instructional materials, and in judging the efficacy of our teaching process, we fall short of our responsibilities as professionals. Indeed, until we accept such a comprehensive and evolving concept of evaluation, we dare give no one a grade but ourselves.

IRENE A. HUBIN

Teacher, Ho-Ho-Kus Public School, New Jersey

69. The Evaluation of Citizenship*

Possibly one of the most difficult problems the typical teacher faces is the evaluation of the complex curriculum known as the social studies. Involved in the evaluation of this subject are not only objective criteria such as grades and arithmetic levels of achievement, but also the large element of subjectivity. The subjective characters of the evaluation may very well take a wide variety of forms. The introduction of subjective evaluations has unfortunately been largely neglected by most writers in this particular field.

Cummings states that,

> The growth of evaluation has been one of the major achievements in American education during the last two decades. Evaluation of citizenship education has been a part of that movement. In general, broad objectives have been agreed upon, and evaluation has been an attempt to discover to what extent these objectives are being reached.[1]

However, research in evaluation discloses that Cumming's statement is subject to some question. Other writers such as Otto contend,

> Unfortunately most current efforts at evaluation of instruction in the social studies are restricted to methods of appraising what children have learned in social studies without also examining and appraising the transfer of these learnings, or of some of them, to the events of everyday living.[2]

Undoubtedly Otto has more particularly appreciated the difficulties involved in the evaluation of the social studies than has been indicated in the rather broad generalization of Cummings.

The social studies encompass a diverse categorization of individual subjects which can be interrelated into a meaningful whole. The subjects included in the social studies have come to mean, "those portions of history, geography, civics, and other social sciences that are selected for

---

Social Studies, 49:96–100, March 1958. Used by permission.

[1] Howard H. Cummings, "Evaluation of Citizenship Education," *Education for Democratic Citizenship*, National Council for the Social Studies, 22nd Yearbook (Washington, D.C., 1951), chap. 10, p. 108.

[2] Henry J. Otto, *Social Education in Elementary Schools* (New York: Rinehart & Co., 1956), p. 465.

use in teaching."[3] In addition the term in many areas also includes, "...
the social sciences, art, literature, music, and even some phases of science."[4] The ultimate goal of the social studies is directed toward generating and improving individual student citizenship.

Progress in the social studies should be evaluated in terms of the teaching objectives. Instruction in the social studies for the purpose of developing:

> Responsible, sensitive, and courageous citizens who will participate intelligently in the solving of problems growing out of their own human relationships and of problems facing society.
>
> Accurate knowledge of man and society. Informed insight into man and society. Those skills essential to acquiring knowledge and insight.
>
> Loyalty to social ideals that forward the dignity of individual men and the brotherhood of all men.
>
> Ability to apply knowledge, insight, skill, and loyalty to daily living.
>
> Familiarity with urgent social problems such as the dangerous spread between mechanical and social invention, provincial nationalism that blocks progress toward "one world," the confusion between education and propaganda, and wastefulness in the use of natural resources.
>
> Personality traits in the child through meeting his needs for exploration, muscle activity, social activity, imaginative activity, and recognition as an individual."[5]

It is evident that evaluation of progress toward such goals will require a broader base than recitations and tests.[6]

The development of an evaluation technique of the social studies subjects is the major objective of this paper. Evaluation consists of the determination of the level of achievement, appreciation, understanding, and accomplishment on the part of the student. As previously indicated, a series of objective criteria is satisfactory but by no means completely indicative as an attainment measure.

"Evaluation includes measurement but it extends far beyond the areas to which objective measurements have been applied.[7]

An attempt to develop subjective criteria for evaluation is presented which will prove more revealing and significant to the teacher for purposes

[3]Ralph C. Preston, *Teaching Social Studies in the Elementary School* (New York: Rinehart & Co., 1956), p. 3.

[4]W. B. Brown, "A New Approach to the Social Studies," *Social Studies*, 27:12–17, January 1936, p. 12.

[5]Preston, *Teaching Social Studies*, p. 294.

[6]*Ibid.*, p. 295.

[7]Edgar Bruce Wesley, *Teaching the Social Studies* (Boston: D. C. Heath and Co., 1942), p. 551.

of more fully ascertaining the true level of achievement on the part of the student.

A brief presentation of some past and unfortunately existing evaluation procedures may well be in order so that a highlighting of current defects can be indicated. Generally speaking a separatist treatment of each of the individual subjects in the broad social studies field has prevailed. Recent advances indicate that a fusionism of these many subjects into a coordinated whole develops a better and more integrated appreciation on the part of the student.[8]

Antediluvian conceptualizations which are largely disappearing from the scene stressed regimentation, rote learning, and memorization of factual data to an extreme degree. Obvious defects in such methodology have been recognized and attempts to correct them have been introduced through the idea of integration or fusionistic philosophies. Obvious defects developed from these conceptualizations which were primarily manifest in the form of lack of student interest, inability to evaluate the overall impact of the several subjects, questionable value to the student, and, in all probability, a complete lack of recall on the part of the student after the passage of a very short period of time.

Presently the trend toward integration of the social studies presents an attempt to counteract the disadvantages inherent in classical doctrines. Most advanced present thought appears to be centered on the philosophy of making the social studies significant, meaningful, and developing better and more informed citizens. These latter developments are definitely worthy of praise as being forward steps in attaining the before-mentioned objectives. However, concurrent with the new philosophy is introduced the problem to which this paper is devoted, namely, that of evaluation. It is admitted that evaluation under classical dogma practices was a much simpler and more objective procedure.

However, evaluation of the social studies under our new integrated and fusionistic teaching methodology does present some extremely complex and, as previously indicated, undeveloped evaluation problems.

Questions such as: How do we weigh the increase or decrease in individual student citizenship? How do we evaluate the impact of integrated social studies on making the student a more understanding and better member of society? What percentage should we assign to a student's grade for the positive factor which could be generated out of a well developed social studies program, namely a reduction in racial discrimination? When do we know, and what percentage should be given to a student's grade to indicate his achievement of attitudes which are socially

---

[8]See Irene A. Hubin, "The Fusion of Social Studies in the Elementary School," *Social Studies*, 48:93–97, March 1957.

harmonious? What grade is assignable to evidences of maturity and ability on the part of the student to appreciate contemporary social structures?

Questions such as these introduce the before-mentioned subjective evaluation factors. No objective type of examination can ever possibly reveal a representative answer to any of the foregoing questions. It can be appreciated that the classical methodology previously indicated is helpless in generating a meaningful answer to any of these questions. From a review of the brief foregoing discussions it appears that the elimination of subjective factors from the grading of social studies achievement is quite impossible. A concentration or a misdirection of emphasis on objective factors will only develop nonrepresentation and probably misleading results.

Evaluation is therefore divisible into subjective and objective grading elements. The objective elements have been classified by several authorities in this field.

Otto mentions that, "In some schools teachers have become so 'measurement conscious' that they have discarded the use of teacher observation as a means of identifying children's problems and noting children's development. In such schools little attention is paid to any information or evidence which cannot be classified, tabulated, and treated statistically. Measurement has an important place in educational work, but so does teacher observation of pupil behavior and performance." [9]

The Association of Social Studies Teachers of the City of New York reveals that,

> Any analysis of examinations currently in use in the social studies would reveal an emphasis on the testing of the mastery of information. Since there is universal acceptance of the wider objectives in teaching to include not only information but also skills and attitudes, an undisputed answer to the query, "What to Test?" should be that examinations must test all the objectives of teaching, information, skills, and attitudes.

The following factors should be considered in order to develop skills and attitudes:

1. Reading and interpretation of graphs.
2. Map making and reading.
3. Use of reference materials.
4. Participation in panel discussions, debates, etc.
5. Writing dramatizations, diaries, etc.
6. Observations as a result of trips.
7. Making of posters, cartoons, graphs, etc. to illustrate some phase of the subject matter.
8. Preparing materials for visual exhibit.

[9] Otto, *Social Education*, p. 472.

9. Preparing outlines and presenting reports.

10. Ability to analyze material being presented with one's own knowledge.

11. Ability to listen to a speaker and determine what to listen for.

12. Ability to make and take notes for later reference and study."[10]

The most outstanding limitation of standardized as well as teacher-made tests is the lack of attention given to the measurement of understanding of concepts and generalizations. [11]

. . . observation of behavior and evaluation in any area becomes difficult without some normative frame of reference and some reasonably objective or tangible criteria.[12]

Evaluation of the social studies program should be carried on as continuously and persistently as evaluation of the child's learning. In fact, the appraisal of outcomes of learning experiences in the social studies inevitably leads to evaluation of the program. Such evaluation, however, is sometimes neglected because comprehensive criteria are not used. [13]

Factual tests are easier to make, easier to score, and, in a sense, easier to defend than any other type of test. [14]

Subjective ascertainment levels are not as easily indentifiable as indicated in the quotes from the above authorities. The subjective evaluation is founded on the interpretative and analytical talents of the grader. Answers to the previously developed questions can only be developed in the light of three basic criteria.

First the student has to demonstrate that he comprehends the basic factual material in the social studies group. Indication of this comprehension ability is developed through the criteria of tests and examinations. This first component of the overall evaluation process is objective in nature.

Subjectivity is introduced in the second and third components in the form of personal judgment. The second and third components of the subjective evaluation process are namely, the application of the learned material and finally a measure of consistency in the application itself.

Individual observation will demonstrate whether or not the student is applying the principles for which he has demonstrated comprehension.

[10] Association of Social Studies Teachers of the City of New York, *A Handbook for Social Studies Teaching,* (New York: Republic Book Co., 1951), pp. 170–171.

[11] Harl R. Douglass and Hervert F. Spitzer, "The Importance of Teaching for Understanding," in *The Measurement of Understanding,* National Society for the Study of Education, 45th Yearbook, pt. 1 (Chicago: University of Chicago Press, 1946), p. 21.

[12] Otto, *Social Education,* p. 483.

[13] John U. Michaelis, *Social Studies for Children in a Democracy* (Englewood Cliffs, N.J.: Prentice-Hall, Inc., 1956), p. 428.

[14] Cummings, "Evaluation of Citizenship Education," p. 101.

The application is demonstrable in a variety of forms. For instance, a student may well be able to correctly answer an examination question such as: Is racial segregation basically undemocratic? Comprehension is demonstrated here. However, the examination answer is not entirely indicative of the final degree of citizenship possessed by the student. Observation of the student in his social environment and contact with others will reveal whether or not a satisfactory degree of comprehension exists.

The point being developed here is that the individual observation of the teacher directed toward uncovering evidences of application or nonapplication is necessary before the ascertainment of a grade can be realistically developed.

The third component of our subjective criteria, namely consistency, is more or less self-explanatory. The comprehension of factual data and its subsequent degree of application has to be consistently applied before a proper evaluation can be determined. A student correctly saying that racial segregation is undemocratic and applying the principle in his social activities must demonstrate a level and degree of consistency before a grader could rank him in the highest stratum of a particular group.

Thus it can be seen that a subjective evaluation incorporates not only objective but also subjective measures which require individual observation. The ultimate goal is to develop better citizens through the consistent application of basic teachings associated in the social studies group.

A selection of three cases with which the writer has had experience is presented in order to further clarify the subjective evaluation technique.

Case A

John, a boy of 12 years of age, demonstrated exceptionally high ability in every examination. His grades in all subjects were A's. He was never absent or late, personable, and at all times a neatly dressed individual. Unfortunately, John was unable to play with other children. He was quite egotistical and the offspring of an extremely wealthy family. Observation revealed that he was extremely class and race conscious, and although a brilliant student, quite unable to get along with any of the other students in the school. He refused to enter into any group activities, would not talk to or associate with any of the other students. He further demonstrated an obnoxious and a superior attitude because of his rather high academic achievements.

This particular case, although far from being typical, is well illustrative of the subjective evaluation that would be involved in determining a grade for citizenship. John received a grade of F in citizenship because he significantly failed to qualify under the subjective components, application and consistency. John knew his work but never applied it and never demonstrated any consistency with respect to such application.

Case B

Mary, 10 years of age, came from a middle class family. Her grades were average. She demonstrated no great ability as an academician yet showed an ability to comprehend subject material of her course work. Observation indicated Mary to be an exceptionally talented and gregarious person. She took part in practically every social activity. She was well liked by her classmates and might be described as a "Popular girl."

Mary received a grade of A in citizenship primarily because observation revealed that she was consistently applying the evidences of her comprehension of social studies course work.

This case shows again the departure from classical dogma in that although being an average student in social studies, she manifested the ability of applying, and applying consistently, the factual information she obtained in her social studies exposure.

Case C

Peter, age 11, was an exceptionally poor student in every respect. He came from an underprivileged family of 2 brothers and 4 sisters. This large family was crowded in a small development home where space was at a premium. His parents were irresponsible. Although he demonstrated mental capabilities in several instances, he was definitely unable to achieve satisfactory grades because of his adverse home environment. Peter, however, did show evidence of extreme degrees of leadership, popularity, and gregariousness in all of his contacts with fellow students.

This case is indicative of the other extreme wherein a child unable to achieve satisfactory grades did excel in citizenship because of his consistency and application of factual material.

Preston suggests the following,

> . . . ways in which teachers may collect information which is necessary for comprehensive evaluation of progress.
> 1. Observation of Pupil Behavior.
> 2. Inspection of Children's Work.
> 3. Study of Results of Teacher-Made Tests. Many teachers have found that it is better to have frequent short tests than infrequent long ones. . . . Objective tests with true-or-false items or multiple-choice items are also suitable and should be occasionally given. . . . Teacher-constructed tests should be corrected and returned to the pupils for discussion. Test results are properly kept as part of the pupil's record.
> 4. Study of Results of Standardized Tests."[15]

[15] Preston, *Teaching Social Studies,* pp. 295–96, 298.

From these cases and the previous discussion certain generalizations can now be developed:

1. The principal purpose of the social studies is to develop better citizens.
2. Objective tests do not reveal citizenship qualities, they merely present evidence indicating memorizational ability.
3. Subjective observation is required in order to evaluate and determine citizenship qualities.
4. Subjective observation is directed toward determining the extent and degree in which a student consistently applies the overall philosophy of the social studies.
5. Evaluation skills can be developed in the teacher through exposure and observation of students in their play, classroom participation, and school environmental situation.

HENRY W. BRAGDON

Editor, New England Social Studies Bulletin

70. Neglected Resource: The Essay Question*

We live in an age when everything conspires to reduce that faculty of attention which is gained by close reading and accurate writing. Since people who can neither read nor write accurately all too often are people who cannot think accurately, no teacher of any academic subject can afford to neglect the first two R's. In history and social studies classes students need unremitting training in how to extract and retain knowledge from the printed page, and in how to read for connotation as well as sense. Equal attention should be paid to a variety of writing exercises: brief summaries or analyses of outside reading, research papers, class reports. This paper will consider a too frequently neglected aspect of this training—the essay test.

The author has yet to meet an independent school history teacher who did not impose written tests, and who did not at least pay lip service to their importance. But the picture is not entirely rosy. In a few schools teachers seem still to be preparing for the College Board Examinations of the early '30's, in which candidates were asked to regurgitate chunks of undigested fact in a series of twenty-minute "essays," starting with a pre-canned biography of Henry Clay, or Alcibiades, or Gladstone as the case might be. This preparation for an outmoded, highly mnemonic type of history is quaintly called "keeping up standards," and is applauded by self-dubbed "patriotic" societies, who fondly imagine that if students go through the learning processes of a generation ago they will also acquire the political and economic philosophy of Calvin Coolidge.

Even where historical training is on a much higher plane, it is apparent that often there has not been careful attention to essay testing. Consider these two questions, both given in good schools to students taking advanced placement courses in American History:

Trace American nationalism from 1815 to 1877. Bring in social, economic, and cultural as well as political factors. (This was one of eight questions in two hours.)

Explain why slavery was the principal cause of the Civil War.

On the face of it the first question is an impossible assignment, particularly in the time allowed, and can only elicit from the student a hurried mish-

*Independent School Bulletin, pp. 59-60, May 1960. Used by permission.

mash of vague, unsupported generalization. The second question at least focuses on a point and demands an argument, but it suggests that there is an official imterpretation of history, which the student had better learn as unthinkingly as he learns the dates of the Presidents. No, these won't do. If you call a test an "essay test," you must see that the student is encouraged to write an essay, which according to the dictionary is a "literary composition, analytical or interpretive in nature."

To illustrate, let us examine a run-of-the-mill question in American history. Note the directions as well as the question itself:

> *Time*: 50 minutes.
> *Directions*: Write good English.
>   You will be graded on:
>   1) organization,
>   2) clarity and validity of general statements,
>   3) wealth of factual material related to the question.
> Trace the connection between the slavery issue and political parties in the period 1840 to 1860.

What does the instruction, "Write good English" mean here? It means at least certain elementary virtues: well-constructed sentences, correct spelling and punctuation, avoidance of slang and abbreviations, attention to accurate expression. Unless these are insisted on all through the school, students will get the notion that they are simply idiosyncrasies of English teachers.

What does it mean that the candidate will be graded on "organization"? Surely it strongly suggests an introductory paragraph of some sort. In this particular question one approach might be to contrast the situation in 1840 when both major issues were avoiding the explosive slavery issue like the plague, and the Whigs won by nominating a war hero who was alleged to live in a log cabin and drink hard cider, to the situation in 1860 when both major parties had broken apart over the issue, and when Lincoln's election was the occasion for secession. How explain the change? A more obvious approach might be to start with the election of 1844, when slavery first began to obtrude in politics, and save 1860 for the final paragraph. The important thing is that there should be a formal introduction which leads the reader into the question. Then the body of the essay should be arranged in some sort of logical sequence so that there is a *flow* of meaning. Each major point deserves a paragraph. To get the point across I tell students that if they don't know how to paragraph, at least indent every sixth to eighth line, and this may deceive the reader.

Now as to "clarity and validity of general statements." This question is more artful than it may first appear. It does not ask something that the candidate can parrot. It demands that he state, and state clearly, a constantly shifting connection between two factors—in other words, that he establish generalizations. No mere recitation of facts about parties and slavery gets any credit at all.

But these generalizations are fruitless unless supported by facts, hard facts. So this question demands them, but insists that they be "related to the question." Students are tempted to parade what they remember, regardless of relevance. In this question, for instance, they fall into what I have nicknamed the "Compromise of 1850 syndrome." Those who suffer from this malady cannot mention an event without telling all they know. In the case of the Compromise of 1850 this means giving all six of its major provisions. When a student falls into this trap, he should also lose credit for organization, because he has not *aimed* his facts at the problem under discussion.

Recently a boy complained that he had been given too low a grade. He had compared his paper with others who had higher grades, he said, and was convinced that he had done as well as they. This was the question:

> Clemenceau has often been referred to as a "hardheaded realist," and Wilson as an "impractical idealist." Explain how far you agree or disagree with these judgments in relation to their ideas as to the treatment of Germany in the Versailles settlement.

The first part of his answer went as follows:

> Before the convention (sic) at Versailles, both Wilson and Clemenceau had shown their hands, deciding, in effect, the fate of the treaty. Wilson, relying on the assumption that the other leaders were as humanely reconcileable (sic) as he, failed to commit Clemenceau and Lloyd George to the kind of treatment for Germany as later (sic) indicated in his fourteen points.

So far so good, except for some awkwardness of expression and an error in chronology, but then follows this paragraph:

> Wilson's fourteen points had a lot of idealistic ideas. One said that tariffs be abolished—they came out higher than before the war. Another point advocated the settling of the North Italian border by self-determination, a bit of wishful thinking in view of the mixture of language and culture in that area. Another advocated the peaceful settlement of all colonial disputes, which could only end up by a divvying between the European victors. There were other settlements hoped for equally impossible, such as Balkan self-determination.
> As to Germany...

And finally he comes to grips with the problem, having wasted his time and mine. He thus suffered double jeopardy: he used up time which might better have been devoted to relevant material, and he lost credit for organization because this miscellaneous information about the Fourteen Points was irrelevant.

There are those who fear that a too steady diet of essay tests will encourage students to "bloviate"—to use the verb immortalized by Warren Gamaliel Harding. The students have a word for it, too: to "shovel." Therefore, goes the argument, there must be "fact tests" to make students understand they cannot get by with mere glibness. But testing for facts in isolation is wrong. It encourages the "quiz kid" mentality, the notion that knowledge of disparate facts is by and of itself a virtue.

There are various ways of testing for fact within the framework of an essay question. One of them is to demand reference to certain relevant items, so:

> Samuel Flagg Bemis, one of America's foremost diplomatic historians, maintains that American acquisition of commitments in the Far East during the years 1898–1900 marked "a great national aberration,"* promising disastrous consequences.
>
> Write an essay arguing *for or against* Mr. Bemis's point of view in the light of later events. In the course of your essay weave in reference to the Open Door policy, the annexation of the Philippines, Theodore Roosevelt's policies toward Japan, the Washington Conference, the Stimson Doctrine, Pearl Harbor, SCAP.
>
> *Aberration: "Act of wandering; deviation, especially from truth, moral retitude, or the natural state."

Still, comes the insistent voice: "I *want to test students on facts.*" Fine, so long as you test on them in relation to trends, ideas, other events. One of the simplest ways of doing this is to ask candidates to explain the connection between two items in juxtaposition, so:

> Explain the relationship between FOUR of the following pairs:
> 1) "Muckrakers" - : : - Theodore Roosevelt
> 2) National Banks - : : - Federal Reserve Banks
> 3) Russo-Japanese War - : : - Root-Takahira Agreement
> 4) "Dollar Diplomacy" - : : - Woodrow Wilson's speech at Mobile, October, 1913.
> 5) Payne-Aldrich Tariff - : : - Underwood-Simmons Tariff

This form can be used to test understanding of ideas, too. Here is another set, from a test on laissez-faire and socialism:

> 1) Ricardo's "iron law of wages" - : : - Marx's theory of "surplus value"
> 2) Paris Commune of 1871 - : : - Syndicalism
> 3) The "economic man" - : : - "the greatest good of the greatest number"

4) "The bourgeoisie are their - : : - Monopoly
own gravediggers."

5) "Religion is the opiate of - : : - Christian Socialism
the people,"

I have written elsewhere about this type of short question that it puts "emphasis on the generalizations which tie facts together, rather than on rote knowledge. Each (juxtaposition) is intended to produce a little essay, in which skill in written expression, judgment, and ingenuity count."

Essay questions take time to prepare, because so many factors must be considered—what the members of a class may be expected to know, what they may be expected to infer from their knowledge, the time allowance, clarity of the directions, and exact expression in the question itself. More often than not, one is unsatisfied, but occasionally a question somehow emerges which stimulates the well-prepared and thoughtful to do their best and at the same time penalizes the lazy and the glib. Such a question, more precious than fine gold, can be used year after year. One is this:

How far do you agree with this statement: "Louis XVI could have led the French Revolution."?

This always seems to produce some superior answers. Perhaps this is because to do well the student must begin by defining two terms, "Louis XVI" and "French Revolution." Do you mean by "Louis XVI" the man himself—timid, well-meaning, surrounded by contrary influences, the prisoner of Versailles, or do you mean someone else who might have held the position, a monarch with vision such as Queen Elizabeth or Henry IV? And what do you mean by "French Revolution"—simply the abolition of certain privileges, or the creation of a new order of society?

Incidentally, an excellent source of essay questions is the Advanced Placement Tests in American and European History, which may be obtained from the College Entrance Examination Board. While these are designed for superior students in college level courses, they suggest ideas which may be adapted for students of less maturity. The history examiners in the Advanced Placement Program have succeeded brilliantly in devising tests which excite students to put their best foot forward, to write with verve and style.

While essay questions generally involve exposition or argument, they can also be used to excite the imagination. This can sometimes be accomplished by the "you were there" type of question. Among the first and best of these in my little treasure trove was one used for several years in an eighth grade class in ancient history:

Assume yourself an Athenian peasant living at the time of Solon. Explain in your own words the effects of the introduction of money, and then of the Solonian reforms, on your life.

This type of question has special virtues when students can read contemporary documents in preparing for it. For instance, those given the question, "Assume yourself to be someone living in 1932, and explain how you would vote," were advised to browse through magazines of the period in order to get some feeling of a time almost as alien to them as the American Revolution. It also seems important that such a question be written in class, within a fixed amount of time. Limited to a single class period, knowing that they must finish somehow, they tend to lose their inhibitions. Sometimes they manage brilliantly. Note how quickly the status of the narrator and the historical setting are sketched in the opening paragraphs of three answers to this question on the 1932 election:

> "Here I am slapping flies on the Capitol steps and sweating with a coupla thousand other guys in the same boat. We came here, us vets, 'cause we didn't know how else to get action. An' we ain't feeling too good about anything right now in the middle of July 19 and 32, and we ain't gonna feel any better if old man Hoover tries to kick us outta town the way they say he's gonna do. . . .". . . . .

> "So you ask me how I'm going to vote this year? Well, I'll tell you, but first you ought to know about me, so I can explain my choice better. I used to work in a factory in Detroit up to a year ago. The plant used to produce auto parts, but it closed down. The big auto plants closed down too. Now I barely got a job. I got a wife and two kids to support, too. Now I'm working for that banker's wife, Mrs. Couzens, as a gardener. It's a lousy job, but it pays $15 a week. . . ."

> 18 Beekman Place,
> New York City,
> October 7, 1932

> Dear Nicky,
> Don't they teach you history at Groton any more? You asked some very foolish questions in your last letter. Of *course* your mother and I shall vote for Mr. Hoover this November. Mr. Hoover represents the Republican party, the party to which your family has always belonged and which acts in your family's interest. With God's help I think Mr. Hoover is perfectly competent to deliver the nation from its present difficulties.
> Franklin Roosevelt *used* to be a gentleman. I graduated when he was in the Fourth Form, and I remember him as a rather handsome boy, quite a good sailor. . . .

In these "you were there" questions, there often emerges some student of previously unsuspected talents who catches fire. Conversely that class of student often classed as "good"—the academic spigot who dutifully opens the cock and pours back what is poured in—often does poorly.

In writing this article I have had the sobering experience of going over scores of old tests and being shocked at the shortcomings of many of them. Sometimes too much was packed in, so that the question resembled that mock debate subject once propounded in the Cambridge Union:

> *Resolved:* That this house, while approving the attitude of the First Lord of the Admiralty toward greyhound racing, supports a policy of unilateral disarmament, and believes that the salvation of the drama lies with the Liberal Party.

Sometimes I was guilty of the very sin I decried early in this article, that of asking students to hand back an argument: "Why is it natural that there should be more sympathy in the United States today for Moslem Pakistan than for Hindu India?" Often the wording was fuzzy or misleading. But such errors may be inevitable, because the fabrication of essay questions is an act of creation, and one's creative powers are seldom at a peak.

A final caution. Since essay questions are designed to induce acts of creation on the part of the pupil, he will vary in the quality of his responses —he will "hit" a question one week and flub it the next. This must be accepted as a fact of life. If your principal aim is uniformity, you will use objective tests. But if you think it vital to train the student to write—and to think—you will give nothing but carefully framed essay tests, and hope that the average of many grades will somehow be a just measure of his achievement.

PAUL L. HANNA

Professor of Social Sciences, University of Florida

71. Improving Classroom Testing: Suggestions from the 1965 NCSS Yearbook*

In reviewing the 1965 Yearbook[1] of the National Council for the Social Studies in search of practical solutions for improving classroom achievement tests, I was struck by the emphasis which author after author placed upon the essentiality of adequate planning.

First, planning necessitates the allocation of sufficient time for designing and constructing the test—and sufficient time means a great deal of time. Thinking through objectives, composing (or even selecting) appropriate test items, assembling a proper number and balance of items into a draft instrument, reviewing the test, and putting it into final form are enormously time-consuming activities.

Second, planning involves a conscious determination of purpose—first in terms of the intended use of the test and then, but not less important, in terms of what is to be tested. The characteristics of tests intended for diagnosis, for measurement of growth, and for ranking students may be quite different but, without clear identification of intended use, the appropriate characteristics are not likely to be attained. Furthermore, a test, if it is to provide meaningful data, must offer evidence concerning some identifiable student behavior. This behavior in the social sciences will have two dimensions—one with reference to some body of subject matter, the other with reference to kinds of learning, to the possession, for example, of knowledge of facts or sources, of understandings, of intellectual skills, or of critical-thinking abilities. A good test must have validity (i.e., relevance to its intended purpose); and reliability (i.e., dependability in the sense that it does a good and consistent job of measurement). Obviously a test is unlikely to possess either of these qualities unless purposes have been thought through and defined in operational terms by the test maker.

Third, planning includes an evaluation of the intended takers of the test. Vocabulary employed and difficulty of items used must be appro-

Social Education, XXX:321–24, May 1966. Used by permission.
[1] Harry D. Berg, ed., *Evaluation in Social Studies*, 35th Yearbook (Washington, D.C.: National Council for the Social Studies, 1965).

priate to the students to be tested. An ideally good achievement test should give the best student an opportunity to demonstrate his superior attainment and allow the poorest student to accomplish something, yet to rank himself properly at the foot of the group. These things can occur only if the test is consciously adjusted to the capacity of its takers.

In addition to the emphasis on adequate planning, the Yearbook suggests strongly the desirability of exploiting the respective strengths of essay tests and objective tests by using both in the total testing program. The essay form offers the possibility of measuring qualities which are necessary attributes of the historian and the social scientist—knowledge, understandings, and skills possessed in depth, the ability independently to organize material, and the capacity to communicate effectively in writing. The objective form can provide wider sampling, establish more nearly identical tasks as a basis for accurate ranking of students, and permit more uniform and impersonal grading.

Robert J. Solomon in his chapter on the essay test offers specific suggestions for the construction of essay examinations. He warns against the habitual use of the essay form to test the recall of memorized generalizations. If these are to be tested at all, the objective form can generally do the job better. So that the essay test may be an acceptable measuing device, Mr. Solomon urged, first, conscious structuring of the individual questions and of the whole test to provide a range of tasks as nearly as possible the same for every taker and, second, extreme care in grading. In essay tests, avoid the overworked direction, "discuss." Be specific; ask the students to list, define, illustrate, explain, defend, compare, differentiate, outline, or summarize. Mr. Solomon also argues that there should be no choice permitted in the items to be answered. He points out that teachers seldom have evidence that alternative questions are of equal difficulty and that students are often incapable of determining for themselves on what items they will perform most creditably. Allowing students a choice of items really means presenting them with different tests. The grading of essay examinations should ideally involve (1) drafting model answers in advance to check on the clarity of the questions, the difficulty of the expected answers, and the time it will take to respond; (2) reading a random sample of answers to check the level of responses and the presence of widespread unexpected interpretations; (3) attempting to avoid identifying papers with their authors; (4) grading question by question rather than paper by paper; (5) grading different questions in different sequences; and (6) periodically rechecking papers graded earlier to see that standards have not shifted during the grading process.

Finally, students should be informed of the ground rules in testing— the time available for the test, the weighting of various items, and whether spelling, grammar, and composition will be evaluated along with social science content.

Specific suggestions for the preparation of objective tests are to be found principally in Harry Berg's chapter on the objective test item and in my chapter on planning, assembling, and administering the objective test, but Henry Dyer's chapter on educational measurement, Hymen Chausow's on evaluation in critical thinking, Maxine Dunfee's on evaluation in the elementary school, and Robert Ebel's on using the results of measurement should not be ignored.

At the outset, it is important to recognize that the objective examination, while highly suitable for the testing of information recall, is by no means limited to this task. Incidentally, when recall is tested, it should be the recall of significant information and broad concepts. The objective test, when properly constructed, can test for understandings, for skills, and for critical-thinking abilities. It can do this through the translation of knowledge into unfamiliar terms, the structuring of problem situations, and the presentation for interpretation of new material in the form of quotations, tables, graphs, maps, etc. Objective items may ask for identification of common elements: for causes, results, conclusions, illustrations, and examples; for the essential as distinguished from the incidental; for the central idea; for assumptions and implications; for the impartiality, relevance, and adequacy of facts in support of a generalization or conclusion; and for the difference between fact and opinion.

The form of objective items to be employed is of far less concern than the content of the items. There is much to be said, however, in favor of the four-response or five-response, multiple-choice form. It is highly flexible in that it can be used either for discrete, self-contained items or for groups of related items dependent upon quoted material. It also lends itself to use either in tests which seek the one "right" answer (often employed with factual material) or in those which seek the "best" answer (highly useful in dealing with understandings and skills).

To assure that the advantage of the objective test in setting the same task for all is really achieved, great care should be taken in the composition of the test items. Clarity and conciseness must be the watchwords. All responses (not merely the first) should follow logically and grammatically from the stem. Responses should parallel one another in phrasing and should, in general be of about the same length. "None of the above" may be an acceptable response when it makes a pertinent point. It cannot logically be used, however, with the "best answer" type of item. Also it should not be used when other choices have already exhausted all *possible* alternatives. "All the above" may have the weakness of providing a clue to students who recognize that two of the other responses are true and, therefore, correctly choose the "all" answer even when they do not know that the remaining one or two answers are correct. This disadvantage can be obviated by specifying alternative combinations such as "1 and 2 above but not 3," "2 and 3 above, but not 1"—or by presenting a series of labeled items in the stem (a, b, c, etc.) and offering varied combinations of these items in the responses.

To be as sure as possible that objective items are testing what the maker intends them to test, all items should be checked for unintended clues such as the use of specific determiners like "never" or "always" in wrong answers, the repetition of key words from the stem in the correct, but only in the correct, response, uniqueness of the correct response while the wrong answers are mere variations of the same idea, over specificity and length in the correct response, and interlocking items in which the stem of one reveals the correct answer of another. Another way in which objective items may go astray and fail to test what is intended is through the presence of nonfunctioning content. Avoid introductory statements which contain intrinsically significant material but which are in fact unnecessary in answering the item in which they appear. Avoid giving so much information in the responses that different test takers may arrive at the correct answers on the basis of different kinds or levels of information or skill. Unless care is exercised, the laudable effort to make items more thought provoking may merely load them with nonfunctioning content and make them *appear* to test things which they really do not test.

Objective items should be recorded in such a way that they can be stored conveniently, filed by category for easy recovery, readily arranged and rearranged in the creation of a test, and broken up for re-use in a new context. These desiderata can be attained by the use of index cards. It is well to double space typed cards and to leave a place at the top of the card for category code, dates of use, and difficulty and discrimination data if these are calculated.

In the actual assembling of an objective test a number of matters should receive consideration.

First, the length of the test should be established. For achievement tests the objective should be to allow every student to consider every item. Since, if there is a wide range of ability and reading speed in the class, this may be impossible to attain and still not have some students finish far too soon, it is acceptable to adjust the length of the test so that between 80 and 90 percent of the takers will complete it.

Second, the difficulty level of the test should be considered. A good test should provide a wide range of difficulty in its items. Theoretically, the mean attained score should be near the middle of the available score range. In practice, when new items are being employed, the classroom teacher can do little more than use his best judgment, trying to avoid items which are patently too easy or too difficult for his students, classifying apparently acceptable items as "difficult," "moderate," or "easy," and placing on his test about an equal number of items from each of these three categories. The difficulty of items which have appeared on a test can be calculated and this information can be recorded for later use.

Third, the discriminating power of items must receive attention. Desirable items for a test are those which properly differentiate students who possess the traits being tested from those who do not. Unfortunately, the only practicable way to check the discriminating power of items is to use them on a test and to analyze their effectiveness. Even worse, the only easily available criterion against which to check these items is the total examination of which they are a part. The classroom teacher, therefore, must again rely in the first instance upon subjective judgment in selecting items that *appear* to be relevant to his test's defined purpose and that *seem* likely to discriminate well. He can, however, weed out from future use items which function poorly. This can be done by calculating a crude index of discrimination by methods suggested in chapters 9 and 10 of the yearbook.

In planning and assembling an objective examination, it is good practice to employ a two-way table of test specifications to assure that the intended coverage of the test in terms of subject matter and student behaviors is adhered to in execution. Examples of such tables appear in chapters 2 and 9 of the Yearbook. The first draft of a test should contain about 10 percent more items than the final test, so that weak or unsatisfactory items may be withdrawn in the course of revision and review without necessitating the writing or selection of new items at the last moment. Items may be assembled at random, in order of increasing difficulty, or in terms of some logical arrangement by subject matter. An effort to arrange a classroom test in order of item difficulty is likely to be frustrated by the inadequacy of data available. If the test is to be used by the students for review and study, the order of subject matter often appears more desirable.

Once the test is assembled, it should be carefully read as a whole to detect clues arising from context, and a key should be made by actually taking the test. This key ought to be checked against the original keying of the items, and discrepancies should be accounted for and reconciled. In the final key, avoid patterned answers in which one position is habitually favored, long consecutive runs of the correct response in the same position, and the consistent use of the same position for the right answer. Finally, other qualified persons—as many as possible—should review the examination, reading it critically and keying it independently. If this is impossible, the test should be laid aside for a time and then reviewed by the maker, who should approach it so far as possible as if it were someone else's creation.

An objective test should be designed and duplicated in such a way that each student may have a clear and conveniently arranged copy. Adequate directions should appear at the beginning of the test, and the system of designating items and labeling responses should be unambiguous. There should be adequate indication of where and how answers are to be recorded. Meticulous proof reading of mimeograph stencils or ditto trial sheets is essential.

The grading of objective tests seems to raise fewer problems than the grading of essay examinations, since it can be done by machine if appropriate answer sheets are used, or almost mechanically by the teacher, a clerk, or by students. Yet certain problems do arise. One pertains to the weighting of items, another to the applying of a penalty for guessing. Concerning the first, the effect of item weighting can be gained, without the complexities in scoring which this causes, by varying the number of items dealing with various behavior traits or subject matter areas. Concerning the second, the possibility of chance success on a five-response, multiple-choice item is small and, if everyone attempts all items, the application or nonapplication of a correction formula makes virtually no change in the rank order of test takers. It appears, therefore, that the ease of grading achieved by ignoring guessing and scoring simply the number of items right justifies this procedure.

Dr. Ebel suggests in the Yearbook that for an objective test there should be prepared a frequency distribution of scores, that the mean of the distribution and the standard deviation should be calculated, that letter grades might be assigned, that the reliability and the standard error of the scores should be calculated, and that all these data should be reported and explained to the pupils. In the best of all possible worlds, where classroom teachers and their pupils had taken college courses in tests and measurements, this would certainly be helpful in creating better tests and making the testing process more meaningful and useful to students. In this imperfect world, I doubt its practicality.

There are, then, some suggestions in the 1965 Yearbook that most classroom teachers will probably not think it feasible to follow. There are many suggestions, however, which are realistic for the use of the classroom teacher in dealing with the ever present and often frustrating task of effective teaching.

part **III**

What Next?

IIIA. Emerging Developments and Suggestions for Change

Teaching and learning are tasks which never end. If the teacher is to be a true professional, he must continue to broaden both his intellectual and his educational horizons throughout his teaching career. Intellectually, he must seek a broader and deeper understanding of the nature and procedures of the social sciences—what questions do they ask, what problems do they face, what methods do they use, what answers do they seek? He must establish a lifetime quest for knowledge as well as for a more thorough understanding of himself and of others. Most important, he must attempt to synthesize what he knows and what he learns into a social theory which helps him explain the world in which he lives.

Pedagogically, he must seek more effective ways of planning and organizing the materials he has to teach and must search for more interesting and vital materials with which to involve students. He must continually try to individualize his instruction so as to maximize the learning of his widely varying types of students. He must try to raise the level of what he emphasizes so that students may develop to their maximum potential. Above all, he needs to evaluate, and reevaluate, what he has taught so as to determine whether or not his students have actually learned what he originally intended them to learn.

All the signs of our time indicate that change and the clash of new developments and new viewpoints with accepted positions will accelerate in the years ahead. It is likely that old answers will be found less satisfactory with each passing decade. In such eras the teacher must actually struggle to keep abreast of happenings if he is to fulfill his challenging role in the most timely fashion.

Under these conditions, then, what specific things can the social studies teacher do in order to maintain and improve his effectiveness in the classroom?

1. He can continue his education. The nature of the social studies curriculum and the teaching assignments in most secondary schools do not allow him to specialize in any one social science discipline. Hence, he needs to broaden his general education in all of the social sciences, as well as the natural sciences and the humanities. He needs to know as much as he can about art, architecture, literature, and philosophy. He also needs to maintain and develop his interest in current affairs, subscribing to as varied a number of periodicals and newspapers as his time and budget will permit. Above all, he must read books—as widely, as rapidly, and as frequently as possible. The social studies teacher can never know "too much."

2. He can grow professionally by increasing his awareness of his profession and the problems it faces. Attendance at local, state, and national conventions of the social studies can help him upgrade his teaching skills. He should participate in workshops, institutes, and other meetings, so as to deepen his ability as a teacher. He may participate in testing the exciting, new-curriculum projects and the striking media now appearing. It is hoped that he will develop the qualities and contacts necessary for cooperation in needed research in his own school and district. He should explore the nature and activities of other organizations which exist to assist and to serve his needs and to promote educational purposes.

3. He can keep informed of recent developments through the literature of his profession. Such journals as *Social Education, The Social Studies, The Journal of Geography, Phi Delta Kappan, The Clearing House,* and others provide information and arguments concerning the role of the school and of the social studies in society. Along with the books in his field, readings such as these will help him decide how the social studies curriculum can meet the problems of the age and will also provide him with specialized suggestions as to new tools and techniques available to improve the quality of his instruction.

Most important, the social studies teacher should strive continually to improve his effectiveness as a catalyst and as a communicator in and out of the classroom. To accomplish this he must continue to grow as a human being—to travel widely, to broaden his areas of knowledge, to seek to meet and to understand as many different peoples as possible, to remain active professionally, and to make a lifetime task of improvement.

As you conclude this book, reflect upon these queries: Which areas of further development merit my initial attention, and why? In what ways can I best join with my colleagues in the evolution of a truly new social studies? What are the steps I should take in a program of personal growth that will lead most directly to my being in reality a master teacher of the social studies?

CHARLES R. KELLER

Teacher and Scholar-in-Residence, Fairfield and Greenwich Schools, Connecticut

72. History and Social Sciences: Reflections and Recommendations*

I have said many times that of all subjects the social studies are most in the doldrums. Mathematics, science, the foreign languages, and English—here there are at the national level significant stirrings. Not so the social studies, though a few individual schools are involved in some interesting thinking and action, especially in regards to Advanced Placement work.

But in this article I stress neither the doldrums nor the motion, although I certainly believe that nothing is as yet going on in our area comparable to developments in other subjects. We badly need a "New History" as well as a "New Mathematics." My aim is to discuss with you some ideas for improving history and the social studies in schools and colleges. I am simply making suggestions, I am not laying down "the gospel according to St. Charles," I am not dictating.

I begin by advocating once again the elimination of the term "social studies" and the substitution of the term "history and the social sciences." I do not seek to argue the point. It just seems to me that "history and the social sciences" is a more exact and hence a more meaningful term. I know that many secondary school teachers think as I do, and I am convinced that there will be the desired cooperation between school and college teachers only on the basis of "history and the social sciences."

Then I suggest that we ask the really basic question: What is it that we want history and the social sciences to do in the educational process? In answering this question we should not claim too much as I think we have in the past. The social studies program approved by the executive committee of the National Association of Secondary-School Principals, for instance, contains the following statement, "Young people who have a rich background in social studies are able to recognize the struggle for freedom when it occurs and to detect, appraise, and overcome the enemies of freedom in whatever guise they appear." Such exaggerated claims harm both the schools and the subjects.

Journal of Secondary Education, 37:263–70, May 1962. Used by permission.

History and the social sciences are subjects with disciplines. What should be their role? I have rethought the question, but I still give the answer which appeared in my article in the September 16, 1961, issue of *The Saturday Review*.

1. To acquaint students with certain facts. There is no other way to deal with these subjects. But not *all* facts and not *only* facts.

2. To give students' minds the particular kind of development which these subjects provide, moving ahead in a sequential manner from course to course. In courses we must stress not only the "what" but also the "why" and the "what of it."

3. To help students understand the past, so that they will realize where mankind has come from, what men's struggles have been, how and why they have done what they have done. Here are roots; here is identification with the past.

4. There are the present and the future too. What are the economic problems, the political problems, the international problems, the social problems? How shall we look at them, where have they come from, what shall we do about them?

5. We live in the United States and have a peculiar obligation to know as much as we can, in no chauvinistic way, about our own country, its past and its present. We live in the world. We must know other countries, their pasts and their presents.

6. We must know men and their roles, forces and their roles, and change which is always with us.

7. We must know the places where men live and move and have their being.

You will notice that I have said nothing about making good citizens or creating democratic attitudes. I assure you that I am for both good citizenship and democracy. But we should rid ourselves of the idea that history and the social sciences have the job of making good citizens. Do any of us really know how to make good citizens? To the extent that we do, all subjects, the home, the church, society, the individuals themselves, and other factors are involved.

And democratic attitudes? I want students to know how American democracy got started, how it has fared through the years, where it stands today. Students should be acquainted with democracy elsewhere in the world, and with governmental forms which are the antithesis of democracy. They should know how our government functions and how other governments function.

Students should develop an enthusiasm, based on reason, for democracy and what it stands for: the individual with rights and duties. They should acquire knowledge of political parties and procedures and obtain information that they will need as future voters. Democracy means responsibilities and duties as well as rights and privileges. We do less talking about the former than we should. Democracy should be something of an absolute in a country where pragmatism is the prevailing philosophy.

Here is the essence of democracy which can and should be taught in courses in history and the social sciences. But attitudes cannot and should not be taught in formal classroom situations. We weaken education when we try to do so. What students should do in schools is to study subjects and become acquainted with facts and ideas. They should learn how to think and to understand. Subjects as such have disciplines which will develop students' minds. Students should learn how to distinguish the relevant from the irrelevant, how to weigh evidence and come to their own conclusions. Then they will develop attitudes for themselves; then hopefully they will become good citizens.

Let us now move on to another question: What can we do to enable students—and remember that I am not limiting myself to students in grades 9–12—to derive greater benefits from, and to enjoy more than they do, the study of history and the social sciences? I shall have several parts to my answer to this question. I shall begin with concepts and the structure of the subjects included in history and the social sciences. Here, I believe, is the essence of the "New History."

For some time I have been bothered by the fact-by-fact approach to history, by the realization that although much was taught to many students, much was forgotten by most of them and too little was retained. In the new mathematics and the new science, I observed, the conceptual approach was employed. Instead of just learning things and then reaching into their memories when the time came to use what they had learned, students were introduced to basic concepts and were then given opportunities to figure out things for themselves. Exciting things were happening in mathematics and science. Why not in history and the social sciences?

Then I read Jerome Bruner's *The Process of Education*, a little book published in 1960 and based on the proceedings of a conference held at Woods Hole on Cape Cod in September, 1959. The conference was concerned with the improvement of science education in the elementary and secondary schools and was attended mostly by scientists, mathematicians, and psychologists. Two historians sat in. I shall not probe too deeply into the conference or Bruner's book. Important is the emphasis put on "giving students an understanding of the fundamental structure of whatever subjects we choose to teach." I shall not be happy until we begin to get at the structure of history and the social sciences and not just the facts and techniques. We must stress fundamentals, believing with Bruner that "understanding fundamentals makes a subject more comprehensible."

I paused long over statements like the following in Bruner's book:

> We begin with the hypothesis that any subject can be taught effectively
> in some intellectually honest form to any child at any age of develop-

ment. . . . [If this hypothesis is true] then it should follow that a curriculum ought to be built around the great issues, principles, and values that a society deems worthy of the continual concern of its members.

Grasping the structure of a subject is understanding it in a way that permits other things to be related to it meaningfully. To learn structure, in short, is to learn how things are related.

Organizing facts in terms of principles from which they may be inferred is the only known way of reducing the quick rate of loss of human memory.

If earlier learning is to render later learning easier, it must do so by providing a general picture in terms of which the relations between things encountered earlier and later are made as clear as possible.

Students should grasp the fundamental concept, for instance, that revolutions are the result of events within the country, events abroad, ideas current at the time, and the effects of these events and ideas on certain people at a certain time, and apply this concept to the American Revolution. They will then understand this Revolution better than if they simply study in a fact-by-fact manner the events leading to the Revolution. Once the basic concept, mentioned by Bruner, that a nation must trade to live, is understood, various eras in American history will be studied quite differently from the way in which they are studied today.

In the recently published "Summary of the Report of the National Task Force on Economic Education" is a section entitled, "Importance of Analytical Concepts and Institutions." I like this statement: "What is needed is an understanding of a few essential concepts and a few major institutions (such as the market place, supply and demand, the corporation, labor unions, profit, wages, and the like), plus an understanding of how these fit together in the functioning of our economy." At the end of each major section of the full report is a brief list of the major concepts and institutions which are considered essential and accessible to high school students.

At present, to too great an extent, we first attempt to fill the minds of students and later we teach them to think, to analyze, to interpret. I suggest that we begin by deciding what concepts we want students to know and by relating just enough facts to the concepts to enable the minds of young people to develop and that later on we help these young people to fill their own minds intelligently and effectively.

It must be very clear that our present textbooks will not do, that in history and the social sciences there must be new materials—just as new materials became essential to mathematics and science. Current textbooks take the fact-by-fact approach. They *tell* students things, with now and again some interpretation. They do not show students how the author got his facts or arrived at his conclusions. Nor do most teachers do this. Students of science have laboratories where they learn how scientists work. We need to develop something similar to laboratories in history and the social sciences so that students may handle the elements and the compounds and the acids of these subjects and see how history and the social sciences are put together. Education in these fields should be inquiry and discovery, not regurgitation as it too often is.

It must be very clear, too, that we must rethink the whole process of teacher education and that we must provide opportunities for present teachers to learn the new approaches, to become acquainted with the new interpretations, and to recharge their intellectual batteries. Good teaching by qualified, informed, enthusiastic teachers is the key to effective education.

"How is your course in American history?" I asked an eighth grader a short time ago. He turned up his nose and remarked wryly that he was doing over again what he had studied in the fifth grade. He was bored by the repetition. Incidentally, he was not bored in mathematics, for he was studying modern algebra in the eighth grade. I refrained from telling him that unless he is lucky he will do American history over again in the eleventh grade and then in college. But he will—unless we do something about it—and fast. We must give up our all-too-common cyclical arrangement of courses and substitute for it a sequential arrangement, with tenth grade readings, subjects, discussions, and tests, for instance, consciously made more demanding and more mature than those of the ninth grade. We have done little to develop sequential thinking and procedure in history and the social sciences. The order in which courses are given makes a difference. We must improve articulation in an area where articulation has been poor and duplication excessive.

Students have been bothered by the fact that we try to cover too much in our courses and classes. We should have courses post-holed for depth, with a few things selected and covered well. Teachers must realize that some of the best teaching is done before a course ever begins, when the teacher decides what to include and what to omit. Essential are the "courage to exclude" and the "imagination to include."

I have now had something to say about concepts and the structure of subjects, new materials, and teacher education, learning how historians and social scientists work, the need for sequential arrangements in history and the social sciences, and for post-holing. I now comment on curriculum planning and suggest courses.

Let me say first that curriculum planning must be at least kindergarten-through-grade-twelve, preferably kindergarten-through-college, for some students even kindergarten-through-graduate school. We must stop the segmentation of education which is too much with us. It did Gaul no good to be divided into three parts; it does education no good to be divided into five parts—or four parts—elementary schools, junior high schools, senior high schools, colleges, graduate schools—with the quintet meeting— not never but hardly ever. A school system has control over twelve grades. Since a few more than 50 percent of our high school graduates continue their education, many of them in four-year colleges, the schools and the colleges should become involved in overall, vertical planning which will wring much water out of "watered education."

I now suggest a set of courses for schools—with some suggestions for colleges. History and the social sciences should begin in the fifth grade. In the earlier grades the emphasis should be on reading, writing, viewing, listening, elementary science and mathematics, music, art, and whatever good things now done in the social studies which help children get ready for the work of grade five. In this grade history and the social sciences can begin to be subjects with disciplines. My suggested course for grades five and six is concerned with men doing things in places—men in different parts of the world and at different times. Here is biography which is an important part of history, and geography in its broadest sense. I want to stress the concepts that men make history, and that time and place are important. This course, hopefully, will capture student interest through exciting action in exciting places.

Then in grades seven and eight would come the introduction of the formal study of history—American history with European backgrounds— with classes meeting three times a week, perhaps, instead of the conventional five. Education needs to be "demonotonized." It should be made clear that all classes do not have to meet five times a week. Somewhere early in the seventh grade the students should *write* history and not just *read* it. Give them material on the Constitutional Convention, for instance, and let them begin to learn how a historian works. And begin to learn, too, that history is not just something that happens in a book. I like American history with European backgrounds because in this way the concept can be developed that the country in which we live has always been in the world.

For grade nine a world history course, not a course that tries to cover everything but one really post-holed for depth. A post-holed world history course can be developed by selecting either certain periods—the fifth century B.C., the twelfth and thirteenth centuries A.D., the Enlightenment, Asia in the twentieth century, etc.—or certain countries or areas, and by studying them intensively. Wires may be strung between the posts by lectures or by readings.

There is much to be said for a continuation of world history in the tenth grade, but, after considerable thought and weighing of pros and cons, I support a course in "The Introduction to the Social Sciences," along the lines, perhaps, of the course now being developed in the Pittsburgh schools. I am a card-carrying historian, but I believe that students must know that there are the social sciences as well as history, that they need to become acquainted with some of the social science concepts—some have certainly been introduced before the tenth grade—and that they should learn how social scientists work. This course is needed in the tenth grade, it seems to me, so that students may do more mature and more meaningful work in the eleventh and twelfth grades.

In grade eleven comes an American history course in which all concepts previously introduced are put to work, which should be post-holed, which may be given a new dimension through the effective use of art and music, which may be an Advanced Placement course. Above all, it must not simply duplicate the seventh and eighth grade course.

And in grade twelve electives. I am thinking of both students and faculty members, of making the final year of high school especially exciting for students, and of giving special opportunities—real morale builders—to teachers. The electives in a school should be chosen according to the number and quality of the students and the interests and ability of faculty members. Here are possibilities: Advanced Placement work in American or European history; term courses in Far Eastern, Russian, or African history; international relations; government, economics, or problems of democracy; or an interdisciplinary humanities course or a course in philosophy—logic for instance—for some students. I have often said that I will not be happy until Plato and Socrates go to high school.

This curriculum is planned vertically. It should be kept flexible so that it will fit the nongraded elementary and secondary schools which already exist and will soon increase in number. By this arrangement of courses the cyclical pattern is voided and the desired sequential element is obtained. All courses should have significant and challenging content; they should be as library-centered as possible. It is hoped that they will capture and retain student interest. Students should have good readings—stirring, exciting books, documents and other source materials, rather than mainly textbooks. I have already mentioned the need for new materials.

There should be change of pace in a course; all assignments should not be the same. Students should do as much independent work as possible, as early as possible. I like classes in which half the students meet on Mondays and Wednesdays, half on Tuesdays and Thursdays, and all together on Fridays. The emphasis should be on learning rather than on teaching, and on analysis, critical and creative thinking, and interpretation. The hope is that students will not just learn facts but will become acquainted with concepts and skilled in ways of thinking which will help them to analyze and come to grips effectively with the new, complex, and difficult situations which they will constantly be facing. The hope is that students will say to teachers, as one group of twelfth graders did to a teacher last June, "We thank you for allowing us to let ourselves go intellectually."

The college curriculum in history and the social sciences—there is no social studies here—needs rethinking and replanning, with looks to the schools and to the graduate schools. Perhaps a new Advanced Placement Program is needed involving colleges and graduate schools, with the colleges doing graduate-school-level work which the graduate schools will recognize with credit and placement.

We need action, intelligent action now—in history and the social sciences—from kindergarten through graduate school. It will take valiant efforts on the part of teachers and administrators—from elementary schools, secondary schools, colleges, and graduate schools. And these efforts will be more valiant—and hopefully successful—if we remember a statement made by Ralph Waldo Emerson: "Every revolution was once a thought in one man's mind, . . . every reform was once a private opinion." And if we agree with William James who once wrote, "If things are ever to move forward, someone must be ready to take the first step and assume the risk of it."

EDGAR BRUCE WESLEY

Emeritus Professor of Education, University of Minnesota

73. Let's Abolish History Courses *

HISTORY AS A COMPILATION

The *World Almanac* is a wonderful compilation. It contains data of various kinds, facts unnumbered, names, figures, tables, lists, and oddities. Whatever one wants to know, he turns hopefully to this inspired book and is seldom disappointed. Every teacher should use it, cite it, and direct students in discovering its potential. A course in the *World Almanac* would no doubt be interesting and unique, but it is scarcely necessary. The book has no structure, generalizations, complications, or conclusions that puzzle the human mind.

The dictionary is a wonderful compilation. It provides words, synonyms, phrases, examples, ideas, limitless information, and unbounded entertainment. Valuable and useful as is the dictionary, a formal course in it is quite unnecessary. By demonstration, explanation, and guidance, the teacher can induce the student to secure the major values of the dictionary. It is a storehouse from which to draw rather than a structure or system that requires study.

An encyclopedia is a wonderful compilation. It contains an inexhaustible store of tried and tested statements, a bottomless reservoir of information, and amazing summations of human knowledge. It is a reliable and stimulating guide to further quests. Every teacher should recommend it and entice students to do likewise, but one needs no formal course in order to use and appreciate its contents. A course in the encyclopedia would be an absurdity.

History is a wonderful compilation. It abounds with useful facts, information, knowledge, and wisdom; it is society's memory, the fulcrum of progress, the sovereign's guide. It is nearly impossible to overstate its social utility, its guidance function, its dramatic appeal, its value as entertainment, and its service as a molder of citizens and soldiers. Every teacher and every student should see, utilize, and appreciate this fund of human achievement, this colossal storehouse, this communicable heritage. No teacher at any grade level, however, should teach a course in history as content. To do so is as confusing, unnecessary, frustrating, futile,

Phi Delta Kappan, XLIX:3–8, September 1967. Used by permission.

pointless, and as illogical as to teach a course in the *World Almanac,* the dictionary, or the encyclopedia. The content of history is to be utilized and exploited—not studied, learned, or memorized.

THE COMPLEXITY OF HISTORY

History is complex and many-sided, ranging from the simplicity of a story that appeals to children to the profundity of an analysis of the parliamentary system. History is past politics, past economics, past sociology, past geography, past anthropology, and past current events. Being the past of everything, it has no vocabulary of its own.[1] All its words are appropriated from other subjects and fields. Being a conglomeration and not an entity, history has and can have no standards that can be described or established. The much-publicized advanced placement program in history proves that any reasonably normal student can learn any kind of history at any grade level in school or college. There are no difficulties or standards. Being only the backward projection of other studies, fields, and areas, history can have no structure, no organization of its own, except a loose and interruptible sequence. History is an echo which can never be faithfully reheard; it is a miscellaneous collection of varying value; it is an unlimited and unbounded chaos. It can be used and exploited, but it cannot be successfully taught or studied as content to be learned.

Continuity, one of the shibboleths of the historian, has only a mythical existence. It is an asserted entity, not an actuality. It grew out of the alleged need to strengthen the record and was not deduced from sources. History provides significant chains of causal sequences but no unbroken continuity. Life and history are alike in consisting of dizzy thrusts forward and sudden sidewise diversions. A whole century is gone from the history of the Roman Republic and the four centuries of the Dark Ages rest in comparative obscurity. Students do not mind the loss of a decade now and then or even a whole century. Seldom does an autobiography have continuity, nor is such unbroken recording necessary or desirable. Yet there is enough continuity in societal living to justify the historian in denying the sharp divisions between ancient and medieval history, between medieval and modern, and between other eras, periods, epochs, and ages.

After centuries of moralizing, the consensus of historians now is that history teaches no lessons for princes or citizens, that it has no laws, generalizations, interpretations or conclusions such as Plutarch and subsequent moralizers proclaimed. History has little guidance value for governments or citizens and no value whatever as a predictor of the

---

[1] Some dead political terms, such as *archon, quaestor,* and *reeve,* and some words connected with feudalism, may be regarded as the peculiar property of history.

future. It speaks like an oracle out of both sides of its mouth at the same time. Sadly enough, some of these summary statements about history run counter to popular beliefs and wishes. They tend to minimize the clear-cut values of history that the public has long accepted. The true nature of history provides one more broken illusion. Even as adults we sometimes wish there had been or will be a golden age.

Thus we see that history is not a simple unadorned tale, no McGuffey formula for national greatness, no easy story on which lawmakers, psychologists, historians, parents, teachers, and pupils can readily agree. Being a mass of materials and documents that requires infinite rework-ing, it really is not very well adapted to children. Since popular demands, prevailing tradition, and extant laws require that simple, condensed, abstract, and sketchy précis be prepared for the schools, the historians and educators have done their best to bridge the yawning gap between the complexities of history and the multiplicities of our moral and civic needs. In fact, these writers, with the generous and imaginative help of the pub-lishers, have done remarkably well. Indeed, some of the charmingly written and tastefully illustrated books almost convince one temporarily that there should be a course in history.

HISTORY AS COURSES AND RESOURCES

It is impossible to teach a course in history without implying that at least some of its content is to be learned or memorized and fed back to the prying instructor at the time of the inquest. Good teachers have long tried to escape from this situation, to evade the curse of content-to-be-learned. Such teachers have compiled lists of minimum dates, names, events; they have tried to identify the fundamental and separate it from the temporary, the permanent from the transitory. Their efforts have met with little understanding, support, or agreement. Curricular laws, patriotic celebrations, and civic traditions conspire to keep teachers from seeing the difference between history as content and history as resource.

The curse of learning content that wrecks courses in history and ob-scures the real values of the subject does not apply to any major extent in other subjects. The pupil sees the necessity of a rule in mathematics, a formula in chemistry, a category in English, a vocabulary in a foreign language. He sees their utility. When he uses the *World Almanac,* the dictionary, or the encyclopedia he does not burden his mind with the thought that he must bring back something in addition to that which he sought. But in history—what shall he do with this list of Roman emperors, this account of the Battle of Actium, the treaties that ended the inter-colonial wars, the names of the generals of the Civil War? They do not answer any question that he has asked, nor solve any problem that he has undertaken, nor further any quest upon which he has embarked. The better student slowly begins to perceive the differences among reading, learning, memorizing, understanding, and utilizing.

Evidence of the unpopularity of history as a school subject is abundant, prolonged, and overwhelming. Nearly a century ago William H. Mace, one of the early students of the teaching of history in America, commented upon the abominable teaching, the wretched results, the outcries and protests of rebellious students. Subsequent studies in goodly numbers have sustained Mace's findings and brought them up to date.

Let us recognize one of the greatest grievances of the student—memorizing. While memorizing names, dates, and events is a time-honored practice, the impossibility of remembering history has been demonstrated again and again, generation after generation. Even college professors of history take notes to class. The need for remembering history has never been established, and whatever need may once have existed has largely disappeared since the invention of printing and other handy methods of duplicating and recording.

Pupil dissatisfaction alone is scarcely sufficient evidence of the failure of history as a school subject, but when successive generations of students and teachers concur in reporting that the wrong kind of history is thrust upon the classes at the wrong grade level for the wrong reason and taught with the wrong kind of equipment in the wrong manner, it is time to lend attention if not credence to the protests and laments of pupils, teachers, supervisors, and divers kinds of observers. History content is a failure as a school subject.

The failure of history as a school subject is more, however, than a pedagogical failure; it is a societal failure. Obstinate students, unaccepted purposes, the absence of motivation, unsuitable materials, unprepared teachers, and dreary, dull, catalogic, inconsequential content all join in explaining in part history's unpopularity. It is probably, however, that the most serious and determinative reason for its failure is the insincere and fraudulent social purposes that force the subject into the curriculum. Every legislature in America believes that the taking of history courses will produce loyal patriots and law-abiding citizens. No proof that this is so has ever been adduced, but this lack of evidence has never deterred the lawmakers from passing a new requirement. The only logical conclusion that an honest, intelligent person can reach is that such laws require and compel the distortion of history in order to achieve its preordained results. In brief, society requires the teaching of history for the sake of inculcating obedience, docility, humility, patriotism, civic virtue, and other desired outcomes. History is merely the incidental means in which these debatable outcomes are embodied. As long as the student senses this duplicity of purpose he will resent history courses.

In this contest between pupils and society, the latter has, of course, the power and tradition to compel pupils at least to enroll in history courses. Since the public has neither the time, patience, humility, nor intelligence to listen to the pupils, the teacher, the educator, or the psychologist, it stubbornly persists in its policy of coercion and compulsion. Since the historians as a group are not interested in the problems of teaching and learning, they have not been seriously interested in grade placement, vocabulary difficulty, or the abstractness of the concepts. They insist that history be taught direct, undiluted, separate from other subjects. This elemental blunder is nearly as serious a handicap to teaching as the legally required hypocrisy.

But the pupil wins a temporary battle. He yawns disconcertingly and otherwise sabotages the course while picking up enough facts to placate the teacher. He also resolves never again to open a history book. That is, never again until as a parent, legislator, or school board member, having forgotten his experiences and forgiven his tormentors, he urges his child to study history and calls upon the schools to establish higher standards.

THE FACES OF HISTORY

Since history is an aggregate rather than an entity, an assemblage rather than an element, let us see how it appears to the four groups most directly concerned with its production, dissemination, and use. Let us look at the faces of history as they appear to 1) the student, 2) the teacher, 3) the historian, and 4) the public. This many-sided examination may help us to see the changing face of history, the changing needs of society, and possibly the need of changing the method and manner of teaching history.

The Student

The first face of history is the one seen in the schools. To pupils history appears to be a mixture of narration, description, and implied, if not always expressed, conclusions. Some of these foreordained conclusions, set up in the name of law, patriotism, national security, and civic virtue, do violence to logic, truth, and common sense. Touched now and then with color, sincerity, and appeal, school history is, however, generally catalogic, tedious, and irrelevant. Students learn slowly that they have to study history because the law, the school board, the administrators, the teachers, and the patriotic organizations say they must. Learning under duress has been repeatedly demonstrated to be wasteful, frustrating, and provocative of hostility and sullenness. The colorful pictures and the wonderful maps in the textbooks do not save the content from being dull and dry. School history fails because it is selected content set out to be learned for preordained purposes. Face one of history is not very appealing.

The Teacher

The second face of history is the one that the teachers see. Many teachers are, like the students, overwhelmed by multifarious facts and bewildering details. Too frequently, they do not know the difference between a significant, inclusive generalization and a routine item. But by far the grimmest visage that history presents to the teacher is its demand that he present the content appealingly, intelligibly, and successfully to the wayward, listless student. So he slowly and reluctantly discovers that his major task is not the handling of history content but the handling of the would-be consumers of history. In brief, he discovers the humiliating fact that he has to teach students and not just history. Hence he seeks to discover or invent devices, tricks, mnemonics, puzzles, games, and methods that will transform a succession of facts into intelligible patterns and meaningful sequences.

This aspect of the teacher's task has been made immeasurably harder by the scornful contempt with which method has long been regarded. In spite of the paramount obligation to try to enlist the interest of the students, the teacher, aided and abetted by college teachers of history, scorns and ridicules method. The humiliating delusion of the 1890's that the historians knew what history should be taught and at what grade level each course should be given has descended upon us again with all the vitality of error.

Accepting the great illusion that history can be taught straight, the teacher nevertheless sees the subject as dim, dreary, and dismal. Facts, facts, facts. Only the exceptional teacher knows more than the textbook contains. Rarely does the typical teacher read beyond the textbook, even more rarely does he attend a professional meeting, and rarest of all does he become a practicing historian. But unless he writes some history—local, minor, or trifling though it be—he cannot teach with any spark of reality or enthusiasm. Sadly enough, the history teacher is about as likely to discuss baseball, automobile racing, or fishing lore as he is to talk about some person, topic, or problem in history. While he is likely to be an improvement over his colleague of twenty years ago, he is still too often a drudge who wishes the history hour were over.

The history teacher knows that something is wrong, and now and then a teacher is perspicacious enough to discard names, episodes, events, epochs, and whole centuries, but he feels apologetic and seldom realizes that he has done an exceedingly intelligent thing. By and large, face two of history is not much of an improvement over face one.

The Historian

History's third face is the one turned toward the historian. Historians are divided and confused as to the purposes and functions of their subject. Some see it as a storehouse of precedents from which one can be drawn that will fit today's situation; some see it as a glorious record of great men, great events, great outcomes—glorious examples suitable for imitation and repetition; some see it as a woeful tale of greed, failure, disaster, and weakness studded with warning signs against repetition; some see it as a vista dome from which to view and plan the future; some see it as merely a harmless and sometimes interesting record to be read for entertainment or, as with King Ahasuerus, to cure insomnia. Historians are almost unanimous in their opposition to curricular laws concerning history, civics, constitutions, special celebrations, and school holidays, because the latter always destroy and defeat the purposes for which they were proclaimed. Historians generally favor the honest use of their subject to promote a reasoned patriotism and good citizenship.

For generations historians have fretted over the problem of what to write. Should they write the plain, unadorned facts or should they select, focus, color, conclude, and recommend? The scientific school led by Stubbs, Maitland, Ranke, and the majority of early American historians tried earnestly to tell the significant facts, believing and hoping that they thus attained truth. Thus the majority of historians for nearly a century tried manfully to be scientific, objective, impersonal, and disinterested. They tried at least feebly to understand and cooperate with the social scientists and to utilize new methods of research and inquiry.

Recently, however, there has been a veritable stampede of historians away from the rigid and exacting standards of the social sciences toward the easy, undefinable, sentimental humanities. This return to the wallows of philosophy, the banalities of the liberal arts, and the nebulosities of the humanities will lead, of course, to the lowering of historical standards. Historians will inevitably minimize facts and maximize interpretations. Such soft history will result in soft pedagogy.

The historians have done their subject a great disservice by seceding from the social sciences and returning to the humanities. This retreat was made in a nostalgic mood to get back to the womb of literature and because of the inability of most historians to grasp and utilize the findings of sociology and economics. A journey from science to sentiment is a lamentable loss to the cause of scholarship.

As a group, historians are realistic, enlightened, sophisticated, and semi-cynical. They seem to have more faith in their art than they have in the institutions they describe, more faith in the value of their writings than in the persons who perform the deeds that are recorded, more faith in history for school children, statesmen, and citizens than in its utility for teachers and historians. They are seldom interested in teaching, and so they have only scorn for the history of education. They loftily assume that scholarship conquers all—all psychological, pedagogical, and personal problems in teaching. In brief, however good they may be as historians they are generally only mediocre at their major work of teaching.

The Public

The fourth face of history is the only one that is assured, untroubled, unwrinkled, smiling. It has no doubts, no self-consciousness, no hesitation. It knows who and what it is and where and for what purposes it is going. It is the face that history presents to the public, and the public consists of parents, alumni, lawmakers, professionals, businessmen, laborers, patriots, and ex-students. Facing its public, history, like Ignorance in *Pilgrim's Progress,* comes bounding down the crooked little lane that emerges from the country of Conceit.

In the eyes of the public, history is filled with nationalistic vitamins; it is the galaxy of national heroes, the repository of national episodes, the concentrated image of our national greatness, the wide platform from which issue sacred documents, great speeches, and sound doctrines. History is the record of our national triumphs; it describes our great presidents and wise statesmen; it portrays successive generations of loyal patriots and fearless warriors; it provides the one-cure remedy, the one-shot weapon, and the one-pellet wisdom that our national impatience requires. History, our history, is to America what the Bible is to Christianity. Let it be required in all schools.

With faith abounding, the public proceeds to embody these assumed values into laws, holidays, ceremonies, oaths, and above all in courses in history—required courses, primarily American but also including state constitutions, state history, and local lore. History is offered and required, not once but three, four, or five times. The public is untroubled about substituting the narrative of American history for the purpose of good citizenship.

TEACHING HISTORY AS A RESOURCE

Since history has great and numerous societal functions and limitless potential for various purposes, and since no course in content is to be given at any grade level, how is the student and future citizen to discover and utilize these values? The answer is brief, clear, and specific: Change the curricular image of history as content to be learned to a resource to be utilized; change from courses to resources. Focus attention upon documents, old and new, public and private. Use extant textbooks for outside reading, for overall guidance, and for guaranteeing a sort of common basis from which all can start. Admit that history contains much debris as well as significant materials. Help the student to see that history is a kitchen midden and not a sacred temple. Present an endless number of topics, projects, problems, issues, themes, current events, local occurrences, and other undertakings that utilize and require the historical approach. In carrying our these undertakings the students will be learning facts, methods, and techniques. They will learn when to go where to find what.

If history is abolished as a course and topics, issues, and problems involving the use of history are substituted, will not many of the larger values of history be lost? What becomes of the long sweep of events that can be seen only in part in a topic? Will there be any continuity beyond a loose sort of sequence? Will the learner ever see time and chronology as a guiding path for understanding events? What becomes of the great laws, generalizations, and synthesizing interpretations that illuminate dark areas of confusion and misunderstanding?

These questions have merit. Merely to contradict them would not satisfy the critics. It should be pointed out, however, that many students who take courses in history do not attain these insights. In fact, many teachers do not have them. The student, depending somewhat upon his ability and curiosity and his readings, may or may not achieve these larger insights, no matter whether history is taught or how it is taught.

Because of its unpsychological presentation, its compulsory aspect, and its hypocritical inconsistencies, history is seriously threatened by the other social sciences. Aggressive committees in all the social sciences are carrying on extensive studies, the general trend of which shows the desirability of teaching more political science, more economics, more sociology, more geography, more anthropology, and more contemporary events in the schools. In looking for places in which to insert these new units and elements, the social scientists have naturally discovered the disproportionate place of history in the curriculum. As new contributions move into the curriculum, some extant content will have to yield, and history appears to be the logical subject to shrink and move over a bit. History is on the way down and possibly out.

It may be that history will disappear from the curriculum altogether. All its values can easily be infused into, or drawn out of, other studies. Only the historian thinks that pure, undiluted, unmixed, uncontaminated history exists and requires rigorous teaching and study. This tantrum-like demand is, of course, unrealistic, unenlightened, and unpsychological. History needs no separate existence for teaching or learning; it is a service study, not a self-sustaining discipline. In fact, it functions most usefully when suffused with other elements and subjects. So it is probable that the demand for its continued separate existence will actually work toward its diminution.

History might be saved and even enriched and extended by merging into the social studies, which could utilize it continuously. In other words, perhaps we should return to the merging of the social sciences as advocated by Harry Elmer Barnes in the early 1920's and to the complete fusion of the social studies as advocated and demonstrated by the late Harold Rugg.

If history courses were abolished in schools and colleges, the societal importance and value of history would not be greatly affected. Society would continue to search the record for guidance, readers would continue to read books on their favorite topics, persons, and subjects, and textbook writers would continue to lead, guide, introduce, explore, and induce readers to read on and on into other books. Historians would continue to produce history in all its bewildering complexity.

The student would be the great beneficiary of the abolition of history as courses. Freed from compulsion, from the futile effort to remember, he would begin to explore history, to see it as a source, to utilize it for answers to his questions, to experience the thrill of discovery, to evolve his own organization of his findings. He would be transformed from a dull underling to a self-directing inquirer. Free to choose among many possible research and reading projects, he would no longer feel a hostility toward history. He might even learn to love it. Who knows—he might become a historian.

MARK M. KRUG

Professor of Education in History and Social Sciences, University of Chicago

74. Bruner's New Social Studies: A Critique*

Many voices have recently been raised to suggest that the emphasis on the teaching of social studies should be on the structure of history and of the social sciences. Advocates of this position take much of their inspiration and rationale from the work of Jerome S. Bruner. Bruner, a Harvard psychologist, maintains that each discipline can best be mastered by teaching the basic organizing principles which, according to his view, form the structure of every natural and social science. These generalizations and broad ideas help scholars, who have invented them, to organize their facts and their respective bodies of knowledge into meaningful and connected patterns. Students who study any discipline by looking at its structure are bound to find the interconnecting spiraling logic of these sets of broad organizing principles.

Bruner and his coworker, Jerrold Zacharias, a physicist of M.I.T., contend that the stress on structure proved to be a great boon for the new mathematics and new physics and that there is no reason to doubt that the same can be true for the social studies. Consequently, both scholars, who are the leaders in Educational Services Incorporated, an endowed corporation, are now hard at work to prepare a new social studies curriculum.

The new curriculum is to be based on Bruner's contention that

the structure of knowledge—its connectedness and its derivations that make one idea follow another—is the proper emphasis in education. For it is structure, the great conceptual inventions that bring order to the congeries of disconnected observations, that gives meaning to what we may learn and makes possible the opening up of new realms of experience.[1]

The implication is that learning one set of broad concepts will logically lead to the learning of a more complex set of conceptual frameworks. Bruner is confident that "any subject can be taught effectively in some intellectually honest form to any child at any stage of development."[2]

*Social Education, XXX:400–406, October 1966. Used by permission.
[1] Jerome S. Bruner, *On Knowing* (Cambridge, Mass.: Harvard University Press, 1962. p. 120.
[2] Jerome S. Bruner, *The Process of Education* (Cambridge, Mass.: Harvard University Press, 1962), p. 33.

It may be of significance to note that in explicating this theory of the structure of disciplines, Bruner uses, almost without exception, examples from mathematics or from the natural sciences. His interpretation of the role and power of the organizing concepts seems to be best understood and related to the function and objectives of the natural sciences. Take, for instance, the statement of Bruner that,

> Knowledge is a model we construct to give meaning and structure to regularities in experience. The organizing ideas of any body of knowledge are inventions for rendering experience economical and connected. . . . The power of great organizing concepts is in large part that they permit us to understand and sometimes to predict or change the world in which we live. [3]

This statement has an obvious relevance to mathematics, physics, and chemistry. The question is whether Bruner in his work on the social studies curriculum will be able to isolate some great organizing ideas in history or the social sciences which will help the students "to understand and sometimes predict or change the world." Once this is done, it remains to be seen whether historians will be ready to accept the structure of history as finally defined by Bruner and his colleagues at E.S.I.

Bruner cannot escape the task of defining the structure of history and of other social sciences because, according to his own conception, curriculum revision calls for two initial steps, the definition of the structure of the discipline by the scholars themselves and the organization of the discovered structure into meaningful patterns of relationships for purposes of classroom instruction. This means that Bruner would have to ask historians to define the structure of their discipline. The few historians who have tried to find some order, rhythm, or structure in history have done so with limited success and usually without the endorsement of their fellow historians. Whether this task can be done by Bruner with the help of several historians who are working with him is very doubtful. The task of identifying even a small number of fundamental ideas in world history and of finding their spiraling relatedness may prove to be formidable, if not forbidding. An example of a great idea in history, cited by Bruner, "A nation must trade in order to live," is so broad and so full of fuzzy implications, that its value for classroom instruction may prove to be as useless as the generalization, "in war there is no substitute for victory" or "appeasement of aggressors does not pay."

If we are to teach the structure of history or of sociology in high school classes, scholars in these disciplines will have to agree on some list of fundamental ideas, basic skills, and methods needed and used by historians and sociologists and then show how these great ideas and skills are related

---

[3] Bruner, *On Knowing,* p. 120.

to one another and how they represent the structure of history and sociology. This has never been attempted by historians or sociologists and I doubt whether many would want to try. Commenting on this question, Professor Fred M. Newmann of Harvard wrote:

> Can a discipline have a structure independent of the scholars' ability to articulate it? An affirmative answer carries with it an implication that some sort of intellectual natural law transcends scholarly endeavor, unaffected by the studies of human beings, *that pre-existing structures are waiting to be discovered.* On the other hand, a negative reply suggests that the utility of structure as a concept depends mostly upon a prediction that scholars will in fact be able to articulate the structure of their field. If the existence of structure is mainly a function of the scholars' ability to construct it, then there is no logical basis for assuming that any given discipline has a structure. [4]

Suppose that some historians, even as respectable and distinguished as those who serve as advisers to Professor Bruner at the E.S.I. Project, would conclude that they have discovered the "pre-existing" structure of history. Would their "discovery" be accepted by their colleagues? Is it probable that an interlocking, logically connected, progressively complex system of fundamental ideas in history, or for that matter in sociology or in political science, could ever be identified? The basic difficulty which apparently does not exist or has been overcome in mathematics and in the natural sciences is the lack of any logical ladder of progression in the study of sociology or history. It is not absolutely essential for a high school student to have had a course in the American Revolution in order to study the Civil War. Children do learn about the Napoleonic Wars without ever having heard of the invasions and conquests of Alexander the Great. It would be rather difficult to formulate a generalization from the Napolenic Wars which would have a logical relationship to the wars of Alexander or the conquests of Ghengis Khan. The same would undoubtedly be true about the broader questions in sociology. It may be possible and profitable to study about the "apartheid policy" in South Africa without any relation, or logically discoverable relatedness, to the situation of Indians in Peru or the Negroes in America. In fact, it can be argued that any attempt, for instructional purposes based on a search for structure, to develop an organizing idea which would relate the study of these three areas would be full of loopholes and misleading.

Even granting for a moment the legitimacy of the contention that the teaching of the structure of the disciplines is the proper emphasis in education, there is a question which would naturally occur to those who have

[4]Fred M. Newmann "The Analysis of Public Controversy—New Focus on Social Studies," *School Review* Winter 1965, p, 413. (italics mine)

taught social studies on a high school level. Would not the teaching of the broad concepts and generalizing principles, even if taught by inventive teachers by the inductive "discovery" method recommended by Bruner, prove to be boring for many students during the long stretch of the school year? Granting that some of the students will, after engaging in an inquiry by imitating the ways of research of sociologists, political scientists, and historians, experience the "thrill of discovery," is it not sensible to assume that many other students would find this intellectual exercise boring and wasteful?

While there is no question that in the search for structure, Bruner's discovery approach is valuable and should have a place in the social studies curriculum and in the lively, dramatic study of history and the social sciences, to build the entire social studies curriculum on the structure theory is fraught with grave dangers. Much in history and in the study of human personality and group interrelationship which cannot and should not be fitted into a structure, or even related to something else, is eminently worthy of teaching to our children. The way a historian or an economist goes about his work is interesting and may occasionally be useful as a mode of inquiry in the social studies class, but equally interesting and equally important is a deductive approach by a scholarly teacher who constructs his lesson by presenting to his students for discussion and analysis conflicting conclusions reached by historians about the causes of the Civil War or about the effectiveness of the New Deal legislation.

Newmann poses a legitimate query to Bruner and his followers. "Why should a general lay population be taught to perform intellectual operations of a nature preferred uniquely by the academic profession? That is, why should all children be taught to ask and answer the kinds of questions that interest historians, political scientists, economists, etc?"[5] It is also disturbing to note that Bruner and the Structuralists in the social studies seem to assume that history and the social sciences each have one structure, when in fact most of them may be examined in terms of several sets or patterns of great conceptual ideas.

Scholars who may eventually be induced to undertake the task of writing complete social studies curricula based on the structure theory will undoubtedly find that historians and social scientists freely borrow ideas, methods, concepts, including fundamental ideas, from one another. Professor Arno Bellack of Teachers College pointed out in his critique of Bruner's theories that

> the social scientists today are characterized by a plurality of methods and conceptual schemes. . . . Instead of a unity of method or a single universal discourse, we are confronted with a vast confederation of

[5] *Ibid.*, p. 414.

separate areas of study. Modes of thinking and analysis differ from field to field and even from problem to problem within the same field. In time, a Bacon of the sciences that bear on social and cultural behavior may emerge, but that time is not yet.[6]

The E.S.I. under the leadership of Professor Bruner has made considerable progress in preparing a new social studies curriculum. A preliminary report on the social studies, published in 1963 by the American Council of Learned Societies and Educational Services, Incorporated, included a basic statement of policy in the preparation of a course of study in the social studies. It reads in part: "history, sociology, anthropology, economics and political science may for convenience be separated as academic disciplines, but they all deal with a single thing: the behavior of man in society. Accordingly, we propose to teach them jointly, not separately."[7] One wonders what the reaction from the academic mathematicians and natural scientists would be to a similar statement: "Mathematics, physics, chemistry and biology may for convenience be separated as academic disciplines, but they all deal with a single thing: man's attempt to understand and to control his natural environment. Accordingly, we propose to teach them jointly, not separately." The outcries of anguish and protest would undoubtedly be overwhelming. And yet, the Structuralists in the social studies do not hesitate to advocate an amalgamation of history and the social sciences and do not seem to be concerned about the protection of the integrity of these disciplines and the reluctance, if not outright opposition of most historians and of many social scientists, to a reductionist synthetic unification.

The E.S.I. group has identified 24 broad generalizations which are to be taught sequentially by using interdisciplinary insights and techniques. Here is an example of one of these generalizations.

"All societies have developed in different degrees of elaboration special institutions for ensuring conformity to other institutions [law] or changing institutions. All ultimately use the threat of force to try to ensure that conformity to institutions shall be rewarding." It is impossible to quarrel with such a broad generalization, but whether it constitutes an organizing, fundamental idea representing the structure of any discipline or the joint structure of history and the social sciences, is another matter. Most scholars would undoubtedly have grave doubts.

Apparently the followers of the structure approach in the social

[6] Arno Bellack. "Structure in the Social Sciences and Implications for the Social Studies Program," in Odegard et al., The Social Studies Curriculum Proposals for the Future (Chicago.: Scott, Foresman, 1963), p. 102.

[7] E. S. I., "A Preliminary and Tentative Outline of a Program of Curriculum Development in the Social Studies and Humanities," American Council of Learned Societies and Educational Services, February 15, 1963, mimeographed.

studies are not as cautious as the scholars in Cambridge. The new social studies curriculum published in 1965 by the Wisconsin State Department of Public Instruction, on which 26 Wisconsin educators worked for three years, set down six major concepts each for history, political science, economics, geography, and sociology. These concepts, the authors claim, are applicable to all mankind. One of the major concepts in history reads: "Human experience is continuous and interrelated. Continuity is a fact of life: there is nothing new under the sun. . . . All men, events and institutions are the outcome of something that has gone before. . . . Man is a product of the past and restricted by it."[8]

Some of the other concepts from history which, according to the Wisconsin guide, are to serve as "a means of organizing subject matter in a most meaningful pattern" are:

> Every effort at reform began as the private opinion of an individual.
> It is difficult to separate fact from fiction. Every writer has his biases.
> Those who cannot remember the past may be condemned to repeat it.
> Facts may often be interpreted in more than one way.
> Nations with great power may not always use it wisely.

A similar concept in political science states, "Governments are established by men. In some situations, people delegate authority; in others authority is imposed."

One could, I hope not too irreverently, comment, "Elementary, Dr. Watson," since some of these generalizations are obvious and even trite. Several of the cited generalizing concepts in history would find little support from professional historians. Certainly, by no stretch of imagination can these statements be assumed to constitute the fundamental concepts in history constituting its structure. The more important concern is the question of how interested high school youngsters are in such high sounding generalizations and whether it is wise to build an entire social studies curriculum around them.

In the E.S.I. Report published in the summer of 1965, Bruner gives a rather detailed description of the new social studies course of study which would be given experimentally in grades 4, 5, and 6, and be entitled simply "man." "The content of the course," Bruner writes, "is man: his nature as a species, the forces that shaped or continue to shape his humanity. Three questions recur throughout, namely: What is human about human beings? How did they get that way? How can they be made more so?"[9]

---

[8] *A Conceptual Framework for the Social Studies in Wisconsin Schools,* Social Studies Bulletin, issued by Angus B. Rothwell, State Department of Public Instruction, Madison, Wis., December 1964.

[9] Jerome S. Bruner. "Man: A Course of Study," in *E.S.I., Quarterly Report* (Watertown, Mass.: Educational Services, Inc., Summer 1965), p. 85. Also in Bruner, *Toward a Theory of Instruction* (Cambridge, Mass.: Harvard University Press, 1966), p. 74.

The course would include a section on language, contrasting how humans and animals manage to send and receive messages, on how language is acquired by young humans and other primates, and the origins of human language and its role in shaping human characteristics. This section, says Bruner, may take a year of study. The second section of the course would deal with "tools." The objective is to give the children an idea of the relation between tools and our way of life. "Our ultimate object in teaching about tools," Bruner writes, "is . . . not so much to explicate tools and their significance, but to explore how tools affected man's evolution." [10] The study about changes in technology and the corresponding changes in society aims to fulfill one of the basic goals of the social studies program; namely, "to get across the idea that a technology requires a counterpart in social organization before it can be used effectively by a society." [11]

The crux of the matter is what is meant by the word "effectively." This statement represents one of the important objectives of the social studies as defined by the E.S.I. group. It is indeed strange and controversial. If one understands the main trend of thought of the atomic scientists as reflected in recent years in the articles that appeared in the *Bulletin of Atomic Scientists,* it is the considered opinion of our leading atomic scientists that we have failed to build a "counterpart in social organization" to deal with atomic technology. However, our society has used atomic energy "effectively" to subdue Japan, to run atomic submarines, ships, and power stations, and to create some kind of equilibrium in the world by the reality of a balance of atomic terror.

The third section of Bruner's new social studies curriculum deals with social organizations. It is aimed at explaining to the children "that there is a structure in a society and that this structure is not fixed once for all." It would seem that even our average students should have little difficulty in grasping this principle which is certainly quite obvious to them from their own gangs, clubs, and school organizations.

The fourth unit is devoted to the theme of child rearing. This study deals with the phenomenon of sentiment in human life which develops during the long human childhood and the influence of the special manner of childhood on future personality development.

The fifth and final section of this course of study aims to develop a world view and deals with "man's drive to explicate and represent his world." "Central to the unit is the idea that men everywhere are humans, however advanced or 'primitive' their civilizations." This seems to be essentially an anthropological unit aimed at proving that all cultures have

---

[10] Bruner, "Man: A Course of Study," in *E.S.I. Quarterly Report,* p. 88.
[11] *Ibid.,* p. 89.

inherent values and that there are no "superior" and "inferior" cultures. The objective is to combat an ethnocentric approach to world cultures.

In explaining why this unit should be taught early on the elementary school level, Bruner presents an idealistic view of world history based on the idea of the rule of reason and the continued progress, which few historians would accept. "We want children," he states, "to recognize that man is constantly seeking to bring reason [sic!] into his world, that he does so with a variety of symbolic tools, and that he does so with a striking and fully rational humanity."[12] Our students will be ready to accept this view only if we impose upon them and somehow enforce a total news-paper and television blackout and also frequently tape their eyes and ears so that they cannot listen to their parents, friends, and casual acquaint-ances. Otherwise, they may tend to believe that, unfortunately, man is not very often successful in bringing "reason into his world."

As for the methodology to be used in this new social studies curriculum, Bruner wants to use three techniques, which seem to be quite unique to the E.S.I. because they bear no resemblance either to the methods of inquiry in history or in the social sciences. The first technique consists of using contrast; the second is the use of especially prepared games that "incor-porate the formal properties of the phenomena for which the game is an analogue." The third is "the ancient approach of stimulating self-consciousness about assumptions—going beyond mere admonition to think."[13]

Little can be said about this new methodology in the social studies because few details have been given as yet. Bruner sees "the most urgent need" to teach the students to use theoretical models which will be "rather sophisticated." Evaluation will have to await the publication of the models, and reports of their application will have to be analyzed. Enough, however, has been published to indicate that once the curriculum (which will include materials, games, films, and models, all prepared under the supervision of academic scholars), is submitted to the schools, the social studies teachers will have little opportunity to exercise their initiative and inventiveness. The traditional autonomy and flexibility of the better trained and more effective history and social studies teachers may be severely curtailed. If past experience is any guide, the more promising young people will refuse to go into social studies teaching where they would serve only as assistants to the curriculum-making and curriculum-evaluat-ing academic scholars. Other teachers will undoubtedly offer passive or active resistance to the new packaged curriculum.

Bruner and his associates are constantly emphasizing the importance

[12] *Ibid.*, p. 92.
[13] *Ibid.*, p. 92.

of the child "doing" mathematics or physics instead of learning about them. The student should "do" the things on the blackboards or in the laboratory that mathematicians and physicists are doing. That sounds reasonable and exciting. But how does this apply to history? Christopher Jencks, in his review of Bruner's book, *Toward a Theory of Instruction,* made an acute observation. "The analogy," he wrote, "between physics and history is at bottom misleading. The men who really 'do' history are not, after all, historians. They are politicians, generals, diplomats, philosophers. It is these people whom the young need to understand, far more than they need to understand the historians who judge them." [14]

All new curricular approaches to the social studies are basically determined by the postulated objectives. It is the objectives set by the curriculum makers that determine the content of the particular courses of study proposed.

Thus, Jerome Bruner hopes to achieve five ideals:

1. To give our pupils respect for and confidence in the powers of their own mind.
2. To give them respect, moreover, for the powers of thought concerning the human condition, man's plight and his social life.
3. To provide them with a set of workable models to make it simpler to analyze the nature of the social world in which they live and the condition in which man finds himself.
4. To impart a sense of respect for the capacities and plight of man as a species, for his origins, for his potential and for his humanity.
5. To leave the student with a sense of the unfinished business of man's evolution. [15]

These objectives deserve some scrutiny. They are truly far-reaching, ambitious, and, frankly, not entirely clear. How does one "give" or "impart" respect or a "sense of respect," and how would a teacher go about measuring whether he has done so? In setting before the social studies teachers the task of stressing the power of man's rational mind (an interesting throwback to the worship of man's rational powers by the philosophers of the Age of Renaissance and Enlightenment), do we not belittle or eliminate the evidence that suggests severe limits to the use of the "powers of thought" in dealing with the human condition? Are the teachers expected to know the state of the "human condition" today and of "man's plight and his social life"? Is this not a tall order? Is this not too much to expect from high school teachers? Would not a world-conclave of scholars have a very difficult time in assessing the human condition and the very complicated plight of modern man? Why should it not also be one of

[14] *Book Week,* February 20, 1966, p. 5.
[15] Bruner, "Man: A Course of Study," in *E.S.I. Quarterly Report,* p. 93.

the objectives in the social studies (if such basic personality changes are indeed feasible) to try to impart a sense of *dis*respect for man's consistent refusal to live up to his potential and for his *in*humanity? An effective and imaginative study of history would certainly be more likely to give the student a more balanced picture of man's virtues and follies.

The Bruner objectives, and especially the last one which aims to leave the student with a sense of unfinished business of man's evolution, have a distinct anthropological flavor. Indeed the whole proposed curriculum is anthropological in its essence. The E.S.I. approach was to be an interdisciplinary one, teaching jointly all the social sciences, but, in fact, there is little of political science in Bruner's curriculum. As for history and geography, they are virtually non-existent. It is curious that the accumulation of a body of knowledge, yes, the acquisition of related and meaningful information, is not mentioned among the objectives. This, of course, is in line with the recent trend of denigrating the importance of the transmission of accumulated knowledge. The stress is on skills, concepts, and, in Bruner's terms, on "workable models." All this is based on the unproven and perhaps unprovable assumption that it is not really important to know much about, let us say, the English Civil War, about the American Revolution, the French Revolution or the Bolshevik Revolution. Bruner and his colleagues seem to say that what a future intelligent man needs to know is the basic concepts and generalizations pertaining to all revolutions, or a workable model of *a* revolution, possess the skills of critical inquiry, and when the need arises, he will merely apply the generalization, the models, and the skills to the study of any revolution he chooses to investigate.

Crane Brinton's careful study, *The Anatomy of Revolution*, has failed to come up with many generalizing principles about revolutions and clearly indicated that the differences and the variables involved in the American and the French Revolutions or between the English Civil War and the Bolshevik Revolution are so great that each of these great events should and deserve to be studied separately. Even if it were possible to construct, in Bruner's words, "workable models to make it simpler to analyze the nature of the social world" and apply them to the study of revolutions, our pupils would be deprived of the opportunity of meeting and living with (through dramatic and effective teaching) such fascinating people as T. R. Roosevelt, Cromwell, Lilburne, Marie Antoinette, Dante, Lenin, and Trotsky.

Questions pertaining to the learning of a body of knowledge (carefully selected and logically connected) are rather simple. Is it or is it not important for high school graduates and college freshmen to know about the Populist Rebellion, the War of 1812, about Daniel Webster and Marcy Tweed, about the Clay Compromise, about the Teapot Dome Scandal, and about the history of Reconstruction? Is it or is it not important for high school graduates to know about Pericles and the conquests of Alexander, about Caesar, the Carthagenian Wars, about Constantine, about Ghengis Khan, the reforms of Ahkbar and the wisdom of Confucius, about Voltaire, Napoleon and Waterloo? The assumption postulated here is that such—and similarly related—knowledge taught in an analytical and interpretative manner, is essential and worthwhile for any moderately educated man. I would shudder to think that a college freshman would have to see a Broadway play to become acquainted for the first time with the women of Troy, the complicated nature of Marat, or the tragic downfall of Charles Dilke. Historical knowledge may, of course, be gained through the partial use of Fenton's inductive method, the public controversy approach of Oliver and Shaver, the traditional chronological approach, the case-study approach, or preferably by a combination of all these approaches.

Some of the new curricula in the social studies, based on Bruner's ideas, have drastically cut the time devoted to United States history and are drawing fire from some right-wing groups. This is unfortunate and it must be resisted as an unwarranted interference with the orderly process of curriculum revision.

However, one would hope that it is legitimate to raise a voice in defense of the teaching of American history as deserving a place of importance in the schooling of young Americans. Chauvinism has no place in the school because it is destructive and because it usually leads to unbridled cynicism. But it is proper to argue that to give the student an understanding and an appreciation of the ideas that brought about the founding of this nation, the men who helped to guide its destiny and to make them aware of the constant struggle for the improvement of the democratic process, are the proper concern of social studies teachers and of the schools. It should be stressed that America must be taught full face, with all the warts showing, and that the teachers are duty bound not to gloss over the weaknesses and imperfections of our government and of our society.

The end result of such teaching of United States history, based on integrity, scholarship, and imagination, will be a sense of pride in the unique genius of the American government and American politics. Dean I. James Quillen of Stanford put it this way:

Through history a student comes to know his nation's ideals and traditions, the nature of its government, and the responsibilities of its citizens. In one sense, history is the door through which an individual can enter the edifice of his nation's culture. Without a knowledge of history, patriotism has no roots and loyalty no bonds tying it to the past.[16]

---

[16] I. James Quillen, "American History in the Upper Grades and Junior High School," in William H. Cartwright and Richard L. Watson, eds., *Interpreting and Teaching American History,* National Council for the Social Studies, 31st Yearbook (Washington, D.C., 1961), p. 347.

Professor Bruner has recently made his position on the place of history in the social studies curriculum in elementary schools and high schools crystal clear. We should be grateful to him for his candor, and if he and his supporters succeed in emasculating or eliminating the study of history from school curricula, no one will be able to say that this was done surreptitiously or without proper warning.

In an article in the *Saturday Review* which the editors described as a preview for his latest book, *Toward a Theory of Instruction,* Bruner relates that his work on a new social studies curriculum has led him to the conclusion that "we are bound to move toward instruction in the sciences of behavior and away from the study of history."[17] The basic reason for the need to shift from history to the behavioral sciences is that history looks to the past, the recent past, and the behavioral sciences prepare the young to grasp and to adjust to the changing human conditions. "Recorded history," says Bruner, "is only about five thousand years old, as we saw. Most of what we teach is within the last few centuries, for the records before that are minimal, while the records after are relatively rich."[18] However, Bruner continues, modern methods of retrieving and storing of information will make it possible to store masses of information and consequently, "a thousand years from now we will be swamped." Because of this specter, if I understand Bruner correctly, we ought to stop the study of history right now because, as he tells us, at that future time there would be little sense to dwell "with such loving care over the details of Brumaire or the Long Parliament or the Louisiana Purchase."

It is quite obvious that Professor Bruner never really enjoyed the study of the dramatic record of the Long Parliament, which had a decisive influence on British political institutions and British democracy, or the study of the brilliant and dramatic exercise of Presidential powers by Thomas Jefferson, whose decision made it possible, in a large measure, for the United States to be the great power it is today. Bruner is disdainful of the record of history which includes only the recent five thousand years. He seems to be much more interested, as his anthropologically-centered curriculum clearly indicates, in teaching about the 500-million-year-old history of the evolution of mammals and man. Without in any way belittling the importance of the study of the origin of the human species, one can and perhaps should argue that the study and the understanding of those "mere" five thousand years are of crucial importance for our young generations if they are to live meaningful and useful lives and if they are to be expected to make an effort to prevent the destruction of the human race in an atomic holocaust.

[17] Jerome S. Bruner. "Education as Social Invention," *Saturday Review,* February 19, 1966, p. 103.
[18] *Ibid.,* p. 103.

Bruno Bettelheim argued that educators should ask the question about what kind of persons we want our children to be, so that they may build a new world, different from the one that we live in, "a world in which they can live in accordance with their full potentialities." Answering the question on how this objective may be achieved, Professor Bettelheim recently wrote:

> Most of all, our schools ought to teach the true nature of man, teach about his troubles with himself, his inner turmoils and about his difficulties in living with others. They should teach the prevalence and the power of both man's social and asocial tendencies, and how the one can domesticate the other, without destroying his independence or self-love. [19]

History is superbly equipped to contribute a great deal to the attainment of these goals in education. It is the business of history to deal with the trials, tribulations, and the inner turmoils of man and the good and the bad in them. Effective history teachers allow their students a glimpse into the tormented soul of Ivan the Terrible and the social and asocial instincts and predilections of the Levellers.

For young people to adapt to changing conditions, Bruner argues, they must study "the possible rather than the achieved. . . . It is the behavioral sciences and their generality with respect to variations in the human condition that must be central to our presentation of man, not the particularities of his history." [20] Thus, Bruner made his choice. Without equivocation and without any attempt to becloud the real issue, he wants the social studies curriculum in elementary and secondary schools to be centered on the concepts and generalizations and skills from the behavioral sciences. He is willing and ready to abandon the teaching of history with its stress on the unique, the separate, and the particular. This is no place to discuss the uses of history. A. L. Rowse and Allan Nevins have done it very well. It may suffice if we observe that if Bruner's ideas on the nature, content, and objectives of the social studies should prevail, elementary and high school students would get only a little of the historical perspective they need to understand today's world and its problems.

Generalizations and generalizing concepts are helpful to scholars as ordering devices, but the world as it impinges on the minds of the young is exactly the historical world of the specific, of the unique, and of the separate. Students want to study about racial problems and about traffic laws in the cities, to learn more about the personality of the man in the White House, and about the nature of the war in Viet Nam because they are per-

[19] Bruno Bettelheim, "Notes on the Future of Education," *The University of Chicago Magazine,* February 1966, p. 14.

[20] Bruner, "Education as Social Invention," p. 103.

sonally, specifically interested in these problems. Teachers of social studies ought to be warned that the making of the study of structure and skills—"skills in handling and imagining, and in symbolic operations"—the principal emphasis in education, as postulated by Bruner, may make much of social studies instruction boring and unrewarding. The elimination of history from the social studies would be an educational and a national disaster.

EDWIN FENTON

Professor of History, Carnegie-Mellon University

75. Social Studies Curriculum Reform: An Appraisal*

If you find new developments in the social studies bewildering, I bid you welcome to a very large club. Experiment has been piled on experiment in confusing disarray. In order to make sense of these changes, I spent a leave from Carnegie Tech during the academic year 1965–66 visiting social studies projects throughout the country and reading the thousands of pages of material they have produced.[1] No generalizations hold for all of the more than fifty social studies projects established during the past five years. They vary in almost every dimension: objectives, teaching strategies, types of materials, patterns of pupil deployment, evaluating instruments. I could cite a half dozen exceptions to every generalization which I am going to make. Let me make generalizations anyway, in order to indicate dominant trends which I have detected.

The purpose of the new social studies is to make the child a useful, independent citizen through helping him attain four types of objectives: attitudes, values, inquiry skills, and knowledge. The major criterion for the selection of content is the structure of the disciplines. The major teaching method is directed discussion. The dominant types of material consist of data in virtually every form except the traditional textbook. Let me discuss each of these four generalizations in turn, leaving the most significant of all—objectives—to the end. I shall begin with structure.

In his influential little volume, *The Process of Education,* Jerome S. Bruner failed to give a clear and specific definition of structure.[2] Although he hints that structure involves both attitudes and inquiry skills, he limits his examples in the social studies to substantive generalizations: "That a nation must trade in order to live." Bruner's definition has touched off heated controversy about whether the social studies have a structure. I have read twenty-seven books and a number of articles written during the past five years about this subject. Most have not been illuminating.[3] The long

*California Social Science Review, 6:23–33, June 1967. Used by permission.
[1] A full account of what I have learned is in my book, *The New Social Studies* (New York: Holt, Rinehart and Winston, 1967).
[2] Vintage Book (New York: Random House, 1963), pp. 6–8 and elsewhere.
[3] Among the best of these volumes are two produced by curriculum projects: Roy A. Price, Warren Hickman, and Gerald Smith, *"Major Concepts for Social Studies"* (Social Studies Curriculum Center, Syracuse University, Syracuse, New York, 1965); Irving Morrissett, ed., *Concepts and Structure in the New Social Science Curricula* (Social Science Educational Consortium Inc., Purdue University, West Lafayette, Indiana, 1966).

lead article by Professor Mark Krug in the September, 1966, edition of *Social Education* is the most recent contribution to the controversy, a contribution which confuses more than it clarifies, because neither Bruner nor Krug has a sound conception of structure.[4]

What is structure? The most useful definition I know, that of Joseph J. Schwab, argues that structure has two parts: ". . . the body of imposed conceptions which define the investigated subject matter of that discipline and control its inquiries," and " . . . the pattern of its procedure, its method, how it goes about using its conceptions to attain its goal."[5] In layman's language, structure consists of a method of inquiry made up of two parts: hypothesis formation and proof process. Let me examine each, beginning with hypothesis formation.

Facts mean nothing by themselves. They assume meaning only as part of each person's frame of reference. The same piece of data can have quite different meanings to two people with contrasting views of the world. Moreover, a person's frame of reference inclines him to notice some facts and to overlook others. Marx's firm conviction that class struggle explained history caused him to select certain facts as he read and to use them in particular ways as evidence for his argument. Adam Smith's dedication to the theory of the free market would condition him to note other facts in the same body of data and to use them as evidence for very different arguments. The way in which a person selects facts to note helps to determine the kinds of hypotheses he forms. His "body of imposed conceptions" conditions him to ask certain questions and to seek answers to particular problems. The pedagogical issue can be stated simply: How can we help a student to develop a "body of imposed conceptions" which will help him to formulate useful hypotheses about a variety of problems?

Bruner's generalizations are not very helpful. Generalizations lead to teaching social studies as product, as information known to scholars which students should learn. One school system after another has indulged in the vain pursuit of a small body of generalizations to cram into children's heads. Professors Hanna and Gross of Stanford University together with ten of their graduate students identified more than 3200 generalizations.[6] Both the California and the Wisconsin State Social Studies Committees have issued well-known lists.[7] None of them is very useful, primarily

[4]Mark M. Krug, "Bruner's New Social Studies: A Critique," *Social Education,* 30:400–406, October 1966.

[5]Joseph J. Schwab, "The Concept of the Structure of a Discipline," in *Educational Record,* 43:199, 203, July 1962.

[6]See a condensation of their work in the following article: Paul R. Hanna and John R. Lee, "Content in the Social Studies," in John U. Michaelis, ed., *Social Studies in Elementary Schools,* National Council for the Social Studies (Washington, D.C., 1962), 62–89.

[7]*Report of the State Central Committee on Social Studies to the California State Curriculum Commission* (Sacramento, 1961); *A Conceptual Framework for the Social Studies in Wisconsin* (Madison, 1964).

because a generalization is inert. Teaching product becomes the major objective, and product in the form of generalizations—many of which may be proved incorrect in another decade or so— are not very useful as a body of imposed conceptions to control inquiry.

The best of the new social studies projects identify the hypothesis-making aspect of structure with concepts. By a concept they mean a category: social class, leadership, culture, or supply-and-demand may serve as examples. A number of curriculum centers have tried to identify a small number of analytical concepts from all the social sciences. Although each has developed a workable list, the lists are not identical. This result suggests that the social studies do not have a single structure inherent in the discipline. Each person brings his own "imposed conceptions" to the task of selecting concepts. Hence, each person has his own structure. The problem for each of us, like the problem for curriculum centers, is to develop a structure based on the social sciences which will help us to analyze problems in such a way that our answers have a high probability of accuracy.

Let me examine the way in which concepts make up a body of imposed conceptions which will help a student learn to develop fruitful hypotheses. Suppose that a student knows four concepts from sociology—social class, role, status, and norms—and wants to investigate a problem in history or in contemporary society, say, to describe the social structure of Boston, Massachusetts, in the middle of the eighteenth century. As he reads diaries, autobiographies, newspaper accounts, and similar source material, his knowledge of social class, status, role, and norms will help to guide his search for data. He will ask himself how many social classes existed in the society. He will try to learn what relative position on the social scale each occupational, racial, and religious group occupied. He will examine the roles of many groups and individuals in society to determine, for example, whether housewives in seventeenth-century New England had the same roles as housewives in our own world. He will be alert to pick up clues about norms, the behaviors expected of various people of different status and roles. Knowing these concepts guides his search for data along productive lines which social scientists have found extremely useful for the scientific analysis of society. Concepts are an extremely useful body of imposed conceptions because, unlike generalizations, they are useful tools of inquiry. Generalizations become ends in themselves; taught properly, concepts become means to an end.

Some concepts are more useful for the analysis of society than others. Let us consider five types as examples: historical periods (the Renaissance), historical topics (the growth of parliamentary government), concepts requiring historical definitions (democracy), concepts involving methods of procedure (multiple causation), and analytical concepts (leadership). Only the last of these five can be used as a source of analytical questions to guide the search for data in any study of any political system at any time or place. Many lists of concepts jumble several types together indiscriminately. With our growing knowledge of the nature and purpose of structure, we should soon be able to do much better, eventually arriving at several alternative lists of analytical concepts which can guide the search for data along productive lines.

Analytical concepts imply questions. Let us use the concept of leadership as an example. Modern political scientists recognize the vital role which leaders play in any political system. They want to know a number of things about political leaders. How are they recruited? What are their personal characteristics? How do they gain and maintain support from their followers? How can a citizen get access to them? The overwhelming majority of analytical questions used in the social studies either come from social science concepts or can be related to social science concepts. Taken together, concepts and analytical questions constitute an extremely useful notion of the hypothesis-forming aspect of structure. They are tools, a part of the process of inquiry. Generalizations, on the other hand, are product and are learned for their own sake.

The remaining part of structure, as Schwab defines the term, consists of proof process. Once a person has developed a hypothesis, he must revise, reject, or validate it. Within the past decade a number of scholars, both within and outside of the curriculum projects, have worked hard to develop schemes of validation. Much of their work stemmed originally from the model of reflective thinking posed by John Dewey in his classic volume *How We Think*.[8] The projects have refined and amplified this model to bring greater precision to the enterprise. They have identified each of the steps in the proof process and devised ways to teach individual skills of critical thinking on which these steps depend.

At Carnegie Tech we have integrated the teaching of structure defined as hypothesis formation and proof process into six major steps. They are:

1. Recognizing a problem from data
2. Formulating hypotheses
   a. Asking analytical questions
   b. Stating hypotheses
   c. Remaining aware of the tentative nature of hypotheses
3. Recognizing the logical implications of hypotheses
4. Gathering data
   a. Deciding what data will be needed
   b. Selecting or rejecting sources on the basis of a statement of the logical implications
5. Analyzing, Evaluating, and Interpreting the Data
   a. Selecting relevant data from the sources

[8](Boston: D. C. Heath and Co., 1933), p. 106.

    b. Evaluating the sources
      (1) Determining the frame of reference of the author of a source
      (2) Determining the accuracy of statements of fact
    c. Interpreting the data
  6. Evaluating the hypothesis in light of the data
    a. Justifying the hypothesis
    b. Modifying the hypothesis
      (1) Rejecting a logical implication
      (2) Restating the hypothesis

The process I have been describing makes structure something useful to teach. A discipline is not so much a body of knowledge as a method of inquiry. Hence, the structure of a discipline is not a group of generalizations; it is a tool which can be used to analyze problems—contemporary, historical, personal—which interest the student. Whether or not the solution he arrives at will be useful will depend upon the skill with which he uses the mode of inquiry, the attitudes he brings to the endeavor, and the knowledge he amasses as he develops and validates his hypothesis.

Let me now turn to teaching strategies. The major teaching method of the new social studies is directed discussion. Most of the projects, however, do not rely solely on one teaching technique. They employ a range of techniques, each one directed toward a specific group of objectives.

Teachers sometimes find it useful to think of teaching strategies as if they were ranged along a continuum. At one end of the continuum lie expository techniques—techniques such as the lecture in which the teacher gives all the cues, that is, all the generalizations and all the evidence for the generalizations which the student is supposed to learn. In most expository classes students listen, take notes, memorize them, and give them back to the teacher often in the same form on examinations or in class discussions.

Several hundred pieces of research done with superior senior high school students and college students indicate that students master just as much content from a discipline by listening to lectures as they do by discussion.[9] Notice several aspects of that statement. The generalization is confined to senior high school and college students and the objective is confined to knowledge of content. Nevertheless, if a teacher's objective is to have students be able to recall or state a definite body of facts and generalizations and the students are fairly sophisticated and at least fifteen years old, then the weight of evidence indicates that the lecture is a suitable teaching technique.

At the other end of the continuum lie discovery exercises in which the teacher gives no cues at all. He provides the data—a group of quotations, some tables, simply an assignment in the library—and then gets out of the way. Classroom interaction proceeds from student to student with the

[9]John W. Kidd, "The Question of Class Size," *Journal of Higher Education,* 23:440–44, November 1952, summarizes the results of some of these studies.

teacher acting only as a referee, leading the students neither by expository comments nor by questions which point the way toward data. I am referring to the sort of discovery exercise described by Byron G. Massialas and Jack Zevin.[10]

I find discovery exercises of this type useful for two purposes. First, they are an excellent evaluating device. If we want to learn whether or not a class can isolate a useful problem from data we can present them with a diary, an autobiography, or a group of tables and see what problem they identify for discussion. If they cannot formulate a worthwhile problem, they have not learned the first of the six steps in the mode of inquiry which I outlined. I'm sure any teacher can think of a number of other variables that could be evaluated in this way. Secondly, discovery exercises like these may encourage the creativity of children because they are challenged on their own to think a problem through. Creativity, however, does not spring full-blown from the mind of a child. The creative historians of recent decades have been among the best trained ones. They are men who know concepts and are in the habit of letting stubborn unexplained facts trigger new analytical questions, and they use these concepts and questions to develop new and interesting hypotheses. Nevertheless, discovery exercises may encourage creative thought by challenging students to use their resources to the limit.

Between these two poles on the continuum lie a variety of techniques which can be described as directed discussion. In directed discussion, the teacher asks questions. He does not give all the cues as he does in expository techniques nor does he withdraw almost entirely from the discussion as in a discovery exercise. Knowing exactly what he wants the student to learn by the end of the class period, he guides discussion by the questions he asks, helping students to learn how to put evidence and inference together in the process.

Directed discussion can be used for a great range of objectives. I find it indispensable, for example, for teaching students to use the mode of inquiry of the social studies, that is, to teach them to develop and validate hypotheses. As the work of Professors Lawrence Senesh at Purdue and [the late] Hilda Taba at San Francisco State College has proved, elementary school students can discover sophisticated social science concepts under the guidance of a skillful teacher.[11] These concepts can later be used as a basis for

---

[10]"Teaching Social Studies through Discovery," *Social Education,* 28:384–87, 400, 1964; reprinted in Byron G. Massialas and C. Benjamin Cox, *Inquiry in Social Studies* (New York: McGraw-Hill Book Co., 1966), pp. 136–52; and in Edwin Fenton, *Teaching the New Social Studies in Secondary Schools: An Inductive Approach* (New York: Holt, Rinehart & Winston, 1966), pp. 255–64.

[11]Lawrence Senesh, "Organizing a Curriculum Around Social Science Concepts," in Morrissett, ed., *Concepts and Structure,* pp. 21–38; Hilda Taba and James L. Hills, *Teacher Handbook for Contra Costa Social Studies, Grades 1–6* (Hayward, Calif: Rapid Printers and Lithographers, 1965).

hypothesis formation. Virtually all of the directors of projects agree that students can best be taught to learn the proof process of history and social sciences through directed discussion. Questioning, challenging, pointing out exceptions to a generalization, introducing new evidence which the students have not read in their homework assignment, a skilled teacher can emphasize over and over again the essential elements of inquiry skills.

Another sort of directed discussion can be used for another purpose: to teach students how to resolve value conflicts. The work of Donald Oliver at the Harvard Curriculum Center has been particularly concerned with this issue.[12] Oliver argues that the essential value of a democratic society is the belief in the dignity and worth of the individual. A truly democratic society tries to align its laws and practices with this value. Yet on many issues contradictory values are involved and need to be resolved. Americans have generally believed, for example, that the owner of a piece of property has the right to sell it to whomever he wishes. At the same time, we also believe that any individual of any race should be permitted to buy property in any neighborhood if he can afford it. What do we do when these two beliefs come in conflict? Which is more important, the property right or the human right? This is the specific sort of value problem which Professor Oliver argues should be discussed in the schools.

Oliver terms his type of classroom procedure Socratic-analysis discussion. He poses an issue such as open occupancy of housing and attempts to clarify both sides of the argument. Questioning one student at a time, he draws from the class the logical implications of each position and eventually tries to get each student to resolve the conflict in terms of a higher value, the dignity and worth of the individual. His objective is to teach students how to deal with public controversies involving conflicting values and conflicting policies. Socratic-analysis discussion in which the teacher plays an indispensable role as questioner and challenger lies at the heart of his teaching technique.

The entire matter of teaching strategies has been confused by the use of a variety of terms, most of which are not defined precisely. In contemporary literature the terms of discovery, inductive learning, inquiry, reflective thinking, directed discussion, Socratic-analysis discussion, and a half-dozen more all are used to describe varieties of directed discussion. Moreover, some teachers believe that people in curriculum projects endorse only one style of teaching to the exclusion of all others. For the Carnegie Tech group at least, this impression is completely wrong. We employ expository teaching for certain content goals with particular student audiences. We use nondirective discovery exercises for other goals, particularly evaluation. We use various sorts of directed discussion for still different purposes. At times,

---

[12] See the excellent account of the rationale for the Oliver project in Donald W. Oliver and James P. Shaver, *Teaching Public Issues in the High School* (Boston: Houghton Mifflin Co., 1966).

in the midst of a directed discussion, we employ recitation techniques to make sure that all the students in the class are dealing with the same body of evidence. Role playing and simulation also play a part in our teaching repertoire. There is no magic road to teaching. There are many roads each appropriate to different goals.

Most of the projects produce elaborate teacher's manuals to accompany their materials. For some of the courses produced at Carnegie Tech, the teacher's manual is as large as the collection of student material. Each manual contains a rationale for the entire four-year curriculum as well as a rationale for the particular course. These documents precede daily lesson plans which state specific objectives for each day's work, note the materials provided, and lay out a detailed teaching strategy which has been tested in the classroom. These elaborate aids are not designed to hamstring teachers; any instructor who wishes to do so may ignore them. Most teachers, however, welcome lesson plans. They provide the essential link between objectives, materials, and teaching strategy and help teachers to grasp principles which may be quite unfamiliar to them.

Now let me turn to teaching materials, the heart of the curriculum revolution. A few reformers still speak naively of "teacher-proof materials," an absurd notion. Teachers who do not understand the principles upon which materials are based can make hash of the most imaginative materials ever created. Moreover, the entire concept of teacher-pooof materials is unsound philosophically. Every teacher should adapt materials and teaching techniques to the particular needs of his own classroom audience. He should also adapt materials to his own personality and style of teaching. All these disclaimers aside, the new materials being produced by the projects stand at the forefront of the curricular revolution.

If the projects are the wave of the future, the textbook is dead. Only one or two projects produce materials in customary narrative textbook form. The rest have either abandoned conventional texts entirely or relegated them to a subsidiary position among a galaxy of diverse materials both written and audio-visual. In the past textbooks have been used primarily to teach the social studies as product. Teachers assigned as homework a few pages from a text. In class the next day they asked questions to determine whether students learned the facts and generalizations which they had studied. Texts remain a good way to convey information to students if the students under consideration are well motivated and have a conceptual apparatus to help them organize data from a textbook in meaningful ways. But conventional texts are not particularly useful for teaching the structure of a discipline nor are they as useful as many other materials to help form appropriate attitudes and to raise issues involving value conflicts.

If the textbook is on its way to the grave, what will replace it? An enormous variety of written, audio-visual, and manipulative materials. As the core of many courses, the social studies projects are putting together extensive collections of source materials each carefully designed for a specific function. Among these materials are diaries, letters, autobiographies, biographical sketches, pieces of fiction, government documents, business records, charts, tables, graphs, secondary accounts written by historians and social scientists—virtually anything, in other words, which contains data about society. For example, both of the one-semester ninth grade courses designed at the Carnegie Tech Curriculum Development Center contain between sixty and seventy readings each intended for one night's homework and one day's class discussion. A reading consists of three parts: an introduction which relates one day's work to that of the remainder of the course, three or four study questions guiding the student to the heart of the issue which is involved, and a document, article, collection of tables, or other written material which raises one or two points for students to think about. In addition to this written material, our project has prepared a large number of transparencies, tape recordings, single concept filmstrips, plays which the students can produce in class, simulations, and supplementary written material to be handed out in class, each piece carefully designed to make a specific point during a specific part of a class discussion. In our tenth and eleventh grade courses three days of source material like this are followed by a summary essay which analyzes in textbook style the main events in the history of western Europe or the United States and links one problem to the next. In this way students gain a grasp of continuity which often disappears when source materials are used entirely by themselves, and at the same time they learn the tools of inquiry through careful examination of documents.

Let me describe several innovations in materials which point in new directions. The Tech Center has developed a number of single concept filmstrips consisting entirely of pictures without captions. These filmstrips can be used to help students develop hypotheses, to give them data from which they can learn a concept, to introduce evidence which supplements written material in homework assignments, or for a variety of other purposes. An example may make the point clear. In our eleventh grade history course, we wanted students to develop a hypothesis about the cause of the Civil War before they began to study the Civil War in written materials. We made a filmstrip out of thirty pictures of maps, largely adapted from Paullin's *Atlas*.[13] The first four maps show physical differences between the North and South—such factors as rainfall, average yearly temperature, soil formations, and so forth. A second series contrasts the economies of the two areas, emphasizing agriculture, industry, trade, and commerce. A third series compares the societies by looking at a number of variables:

[13]Charles O. Paullin, *Atlas of the Historical Geography of the United States* (Washington, D.C.; Carnegie Institution of Washington, 1932).

number of slaves, number of immigrants, religious affiliation, number of colleges, and so forth. Finally, the fourth section concentrates on votes on various sectional issues beginning with the Missouri Compromise. At the end of each section of the filmstrip we ask students to write a couple of sentences indicating whether or not they see any major differences between the North and the South. For class preparation on the following day they are told to write a hypothesis from their notes on the subject, "What caused the Civil War?" They then spend the following three weeks in homework assignments and class discussions refining and altering the hypotheses they developed from the maps and discussing the advantages and disadvantages of beginning with a hypothesis based on such limited and controlled data.

Instead of single concept filmstrips, a number of projects have been developing film loops. A film loop consists of a continuous circle of film which projects through an 8mm. silent projector. Most of them last only four or five minutes. They are particularly useful, in my judgment, for helping students develop one single idea clearly. Suppose, for example, that a teacher wanted students to grasp the idea of cultural diffusion, the process by which ideas, institutions, techniques, and so forth are transferred from one culture to another. He might begin a loop with two-and-a-half minutes of film illustrating life in a major western city. The film would include pictures of housing, commerce, industry, transportation, clothing, recreation, and so forth. The next two-and-a-half minutes could be devoted to similar pictures from a city in a developing country. The teacher might then ask students which aspects of western culture had been diffused to the non-western city and encourage them to speculate about why some had been and others had not. He might also encourage students to think about the ways in which the culture of the west had been carried to other lands. An exercise such as this one encourages the student to observe carefully; it challenges him to be creative; it teaches him the concept of cultural diffusion; it breaks the deadly monotony of classroom recitation; it may even teach him how to look with a new perspective at his own city and at other cities when he sees them on television or on summer travel.

"But what's it all for?" you may well ask. What are the objectives of the new social studies? I have already suggested their essential purpose: to help the child develop into a useful, independent citizen. This general objective can be divided for purposes of discussion into four major parts: attitudes, values, inquiry skills, and knowledge. Let me get at each in turn.

A useful independent citizen has a set of cooperative attitudes towards society. He is a participant in politics, anxious to pull his oar. He wants to hear all sides of a debate and to make up his mind about an issue through a rational decision-making process. The new social studies tries to generate these attitudes and a number of others like them.

Many attitudes develop through the way in which a class is taught.

Calling on students whether or not they have raised their hands indicates that a student, like a citizen, should participate actively in the learning process. Requiring students to use a mode of inquiry from history and the social sciences may teach them to prefer a rational decision-making process to authority or superstition as a test for truth. Notice that these attitudes result from conduct in the classroom, not from the choice of teaching material. How silly talk of "teacher-proof materials" is in this context!

Many of the social studies projects assume a basic ethic based on the dignity and worth of the individual. With the exception of this basic value —and in a few cases without even this exception—the projects do not try to get students to internalize a specific set of policies toward controversial public issues. Instead the projects present materials and teaching techniques which consistently challenge students' values and encourage them to reflect upon them in the light of evidence. The goal is not consensus; the goal is reflection. If at the end of the year a student emerges with the same values he held at its beginning, he will still have amassed a body of evidence for his position, evidence which may support him in a crisis. He will also have learned something about techniques by which he can test his values. If, on the other hand, he finds that some of the values he held could not stand the test of evidence, he can abandon them for others. In either case he will be better off. By consistently raising issues involving values and by subjecting them to discussion under the rules of evidence, the projects are attempting to develop citizens who know where they are going in a world buffeted by change.

The projects are also trying to teach these students the skills of inquiry essential for independent learning. Robert Oppenheimer suggests that the total quantity of knowledge in the world doubles with every decade. Much of what we now accept as true will probably be proved wrong in the future. Learning a body of facts and generalizations cannot equip children to live intelligently ten or twenty years hence. In order to help them cope with the knowledge explosion, we must teach them how to learn for themselves. They must know how to inquire in a disciplined way to avoid being abandoned like worn-out automobiles on the human scrapheap.

Hence, the emphasis on inquiry skills, a phrase which, as I define it, is synonymous with structure. A child well-equipped with the skills of inquiry can develop hypotheses, drawing upon the conceptual apparatus which he has learned. He can also use a proof process with which he can validate, revise, or abandon the hypothesis he has formed. This mode of inquiry is a tool with which he can learn in the future. The facts gleaned from textbooks often disappear from a child's memory bank within a few weeks after the examination. The skills of inquiry, however, persist longer and are far more useful. Perhaps the major difference between the objectives of the new social studies and the old lies in the area of inquiry skills. In the past, courses of study have always bowed to something called "critical thinking." The new projects put inquiry in the forefront of their objectives. No one who cannot inquire independently and critically can survive well in the modern world.

Finally, let me turn to the last objective, knowledge of content from history and the social sciences. In the past what a textbook author thought was important was the major guide to content in the social studies. Teachers "covered the course;" students "read the whole book;" what lay between those grey flannel covers *was* the social studies to millions of children. The projects are much more self-conscious in their choice of criteria for the selection of social studies content. Most of them combine four criteria: what will help a student grasp the fundamental conceptual apparatus of a discipline; what interests a child and what he needs; what will help a student understand and cope with contemporary problems; and a certain indispensable corpus of knowledge which the curriculum developer feels every educated and intelligent American citizen should know. Establishing four criteria such as these implies an end to the dogma of coverage which is a ridiculous dogma to begin with. The projects leave out vast quantities of material which has been covered superficially and often badly in the past. Better to do a few things well, they argue, than to do more things poorly. Clearly a new day is coming.

Materials from the social studies projects have not yet been published commercially except in experimental units and a few paperback volumes. Within the next two or three years, materials will hit the market in a flood. It's time to get ready for them. I'd suggest several courses of action for any school system. Try to get teachers to an NDEA summer institute, many of which are stocking the materials from the projects which are already available. Buy the four new methods books which have come out during the past year or will appear next year for the professional book shelf in each social studies department and encourage teachers to read them.[14] Get hold of experimental editions from the projects.[15] Lists of these materials will appear from time to time in the pages of *Social Education*. Get a classroom set from a project and try it out on your own students to see how you like it before you plunge blindly into a new way of teaching. Start to work on your school administrators; let them know that you will need more money for materials, that you will require more audio-visual equipment, that every school should have a department chairman who devotes at least half of his

[14]See the volumes by Cox and Massialas, Fenton, and Oliver and Shaver cited above. A revision of the Hunt and Metcalf text, *Teaching High School Social Studies,* was published by Harpers in 1968.

[15]For example, experimental units from the Carnegie Tech project for the ninth, tenth, and eleventh grade courses are available free of charge in classroom sets from Marketing Manager, Social Studies, Holt, Rinehart & Winston, Inc., 383 Madison Avenue, New York, New York 10017.

time to keeping up with what's going on in the curriculum projects and to communicating this information to his colleagues. Finally, look at the new materials critically. Each teacher knows his own student audience far better than a college professor in a curriculum center. Decide which materials are most appropriate to your students and to their needs. Adapt what someone has written to your own particular circumstances. Keep the independence which teachers have always had to set their goals and choose their materials and ways of teaching for the needs of the boys and girls who are their charges. This is the thrill and glory of teaching. Don't let them take it away.

RICHARD E. GROSS

Professor of Education, Stanford
University

DWIGHT W. ALLEN

Dean, School of Education, University
of Massachusetts

76. Time for a National Effort To Develop the Social Studies Curriculum*

Two major problems have plagued the social studies curriculum for nearly half a century. We must solve these problems by enabling teachers properly to: (1) teach the essential, updated content and approaches found in history and the social science disciplines, and (2) carry out this instruction in the most appropriate organizational framework.

In these two areas it is time to stop playing blindman's buff. In this heartland of socio-civic education in American schools, we must shame-facedly admit that we have been driving a troika on a circuitous, repetitive, and ill-marked course. We have been saddled with three poorly-teamed steeds named tradition, prosaism, and improvisation. A long overdue at-tack upon the problem of revitalizing the social studies can now become a reality. There is no need to elaborate on the need for a new program. Authorities are continually sounding calls for such action, but up to the present no really significant or grand examination and trial have been possible.[1]

We are proposing the establishment of a national research center for social studies and a comprehensive, coordinated assessment of the social studies curriculum and instruction by a national commission responsible for planning alternative social studies programs, grades K through 14.

Recent proposals[2] add up to little more than a gigantic kettle of *bouilla-baisse*. Unless definite steps are taken to collect, synthesize, and publicize

---

*Phi Delta Kappan, XLIV: 360–66, May 1963. Used by permission.

[1]Recent evidence of the unrest and varied proposals for reconstruction are found in sources such as the following: R. E. Gross and L. D. Zeleny, *Educating Citizens for Democracy,* (New York: Oxford University Press, 1958), pp. 5–9, 68–69, and 78–80; C. R. Keller, "History and Social Sciences: Reflections and Recommendation," *Journal of Secondary Education,* May 1962, pp. 263–70; and Franklin Patterson, "Social Science and the New Curriculum," *The American Behavioral Scientist,* November 1962, pp. 28–31.

[2]See two articles: R. E. Gross, "Emerging Horizons for the Social Studies," *Social Education,* January 1960, pp. 21–24, and L. S. Kenworthy, "Ferment in the Social Studies," *Phi Delta Kappan,* October 1962, pp. 12–16. More details on several of the larger projects are found in Edwin Fenton's section in *The Changing College Preparatory Curriculum* (Princeton, College Entrance Examination Board, 1962), pp. 45–51, and Dorothy Fraser, *Current Curriculum Studies in Academic Subjects,* Project on Instruction, National Education Association (Washington, D.C., (1962), Chapt. 6.

significant recent innovations, there is grave danger that the results may see minimal application in school social studies programs that already lag in a doldrum unbelievable to any perceptive outside viewer. The impact of so many unrelated studies can also be a prelude to unfortunate power struggles among the discipline areas, agencies, foundations, and publishers involved.

DEVELOPMENTS IN SOCIAL SCIENCE DISCIPLINES

Scholars in history and the social sciences are busy with projects important to social studies teaching. Two significant anthropological projects related to the lower school curriculum, headquartered at Harvard and Chicago, are now moving ahead. The American Sociological Association has a committee interested in developing a high school course. In economics we have just had the Task Force Report and the national TV program in economic education. The Joint Council on Economic Education has made valuable contributions. Another approach to economics in the elementary curriculum is being developed in Indiana schools by a group at Purdue University. A model course in geography is being produced by teachers cooperating with professional geographers. Historians, psychologists, and political scientists are reported about to launch national studies, producing new units, prototype courses, and new teaching materials.

Social science groups continued to discuss the merits of separate discipline approaches versus integrated courses, and some now wish to explore more deeply this still unsettled issue. Others are concerned with the designation of essential generalizations in each of the social science disciplines. Here there has been considerable exploration; valuable work has been conducted through projects and doctoral studies at Boston University, Harvard, and Stanford, among others; at Stanford 3,700 generalizations drawn from basic social science publications have been identified. School systems such as Portland, Oregon, at the local level and California at the state level have attempted to identify generalizations as major goals in new courses of study. The National Council for the Social Studies and the American Council of Learned Societies have recently published a series of papers dealing with these fundamentals.[3] Other similar studies are promised. In this one important area of concept identification much effort has been duplicated and results have generally not been employed to reinforce later studies. Leading social scientists meeting at the Center for Advanced Study in the

[3]For one sample list of these basic ideas or generalizations from history and the social sciences, see the recent *Social Studies Framework for the Public Schools of California,* California State Department of Education, June 1962, pp. 89–109. The National Council for the Social Studies and the American Council of Learned Societies sponsored *The Social Studies and the Social Sciences* (New York: Harcourt, Brace, and World, 1962), 303 pp.

Behavioral Sciences at Stanford in December, 1962, expressed unanimous agreement on the need to provide a national clearing house for the exchange of information about their various studies and projects.

OTHER SOURCES OF TRIAL AND EXPERIMENTATION

New courses of study are being launched in endless and overly repetitive succession not only by local school systems and state departments of education; other sources are now entering the fray. While publishing houses bring out entire series of books for both elementary and secondary social studies curriculum, additional courses of study are now to come from the new Council for Public Schools in Boston, while the Civil Liberties Education Foundation promises to reform the social studies curriculum in the next two years! Educational Services, Inc., has recently received a million dollar grant to develop experimental courses and related materials in humanities and the social studies that will aim to renovate the entire elementary and secondary program. The North Central Association's Foreign Relations Project is moving into the area of curriculum revision in the social studies; the Robert Taft Institute of Government has just concluded a survey of citizenship education in New York and is pledged to carry on other such studies; and the Tufts University Civic Education Center is working with nine eastern states in a variety of valuable curriculum projects.[4]

Numerous other independent and more limited curriculum studies can be cited that threaten to add to the conglomeration. Social studies programs will be affected by the advanced placement courses of the College Entrance Examination Board and by the growing demand for state tests, as well as by curriculum changes through fiat, that devastating prerogative of state legislatures. New courses on film and TV can also be influential in either a divisive or unifying way. With increased funds becoming available for social studies research from the United States Office of Education (Project Social Studies) and the National Science Foundation, there will undoubtedly be a further increase in studies and projects.

A NATIONAL RESEARCH CENTER FOR SOCIAL STUDIES

If past history is repeated, much of this activity will come to naught. Even the valuable contributions may well be lost to the mainstream of so-

[4] See *Points of Take-off for the Social Studies*, NCA Foreign Relations Project, 1961; *Citizenship Education in the High Schools of New York State*, The Institute, 1962; and *The Nine States Youth Citizenship Project*, the Commissioners of Education of the Northeastern States, Tufts University (brochure, n. d.).

cial studies education as the results take final form in a dissertation, monograph, limited local publication, or in a professional journal of small circulation. Therefore, we are proposing first of all the immediate establishment of a National Research Center for Social Studies, Grades K–14, to initiate two major projects essential for the elimination of the persistent problems stated at the beginning of this article.

The center would act to classify, summarize, and report the pertinent research. There is at present no single source of information to which researchers, school administrators, curriculum workers, publishers, teachers, and others interested in the social studies can turn for statements on recent or planned developments. There is a great need for a national clearing house to cooperate with institutions of higher learning, school systems, public agencies, professional organizations, and foundations in reporting results of the expanding experimentation, trial programs of study, new instructional materials, and emerging methods of approaching subject matter such as team teaching, flexible scheduling, and individual study programs.

In the first instance, therefore, the center should serve as a much needed marshaling base for the collection and organization of data fundamental to any comprehensive rethinking of the social studies curriculum. The center should also provide information needed by persons interested in developing new social studies curricula.

A second major role for the center should be proposing and initiating research that is shown to be needed as a result of the center's gathering and classifying activities. In spite of all the recent social studies experimentation, there is a great need for much more research and for improved experimental designs.[5]

In keeping abreast with research in the social studies field, the center would become a source of proposals for experiments needed to fill the evident gaps in information about curriculum and instruction. As one example, following the examination of all available research by the center's staff, it may become apparent that only a handful of studies have been conducted on the organization of instruction in contemporary affairs. It may also have become clear to the center that teachers are giving more time to current events but that both teachers and pupils are highly dissatisfied with the results. The center might then propose appropriate research and perhaps carry out trials or pilot studies in this area. These may be planned with local school districts, state departments of education, educational associations, or cooperating colleges and universities.

[5]For a critique of some aspects of current research in the field, see B. G. Massialas, *Research Prospects in the Social Studies,* Bulletin of the School of Education, Indiana University, January 1962. For a discussion of the difficulties of research dissemination. see R. E. Gross, "Research Needs in Social Studies Education," *Social Education,* December, 1961, p. 401.

The degree to which the center could actually sponsor and carry out such experimentation would depend upon its resources in money and staff. The center would eventually need a large full-time and part-time staff. Even with panels of part-time experts and specialists to advise and help plan its endeavors, we envision a planning period of at least two years. This would be followed by another period of several years for the development of desired pilot studies and the initiation of research projects essential to gaining a full picture of the current status of social studies curriculum and instruction in the United States. All of this must be coordinated with the major effort that must be made to develop an integrated social studies program, grades K-14. The examination of three or four basically different curriculum designs should involve a large number of representative school districts in several states, and may well require fifteen years, the involvement of the entire profession, and the expenditure of millions of dollars.

Ideally, therefore, along with the establishment of the proposed Research Center for the Social Studies, extensive funds should be made available simultaneously to launch the National Curriculum Study Commission in the Social Studies. The facilities and resources of the research center could be used for these activities and the efforts and findings stemming from the first several years' work of the center can be coordinated with the plans of the Commission whose major responsibility would be the mounting of a massive nationwide organization and exploration to test the several alternative models of plausible social studies curricula.

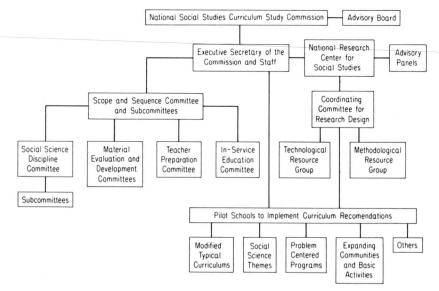

FIGURE 76-1

Space is not available to present the specific elements of the proposed study commission and its structure and functions, as developed by the authors. They have prepared a detailed description of the design, various committees, pilot projects, and activities of the contemplated commission, and will be happy to share this with interested colleagues who contact them. The accompanying diagram indicates elements and relationships in the proposal.

Alternative Curriculum Models

The commission would not need to start from scratch in planning its "grand examination." A number of designs for model social studies curricula have been proposed in the past, but most of them have never been adequately tested. In 1939, for example, the National Council for the Social Studies gathered fifteen provocative proposals for an experimental social studies curriculum, but this was never followed up with any actual trial.[6] In November, 1962, an ad hoc committee of the council submitted a substantial proposal.[7] The commission would have no difficulty in finding grade placement suggestions. These vary from such fundamental contributions as the "social processes approach" developed many years ago by Marshall and Goetz[8] to the earlier problem-centered programs suggested by John Dewey and Harold Rugg.[9] Needless to say, these have never been given an adequate trial. It is now time to map the course and to replace the three steeds—tradition, prosaism, and improvisation—with a soundly constructed and tested program of studies.

The Modified Typical Curriculum

The commission might well be advised to begin its list of alternative framework proposals with a modified typical program that incorporates much of what is now familiar and deemed to be satisfactory social studies offerings. Some obvious but minimal alterations in usual state and local programs are called for if we are to frankly meet the commonly perceived objectives of the social studies. In such a curriculum, administrators, teachers, and parents will feel more secure, there will be less need for extensive teacher retraining, and currently available materials and instruc-

[6]James A. Michener, ed., *The Future of the Social Studies,* National Council for the Social Studies, Curriculum Series no. 1, (Washington, D.C., 1939).
[7]"The Social Studies and the National Interest," ad hoc committee report, The National Council for the Social Studies, November 1962, mimeographed.
[8]L. C. Marshall and R. N. Goetz, *Curriculum-Making in the Social Studies,* Report of the Commission on the Social Studies, pt 13 (New York: Scribner's, 1936).
[9]See summaries of their recommendations in R. E. Gross, R. H. Muessig, and G. L. Fersh, eds., *The Problems Approach and the Social Studies,* National Council for the Social Studies, Curriculum Series no. 9, rev. (Washington, D.C., 1960).

tional media may meet most needs. The following is suggested, therefore, as a modified typical program for initial testing by the Commission:

> Grades K–1—Studies of Home, School, Neighborhood, and Community
>
> Grade 2—Our Community: Producing, Processing, and Marketing Relationships
>
> Grade 3—Growth and Change Affect Our Citizens and Institutions
>
> Grade 4—Our State and Region: Backgrounds, Characteristics, Peoples and Problems
>
> Grade 5—The Development of the United States and Its Canadian Neighbor
>
> Grades 6 & 7—Latin America, Eurasia, and Africa (a two-year geographically-centered sequence with units on representative regions and nations)
>
> Grade 8—Introduction to Human Culture (first semester); The Citizen and His Government (second semester)
>
> Grade 9—The History of Selected Key Eras, Peoples, and Nations (depth studies)
>
> Grade 10—United States History (emphasis since 1890)
>
> Grade 11—Economic Opportunities and Problems in the United States and the World
>
> Grade 12—Contemporary Problems: Local to International (primarily political and social)
>
> Grades 13 & 14—Western Civilization, plus selected social science electives

This modified program permits fuller introduction of all of the major social sciences than is now possible, primarily through the elimination of the usual eighth grade American history offering. It provides for a more logical sequence than is now often found, and a more comprehensive treatment of other areas of the world, as well as of the social sciences.

The Social Science Themes Curriculum

A second and bolder option is suggested next for those who desire timely, unifying, but related themes that move away from the present unsatisfactory scope and sequence.

Operating on the assumption that there are few limitations on what can be taught to any student at most ages in an intellectually honest form, we suggest the building of a curriculum that provides a systematic overview of the social sciences by using the disciplines themselves as underlying themes. Inherent in the design of such a curriculum are the criteria of producing desirable social behavior, identifying generalizations regarding human relationships and institutions, and developing an appreciation of scholarly inquiry. This experimental curriculum would focus upon a central theme for

period blocks of several years that should provide for the systematic introduction of the various social science disciplines. To achieve these ends the
following themes are proposed.

Grades 1 through 3—*Anthropology*. The introduction of culture as a
key to understanding people. Emphasis in these grades can be cultural
diversity and change, and the importance of judging other people by the
standards of their own culture. Allied with the anthropological theme, the
other disciplines can be reflected in such topics as "how man makes a
living," "how men work together," or "how man attempts to modify his
environment."

Grades 4 through 6—*Geography*. The use of the area-culture approach
can provide a vehicle for correlating the social sciences. The very nature of
geography, which draws upon the various disciplines of the social and
natural sciences, is a natural avenue for understanding the full perspective
and scope of the social sciences.

Grade 7 through 9—*History and Sociology*. World history in a geographic setting, with attention to the non-Western world will present the
chronology of human experience and the universal condition of change.
Sociology will emphasize man's social structures, their functions, and the
responsibilities inherent in the varied roles man plays in society.

Grades 10 and 11—*Political Science and Economics*. This course is to
be divided into two parts, the tenth grade to treat U.S. history from the
founding of the nation until the end of Reconstruction in 1876. The eleventh
grade will treat U.S. history from 1876 to the present. The content of the
10th grade lends itself to the introduction of political science. The structure and function of government and the obligations of citizenship can be
pursued in far greater depth than has been possible in the past.

The period after Reconstruction, marked by the transition of the nation
into an economically maturing urban society, presents an avenue for introducing economics in a meaningful way. Units emphasizing the goals of
economic welfare, stability, and the role of economic change as it influences
other aspects of society can be taught profitably against a backdrop of the
remaining social sciences.

Grade 12—*The Methodology of the Various Disciplines*. This
group of elective offerings is designed for students of varying abilities and
is open to tenth and eleventh graders with particular interest and talent in
the social sciences. Course content is designed to meet advanced placement
requirements. Courses in depth would be offered in psychology and
philosophy as well as those disciplines previously cited. History, as an example, would emphasize familiarity in research methodology and historiography in teaching students to make critical assessments regarding the
finality of knowledge and human behavior. In all cases students moving on

to college will be prepared to begin earlier specialization in chosen social science areas.

The systematic development of themes organized around the social science disciplines can produce a social studies curriculum which exploits a categorization of learning that can be applied at increasing levels of sophistication. The student should emerge from such a curriculum with a fundamental intellectual preparation that can sustain him in higher education or in the world of work and citizenship.

Expanding Community—Basic Activities

Other possibilities need to be examined in providing possible frameworks for the social studies. One of our colleagues, Paul R. Hanna, has crusaded for a program concentrating on ten "basic human activities" within concentric circles of the expanding communities of men.[10] Hanna has suggested the following lists as the basis for a scope and sequence model. He and his students have already been carrying on a systematic exploration of this theory, which deserves further testing.

Basic Human Activities

1. Producing, Exchanging, Distributing and Consuming Food, Clothing, Shelter, and Other Consumer Goods and Services
2. Communicating Ideas and Feelings
3. Organizing and Governing
4. Transporting People and Goods
5. Protecting and Conserving Human and Natural Resources
6. Creating Tools, Technics, and Social Arrangements
7. Providing Recreation
8. Expressing Religious Impulses
9. Expressing and Satisfying Aesthetic Impulses
10. Providing Education

Expanding Communities of Men

1. The Family
2. The School Community
3. The Neighborhood Community
4. The Local, County, and Metropolitan Communities
5. The State Community
6. The Region-of-States Community
7. The National Community

[10]One of the more complete presentations of this approach is found in Hanna's chapter, "Society—Child—Curriculum," in C. W. Hunnicutt, ed., *Education 2000 A.D.*, (Syracuse; Syracuse University Press, 1956), pp. 165–99.

8. The Emerging Inter-American Community
9. The Emerging Atlantic Community
10. The Emerging Pacific Community
11. The World Community

Other alternative schemes such as a problem-centered framework could be presented to the commission or developed by one of its committees, but eventually the commission would have to decide upon three or four most plausible models for its "grand examination." It would, meanwhile, have carried out related pilot projects, produced needed materials, and made arrangements with school systems for the long-term trial of the proposed alternative programs. For alternative proposals, see *Social Education,* April, 1963.

To create the commission, the cooperation of related organizations will have to be obtained. Such a national study commission cannot be brought to full bloom in a few months' time. The effort must be planned by top-flight persons in the field with interest and time to launch the project. Some of these individuals should probably be assigned to the advisory board (several may also be assigned to the commission) as liaison personnel with the groups they represent, such as: The National Council for the Social Studies, The American Association of School Administrators, The American Council of Learned Societies, The Social Science Research Council, and important regional associations such as the Middle States Council for the Social Studies, The North Central Association, and the Nine States Youth Citizenship Project. Additionally, various academic societies and supporting agencies such as the American Economic Association, The Service Center for Teachers of History, The College Entrance Examination Board, the U. S. Office of Education, and the National Science Foundation, as well as state groups such as departments of public instruction and teachers associations, will have to be consulted and should be represented on the advisory board. It is imperative to have broad understanding and acceptance as a prelude to any successful venture into the field of socio-civic education on the scale we have envisaged.

We have attempted to outline a dual-phased approach to the remapping of the social studies program in American schools. We hope that those in agreement and those who oppose any elements of our proposal will speak up, before some immediate next steps are taken. The difficulties are many and obvious. Our intent here is to underscore the need and the potential. Exchanges of opinion and controversy will be all to the good, as important persons and agencies must be convinced of the rising need for a monumental assessment of curriculum and instruction in the social studies. As people suggest modifications and as recognition of the problem grows, there will be increased possibility of gaining the vast financing this project demands.

TWO AGENCIES TO SOLVE TWO MAJOR PROBLEMS

This article began by citing the two major problems besetting the social studies: the lack of agreement on the essentials to be taught, and ignorance of how to structure and approach these learnings. We believe a National Research Center for the Social Studies will serve to bring needed answers to a number of key queries in the first problem area. To ascertain the most effective approach for an updated social studies curricular framework, the establishment of a National Social Studies Curriculum Commission is crucial.

These institutions and the "grand examination" of the social studies that we have proposed they conduct as an integrated national effort can provide the bases for a new map of the social studies. Professionals at all levels and concerned institutions and agencies throughout the land must become close collaborators if we are to realize the full potential of national endeavor in social studies curriculum development. The time is ripe. Let us seize this opportunity.

Index

Gantert, Robert L., 74
Gardner, John W., 160
Garfield, Deborah, 163
Gay, John, 330
Gemeinschaft, 14
Generalizations, 4
Geography
  cultural, 58
  in the curriculum, 58
  ecological dominant, 59
  globalism, 62
  law of comparative advantage, 60
  life-layer, 59
  perpetual transformation, 60
  perspective, 112–113
  regions and regionalizing, 61
  relative location, 62
  round earth on flat paper, 61
  spatial interaction, 62
  trilogy of, 58
Gesellschaft, 14
Getzels, J. W., 304
Gibel, Dederer, 107
Giffin, Ken, 199
Gifted students
  case study, 452–453
  common approaches assessed, 449
  evaluation, 453
  homogeneous grouping and enrichment
    programs, 449–452
Glaser, E. M., 228
Glenn, John, 155
Goals, American, 50–53
Goetz, Richard N., 10, 559
Golden, Harry, 135
Goldstein, Joseph, 238
Goodnow, Jacqueline J., 242
Gorman, B., 232
Greene, Homer, 350
Grodzins, Morton, 107
Gross, Richard E., 38, 74, 130, 195, 228,
  308, 374, 378, 480, 542, 554, 557,
  559
Group dynamics, 181; *see also* Group
    work and Group process
  individual differences, 427
Group process, 181; *see also* Group work
    and Group dynamics
Group work, 181; *see also* Group
    dynamics and Group process
  buzz techniques, 182–187
  evaluation of, 189–193
  long-run, 187–189

Group work (*continued*)
  reasons for use, 181–182
  reporting, 193–194
  short-run, 182-187
Grow, Julian F., 62, 63
Gruntwig, Bishop, 12
Gulley, Halbert E., 293

Hanna, Lavone, 236
Hanna, Paul R., 542, 562
Hanson, J. W., 235
Harris, Chester W., 38
Harvard Center of Cognitive Studies, 86
Harvard Curriculum Center, 547
Harvard Social Studies Project, 348
Heenan, L. D. B., 276
Heilbroner, Robert, 107
Henderson, Kenneth, 241, 242, 243
Henry, Ralph S., 74
Herbart, 135
Hickman, Warren, 541
Hill, James L., 546
History
  aids attainment of educational goals,
    539
  as courses and resources, 519–521,
    524–526
  as seen by historians, 523–524
  as seen by public, 524
  as seen by students, 521–522
  as seen by teachers, 522–523
  classificatory terms of world, 27
  complexity of, 518
  concerns of, 30
  evaluation in world, 28
  four periods of American, 40
  in the curriculum, 32, 37
  nature of generalizations in American,
    46
  not a content course, 517
  not a social science, 101
  organization within cycles of American,
    41
  relationship to social sciences of world,
    30
  role of, 116
  selection of content in American, 43
  testable propositions in world, 28
  three-cycle approach to American, 37
  truth claims of world, 27
  use of music in teaching, 334–340
  use of novels in teaching, 318
  use of poetry in teaching, 327–333
Historians, and behavioral sciences, 31

Students, motivating, 175
  results of ridiculing, 176
Suchman, J. Richard, 224
Swift, L. F., 245

Taba, Hilda, 49, 546
Taylor, Harold, 160–161
Taxonomy
  analysis, 205
  application, 204
  comprehension, 204
  evaluation, 205
  knowledge, 203
  synthesis, 205
Teacher education, world history, 35
Teaching units; see also Units
  definition, 207–208
  individual differences, 425–426
  rationale for use, 208–209
Team teaching, 195
  advantages of, 196
  arguments against, 197
  definitions, 196
Technique, definition, 15
Textbooks
  bleak future in new social studies, 548
  essential understandings of, 463–365
  a teacher's tool, 460
Thompson, Warren, 106
Thomson, Scott, 199
Thorp, Willard, 323
Thrower, N. J. W., 278
Thursfield, Richard E., 473
Todd, Lewis Paul, 9
Toynbee, Arnold, 328
Trial by newspaper, 52
Trow, Martin, 104
Trump, J. Lloyd, 196
Turner, Gordon B., 18

United States history; see History
Units, model, 308–314; see also Teaching
  units
U.S. Office of Education, 643

Value systems, 16
Values
  clarification through current affairs, 382
  conflict in, 16
  Educational Policies Commission's list
    of, 375
  how to teach, 376–380
  teacher personality in teaching and,
    380–381
  teacher reticence to teach, 374
Verba, Sidney, 55

Wallick, Ray G., 79
Warntz, William, 277
Watson, Richard L., 72
Weingrod, Alex, 72
Wells, Charles A., 383
Wesley, Edgar Bruce, 39, 485
Weston, Grace, 238
Whitehead, Alfred North, 66
Williams, Jr., F. E., 235
Williams, Jr., Robin M., 155
Williamson, Dale, 239
Wilson, Mary C., 433
Wolfe, Thomas, 9
Wood, Charles L., 79
World history; see History
Wright, Grace S., 38
Wright, J. K., 278
Writing skills
  and objective tests, 261–262
  taught through history courses, 261

Young, Marian A., 475
Yuker, H. E., 280
Yutang, Lin, 155

Zacharias, Jerrold, 527
Zeitgeist, 10, 329
Zeleny, Leslie D., 74, 130, 554
Zevin, Jack, 546
Zimmerman, Erich, 60